THE ONLY OPTIONS TRADING
BOOK YOU'LL EVER NEED

A Complete Step-by-Step Tutorial for Entry-Level Option Traders
A Comprehensive Option Strategy Reference for Experienced Traders

A comprehensive option handbook including:

- Why Trade Options?
- Financial Leverage
- Rewards and Risks
- Brokerage Selection
- Trading Platforms
- Equipment Planning & Backup
- Internet & Smartphone Connections
- Order Routing
- Technical Analysis
- Chart Types and Patterns
- Chart Studies and Odds Enhancers
- Option Trading Strategies and Goals
- Setup Parameters
- Scanning for Trades
- Trade Evaluation
- Option Trade Entries
- Risk Management
- Possible Outcomes
- Trading Options on Futures
- Trading Options on Small Accounts
- Option Strategy Quick Reference
- Evaluations (What You Learned)
- Option Terms and Definitions
- And much, much more...

THE ONLY OPTIONS TRADING BOOK YOU'LL EVER NEED

Earn a steady income trading options

Russell Allen Stultz

Library of Congress Cataloguing-in-Publication Data

Stultz, Russell Allen
The Only Options Trading Book You'll Ever Need — a complete step-by-step tutorial for entry-level option traders / a comprehensive option strategy reference for experienced traders
Includes Index
ISBN 1-945390-11-5

For more information, send e-mail to ntxisc@gmail.com
or mail:
Option Trader
4217 Country Club Drive
Plano, Texas 75074

Foreword by Donald E. Pearson, M.D.

An Unusual Journey — Our journeys began as grammar school buddies many years ago. Growing up at that time was sand lot baseball, summers at the beach, and exploring this new world. Russ and I last saw each other at our high school graduation. Subsequently, we traveled different paths on life's journeys.

At a recent high school reunion we met again. Russ had spent many years in the publishing business and was an accomplished and respected author and instructor. This involved didactic teaching, inspiring students and writing, with more than 50 published books under his belt. He also had formal training and extensive experience in options trading and taught and lectured on the subject. Thus, Russ brought a unique set of credentials together to formulate a guide and reference book on options trading.

My journey was quite different. I had been practicing Orthopedic Surgery and teaching post-doctoral residents. But my interest in option trading was ignited with our chance encounter at a class reunion. Soon, I was beginning to realize that I was entering a whole new world, new skills, even a new language: option chains, the "Greeks," iron condors, twisted sisters.

There were no familiar areas upon which to start my learning process. This mysterious and daunting world was uncharted.

Amazon supplied me with the first book on options which I anxiously studied. Something was missing. I went back to Amazon time and time again until I had covered 6 books, 2 newsletters, and several handbooks. Each of them had some "take away," but none prepared me to trade, or alerted me to the many inherent risks involved in active trading.

Thus, Russ saw the challenge to create a handbook for beginners and a reference book for more experienced option traders. He did a masterful job. His book provided me with the information, jargon, and step-by-step instructions I needed to begin trading options. This book filled the gap, taking me from knowledge to application!

I flippantly said, "If Russ can teach me option trading, I'm going to teach him how to replace a hip." I'm not sure he wants to collect on that deal!

And now as our journeys continue, I am pleased to introduce to you a book that delivers its promise and to its author, my long-time friend and colleague, Russell Stultz.

Donald E. Pearson, M.D.

ACKNOWLEDGEMENTS

My deepest gratitude to the many contributions made by more than a dozen experienced option traders who reviewed and provided invaluable feedback and many excellent suggestions during the development of this book. Your many compliments with regard to the value and unique format of this book spurred me on to its completion.

I also wish to acknowledge the more than 400 members of the North Texas Investment Strategies Club (NTXISC) and the West Plano IBD Meetup for their encouragement and useful feedback. A special thanks to Mo Fatemi, founder of the West Plano IBD Meetup group, and active option trader Rick Comer. Both highly respected and exceptional options traders themselves, they each spent many days examining and commenting on the hands-on option trading activities within chapters 14 through 16. It was with much assistance from a large community of active option traders that this book earned its title, *The Only Option Trading Book You'll Ever Need*.

My thanks to both TD Ameritrade and the Chicago Board Options Exchange, Incorporated. They were kind enough to permit me to capture and use a total of approximately 200 screen illustrations contained in this book.

Last, but certainly not least, my thanks to my good friends Herm Deary and Dr. Donald Pearson. Both proved the value of this book. Neither had ever traded options, but both were motivated to learn. Herm saw options terminology as a foreign language. The universe of short puts, long calls, strike prices, vertical spreads, and the "Greeks" made no sense. Don read six competing option books cover to cover without entering a single trade. None of these option books put theory into practice. I shared copies of early manuscripts of this book with both Herm and Don. After only a few months, both began to earn incomes as active option traders. It worked!

PREFACE
THE ONLY OPTIONS BOOK YOU'LL EVER NEED

Knowledge is easy. The application of knowledge requires some work. This book is designed to take you to an application level and beyond. It describes ways you can use stock, ETF, financial index, and futures options to produce a steady income. Unfortunately, seasoned traders use a specialized vocabulary which many aspiring traders find daunting, if not completely unintelligible. This is particularly true among option traders. Perhaps they know too much, which can make it difficult to simplify. I once asked a seasoned option trader how to structure a "covered put." After his explanation, I was totally confused. Not wanting to seem ignorant, I accepted his description and retreated — still not knowing what a covered put looked like, or understanding how to structure one. It's possible that you, as my reader, don't know a *put* from a *call*. Perfect! I assure you that you'll know quite a lot about puts and calls when you finish reading this book.

So a primary goal in writing this book is to clarify the confusion and obscure terms by explaining everything in plain language. You'll also find a substantial amount of information about how the market works and how to use the underlying charts, readily available options information, and other common metrics, referred to as "odds enhancers," to scan for trade opportunities.

In particular, you'll be stepped through the use of financial tables, called *option chains*. These are at the core of every option trade. You are also guided through the creation and use of watch lists in order to minimize risk through diversity. You can use these watch lists in concert with the underlying option chains, price charts, and other readily available data, such as market volatility, an option contract's time in force, and its daily average price range, to find option trade opportunities. Numerous trade examples with possible outcomes and trade maintenance techniques are provided for use as models for your own trade setups and risk management strategies.

We've all heard how gambling casinos make money by leveraging what is known as "the house odds." Wouldn't it be great if you could leverage those house odds in your own trading activities? Well believe it or not, you can minimize your own trading risk by using readily available statistical probabilities in addition to learning how to use a variety of other "odds enhancers." The information within this book shows you how to determine your risk level before you enter a trade. This practice gives you the house odds you need to pick more winners than losers.

Of course investment income requires that you have a brokerage account. Several of today's millionaires, such as well–known options trader and retired airline pilot Chuck Hughes, started trading with less than $5,000 in their accounts. One lady named Karen began trading options in 2007 with $10,000 of her own money. After several months of proven success she received another $600,000 from several investors who trusted her option investment strategies. Karen made $41 million in three short years trading options on the financial indices including the S&P 500, NASDAQ, and the Russell 2000. Today Karen's account is approaching 300 million dollars — all from trading options! With a $500,000 brokerage account you can make $1,000 a day if you achieve an annual return of 50%. Sounds impossible doesn't it? But it's not. Many active investors achieve steady annual returns in excess of 60%.

If you're a novice trader this book provides a substantial amount of information to help you understand market dynamics. And even better, it includes dozens of illustrated hands-on learning activities. The book shows you how to use readily available market information to scan for and select high-probability, winning trades. If you are already a serious options trader, this book may give you some new ideas that may enhance some of your own trading practices. Ever do a *covered strangle* or a *Gamma–neutral/Delta–neutral options spread*? Yeah, they're in here too. Or perhaps you can give this book to a friend or family member to help them better understand market dynamics and to introduce them to many of the available online analysis tools. Among these tools are price charts — the "windows to the market."

DISCLAIMER

Trading and investing always involves risk. Any money traded or invested can be lost. You alone are responsible for any trading or investing activity that you undertake. Neither the author or the publisher are licensed, qualified, or authorized to provide trading or investing advise nor will they assume any responsibilities for your actions. Hence, by reading this disclaimer and the information within this book, you understand that there is always risk involved in trading stocks, exchange traded funds, financial indices, bonds, option contracts, futures, and the foreign exchange currency market. The author and publisher make no representations or warranties for your trading success nor will they be held liable for your actions.

thinkorswim® is a registered trademark of TD Ameritrade
TradeMonster® is a registered trademark of OptionsHouse, Inc.
TraderWorkstation® is a registered trademark of Interactive Brokers, Inc.

CONTENTS

Contents

Contents

1 INTRODUCTION

About this Book

There are many option books for both beginners and advanced option traders. But there is none like this one! This one starts at the beginning and progresses to an advanced level. Unlike all the other books, this one guides you through dozens of hands-on option trades — step-by-step.

Options come with a lot of baggage — dozens of specialized terms, like long and short positions, puts, calls, strike prices, and the list goes on. And there are dozens of option trading strategies. This book includes more than sixty. Moreover, this book doesn't assume you know anything about the dynamics of the financial markets or even how to use a price chart. But this book teaches you all of these things, and much, much more. The goal is to take you from a novice to a professional option trader. Your trades will be based on sound trading rules rather than tips, hunches, or emotion. Here's a partial list of what you will learn:

- Vocabulary — those terms and concepts used by professional traders
- Why most experienced traders prefer options
- Factors to consider when selecting a broker

- How the financial markets work
- How to use price charts and popular chart studies, called "odds enhancers"
- Market research techniques
- How to determine oversold at demand/support and overbought at supply/resistance
- The development of watch lists (tables of tradable stocks, exchange-traded funds (ETFs), financial indexes, and futures
- How to develop and use trading rules to limit risk
- How to determine probabilities for success before you trade
- How to manage working trades and when and how to exit
- How to use protective stops and profit targets
- How to enter and manage more than thirty option strategies
- And sixteen *What did you learn* activities to check your progress

You'll also find that new terms are defined as encountered. So you won't have to jump to the terms and definitions appendix when you encounter an unfamiliar term.

Earn $1,000/Day

When this book was conceived the working title was *Earn $1,000/ Day Trading Options*. But as the book progressed, its coverage became comprehensive. So a book originally intended to teach option basics morphed into a complete options tutorial and a comprehensive strategy reference. And as the title implies, it's likely that this is the only option book you'll ever need.

The original *Earn $1,000/Day Trading Options* title was based on a comment made by one of my option trading friends. For several years he earned $1,000 every trading day of the year selling "covered call" option contracts. But it would be dishonest to make this claim for every option trader. It requires study, time, practice, and discipline to become a successful option trader. Being able to earn

$1,000 on each of the 252 trading days of the year is certainly possible, because it happens — a lot. But the probability of achieving this level of success is entirely up to your willingness to invest the time it takes to learn how options work and when and how to trade them.

You must also become familiar with chart analysis, trade scanning techniques, and statistical probabilities, all of which are covered in this book. And of course, you must have a brokerage account that supports your trading strategies. You can't buy $5,000 worth of stock in a $500 account. But you can use options to control $100,000 worth of stock with a $10,000 account. This book explains how this is done.

Once you learn how options work, you must develop and refine a set of trading rules and risk management guidelines. This book was written to help you achieve this too.

These are just some of the topics included within the pages of this book. There are many more. And none of the information is obscure or secret practices known only to experienced option traders. There are no exclusive options trading clubs or secret handshakes. But dozens of straightforward, popular practices learned and used by today's successful option traders are included for you to take away and keep for just the price of this book.

Most option traders who earn $1,000 or more per day are just regular people like you and me. They're not "trading legends" like Karen and Chuck, who were mentioned in the preface and again in the following Successful Traders paragraph. They are hard-working journeymen who have developed a catalog of trading skills. They adhere to a set of rigid trading rules developed over several years of trading experience. They use time-tested strategies, conduct careful analyses, and only enter trades that fit their rules and are well suited to their trading styles, risk tolerances, and personalities. And they make good livings as full- or part-time *professional traders*. They're professional because their trading is a highly disciplined, rules-based business.

Very few professional option traders enter trades every trading day of the year. Of course there are day traders, called *pattern day traders*, who specialize in trading stocks, ETFs, futures, and foreign exchange currencies. Pattern day traders are defined by the Financial Industry Regulatory Authority (FINRA) as those traders who enter four or more trades within five business days. They are required to maintain a balance of at least $25,000 in a *margin* account. A margin account permits traders to borrow trading funds from their brokerage. Their borrowed funds are collateralized by the stocks and cash (or *equity*) held within their accounts. The alternative to a margin account is called a *cash account*. You'll learn all about account types in chapter 4.

Tens of thousands of day traders spend hours each day entering and exiting dozens of daily trades as they watch the prices of underlying stocks or exchange traded funds (ETFs) oscillate up and down throughout the day. (An ETF is a managed fund that contains a "basket" of related stocks.) Day traders enter and exit dozens of 50- to 200-share daily trades in their efforts to make 5 to 10 cents per share per trade. They typically make as many *short* trades (sell stocks in anticipation of price drops) as they do *long* trades (buy stocks in anticipation of price rallies). Only a few day traders specialize in option trading, although many trade futures and foreign exchange (forex) currency pairs. (More about these later.)

Their trading regimen resembles gamblers in a casino, feeding the slots or betting a series of blackjack hands. Some practiced day traders are quite successful, while others fail as their accounts fall below the $25,000 minimum account balance required by FINRA.

Most option traders study the market and then make several trades at a time. This may take from 15 minutes to a few hours per trading session depending on the time spent in analysis and the number of trades typically entered. Then they let their trades *work*. Although they may watch their working trades every day, they often go for days without a single mouse click. A trader that enters and exits several trades each week or month is referred to as a *swing trader*. Some attribute the name to trading "swings" in the prices of the underlying securities. Traders who become fatigued from day trading often convert to swing traders. Swing traders typically trade for price moves of several dollars. Swing traders often make as much or more income than day traders with much less time and effort.

Professional and Novice Traders

Every trade involves moving money from one trader's account to another's. Therefore every trade consists of a buy order and a sell order that are exercised between a willing buyer and a willing seller.

> **Terminology Note:** The terms *bid* and *ask* can be confusing. A willing stock buyer typically places a bid at or slightly below the current price, while a willing stock seller places an ask at or slightly above the current price. In contrast, bid is used to sell an option and ask is used to buy an option. Because this book is about options, bid and ask hereafter relates to options transactions: Bid = sell and Ask = buy. (Confusing, isn't it?)

As mentioned, a buyer and a seller are involved in every trade. And whether they consistently "win" or "lose" has little to do with luck and lots to do with skill. You should know that there is a difference between investors and traders. Investors typical buy and hold assets expecting their assets to appreciate in value over months and even years. Most active traders enter buy and sell orders either daily or every few days in an attempt to *scalp* short term profits. They buy and sell stocks, ETFs, bonds, option contracts (all classified as equities), futures contracts, and foreign exchange currency pairs. *Professional* traders leave little to chance. They know how the market works, develop trading rules based on both study and experience, and rarely dabble in high-risk, low-probability trades. They know the difference between random chance, or "coin flips," and statistical probability.

Professional Traders

Professional traders make their living by taking money from "novice" traders. Professional traders are educated in how to analyze the probability for success well in advance of entering their trades. They develop a set of time-tested trading rules and follow those rules, avoiding the influence of "hot stock tips" or personal emotion. In their trading they become familiar with stock and ETF symbols that represent companies and funds. Each symbol is commonly referred to as the *underlying*. Professional traders study historical price charts for selected symbols, such as AAPL (Apple), ALK (Alaska Airlines), and SPY (the S&P 500 SPDR ETF). They study historical price levels and apply mathematical "odds enhancers" to increase their probability for successful trade outcomes. They use trading rules that include the amount of money they're willing to risk, whether the underlying is currently oversold or overbought, and some even study the current condition of the company or market sector to which it belongs. But more importantly, they evaluate the current market sentiment. And market sentiment, rather than company earnings or its balance sheet, has the most influence on the rallies and drops in the price of a company's stock.

Market sentiment creates *volatility* — high frequency trading. Prices are driven up or down by trader sentiment (or emotion). A company's overall financial condition may remain constant for a year, a month, or a week, while the price of its stock rallies and then drops for no apparent reason. Sentiment is not rationale. This makes it considerably more difficult to measure than a company's financial statement. So volatility is the most influential factor in pricing. We discuss the impact and measures of both historical and implied (or current) volatility — both extremely important to traders — later in this book.

Professional traders also understand the importance of supply and demand. An imbalance in the supply and demand of any commodity establishes value. For example, an oversupply of energy causes a decline in the price of fuel. An undersupply increases demand and causes prices to rise. Supply and demand also operates in the pricing of stock — perhaps even more so than with commodities. If traders begin to sell a stock, the excess supply drives the price of the stock down until it finds a level of "equilibrium." When many traders are actively buying a stock, the extra demand for the stock increases the stock's price. Professional traders know this quite well. They take advantage of supply, demand, and equilibrium. They count on it and use it as a basis for entering and exiting trades. This book discusses the principles of supply and demand, which to most entry level traders is rarely even considered.

Amateur Traders

Most amateur traders view the market as they would a gambling casino. They place a bet on a symbol — often because they feel lucky, heard it mentioned on television, or received a recommendation from a friend. It's the amateur traders who feed the professional traders. And until they are educated about market dynamics, chart analysis, and statistical probabilities, they will continue to feed the professionals. Professionals need and rely on the amateurs.

Novice traders often look at charts to find prices that are either rallying or dropping. When they see a rally, they jump in with buy orders looking for the rally to continue unabated. This is usually buying at a price in which supply quickly becomes greater than demand. Novice buyers create oversupply. The rally screeches to an abrupt halt when supply and demand are out of balance. All the while the professional traders are waiting. Their chart analysis shows them where prices are most likely to reach equilibrium and reverse direction. They patiently wait at either the bottom of a price drop or the top of a price rally, while the novice traders chase the rallies with buy orders and follow the price drops with sell orders.

Many people with sizable accounts use financial managers rather than attempting to trade the market themselves. They realize their limitations. So they delegate the management of their money to an individual money manager or financial management company. Some are satisfied with a 4% to 6% annual return net of management fees, in spite of a 3% to 5% annual loss caused by inflation.

A fortunate few who recognize their own limitations and the poor return they receive from their money managers choose an alternate strategy. Some find they can do much better buying medium- to high-yield dividend stocks. Of course there is always a degree of risk from declines in underlying dividend stock values. On the upside, they no longer have to pay management fees. And the dividends are typically reliable from old-line companies and well-managed master limited partnerships (MLPs).

Still others opt for market education. Although only a handful, these individuals are ambitious enough to invest the time and tuition expense to learn how the market works and how they can exploit that knowledge to manage their own money. These individuals learn much of what's written on the pages of this book.

It is said that no one cares about your money as much as you do. Perhaps this is the most compelling incentive to learning how to buy and sell stocks or even better, how to trade options.

Successful Traders

Consider what the following three people have accomplished. Probably like you, all three started from scratch. All spent time and energy studying the market, developing trading rules, and operating in a highly disciplined, business-like manner.

Floyd Earns $1,000 per Day Trading Options

Floyd is a close personal acquaintance of one of my best friends and golfing buddies. My friend mentioned that Floyd had quit his job in his early forties and now made a good living trading the market. He had no idea what Floyd was doing or, for that matter, what he traded. But whatever it was, Floyd was making a very good living at home.

We were teeing up on a long, uphill par three and waiting for the group ahead to clear the green. "Herm tells me you're a trader, Floyd," I said. "What kind of trading do you do?"

"I trade covered call option contracts. When I began trading my goal was to make at least $1,000 each trading day. I'd start in the morning when the market opened, and I was always done before lunchtime. Then I'd have my afternoons free to run errands or play a round of golf."

NOTE The covered call option strategy is explained in detail in chapter 14.

"How many stocks do you watch?" I asked.

"I usually keep a list of between 50 and 60 stocks. Sometimes they get called away, but I keep an eye on them and then get back in when it makes sense. And I'll add new stocks to my list and take others off when they don't offer the return I want."

The group in front of us cleared the green and we continued our round. But Floyd's story definitely planted some seeds. I needed to learn even more about options. Although my dividend stocks were yielding more than a 12% annual return, and I was also dabbling in a few simple option trade strategies at the time, I decided it was time to learn much more about options. I enrolled in intensive technical analysis, options, advanced options, and futures courses. I've been an active trader ever since. I continued to learn and trade and learn. And now I teach options.

Karen Made $41 Million Trading Index Options in Three Years

Karen "Supertrader" is what she's called in her interviews. You can watch those interviews on YouTube using the following links, which were available when this book was written.

1. https://www.youtube.com/watch?v=cXy9HoWX0es
2. https://www.youtube.com/watch?v=BquDGE9KxZQ
3. https://www.youtube.com/watch?v=8yt51STpZ5I
4. https://www.youtube.com/watch?v=586eEoOL_i4

Also try Googling *Karen Supertrader* if necessary. As you'll see from the videos, after retiring from her accounting job at a brick and mining company in North Carolina, Karen took several trading courses from TD Ameritrade's Investools educational and market research subsidiary. She began trading with $10,000 of her own money. A little less than a year later, she reluctantly agreed to accept approximately $700,000 from others, including her old boss, who saw her option trading success. By developing a rules-based trading system, Karen was able to make $41 million dollars trading financial index options that included the S&P 500, NASDAQ, Russell 2000, and a few others. As you will see in the above mentioned YouTube videos, Karen works in a Nashville office of six. She and four others are full-time traders and one staffer keeps the books. By the fall of 2015, just eight years after she began trading options, Karen's income was approaching 300 million dollars. Unfortunately, in 2016, the SEC began investigating irregularities in bookkeeping practices. However, this does not minimize the income achieved through options trading.

Chuck (Seven-Time World Champion Trader)

Chuck retired from his job as a commercial pilot while still in his early 40s. He'd been trading the market for a while and decided that he could achieve financial security for himself and his family by quitting his job and going into full-time trading. He started his trading with a $4,600 trading account. Chuck developed and meticulously followed a set of option trading rules that he developed himself.

In his first two years of full-time trading, Chuck earned over $460,000 in trading profits. Like most of us, Chuck's goal was to achieve some level of financial security. But he surpassed financial security by achieving substantial wealth. Chuck entered and won or placed in several international trading competitions using his trading system — which, like Floyd's, was originally based primarily on simple covered call options. As previously mentioned, trading covered calls is described in detail in chapter 14.

Is It Really That Easy?

Not everyone is a "natural" trader, just as not everyone can sing on key or drive a golf ball straight down the middle of the fairway. Achieving a high level of success requires a strong desire, ability, knowledge, lots of practice, and discipline. This book guides you through a number of processes that teach you the mechanics of trade analysis, scanning, and rules-based trading setups. All require practice. The rest is up to you.

Fortunately, most trading platforms offer simulated or *paper* trading. Some, like thinkorswim®, also provide *back trades*. This feature permits users to examine historical market data on thousands of stocks, ETFs, and financial indexes (like the S&P 500 or NASDAQ). Several years of daily open, close, high, and low prices are available. A calendar lets you walk through each day of an entire trade from entry to exit. This data permits users to test option trading strategies, including the trading setups, to see how they would have actually performed. So before you begin putting real money on untested trades, you can see how they would have performed using actual daily price data. Of course historical prices are not predictors of future prices. You'll find more information about price levels and analysis in chapter 7.

It Takes Money to Make Money

The old saw "it takes money to make money" is not without merit, especially for those who invest in the financial market. As a trader, especially an option trader, your goal is to grow your account. If you spend the option trading income that flows into your account, you'll never see progress. So do whatever you can to preserve and grow your capital. As your account grows, your income will grow because you'll be able to make larger trades with larger returns.

If you're familiar with the *Rule of 72*, you understand that a 10% interest rate doubles an investment in 7.2 years. Of course, if you withdraw money from your account, doubling your money in 7.2 years can never happen. But if you're satisfied with a 10% return on your account, you may want to consider holding a basket of dividend stocks. However, those stocks may decline in value. And annual inflation will also punish you — both result in a loss of principle value.

Account Size

A 5% return on a $10,000 investment is $500, while the same 5% return on a $500,000 account is $25,000. It's obvious that your income potential is multiplied by the size of your account. It follows that one of your goals should be to increase the size of your account. That's precisely what Floyd, Karen, and Chuck did. And as their accounts grew, their return on capital grew in proportion. Today, Karen and her staff trade 2500 option contracts at a time. There's 100 shares in a standard option contract. This means they're trading 250,000 shares in a single trade!

Return Potential

A large trading account provides more opportunity for income. The potential for a higher return increases as the size of the account increases. You can make more trades and larger trades to increase your income. And making more trades also increases your ability to diversify. That is, you can trade a greater number of underlying symbols. This spreads your risk. Growing your account adds both flexibility and trading "muscle." So your number one goal is to grow your account for diversification and to reduce risk.

Risk Management

Risk management is always a top trading priority. First, determine the amount of money you are putting at risk for every trade you make. Here's a simple example. You buy 100 shares of XYZ stock for $30 per share and simultaneously enter a $28 "good till canceled" protective stop. (The common acronym for good till canceled is GTC.) Entering a buy order and a protective stop at the same time is called a bracketed trade. Some traders enter a third leg as a profit target. Bracketed trades are alluded to several times later in this book.

> Good till cancelled (GTC) and stop orders were discontinued by both the NYSE and NASDAQ stock exchanges effective March 16, 2016. However, both GTC and stop orders are still maintained on your broker's trading platform and exercised as before.

Some of us have heard stories about people who "bet the farm" on one or two stocks and lost everything. So in addition to understanding how much money a trade can lose, diversity is also a recommended risk management policy. This book presents much more information about risk management — always a vital part of your trading strategy and account management.

Trading as a Full-Time Job

If you haven't already read the disclaimer in the front of this book, you should. It tells you that trading can be risky, and that you are personally responsible for every trade you make. Having said this, if you understand how the market works through education and experience and develop one or more high-probability trading strategies, you can be successful. Your trading can even become a full-time occupation, and you won't have to make those daily round-trip drives to your workplace.

However, there are several full-time traders who have decided that they need the freedom from distractions during trading hours. Trading at home can be chaotic as you're constantly barraged by interruptions from your mate and the kids. So if you're unable to concentrate on your trading activities, you may want to find another location in which to operate your trading business.

Investor Education

There are many trading education resources. And, of course, there are many books. (But none quite like this one!) Investment courses are offered by brokerages, private companies, community colleges, online learning websites, and investment seminars.

Option Books

Trading options can be a complicated topic. That's why so many books have been written on the subject. As with all books, some are instructive while others seem to confuse their readers rather than to clarify. Lawrence McMillan's *Options as a Strategic Investment* and Joe Duartee's *Trading Options for Dummies* can both be instructive. Unfortunately, many option books start using the obscure option terminology on page 1 without clarifying examples. And the trades are described in narrative rather than in a step-by-step "learn-by-doing" sequence. You've already noticed that this book hasn't buried you in jargon. It does mention covered calls as something that is clarified in a later chapter.

Before you can be a successful option trader, you must know something about how the market works. More precisely, you must develop a foundation in how to:

- Read price charts
- Understand the effect of volatility and time on risk
- Understand and apply technical studies
- Construct watch lists

- Scan for trade setups
- Understand trade types and durations
- Understand option contracts, obligations, rights, risks, and rewards
- Know what *calls* and *puts* are and how they respond to changes in prices
- Be familiar with *option chains* (financial tables that correspond to option contracts)
- Learn option terminology
- Know how the *Greeks* work (values listed in the columns of option chains)
- Use readily available statistical probabilities
- Understand the effect of open interest and current trading volume
- Learn to choose option trading strategies that suit current market conditions

As you can see from the above list, you must be able to develop a fact-based bias about the underlying optionable stock, ETF, financial index, or future. Only then should you consider the option trade itself.

Unlike the other books, this is a hands-on tutorial rather than just a narrative. To achieve a thorough understanding of option trading, the book includes more than thirty carefully designed hands-on analysis, scanning, and trading procedures. These procedures include goals, setups, scanning, trade entry, clarifying option chain and risk graph illustrations, and trade management techniques. The illustrations were captured from TD Ameritrade's thinkorswim® trading application. But if you are not a thinkorswim® user, you can still examine charts, option chains, and risk graphs on your own brokerage's website. Or you can use sites like stockcharts.com and finance.yahoo.com. The Yahoo site lets you examine option chains for most symbols, and you can even create and store your own watch lists on Yahoo's site as well as several others.

Trading Education Providers

There are several good trading education companies, as well as educational websites. A few of these are listed below. You can also Google entries like "stock market education," "technical analysis," "candlestick charts," or "option education."

Investools

Investools, a subsidiary of TD Ameritrade, provides both online and live training programs. The author has taken both live and online Investools courses and found them to be both useful and professionally designed. Investools also provides a number of excellent analytical tools. A "Big Chart" interface breaks down which market subsectors are currently "in favor," which are "out of favor," and which subsectors are in transition. Specific stock symbols that comprise each of the market subsectors are also listed. Supporting charts with oversold/overbought indicators plus several other popular technical studies are displayed. Ranking information is also provided for each of the underlying stocks to provide insight to metrics such as trends in sales, revenues, and financial strength or weakness.

Brokerage-Supplied Education

Many brokerages provide online trading education and platform training in the form of webinars and online instruction. For example, TD Ameritrade's thinkorswim® trading platform provides access to a large number of webinars that can be viewed either live or from a list of archived presentations. Many brokerages, including but certainly not limited to Fidelity, Charles Schwab, Interactive Brokers, and OptionsHouse, also provide trading education. Many offer live coaching as well.

Online Trading Academy (OTA)

The author attended several trading courses at the Irving, Texas branch of the Online Trading Academy. OTA is the official training company of the NASDAQ and Singapore Stock Exchange, among others. Based in California, it has 31 training centers worldwide in locations like Tokyo, London, and Dubai in addition to several U.S. branches. To their credit, the courses were outstanding in content, delivery, and supporting class materials. The courses included both platform instruction and hands-on learning using a PC-based trading application provided by the Florida-based TradeStation brokerage.

Although OTA recommends use of the TradeStation application, the TD Ameritrade's thinkorswim® platform was used by one of OTA's highly qualified options class instructors. That instructor, who makes his living trading options, preferred thinkorswim®'s options trading interface over all others he's examined. Another options instructor stuck with TradeStation's options interface, which supported both classroom instruction and options trading quite well. The author has used the downloadable TradeStation, thinkorswim®, and Traders Workstation applications in addition to web-based applications from Option House's (TradeMonster), E★Trade, TD Ameritrade, and Scottrade. All are suitable for most traders. Although all option chains are not identical in look and feel, once you understand how to use one, most are quite adequate for your options trading needs.

Community College Courses

Some community colleges offer courses in different trading venues that include stocks, options, and futures. I know a few people who have taken a community college course in trading options and never learned enough to test their newfound knowledge. Perhaps that was the problem. They never moved from the basic knowledge level to the application and analysis levels. This is a common problem with books that describe trading. While background knowledge is important, it doesn't compare with hands-on trial and error. So graduates of these courses are often unable or unwilling to risk a trade.

Online Training and Financial Sites

There are several websites that provide courses in trading. Many focus on the use of price charts, chart patterns, and the stock market. Some provide good narratives on option strategies and provide examples with *risk profiles* (diagrams that show an option trade's potential for profit or loss based on the price movement of the underlying stock, ETF, future, and financial index — all considered "equities." The use of risk profiles is introduced and described in some detail in chapter 14.

A partial list of websites is presented in the following paragraphs. All were valid when this book was written. Consider Googling OPTION EDUCATION to find these and several other useful sites.

Chicago Board of Exchange — The Chicago Board of Exchange website is available at cboe.com. It includes a wealth of useful information for option traders, all available at no charge. Included are education, lists of weekly options (option contracts that expire each Friday when the market closes), a margin calculator (many traders borrow margin from their brokerage for trading; the margin is collateralized by stock held in the trader's account), and much more. The CBOE is responsible for maintaining and providing live options data that is used by their client brokerages. Among its functions is the calculation and delivery of option pricing, called *premium*.

Investopedia.com — Investopedia provides an expansive website on investing and trading. The options section is accessed using http://www.investopedia.com/tags/options/. Numerous option setups with supporting narrative and risk profiles are available.

Tastytrade.com/tt/learn — This is an excellent website for both learning and commentary by experienced traders. Both live and archived trading shows are available.

Alpha7 Trading Academy — This is another site that offers market trading courses with access to online coaching and a chat room. You can examine it at https://alpha7trading.com. Although the author read the information posted on their website, he is not familiar with their training program and therefore cannot comment.

AlgoTrading — This site teaches mathematical algorithms used in stock scanners. The algorithms are intended to search and return a list of those stocks that meet certain price and volatility patterns. The training is intended for experienced traders who want to learn how to write scanning code.

Trade2win.com — This site provides a substantial amount of options information and forums for option traders.

Finviz.com — This is a popular financial research site that is available at no charge. It includes *heat maps* that show red, yellow, and green symbol swatches to indicate price drops, neutrality, or rallies for underlying symbols. Stock charts and lists of both high and low performing symbols are also provided.

Finance.yahoo.com — This is a free financial research resource that provides financial reports, analyst opinions, insider transactions, and option chains on thousands of underlying symbols. You can also create and use your own personal watch lists. Other websites from sources like Google and Microsoft provide similar information.

Marketwatch.com/optionscenter — The Marketwatch site includes a substantial amount of financial information at no charge. One of its features is the ability to view option chains for selected symbols. As with the Yahoo website, you can also create your own personal watch list on this website.

Stockcharts.com — Examine stock charts by symbol, current prices, *heat maps* (rallying and dropping prices by symbol), common stock chart patterns, and more.

Others — There are many other options-specific websites that can be Googled. Type words like **trading**, **options**, **stock charts** to view a long list of option- and chart-related websites.

Trading in Isolation

Trading in isolation is a lonely activity. It involves sitting in front of a computer and examining charts in an attempt to find reasonable trades. Not only is it lonely, it can be deadly boring, exhausting, and drives some people whacky. Without someone there to discuss prospective trade candidates or strategies, your trading is done in total seclusion. There's no one to listen to your ideas or to provide you with constructive feedback. This is the way most people trade — alone — unable to discuss ideas or learn from the experience of others.

Trading Within a Community of Traders

In my first technical analysis course the instructor emphasized the need to trade in a community of active traders. Learn, teach, and share with each other to see what's working and what's not. That was good advice. We passed around a sheet of notebook paper to see how many students might be interested in forming a group. We decided to meet and share on the last Saturday of each month. Almost everyone signed up. That was a few years ago. Our group of more than 150 members merged with a similar group. We now have more than 450 members who can attend our monthly meetings.

Trading Clubs (IBD, DOC, NTXISC, etc.)

The trading club mentioned above was named the North Texas Investment Strategies Club (ntxisc.org), which merged with the Investor's Business Daily "Meetup." The Dallas Options Trading

Club is another popular regional trading club that specializes in options. The members of these groups find them useful as a continuing source of education and fellowship.

Small Groups

You do not need a large group of traders to form a group. There are hundreds of small groups of active traders that meet periodically at places like Starbucks, Panera Bread, or in restaurant meeting rooms like IHOP or Denny's. A common factor is access to Wi-Fi and a way to show computer screens, either up close for small groups or projected for larger groups. If you're trading in isolation and have friends who are also traders, consider contacting them for a meet. Your small group may grow into a large one. You can also Google trading groups to see if one already exists in your area.

What You Learned

Questions are included at the end of each chapter for your use. Answer keys to the question are available in the appendix of this book. There are no "trick questions," as every answer can be found within the pages of this book. Without determining what you either learned or already know, it's difficult to know if you're ready to apply your knowledge to trading and managing working option contracts. As emphasized several times, begin with simulation. Almost every trading platform provides *paper* (or simulated) *trading*. Simulation is an excellent way to test the option trading strategies described in chapters 14 and 15. By trading on paper, you will learn the steps involved in entering and monitoring working trades. You will even see the profits and losses for each trade. Your goal is to find those strategies that work best, and to develop a trading style. Many who trade options avoid the ownership of stock. They collect premium by using short puts and strangles, iron condors, diagonal spreads, and long straddles on volatile stocks. With the exception of being done in isolation, it can even be more fun than Monopoly.

What did you learn in chapter 1?

1. Is it possible to earn $1,000/day trading options? ☐ YES ☐ NO
2. How many trading days are in a calendar year?
3. Traders who enter 4 or more trades within 5 business days are _____ _____ traders, and must maintain a minimum margin account balance of $ _____.
4. Every trade involves the transfer of money from one trader's _____ to another's.
5. Every trade includes a buy and sell order between a _____ _____and_____ _____.
6. In option trading, Bid = _____ and Ask = _____.
7. A trader is said to *scalp* working trades for short-term _____.
8. Professional traders make their living by taking money from _____ _____.
9. Professional traders develop and then use time-tested_____.
10. Novice traders typically buy when prices are _____ and sell when prices are_____.
11. Floyd made $1,000 per day trading _____ _____ options on a list of stocks.
12. Karen made $___ _____in three years trading financial index options.
13. Chuck won international trading competitions __ times by trading options.
14. It takes _____ to make money.
15. _____ _____ is always a top trading priority.
16. Trading involves _____.
17. Who is responsible for the outcome of trades? _____ _____ .
18. Develop a fact-based _____ before trading.
19. Most brokerages provide _____ and platform training.
20. To find option education, do a web search on the words _____ _____.

2   WHY WE TRADE OPTIONS

Financial Leverage

Simply stated, financial leverage is using an investment instrument that provides a higher rate of return using a smaller amount of money. Trading options offers substantial financial leverage. This is precisely why trading options is so popular among so many experienced traders. For a few hundred dollars an option trader can control the price movement in shares of stock worth tens of thousands of dollars. If the price of the underlying stock rallies or drops — in accordance with the trader's analysis — the return on a few hundred dollars can be in the thousands of dollars. Indeed, this is leverage!

It's About Premium!

Options are financial derivatives of stocks, exchange traded funds (ETFs), financial indices, like the S&P 500 (symbol SPX), and futures. (Stocks and ETFs are referred to as equities). Instead of buying or selling a stock or an ETF, option traders buy and sell option contracts by paying or receiving premium — the current value of an option contract at a given option price. Option buyers pay premium while option sellers receive premium. This premium value is mathematically derived from the current market price and trading volume of the underlying equity. Option premiums increase and decrease as the price of the underlying equity fluctuates up and down. It follows that option traders, just like stock traders, want to buy low and sell high. Or, the option seller wants to sell high and buy back low and keep the difference as profit.

Consider the premium homeowners pay for an insurance policy. A homeowner may pay $2,000 each year for homeowner's insurance on a $500,000 house. If the house is destroyed by a storm during the life of the insurance contract, the homeowner receives the face value of the policy. For a $2,000 premium the homeowner receives $500,000. But if the same storm strikes the day after the policy expires without the homeowner's renewal, the insurance company is "off the hook," and the homeowner receives nothing.

Another dynamic of insurance policy premium is how it drops in value with time. Six months after the same homeowner paid $2,000 in premium he decides to sell his house and move to another state. The insurance company returns the value left in his policy, which would be around $1,000.

Option contracts work this way too. Every option contract has an expiration date. As an option contract nears its expiration date, a dramatic drop in premium value occurs. Option premium behaves like insurance premium. As an option contract nears expiration, the premium is reduced to a fraction of its original value. Hence, passing time is the option buyer's enemy, while nearing contract expiration benefits the option seller.

Option premium sellers, called "option writers" (like insurance policy writers), collect premium from option buyers on the opposite side of their trades. Their goal is for the option contract's premium value to either decline or to expire worthless at the contract's expiration date. Option sellers typically choose option contracts that expire within a matter of several days to weeks. Too much time gives their position time to turn against them. Premium values decline with time and as the price of the underlying equity either drops or rallies in favor of the option trader's position. (This varies based on the trader's strategy and position, which is discussed in detail a little later.)

Option premium buyers look for trades in which they can buy low and sell high. An option buyer has a strong directional bias. The buyer wants the price of the underlying equity to make a strong price move in his or her favor. For example, a buyer may be willing to pay 50 cents per share in premium with a goal of selling the position for $1.00 per share — a 100% return in profit. Because time is an option buyer's enemy, buyers normally select option contracts that expire in more than 90 days. Some buy option contracts on up-trending stocks that expire in more than a year, called LEAPS (Long-Term Equity Anticipation Securities). Buying LEAPS options gives the underlying equity a year or more to move in the buyer's favor. Buying short-term option contracts increase the buyer's risk; the option's premium declines rapidly as it approaches contract expiration. This greatly reduces the probability of the price of the underlying security making a strong enough price movement to benefit the buyer's position.

Premium values are displayed on financial tables called *option chains*. You'll notice Bid, Ask, and Mark columns. Before the automation of option values, individual traders (bidders and askers) negotiated option prices. The Mark (market price) is now derived using mathematical equations that include numerous variables linked to the underlying security's market price, trade *volatility* (the current buying and selling volume), time remaining till expiration, and the current interest rate. An illustration of an option chain is provided in the next paragraph. Note that the data changes instantaneously with price movements and trade volatility of the underlying.

Pulling Back the Curtain — The Option Chain

Before examining two option trade examples, a simple option chain illustration is provided in figure 2–1. Traders use option chains to evaluate and trade option contracts. As mentioned, option chains are financial tables that display option contract expiration dates and premium values that exist above and below the current price of the underlying equity. Each listed price is called a *strike price*. Strike prices are displayed vertically down the center of the table. The strike price that is closest to the current price of the underlying equity is said to be *at the money* — just another example of option trading jargon. Look at the following illustration and the terms that correspond to the numbered keys.

Figure 2–1. A Simple Option Chain Example for Stock Symbol DAL

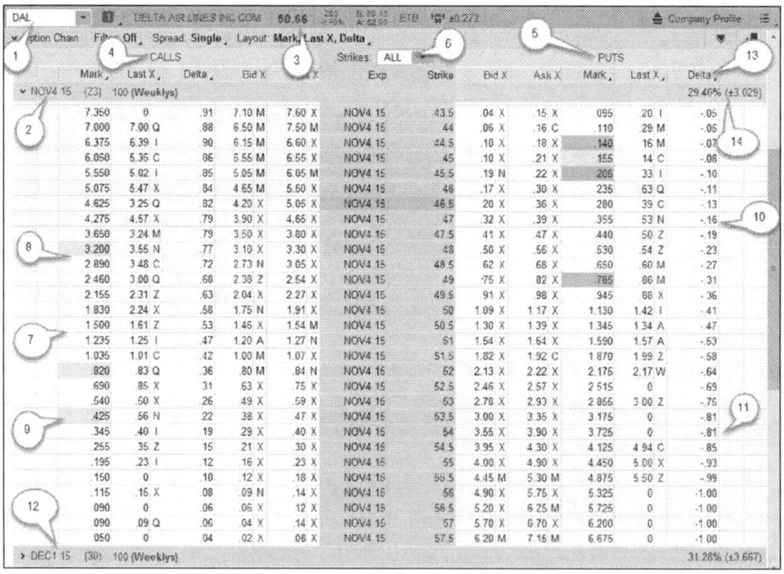

DAL | DELTA AIR LINES INC COM 50.66 | ETB | Company Profile
Option Chain | Filter: Off | Spread: Single | Layout: Mark, Last X, Delta
Strikes: ALL

CALLS Mark	Last X	Delta	Bid X	Ask X	Exp	Strike	PUTS Bid X	Ask X	Mark	Last X	Delta
NOV4 15 (23) 100 (Weeklys)											29.46% (±3.029)
7.350	0	.91	7.10 M	7.60 X	NOV4 15	43.5	.04 X	.15 X	.095	.20 I	-.05
7.000	7.00 Q	.88	6.50 M	7.50 M	NOV4 15	44	.06 X	.16 C	.110	.29 M	-.05
6.375	6.39 I	.90	6.15 M	6.60 X	NOV4 15	44.5	.10 X	.18 X	.140	.16 M	-.07
6.050	5.35 C	.86	5.55 M	6.55 X	NOV4 15	45	.10 X	.21 X	.155	.14 C	-.08
5.550	5.02 I	.85	5.05 M	6.05 M	NOV4 15	45.5	.19 N	.22 X	.205	.33 I	-.10
5.075	5.47 X	.84	4.65 M	5.60 X	NOV4 15	46	.17 X	.30 X	.235	.63 Q	-.11
4.625	3.25 Q	.82	4.20 X	5.05 X	NOV4 15	46.5	.20 X	.36 X	.280	.39 C	-.13
4.275	4.57 X	.79	3.90 X	4.65 X	NOV4 15	47	.32 X	.39 X	.355	.53 N	-.16
3.650	3.24 M	.79	3.50 X	3.80 X	NOV4 15	47.5	.41 X	.47 X	.440	.50 Z	-.19
3.200	3.55 N	.77	3.10 X	3.30 X	NOV4 15	48	.50 X	.56 X	.530	.54 Z	-.23
2.890	3.48 C	.72	2.73 N	3.05 X	NOV4 15	48.5	.62 X	.68 X	.650	.60 M	-.27
2.460	3.00 Q	.68	2.38 Z	2.54 X	NOV4 15	49	.75 X	.82 X	.765	.86 M	-.31
2.155	2.31 Z	.63	2.04 X	2.27 X	NOV4 15	49.5	.91 X	.98 X	.945	.86 X	-.36
1.830	2.24 X	.58	1.75 N	1.91 X	NOV4 15	50	1.09 X	1.17 X	1.130	1.42 I	-.41
1.500	1.61 Z	.53	1.46 X	1.54 M	NOV4 15	50.5	1.30 X	1.39 X	1.345	1.34 A	-.47
1.235	1.25 I	.47	1.20 A	1.27 N	NOV4 15	51	1.54 X	1.64 X	1.590	1.57 A	-.53
1.035	1.01 C	.42	1.00 M	1.07 X	NOV4 15	51.5	1.82 X	1.92 C	1.870	1.99 Z	-.58
.820	.83 Q	.36	.80 M	.84 N	NOV4 15	52	2.13 X	2.22 X	2.175	2.17 W	-.64
.690	.85 X	.31	.63 X	.75 X	NOV4 15	52.5	2.46 X	2.57 X	2.515	0	-.69
.540	.50 X	.26	.49 X	.59 X	NOV4 15	53	2.78 X	2.93 X	2.855	3.00 Z	-.75
.425	.56 N	.22	.38 X	.47 X	NOV4 15	53.5	3.00 X	3.35 X	3.175	0	-.81
.345	.40 I	.19	.29 X	.40 X	NOV4 15	54	3.55 X	3.90 X	3.725	0	-.81
.255	.35 Z	.15	.21 X	.30 X	NOV4 15	54.5	3.95 X	4.30 X	4.125	4.94 C	-.85
.195	.23 I	.12	.16 X	.23 X	NOV4 15	55	4.00 X	4.90 X	4.450	5.00 X	-.93
.150	0	.10	.12 X	.18 X	NOV4 15	55.5	4.45 M	5.30 M	4.875	5.50 Z	-.99
.115	.15 X	.08	.09 N	.14 X	NOV4 15	56	4.90 X	5.75 X	5.325	0	-1.00
.090	0	.06	.06 X	.12 X	NOV4 15	56.5	5.20 X	6.25 M	5.725	0	-1.00
.090	.09 Q	.06	.04 X	.14 X	NOV4 15	57	5.70 X	6.70 X	6.200	0	-1.00
.050	0	.04	.02 X	.08 X	NOV4 15	57.5	6.20 M	7.15 M	6.675	0	-1.00
DEC1 15 (30) 100 (Weeklys)											31.28% (±3.667)

For illustration purposes only.

Figure 2–1 Key

1. Symbol of the underlying equity (stock, ETF, financial index, future)
2. Option contract expiration date and number of days that remain till contract expiration
3. Current price of the underlying (the "at the money" price, abbreviated ATM)

4. Calls★: The left-hand side of the option chain lists call contract values (Call premiums increase as the price of the optioned security increases.)

5. Puts★: The right-hand side of the option chain lists put contact values (Put premiums increase as the price of the optioned security decreases.)

6. The number of available contract (or "strike") prices to display; ALL list all available strike prices

7. The closest price to the market price of the underlying security is referred to as being "at the money"

8. In the money (ITM) call contracts: call strike prices below the current price of the underlying

9. Out of the money (OTM) call contracts: call strike prices above the current price of the underlying

10. Out of the money put contracts: put strike prices below the current price of the underlying

11. In the money put contracts: put strike prices above the current price of the underlying

12. The next available option contract expiration date; click to expand and view the next option chain

13. Option chain column headings. Several more useful headings are examined in later chapters.
    a. Bid: selling price of a call (left-hand half) or a put (right-hand half)
    b. Ask: buying price of a call or a put
    c. Mark: The selected option's "market" (premium) price; midway between the Bid and Ask
    d. Last: The last price at which the selected call or put contract traded
    e. Delta: A decimal value that corresponds to the change in an option's price (premium) as compared to a $1.00 change in the price of the underlying stock, ETF, index, etc.

14. The current implied volatility percentage and (± value) is a measure of how much the price of the underlying optioned security is expected to move over the selected period of time; historical volatility measures actual volatility statistics over the same period.

The preceding illustration and terminology introduces you to some of the jargon commonly used by option traders. A few clarifying trade examples follow to illustrate the benefits of trading options. In chapters 14 and 15 you'll learn much more about the use of option chains and how they're used to trade options through a series of hands-on practice activities.

Example 1

Let's look at an example that illustrates financial leverage. A trader studies the price charts and finds a $50 stock that is presently oversold. It is sitting at a historical low, and the company is in a market sector that has recently fallen from favor. But other stocks in the same market sector are beginning to regain favor. Our trader expects the professional institutional traders to buy a few million shares within the next week. The trader's chart analysis supports a price rally from $50 to occur. This price is clearly a historical support level.

The trader buys 100 shares of the $50 stock for $5,000. The stock rallies to $54 and the trader decides to take a profit of $400 (less the commissions, of course). The return on the $5,000 investment is $400, or 8%. Not bad! Now let's look at the same 100 shares as an option contract.

Each standard option contract represents 100 shares in the underlying stock. And every option contract expires on a specific date. The market price (or *Mark*) of $50 call options is $1.00. (As you know, the option's price is referred to as premium — what traders pay when they buy an option or what they receive when they sell an option.) As before, the trader buys one $50 call option contract for $100; the selected contract expires in 90 days. The trader has given the option contract three months to work in his favor. Within eight days the $50 stock rallies to $54. As the price of the stock rallies, the corresponding market volatility increases with brisk trading activity. The higher volatility increases the option's premium. The option trader sells the $50 option contract for $2.00 to close his position. (Recall that the standard option contract represents 100 shares of the underlying stock.) In eight days the trader has doubled the $100 investment. Instead of making an 8% return by purchasing the stock, the trader makes a return of 100% by purchasing the $50 call option. And the trader makes that return in eight short days.

Trading the stock:
Buy 100 shares of stock at $50/share = $5,000 investment
Sell 100 shares of stock at $54/share = $5,400 return (8% return on investment)

Trading the stock option:
Buy 1 $50 100–share option contract at $1.00/share = $100 investment
Sell 1 $54 100–share option contract at $2.00/share = $200 (100% return on investment)

Controlling $5,000 with $100

Also notice that the trader controlled $5,000 worth of stock with a $100 investment. This is leverage! And by trading more option contracts on several different stocks, ETFs, or futures, it's quite possible to reach that $1,000 per day goal.

Flexibility

In addition to financial leverage, traders often enter two or more positions (or legs) within a single option trade. And because it's a single order, they pay one commission! Now look at Example 2.

Example 2

In Example 1 the trader bought one $50 call contract for $100 ($1/share) that expired in 90 days. And he simultaneously sold another $58 option contract that expires in two short weeks. Option contract sellers (writers) receive premium from buyers on the other side of their trades. When our trader sold one $58 call contract he received $0.40 per share × 100 shares for a $40 credit. This little credit in premium reduced the cost of the trade from $100 to $60. Examining both legs of this trade, the trader paid $100 for the $50 call he bought at $1 per share and received $40 for the $58 call contract he sold.

Selling the $50 call contract for $2 per share added to the $40 premium received by selling the $58 call returned a total of $240 on a net investment of $60. This is a whopping 333% yield and illustrates the power of both financial leverage and flexibility provided by options.

Calls and Puts

Both of the preceding examples are based on call contracts. All option strategies involve either buying or selling calls, puts, or a combination of calls and puts. A few strategies also involve buying or selling (shorting) shares of stock. Calls increase in value when the price of the underlying equity rallies. Calls decrease in value when the price of the underlying equity drops. Conversely, puts increase in value when the underlying stock price drops and decrease in value when the stock price rallies. This lets you trade options regardless of where the market is going.

In the preceding examples both option trades involved call contracts, because the trader expected the stock to experience a price rally. More specifically, trading two or more option contracts, or legs, within the same transaction is called a *spread*. Also, when the trader analyzed the price movement and direction on the underlying price charts, it seemed unlikely for the $50 stock to rally more than $5 or $6 in a two-week period. So the $58 call leg was sold for $40 to offset the cost of the $50 call purchased.

Buy, Sell, or Buy and Sell

One of the most attractive features of option contracts is that you can buy and sell either or both puts or calls — all depending on what you expect the underlying's price to do, i.e., rally, drop, or remain neutral (also called moving sideways).

To be a successful trader your expectations must be based on careful analysis rather than on a hunch. Analysis is something that many option books omit. But this book provides a substantial amount of information on how to analyze price charts in order to develop a reasonable bias on price movements. Being able to develop a rational expectation of a price rally, drop, or price neutrality are vital to trading success. In addition to developing a directional bias, option traders examine current volatility and mathematical probability data, also important factors.

Recall how the structure of the second example bought a $50 call and sold a $58 call. Some refer to this structure as a *bull call spread*: buying one $50 call contract for $100 and selling one $58 call contract for a $40 credit. Recall how the $50 contract bought expired in 90 days, while the $58 contract sold expired in two weeks. Having different expiration dates makes the trade a calendar spread — two legs with two different contract expiration dates. So we could call it a *bull call calendar spread*.

But for the time being option strategy names are of little importance. The important thing is to know how a price movement in the underlying security, typically stock, can impact each leg of a trade. So don't worry about the names of spreads. They have names like strangles, straddles, iron condors, collars, butterflies, straps, and dozens more. These are only labels, and these labels will not tell you how each leg of a trade is affected by price movements of the underlying. Once you know how options work, you'll be ready to apply your knowledge to trading. And the many strange-sounding strategy names will become quite familiar with use.

Built-In Hedging Strategies

An attractive feature offered by options is that several strategies offer built-in risk management. This is referred to as hedging. A perfect hedge is said to return 100 percent of your investment, less commissions in case an investment fails to produce the desired results. Realistically, most hedges are considered "insurance" and are used to manage your level of risk by minimizing a possible loss from a trade that goes against you.

A simple example of a stock hedging strategy is when a trader buys a $25 stock and enters a protective stop loss at $24. This limits the maximum loss to $1.00/share if the stock price drops in value. Even if the stock price eventually falls to $15, the $24 stop loss triggers a sell order and the trader only experiences a $1.00 per share loss. At least this is the intended outcome.

Many option strategies include built-in hedges. Like protective stop losses with stock, these can limit a trader's loss. Let's look at a simple example. A trader sells a call option contract and collects a premium of 50 cents per share. As a hedge, the trader also buys a call contract at a slightly higher strike price for 20 cents in premium. The trade nets 30 cents of premium income. This is like buying "insurance" in case the price of the underlying rallies beyond expectations. The insurance leg is used like a protective stop and minimizes loss.

Having a hedge lets you calculate the potential loss before entering a trade. Several other hedging strategies are examined in the chapters that follow.

Rolling for More Profit

There's buying, selling, and *rolling*. Although we've briefly looked at buying and selling, check out rolling. Can we roll our stock trades for more profit? That would be nice, but it simply isn't done. But rolling is regularly done by option traders. Of course you can enter protective stops and profit targets on stock that work until they're triggered. But compared to options, stocks are inflexible. Options provide traders with many more choices and strategies. In fact, some traders use the *collar* options strategy or buy put options to hedge against a drop in the underlying stock's price. But here the narrative is restricted to options.

The ability to roll an option's position is a powerful tool commonly used by option sellers. Rolling from one trade into another is done for different reasons. Option trades are regularly rolled from the current contract expiration to the next expiration date for maintenance purposes, described below. For example, if the strike price of an option positon is *breached*, the seller can buy to close the threatened position and simultaneously sell an identical number of contracts at a safe option (or *strike*) price that expire at a later date. Or rolls are used to collect more profit by closing a profitable position and then selling it again at a later contract expiration date.

Looking at a roll to increase profit, assume you sold either a call or put contract for a $1.00 per share in premium income. When sold, the contract expiration date was four weeks out. After three weeks, the price of the underlying is still close to its original price. With only a few days remaining until contract expiration, the premium has declined to 15 cents from the passage of time, or "time decay" described later. You look at a later contract expiration date, say 30 days out, and notice the premium is hovering around $1.00 again. So wouldn't it be nice if you could pay 15 cents to close your original contract and sell the new one for another dollar? Well this is a typical example of a roll for even more profit. You can roll your position by buying back your original contract, which only has a few days remaining till expiration. At the same time, you sell another option contract that expires in four weeks for another $1.00 per share. So you've netted 85 cents on the first trade, and collect another $1.00 on your new trade. These are two ways to benefit from a roll. And you can just "keep rolling along!"

By rolling from one contract into another, you continue to collect premium over time. In addition, the roll (called a diagonal or calendar spread) is a single transaction. You pay a single commission for two transactions — entering a *buy to close* order on one position and simultaneously entering a *sell to open* order on a second position. Note that diagonal spreads typically include two consecutive expiration dates; a calendar spread skips over the next expiration date to one that expires even farther out in time.

As a preview to what's presented in a substantial amount of detail in later chapters, a few trade examples are provided to show you the steps involved in rolling a current position. Examine the drop-down menu in figure 2–2.

Figure 2–2. Typical Short-Cut Menu Used for Order Management and Analysis

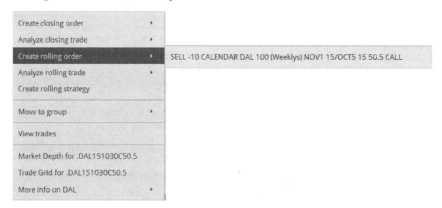

For illustration purposes only.

This shows how a trading platform is used to select an option on stock DAL held within the trader's account. Right-clicking on a listed stock produces a short-cut menu shown. Clicking **Create rolling order** opens a fly-out box that permits the trader to close the front position and sell a later one. Looking at the

default information in the fly-out box, the default roll would do
the following:

1. Sell to open 10 100-share 50.5 option contracts on stock
    DAL that expire the first Friday of November (represented by
    NOV1).
2. Buy to close an equal number of DAL option contracts that
    expire on the fifth Friday of October (represented by OCT5).

Clicking the fly-out box displays the Trade dialog with the corresponding DAL option chain and an order entry bar. The bar is
shown in figure 2–3.

Figure 2–3. A Typical Order Entry Bar Showing a Rolling Order

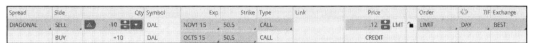

Spread	Side		Qty	Symbol	Exp	Strike	Type	Link	Price			Order	↻	TIF	Exchange
DIAGONAL	SELL		-10	DAL	NOV1 15	50.5	CALL		.12	LMT		LIMIT		DAY	BEST
	BUY		+10	DAL	OCT5 15	50.5	CALL		CREDIT						

For illustration purposes only.

Notice the default roll only provides a credit of 12 cents (the Price).
The trader can modify the expiration (Exp) date and/or adjust the top
Strike price on the top order line to achieve more premium income.
Notice how the option Spread is labeled DIAGONAL. A diagonal
spread rolls into the next available option expiration date. This trade
is a diagonal spread because it rolls from the last Friday in October to
the first Friday in November (Oct5 to Nov1). The trader may decide
to change the NOV1 15 expiration date to the NOV2 15 expiration
date — two expiration dates away. This subtle adjustment changes the
spread name from *diagonal* to *calendar*. Both work identically except a
calendar spread expires at a later date. Adding more time to an option
contract increases premium. However, the extra time gives the trade
more time to work against the trader. This increases risk. Reward is a
function of risk, hence the higher premium.

The trader might also bump up the CREDIT (the price) from 12 cents to 20 cents. But if the price is too high, the trade will not fill and the order will expire unfilled when the market closes at the end of the day. (Notice DAY at the right edge of the order bar tells the trader that the order is good for the current day.) In any event, before entering a trade like the one described here, it's vital to understand the risks associated with longer time periods and vulnerable strike prices. These issues are described in substantial detail beginning in chapter 7.

Trade Maintenance with Stops and Rolls

In addition to rolling out for increased profit, you can also use rolls for trade maintenance. If you find an option trade approaching a loss, it's possible to roll into a new contract that expires at a later date. For example, you may roll a losing position into a *calendar spread* in which you buy back a losing position and sell a new one for either more premium income or for safety. The premium received from selling the second contract offsets part or all of the cost to buy back the original position. You can also *roll up* by simultaneously closing one position and opening a safer position on the same option contract. Option contracts that were bought can also be rolled. Remaining premium can be applied to the roll to offset the new (rolled into) position. But this action may result in further loss. So experienced traders study possible outcomes before spending more money on a bad position.

It's also possible to set stop losses on option contracts. For example, a Bid, Ask, or Mark price can be used to trigger exits from working positions. If the current Mark value of the premium pierces $0.20, an option buyer may want to exit by issuing a sell to close order, while an option seller may want to issue a buy to close order. Like putting protective stops on stocks, option contracts can also be stopped out based on an underlying value. For example, a sell or buy order can be set up to trigger based on any one of several underlying option chain values.

As alluded to earlier, a Delta-triggered stop on an option position might be triggered if the Delta value of a working option becomes "At or below" or "At or above" a specified value. This type of stop triggers a "buy to close" or "buy to open" order in the event Delta pierces a specified value. Delta values are explained briefly later in this chapter and in even more detail in chapter 12.

Although a trader may suffer a loss on the trade, the Delta- or Mark-triggered stop can limit losses and prevent a trade from "blowing out an account." Delta-triggered stops are described in more detail near the end of chapter 14 where trading options on the financial indexes, such as the S&P 500 (symbol SPX), the NASDAQ (symbol NDX) or the Russell 2000 (symbol RUT) are discussed.

Some Terminology: Buying an equity or an option contract is referred to as taking a *long* position. Selling is called taking a *short* position. "She went long on a $50 IBM call" means a trader bought an IBM $50 call contract. "He entered a short $58 IBM call" means a trader sold an IBM $58 call contract. Plus (+) and minus (−) signs are notation used to represent long (+ = buy) and short (− = sell) positions.

The expression **+5 FDX May 2017 50.0 Call @ 2.40** represents buying 5 FedEx $50 call contracts (500 shares) for $2.40 per share that expire on the third Friday of May 2017. Similarly **−3 FDX Apr2 2017 58.0 Put @ 0.85** represents selling 3 $58 put contracts (300 shares) for 85 cents per share that expire on the second Friday of April 2017.

The number following the month abbreviation is used with weekly options that expire at market close of the indicated week. For example, Apr1 is the first Friday of April. Apr2 is the second Friday of April. Apr4 is the fourth Friday of April. When a month is displayed without a number, it means the third Friday of the month — referred to as *expiration Friday*. Prior to the introduction of weekly option contracts, all traditional option contracts expired on the third Friday of the month, hence the term "expiration Friday."

But option traders should know that in spite of the option contracts' officially closing at 4 p.m. on the third Friday, the underlying stock continues trading until the after-hours market closes at 9 p.m.

Extended Trading Hours include pre-market hours from 4:00 a.m. to 9:30 a.m. and after-hours trading from 4:00 p.m. to 8:00 p.m. All times are Eastern Standard Times. These hours exclude special holiday hours.

Third Friday expirations are settled on the following Saturday at 11:59 a.m. Although this is an obscure nuance, it's possible for a trader to exercise an option by contacting the responsible market maker with instructions to exercise the contract if it has rallied or dropped in his or her favor. (Market makers are firms that match buy and sell orders.) Although a rare occurrence, it is important to know what can happen on a third Friday contract expiration, particularly with a long call position that is experiencing a dramatic rally at market close.

Mini Options also exist. These represent 10 shares of the underlying rather than the traditional 100 shares. Mini's were introduced to fit the budgets of traders with smaller accounts.

A.M. Expirations: Most traditional and weekly option contracts expire upon Friday's market close at 4 p.m. The CBOE also offers AM, Tuesday, Wednesday, and Thursday expirations on the SPX financial index, i.e., SPX AM and SPX W options. (See the www.cboe.com website for details.)

Access to Pertinent Information

The amount of supporting information available on an option chain is another reason that option traders are drawn to the option trading venue. Most trading platforms permit traders to add a substantial amount of valuable information to their option chains. You may want to add some of the following columns in order to have a clearer understanding of your probabilities for success. Note that each of the values are listed at every strike price within an option chain. Below are brief descriptions of some of the information available on an option chain. Their use is discussed in detail in chapters 11 and 12.

- Last — The cost (premium) of the most recent put and call trade at each strike price.
- Open Interest — The number of working orders (never trade options with weak open interest). Summing open interest for both calls and puts at all strike prices should total a few thousand. This shows a strong interest level in the selected symbol.
- Probability ITM, OTM, Touching — These are values showing the statistical probabilities of a strike price reaching the market price of the underlying, or becoming *at the money*. ITM is *in the money*, OTM is *out of the money*, and *Touching* is the probability of a strike price reaching the market price of the underlying for the duration of the contract. The probability values are expressed as percentages. Each is based on the time remaining till expiration and current market volatility. A Prob. ITM value of 20% means there's an 80% chance for the strike price to be *out of the money* at contract expiration. Option traders examine probabilities. Some trading platforms do not include Probability ITM or Touching. Without these, option traders either use Probability OTM or a value labeled Delta, which is included on option chains and is approximately equal to the Probability ITM value. Unfortunately, most stock traders are unfamiliar with option chains, so they rarely avail themselves of this valuable information.
- Theta — Theta values tell option traders the amount of premium (option value) that is exiting with the passage of each day.

Theta, which is expressed in dollars and cents, increases as the option contract nears its expiration date. Hence, option premiums lose value rapidly as the option contract nears expiration. A Theta value of .09 tells an option trader that the option contract is losing 9 cents per day per share or $9.00 per day per contract with the passage of each day.

- Delta — The amount of change in the option's premium value relative to a $1.00 change in the price of the underlying. For example, a Delta value of .30 tells traders that a change of $1.00 in the underlying changes the option's premium by 30 cents.

- Vega — A measure of volatility. Vega influences the value of premiums more than any other factor. As volatility increases, risk increases. Increased risk drives up option premiums.

There are many more indicators that can be added to an option chain, but the ones listed above are usually sufficient. Note the *Greek* letters *Theta* and *Delta* are used by mathematicians to represent English words like **time** and **difference**. *Vega*, for **volatility**, is not a Greek letter, but the mathematical constant *Vega* has been in use since 1973 to represent volatility — a variable used in the original *Black-Scholes* formula used to calculate option premium values.

What did you learn in chapter 2?

1. Financial leverage provides a bigger _____with a smaller amount of _____.
2. Options are financial _____ of other equities and indexes.
3. Option traders buy and sell option contracts by paying and collecting _____.
4. _____ _____ are financial tables used to enter and exit option contracts.
5. Every option contract has an _____date.
6. The left-hand side of an option chain lists _____ and the right-hand side lists _____.
7. The closest option price to the market price of the underlying security is said to be ___ _____ _____.
8. Abbreviations: ITM = __ ____ _____, ATM = ___ ___ _____, OTM = ____ __ ____ _____.
9. Example 1 in chapter 2 compares a stock trade to an option trade. The stock trade returned 8% on the investment while the option trade returned _____%.
10. Options offer both financial leverage and _____.
11. What is a *spread* as applied to options? An option trade having two or more _____.
12. Time decay causes the price of option premiums to_____.
13. Simultaneously buying-to-close an option and selling-to-open a new position is referred to as _____.
14. Rolls are used to increase profit. They can also be used for trade _____.
15. Taking a long position means to _____ a stock or an option contract.
16. Standard day trading hours begin at _____ a.m. and end at _____ p.m. Eastern Time.
17. Standard option contracts include 100 shares; mini option contract include ___ shares.

18. Open Interest is the current number of _____ _____.

19. Probability ITM is the statistical probability of an option price becoming ___ ____ _____ at or prior to contract expiration.

20. The value of _____ is a measure of premium exiting an option with each passing day.

3   TRADING PREPARATION

Essential Knowledge

For the purpose of discussion, we'll use the term *equity* as a general term for stock, an ETF, a financial index, and cash. All are considered equities. All can be either directly or indirectly held in a trader's account. Options are financial derivatives of equities. Therefore, the performance of options is tied directly to the performance of the underlying equity.

Successful equity traders know how to time the market. Through analysis of price charts and underlying price patterns, the use of mathematical studies, and relevant economic news, they know when to buy and when to sell. Their chart studies influence their disposition toward the timing of a rally or a drop in the underlying equity's price. They enter their trades based on the results of these studies.

It follows that option traders must know what equity traders know, because their option trades are linked directly to the price movements of the underlying equities. In other words, their expectations of price direction and scale should be based on the same time-tested analytics that equity traders use.

Beyond using basic chart analysis and the application of mathematical studies, successful option traders must also be intimately familiar with the information available within option chains. And they must know exactly how option contracts work in addition to understanding the obligations of option buyers and sellers.

Like equity traders, option traders always have a bias relative to a potential price breakout, either up or down, or for the underlying equity to remain within a narrow price range. These price actions and corresponding market volatility influence the option strategy a trader is likely to use.

Preparation

Before you can trade options you need a brokerage account. Your broker should provide access to trading using either an online, web-based trading application or by providing a downloadable trading application. While there are several good trading applications, the screen shots were taken from the Windows-based thinkorswim® trading application from TD Ameritrade. But nearly every trading application provides access to option chains, charts, and watch lists. This is true for many applications designed to run on Macintosh computers, i-Pads, i-Phones, Android tablets and smartphones, and Windows smartphones.

Once you begin trading in earnest you are going to want a large screen. In fact you may wish to have two to four screens. Multiple screens permit you to synchronize and view watch lists, charts, option chains, and account positions at the same time. The author uses a fast Windows 10-based tower PC computer with two graphic cards and four high-definition monitors. He is connected to the Internet over a high-speed fiber connection. He has three backup devices consisting of a Windows 10 Notebook PC, an Android smartphone that runs TD Ameritrade's mobile trading app, and an Apple iPad tablet.

Setting up your trading tools and applications may be the easiest part of your preparation. Your computers and backup systems can be set up within a week or two. The most important and rigorous part of your preparation is learning how to trade. This book will guide you through the analysis, scanning, and trading processes.

These processes are supported by a combination of narrative and hands-on learning activities supported by annotated screen captures that illustrate the processes used to find, enter, monitor, manage, and close trades. Carefully read the narratives and perform the procedural steps until you're comfortable with the scanning and trading processes. A set of fundamental trading rules are included. Use these as guidelines to develop rules of your own that fit your account size, trading level (or permissions), and risk tolerance.

In regard to your trading level, you must be able to convince your brokerage that you are qualified to trade options. This requires option trading experience. Some brokerages grant permissions based on years of experience. Others require you to pass option tests. Each brokerage grants different levels of trading permissions. Low level trading permissions allow simple, low-risk trading strategies. The highest option trading levels permit the riskiest of option strategies. This includes permission to sell *naked puts* and/or *naked calls*. Naked (also referred to as *uncovered*) involves a high-risk option trade that is not secured (or *covered*) by underlying shares of stock in the trader's brokerage account. When a naked call position is exercised, the trader must acquire and deliver shares of stock or cash to the buyer on the opposite side of the trade. When naked puts are exercised, the stock is put to the trader at the option (strike) price. The trader may pay $50 per share for stock having a market value of $40 per share. When selling uncovered index options, such as the S&P 500 financial index (symbol SPX), the trade is cash settled. When exercised, the trader must deliver cash to the buyer at the current market price; the buyer pays the seller at the option price. The difference may be thousands of dollars.

These *naked* puts and calls are high-risk, high-reward positions that must be carefully monitored. Depending on the number of contracts traded, a single cash-settled naked put option contract on a financial index, such as the NASDAQ or S&P 500, can carry a risk in the tens of millions of dollars. Don't let this scare you. You can't be forced to trade cash-settled option contracts. However, you should know about them and how they work, whether you use them or not. Many people run in terror when they hear about high-risk option trades like these. They're told that options carry substantial risk. And of course they can if the trader doesn't understand how they work.

A close friend told me that he used to trade options until he lost his entire account on a bad trade. It seems that he invested his entire holdings by buying call contracts that were slightly out of the money (above the price of the underlying stock). Within a day of his trade, the underlying stock dropped precipitously. His call premium plummeted as his position (strike price) got farther out of the money with each passing day. He watched his premium drop to less than ten cents per share. But he held on in hopes of a rally. His contract finally expired worthless. He closed his brokerage account and retreated. Apparently my friend didn't understand how options work nor did he have any risk management rules. The operation of options and trade management, including risk management, are both emphasized in this book. Too bad my friend didn't have this book prior to entering that fatal trade.

If you plan on trading a qualified retirement account, like an IRA, you should know that the Securities and Exchange Commission (SEC) disallows any trade that carries unlimited risk. This limits the option strategies you are permitted to use within a qualified retirement account. Having said this, many traders grow their retirement accounts by buying strong stocks and ETFs in concert with stock-covered and cash-covered option contracts. Of course this SEC rule prevents option traders from entering naked option contracts or using other strategies that can result in an unlimited loss.

Terminology and Definitions

Some of the terms and definitions contained in the following paragraphs have already been introduced. A glossary of terms and definitions is included in the appendix at the back of this book. The goal of this section is to introduce common terms that may help you in your communications with other traders, whether they trade stocks, options, futures, or the foreign exchange (FOREX).

Financial Market Terms

A growing number of financial networks use dozens of common stock market terms every day of the week. These terms are much more familiar to most than the more obscure terms, concepts, and strategies used by option traders. Of course there is a substantial overlap, because as you now know, option contracts are derivatives of stocks, ETFs, financial indexes, and ETFs.

Bearish and Bullish

The bulls and the bears have been talked about for years. *Bullish* people anticipate market growth and a strengthening economy. We say they have a *bullish* bias. *Bearish* traders anticipate a declining market and a weakening economy.

They have a *bearish* bias. Both traits are often referred to as *trader sentiment*. It's trader sentiment that drives short-term prices up and down in spite of the financial condition of the underlying enterprise. Emotion reigns!

Having biases based on rational price analyses can lead to profitable trades. Before trading either a stock or an option contract, experienced traders develop a bullish or bearish bias based on analysis. Getting tips from one of the talking heads that appear on those high-definition flat-screens (and that babble on to fill air time) is not a recommended way to develop bias. Instead, learn how to mine for yourself by analyzing price charts. Look at the long- and short-term price trends. Apply available mathematical studies that show current implied volatility, the average price range of the underlying, the current oversold or overbought condition, and the underlying's proximity to historical support or resistance levels. There are many powerful chart studies that are useful in helping you develop a bullish or bearish bias.

Often the behavior of the underlying is indiscernible. Its price charts are choppy or scattered, making it impossible to develop a strong bias. Leave it! Continue to search for a price pattern that provides clarity. Look for distinctive patterns and underlying studies that signal price breakouts or sideways moves that are well suited for certain option trades.

In contrast, the talking heads give trading advice that's usually based on a company's fundamentals. They invite company CEOs to extol the positive attributes of the company and its future outlook. This can be useful information for buy-and-hold stock and ETF traders or option traders who buy and hold LEAPS (long term option contracts). But underlying company fundamentals are not strongly coupled to short term price movements. Short term prices are influenced by trader sentiment, which translates to current volatility (referred to as *implied volatility*). And trader sentiment can often be irrational. Novice traders follow the herd; professional traders lead the herd.

Long Stock

Traders take a long position in a stock trade when they buy a number of shares in that stock. An example of a long stock position would be if a trader buys 100 shares of a $50 stock and then sells the stock when it rallies to $55 for a profit of $500.

Short Stock

Traders short a stock by selling it and then buying it back after a drop in price. For example, if a trader shorts 100 shares of a $50 stock and then enters a *buy-to-cover* order when the stock drops to $45, the trader collects the $5.00 per share, or $500. Shorting a stock pays the trader the difference in the price drop for each share of stock sold (or *shorted*). Shorting stock is financed by the trader's *margin account*, without which shorting stock and other securities couldn't exist.

Price Movements

Traders watch the price charts for signals, of which there are many. Price trends, chart patterns, candlestick chart shapes, price break-outs, and moving average crossovers are just a few of the signals traders look for.

Most trading platforms offer several chart types. For years traders looked at line charts and bar charts. Japanese candlestick charts were adopted in the 1990s. These were developed by Japanese traders in the early 1700s to chart the price of rice futures. Because they are visually superior to the traditional bar and line charts that were in use for many years in western financial markets, candlestick charts were quickly adopted in place of bar charts. However, line charts are still in daily use by many traders, as they reveal long-term price trends, reduce noise, and amplify price breakout signals.

Following are examples of a line chart, bar chart, and a Japanese candlestick chart. As you quickly see, candlestick charts are easier to read. The bottom and top of each candle shows the opening and closing price for the selected time interval. The width of the candle body corresponds to the selected time interval, i.e., week, day, hour, minute, etc. A green or hollow candle has a closing price that is higher than the opening price. Red or black candles designate a price drop from the time interval's opening price to its closing price.

There are also *tic* charts. Tic-based charts print a candle after a specified number of trades are transacted. For example, one tic may represent a series of 300 trades. Normal time-interval charts print a candle for a single trade or a thousand trades. So it's important to put volume bars on time interval charts to improve understanding.

Figure 3–1. Price Chart Examples

Line Chart	Bar Chart	Candlestick Chart
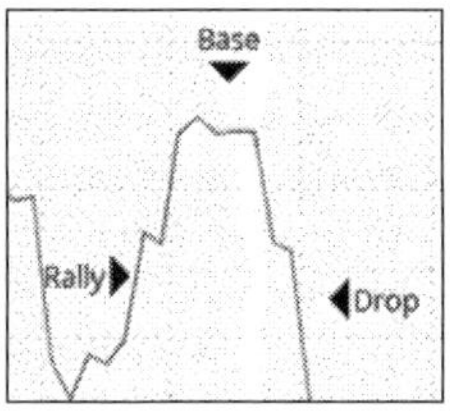	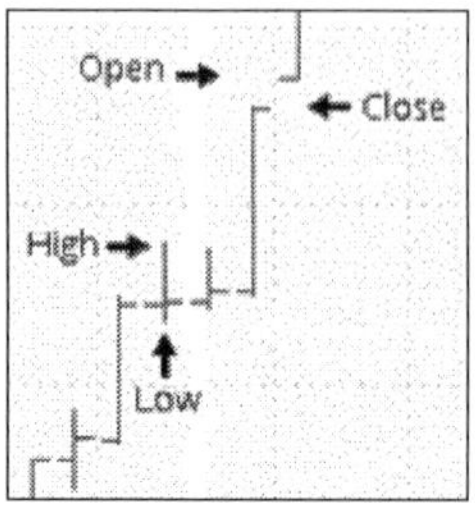	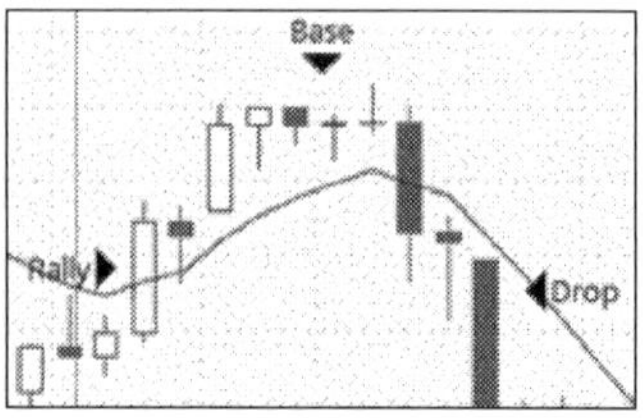
Summarizes directions of price movement across a selected calendar. Daily open, close, high, and low values are unavailable.	Shows open and close tickmarks. Top and bottom of lines (or "bars") show highs and lows for selected time interval.	Green (unfilled) candles show price rallies, red (or black) show price drops, tops and bottoms of shadows ("wicks") show highs and lows for the selected time interval.

The tips of the top and bottom candle *shadows*, that resemble candle wicks, show the high and low price during the selected time interval. So each candle and its shadows show the open, close, high, and low price that correspond to the selected time interval.

Following are simple illustrations of a line chart, bar chart, and candlestick chart.

Breakout

Price breakouts are usually the result of a compression and then an expansion in volatility. Volatility is a measure of the buying or selling volume that corresponds to current trading activity. Excessive buying or selling causes price breakouts. Price breakouts are directional — either upward or downward. Trading a price breakout in its early stages is something professional traders exploit. Institutional traders (who are pros) often buy or sell a few million shares at a time. This often causes a price breakout. Once the price is driven up or down by their buying or selling action, the institutional traders take their profit by entering an opposite trade. This pushes the price back in the opposite direction. So a big "player" can sometimes trade enough volume to whipsaw the market up and down to the institution's advantage. Their ability to influence price movement depends on *market depth*, described later in this section. As a trader your job is to examine the charts to understand what's happening. Then trade with the pros rather than trading against them.

Rally, Base, Drop
Notice the *candlestick* chart illustration to the right. (Candlestick charts and their use is described in much more detail in chapters 7 and 8.) A rally is an upward price move-ment. The long rally can-dle at the left illustrates

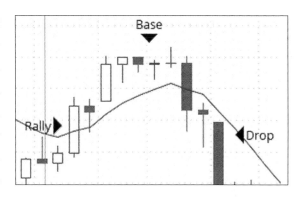

this movement on a chart. At the end of the rally, the price begins to move sideways. This is called *basing*. Then the price turns downward, or *drops*. The entire price formation is referred to as a "rally-base-drop."

Other formations include descriptive terms such as: drop-base-rally, rally-base-rally, drop-base-drop, rally-drop, and drop-rally. Each of these price formations is created by trader action rather than changes in the financial condition of the underlying company. Emotion drives markets!

Trend
With very few excep-tions the market prices of equities have directional *trends* over time. Prices may trend upward (bull-ish), downward (bearish),

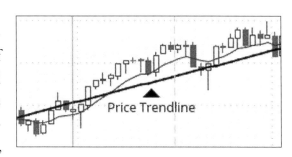

or sideways (neutral). Experienced traders most always consider the underlying's price trend and chart pattern before constructing a trade. The trendline on the preceding chart is a *linear regression trendline* study. This tells traders that the price of the underlying has been increasing over time with a series of higher highs and higher lows.

It's important to look at price trends across different time intervals to understand the long-term outlook. Many traders begin by looking at weekly charts in which each candle represents one week. This is followed by examining one-day, one-hour, and 30-minute charts. Entering a counter-trend trade is discouraged unless a resistance or support level is being approached. But this must be done based on historical price actions. Otherwise, the trader may be "betting the farm." Be sure to study the corresponding charts and price trends in advance of entering a trade. This practice is detailed in chapters 7 and 8.

Moving Averages

Most traders put some kind of a moving average study on their charts. The 9-, 15-, 20-, 50-, and 200-period simple moving averages are common. (The abbreviation SMA(15) represents a 15-period simple moving average.) An SMA(20) represents the simple moving price average over 20 weeks, days, hours, etc., depending on the chart interval in use. Exponential moving averages are weighted to show the most recent price averages. The number of SMA periods used should correspond to your planned trading strategy and the length of time you intend to retain the underlying security.

Crossovers

A price crossover exists when the price of the underlying crosses above or below an SMA plot. Another type of crossover occurs when one chart plot crosses another. Because the SMA plot is like "gravity," the price is likely to return and continue oscillating around its historical moving average. If you catch the move early, a breakout may occur. Even when a price crossover is expansive, the price is likely to return to its moving average, especially when shorter term moving averages are used. Because the SMA period corresponds to the underlying chart's time period, be sure to use moving average lengths that correspond to your trade's time-in-force. If you buy and sell every one or two weeks, you may want to consider an SMA(9) on a daily chart, i.e., one candle per day. But keep in mind that the time interval dictates the shape of the SMA plotline.

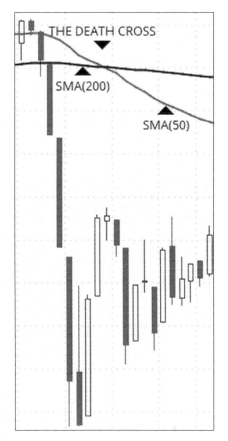

Many traders watch financial indexes like the S&P 500. This index is comprised of the average price movements of 500 large company stocks. The stocks of companies having market capitalizations of at least $10 billion are called *large caps*. Some traders put both the SMA(50) and SMA(200) on their S&P 500 index charts. When stock prices are trending upward, the SMA(50) remains above the SMA(200) on a daily chart. However, traders become concerned whenever the SMA(50) crosses and then drops below the SMA(200). This cross-over is commonly called the *death cross*, and signals a downturn in the market.

Experienced technical analysts watch many different *chart studies* to develop a strong bias about price moves as well as the near-term direction of the overall market. Over time and with practice, they develop a sense of what is about to occur and trade accordingly. Their successes are based on both chart studies and mathematical probabilities, referred to as "odds enhancers." Chapters 7 and 8 examine several of the popular chart studies used by traders.

Volatility

The popular *Bollinger Bands* study, which was devised by John Bollinger in the 1980s, tracks current volatility. When current volatility, referred to as *implied volatility*, exceeds the historical volatility of an underlying security, the buying or selling volume is higher than its historical average.

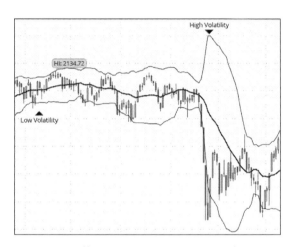

For illustration purposes only.

This drives the price of the underlying either up (high-volume buying) or down (high-volume selling).

Notice the Bollinger Band envelope. The default center line is an SMA(20). The outside lines are two standard deviations above and below the SMA(20) centerline. Standard deviation tracks the average number of data points produced by trading activity. High activity increases the width of the external envelope. When the envelope collapses, traders anticipate a breakout. They know the envelope will likely expand back to its original (historical volatility) plot. When the volatility is high, the bandwidth widens, and traders expect the envelope to collapse.

Recall the previous discussion about calls and puts. Call premiums increase as the price of the underlying rallies; put premiums increase as the price of the underlying drops. When the chart signals a pending increase in implied volatility, it's time to examine the underlying's option chain for a trading opportunity. If the stock is on the edge of a price rally, you may wish to buy the stock and sell an *out of the money* call contract (a "covered call"). There's much more information about covered calls and many other option strategies in chapters 14 through 16.

Historical Volatility (HV)
Historical volatility measures the average daily buying and selling activity of an underlying equity over one year's time. A stock with a high historical volatility value has a high degree of trading activity and corresponding price swings. High volatility adds risk or opportunity, depending on your option strategy. While volatility increases option premiums and possible profit, it can be a double-edged sword. You may buy a stock and sell call options for a substantial premium. If the underlying stock plummets in value, the trade will result in a major loss — from the drop in stock price. You may make money on the sale of you option contracts, while losing much more from the drop in the underlying stock price. Be careful!

Implied Volatility (IV)
Implied volatility reflects current trader sentiment, and is the estimated volatility of a security's price. In general, implied volatility increases the most when the market is bearish. This is because investors tend to believe the underlying's price will drop faster than it will rally. Extraordinary buying and selling increases implied volatility, which is carefully watched by experienced traders. Because implied volatility will normally return to historical volatility levels, many traders scan for stocks and ETFs with high IV and corresponding higher than normal option premiums. They know that the IV will return to its HV. A combination of lower volatility and the passage of time reduce option premiums. This also dampens the effect of potential price rallies and drops in the underlying.

Implied volatility doesn't predict the direction of price changes — the price may rally or it may drop. More stable prices exist during periods of low volatility. There are option strategies that take advantage of both high and low volatility situations.

Always remember that implied volatility is about probability: an estimate of future prices. But it's never a guarantee. Even though most experienced traders consider volatility when entering an option trade — and their reliance on volatility actually impacts underlying prices — they understand that an option's price may not follow the most likely pattern. However, when entering a trade, it helps to understand the actions other traders are most likely to take. Remember, they are looking at the same charts and option chains that you're using. Knowing that implied volatility is strongly coupled to market sentiment, a trader's probability of being right is enhanced.

Market Depth

You can think of market depth as the number of shares of an underlying financial equity that can be bought or sold to move the underlying price by an observable amount. Consider buying or selling 100 shares of stock in which five million shares exist. Your 100 share transaction doesn't cause the price to fluctuate. An institution decides to buy or sell 500 thousand shares of the same stock. This will undoubtedly move the price of the underlying.

Let's say you own 15,000 shares of a $12.00 stock and decide to place a stop loss to sell the stock if it drops to $10.50. A market order sells all 15,000 shares if the price touches your $10.50 stop price. The market order will continue to sell your stock until all shares are sold. However, this action can influence market depth, so the final shares of your stock will likely be sold for far less than the $10.50 stop price. This is a "you just shot yourself in the foot" situation. Your trade affected the market depth, and by selling 15,000 shares you caused the price of your own stock to drop dramatically.

Instead of a market order, use a limit order. This limits the selling price of your shares to $10.45 or more. Therefore, your shares "trickle out" at the $10.45 stop price. From this example you should understand that the number of shares it takes to move the price of the underlying is an indication of market depth.

You can view market depth on many trading platforms. It is shown in Bid and Ask columns for each of the listed exchanges.

NOTE As mentioned earlier, the terms Bid and Ask used for trading equities are the opposite of Bid (sell) and Ask (buy) used with options. This distinction becomes relevant when you begin trading option contracts.

Liquidity and Liquidity Risk

There are two kinds of liquidity — *funding liquidity* and *market liquidity*. Corporate treasurers worry about funding liquidity. A primary concern is having enough cash on hand to pay the current bills. To survive, many companies negotiate lines of credit with banks to meet short-term debt. Banks are concerned with having enough liquidity to make customer loans. Although it's good to know about funding liquidity, as a trader your primary concern is about market liquidity.

When ample market liquidity exists, trades execute quickly because there's plenty of open interest in the underlying equity. As a general rule, S&P 500 stocks trade quickly because of the high liquidity. Treasury bonds also have high liquidity and can be bought or sold within a matter of seconds.

In contrast, you can be punished by choosing a symbol with little trading volume. If the current open interest is weak, you may be "stuck." Your sell orders on low liquidity stocks may not trigger. You may find these orders expiring unfilled day after day. Other traders are simply not interested in your sell order, because they're not even looking at the stock or option contracts. Some people refer to these symbols as "tar babies." They cling to you like sticky tar because there's no liquidity.

As one of your cardinal trading rules, be sure to examine both trading volume and open interest prior to committing to a trade. ALWAYS ensure that ample liquidity exists by checking average volume and/or current open interest before entering a trade.

Exchanges

A stock or financial securities exchange may be a physical location where traders conduct their business on a trading floor, an electronic exchange that processes buy and sell orders over a communication network, or both. Financial exchanges exist all around the world. The New York Stock Exchange (NYSE), the NASDAQ, the Toronto Stock Exchange, and the Singapore Stock Exchange are just a few examples of the many exchanges located around the world that process buy and sell orders. We can check the current performances of the overseas exchanges on the Internet or on several of the financial television channels. Among these overseas exchanges are the FTSE (London), DAX (Frankfurt), CAC (Paris), and the NIKKEI (Tokyo). Current exchange prices in addition to the day's gains or losses are posted by CNBC, Bloomberg, and the Fox Business Channel, among others.

A variety of security classifications are transacted by stock exchanges. This includes stock issued by exchange-listed companies; unit trusts; derivatives (options are examples of derivatives); pooled investment products (ETFs, bond funds, etc.), and bonds. These exchanges function as a "continuous auction" in which buyers and sellers enter into trading transactions. As mentioned, these transactions can be done by people on the exchange trading floor. But more often, the transactions are processed electronically.

To trade a security on an exchange, it must be listed by the exchange. While trading records are maintained at central exchange locations, trading activity is rarely linked to the trading floor. The electronic communications trading networks in use today have reduced transaction costs and increased the speed at which trades are transacted. The time from order entry to order fulfillment is completed within a matter of a few seconds.

There was a time when a client phoned in their orders to a local brokerage office. That order was entered into a primitive proprietary network connected to an exchange. Order execution could take as much as a few hours. Over the past several years, electronic communication networks have shifted trading volume from the traditional stock exchanges to online brokerage houses. Most brokerages have direct high-speed connections into the exchanges.

In addition to specializing in stocks, ETFs, and bonds, some exchanges specialize in certain financial instruments. For example, there are a number of exchanges that specialize in options, futures, foreign currency exchange, and commodities. These include:

- Chicago Board of Trade
- Chicago Mercantile Exchange
- Hong Kong Mercantile Exchange
- Kansas City Board of Trade
- London Metal Exchange
- London International Financial Futures and Options Exchange
- New York Mercantile Exchange
- Tokyo Commodity Exchange

Regardless of which exchange is used, all are responsible to ensure fair trading. All are required to submit periodic financial reports and are regularly audited by governing regulatory agencies.

Market Makers

Market makers are dealers who specializes in matching buy and sell orders for financial securities. Their customers are brokerages who use market makers to route client orders to the responsible exchange. Market makers compete for orders by providing price quotations. They make their profit on what's called a bid-to-offer spread. That is, they buy and sell securities for a small incremental profit. The spread is the difference between what they pay for a security and what they sell it for.

The New York Stock Exchange (NYSE) and American Stock Exchange (AMEX) are just two of several exchanges that have *designated market makers*. These market makers represent specific securities. Market makers provide liquidity to the securities market. They take both sides, i.e., the buy and the sell sides, of the trades for which they're responsible. This includes taking a short-term buy or sell position when imbalances exist in the current number of buy and sell orders. This gives the market maker an informational advantage that usually leads to more profitable trades by the market maker.

Other stock exchanges, such as the NASDAQ Stock Exchange, use multiple market makers. Several of these market makers may list the same securities. These market makers must stand ready to buy and sell at their quoted bids and offers throughout each trading day. There are times when a trader who specifies "Best" on his trading platform buys from one market maker and sells to another. For example, in an option spread with two or more legs, it's possible for multiple market makers to be involved in the same trade. Market makers are selected based on the prices they quote. Some option chains list a small alphabetical letter next to bid and ask prices that designate the source.

Several financial brokerages double as market makers. Some traders view this as a conflict in interest, if not a distraction. They prefer order takers rather than order makers. As traders we want a competent clerk who performs the administrative work involved in executing our trades.

Although multiple market makers may not benefit from the advantages held by those who have a "lock" on a list of securities, they do have the ability to short (sell) stocks without borrowing against their short positions (see Long Stock and Short Stock above). Since they process stacks of buy and sell orders, they know exactly what is being bought and sold in real time. This gives them a definite advantage. Designated market makers engage in *naked* (uncollateralized) trades based on this knowledge. Selling naked options was once a lucrative revenue generator for all market makers. However, regulations have been introduced that attempt to restrict a market maker's "unfair advantage."

Electronic Communication Exchange Networks (ECNs)

Electronic communication exchange networks (ECNs), also called alternative trading networks, are networks that support stock and currency trading outside the traditional stock exchanges. These are passive computer-driven networks designed to match limit orders. An ECN's per share transaction fees are typically quite small. Fees are collected from both buyers and sellers to support the cost of the network. These networks distribute market maker orders to third parties. Large orders are often executed incrementally either until they are filled or when the offer price becomes invalid. This may result in partial fulfillment or in negotiation between the participants.

The first ECN, Instinet, was created in 1969. Since then many more have surfaced. ECNs increased the competition between trading firms. This was a direct result of the ECNs' reduced transaction costs. These reductions were a major benefit to traders. Market makers gain full access to their order books, and offer order matching outside of traditional exchange hours.

Originally ECNs were considered *closed book*. They restricted participant use to their networks. Today, most if not all ECNs are *open book*. This minimizes fragmented liquidity by integrating ECN orders with other ECNs or market makers. Obviously, this increases the overall pool of orders and expedites order execution — a major boon for traders.

For us to gain access to the services of an ECN, the ECN must have an account with our broker. Many brokers have access to multiple ECNs as a service to their clients. ECN subscribers send orders to their ECNs over their network connections. The ECN matches sell orders to buy orders for fulfillment. Unmatched orders are posted for other subscribers to view and process. Individual buyers and sellers are anonymous. Trade reports list the ECN as the involved party.

When substantial separation exists between the buying and selling price, negotiations often follow. ECNs offer electronic negotiations in order to arrive at a reasonable trade price. More complex negotiations can draw agents into the process. These agents argue the offers and counter-offers in an attempt to reach a fair price.

Order Routing

Exchanges, market makers, and electronic communication exchanges are rarely described in trading books. So most traders are unfamiliar with what happens when they send an order to their broker. Most simply don't know where market makers or electronic communication exchange networks (ECNs) fit into order routing. So a brief overview of how orders are routed is summarized for you here.

1. Trader places order with broker.
2. Broker determines order routing based on available sources and order size.
3. Broker chooses from one of the following:
   a. Order goes to the trading floor of the exchange (like NYSE or NASDAQ).
   b. Order goes to a regional exchange for processing.
   c. Order is routed to a market maker if:
      1) The market maker entices broker with an incentive (lowest current price).
      2) The broker is not a member firm of the exchange, while the market maker holds exchange membership and has full trading access.

d. Broker uses *internalization* — This is possible if the broker holds inventory in the security. Internalization promotes the fastest execution, and the brokerage also receives the spread normally received by market makers.

e. Broker routes order through an ECN, which automatically matches buy and sell orders for a small transaction fee. ECNs use software that programmatically process limit orders, and that negotiates bid and ask values to achieve a "fair price."

Figure 3–2. Simplified Order Routing Diagram

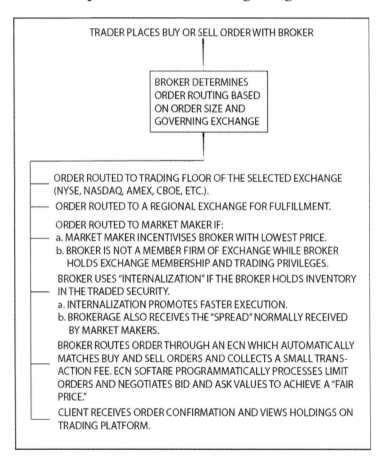

Broker Obligations:

Brokers are required to give investors the best possible order execution. They are duty-bound to negotiate the best possible price for their clients, although some suspect finagling in the broker's own interest.

In reality, brokers try to execute trades in the best interest of both their clients and themselves. However, the SEC has regulations that tilt trades in favor of clients through financial reporting and periodic audits.

Order Execution Speed:

The speed of order execution depends on the type of order submitted and current volatility.

Market orders are used by traders who want the fastest possible execution, regardless of the trade price. Protective stops are market orders.

Market buy orders typically execute at prices higher than limit buy orders. It follows that market sell orders execute at prices lower than limit sell orders.

However, a risk associated with limit orders is that they may not be filled at all. If a day order remains unfilled through market close, the order is automatically canceled.

Diversification

Many traders think they're *diversified* when they own a collection of a dozen or more stocks. However, holding a dozen or more stocks is not diversification. It's just a list of stocks. Diversification involves owning a portfolio of securities that reside in different market sectors. If the stocks are in a broad mix of market sectors, like energy, financials, health care, industrials, materials, and telecommunications services, then you can claim diversification.

Financial managers like diversification because they know that one market sector can be in favor while another may be in decline.

The stock prices within the sectors seem to "follow the pack." When a sector falls from favor, the underlying industries and participating companies usually suffer corresponding declines. Within the ten general *market sectors* listed below, there are 196 *industries*. So there can even be a degree of diversity within a market sector.

Market Sectors

Following is a list of eleven different market sectors:

Market Sectors

Basic Materials	Health Care
Capital Goods	Technology
Consumer Discretionary	Telecommunication Services
Consumer Staples	Transportation
Energy	Utilities
Financial	

Within each market sector are industries. For example, the industries that fall into the energy sector are listed in the following table.

Energy Sector Industries

Coal & Consumable Fuels	Oil & Gas Exploration & Production
Integrated Oil & Gas	Oil & Gas Refining & Marketing
Oil & Gas Drilling	Oil & Gas Storage & Transportation
Oil & Gas Equipment & Services	

It's interesting to note that profitable industries within a sector often fall victim to trader sentiment relative to the sector to which the industry belongs. An example of this is in the energy sector shown in the table. When the price of crude dropped to near-record lows in the summer and winter of 2015–16, the stock prices of Oil & Gas Storage & Transportation companies fell right along with the drilling, exploration, and refining industries. This was in spite of the fact that the prices charged for storage and transportation are not dependent on the price of the product in their storage tanks or pipelines. This demonstrates how trader sentiment washes across all industries within a depressed market sector.

You can Google market sectors and industries to find lists. Most brokerages provide online resources to help you find popular market sectors. The TD Ameritrade brokerage provides research information from its Investools subsidiary. In particular, examine the sector ranking in the Investools' Big Chart and the Industry Groups.

The Big Chart ranks industries by current trader sentiment, and provides price charts and performance scores for each symbol listed. Other brokerages provide similar information, so be sure to explore your brokerage's website to find rankings by market sector and industry.

Economic Data and Reports

There are many economic data reports available to traders. Just a few examples of these are listed in the following table.

Financial Reports

Business inventories	Home builders' index
Capacity utilization	Industrial production
Consumer credit	Job openings
Consumer price indexes	Producer price index

Consumer sentiment	Retail sales
Existing home sales	Weekly jobless claims

Numerous websites provide economic report calendars as well as current economic and financial reports. Traders use these reports to develop market bias, i.e., rallies in the financial indexes follow good news; drops follow bad news. However, there are instances in which market sentiment seems to ignore the news.

Traders also watch the early morning gains and losses on the overseas exchanges including the FTSE, CAC, DAX, and NIKKEI mentioned earlier. They also look at index futures (called *e-mini* futures) that track the Dow-Jones Industrial Average, S&P 500, NASDAQ, and the Russell 2000. Futures traders buy and sell the *e-mini* futures (the financial index futures) along with currency and commodity futures 24 hours per day. The futures market trades around the clock, closing on Friday evenings and reopening for business on Sunday afternoons.

But in spite of all this economic data and the trends seen in futures and the foreign exchanges, traders are never certain about how the economic data will ultimately affect the market. They may see a few hours of declines only to see the market reverse direction and rally in the afternoon hours.

Many traders develop trading hour rules. They avoid trading during the first and last hour of the trading day and during the lunch hours of 11:30 to 1:00 Eastern Standard Time. Others look for overnight gaps and put on trades in anticipation of "closing the gap" with a fast price recovery.

To find current economic data and report schedules, you can Google "economic data." You can view economic data produced by the U.S. Economics & Statistics Administration government at www.esa.doc.gov. Here's a brief list of sources.

Some U.S. Government Economic Data Websites

Website	Description
www.esa.doc.gov/reports	U.S. workforce statistics
www.bea.gov	Bureau of Economic Analysis
www.census.gov/econ/	Census Bureau's economic statistics
www.bis.gov/news.release/	Bureau of Labor Statistics
www.whitehouse.gov	Economic indicators
www.treasury.gov	Economic indicators

A list of economic reports produced by the U.S. government is also available from Wikipedia.org at https://en.wikipedia.org.

Stock Categories

Stocks are classified by the market capitalization of the company. Market capitalization (often called the "market cap") is the total dollar value of the company's outstanding shares of stock. If a company has issued one million shares of stock currently worth $10 per share, the company's market cap is ten million dollars. This is considered the "market value" of the company, which is different from the "book value." Most of us have heard the terms large cap, mid cap, and small cap. The following table defines these terms.

Term	*Market Capitalization*
Large Cap	More than $10 billion
Mid Cap	From $1 to $10 billion
Small Cap	Less than $1 billion

There are also *penny stocks*. These are stocks having a value of less than $1.00 per share. They are also called *pink sheet* and *over-the-counter* (OTC) stocks. There are market makers that specialize in penny stocks. A daily publication is produced by the National Quotation Bureau that lists the bid and ask prices of penny stocks. The paper is pink, hence the name "pink sheet." Penny stock symbols end with the letters "PK" for "pink."

Penny stock companies do not meet the minimum Federal Securities and Exchange Commission (SEC) requirements, and they do not file with the SEC. Companies in this category rarely have more than a few million dollars in assets. A penny stock company could drop out of sight in a matter of days. Therefore, they are considered high risk. Serious traders rarely consider penny stocks. In addition, because penny stock companies are unregulated, they are subject to fraud. In contrast, high-value public companies are scrupulously audited.

Because of the high level of risk, penny stocks are disallowed by brokerages as collateral for account margin. (Margin and its use are discussed in the next chapter.) If you are unfamiliar with a penny stock company, beware!

Trading Days and Hours

The New York Stock Exchange is open 252 days per year from 9:30 AM to 4:00 PM Eastern Time. The exchange is closed on weekends and also honors most of the following holidays. Extended trading hours range from 4:00 a.m. until 9:30 p.m. EST.

Holidays Observed by the NYSE

New Year's Day	*Independence Day	Labor Day
Martin Luther King, Jr. Day	Good Friday	*Thanksgiving Day
George Washington's Birthday	Memorial Day	*Christmas Day

★ Some exchanges close early on the days prior to some holidays.

Market Venues (The Four Pillars of Wealth)

There are four market venues. Some refer to these as the *four pillalrs of wealth*, although they can also be pillars of financial doom — especially if you are not a practitioner of risk management. All four venues are heavily traded. Of course this book targets option trading, but it's instructive to have some understanding of what else is traded across the various financial markets.

Equities

The term *equities* refers to stocks, ETFs, options, and futures. Cash is also equity. In fact, cash is a declining equity as inflation reduces the value of cash by 3% to 4% per year. Here, we focus on financial instruments that are bought and sold.

Stocks

A company's stock is a security that conveys ownership in a corporation. There are often two types of stock: common stock and preferred stock. Each share of stock represents a claim on both the corporation's assets and its earnings. If you own ten thousand shares of a corporation's common stock that has issued a total of one million shares of stock, you own one percent of the corporation's assets and earnings. The owners of common shares of stock can vote their shares by attending the company's annual shareholder meeting or they can vote electronically. In contrast, preferred stock shares rarely carry voting privileges.

Companies that pay dividends to their shareholders make periodic monetary distributions based on a per-share amount. There are monthly, quarterly, semiannual, and annual dividend schedules. Some companies occasionally pay *special dividends*. Since company executives are most often major shareholders, the ordinary and special dividends enrich them.

Each dividend distribution begins with an announcement date followed by an execution date, a record date, and a distribution date. On the announcement date the corporation communicates the dividend amount, execution date, record date, and distribution date. Dividend funds are set aside on the execution date. Shareholders must own the stock on the date of record to be eligible for the dividend payment. The record date is typically two business days following the execution date. Dividends are transferred to shareholder accounts on the distribution date. Preferred shareholders most often receive dividends before the shareholders of common stock. Hence, the term "preferred" or *preference shares*.

If a corporation files bankruptcy and is liquidated, shareholders must wait to receive the proceeds from company liquidation after all monetary claims are settled by the courts. This transaction is often delayed by lawsuits and other filings before a final value for the liquidated assets is determined. In the case of bankruptcy, preferred stock shareholders are paid from the company assets prior to common stock shareholders.

Options

Options are also classified as equities because they have monetary value. As mentioned in chapter 2, options are a financial derivative of a stock, ETF, financial index, or a futures contract. Most options are bought and sold in 100-share contracts, although there are also mini option contracts comprised of 10 shares. This book focuses on the standard 100-share option contract, although both standard and mini option contracts work identically.

Option contracts are bought and sold by traders for many reasons. Financial leverage, flexibility, and the availability of pertinent information were all discussed in chapter 2. The ownership of an option contract within your brokerage account has value, and is therefore an equity, just as stock and ETF shares are equities.

Futures

Futures contracts have monetary value in the same way that option contracts do. Futures traders buy and sell a variety of futures types including futures on financial indexes, precious metals, currencies, agricultural products, livestock, and energy (gas and oil). Futures traders use account margin as a financial guaranty for their participation in the futures market.

Futures contracts have their roots in Ancient Greece, where grain farmers sold their crops several months in advance of the harvest to dealers and processors. The producers are assured of an acceptable price for their work product, while the dealer/processors know their costs in advance of delivery. Futures have been in use to assure supply and to regulate costs since the time of Aristotle in the 3rd Century BC. The Japanese were trading rice futures as early as the year 1710. The candlestick price charts in use today were developed by Japanese rice futures traders. Today about eighty percent of futures contracts are negotiated between producers and dealer/processors. In 1848 the Chicago Board of Trade was formed to regulate futures within the United States. Today the Chicago Board of Trade is the largest futures exchange in the world.

Just a few examples of agricultural producers include grain and pig farmers. Processors include companies like Kellogg, General Mills, Tyson, and Cargill. But of course futures are also used to regulate the mineral, energy, timber, and currency markets. About 20 percent of futures contracts are bought and sold by speculators. Futures speculators must sell their futures contracts prior to expiration or they may be obligated to accept delivery on a boxcar load of grain or live hogs.

Producers want to know what kind of price they'll receive for a soybean crop. They need to negotiate the future price before they buy the seed and plow, plant, fertilize, and harvest. If the price is acceptable, the producer buys the seed. The processor must know what price will be paid for the soybeans. The processor must calculate the delivered price of the soybeans, storage, processing, packaging, warehousing, and distribution costs. Knowing this, the producer can build in the necessary profit margin and set a fair price that is acceptable to his wholesalers.

Each future type has a market symbol. Below are just some; there are many more for national currencies, bonds, and other metals like palladium (PA) and platinum (PL).

Partial List of Commodity Futures Symbols

AG	Silver	FV	Treasury Notes, 5 Year	LC	Live Cattle
C	Corn	GC	Gold	LH	Live Hogs
CC	Cocoa	HG	Copper	HU	Unleaded Gasoline
CL	Crude Oil	HO	Heating Oil	S	Soybeans
CT	Cotton	KC	Coffee	SB	Sugar
DX	U.S. Dollar Index	KW	Wheat	SV	Silver
FC	Feeder Cattle	LB	Lumber	TY	Treasury Notes, 10 Year

The above futures symbols are appended with one of the following letters and the year to designate the expiration month and year of the futures contract. For example the cotton futures contract symbol that expires in December 2016 is CTZ16. Just as in stocks, the buyer of a futures contract is said to be long and the seller is said to be short.

Contract Expiration Symbols

F – January	J – April	N – July	V – October
G – February	K – May	Q – August	X – November
H –March	M – June	U – September	Z – December

Financial Index Futures (the e-minis)
Many futures traders specialize in trading financial index futures. These involve the S&P 500, the NASDAQ, the Dow Jones Industrial

Index, the S&P MidCap 400, and the Russell 2000. The following five index futures are called the *e-minis*. Symbols used are:

E-Mini (Financial Index) Futures

Contract	Symbol	Contract Size	Tick Size	Contract Months
S&P 500	ES	$50	$12.50	H, M, U, Z
NASDAQ	NQ	$20	$5	H, M, U, Z
DJIA	YM	$5	$5	H, M, U, Z
Russell 2000	TF	$100	$10	H, M, U, Z
S&P MidCap 400	EMD	$100	$10	H, M, U, Z

The e-mini trading venue can resemble a casino. Look at the S&P 500, symbol ES. If a trader buys ten S&P 500 e-mini contracts and it rises 3 points, the trader is at $1,500 in profit ($50 × 3 points × 10 contracts). This is a tempting scenario, especially if you like a lot of action.

Most e-mini futures traders use *bracketed trades* that include a limit entry order, a protective stop, and a profit target. A long position (the trader buys) might include a protective stop some 2 to 3 points below and a profit target 4 to 6 points above. Consider the following Active Trader (a typical *order ladder*) illustration in figure 3–3. This trade is comprised of:

A limit order to buy ten e-mini futures contracts on the S&P 500 (symbol ES)
A protective stop 1 point below the limit entry
A profit target that is 3 points above the price of the limit entry

Figure 3–3. A Trading Ladder

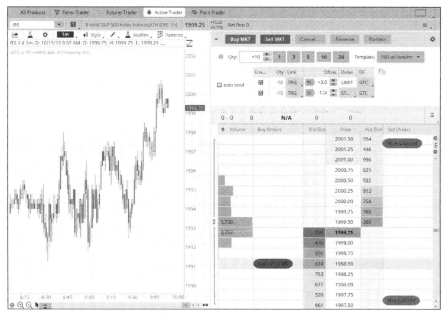

For illustration purposes only.

If this order is stopped out, the trader will lose $500 (1 point ×
10 contracts × $50/point). If the S&P rallies to the trader's profit
target three points above the entry, the trader earns $1,500 in profit
(3 points × 10 contracts × $50/point). Note that on the ES there
are four ticks per point. Each tick has a value of $12.50. Orders and
stops can be set to either tick or point values.

Looking at a 1-minute chart, the trader watches the upticks and
downticks on the *trading ladder* as the price oscillates either above
or below the limit entry price. Money is rapidly gained and lost
before the trader's eyes. Finally, if the trader doesn't intervene with a
manual exit, the trade either sells for a profit or stops out for a loss.
This is what life can be like in the world of e-mini futures. The trading ladder is also used by day traders in support of fast entries and
exists on stocks and ETFs.

Currency Futures

Traders also buy and sell currency futures in the same way they trade other securities. A trader must have special knowledge and understand those economic actions that influence valuations of specific currencies. It requires months of observation to understand currency dynamics. For example, how will a strengthening dollar affect the value of the Yen, the Euro, or the Canadian dollar? When the dollar weakens, which currencies strengthen the most? These are simple questions, yet they are strategically crucial to the success of a currency futures trader.

Regardless of the underlying future, there are always the price charts. These provide a window to the market. Learning how to use the charts, regardless of the underlying financial instrument, provides indisputable facts about trader sentiment that often corresponds to historical events and sentiments.

Commodity Futures

What will the crop yield be like this summer? When is the best time to buy futures contracts on corn, wheat, soybeans, or rice? How much influence do long-range weather forecasts have of futures prices. What about the cost of fuel? If a crop is abundant, will the futures prices drop? If the crop yield is poor, will some futures prices rally? All these factors, and many more, influence futures prices. This is also true of livestock and cotton futures. Again, study the market. Read economic reports and understand how weather, governmental policies, crop reductions, reallocation to ethanol, or a leveling off of demand can affect the price of commodity futures.

Although there may not be as many speculators in many of the commodity futures as there are in the e-mini futures, there are still rallies and drops during each trading day. ALWAYS study the price charts! The charts are superior to random speculation. Develop a bias based on the charts and trade accordingly. Keep meticulous records so you can track your successes and failures. Then refine your analysis strategies as needed.

The Foreign Exchange (Forex or FX)

While stocks trade in the tens of billions of dollars each day, the foreign exchange market, or *forex*, trades about 2.5 to 3.0 trillion dollars each day. It is by far the largest trading venue in the world. The forex market is open 24 hours per day five days per week. It is dominated by institutional traders who compete for pennies while trading millions and tens of millions of *currency pairs*.

Forex trading involves buying one currency and selling another. The two currencies involved in the trade are called a *currency pair*. Each currency has a unique three-character symbol. A popular pair is the Euro and US dollar, symbol EUR/USD. A list of currency pairs is provided in the table following the trade example.

The first symbol is called the base currency and the second symbol is called the quote currency. If the EUR/USD = 1.24000, the base currency (EUR) is worth $1.24000 US dollars. The trader must pay $1.24 for each Euro bought. If this exchange rate is maintained, the trader would receive $1.24000 when the Euro is sold. Here's a simple example of a forex transaction.

1. A trader believes the Euro will rally against the dollar (the quote currency).
2. The trader buys 10,000 Euros (the base currency) for $12,400 USD (the quote currency).
3. The EUR rallies against the dollar to $1.25500 USD.
4. The trader closes the position with a sell order and profits $0.015 (or 1.5 cents per Euro).
5. The trader's profit is $150.00 less commissions.

As you can see the trader risked more than $12,400 on this trade for a $150 return. This is a 1.2% return. To make a substantial amount of money on the forex market, the trader must be right. And millions of dollars must be exchanged. Many large banks trade the foreign exchange. This explains the huge volume that is traded every day in forex trading venue.

Following is a list of forex symbols used by currency traders.

Foreign Exchange (Forex) Currency Pairs

EUR/ USD	Euro / US Dollar	USD/ GRD	US Dollar / Greek Drachma
USD/ JPY	US Dollar / Japanese Yen	USD/ SEK	US Dollar / Swedish Kroner
GBP/ USD	British Pound / US Dollar	USD/ NOK	US Dollar / Norwegian Kroner
USD/ CHF	US Dollar / Swiss Franc	USD/ DKK	US Dollar / Danish Kroner
USD/ CAD	US Dollar / Canadian Dollar	USD/ FIM	US Dollar / Finnish Markka
AUD/ USD	Australian Dollar / US Dollar	USD/ NLG	US Dollar / Dutch Guilder
EUR/ JPY	Euro / Japanese Yen	USD/ MXN	US Dollar / Mexican Peso
EUR/ CHF	Euro / Swiss Franc	USD/ BRL	US Dollar / Brazilian Real
GBP/ CHF	British Pound / Swiss Franc	USD/ IDR	US Dollar / Indonesian Rupiah
GBP/ JPY	British Pound / Japanese Yen	USD/ HKD	US Dollar / Hong Kong Dollar
CHF/ JPY	Swiss Franc / Japanese Yen	USD/ SGD	US Dollar / Singapore Dollar
NZD/ UZD	New Zealand Dollar / US Dollar	USD/ CZK	US Dollar / Czech Kroner
USD/ ZAR	US Dollar / South African Rand		

Like stock, option, and futures traders, forex traders also use the price charts to see trends and levels of price support and resistance. And as with the other traders, the price charts provide a basis for the forex trader's directional bias. The charts point to appropriate entry and exit levels for each of the currency pairs being considered.

Option Derivatives

Not all financial securities are optionable. This includes stocks, ETFs, and futures. When you try to view an option chain for a non-optionable symbol, your trading platform will display a message that tells you there are no options available for the symbol. For example, the symbol TNH (Terra Nitrogen) returns the following message.

Figure 3–4. Instrument Has No Options

For illustration purposes only.

Stocks

You can open an option chain on your trading platform. Open the chain, enter a stock symbol, and display one or more contract expiration dates. Looking through a series of expiration dates helps you determine available premiums and risks. Always consider the rule to sell option contracts inside 60 days and buy option contracts outside 90 days. Both limit your risk.

The option chains may display both weekly and monthly expiration dates when both exist. However, many symbols offer only monthly option contracts. Many traders who specialize in selling option contracts for premium income build watch lists that are restricted to stock, ETF, financial index, and futures symbols that have weekly option contracts.

ETFs

Options can be traded on exchange traded funds in the same way as on individual stocks. Many traders like index ETFs such as SPY (SPDR S&P 500 ETF). The QQQ and IWM are also popular optionable ETFs. ETFs are popular because they offer diversity across a range of underlying stocks. An option chain for the QQQ is shown in figure 3–5.

Figure 3–5. An Option Chain for the QQQ Exchange Traded Fund (ETF)

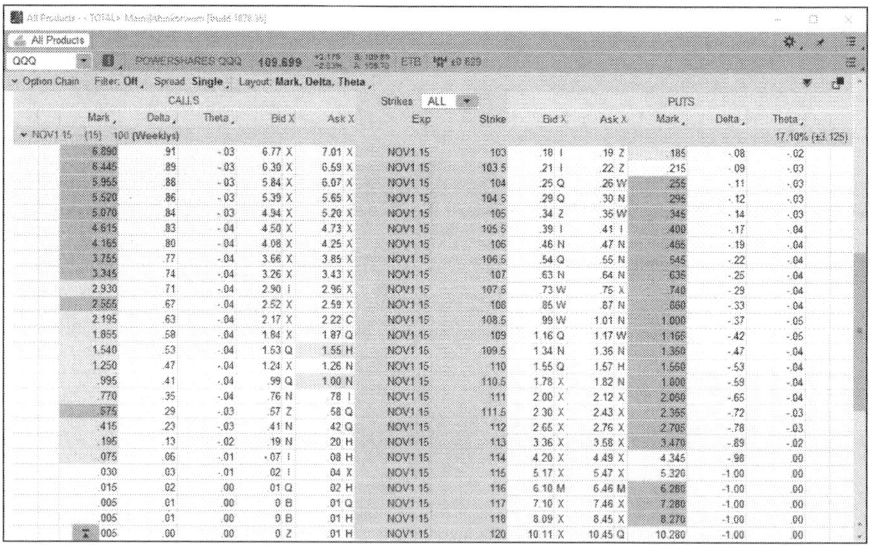

CALLS Mark	Delta	Theta	Bid X	Ask X	Exp	Strike	PUTS Bid X	Ask X	Mark	Delta	Theta
6.890	.91	-.03	6.77 X	7.01 X	NOV1 15	103	.18 I	.19 Z	.185	-.08	-.02
6.445	.89	-.03	6.30 X	6.59 X	NOV1 15	103.5	.21 I	.22 Z	.215	-.09	-.03
5.955	.88	-.03	5.84 X	6.07 X	NOV1 15	104	.25 Q	.26 W	.255	-.11	-.03
5.520	.86	-.03	5.39 X	5.65 X	NOV1 15	104.5	.29 Q	.30 N	.295	-.12	-.03
5.070	.84	-.03	4.94 X	5.20 X	NOV1 15	105	.34 Z	.35 W	.345	-.14	-.03
4.615	.83	-.04	4.50 X	4.73 X	NOV1 15	105.5	.39 I	.41 I	.400	-.17	-.04
4.165	.80	-.04	4.08 X	4.25 X	NOV1 15	106	.46 N	.47 N	.465	-.19	-.04
3.755	.77	-.04	3.66 X	3.85 X	NOV1 15	106.5	.54 Q	.55 N	.545	-.22	-.04
3.345	.74	-.04	3.26 X	3.43 X	NOV1 15	107	.63 N	.64 N	.635	-.25	-.04
2.930	.71	-.04	2.90 I	2.96 X	NOV1 15	107.5	.73 W	.75 X	.740	-.29	-.04
2.555	.67	-.04	2.52 X	2.59 X	NOV1 15	108	.85 W	.87 N	.860	-.33	-.04
2.195	.63	-.04	2.17 X	2.22 C	NOV1 15	108.5	.99 W	1.01 N	1.000	-.37	-.05
1.855	.58	-.04	1.84 X	1.87 Q	NOV1 15	109	1.16 Q	1.17 W	1.165	-.42	-.05
1.540	.53	-.04	1.53 Q	1.55 H	NOV1 15	109.5	1.34 N	1.36 N	1.350	-.47	-.04
1.250	.47	-.04	1.24 X	1.26 N	NOV1 15	110	1.55 Q	1.57 H	1.560	-.53	-.04
.995	.41	-.04	.99 Q	1.00 N	NOV1 15	110.5	1.78 X	1.82 N	1.800	-.59	-.04
.770	.35	-.04	.76 N	.78 I	NOV1 15	111	2.00 X	2.12 X	2.060	-.65	-.04
.575	.29	-.03	.57 Z	.58 Q	NOV1 15	111.5	2.30 X	2.43 X	2.365	-.72	-.03
.415	.23	-.03	.41 N	.42 Q	NOV1 15	112	2.65 X	2.76 X	2.705	-.78	-.03
.195	.13	-.02	.19 N	.20 H	NOV1 15	113	3.36 X	3.58 X	3.470	-.89	-.02
.075	.06	-.01	.07 I	.08 H	NOV1 15	114	4.20 X	4.49 X	4.345	-.98	.00
.030	.03	-.01	.02 I	.04 X	NOV1 15	115	5.17 X	5.47 X	5.320	-1.00	.00
.015	.02	.00	.01 Q	.02 H	NOV1 15	116	6.10 M	6.46 M	6.280	-1.00	.00
.005	.01	.00	0 B	.01 Q	NOV1 15	117	7.10 X	7.46 X	7.280	-1.00	.00
.005	.01	.00	0 B	.01 H	NOV1 15	118	8.09 X	8.45 X	8.270	-1.00	.00
.005	.00	.00	0 Z	.01 H	NOV1 15	120	10.11 X	10.45 Q	10.280	-1.00	.00

For illustration purposes only.

Futures

You can also trade options on futures contracts. Some traders are drawn to futures options and there are even a few books about trading options on futures contracts. Obviously, traders should understand how futures work before they step into buying and selling options on them. Figure 3–6 is an example of an option chain on the S&P 500 e-mini symbol ES.

Figure 3–6. An Option Chain for the S&P 500 Futures Contract (Symbol ES)

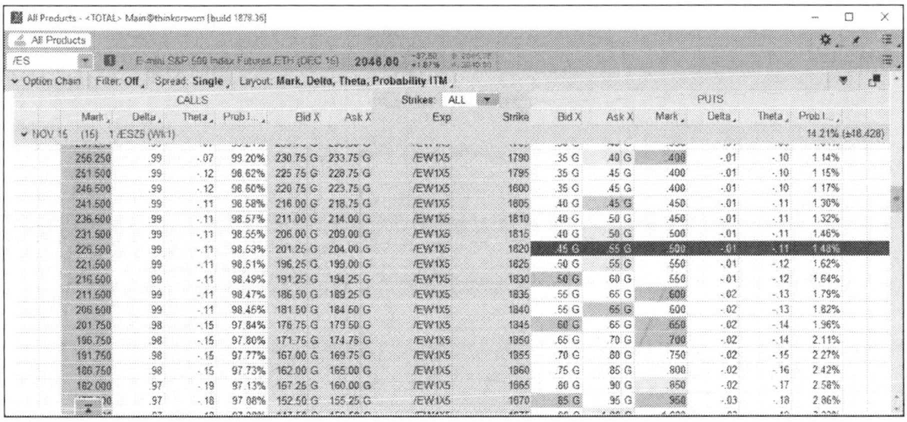

For illustration purposes only.

Notice the option contract expires on NOV 15 which has 15 days remaining in the option contract, designated by the number within parenthesis to the right of the contract expiration date of NOV 15 (15). You can see that the S&P 500 is presently trading at 2046.00. An 1820 put is highlighted. With the Mark (market price) currently listed at .500, selling 10 1820 put contracts earns the trader $250 in premium with 50 shares per option contract. What's that? Did you say fifty shares? Yes, an option contract on the ES futures is 50 shares per contract. So there are some differences in the number of shares in addition to the commissions paid. However, the options work just like other options, and the same strategies are used.

Notice the rightmost column labeled **Prob. I....** The value 1.48% is the statistical probability of the S&P 500 e-mini reaching the 1820 *strike price* (becoming in the money) during the term of the contract. This tells the trader that there is a 98.52% probability of seeing the option contract expire worthless. A profit of $250 is highly likely.

You should be aware that option contracts on futures and financial indices, like the NASDAQ or Russell 2000 index, are cash settled. There are no shares exchanged in these transactions. If you must buy to close a working order, you will pay cash since there are no stock or ETF shares involved.

Financial Indexes

As just mentioned, financial index option contracts are cash settled. Figure 3–7 shows an option chain for the S&P 500.

Figure 3–7. An Option Chain for the S&P 500 Index (Symbol SPX)

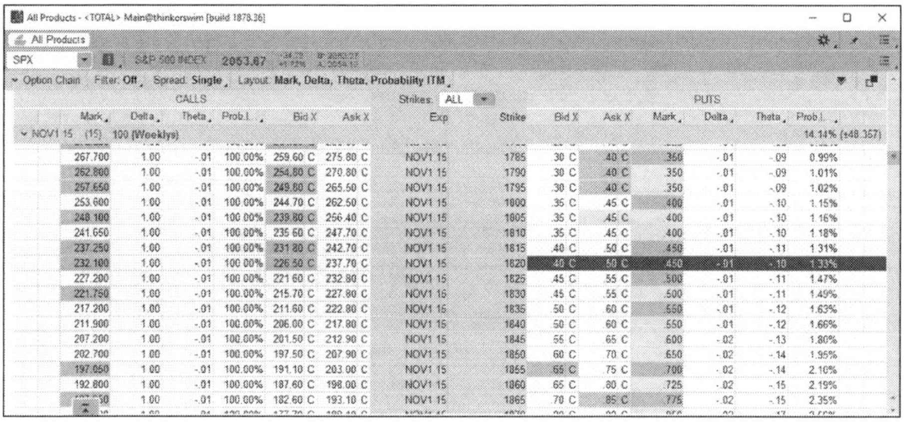

CALLS Mark	Delta	Theta	Prob.I...	Bid X	Ask X	Exp	Strike	PUTS Bid X	Ask X	Mark	Delta	Theta	Prob.I...
267.700	1.00	-.01	100.00%	259.60 C	275.80 C	NOV1 15	1785	.30 C	.40 C	.350	-.01	-.09	0.99%
262.800	1.00	-.01	100.00%	254.80 C	270.80 C	NOV1 15	1790	.30 C	.40 C	.350	-.01	-.09	1.01%
257.650	1.00	-.01	100.00%	249.80 C	265.50 C	NOV1 15	1795	.30 C	.40 C	.350	-.01	-.09	1.02%
253.600	1.00	-.01	100.00%	244.70 C	262.50 C	NOV1 15	1800	.35 C	.45 C	.400	-.01	-.10	1.15%
248.100	1.00	-.01	100.00%	239.80 C	256.40 C	NOV1 15	1805	.35 C	.45 C	.400	-.01	-.10	1.16%
241.650	1.00	-.01	100.00%	235.60 C	247.70 C	NOV1 15	1810	.35 C	.45 C	.400	-.01	-.10	1.18%
237.250	1.00	-.01	100.00%	231.80 C	242.70 C	NOV1 15	1815	.40 C	.50 C	.450	-.01	-.11	1.31%
232.100	1.00	-.01	100.00%	226.50 C	237.70 C	NOV1 15	1820	.40 C	.50 C	.450	-.01	-.10	1.33%
227.200	1.00	-.01	100.00%	221.60 C	232.80 C	NOV1 15	1825	.45 C	.55 C	.500	-.01	-.11	1.47%
221.750	1.00	-.01	100.00%	215.70 C	227.80 C	NOV1 15	1830	.45 C	.55 C	.500	-.01	-.11	1.49%
217.200	1.00	-.01	100.00%	211.60 C	222.80 C	NOV1 15	1835	.50 C	.60 C	.550	-.01	-.12	1.63%
211.900	1.00	-.01	100.00%	206.00 C	217.80 C	NOV1 15	1840	.50 C	.60 C	.550	-.01	-.12	1.66%
207.200	1.00	-.01	100.00%	201.50 C	212.90 C	NOV1 15	1845	.55 C	.65 C	.600	-.02	-.13	1.80%
202.700	1.00	-.01	100.00%	197.50 C	207.90 C	NOV1 15	1850	.60 C	.70 C	.650	-.02	-.14	1.95%
197.050	1.00	-.01	100.00%	191.10 C	203.00 C	NOV1 15	1855	.65 C	.75 C	.700	-.02	-.14	2.10%
192.800	1.00	-.01	100.00%	187.60 C	198.00 C	NOV1 15	1860	.65 C	.80 C	.725	-.02	-.15	2.19%
[illegible]	1.00	-.01	100.00%	182.60 C	193.10 C	NOV1 15	1865	.70 C	.85 C	.775	-.02	-.15	2.35%

For illustration purposes only.

For comparison to the S&P 500 futures contract just shown, the same 1820 put is shown. Notice that the Mark (premium value) is within 5 cents of the option contracts for the ES futures. Trading ten contracts returns approximately $450 in premium. Notice the Probability In the money is 1.33%, giving the trader excellent odds for a successful outcome. Having these statistics provides us with odds for success — another reason to like options!

Active option traders might make both of these trades for $700 in premium income. Not a bad day's work. But be aware that experienced traders monitor their trades as they work. If threatened by a precipitous drop in the value of the S&P 500, they will be well advised to buy back their option contracts for a loss, or buy insurance legs one or two strikes below.

Another consideration is the trader putting two trades on essentially the same underlying instrument. Buying 20 contracts on either the ES futures or the S&P 500 index would essentially be the same trade. So by trading both the ES and S&P 500, the trader is paying two commissions and is not spreading risk across two diverse instruments.

Because the commissions are reduced on the SPX, selling 20 1820 put contracts would earn $900 less a small commission and *exchange* fees.[*]

---

[*] A small exchange fee is paid to the managing option exchange, such as the Chicago Board of Exchange (CBOE), for each contract sold or bought.

What did you learn in chapter 3?

1. Options are financial _____ of equities.
2. In addition to a primary trading computer, traders should also have one or more _____ systems.
3. Every trader should have a set of _____ rules.
4. People who anticipate market growth or a price increase have a _____ bias.
5. The terms long and short mean _____ and _____.
6. Bar charts were replaced with Japanese _____ charts in the 1990s.
7. Institutional traders often buy or sell a few _____ _____ at a time.
8. Three terms used to describe price dynamics include rally, _____, and _____.
9. Standard deviation tracks the average number of data points produced by _____.
10. Call premium increases as the price of the underlying _____.
11. The number of shares required to move the price of a security is called _____ _____.
12. When market liquidity is high, trades execute more _____.
13. There are both physical securities exchanges and _____ securities exchanges.
14. A market maker is a dealer who matches _____ and _____ orders.
15. ECNs support trading outside traditional stock exchanges and are designed to match _____ orders.
16. Holding a dozen or more stocks is not _____.
17. Within each market sector are _____.
18. Most experienced traders study economic _____ and _____.
19. Penny stocks are also called _____ sheet and _____ _____ counter stocks, are not regulated, and are considered risky.
20. Not all financial securities are _____.

4 YOUR BROKERAGE ACCOUNT

Choosing your Broker

Choosing and using a financially sound and responsive brokerage should be a high priority for every trader. And that brokerage should provide access to every trading venue: equities, options, futures, or forex. There are many brokerages running slick TV ads that do not qualify. When you examine the list of financial products served by brokerages, you may be disappointed. Some well-known brokerages support stocks and options. But they do not offer futures or foreign exchange. So walk away and keep looking.

Many who are new to trading select a brokerage because they know someone who has an account with that particular brokerage. But this is not how you should choose your brokerage, particularly if you are an entry-level trader. Conduct some research before you make a final decision. You want to choose a brokerage that fits your investment and trading style. This may not be the same as your friend's.

Fortunately, you can use the Internet to evaluate brokerages. A website provided by the Financial Industry Regulatory Authority (FINRA) provides a substantial amount of information about the conduct of both individuals and firms. Of course, it essentially lists regulatory citations, and never makes recommendations or posts complimentary comments. The listed regulatory citations are mostly for failures in oversight or careless trading practices. Corresponding fines are also listed. You can read these to find FINRA citations similar to the following:

> FINRA RULE 2010, NASD RULE 2320 - BROKERAGE NAME LISTED HERE TRANSACTIONS FOR OR WITH CUSTOMERS, FAILED TO USE REASONABLE DILIGENCE TO ASCERTAIN THE BEST INTER-DEALER MARKET AND FAILED TO BUY OR SELL IN SUCH MARKET SO THAT THE RESULTANT PRICE TO ITS CUSTOMERS WAS NOT AS FAVORABLE AS POSSIBLE UNDER PREVAILING MARKET CONDITIONS.

As mentioned, individual investment counselors are also registered with FINRA. This permits you to see a list of former employers, the time a counselor has been working with financial securities, and any past FINRA citations that may exist.

You can also check out stocktrading.net for a list of the top five option trading companies, although some traders might not agree with some of the companies listed. In fact, some highly rated companies have deplorable trading platforms. So be thorough in your research. You'll also want to compare commissions and option exchange fees.

Barrons.com, from the publisher of *Barrons* magazine, provides an online list of *Best Online Brokers*. An example of Barrons' 2014 online broker list is shown in figure 4–1.

Not all websites agree on the rankings of online brokers. When this book was written, *Kiplinger* ranked the following ten brokers in first to last order:

Company	Minimum Deposit	Stock Trade Fee
Optionshouse	$0.00	$4.95
Scottrade	$2,500	$7.00
Charles Schwab	$1,000	$8.95
E★Trade	$500	$9.99

OptionsXpress	$0.00	$8.95
Fidelity	$2,500	$7.95
TradeKing	$0.00	$4.95
Interactive Brokers	$10,000	$0.0050/Share
Merrill EDGE	$0.00	6.96
TD Ameritrade	$0.00	$9.99

Figure 4–1. Sample Rating List of Online Brokers from the *Barrons* Website

Barron's Best Online Brokers of 2014

Interactive Brokers again leads this electronic pack, with tradeMonster, Place Trade, and TD Ameritrade also picking up 4½ stars.

Broker	Trading Experience & Technology	Usability	Mobile	Range of Offerings	Research Amenities	Portfolio Analysis & Reports	Customer Service & Education	Costs	Total	Stars
Interactive Brokers	4.8	4.5	4.7	3.8	4.8	5.0	4.6	4.5	36.7	4.5
tradeMonster	4.6	4.9	5.0	4.3	4.9	4.9	4.9	2.6	36.1	4.5
Place Trade	4.8	4.6	4.7	3.9	4.8	5.0	4.8	2.5	35.1	4.5
TD Ameritrade	4.2	4.6	4.7	4.5	4.9	4.7	4.8	1.7	34.1	4.5
TradeStation	4.7	4.4	3.7	3.9	4.4	4.5	4.8	2.6	33.0	4.0
optionsXpress	4.0	4.4	4.5	4.2	4.9	4.8	4.6	1.5	32.9	4.0
OptionsHouse	3.8	4.3	4.6	3.5	4.3	4.3	4.5	3.2	32.5	4.0
TradeKing	3.5	4.3	3.9	4.1	4.6	3.6	4.7	2.6	31.3	4.0
Fidelity	3.6	4.0	4.3	4.0	4.8	4.6	4.6	1.3	31.2	4.0
E*Trade	3.4	4.0	4.4	4.3	4.7	4.5	4.8	0.7	30.8	4.0
Merrill Edge	3.0	3.9	4.2	3.3	4.6	4.5	4.5	2.8	30.8	4.0
Charles Schwab	3.2	4.2	3.9	3.7	4.5	4.3	4.7	1.1	29.6	4.0
Scottrade	2.9	3.6	3.7	3.1	3.8	3.5	4.5	1.2	26.3	3.5
Lightspeed Trading	4.1	4.1	0.0	2.3	3.4	2.4	3.8	4.0	24.1	3.0
Livevol	3.2	3.6	4.6	2.1	2.7	1.9	2.7	3.2	24.0	3.0
SogoTrade	2.6	3.2	2.4	2.9	3.0	2.1	2.9	2.9	22.0	3.0
Capital One ShareBuilder	2.4	3.6	2.6	0.9	2.9	2.7	4.2	1.8	21.1	2.5
eOption	2.1	2.7	1.3	3.0	3.0	1.9	1.8	4.2	20.0	2.5
TradingBlock	2.8	3.6	0.0	4.1	2.6	2.3	2.9	1.6	19.9	2.5
Kapitall	1.1	3.8	0.0	0.8	1.7	2.2	3.2	1.5	14.3	2.0

Charts like these never tell the entire story. And like so much Internet content, they are often misleading. It is obvious that the range of securities supported in addition to the sophistication of the trading platforms were ignored. The Kiplinger rankings are far from accurate when you consider the breadth of services, platform technologies, number of branch offices, availability and quality of customer support, and more.

In the author's opinion, TD Ameritrade's thinkorswim® platform would rank #1 for trading options and stocks. It has the most extensive feature set. And TradeStation, which is superior to many of those listed, wasn't even included. Furthermore, a trade that costs $0.0050/share looks good at first glance. But a 4,000-share trade costs $20 in commissions. Most experienced investors know brokerages will likely reduce their commissions and exchange fees to meet competition. This is especially true for high net worth clients and/or high-volume active traders.

Full-Service and Discount Brokers

Full-service brokers typically provide financial investment counselors. The counselors may suggest financial securities products, managed funds, or recommend investment management companies with which they maintain business relationships. These full-service brokerages also provide research and education to their clients. The fees charged by full-service brokers are usually higher than those charged by discount brokers. Required minimum account deposits may also be higher than those required at discount brokerages. In addition, the maintenance of a minimum account balance may be required.

Discount brokerages also require a minimum account deposit and the maintenance of a minimum account balance. This can range from $500 to $1,000. And experienced active traders who manage their own trading activity have little interest in receiving trading advice from an investment counsellor, who may not have as much trading experience or knowledge as their clients.

Many old-timers have clear recollections of their dealings with the traditional brick and mortar brokerage houses and the so-called "stock brokers" in their employ. They'd look at the lists of stocks in the daily news or the *Wall Street Journal*. When they spotted a trade opportunity, they'd phone their broker to put on a trade, and pay a $70 commission. They also remember receiving phone calls from their broker who had been advised by the "boys in New York" to solicit their clients to buy shares of stock that was part of an issue that their brokerage house was promoting. Some clients wised up and referred to these stocks as the "stock *de jour.*"

This was an unscrupulous "pump and dump" practice used by brokerages to increase the sales of an underlying stock held within the brokerage's own portfolio. Once the solicitations drove the price up as a result of the sudden influx of buy orders, the brokerage dumped the stock for a profit, leaving their clients "holding the bag." Obviously, they couldn't do this every day, and it didn't take long for regulatory agencies and clients alike to catch on. But according to many, this actually happened. Today, the regulatory agencies watch for these kinds of practices and levy heavy fines when detected. As you can see from the FINRA citation shown earlier, even minor infractions are caught and penalized.

But stories like these often drive traders to the discount brokerages. All an experienced trader wants, or needs for that matter, is access to the market through a full-featured, reliable trading platform, reasonable commissions and exchange fees, and fast execution times.

Develop a checklist that evaluates prospective brokerages. Look for the following, arranged in no particular order:

- Account types (Brokerage, IRA Rollovers, checking, bill pay, savings, money market, etc.)
- Minimum balance requirement
- Transaction fees
- Margin interest rate
- Supported trading venues (equities, options, futures, and/or forex)
- Execution speed
- Access to different trading venues
- Trading platforms (online for PCs and/or Macintosh Computers)

- Trade scanning engine(s)
- Market research (either web-based or trading platform-based)
- Account access via brokerage website
- Trading via brokerage website
- Earnings and dividend releases
- Mobile trading apps (iPhone, Android, iPad, Android Tablets, Windows Mobile)
- Paper (simulated) trading for practice
- Back trades (testing strategies with historical pricing data)
- Support (online chat, telephone, e-mail, and text messaging)
- Training (live and/or online)
- Complete financial reporting (monthly, year-to-date, prior years, 1099s, IRA minimum required distribution calculations, commissions paid, margin fees, etc.)
- Nearby branch offices

Financial Security and Stability

When opening an account, you may want to know who is underwriting the security of your account in addition to the maximum amount protected. Congressional action in 1970 requires all brokerages to register with the Securities Investor Protection Corporation (SIPC). The SIPC is to brokerages what the FDIC is to banks. The SIPC protects the brokerage accounts of each customer. If the brokerage firm is closed due to bankruptcy or fraud, the SIPC protects customer assets up to $500,000 in securities and $100,000 in cash. If your accounts exceed these insured values, you may want to consider distributing your funds across more than one brokerage, although very few investors actually do this.

Although the SIPC protects against bankruptcy and fraud, it doesn't protect against market losses caused by a decline in security values. If a brokerage firm does fail, the SIPC works to merge the failed brokerage into a successful brokerage. Failing this, the SIPC will transfer a client's securities to another firm. If stocks or bonds are missing from an investor's portfolio, the SIPC will rebuild port-folios by replacing every missing share of stock or bond, penny for penny, up to the insured limits.

Many investors never consider what can happen to their account holdings in the event of a *run* on the financial markets or an institu-tion. What effect can this have on the stability of your broker, also called *broker-dealer*?

It's somewhat reassuring to know that during such conditions insurance is extended and liquidity facilities are created to back depositor accounts. The Securities and Exchange Commission (SEC) has instituted several reforms on liquidity. These liquidity reforms ensure that each broker-dealer maintains a suitable reserve to cope with inordinate levels of client withdrawals.

In spite of these regulations, short-term unstable funding can prevent broker-dealers from order fulfillment. This can be due to a short-term lack of funds required to carry temporary imbalances in the volume of buy and sell orders. This impairs the ability for traders to buy and sell a wide variety of stocks and bonds. It can also have the effect of bringing trading to an abrupt halt.

Many investor-traders remember the failures of broker-deal-ers Lehman Brothers and Bear-Sterns during the housing mort-gage fiasco of 2008. As a result of the lessons learned then, many broker-dealers have increased their capital holdings, increased liquidity, and reduced their holdings in risky assets. All of these policies are attempts to protect themselves against the reoccur-rence of events like those that brought down these huge broker-age houses.

As the holder of a brokerage account, you should know that the potential for broker-dealer failures still exists. Although the broker-dealer's reliance on wholesale funding works 99% of the time, there's still that 1% chance of failure. Both broker-dealers and banks have been encouraged to form either asset-rich bank holding companies or intermediate holding companies to help spread capital risk.

Broker-dealers typically find short-term security by negotiating repurchase agreements with underwriters, such as money market funds. This provides the financing needed by broker-dealers to fund their transactions. In exchange, the underwriters receive reasonably low financing fees. The money market funds, among a few others, avoid long-term, risky securities. They happily settle for shorter term, low-risk securities with less vulnerability to a potential market run.

Minimums

As you can see from the preceding table that follows figure 4–1, minimum deposits and account sizes vary from $0.00 to $10,000. If you're younger than 30 years old and have not yet accrued several thousand dollars to invest in the market, your choice of a broker based on the minimum required deposit may have a high priority on your checklist. And the size of your trades will also be governed by your account size. But even if you have only a $1,000 account, it may be possible to begin trading some mini option contracts. The key is to learn how to trade and what to trade, based on your asset base.

Consider holding a garage sale and sell that video game console and all the games that have cost you thousands of hours in wasted time. Then use the same amount of time to make an income by finding, entering, and collecting money from high-probability option trades.

Withdrawals

Although the money in your brokerage account belongs to you, it can be hard to withdraw. Some brokers charge fees for withdrawals. There are also instances when a needed withdrawal can reduce your account balance below the required minimum. When this happens, the brokerage is flagged and an automatic response is produced that explains your situation.

Before you open an account, be sure you understand the rules related to withdrawals and minimum balances. Otherwise, you may be in for an unpleasant surprise. In your anger, you may decide to close the account in order to have access to your remaining account balance. This may trigger a penalty fee. Again, know the rules and read the account agreement — especially the part about account withdrawals, closure, and fees.

Market Venues

What are you going to trade? Are you just going to trade stocks and options? How about looking at the futures and foreign exchange markets? Some traders make substantial income from these venues. Therefore, look at what the brokerage offers relative to trading. Even if you are not planning to trade foreign exchange currency pairs, you might want to try it in simulation (*paper money*). So consider a brokerage that provides trading access to all four *pillars of wealth*.

Commissions and Fees

Every brokerage has a published schedule of commissions and fees. But you may talk to people who trade at the same brokerage you use who pay a lower commission than you do. This is also true of the exchange fees paid for options and futures contracts.

Commissions

If you only make an occasional trade, expect to pay the published commissions. As mentioned earlier in this chapter, if you are a high-volume active trader, your brokerage will likely consider a reduction in the commissions you pay. After all, they don't want your account or your high trading volume to go "across the street" to the competition. So talk to your investment counsellor or call the brokerage on the phone. Ask them to check your trading activity and explain that you need a lower commission. If they see that you're a high-volume trader, they'll have an incentive to lower your rate. They'd rather make fast nickels than slow dimes, or for that matter, lose you as a client.

Meeting Competition

You've negotiated a reduced commission rate from your current brokerage. Then you decide to transfer your account to another firm that offers a better trading platform or has a nearby branch office. Be sure to tell the new brokerage what you currently pay in commissions before you make the change. Most brokerages will gladly meet the competition to get your account. In fact, they will even make the account transfer for you. All stocks, bonds, and cash will be transferred for you. Even pending dividends will be swept into your new account, although this can take a few weeks to complete.

When an account closing fee is required by your old brokerage, the new brokerage will often pay that fee for you. This is a common practice and eliminates any costs associated with your transfer.

What You Pay

Each trade you make carries a corresponding commission that is paid to your brokerage. Option trades carry per-contract exchange fees on top of your commissions. If you're a high-volume trader, it's your job to negotiate the best commission rate and a reasonable exchange fee.

Per Trade

Consider the commissions you pay to your brokerage as part of the normal cost of doing business. The commissions paid for each trade, whether 100 shares of stock or 10,000 shares, usually ranges from a few dollars to $10.00. Of course this depends entirely on the brokerage you're using. The commissions you pay are part of your overhead structure. A fixed cost per trade increases the pro rata share of overhead on small trades. For example, small 100-share trades carry more overhead than 300- to 1,000-share trades. Always consider your overhead as a part of the cost of your trading business.

If you buy ten $25 shares of stock, a $10 commission represents 4% of the cost of your trade. A $6.99 commission is 2.79% of the cost. It behooves you as a trader to reduce your overhead. Making a larger trade reduces your overhead, just as reducing the commission does. So watch your commissions in relation to your trade size, as you are penalized by the commissions you pay on small trades.

Per Option Contract

Exchange fees can run from 50 cents per contract to $1.50 per contract. These fees are always paid on a per contract basis. The Chicago Board of Exchange publishes an 18-page downloadable schedule of exchange fees for Equity Options. The schedule also includes the financial index symbols RUT, SPX, SPXW, SPXPM, OEX, XSP, and VIX at the following web address:

http://www.cboe.com/publish/feeschedule/CBOEFeeSchedule.pdf

The underlying exchange fees charged to your brokerage vary from stock options to financial index and futures options. The Options Clearing Corporation (OCC) oversees options and futures trading. You can visit the OCC website at:

www.optionsclearing.com

The OCC is the world's largest equity derivatives clearing house. The OCC operates under the jurisdiction of the SEC and the Commodities Futures Trading Commission (CFTC). The OCC acts as both the issuer of and guarantor for option and futures contracts. It clears transactions for put and call options, stock indexes, foreign currencies, interest rate composites, and single-stock futures.

The OCC's stated mission is to provide market participants with innovative risk management solutions and efficiencies in the clearing and settlement of options, futures, and other financial transactions. The OCC also provides educational videos on options and futures in addition to daily market data on option volume and open interest.

Margin

Margin accounts are offered by brokerages. A margin account allows investors to borrow money from the broker in order to purchase a security or take a position in an option trade. If you have a margin account, as you probably do, the margin you borrow for your trading is collateralized by securities and cash held in your margin account. The alternative to a margin account is a cash account. Holders of cash accounts must pay the full amount for the purchase of securities. The account owner's brokerage cannot extend credit within these accounts.

Standard Margin

Standard margin is available to brokerage accounts at no extra charge. Consider the following example of how margin may be used. A trader wants to purchase 100 shares of stock. The trader uses cash for the first 50 shares and borrows the rest from the broker to buy the remaining 50 shares. This is a typical use of margin. As mentioned earlier, borrowed margin is collateralized by securities held in the trader's account, which may include the shares of stock being purchased. The broker charges interest for the borrowed money at annual interest rates that range from 1.58% (Interactive Brokers) to 9.00%. The rate can be incrementally adjusted downward based on account size.

If you decide to sell several hundred shares of one stock and buy another, without margin you would have to wait for your stock sale to settle and the cash proceeds from the sale be deposited in your account. This is called a *cash account* as compared to a *margin account*. All this may take a few days to happen. Once the proceeds of the stock sale are received, you can buy the second stock. But that stock may have increased by $2 or $3 per share over the two- to three-day waiting period. By using margin, you can sell the first stock and buy the second stock in less than a minute. The borrowed margin will cover the cost of the second stock even before the first stock order is filled.

Fledgling traders may want to tread lightly before they begin using account margin. If a trader buys stock on margin and the value of the trader's account suffers a substantial loss from a market downturn, the trader can be required to either deposit more funds or sell securities held in the account, which may be those just purchased with margin. If the trader cannot be reached during such an event, the brokerage is required to rebalance the account by selling securities within that account. Although margin can be a powerful trading tool, it can also turn on the trader and force stock sales or the closing of option contracts that would otherwise never be considered.

The interest rate charged on margin varies widely from one broker to the next. When writing this book the author checked the interest rates charged by various brokerages. Interactive Brokers was 1.58%, OptionsHouse charged 4.00%, and TD Ameritrade's maximum rate was 9.00%. If you plan to make extensive use of margin, the margin interest rate can be a deciding factor in choosing your brokerage. But the standard rates can be negotiated based on account size and trading volume. You should also recall from earlier remarks, the value of penny (OTC) stocks is never marginable due to the high risk associated with these unregulated securities. This is another reason to avoid penny stocks.

Portfolio Margin

Qualified traders with extensive experience can apply for and secure *portfolio margin*. Some brokerages grant portfolio margin based on years of experience. Some require their clients to take a test to demonstrate their option knowledge. Brokerages also require a minimum account balance for portfolio margin eligibility. To name a few, Interactive Brokers requires a $100,000 account balance while TD Ameritrade requires $125,000. With portfolio margin a trader is at the highest trading level permitted by a brokerage. The trader is unrestricted in the option strategies permitted, which includes those carrying the highest level of risk.

Portfolio margin grants significantly lower margin collateral than standard margin. Instead of receiving 50% margin collateral on the securities held within a client's account, client's with portfolio margin can borrow up to 85% of the value of qualified securities within their accounts. This increases the trader's leverage on unsecured trades, such as selling uncovered (*naked*) call or put option contracts on one of the popular financial indexes or futures contracts. Trades like these are explored in detail beginning in chapter 10 and again in chapter 14.

Trading Platforms

As a trader you must have access to both a trading application and your account information. Every modern brokerage offers both. Of course, some are better than others. And there are both browser-based and application-based trading systems. For example, the OptionsHouse discount brokerage offers the TradeMonster® browser-based trading application plus mobile apps that run on smartphones. TradeMonster includes access to charts, chart studies, and the trader's account information. Charles Schwab, TD Ameritrade, TradeStation, and Interactive Brokers, among others, all offer downloadable computer-, tablet-, and smartphone-based applications. To mention four such applications, Charles Schwab offers OptionsExpress®, which was specifically designed with option traders in mind. TD Ameritrade offers thinkorswim®, which includes a powerful option trading interface. The Trader Workstation from Interactive Brokers is another trading platform specifically designed for option traders. TradeStation is yet another excellent trading application with a trading ladder that supports chart trading. TradeStation's charts, chart studies, and drawing tool set are outstanding. All these are extremely robust trading applications. Most provide access to all four trading venues: equities, options, futures, and forex.

Most of the screen shots within this book are from TD Ameritrade's thinkorswim® application. It was selected because of the ability to adjust colors and the many features provided that were ideal for use with this book. The TradeStation, Trader Workstation, and TradeMonster were also examined. Although all are excellent trading platforms, other considerations, including familiarity, led to the use of thinkorswim® for the purposes of writing this book.

Summary reports are viewable on all of the applications mentioned. Detailed financial reports, including 1099s, are both viewable and downloadable from all of these brokerage websites. This is true of every brokerage that provides both downloadable computer, tablet, and smartphone applications and browser-based trading applications.

Many brokerages include browser-based trading applications. This is true of TD Ameritrade, Scottrade, E★Trade, and Charles Schwab to name a few. Both TD Ameritrade and Charles Schwab accommodate trading on their websites as well as providing computer- and smartphone-based trading applications.

Stock and Option Scanners

The trading platforms from TradeStation and TD Ameritrde (thinkorswim®) both support equities, options, futures, and forex. And both include sophisticated stock scanners. This feature permits users to specify several search parameters in order to produce a list stocks (or *watch list*) that meet the established criteria. Thinkorswim® also boasts an adjustable *Options Hacker* and *Spread Hacker*, shown in figure 4–2, used for the same purpose.

Figure 4–2. The thinkorswim® Stock, Option, and Spread Hackers

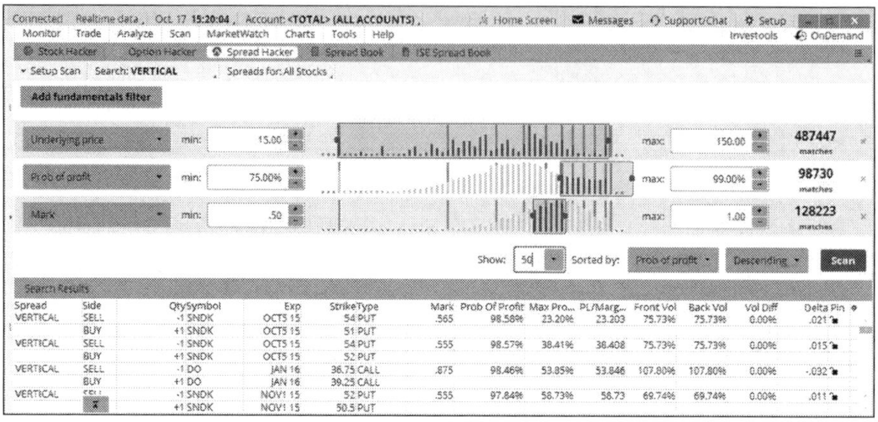

For illustration purposes only.

Simulated (Paper) Trading) and Back Trading

Simulated trading, also called *paper trading*, is another popular feature commonly used by new and intermediate traders. Paper trading provides an opportunity to test different trading strategies with "play money." The thinkorswim® platform also includes a *thinkBack* feature for what are called "back trades." This tool provides several years' worth of daily financial data for thousands of stocks, ETFs, and financial indexes. The thinkBack interface includes an option chain, a calendar, an order bar, and a price chart. Traders can enter option trades that begin and end on selected dates in the past. This produces actual trade outcomes based on historical prices. The chart shows a profit and loss line throughout the duration of the back trade. Users can slide across the chart to see each day's gain or loss. They can also click on the calendar to increment the progress of the underlying trade within the option chain, where the daily Bid, Ask, and Mark (premium value) are shown. Figure 4–3 shows a sample thinkBack screen.

Figure 4–3. Testing Option Strategies with thinkorswim®'s thinkBack

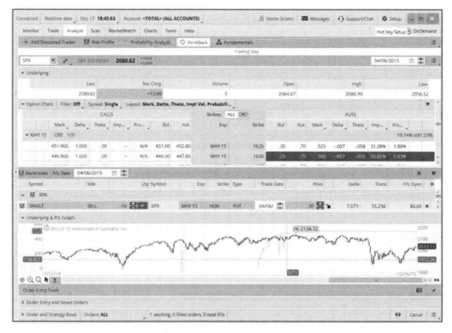

For illustration purposes only.

Other Features

Full-featured trading platforms, especially ones like thinkorswim®, have evolved over a period of many years. They continue to be periodically enhanced and updated. The thinkorswim® trading application was originally developed and released in 1999 by Tom Sosnoff, a Chicago-based options market maker. Because Sosnoff specializes in options, thinkorswim® is well suited to option trading. But the platform is used for much more than options, as it supports the equities, futures, and forex trading venues quite well.

Watch Lists, Synchronizing, Dynamic Scanning

As an active trader you will develop your own *watch lists*. Watch lists are tables of stocks and/or ETFs and financial indices that fit certain parameters or belong to specific market sectors or subsectors. For example, you may wish to view stocks or ETFs that make dividend distributions, like the one shown below. The column headings shown, such as Impl Vol, ATR, Volume, Div, and Div Freq are added by the user, while other default watch list columns are often removed. The symbols within circles pop up dividend, shareholder communication, and earnings release dates.

Symbol ▲		Last	Net Chng	Impl Vol	ATR	Volume	Div	Div Freq
AAPL		115.47	+1.71	32.69%	2.46	40,826,329	.52	Q
AGNC		19.14	+.06	18.65%	0.23	2,908,622	.2	M
BBEP		2.4700	-.01	73.48%	0.19	1,030,029	.0417	M
BPT		42.39	+.62	44.76%	2.03	86,798	.703	Q
CLMT		26.14	+.01	42.07%	0.92	146,170	.685	Q
CYS		8.10	+.13	19.17%	0.14	2,474,893	.26	Q
DOM		1.0950	-.0114	163.84%	0.15	49,512	.0988	Q
DX		6.795	+.035	N/A	0.12	165,085	.24	Q
ERF		5.22	+.09	65.79%	0.37	1,653,717	.05	M
ETP		44.19	-1.34	34.89%	1.56	4,868,209	1.035	Q
EVEP		6.63	-.08	82.11%	0.56	335,154	.5	Q
FSC		5.55	-.14	42.37%	0.16	2,042,182	.06	M
FXCM		9.58	-.33	107.74%	0.67	41,567	N/A	--
HDV		75.49	+1.55	9.74%	0.94	280,602	.7222	Q
HTS		15.895	+.095	18.46%	0.22	492,558	.45	Q
KCAP		5.08	+.01	++	0.15	147,099	.21	Q
LGCY		4.53	-.03	100.28%	0.53	1,077,738	.35	Q
LINE		2.7100	-.04	138.10%	0.26	2,138,242	.1042	M
LRE		106.21	0	++	10.72	0	0	--
MEMP		5.86	-.17	82.74%	0.47	435,085	.55	Q
MMLP		28.52	-.25	31.13%	1.01	132,821	.8125	Q
MTGE		14.80	+.05	18.95%	0.2	530,951	.4	Q
NLY		10.20	+.02	19.14%	0.15	6,960,370	.3	Q
NMM		7.57	-.16	66.03%	0.45	548,711	.4425	Q
NRZ		12.535	-.255	28.91%	0.37	1,978,123	.46	Q
NS		48.94	-1.30	41.54%	1.61	285,093	1.095	Q
PHK		8.26	+.09	N/A	0.19	435,497	.1035	M
PNNT		6.99	+.03	27.79%	0.18	304,792	.28	Q
PSEC		7.37	-.04	23.35%	0.14	2,156,907	.0833	M
PWE		1.1300	+.03	112.86%	0.1113	4,471,342	.01	Q
SFL		17.365	+.135	33.42%	0.35	511,320	.44	Q
SXE		5.2500	-.07	76.48%	0.4039	55,231	.4	Q
TAXI		8.39	+.06	61.41%	0.33	198,023	.25	Q
TCAP		17.4701	+.0101	38.42%	0.56	69,992	.54	Q
TNH		111.19	-.74	N/A	3.1	9,762	2.36	Q
TOO		16.21	+.25	35.55%	0.68	426,548	.56	Q
VIX		14.80	-1.90	98.11%	2.49	0	N/A	--
VNR		8.73	-.17	70.96%	0.67	719,104	.1175	M
WHZ		1.83	-.01	106.64%	0.13	91,716	.1586	Q
WIN		7.51	+.01	72.12%	0.37	1,983,038	.15	Q
WMC		11.90	+.19	19.34%	0.26	421,431	.6	Q

For illustration purposes only.

Another watch list could list stocks that offer weekly option contracts. But because there are more than 400 *weeklys*, you will want to pare the list down. For example, based on your personal experience, your list may include only stocks with prices from $25 to $100. Your platform should permit you to sort the *Last* column (the most recent price) so you can delete those stocks that fall outside the desired price range.

You can also export watch lists to an Excel-compatible file. Opening the list in Excel permits you to sort and parse the data. Once you have your symbol list, keep the column of symbols and delete all other rows and columns. Then import the symbols back to a new, blank watch list. The trading platform automatically fills the underlying data for each of the remaining symbols in the list. Exporting and importing watch lists and other information within a trading platform is a useful feature that is learned with a little practice.

Synchronizing a watch list to an option chain and a chart is also a handy feature. For example, when you click on a symbol within your watch list, a corresponding chart and option chain should instantly access the underlying data for the selected symbol. This makes trade scanning much easier. Otherwise, you would have to open each chart and option chain window independently and then type the symbol in each — a slow and rigorous process.

Some platforms also provide *dynamic scanning*. TradeStation calls this *Radar*. This process begins with establishing parameters, like a price range, current volatility, and trading volume values. The dynamic scanning feature adds and removes symbols to and from the watch list as they come into and fall out of favor — dynamically. This is a useful, time-saving feature because it restricts those symbols displayed in the watch list to just those that meet your parameters.

Charting, Chart Studies, and Drawing Tools

All trading platforms provide price charts. Of course some are better than others. You should be able to look at a variety of chart types that include line, candle, bar, and area charts among others. Below is a chart setting dialog that shows several different chart styles.

You should also be able to change time intervals from week, day, hour, and minute. Some applications support time intervals down to seconds and even "tics." Another handy charting feature is the ability to view multiple chart windows at the same time.

Figure 4–4. Chart Settings

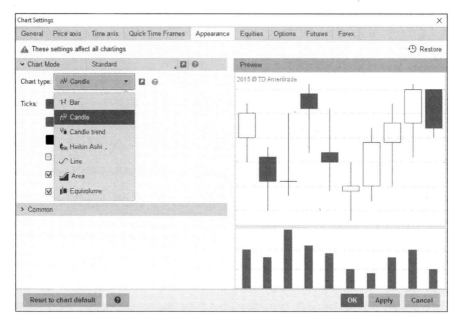

For illustration purposes only.

There are also "libraries" of *chart studies* that include most of the popular studies such as moving averages, Bollinger bands, trend-lines, oversold/overbought oscillators, and average true range (the average daily price movement over a specified number of days, such as 9 or 14). This was briefly discussed earlier. There are approximately 750 such studies, some of which are copyrighted. But most trading platforms provide from one to several hundred from which to choose, including the most popular studies. This is typically more than ample, as most traders use only a half-dozen to a dozen chart studies, but never that many at the same time. Displaying six studies at a time can create a substantial amount of clutter on a chart. But to traders that use them, each study provides meaningful guidance.

Finally, charts should also incorporate a set of drawing tools. Drawing tools are used to annotate charts with entry, stop, and target lines and notes. Some traders like to draw *Fibonacci* retracement lines or add the *Floor Trader Pivot Points* study to their charts. These are quite meaningful to many traders. Both of these studies are examined within chapter 8.

Option Tools and Strategies

Most trading platforms used to buy and sell options incorporate a drop-down list of common option strategies. These strategies can include between one and four "legs." For example, a trader may construct a *vertical spread* comprised of a near the money long call and an out of the money short call. (As you now know, long is buy and short is sell.) Remember the *covered call* discussed earlier? This strategy, also referred to as a *covered stock*, buys stock and sells an equal number of out of the money call shares. (Buy 500 shares of stock and sell 5 option contracts for the same symbol at the same time, that is, in a single transaction.)

Figure 4–5 shows two groups of option strategies. One is from TradeMonster and the other from thinkorswim®.

Figure 4–5. Typical Option Strategies Available on a Trading Platform

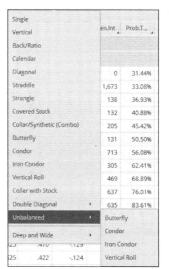

For illustration purposes only.

Another popular option strategy used by many traders is called an iron condor. (The *risk profile* graph of an iron condor resembles a big bird.) Of course you are not expected to understand how this option strategy works yet. But you will know exactly how it works and what to expect by the time you finish reading this book. You will be guided through the setup and entry steps for this and numerous other option strategies. You'll also understand what can go wrong — because it can!

The iron condor simultaneously sells and buys both puts and calls. If one option contract is being traded, one out of the money put and one out of the money call are sold. (We call this a short put and a short call, right?). Then a slightly farther out of the money put and call are bought. The long legs are typically one to three strikes farther out of the money than the short legs. This is all done at the same time and you pay only one brokerage commission for all four legs. However, you must pay exchange fees for each option contract. In the case of ten contracts — 1,000 shares — you must pay exchange fees for 40 option contracts, i.e., ten contracts multiplied by four *legs*.

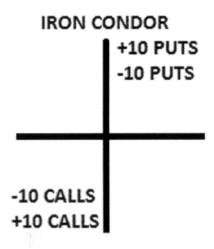

The trader receives premium for the put and call sold, and pays premium for the put and call bought. Obviously, the trader's goal is to collect more premium than spent. If the premium paid is 40 cents and the premium received is 80 cents, the trader nets 40 cents in premium per share for 1,000 shares (ten contracts). Hence, the iron condor is a *credit spread*. If the underlying never reaches the strike prices of the short put or short call prior to contract expiration, the contracts *expire worthless*. The trader's final profit is $800 from 40 cents per share × 2,000 shares (1,000 puts plus 1,000 calls) counting both the puts and calls.

Why would a trader spend the extra 40 cents to buy the puts and the calls? This seems like a total waste of money! The answer: These option legs serve as a hedge, sometimes called "insurance," against a strong rally or precipitous drop in the price of the underlying. They protect against a major loss. If the strategy works as intended, the trader can only lose the difference between one of the put and call pairs.

Figure 4–5 illustrated a series of option spreads. One is from the TradeMonster® platform and the other from the thinkorswim® platform. Notice the *iron condor* spread exists on both. Traders can also create "custom" trades to achieve variations of the underlying default strategies provided within these platforms.

Trading Methods

Simple option trades are entered directly from the underlying option chain by clicking a value within the Bid (sell) or Ask (buy) column adjacent to (that is, on the same row) as the selected option (or *strike*) price. This displays an order bar on which you can make adjustments in the number of contracts, strike price, the premium price, and expiration date(s). You can also add protective stops and fashion the order as a limit or market order and set the order duration to a Day order or a Good Till Canceled (GTC) order. There's more information related to order types and durations in chapter 9.

Trade Ladders for Stock and Futures Traders

A trade ladder is comprised of three vertical columns. A center column lists price levels from high to low. A green vertical column to the left-hand side of the price column is clicked to enter buy orders. A red column on the right-hand side of the price column is clicked to enter sell orders. Figure 4–6 illustrates the thinkorswim® Active Trader interface. It also includes a price chart, and other features including a dialog that can be used to set up bracketed trades. Figure 4–6 shows a bracketed trade with a protective stop $1.00 below the limit entry and a profit target $3.00 above. This is an example of a 3:1 reward-to-risk ratio.

The Active Trader's price chart time interval and chart style are adjustable. Users can also add and remove supporting chart studies and drawing objects. As previously described, bracketed trades are typically comprised of three legs: a limit order, a protective stop, and a profit target. When either the buy (green) or sell (red) column is clicked, an Order Confirmation dialog appears so you can verify the details of your order. Clicking **Send** transmits the order to your brokerage.

Figure 4–6. A Trading Ladder being used to Send a Bracketed Limit Order

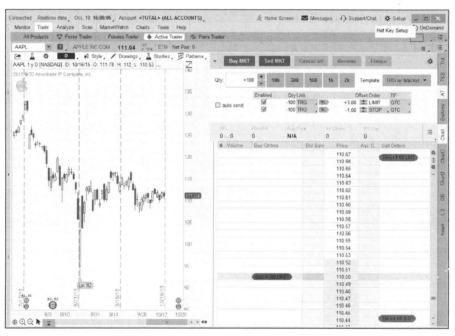

For illustration purposes only.

Figure 4–7. An Order Confirmation Dialog

Order Confirmation Dialog	✕
	☐ Auto send with shift click 🖨
#1 Order Description	BUY +100 AAPL @110.50 LMT GTC [TO OPEN]
#2 Order Description	SELL -100 AAPL @TRG+3.00 LMT GTC TRG BY #1 OCO [TO CLOSE]
#3 Order Description	SELL -100 AAPL STP TRG-1.00 GTC TRG BY #1 OCO [TO CLOSE]
Cost of #1 Order including commissions	$11,050.00 + $5.00 = $11,055.00
Cost of #2 Order including commissions	credit $11,104.00 - $5.00 = credit $11,099.00
Cost of #3 Order including commissions	credit $11,104.00 - $5.00 = credit $11,099.00
Cost of Trade including commissions	$11,050.00 + $5.00 = $11,055.00
Buying Power Effect	($1,662.50)
Resulting Buying Power for Stock	$1,005,895.62
Resulting Buying Power for Options	$1,005,895.62

Single Account ▾   Account: ☐ Save last used mode

Note for this order

Delete   Edit   Save   Send

For illustration purposes only.

Figures 4–6 and 4–7 show a trade setup in which the price of AAPL must drop to $110.50 to trigger the working limit order. Day and futures traders often suppress the preceding Order Confirmation Dialog shown in figure 4–7 to save time. They want to send the order instantly as soon as they click a price level on the order ladder. Any unnecessary delay could be costly as prices can change within a fraction of a second. Notice that a target price on line #2 and a stop price on line #3 of the Order Confirmation Dialog are also being sent. For example, the trader may want the stop to be $1 below the profit target $5 above entry. Remember, the trader can choose to go either long (buy) by clicking a green rung, or short (sell) by clicking a red rung. The system automatically adjusts the stop and target positions based on a buy or sell order. No additional adjustments are required for a long or short order.

Of course you would short stocks when you anticipate a price drop. Shorting a stock is financed by margin. This is also referred to as a *short sale*. Consider the following example of a typical short sale.

1. HLF is presently selling at $51 per share.

2. Your chart analysis reveals a high probability of a drop in the price of HLF.

3. You open the Active Trader and select symbol HLF to view the chart and trading ladder.

4. You set up a bracketed trade with a −$1.00 protective stop at $1.00 and a +$5.00 profit target.

5. You set the number of shares to 200.

6. Then you click the red $50 trading ladder rung to enter a limit sell order (a *short sale*) and send the order; your bracketed limit order is now working, but not yet filled.

7. HLF drops to $50 and your short order is triggered and filled.

8. HLF continues dropping and reaches $47.50. You slide your stop down to $48 to ensure a $2 gain per share in case HLF begins to reverse its downward trajectory.

9. HLF keeps dropping and pierces your $45 stop, at which time a "buy to cover" order is triggered by the $45 limit order that exists at your profit target.

10. You're out! You made a $5 per share profit or $1,000 for the 200 shares you *shorted*.

If HLF had rallied by $1 or more, the $51 protective stop would have triggered. This scenario results in a $200 loss. In the example $200 was risked to make $1,000 in profit. The 5:1 reward–to–risk ratio worked. But experienced traders have learned to be more conservative in the placement of their stops. This is especially true of day traders who constantly scalp. They often use 1.5:1 and 2:1 reward–to–risk ratios. Having stops that are too "tight" are triggered by normal upward and downward price transients. So a $2 stop and a $4 target would be more common.

For buy and hold stocks and swing trades, "good till canceled" protective stops are typically placed between 7% and 10% from the price of the underlying. The stops are adjusted every few days to follow profits. In the case of a rallying or dropping stock, a *trailing stop* is sometimes used. A trailing stop automatically follows the price. For example, a $1.00 trailing stop on long stock trade (a stock you bought) follows the upward price trajectory until the price ends its rally and retreats. When it retreats from the high point by $1.00 (the amount of the trailing stop) the stop automatically triggers a sell order.

Many active traders avoid the use of trailing stops. They prefer to watch the price action and intervene manually. These traders do not want to lose the profit potential of upward trending stocks that experience a brief pullback and consolidation, only to resume the upward trend.

Occasional pullbacks are always expected. Many draw profit target lines on their charts as part of their normal trading setups. Some use Fibonacci retracement or pivot point lines, both described in chapter 8.

Chart Trading

The thinkorswim® and TradeStation platforms permit working stops and targets to be slid up and down on either the trading ladder or on the accompanying chart. When a trade fills, the entry, stop, and target positions are shown as lines and bubbles on both the chart and the ladder. This provides a visual representation of the working trade and is a powerful trade management tool.

Mobile Platform Apps

Many traders use mobile apps to enter and exit trades and to monitor their positions. Mobile apps are particularly useful when a trader is away from home or office, where trading normally takes place. There are some traders who do all their trading on a smartphone.

When choosing a brokerage, be sure to check out the availability of their mobile apps. The apps should provide access to closing and rolling both stocks and options. And the app should be intuitive. Having access to your account on a 24x7 basis can be vital to your success.

Access and Support

Technical and account support are both important to active traders. In the early stages of trading, you may have questions about how to perform certain operations. There are times when all you require is for someone to answer a few questions. But there are occasions when you may require guidance through a complex, multi-stepped process on your trading platform.

Internet Support

The support team within many brokerages can take control of your computer for the purpose of viewing and highlighting areas on your screen. As a technician talks to you over the telephone, he can walk you through each step of a transaction by pointing to or circling buttons or menu items.

Wait times must also be considered. If you have to wait more than a few minutes for assistance, it may be too late, particularly if you're trying to reach the trade desk. So be sure to check out typical wait times for support before electing your brokerage. Find others who are using the brokerage you're considering to determine their experience.

Branch Offices

It can be convenient for your brokerage to have a nearby branch office. There you can discuss account issues, commission rates, and exchange fees; obtain forms; and even get advice from an investment counsellor. But as a self-directed active trader, most of your conversations will be administrative in nature. Nevertheless, check out access to local brokerage facilities.

Education

Next to trading support, trading education is something that can be useful to new traders. Examine the websites of prospective brokerages. Look for education offerings, both live and online. If you're curious about the futures or forex markets or want to know more about chart analysis, you may be able to take either online or live training courses. TD Ameritrade's Investools subsidiary offers both, while Online Trading Academy is a training company that specializes in hands-on classroom instruction. Although tuition is required for high quality instruction, the tuition students pay is often returned through improved trading income.

What did you learn in chapter 4?

1. Not all brokerages offer all trading _____.
2. Full-service brokerages typically charge _____ transaction fees than discount brokerages.
3. Develop a _____ for evaluating your brokerage.
4. The _____ protects brokerage accounts much like the FDIC protects bank accounts.
5. SEC reforms on _____ ensure that broker-dealers maintain suitable reserves.
6. Active traders may be granted lower brokerage _____ and _____.
7. When buying or selling option contracts, two charges exist: a _____ and _____ fees.
8. The _____ oversees options and futures trading.
9. A _____ account allows investors to borrow money from the broker.
10. Brokerage margin accounts _____ the time required for a trade to settle.
11. Penny stocks cannot be used as collateral for _____.
12. Experienced traders with high-dollar accounts may apply for _____ margin.
13. A stock or option _____ lists stocks that meet one or more established criteria.
14. A _____ _____ uses historical market data.
15. A table of stocks used by traders to scan for trades is called a _____ _____.
16. A d_____ watch list (sometimes called *radar*) automatically adds and removes symbols according to the scan criteria.
17. The _____ chart type is the most popular in use today.
18. A _____ trade includes a limit entry, a protective stop, and a profit target.

19. What is chart trading? Setting and moving _____ and _____ directly on a price _____.

20. Many traders use _____ to enter, manage, and exit trades.

5 TRADING IS A BUSINESS

Introduction

A common characteristic found among successful full-time and part-time traders is commitment and discipline. As this chapter title says, trading is a business. NEVER treat trading as a casual hobby. Otherwise, you're probably wasting both your money and your time.

Setting Up

When setting up any business, including a trading business, there are many things to consider. First, you must know how your business works. That is, you must understand how the market works, be familiar with the various trading venues, and know which ones work best for you. Your trading business must be properly equipped. It requires a reliable broker that ranked high on your evaluation checklist. It must have reliable trading equipment and a full-featured trading platform connected to a reliable trading infrastructure on which to trade. Finally, the business requires fast and dependable access to the resources of your brokerage. And, of course, your business must be capitalized sufficiently to support your trading activities.

In addition to knowing what, where, how, and when to trade, know yourself. Conduct a self-evaluation to see how you cope with stress. None of us thinks in precisely the same way nor do we react to stressful situations identically. If you're about to lose a bundle, do you panic, choke, or do you calmly confront the situation with a plan and steady resolve? Full-time traders must know themselves, because failure is not an option.

Daily Activities

Begin each trading day before the market opens by conducting a careful analysis. Check the news and then scan for those trade setups that fit your trading style. Check the charts for trends and patterns like those described in chapter 7. Find those breakout opportunities. Use this information to develop a daily watchlist. When the market opens, you're ready! Your trades will be well planned and rational.

Then stop trading at a regular time. Never overtrade. Fatigue is your enemy. It blurs your judgment and contributes to faulty decisions. Although option trading is not terribly complex, when you're fatigued it's easy to miss something as simple as open interest or a suitable expiration date. Ask any longtime option trader. These things happen. And they happen more often near the end of the trading day. So consider these daily activities:

- Begin early while your mind is fresh and uncluttered.
- Plan your trading day.
- Check the financial news.
- Set up your trades (begin with the previous afternoon's ideas).
- Re-evaluate and then enter your trades.
- Examine and take profits from currently working trades.
- End the trading day by scanning for the next day's trade candidates.
- Close up shop on schedule.
- Walk away.

Education and Practice

You might consider yourself ready to begin trading when you finish reading this book and have:

- selected and funded a brokerage account.
- familiarized yourself with a trading platform
- performed the practice activities
- developed trading rules
- understand risk management

If you've also taken one or more live or web-based trading courses — even better! Having invested the time and money to accomplish these steps indicates that you're committed.

So now it's time to expand your practice using live market data. Be sure to spend a few weeks or perhaps even a month entering and monitoring simulated trades. You can do this using your brokerage's paper (simulated) trading feature. In addition to trading the actual prices of real symbols, you'll become much more familiar with your brokerage's trading platform.

An important goal you'll achieve through your practice is to find those trading strategies that work best for you. You'll encounter some that seem to work well most of the time and others that are not comfortable, rarely work, or both. After testing several strategies, settle on two or three with which you're most comfortable. Establish rules for each (see chapter 13). Then consider "going live." You should know that even the most experienced traders rarely trade more than a few strategies. Consider Chuck and Karen. Although they both know many trading strategies, Chuck is a "covered call" and "debit call spread" guy." Karen likes to sell index options. They've figured out their trading rules and have found their comfort zones, so that's what they do.

Temperament

Emotion has led many traders to the poor house. They are euphoric when a trade succeeds, and become angry or depressed when they experience a losing trade. They blow out their accounts by ignoring their risk management rules. They become too aggressive, overtrade, attempt to get revenge by fixating on a losing symbol, or slide protective stops hoping for a reversal that never comes until they lose everything. These are some of the ways traders can ignore their risk management rules to their detriment. They simply can't let go. As a trader, remember that some trades win and some lose. But good traders move on to the next trade. Celebrating or fretting is a total waste of time.

It's been said that women are better traders than men. Some psychologists tell us men as a group are naturally more competitive. They want to "win," so they approach trading as a competition. Their "gamesmanship" motivates them to "beat" those traders on the other side of their positions. They need the thrill of winning and may even do a "high-five" when a trade becomes profitable. But they'll often choose risky trades that carry a high potential for reward, but that also carry a high degree of risk. After all, it's a high-reward, high-risk "game." But it's not a game. It's a business!

Of course there are also some very competitive women. I know some. For example my daughter received college scholarships in athletics. She's extremely competitive in sports. But she's one of the most conservative traders I know. Women aren't that interested in playing and winning the trading game. They tend to be very businesslike in their trading regimen. While the "alpha trader" is venting aggression on a few high-risk, high-reward positions, conservative traders are busily making income from a series of high-probability, low-risk trades. These traders tend to rake in profits day in and day out — making fast nickels rather than slow dimes. The few losers encountered typically represent a small percentage of a conservative trader's activity. And their risk management rules are working. Small, controlled losses tell traders they're succeeding.

As mentioned in the preceding practice paragraph, find a few winning strategies with which you're comfortable — the ones that seem to work in your favor most often. Then hammer them for a steady stream of incremental returns.

Selecting and Setting up Your Equipment

You can use a PC, a Macintosh, or a tablet computer when using a browser-based trading platform. If using a downloadable trading platform such as thinkorswim®, TradeStation, or Traders Workstation, you may prefer a Windows-based personal computer running Windows with multiple display adapters.

A computer with a fast processor, eight or more megabytes of memory, and ample disk space is recommended. An Intel core i5 4th generation or better processor or one of AMD's FX-8300 8-core or Opteron series processors are also more than adequate. Even slower processors will certainly do the job. If you're using an expandable tower or desktop PC, consider adding a second graphics card. With two modern graphic cards that feature HDMI, DVI, and SVGA outputs, you can attach four separate displays. This permits the simultaneous display of account positions, watch lists, charts, and option chains.

Of course four separate displays aren't necessary to see four different windows. Experienced PC users can quickly jump from one window to the next by pressing the **Alt+Tab** keys. If you're using a notebook PC and its built-in display, the Alt+Tab combination is your ticket to a fast review of three, four, or even more active windows!

You will also use your web browser to access your brokerage's website. There you can examine your monthly and year-end reports, exchange secure messages with brokerage personnel, and transfer funds between your brokerage and your bank. Many other resources exist on brokerage websites such as research information and browser-based trading systems.

There are several applications to consider. For example, Microsoft Excel is useful for downloading and uploading watch list and trading data between your trading platform, the brokerage website, and your computer. You'll also want to learn how to use available graphic applications, such as something as simple as Windows Paint, to capture, edit, and even print screen shots for your records. Microsoft Word is also useful if you want to assemble a collection of screen captures, annotate them, and save them to a file for later reference.

Location

Also consider your trading location. It should be isolated and quiet. The last thing an active trader needs is distractions or constant interruptions. When trading from home, barking dogs and squalling children can be a major barrier to concentration. Some traders actually rent office space and go to work every day just as they would for a normal 8:00 to 5:00 job.

Although this may sound extravagant, think of what these fulltime work-away-from-home traders learn. They work at trading all day long, developing trading rules, testing them, and constantly refining them. They continuously examine a variety of chart studies, find the ones that work, and eliminate the ones that don't. Over time both their trading knowledge and trading skills improve. So they either become master traders or they discover that they are not well suited for a full-time career as a trader.

Connections

Trading requires sending buy and sell orders throughout the day and watching the market in real time. Therefore, it's essential to have a reliable connection to your brokerage. And you should also have a backup plan.

Internet

Your Internet connection to your brokerage must be both reliable and continuous. Many of us have experienced intermittent Internet services. These unreliable connections may require us to reboot our routers several times each day. If you haven't experienced this kind of service, you're lucky. But maybe you've experienced a router failure at your favorite Wi-Fi coffee boutique. Even when you ask the clerk behind the counter to check and reboot the router, they never seem to understand. For some reason they always seem to think that they've got to call a far-away computer technician, when all that's required is an unplug-replug operation. This cycles the power and resets the router, which usually resumes normal operation.

If your Internet service is like the one described here — with constant downtimes and resets — find another service provider. The last thing you need is not being able to get out of a trade that's going against you or getting in one you want. You may be losing money with each passing second without a way to "stop the bleeding."

Telephone

There's always the telephone! Many people have canceled their landline service and use their cellular phones or tablet computers for just about everything. Be sure to download the smartphone trading application from iTunes, the Android Play Store, or the Windows app store. Then spend whatever time is required to learn how to place, monitor, and exit orders. This is your first line of defense in case your Internet connection or power fails. Even when Wi-Fi is down within your trading facility, thankfully your smartphone's connection to a cellular tower goes around Wi-Fi.

Your telephone provides another level of backup. Keep the number of your brokerage's trading desk in a convenient place. Be ready to call your broker with instructions if your connection goes down and you're either missing a good trade or a working trade is currently going against you.

Of course you won't know what's happening within the market when you can't view watch lists or working trades on your computer. So consider staying in touch with your positions on your smartphone.

Using the Branch Office for Backup

Recall that one of the items on the brokerage checklist was having a nearby branch office. Every office has a connection to the trading application. You can visit almost any branch office and find one or more computers in the lobby. There you can launch the trading application, enter your username and password, and access your account. So in the event of a total blackout at your primary trading location, make a beeline for your branch office as a backup resource.

And keep the phone numbers of your brokerage's primary headquarters, its trading desk, and the number of your local branch office close by. If you carry a smartphone, put your brokerage's contact information on your contacts list. You should also consider writing the contact information on a card and keeping it in your wallet or purse.

What did you learn in chapter 5?

1. Trading is a _____.
2. Trading is not a _____ _____.
3. Your trading equipment MUST be _____.
4. Ensure you have fast access to your _____.
5. Do your market analysis and find potential trades before the _____ _____.
6. Quit trading at a _____ _____.
7. During your simulated trading experience, find out which trades _____ _____.
8. Establish _____ for each trading strategy. (See setup parameters in chapters 14 and 15.)
9. Find and trade in your _____ _____.
10. Traders blow out their accounts by ignoring their _____ _____ rules.
11. Revenge _____ is irrational.
12. Find the trades that work. Then _____ for a steady stream of incremental returns.
13. Separate multiple displays are _____ _____.
14. Microsoft Excel is useful for _____ and _____ watch lists and trading data.
15. You should have a _____ connection to your brokerage.
16. You should have a _____ _____.
17. If your Internet service is intermittent, find another _____ _____.
18. Be sure to download the _____ _____ _____.
19. Put your brokerage's _____ _____ on your smartphone in case of emergency.
20. Your brokerage's local branch office is another _____ resource.

6 TRADING STYLES AND DURATIONS

Introduction

A trader's style includes the number of days and amount of time spent trading, the particular markets traded, and of course, the number of trades and average duration of each trade. But a trading style that is well suited to one trader may be extremely stressful to another. Consider day trading. Many day traders enjoy the high-volume action of constantly attempting to scalp small profits from several working trades. They trade long and they trade short based on what the charts tell them. But many traders find day trading much too demanding. The expression "know thyself" is something every trader must learn.

Of course different trading styles are better suited to some markets than to others. However, this book is about option trading, the study of price charts, watch lists, and option chains. This chapter briefly describes trading styles that correspond to the equity and option markets. It also briefly examines options on futures. But futures and forex trading is a different book.

Day Traders (Intraday Trades)

Day traders are often called *market scalpers*. Scalpers take quick profits on sudden price rallies and drops (or price *breakouts*). They focus on fast-moving, highly volatile stocks, ETFs, and the e-mini futures. (Recall that the e-minis were listed in chapter 3, and are fast-moving financial index futures.)

Day traders seem to thrive on constant trading activity. Some might conclude day traders are the kind of people who like to spend hours on end at the casino gambling tables or sitting in front of a slot machine. But their trading results are typically better than their gambling results, because they employ trading rules. They understand the difference between high-probability trading and gambling based on random chance. One is a business; the other is a form of entertainment.

Day traders are interested in fast price movements. They thrive on volatility. They determine the current price trend and look for the most recent price support and resistance levels. Some use Fibonacci retracement lines to place entries and exits, Floor Trader Pivot Point lines that show support and resistance levels, and other studies to help them determine the best place to put a limit entry, a protective stop, and one or more profit targets.

Most follow multiple stocks and/or futures at the same time. And they keep their hand on the mouse and follow the action on the price charts, ready to scalp and exit in an instant in response to a sudden spike or drop on a price chart.

The underlying equities they follow are usually volatile because there's a lot of open interest. Those trading the underlying can be buying, selling, or both. Day traders use trading ladders and short-interval charts to see where the current open interest resides. This helps to develop a bullish or bearish bias before placing a buy or a sell order.

Day traders watch daily, hourly, five-minute and 1-minute price charts. A trading ladder interface, like those provided in thinkorswim® and TradeStation, are the ideal trading tool for day traders. They can slide stops on either the chart or the ladder and scalp for profit with a single mouse click.

Swing Traders (Two or More Days)

There are those who prefer to put on several trades at a time and then walk away while their trades work in the market. These are called *swing traders*. Many who have tried their hand at day trading become swing traders. Day trading is a full-time job. And it can be exhausting. Moving from day trading to swing trading is only natural.

Swing traders can use the same price charts and analytical skills as day traders to find high probability trades. Price trends, moving averages, and many of the other chart studies can be even more useful on longer term trades having durations that range from overnight, several days, weeks, or even a few months. Swing traders are rarely scalpers. They tend to make bigger trades and let them work over longer periods of time. They expect to make hundreds or thousands of dollars rather than scalping for $25 to $50 per trade.

Swing traders begin by first examining weekly price charts. Then they move to shorter interval charts in which each candle represents one day, one hour, and finally several minutes. Swing traders may finally examine a 15-minute chart to see what the price has done over the past few hours. The key is to follow a set of trading rules that guide them through the entire analysis and trading process. Only after the swing trader is satisfied with the trade's probable outcome do they submit an order to their broker.

Long-Term Traders (One or More Years in Duration, i.e., LEAPS)

Long-term traders buy and hold stocks, ETFs, bond funds, and option contracts for extended periods of time — usually in excess of a year. Some of these traders collect dividends for periodic monthly and/or quarterly income. And some trade *long term equity anticipation securities* (LEAPS) option contracts.

LEAPS were introduced in 1990 specifically for option traders. Many option contract expiration dates were extended to two years.

Long-term option contract traders study the same charts that buy-and-hold stock traders use — typically the monthly, weekly, and daily charts.

They also examine the financial reports provided by the underlying companies. Before making a long-term financial commitment that could approach many thousands of dollars, it's only prudent to conduct careful technical and fundamental analyses. Look at profit and loss and income statements, quarterly and annual sales growth, current debt, cash on hand, ownership, and insider transactions (buying and selling shares of stock by company executives). Even check the performance of peer companies and compare their stock price trends to the ones you're considering.

Example:

Based on her extensive study, a long-term-style trader believes that the price of a certain stock, which is presently trading at $50, will experience a $20 increase in price to at least $70 over the next two years. This is based on her financial analysis and chart studies. A few peer companies with approximately the same market share and sales revenue are presently trading between $80 and $90 per share and the price of their stocks are both trending upward.

She decides to buy ten $53 call contracts that expire in two years. She must pay $3.00 in premium per share — a total cost of $3,000. Within five months the underlying stock reaches $70 and the $53 calls are now deep in the money and worth $14.50 per share in premium. Our trader sells her ten $53 call contracts for $14,500 and collects $11,500 in profit. That's 483.33% in profit in five months, less a small amount in commissions and exchange fees.

REMINDER: When buying an option contract, time decay always erodes premium value. The daily decline in premium value associated with time increases as option contracts draw closer to the option contract's expiration date. As a trading rule it is important to buy long-term option contracts (90 days or more till expiration) and sell short-term option contracts (less than 60 days till expiration). In the above example there were still 19 months left (24 months minus 5 months) when the trader decided to sell her $53 option contracts for profit. With roughly 570 days remaining till expiration, decay in premium is insignificant. In fact, with that much time remaining until expiration, the time decay will likely be inconsequential.

Figure 6–1 shows an option chain that corresponds to the $74.46 ETF, symbol HDV. Notice that two expiration dates are shown. The NOV 15 contracts have 30 days remaining, while the May 16 contracts have 212 days remaining.

Figure 6–1. Option Chains for a $74.46 ETF

HDV ISHARES CORE HIGH DIVIDEND ETF 74.46 NTB

Option Chain Filter: Off, Spread: Single, Layout: Mark, Delta, Theta

	CALLS					Strikes: ALL		PUTS				
	Mark	Delta	Theta	Bid X	Ask X	Exp	Strike	Bid X	Ask X	Mark	Delta	Theta
NOV 15	(30) 100											9.20% (±1.591)
	7.400	1.00	.00	5.90 C	8.90 C	NOV 15	67	0 C	.60 C	.300	-.10	-.02
	6.400	1.00	.00	4.90 C	7.90 C	NOV 15	68	0 C	.60 C	.300	-.11	-.02
	5.450	1.00	.00	4.00 C	6.90 C	NOV 15	69	0 C	.65 C	.325	-.13	-.02
	4.450	1.00	.00	3.00 C	5.90 C	NOV 15	70	0 C	.70 C	.350	-.15	-.02
	3.525	.90	-.01	2.25 C	4.80 C	NOV 15	71	0 C	.75 C	.375	-.18	-.02
	2.700	.79	-.01	1.40 C	4.00 C	NOV 15	72	0 C	.85 C	.425	-.23	-.02
	1.800	.71	-.01	.65 C	2.95 C	NOV 15	73	.05 C	1.05 C	.550	-.31	-.02
	1.100	.56	-.01	.60 C	1.60 C	NOV 15	74	.25 C	1.25 C	.750	-.45	-.02
	.550	.37	-.01	.05 C	1.05 C	NOV 15	75	.65 C	1.70 C	1.175	-.66	-.02
	.360	.25	-.01	0 C	.70 C	NOV 15	76	.60 C	3.10 C	1.850	-.88	-.01
	.275	.18	-.01	0 C	.55 C	NOV 15	77	1.35 C	4.10 C	2.725	-1.00	.00
	.275	.15	-.01	0 C	.55 C	NOV 15	78	2.30 C	5.10 C	3.700	-1.00	-.01
	.275	.14	-.01	0 C	.55 C	NOV 15	79	3.20 C	6.10 C	4.650	-1.00	-.01
DEC 15	(58) 100											10.17% (±2.429)
FEB 16	(121) 100											12.07% (±4.151)
MAY 16	(212) 100											12.43% (±5.657)
	7.400	1.00	.00	4.90 C	9.90 C	MAY 16	67	.05 C	5.00 C	2.525	-.28	-.01
	6.400	1.00	.00	3.90 C	8.90 C	MAY 16	68	.05 C	5.00 C	2.525	-.30	-.01
	5.400	1.00	.00	2.90 C	7.90 C	MAY 16	69	.05 C	5.00 C	2.525	-.32	-.01
	4.600	.84	.00	2.10 C	7.10 C	MAY 16	70	.05 C	5.00 C	2.525	-.35	-.01
	3.700	.78	.00	1.20 C	6.20 C	MAY 16	71	.05 C	5.00 C	2.525	-.38	-.01
	3.000	.67	.00	.50 C	5.50 C	MAY 16	72	.05 C	5.00 C	2.525	-.42	-.01
	2.525	.57	.00	.05 C	5.00 C	MAY 16	73	.20 C	5.10 C	2.650	-.48	-.01
	2.525	.49	.00	.05 C	5.00 C	MAY 16	74	.60 C	5.60 C	3.100	-.54	-.01
	2.525	.44	-.01	.05 C	5.00 C	MAY 16	75	1.20 C	6.20 C	3.700	-.60	-.01

For illustration purposes only.

The Theta (time decay) column lists the amount of premium value that is exiting each day. A Theta value of .05 represents a loss of $5.00 per day per 100-share option contract. Notice that Theta is .00 at both of the highlighted $70 strike prices — one with 30 days remaining and the other with 212 days remaining. Also notice the Mark values in the highlighted rows (at the $70 strike prices). With 30 days left, the premium value of the NOV 15 $70 strike is $4.45 and the MAY 16 $70 premium value is $4.60 — only 15 cents difference in spite of the 182 day difference till expiration (212 days − 30 days).

Did our trader "jump the gun" by selling her $53 call too early? Perhaps she did. But we don't have all the relevant information. The market sector may have been falling out of favor. Maybe the price charts signaled the current price was at resistance levels, and ready to drop — especially if she was convinced that the institutional traders were poised to take profits.

U.S. TAX IMPLICATIONS: If the above trade is done inside a qualified retirement account, such as an IRA rollover account on deposit with a brokerage, the profit is treated as tax free income. The funds within qualified retirement accounts are only taxed when withdrawn.

If the trade is made in a traditional brokerage account, the profit is treated as a short-term capital gain — which is taxed at the same rate as ordinary income. If the position is held for twelve months or more, profits receive long-term capital gains treatment. However, each trader must do the math to determine if the capital gains tax reduction offsets the loss from time decay. The prevailing tax bracket is also a factor. As mentioned, the decision to take profit must also encompass market outlook — what is revealed on the underlying price charts.

If the stock price remains close to its current value, the premium will experience a small drop in value with each passing day. If the stock price continues to rally, the profit less taxes may encourage the trader to hold the position. If the stock price stalls and begins to drop, the trader's option premium will also decline with the stock price. Time to exit!

What did you learn in chapter 6?

1. Trading style includes the days and amount of time spent trading, the markets traded, and the average _____ of each trade.

2. A trading style that may be well suited to some traders may be too _____ for others.

3. Different trading styles are better suited to some _____ than others.

4. _____ are traders who take quick profits on sudden price breakouts

5. Day traders are _____ traders.

6. Gambling is a form of _____; trading is a _____.

7. Day traders thrive on _____.

8. Some day traders use Fibonacci retracement lines for the placement of _____ and _____.

9. Floor trader pivot point lines show _____ and _____ levels.

10. These traders make common use of protective stops and one or more _____ _____.

11. Most day traders keep their hand on the _____, ready to scalp and exit in an instant.

12. A trader whose trades remain active for two or more days is called a _____ trader.

13. Swing traders use the same _____ _____ and analytical skills as day trades.

14. Swing traders typically begin their research by looking at _____ price charts.

15. A key is to follow a set of _____ _____ to guide them through the trading process.

16. Long-term traders buy and _____ securities for extended periods of time.

17. A LEAPS trade typically remains active for more than a
    _____.
18. When buying an option, time decay erodes _____.
19. The Greek symbol _____ is a measure of time decay.
20. Trade income received inside an IRA or 401K account is tax
    _____.

7 PRICE CHARTS — WINDOWS TO THE MARKET

●●●●●●●●

Does Technical Analysis Really Work?

This topic has been debated for years. Proponents of both sides of the issue seem to be convinced they're right. The critics of technical analysis rarely understand how the chart technicians use their tools for trading. Technical analysis (sometimes confused with *fundamental analysis*) works with randomly generated data based on trader sentiment. Critics of technical analysis believe the measure of trader sentiment is based on random, unreliable, and unreasonable emotions, and therefore highly unreliable.

At the core of technical analysis is an intensive study of market price movements over time. Obviously, the analysts examine history — price movements and volatility that happened an hour, a day, or perhaps several months ago. Some even look back several years. While technical analysis is the study of the market, fundamental analysis examines the underlying financial strengths and weaknesses of companies. As mentioned in chapter 1, a company's fundamentals often have little bearing on the price of its shares of stock.

Technical analysts consider price, trading volume, and current market volatility. These factors all relate to historical price movement and volatility, and they impact the supply and demand for a company's stock. Some skeptics find it impossible to believe that past prices can in any way be indicative of future prices.

As someone who has likely bought a stock, you know how you feel when you watch the price of your stock either rally or drop. It can put you on an emotional roller coaster. This is an excellent determinant of how price changes can impact the future behavior of traders. They judge performance by comparing the current price of their stock to what they originally paid for it. So it would be folly to think that past prices have little or no relationship to how a stock may trade in the future. Historical prices may not align themselves precisely with future prices, but they are by far the most realistic way we as traders can calculate market supply and demand. And technical analysists rarely claim that their predictions are iron clad. None of us believe this.

Through technical analysis we try to find the most probable trade setups based on both what the market has done in the past and what it is presently doing. We're searching for clues — not just one, but several. If our clues are in agreement, then the probability of being right in our bias is much better.

There are some financial models that attempt to disprove the usefulness of technical analysis. Two such models are called the *Gaussian Random Walk* and the *Efficient Market Hypothesis (EMH)*. Both of these models disavow the usefulness of technical analysis. Proponents believe that it is useless to search for undervalued stocks or try to predict trends in the market through either fundamental analysis or technical analysis. However, fundamental analysis has been in extensive use for many years by hundreds of successful fund managers. And over the years it has proven itself to work quite well.

Without fundamental analysis, they'd be "twisting in the wind." It's interesting to note that those critics of technical analysis are softening. Independent studies show that traders who use technical analysis outperform those who don't — by a broad margin.

Finally, if technical analysis didn't have merit, none of the institutional traders would be using it. It's true that most institutional traders are also fundamental analysts. They buy and hold large baskets of stock for mutual funds, bond funds, and large institutional investors, including insurance company annuity and retirement funds. But some of the most successful fund managers also use technical analysis. Those using technical analysis are being rewarded through better returns for their clients. These funds tend to weather downturns in the market through short sales and hedging. During the same periods, those funds that base their investing practices purely on fundamental analysis experience dramatic downturns in the value of their funds. Buy and hold doesn't work well in declining markets. Of course, they are convinced that they will recover when the market rallies back. But they've missed their window of opportunity to exploit the downturn, and they simply wait (and hope) for change as they watch the value of their funds diminish. Perhaps this serves to illustrate the difference between buy-and-hold investors and active traders.

Candlestick Charts

Candlestick charts were used by Munehisa Homina, a Japanese rice futures trader, in the early 18th century. They were studied and then introduced into the western financial markets by Steve Nison, after studying their use and interpretations by Japanese traders. Mr. Nison brought candlestick charting to the United States in the 1990s. Today, they are the primary chart style in use by traders. Prior to using candlestick charts, the bar chart was the most common chart style in use.

But because candlestick charts can be read and interpreted at a glance, they quickly came into vogue. The interpretation of candlesticks was briefly introduced in chapter 3. Figure 3–1 compares candlestick, line, and bar charts. Here in chapter 7 much more information about candle names and popular interpretations is provided. It's interesting to see why traders spend so much time examining and interpreting the shape of candles and the patterns of price charts.

Figure 7–1. Interpreting the Colors and Parts of Candlesticks

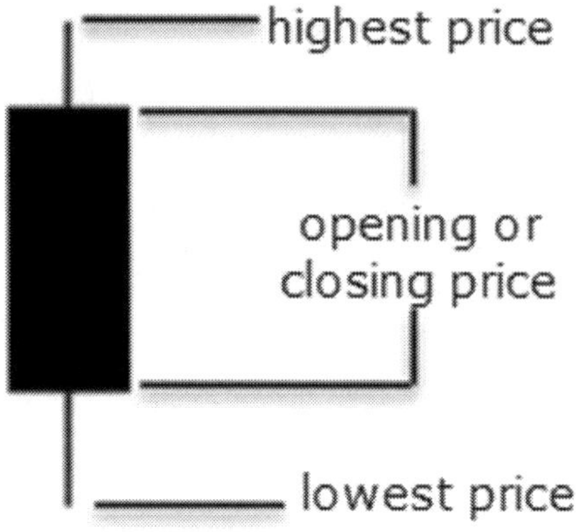

highest price

Green:
Open Low,
Close High

opening or
closing price

Red:
Open High
Close Low

lowest price

Interpretation — Open, Close, High and Low

As discussed in chapter 3, the candle wicks that usually protrude from the top and bottom of candle bodies are called *shadows*. The colored rectangle is the candle *body*. Green or white candle bodies indicate a price rally (lower open, higher close). Red or black candles indicate a price drop (higher open, lower close.) The body width represents the selected chart interval. In other words the width of each candlestick represents one hour when a one-hour chart interval is in use. So the body width of a candle can represent a week, day, or perhaps five seconds. As previously mentioned, tick charts are different.

Each candle within a tick chart represents a specified number of trades. For example, one candle may represent 150 individual trades (or "ticks") on the selected security. The number of ticks per candle is adjustable by the trader, where typical tick values range from 1 to perhaps 4500 ticks per candle. An extremely large number of ticks combined with a high volume histogram indicate buying or selling by institutional traders. Low volume points to transactions by amateur traders. A surge in activity on a tick chart signals price breakouts before they can be detected on a time interval chart. The trajectories provided by tick charts present more details than do time interval charts. For more information on tick charts, check out the website: http://www.emini-watch.com/emini-trading/tick-charts/. As you will see there, tick charts produce trading details that would otherwise be missed on time interval charts.

When to Use Price Charts

Price charts help us find market supply and demand levels. A supply level is where the number of shares being sold exceeds the number of shares being bought. This creates a surplus in shares and drives the price of the underlying stock down. The demand level is where the number of shares being bought exceeds the number being sold. The increased demand drives the price of the underlying stock up. Being able to use the charts to find price turning points (a reversal in supply and demand) is every chart analyst's goal. Of course this takes both study and practice.

Every bona-fide security that's traded within an exchange has a symbol. And each symbol has a corresponding price chart. When you set up your trading application, spend some time familiarizing yourself with the charting features. Be sure you know how to:

- Adjust your chart styles to both candlestick and line chart patterns.
- Adjust the candlestick colors to green (rally from open to close) and red (drop from open to close).
- Select different time intervals (Month, Week, Day, 4-Hour, 1-Hour, 30-Minute, 1-Minute, Tick, etc.)
- Use drawing tools to annotate your charts with price level lines, trendlines, text, and arrows.
- Add and modify chart studies such as simple moving averages, trendlines, Bollinger bands, etc.
- Put your chart in a window for quick access.
- Learn how to display multiple chart windows at the same time using different time intervals or on different equity symbols. (This is called a *flexible grid*.)

These features are accessed in either drop-down lists or settings dialogs. So once you've learned your way around your charting features, keep your charts handy so you can study price dynamics — rallies, drops, patterns, and historical support and resistance levels. Many of these are introduced in this chapter and expanded in chapter 8.

You will also want to learn how to access watch lists and the option chains to view the data that corresponds to the symbol of interest. Figure 7–2 illustrates a typical trading application setup with a chart, watch list, and an option chain.

Figure 7–2. Typical Setup to Access a Watch List, Option Chain, and Chart

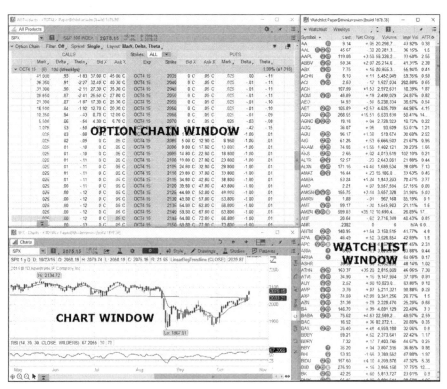

For illustration purposes only.

Setup Tips: Unless you have a large high-definition monitor, consider the following:

- Use three or four monitors to view all windows at the same time in full screen views.
- In a single display, make each window full-screen and then rotate between them by clicking on the task bar or by pressing **Alt+Tab** to rotate from one window to the next.
- Ensure your watch list, chart, and option chain is synchronized, i.e., showing data for the same symbol (unless scanning multiple symbols in a flexible chart). Synchronizing is automatic on many applications like TradeMonster and Traders Workstation.

Note To synchronize symbols across the three windows in thinkorswim® and TradeStation®, use the drop-down color pallet. Looking at figure 7–2, notice the square boxes to the right of each symbol on the option chain and chart windows. The same square box (or numbered color pallet) is shown above the Volume column. When synchronization is active, clicking a symbol on the watch list automatically accesses the corresponding data on the chart and the option chain. This works in the same way when you type a symbol in either the chart or option chain window.

In addition to learning how to use your charts, you must also learn how to create watch lists and how to add useful columns within your option chains. Some of these operations are performed in the trading activities within chapter 14. You may also want to read online platform tutorials, help information, and educational videos provided by your brokerage.

Candlestick Patterns

There are many and varied candlestick shapes. Some traders, including Steve Nison, believe that the shape of a candle is a predictor of a future price action. Below are a few examples of the names given to candles of different patterns or shapes.

- **Doji:** The doji is formed when the opening and closing price of the underlying is the same. The length of the upper and lower shadows may vary, and the resulting candlestick may resemble a plus sign, an upright cross, an inverted cross, a shooting star, or a "T." The doji candle conveys indecision on the part of buyers and sellers. While the open and closing prices are the same, the shadows track the high and low prices for the selected time interval.

- **Dragonfly Doji:** Pictures a high opening and closing price at the same level, indicating indecision and agreement among both bears and bulls.

- **Gravestone Doji:** This opened, rallied, and closed back at the opening price. When at the top of a bullish run nearing historical price resistance, the gravestone doji signals the formation of a bearish sentiment.

- **Hammer:** A hammer candlestick forms when the price of the underlying experiences a substantial drop upon open. Then the price rallies back and closes above the low of the selected time interval. The hammer candlestick resembles a hammer or a square lollipop with a long stick. The hammer candlestick is also called a *hanging man* when it forms during a price rally. The length of the wick should be twice the length of the body.

- **Inverted Hammer:** The inverted hammer is identical in appearance to the shooting star, shown here, except the inverted hammer appears at the bottom of a bearish trend and is preceded by a dropping candle and followed by a rallying candle.

- **Shooting Star:** The shooting star is formed by a price rally and reversal. This pattern is formed when a price opens high, trades even higher, and then closes below its opening price. It looks just like the inverted hammer except it is bearish. As with the hammer and hanging man, the wick should be twice as long as the candle body. The shooting star gets its name from the body and long tail.

- **Engulfing Pattern:** The engulfing patterns shown here are both considered reversal patterns. The first candle pair is a bullish engulfing pattern, because it signals an immediate change in sentiment. The first candle is bearish. The 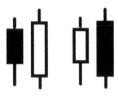 closing price gaps down to the opening price of the second candle, which rallies and closes substantially higher. The second pair signals bearish sentiment. The first candle is bullish only to gap up to the opening price of the second black (or red) candle. The price then retreats and closes lower.

- **Dark Cloud:** This pattern follows a series of upward trending candles and then signals an abrupt change in trader sentiment — from bullish to bearish. The last candle — a long red candle, opens above the previous close signaling a gap. Initially, it looks like a continuation of the upward trend. But when it falls and closes somewhere in the bottom half of the previous candle, the price is poised for a strong reversal.

- **Piercing Line:** This pattern is similar to the dark cloud, except it signals a reversal at support from a downtrend of lower lows and lower highs. Notice how the last candle closes well above the midpoint of the preceding bearish candle, piercing the centerline.

- **Bull and Bear Kickers:** These are both strong reversal pattern candles that include a full-bodied candle well above or below the previous candle. Both require a price gap from the previous candle's closing price to

the last (kicked) candle's opening price. The last candle looks like it was kicked in the opposite direction of the previous trend. A bull kicker is shown here.

- **The Harami** resembles a mother candle followed by a baby candle. Hence the Japanese word *harami* for pregnant woman. The harami is another price reversal signal, and traders anticipate a price turn in the opposite direction of the preceding trend. When preceded by a bearish trend, the baby candle is seen as a signal for a reversal back to  an uptrend when the price gaps from the mother candle's closing price up to the baby candle's opening price. This is shown in the accompanying illustration. The exact opposite is true when this happens in a bull-ish trend.

- **Morning and Evening Star Doji:** These are also both trend reversal pattern signals. The morning star is shown at the left, and the evening star is shown at the  right. Both simulate a reflection of the preceding trend. Both tell traders that the trend is losing strength, and a reversal is likely to happen. The morning star often interrupts a bearish trend, and is followed by a long rally candle. This is a strong indication that a rally has begun. The evening star signals an endpoint to a bullish price trend. The evening star is typically followed by a long dropping candle, signaling the beginning of a downward price reversal.

- **Abandoned Babies:** The location of the abandoned baby candles signal the end of a rally or a drop. When the small candle, often a doji or narrow spinning top, gaps below the close of the previous candle, selling has lost strength. When the price has dropped to a sufficiently low level, traders step in and validate a support level through buying, especially the institutional buyers who drive the price back into an upward price trend. The reverse is true with the bearish version of the abandoned baby. Selling

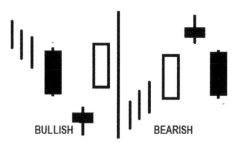

begins and the price begins to drop. The abandoned baby is often followed by a long candle that confirms the trend reversal.

- **Spinning Tops:** Spinning tops can occur almost anywhere on a trendline. They are seen as an indication of trader indecisiveness, but are not seen as either a strong reversal or consolidation signal. They do signal a reduction in current volatility, and may be followed by a price breakout.

- **Three Black Crows:** Many swing traders consider a sequence of three tall red or black daily candles as a strong signal — particularly at the top of a rally. This is particularly true when both the opening and closing price of the first black crow are lower than the opening and closing price of the previous white candle. If the following two black crows also have lower lows and lower highs, the trend reversal is in motion and traders look for bearish-style trades.

- **Three White Soldiers:** This is the opposite signal of three black crows, because traders see the three soldiers as the end of a bearish trend and the beginning of a fresh price rally. As with the black crows, traders look for three long white or green candles with higher highs and higher lows — a strong signal for a bullish trade setup such as a bull call or a bull put spread, both of which are detailed in chapter 14.

You can find additional candlestick patterns by Googling *candlestick patterns*. This will list a number of websites that picture and describe candlesticks and patterns within which they often appear. The above patterns are provided to familiarize you with prominent ones. But the context in which the candlesticks appear is quite useful as trading signals. Beyond the shape of individual candlesticks, all experienced chart traders look for patterns made up of a series of candlesticks. Traders call these patterns by different names such as double tops, head and shoulders, falling wedges, ascending triangles, and cup and handles to name just a few. Many of these patterns are pictured and briefly described within this chapter.

Some form bullish, bearish, or neutral biases from the candle shapes. Consider the following candlesticks and see if you agree with the descriptions. (Red or black candle bodies tell us that the closing price is lower than the opening price for the measured interval; green or white candle bodies represent a higher closing price than the opening price)

Figure 7–3. Candlestick Interpretations

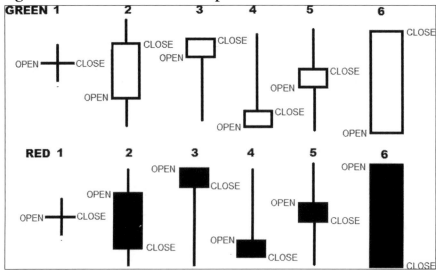

Legend

Green 1	Neutral	Red 1	Neutral
Green 2	Bullish	Red 2	Bearish
Green 3	Bullish	Red 3	Bullish (if close near open)
Green 4	Bearish (if close near open)	Red 4	Very Bearish
Green 5	Neutral	Red 5	Neutral
Green 6	Bullish	Red 6	Bearish

You may wonder why Green 3 isn't very bullish when you compare it to Red 4, which has an identical shape. As explained earlier, traders are aware how the market drops much faster than it rallies. This negative bias influences their outlook. It is somewhat natural to be *very* bearish for a dropping candle versus being mildly bullish for the same shaped rallying candle.

Finally, a single candlestick never tells the entire story. Patterns created by multiple candlesticks strung across a chart present a much clearer view of current supply and demand. So a single candle should rarely, if ever, be your signal to trade. Always look at each candle *in context* with those surrounding it. Determine if a doji, hanging man, morning star, etc. is at supply or demand based on its surrounding candles.

Using Different Time Intervals

As mentioned earlier, experienced traders who wish to study the price charts of one or more symbols are rarely satisfied with a single time interval. For example, a day trader wouldn't use a weekly chart as a basis for an intraday trade — one he or she wishes to enter and exit within a matter of minutes to a few hours. Nor do experienced traders just examine 1-minute charts. Neither reveals the "nature of the beast" relative to the time the trader plans to remain in the trade.

Experienced traders always examine multiple charts. They may move from a week, day, hour, and 15-minute chart to better understand current price trends, historical price patterns, support and resistance levels from highs and lows, and repetitive turning points from demand to supply and back again to demand. This serves as background relative to what is likely to happen in the future.

Many traders display multiple chart windows at the same time — perhaps a week, day, hour, and 15-minute chart. Some especially like to use line charts with the weekly interval. Notice how easy it is to see the price trend on the line chart shown in figure 7–4.

Figure 7–4. A One-Year-Long Daily Line Chart

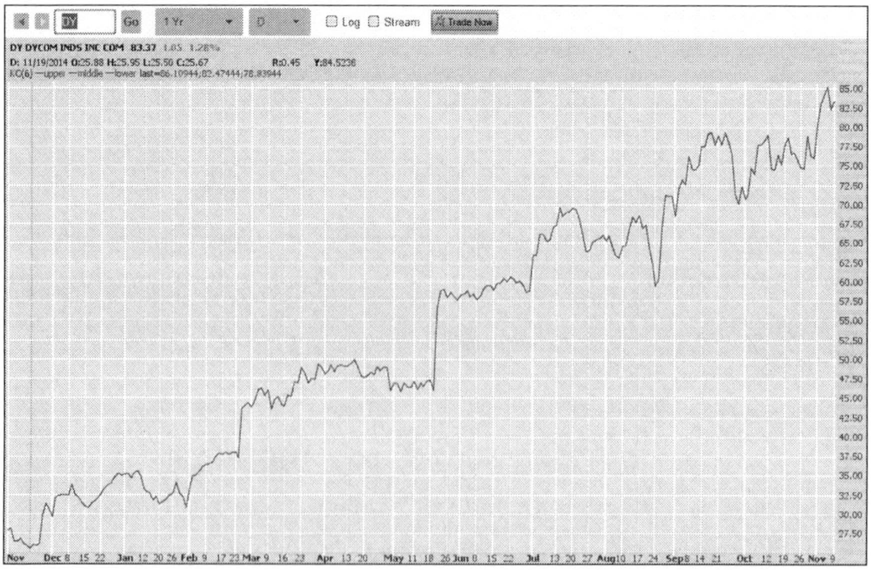

For illustration purposes only.

As you can quickly see, the DY stock has a steady upward price trend with periodic pull-backs and breakouts. Default line chart settings use the daily price close values. Some call this a "daily moving average." Using a line chart on a year-long daily chart quickly shows the price trend over the past 12 months. Figure 7–4 illustrates how the line chart provides a clean presentation. Of course you can use shorter term charts to find more recent 6- to 3-month trends.

Always begin your analysis by finding the trend. It is said, "The trend is the trader's friend — till the end." Finding the price trend is always the first thing to determine on an underlying symbol. Next, the candlestick charts are used to find specific price patterns. These serve as entry and exit signals for trades. Many of the more popular patterns are illustrated and described within the remainder of this chapter.

After viewing the weekly and daily charts, the hour or 15-minute chart might be expanded to full screen for a closer look. Finally, if a price pattern of interest is found, the trader can draw limit entry, protective stop, and profit target lines on the chart that correspond to reasonable trade levels. In the early stages of trading, you may wish to snag a screen shot and save it for later reference. Then keep a record of your setup and the trade's final outcome to see how it worked. If just getting started, you are encouraged to do this in simulated *paper money* mode. Annotate the chart to show your trading rationale. Include a description of your trade setup:

- Symbol and current market price
- Entry date
- ± Shares
- Limit entry price, protective stop price (or %), and profit target price
- Exit date
- Outcome: market price, profit/loss

If trading an option, jot down the following:

- Symbol, current market price, current IV%
- Avg. Daily Trading Volume
- Entry date
- Contract expiration(s), date(s), and day(s)
- Option strategy name
- Leg(s): No. and strike prices of ± Puts, ± Calls
- Premium(s) received/paid at each leg
- Open interest(s) (at each leg and overall)
- Prob. ITM/Touching at each leg
- Theta value(s) at each leg
- Exit date(s), types, and P/L of each
- Market price at exit(s) or roll(s)

Little by little your charting skills and trade selections will improve with practice. When it starts working, you're ready to "go live" with real money.

Determining the Price Trend

Every serious chart technician begins by looking for a security that exhibits an undeniable long-term price trend. Finding a trend is rule number one. The trend sets the long-term outlook for following price movement. The trend varies from chart to chart. While a weekly interval chart may show a steady upward long-term trend, the day or hour charts may show a strong downward trend indicating an intermediate or short-term price reversal.

Trends are computed by averaging the values of the highs and the values of the lows over time. Essentially, the trend of a stock that is rallying is determined by a long series of higher highs and higher lows. Look at figure 7–5.

Figure 7–5. Higher Highs and Higher Lows Form an Upward Trend

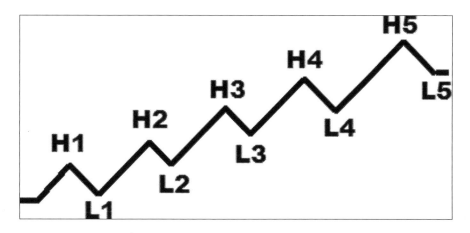

Trend durations vary from short, intermediate, and long term. Trends can last from two days to a month (short), a month to a year (intermediate), and more than a year (long term). Knowing both the direction of a trend and the expected duration are both critical toward your trading success. It is possible for a trend to be upward, slightly upward, sideways, slightly downward, and downward as shown in the adjacent illustration.

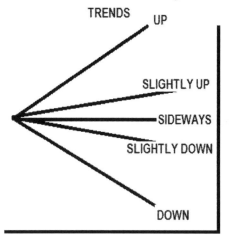

Line charts, like the bullish example shown in figure 7–4, are excellent for looking at long-term price trends. Seeing what the stock has done for the past one to five years is instantly revealed by a line chart. Line charts also show support and resistance levels. This is done by drawing lines across the highs and the lows to see where prices have historically made reversals.

A downward (bearish) price trend is comprised of a sequence of lower lows and lower highs. As a rational trader you would usually be reticent to "trade against the trend." This is especially true of buy-and-hold, long duration trades. Although fundamental analysis examines balance sheets and income statements, they also study long-term trends. However, as an active trader, the current trend is only one of several factors you examine. But as a general rule you should avoid "counter-trend" trades. If the underlying's price has been dropping steadily over a series of long- to short-term price charts, it wouldn't make much sense to buy it, unless.... Are there exceptions to the "don't enter a countertrend trade" rule? It's possible, but rarely advisable.

It is possible for the price of the underlying to be entering a historical support level, which some call a *demand zone*. This is where supply (selling) turns into demand (buying). The Online Trading Academy (OTA) teaches students to look for areas of support and resistance referred to as demand zones (historical support) and *supply zones* (historical resistance). Moreover, there are numerous youtube.com videos and websites that describe methods used to find supply and demand zones on charts. At the time this book was written, a few of the websites that discussed demand and supply zone trading included:

- thepropervillains.com
- traderkingdom.com
- dukascopy.com
- and others.

As you already know from the discussion in chapter 3, many traders put simple moving average (SMA) lines on their charts. This is a price smoothing study based on the average price points of the underlying stock over the previous 9 candles. They tend to look at the SMA as "gravity" and assume the price will return to its upward, downward, or sideways trajectory represented by the SMA line. A down-trending stock may suddenly break out for an even steeper drop in price. Some traders view this as a buying opportunity, thinking the price will return up to the SMA line. This would be a countertrend trade. Is this the way to trade? Perhaps some nod their heads in agreement. But other chart technicians want additional confirmation. For example, what's the overall chart pattern? Has this happened before? Is the price at a historical support level, and where will supply turn back into demand? These are just a few considerations — something examined in more detail in chapter 8.

Developing a Bias (Bearish, Bullish, or Neutral)

At a recent Dallas-area technical analysis seminar conducted by TD Ameritrade's Investools education subsidiary, the instructor — a fellow named Dave Johnson — offered the following advice as the seminar drew to a close:

I trade what I see, not what I think, not what I fear, not what I feel, not what I hear, not what I hope.

The talking heads on TV make statements like, "It's not apparent as to what the market will do today," and "I feel bearish right now because of what's happening in the technology sector." First, it's never apparent as to what the market will do on any day. And it is ludicrous to believe that the bearish feeling of a commentator has any bearing whatsoever on what will happen in the market. Commentators are wrong as often as they're right — their commentary is often just meaningless dribble. Therefore,

TRADE WHAT YOU SEE!

Before entering a trade, it's important to develop a bias based on what the charts show you. Begin by examining price trends across different time intervals. See if you can determine where the price is likely to go based on the trend and historical and current levels of supply and demand. Although this process is described in more detail in chapter 8, for now you should understand that examining the charts is always an important first step in your analysis. Is the stock rallying, dropping, or moving sideways? Can you tell if it is presently oversold or overbought? What's the average daily price movement — in other words, how much is the price likely to move, regardless of direction? Is it ready for a breakout based on current volatility and the average daily price range? Are there more buyers or more sellers? How does the current trading volume (*implied volatility*) compare to the historical trading volume (*historical volatility*)? All of these questions can be answered on your charts, watch lists, and option chains during market hours. And all of these questions are addressed in chapter 8. There, you are introduced to a number of popular chart studies. These will help you validate what you're seeing on your price charts. They enhance your odds for successful trading outcomes.

Support and Resistance Levels

Support and resistance levels are price points located near the bottom and top of a stock's price range. Unless some unusual event drives a price down or up beyond its usual trading range, you can think of support and resistance levels as the lowest and highest prices within which a particular stock seems to remain. For example, a trader may notice that the price of HA remained between $19.80 and $26.00 from mid-March through September of 2015. The price tested these levels several times, but never dropped below $19.80 or above $26.00. From this, the trader concludes that $19.80 is HA's support level and $26.00 is its resistance level. This is shown in figure 7–6.

In addition to support and resistance at fixed price levels, you can also draw support and resistance trendlines at the bottoms and/ or tops of either price rallies or drops. Figure 7–7 illustrates support and resistance trendlines on HA's price chart.

Figure 7–6. Fixed Support and Resistance Levels Drawn on a Chart

For illustration purposes only.

Figure 7–7. Support and Resistance Trendlines Drawn on a Chart

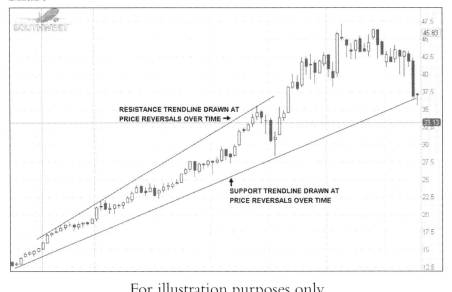

For illustration purposes only.

Applying Historical Support and Resistance Levels

Both fixed support and resistance levels and support and resistance trendlines become stronger over time as the price tests and then reverses direction away from an established level. Traders often use proven support and resistance levels and trendlines to determine both a trading strategy and a trade's entry price. For example, a trader may place a limit sell order to short the stock at or just above a proven resistance level, or a limit buy at or just below a proven support level.

Traders place their limit entries as follows:

1. At or very near the support or resistance level prior to the price reaching the level
2. Just below or above the support or resistance level in anticipation of a new low or high — this is a more conservative entry.
3. Entry after a price reversal — this would be called a "confirmation entry."

Figure 7–8 is an example of a trade that uses a $32.00 support level that has been tested multiple times over the past several weeks or months. Notice that it uses the typical bracketed trade comprised of a limit entry, a protective stop (for risk management), and a profit target.

Figure 7–8. Trading at a Support Level

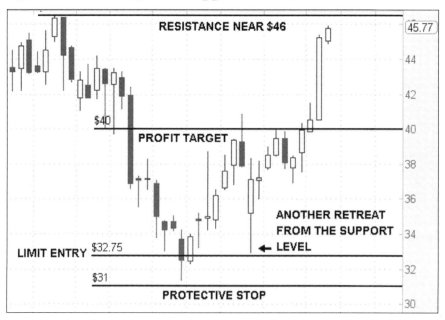

For illustration purposes only.

The profit target is $7.25 above the limit entry. This trade has a 4:1 reward-to-risk ratio, exceeding the usual 3:1 and 2:1 ratios often used by traders. Notice that after profit is taken, the sellers enter the picture producing supply. This reverses the price direction, which drops back near the original support level. Buyers return and the increase in demand results in another rally. Notice how the price rallies back to $45, which appears to be a resistance level.

Demand and Supply Zones

Chart traders have used what are referred to as demand and supply zones for several years. One trader that goes by the name of Keyser Soze (a name used for the antagonist in the 1995 film *The Usual Suspects*) presents several interesting examples of finding and drawing supply and demand zones in a series of YouTube videos. If you can tolerate Mr. "Soze's" R-rated language, you will see how he finds and uses these zones for his trading. Mr. Soze appears to trade in both the forex and futures markets. In any case, you already know that chart technicians analyze charts in essentially the same way for all trading venues. Therefore, knowing how to use charts has value for trading stocks, options, futures, and forex.

If you watch Mr. Soze's technique, you quickly see how he looks for and finds "engulfed" candles. Figure 7–9 shows a typical engulfed candle pair.

It's possible, even likely, to find many engulfed candle pairs on a chart — especially weekly and daily charts. Engulfed candle pairs that exist near support and resistance levels are seen by many as good signals for future trade setups. Also look for supply and demand zones near a rally-base-drop formation (to form a supply zone) or a drop-base-rally formation (to form a demand zone). In addition, look for dojis, spinning tops, hammers, gravestones as confirmation for a potential price reversal.

Figure 7–9. Using an Engulfed Candle Pair to Find a Supply Zone

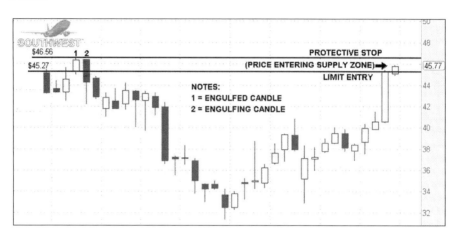

For illustration purposes only.

Notice that you can draw the lines that form your zone from a candle's opening price to either the candle's closing price level or to the tip of the shadow. The line used to form the protective stop is the most important. This line is used for risk management. Look at the average daily price movement to help you decide on your stop price. The average true range (ATR) study discussed in chapter 8 is often quite useful. Overly conservative stops typically "stop out" soon after the limit entry is triggered by the price entering a demand or supply zone. Excessively loose stops may lose more money, but they provide more room for the price to reverse direction before the stop is triggered. Using a mathematical chart study like the ATR can be quite helpful.

The Bull Flag and Bear Flag

It's quite common to see a price pullback from a dominant trend only to be followed by an abrupt move back to the trend. When in a long-term upward trend, the pullback and reversal is referred to as a bull flag. You can guess what a bear flag pattern looks like. Figure 7–10 illustrates a bull flag — a brief reversal from the dominant

Figure 7–10. A Bull Flag (Signals an Entry Opportunity for a Bullish Trade)

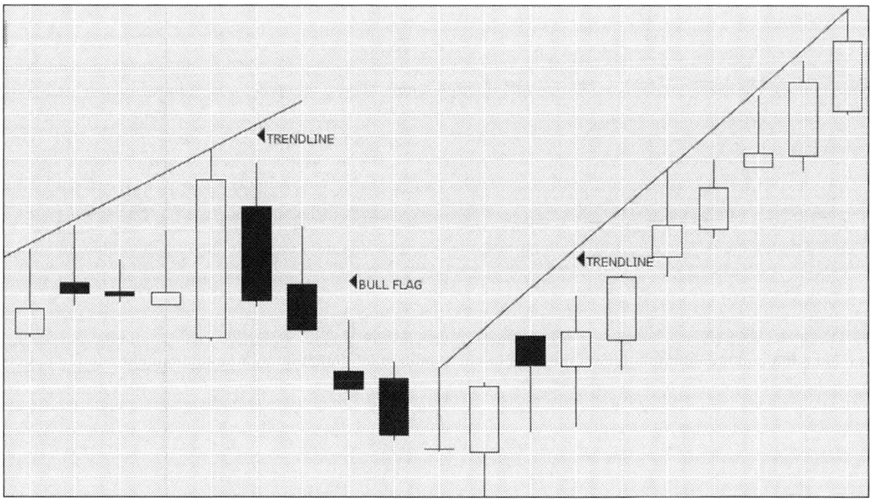

For illustration purposes only.

price trend that lasts for roughly one week and then a resumption of the upward trend. Notice the gravestone doji in figure 7–10 — a candle formation that signals a price reversal and is frequently seen at support levels.

Popular Chart Patterns

As mentioned near the beginning of this chapter, there are many traders who look at individual candle shapes like the doji, hammer, and a long, shadowless body in anticipation of a bullish or bearish price reversal, such as the bull or bear flags described above. These are seen as signals for a price breakout that leads to a rally or a drop. As suggested earlier, one candle can rarely reveal longer term supply or demand for an underlying security. It must be viewed in concert with surrounding candles.

Many traders look for chart patterns formed by a series of several dozen candlesticks. They step back from the trees and look at the forest. These traders "see" rallies, drops, and reversals based on peaks, valleys, or wedge- and cup-shaped formations. The Internet is packed with information on chart patterns. Here, several popular patterns are briefly examined. This is intended to provide some basic knowledge about chart patterns and how they are interpreted by tens of thousands of traders.

How Reliable Are Chart Patterns?

Be aware that the following chart patterns often fail to work. In fact it would be naïve to believe that all of the chart patterns about to be examined are ironclad. There's a good chance that even the most popular patterns will fail to fulfill a trader's belief in them. Traders who bet on any of these patterns without knowing the statistical probabilities for success are gambling. So you are advised to never risk money on chart patterns without going through an analysis of successes and failures. You may find through several hours of testing with back trades, where back trades are based on actual historical price data, the popular patterns fail as often as they succeed.

Consider the highly touted double top formation. Is it a highly reliable signal for a trend reversal? Or is it a random formation created by thousands of buy and sell orders entered by hundreds of uneducated traders who rarely, if ever, even look at price charts.

To reiterate, the only way to check the reliability of the double top reversal pattern is to perform a statistical analysis of fifty or more trades based on a pattern. Use the double top and record the outcomes. If the resulting price movement follows expectations two thirds of the time, you may be on to something. If not, do something different, such as finding proven levels of support and resistance and corresponding supply and demand zones. There, too, you can verify your win–loss record to develop statistical reliability. Historical levels of price reversals back to the dominant trend are much more reliable.

Play Safe with Bracketed Trades

In combination with finding entry levels based on supply or demand, you can also employ reward-to-risk ratios in each of your trades. If you can maintain a 3:1 reward-to-risk ratio, you should make money when you're right four out of ten times. Consider ten trades. Your average trade uses a $1 protective stop from your limit entry and a $3 profit target. If you are successful four times and lose the other six times, you still earn 66.66% in profit as follows:

Your income is 4 × $3 = $12.
Your losses are 6 × $1 = $6.
Your profit is $6 — a 50% profit.

Now consider a 2:1 ratio in which your protective stop is still $1 and your profit target is $2. Again, you are successful four times and lose the other six times. Using the 2:1 reward-to-risk ratio, you will still make a nice profit:

Your income is 4 × $2 = $8.
Your losses are 6 × $1 = $6.
Your profit is $2 — a 25% profit.

If you're good at finding valid supply and demand zones, and you're right one third of the time, you earn more than you lose. All that remains is to learn how to find these evasive zones — where an imbalance in supply and demand occurs and a reversal in price is imminent. Even before you develop your trading skills, using the reward-to-risk ratio with a profit target and protective stop enhances your odds for success.

Reversal Patterns

Reversal patterns typically show indecision on the part of buyers and sellers. The patterns tell chart technicians that either flight from (creating a surplus in supply) or attraction to (creating demand) in the underlying equity is either occurring or about to occur. These reversal patterns include names like double tops or bottoms, triple tops or bottoms, head and shoulders, and wedges.

Double Top

The double top is a price reversal pattern. It is bearish because it predicts a price reversal from a rally to a drop. Top 1 and top 2 in figure 7–11 mark the double top. This formation usually occurs after a sustained price rally. Although the first peak is normal, it sets the stage. When followed by a trough and then another lower peak, the double top is formed. Notice in figure 7–11 how the second top (2) is followed by a precipitous price drop as selling activity increases. If enough traders believe a double top to be ominous, some might believe the pattern motivates selling rather than a rational financial event.

Figure 7–11. Double top Reversal Pattern

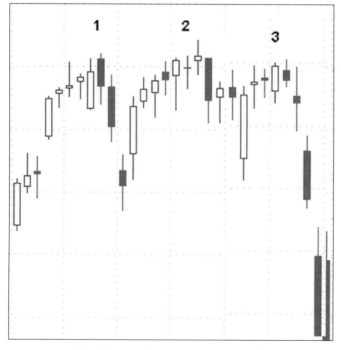

For illustration purposes only.

Double Bottom

As you can imagine, this is a reversal pattern with a bullish bias. It is a mirror image of the double top reversal.

Figure 7–12. Double Bottom Reversal Pattern

For illustration purposes only.

Triple Top and Triple Bottom

The triple top and triple bottom formations are both considered strong reversal patterns by many traders. Double and triple tops indicate a series of stalled rallies and drops. Buyers and sellers are indecisive — perhaps even timid. In the case of the tops, they finally give up and retreat from the underlying stock by selling, which creates a surplus in supply. Figure 7–13 shows a triple top pattern; the tops are numbered 1, 2, and 3. The opposite is true at the bottom. There, traders see the price levels constantly testing support and retreating to the upside. This encourages buyers to enter to create sufficient demand to result in a rally.

Figure 7–13. The Triple Top Reversal Pattern (Bearish)

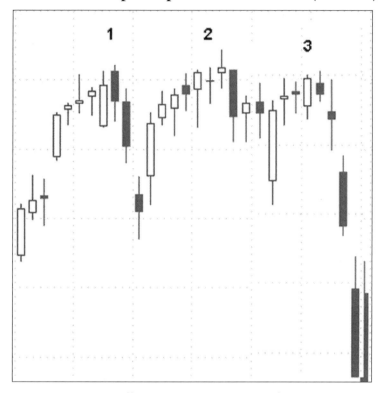

For illustration purposes only.

Head and Shoulders Top and Bottom

This is another bearish reversal pattern that anticipates a price stall, a period of indecisiveness, followed by a selloff that creates surplus supply and a corresponding price drop. It has a center peak (the head) flanked by left shoulder and right shoulder peaks and a horizontal "neckline" located at the bottom of the troughs located between the head and the two shoulders. The bearishness of this pattern increases with the downward slope of the neckline. This pattern often follows a long price rally in which the underlying stock reaches an oversupply condition. The novices continue to buy while the professionals begin selling. The bears follow the downward price movement with strong selling, creating excess supply and a corresponding drop in price.

Figure 7–14 Head and Shoulders Top Pattern (Bearish)

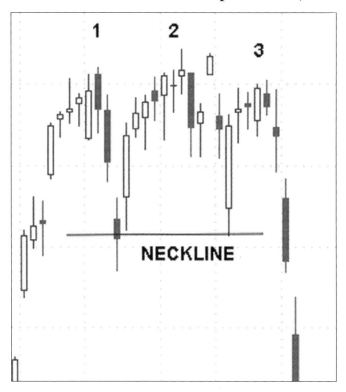

For illustration purposes only.

Head and Shoulders Bottom

The head and shoulders pattern can also occur at the bottom. This is the "flip-side" of the head and shoulders top making it a bullish reversal pattern. It works in precisely the same way as its first cousin — the head and shoulders top. This pattern typically follows a sustained drop in price. The excess supply depreciates the price. The oversold, cheap supply condition brings buyers back into the market. As you would expect, fresh demand results in a price rally as the price bounces off a support level from an increase in buy orders. Because the double top, double bottom, and the head and shoulders patterns are easy to spot, many traders time their entries around these four formations.

Falling and Rising Wedge

These are both reversal patterns. The falling wedge is bullish in anticipation of a rally. The rising wedge is bearish and signals a price drop to follow. Figure 7–15 illustrates the falling wedge pattern. Notice how the wedge is formed by progressively narrower drops and rallies until a bottom support level is reached. This is where a sustained level of demand occurs and is followed by a significant rally.

Figure 7–15. The Falling Wedge Reversal (Bullish)

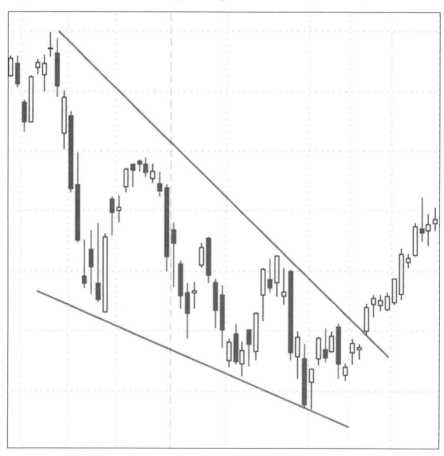

For illustration purposes only.

Rounding Bottom (also called Saucer Bottom)

This is a bullish formation that is best suited to weekly price charts. The formation, which looks like a saucer, is shown in figure 7–16. This pattern signals a turn from a sustained price decline. The low price creates demand and entices buyers to enter the market. The rally that follows makes this a bullish pattern.

Figure 7–16. Rounding Bottom or Saucer Pattern

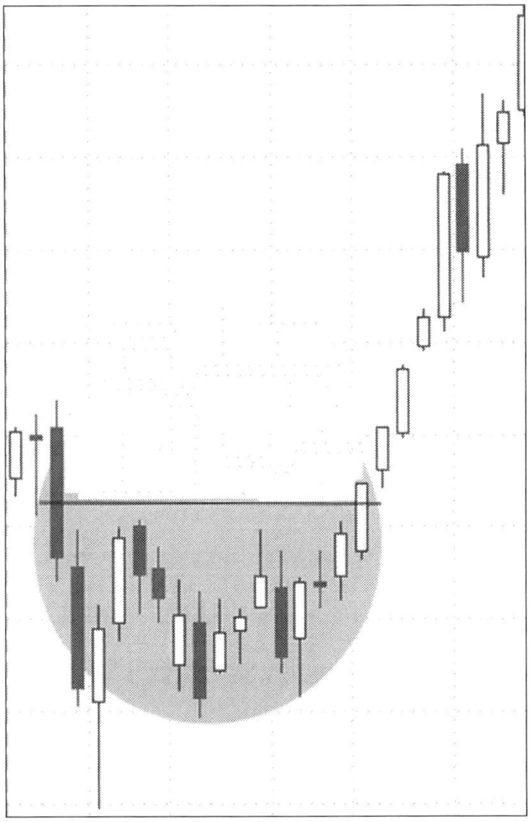

For illustration purposes only.

Bump and Run

The bump and run reversal pattern has a lead-in period that may last a month or even longer. But you can look for this pattern on daily, weekly, and even monthly charts. The trendline at the bottom of figure 7–17 shows the lead-in activity. Volume is typically normal during the lead-in phase. Notice that the price drops and "bumps" the lead-in line and then begins to rally on a steeper slope, indicating an increase in buying volume. According to a chart guru named Bulkowski, the lead-in trendline should be between 30 and 45 degrees. Of course squeezing a chart can change this angle, so be sure to view your chart at full scale. The steeper trendline illustrates what is called the "bump" phase of this pattern. As you can see, it is steeper than the lead-in trendline, and typically rises to an angle of around 50 degrees. Don't bother to take out a protractor — simply approximate the angles of the lead-in and bump lines. The upper trendline may be broken by a reversal and then a retracement toward resistance. This is where the bears enter and begin to retreat from the excess in supply by selling. This increase in selling activity creates a surplus, causing a drop in the price of the underlying.

Figure 7–17. The Bump and Run Pattern (Bearish Reversal)

For illustration purposes only.

Continuation Patterns

Think of continuation patterns as normal periods of consolidations followed by a resumption of the original price trend. This is why the term *continuation* is used rather than *reversal*. Continuation patterns can be either bullish or bearish, based on the original trajectory of the price. Some continuation pattern names are *flags*, *triangles*, *rect-angles*, and *cup and handle*. The remainder of this chapter examines several common continuation chart patterns.

Flag or Pennant

The flag pattern (sometimes called "pennant" when the right side of the formation is narrow) marks a small pause in a rally or a drop for consolidation. The consolidation almost always follows a period of unusually high trading volume, which marks a central point in the price move of the underlying. In an upward trend, the flag is marked by a continuous rally, a period of basing, and then a continuation of the rally. Trading volume declines during the basing period, only to resume in support of a continued rally.

Notice how strong volume, shown at the bottom of figure 7–18, is supporting a nice price rally. Then basing occurs during a period of consolidation with an expected decline in trading volume, as seen at the bottom of figure 7–18. This is followed by continuation of

Figure 7–18. A Bullish Flag Pattern Formed by Rally-Base-Rally Candlesticks

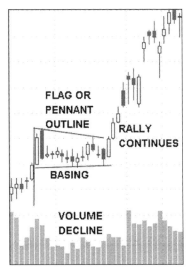

For illustration purposes only.

the rally. This is a typical flag formation with a bullish bias. The same flag formation, only in the opposite direction, forms a bearish flag. When bearish, selling volume is high, declines, and then increases again as traders resume selling activity.

Symmetrical Triangle

The symmetrical triangle is another base and continuation pattern. The one shown is bullish because at least two highs and two higher lows exist. The higher lows are represented by numbers 2 and 3 below the bottom trendline of figure 7–19. The lower portion of this formation resembles a narrowing wedge because it's wider at the beginning than at the end. Notice that the trendlines are parallel to each other. This pattern typically forms over a period of a month or more. Trading volume often declines as prices begin to make smaller than usual drops and rallies. When basing does occur, it is typically quite narrow. After some price consolidation, the rally (or drop in the case of a bearish formation) typically resumes from continued demand and the price continues on its original trajectory.

Figure 7–19. A Symmetrical Triangle Formation (Bullish Pattern Shown)

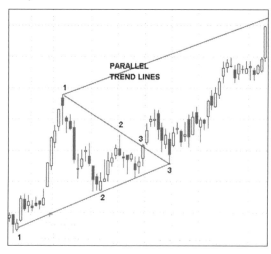

For illustration purposes only.

Ascending and Descending Triangle

The ascending triangle is made up of a series of peaks and valleys that have a directional trend. A bullish ascending triangle pattern is characterized by progressively higher lows and a series of highs that are essentially parallel to each other. Hence, the market action is a rally to a fixed level of resistance, a pullback followed by another rally to resistance, and a slightly shorter pullback. This process continues until the price resumes its rally (or drop) in the original direction. Figure 7–20 illustrates a bullish ascending and descending triangle.

Figure 7-20. The Ascending and Descending Triangle (Bullish Example)

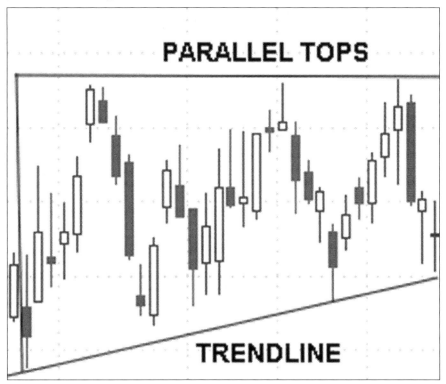

For illustration purposes only.

Rectangle

The rectangle continuation pattern is another pause in a trend for consolidation. This pattern is formed by two highs and two lows within either a rally or a drop series. The underlying volume typically retreats during this consolidation. When the buying or selling volume returns to normal, the price continues on its original path. Of course buying pushes prices up and selling pushes them down.

Figure 7–21. The Rectangular Continuation Pattern (Bearish Example)

For illustration purposes only.

Price Channel

This continuation chart pattern slopes either upward or downward within an angular channel formed by an upper trendline and a lower channel line. The lines represent price resistance levels at the top of the candles and price support levels at the bottom. The direction of the slope indicates the bullish or bearish trend. For example, a downward slope indicates a bearish bias. The main price channel trendlines require two or more price points to plot. Of course even more price points are better. The parallel channel lines exist at the bottoms of two or more low points. Breaking out of either of the trendlines or channel lines indicates a bullish or bearish breakout, where the bias depends on the direction of the breakout. Some traders use these channel and trendlines as support and resistance levels and trade accordingly. For example, if the price touches a channel line, they anticipate a reversal into a rally. Touching the trendline predicts a drop from supply (resistance). Traders who use price channel patterns watch for the price to approach either of the two price channel lines.

Figure 7–22. Bullish and Bearish Price Channel Lines

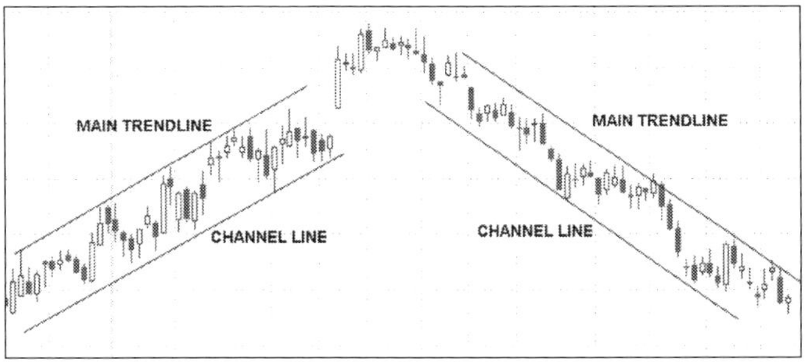

For illustration purposes only.

Measured Move — Bullish or Bearish

A measured move continuation pattern typically forms over a period of several months. This pattern can be either bullish or bearish. In a bullish measured move, there is a rally, basing, and then a gradual drop. This is followed by a resumption of the rally. Like some of the other chart patterns, it is difficult to know when this pattern is forming until you can see the third phase once it forms. This trend traditionally begins as a correction from a reversal in price. It is common for consolidations to occur during both long-term rallies and long-term drops. The measured move pattern is a typical example of consolidation and then resumption of the dominant trend. Trading volume from selling drops at the beginning of the reversal and then increases as the price resumes its direction and exits the measured move pattern.

Figure 7–23. The Measured Move Pattern (Bullish Example)

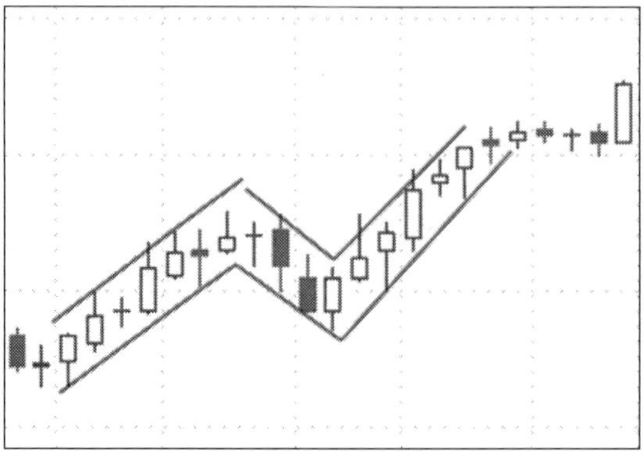

For illustration purposes only.

Cup with Handle

This is a bullish continuation pattern that some traders look for and use during a lengthy price rally. Both the cup and the handle patterns represent a consolidation rather than a reversal. Traders anticipate a price breakout following the brief pullbacks that form the cup with handle pattern. As you can see in figure 7–24, the pattern includes two distinct parts: a cup that represents the first pullback and a handle that represents a second, smaller pullback. The cup resembles the rounded bottom reversal pattern described earlier. Recall that the rounded bottom pattern wasn't followed by a handle that represents retesting before continuing the rally. As shown in figure 7–24, when the cup pattern is completed, a "handle" forms at the trailing side of the cup. A retreat from the bottom of the handle signals a resumption of the rally.

Those who describe this pattern believe that the pullback that forms the cup's depth should never exceed 1/3 of the rally leading up to the pullback. The same is true for the handle, that is, it should not exceed 1/3 of the drop that forms the cup. Cups can represent several months in duration, while handles typically range from a week to a month in length.

Figure 7–24. The Cup with Handle Pattern (Bullish)

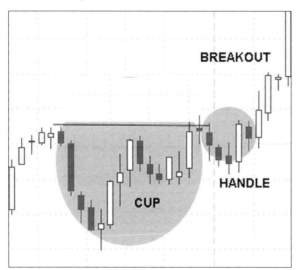

For illustration purposes only.

These are not the only chart patterns in use today, but they do represent several of those used by chart traders. The next chapter presents a collection of popular chart studies that are in common use by professional traders. The studies are used because traders believe mathematical chart studies enhance their odds for successful trades. Once you are familiar with these technical studies and see how they work, you will be ready to begin using them on your charts to help you develop a rational directional bias and to determine where and when to enter your trades.

Chart Patterns versus Supply and Demand

Before leaving this chapter, be advised that there is nothing magical about chart patterns. They are not the Holy Grail for trade entries or exits. Buying and selling "in the middle" of a price chart, far above support and far below resistance, is where the rookies trade. Professional traders who are chart technicians make their livings trading near support and resistance at the top and the bottom of their price charts (the same price charts you see). This is where supply and demand exists. This is where traders buy wholesale and sell retail. So never look at a chart pattern in isolation. A perfect double bottom well above historical support may be in consolidation only to continue on its downward journey toward support.

Use patterns as signals. But put your weight on price trends, historical support and resistance levels, and current trading volatility. Enhance your trading by applying one or more technical studies like those introduced in the following chapter.

What did you learn in chapter 7?

1. Technical analysis is used with randomly generated data based on _____ _____.

2. Examining a company's underlying financial condition is part of _____ analysis.

3. The study of _____ _____ data is useful for predicting future price movements.

4. The Gaussian Random Walk and EMH disavow the usefulness of _____ _____.

5. Japanese candlestick charts were first used with Japanese _____ _____.

6. A single candlestick shows four price levels:_____, _____, _____, and _____.

7. Use multiple charts having different _____ _____.

8. A doji candlestick is formed when the opening and closing price are the _____.

9. Some traders use the shapes of _____ to predict a price reversal and breakouts.

10. Finding a definite price _____ is an important first step in chart analysis.

11. A sequence of lower lows and lower highs indicates a _____ price trend.

12. A historical support level is also called a _____ zone.

13. Trade what you _____, not what you think, fear, feel, hear, or hope.

14. Stock prices tend to remain between established _____ and _____ levels.

15. Securities are _____ at resistance and _____ at support.

16. In an upward-trending stock, a bull flag signals an _____ _____ for a bullish trade.

17. It would be naïve to believe that popular chart patterns _____ _____.

18. Two classifications of chart patterns are _____ and _____ patterns.
19. The double top, triple top, and head and shoulders are all _____ patterns.
20. The bullish flag and cup with _____ are continuation patterns.

8 TECHNICAL ANALYSIS USING CHART STUDIES

Introduction

The previous chapter introduced you to the diversity that exists between chart technicians and their skeptics. It also reiterated the importance of price trends. Several candlestick shapes, their names, and the corresponding expectations were also discussed. And you read how many chart technicians use the shapes of candles to predict a price breakout into either a rally or a drop. Chapter 7 also explained the rationale for the interpretations of each of the chart patterns. While knowing the shapes, names, and expectations of candlesticks and chart patterns is important to traders, there are many more useful chart tools. These are regularly used by experienced traders to enhance the outcomes of their trades. These are mathematical studies that are frequently added to price charts. These studies are applied to confirm the trader's bias, and to increase the probability for a successful outcome.

This chapter builds on the candle shapes and patterns learned in chapter 7. It drills down even deeper into chart analysis. It introduces and describes numerous popular chart studies, commonly referred to as "odds enhancers." Some chart traders often add and leave their favorite chart studies on their charts as permanent "fixtures."

The chapter also examines the concepts of support and resistance and supply and demand. Integrating chart trends, candlestick and chart patterns, and technical chart studies provides a substantial amount of detailed information about what prices are doing and are about to do. Combining all of these analytical tools provides a powerful trading "toolbox" chock full of useful information — a prerequisite to becoming a successful trader. With this toolbox you can begin trading based on what you see.

Trends, Breakouts, and Momentum

Even people who are unfamiliar with how to use price charts can look at one and see price rallies, price drops, price reversals, and perhaps even more. Even if they don't know what the volume bars mean at the bottom of a chart, or the vertical lines that represent expiration Fridays (used with monthly option contracts), they can see where the price was and where it seems to be heading. The novice trader usually buys stocks based on the direction of the underlying's price. If they only knew how to use a bracketed trade, they might make some money. But they typically enter a market order (as compared to a limit order) and take what the market gives them..

Professional traders depend on this, as novice traders typically buy near the end or immediately following a rally, and sell at the end or after a decline — always a bit too late, and often just in time to see a reversal against their positions. This is because they buy at price levels where supply exceeds demand or, more rarely, sell where demand exceeds supply.

Why "more rarely?" Many who are new to the market are unfamiliar with the steps required to short a stock. They are unaware that it's possible to sell (or short) a stock they don't currently own in their brokerage account and then close their short order at a lower price for profit. Selling and then buying back — called *buy to cover* — at a lower price is done on a regular basis. If you are not familiar with how shorting a stock or ETF works, check this brief explanation.

How to Short a Stock

1. Sue has a standard margin brokerage account.
2. She finds three black crows on XYZ's price chart; it has begun to drop just above $50.
3. Sue decides to use account margin to short (sell) 100 shares of XYZ.
4. For protection, Sue places a protective "buy-to-cover" market stop order at $51.25.
5. She also places a "buy-to-cover" limit stop order at $46.00 as her profit target.
6. Her entry has a 3.2:1 reward to risk ratio (risks $1.25 for a $4.00 profit).
7. XYZ drops to $46; this triggers Sue's profit target for $400 in profit.

Trends

Chapter 7 included trendlines on several of the charts. Recall that a trendline is drawn as a line parallel to the candlesticks. An uptrend is formed by the price swings from a series of higher highs and higher lows. A downtrend is formed by a progression of lower highs and lower lows. Figure 7–4 and 7–5 illustrated uptrends.

Also recall how the trend is the single most important factor to consider when trading, because it is the direction of trading. And never look at a single interval chart. Always examine price trends on several charts, from long to short intervals. It's common to see a weekly chart in a down trend, while a daily or hourly chart is in an uptrend. This is why we examine a series of charts rather than just one.

Breakouts

A breakout occurs when a price exits the prevailing trend by suddenly changing direction either upward or downward. Knowing when a price breakout is about to occur is a major advantage. The trader can either buy or sell short to take advantage of the forming price action. Setting a "trap" in the form of a limit entry near the breakout price can maximize profits. An active trader will set a profit target and manage the working trade. If it moves in the desired direction, these traders begin sliding both protective stops and profit targets to "let the profits run." If the trade goes against them and their protective stop is triggered; they're out. However, their trade setup worked because the amount lost was acceptable based on their trading rules.

In addition to looking for a breakout on an underlying chart, watch volume, price ranges, and current volatility. There is an interesting chart study called the "Trade-the-Market-Squeeze" (TTM_ Squeeze) that was developed by an active trader and instructor named John Carter. The TTM_Squeeze is used to find price breakouts when trading volatility falls inside 1.5 of the 14-day average price range (ATR) of the underlying security. The TTM_Squeeze study also predicts the direction of the breakout, which makes it all the more valuable to those who use it.

Momentum

Momentum is the speed at which the market moves. The ability of the market or an individual stock to sustain an increase or decrease in price is a measure of *market momentum*. Momentum is measured by calculating price change over a specified period of time. Momentum is the direct result of the increase or decrease in trading volume and is measured in terms of *volatility*. High trading volume (volatility) increases momentum. And momentum decreases with a corresponding reduction in trading volume. Obviously, an increase in the volume of selling pushes prices down; high buying volumes push prices up.

There are a number of available momentum studies to measure relative strengths. These compare the momentum of an individual stock to the momentum of the index (or sector) to which it belongs. For example, when the momentums of AAPL and the S&P 500 index are compared, relative strength is revealed. As described in the following note, we call this *beta weighting*. Also recall that the beta value of every index is 1.0. This is the current combined volatility average of all stocks and ETFs that comprise a financial index.

Charting technicians (or *technical analysts*) put momentum studies on their charts to determine when a stock is oversold or overbought compared to the index to which it belongs. Four such "odds enhancers" include the relative strength index (RSI), commodity channel index (CCI), the Stochastics Oscillator, and the moving average convergence-divergence (MACD). All of these *momentum oscillators* are explored in more detail within this chapter.

> **NOTE** As mentioned, the *beta* weighting of a stock compares an individual stock's volatility to the volatility of the market to which it belongs. Every market index or sector carries a beta value of 1.0. For example, the S&P 500 stock AAPL had a beta weighting of 0.52 when this note was written. This tells us that AAPL had roughly half the volatility of the index's average. At the same time, the SPY ETF had a beta weighting of 1.033 — very close to the index average, which is expected because the SPY is an S&P 500 index ETF. The beta weighting value changes as buyers and sellers enter and exit the market. It's entirely possible for the beta value of 0.52 to move to 2.0 or even higher during high periods of trading volume.

The preceding note mentions indexes and *sectors*. The following table lists nine ETFs comprised of stocks within specific market sectors.

Market Sector ETFs

XLB	Basic Materials	XLI	Industrials/ Transportation	XLM	Utilities
XLE	Energy	XLK	Technologies	XLV	Healthcare
XLF	Financial	XLP	Consumer Staples	XLY	Consumer Discretionary

Open, Close, High, Low

Chapter 7 presented several candlestick patterns in addition to describing their meaning. Recall a candle is comprised of a green (or white) or red (or black) colored body and a top and bottom shadow resembling the wicks of an ordinary wax candle. The ends of the body represent the opening and closing price and the tips of the shadow represent the high and the low for the selected chart

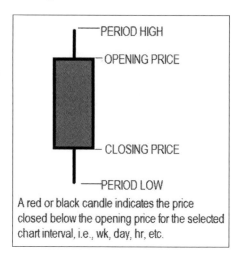

A red or black candle indicates the price closed below the opening price for the selected chart interval, i.e., wk, day, hr, etc.

interval. The red candle in adjacent illustration provides a review of how a candle is interpreted. A green or white candle tells us that the price closed higher than it opened for the designated chart interval.

Popular Chart Studies

There are hundreds of chart studies used by chart technicians. These studies provide clues to things like momentum, price averages over different time frames, current volume, volatility, pending breakouts, and more.

Many of these are available on your trading platform. Interactive Broker's Trader Workstation includes about a hundred. The thinkor-swim® trading application provides several hundred.

Volume and Open Interest

You can display trading volume on your charts as bar charts that rise from the bottom of your chart window. As you can see in figure 8–1, trading volume corresponds to price levels. Volume peaks during strong rallies and drops during basing. Volume always swings back and forth from low to high or high to low — something you can count on. So when the trading volume is unusually low for an actively traded stock, you can anticipate a return to normal trading volume or perhaps even higher.

Figure 8–1. Volume Bars Shown on an AAPL Chart.

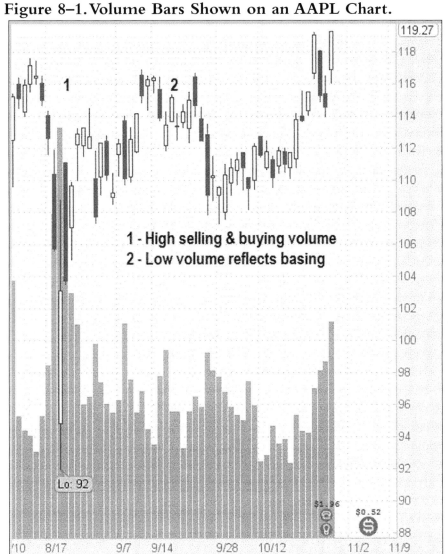

1 - High selling & buying volume
2 - Low volume reflects basing

For illustration purposes only.

Open interest is the number of option contracts that have been settled for a specific optionable equity (stocks, ETFs, financial indices, or futures). Open interest can be displayed at every strike price and for every call and put contract on the underlying option chain. Open interest is extremely important to option traders. Without open interest, working option orders may never be filled. These orders are likely to expire at the end of the day when the market closes and trading ends.

Moving Averages (Simple, Exponential, Triangular)

Many traders put one or more moving average plots on their charts. One of the characteristics of moving averages is smoothing. Moving averages are lagging indicators that take the "hash" out of price fluctuations. They plot the average closing prices over the specified time interval — days, hours, etc. For example, a 20-day simple moving average — abbreviated SMA(20), adds the closing prices of the previous 20 days, including the current day, and divides by 20. Moving average plotlines reveal the price trend. Many consider price swings above and below the moving average line as a signal for entry or exit.

There are generally three types of moving averages: simple moving averages (SMA), exponential moving averages (EMA), and triangular moving averages (TMA). These moving averages are sometimes the only lines on a price chart. However, there are several other chart studies that are based on the moving average plot. For example, the Moving Average Convergence Divergence (MACD) is dependent on moving average plots, as are Bollinger bands and Keltner channels, to name three.

Calculations

On a day interval chart, the default 9-period simple moving average, abbreviated SMA(9), uses the closing prices of the nine most recent trading days. This is calculated by taking the sum of the closing prices and dividing by 9. This process readjusts each day using the average closing prices of the preceding nine-day period. An SMA(15) uses the same calculation, except for 15 days (three weeks). The simple moving average study is adjustable as follows:

- Change the number of periods to plot.
- Change the price value being plotted from close to open, high, low, open, close, H+L/2, etc.
- Change the displacement in bars, where each bar is equal to the number of days in a day chart. A positive value represents a backward displacement.

Figure 8–2. An SMA(9) and SMA(50) Crossover

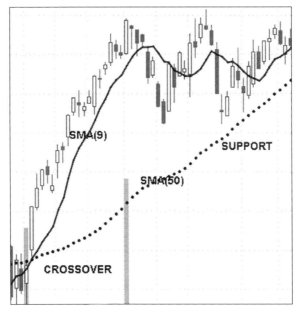

For illustration purposes only.

Some traders look for moving average crossovers. This is done by using a short-term and a long-term SMA at the same time. For example, a rising moving average signals an uptrend. Figure 8–2 shows the SMA(9) crossing above an SMA(50) plot. Notice that the SMA(50) appears to form a price support level.

The exponential moving average (EMA) is the most popular short-term moving average used by chart traders. The EMA places more weight on the most recent price points. This reduces the amount of lag, although an EMA is still a lagging indicator. According to several sources, the 12-period EMA, written EMA(12), and the 26-period EMA, or EMA(26), are the most popular. Some traders use longer term EMAs when searching for long-term price trends. The EMA is also used to create other chart studies. Two examples are the MACD, discussed below, and the Percentage Price Oscillator, PPO.

The triangular moving average (TMA) is another plot that accentuates the center values of the most recent series of price points. It is a double-smoothed simple moving average of the specified number of preceding price points. For example, the most recent nine candles are included in the TMA(9). The term *double-smoothed* means the plot is the SMA of the SMA, which removes the choppiness that is often seen in similar SMA and EMA plots.

Moving Average Convergence Divergence (MACD)

The MACD study is a derivative of the EMA(12) study. It is based on the closing prices of the underlying's moving averages. This indicator tracks EMA crossovers. Looking at figure 8–3, notice how the EMA(12), represented by the solid plot, crosses EMA(26) represented by the dashed plot. Traders interpret a buy signal when the EMA(12) crosses above the EMA(26) and a sell signal when it crosses below the EMA(26). Notice the small bars that extend above and below the zero line. Bars that begin to extend below the zero line signal divergence from the trend — a potential breakout and buying opportunity may be forming; bars that are above the zero line signal a continuation of the trend. When exceptionally wide separation exists between the two plots, traders expect the two plot lines to converge. The clarity of these signals makes the MACD a popular study among traders.

Figure 8–3. The Moving Average Convergence Divergence Study

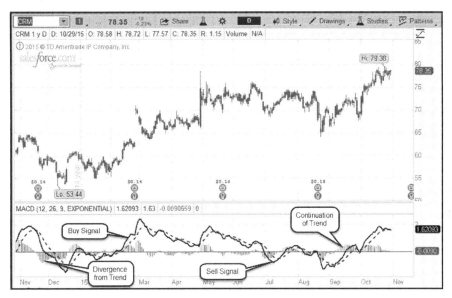

For illustration purposes only.

More Oversold/Overbought Studies (RSI, CCI, Stochastic Oscillators)

Many chart traders consider these momentum oscillators (or *studies*) to be vital additions to their charts. Some even put two or more on their charts. Figure 8–4 illustrates all three.

Figure 8–4. Oversold/Overbought Momentum Studies

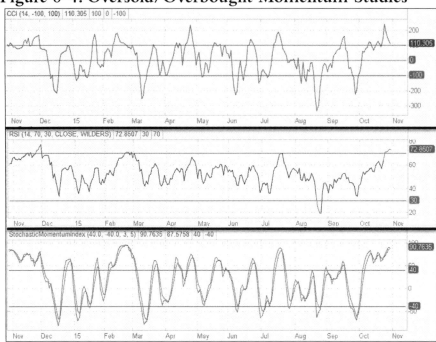

For illustration purposes only.

These studies were briefly referenced in the preceding momentum paragraph. CCI stands for Commodity Channel Index and RSI stands for Relative Strength Index. Because all three serve the same purpose, the one used depends almost entirely on a trader's personal preference. Looking at the plots in figure 8–4 you quickly see that all three provide nearly identical information, which is a sense of current momentum. There is at least a 70% correlation between the three.

The price chart above these indicators will closely resemble the momentum plots upward and downward of these studies. The ability to quickly glance at a plot at the bottom of a chart to determine the current momentum is certainly useful. With a quick peek a trader can qualify or disqualify a stock or ETF. If discouraged by either an oversold or overbought plot, the trader can either quickly move on or stop for a closer look. But the plot is not the end of the story. The dominant trend, chart patterns, and historical support and resistance levels must also be taken into account.

Although the high and low values of these studies are similar, there are minor differences. For example, the CCI and RSI studies both include the most recent 14 candles. The CCI study oscillates between −100 and +100, making the zero line neutral. The default range of the RSI chart is between 30 and 70. The StochasticMomentumIndex (SMI) ranges from −100 to +100 and is based on the most recent 40 candles. The underlying calculations for the SMI are more complex than either the CCI or RSI. The SMI computes the difference between the closing price relative to the high-low range's midpoint rather than just the range itself. This difference returns a higher value, which is why the scale ranges from −100 to +100 from bottom to top. A buy signal is produced when the SMI crosses below the −40 level, and a sell signal is produced when the plot crosses above the +40 level.

There is also a StochasticFastOscillator oversold/overbought study. This momentum study also displays a scale ranging from 0 to 100. If the plot crosses below 20 it is interpreted as a buy signal; crossing above 80 is a sell signal. This plot makes use of the last ten bars in addition to the highest price point of the last three candles. Some traders use this momentum oscillator for shorter term trades ranging from one day to one week in duration.

So which one is best? To avoid taking a lengthy and perhaps confusing "walkabout" through the sequence of momentum oscillators, consider taking a brief look at each and make your decision. But don't clutter your charts with more than one. In a recent straw poll among a group of active traders, most preferred the MACD over the other momentum studies. They particularly liked the divergence bars and watch them for price reversal signals. So start there and learn how to use the divergence and convergence bars in conjunction with your candlestick charts.

Figure 8–5. Market Forecaster Study with Three Plots

For illustration purposes only.

Market Forecast Study

The Market Forecast Study is yet another momentum study. Like the other momentum studies just described, this study is also displayed at the bottom of your price charts. The "factory default setting" displays three lines: Momentum (red), Near Term (blue), and Intermediate (green). The three lines can be more confusing than helpful, as shown in figure 8–5.

Users of this study often remove the red and blue lines and leave the green (intermediate) line for clarity, as shown in figure 8–6.

Figure 8–6. Market Forecaster Study with One Intermediate Plot

For illustration purposes only.

Removing the "noise" created by the red and blue plots makes this study easier to use. The Market Forecast study uses the scale to the right, which ranges from 0 to 100 with 25-unit increments. Some call the Market Forecaster their "seat belt" and use it to avoid a trading "wreck." When the green plot line drops below 80, it signals caution. If it drops below 50, it signals SELL! as a precipitous drop is looming. As seen in figure 8–6 above, which is a weekly chart ranging from 2006 to 2015, the crash of 2008 was signaled well in advance. Traders using the Market Forecast study would sell and then buy back once the green line moved back above 50. But the traders must also see confirmation on the corresponding price chart, as it must be in agreement with the Market Forecast study.

Average True Range: ATR(n)

The average true range indicator is another price momentum study. It is most often set to evaluate the last 14 candles on a daily chart. It is also called the ATR(14) Wilder, named after its developer, Mr. J. Welles Wilder. Hence, each candle represents one day. This provides the average price range from opening to closing prices over the specified number of candles — typically 14. The average price range is computed using the greatest absolute value found in one of the following differences:

- today's high and today's low,
- yesterday's close and today's high, or
- yesterday's close and today's low.

Because the trader is looking for daily price changes, negative and positive values are ignored. Therefore, only absolute values are used in the calculations. In an ATR(14), these daily calculations are averaged over the last 14 candles in the daily chart.

Many traders consider the ATR(14) in their trading. First, they want enough price momentum (or movement) to justify an entry.

The ATR(14) value is often used when choosing a protective stop. Traders often consider the ATR(14) value when choosing the placement of a protective stop below/above the limit entry price.

Trends and Trendlines

As you know, trendlines, already discussed extensively, are extremely important to chart technicians. Over long chart intervals, trendlines show us the historical movement of the underlying's price. Has the price been experiencing a gradual rise or fall over a long period of time? Has it been moving sideways with intermittent rallies and drops around what appears to be a central axis? You may look at a 15-minute chart and see a downward sloping trendline. But a day or a week chart interval may reveal that the price has been in a consistent uptrend. This illustrates the need to examine charts from progressively long to shorter intervals to see the dominant, long-term trend.

The linear regression trendline is quite useful in determining the price trend. This study plots the trend for the current chart interval. The trendline is derived using what mathematicians call a *linear regression analysis*. This analysis uses all past prices using the "least squares" method. The trendline calculation is usually based on the closing prices of each candle in the series. However, this can be changed to the average daily price of each candle by summing the high and the low and dividing by 2. The least squares method involves an algebraic equation that was developed in the early 1800s for use in linear regression analysis.

The two charts shown in figure 8–7 contrast two linear regression trendlines for the same stock over two chart intervals — a daily chart and a 15-minute chart. Although the 15-minute chart might lead a trader to believe that the stock price is trending downward, it's apparent that it is has actually been steadily trending upward over the past year. Figure 8–7 illustrates the importance of looking at multiple charts from long to short time intervals.

Figure 8–7. Linear Regression Trendline on a Day and a 15-Minute Chart

For illustration purposes only.

Volatility

Levels of volatility are derived by measuring the price points of all the orders related to an underlying equity for a specified period of time. Volatility is either based on the trading volume for a selected security or its deviation from the market index to which it belongs. Traders compare current (or *implied*) volatility to *historical* volatility to determine if trading activity is unusually high or low when compared to historical order volumes.

When current volatility is higher than historical volatility, the price of the underlying security is either rallying or dropping from higher than usual buying or selling. As you develop your option trading rules, volatility is one of the most important measures to consider — especially implied volatility percentile and rank. Experienced traders view implied volatility as a measure of current trader sentiment.

Historical Volatility

Historical volatility uses twelve months of data points derived from the price movements of the underlying. Notice a custom volatility chart study at the bottom of figure 8–8. This study breaks down implied volatility percentage levels into 20-percentile increments across a one-year period. The light solid line represents historical

Figure 8–8. A Custom Volatility Study Showing 20% Quintiles

For illustration purposes only.

volatility. The dotted line traces implied volatility. Many option traders select option strategies based on current implied volatility levels. Some even consider the 20% levels shown at the bottom of figure 8–8 to select specific option strategies that are well suited to a specific IV quintile.

Implied Volatility

With a basic understanding of the difference between historical and implied volatility, we'll examine how the implied volatility is derived. Implied volatility is an excellent measure of current trader sentiment because it reveals unusually high or low trading activity — but this may be short lived. The level of trading activity can stall and turn on a dime. So entering a bull or a bear trade strategy is typically done quickly, before the "pendulum" begins to swing away from the opportunity. Look at the option statistics shown in figure 8–9.

As mentioned, IV is the measurement of current market sentiment.

Historical volatility (HV) is the measure of a security's potential price movement based upon the historical range of price movements of the selected security.

When current volatility is halfway between the 52-week HV High and the 52-week HV Low, the Current IV Percentile would be 50%.

If the current volatility is presently at the 52-week HV High, the current volatility would be 100%. Conversely, if current volatility is equal to the HV Low, it would be 0%. When current IV% exceeds 100%, it has exceeded historical volatility.

The acronym VWAP shown at the bottom of the volatility measures stands for *volume-weighted average price*. The VWAP is a measure of the underlying's price based upon the number of shares or contracts traded at different prices. In other words, it is the weighted average price at which most of the trading has occurred.

The center section of figure 8–9 provides a summary of all the option trades recorded for the current date. Notice how this data is broken down into different classifications. For example, the number of trades at or below the current BID price (sell orders), at or above the ASK price (buy orders), and Between the Market orders (orders that settled between the BID and ASK prices — this value shows a combination of option spreads and those orders that settled between the BID and ASK prices, such as at the Mark price. The Delta between is the sum of all Delta values involved in the day's cumulative option trades separated into 20% quintiles.

The rightmost section of figure 8–9 provides the current *Sizzle Index* data. The sizzle index is the ratio of the current day's volume for all options traded on the underlying compared to the average volume of all options traded for the previous five days. A sizzle index of 1.0 indicates options are currently being traded at the average of the last five days. Similarly, the call and put sizzle indexes measure the call and put volumes compared to the average volumes over the most recent five days.

Finally, volatility sizzle measures the current day's volatility index compared to the average volatility of the last five days trading activity. Stock sizzle measures the same five-day average of the underlying stock itself.

When implied volatility is greater than 50 percent, traders check the corresponding charts and option chains for higher than usual premium values. High implied volatility percentile levels elevate option premium levels, which can make them a trade target. You can examine some or all of these volatility statistics within most option trading platforms.

Figure 8–9. Volatility Statistics

AAPL APPLE INC COM 116.585 ETB NASDAQ +0.66 Company Profile

Today's Options Statistics

52 week IV High:	0.623
52 week IV Low:	0.192
Current IV Percentile:	10%
52 week HV High:	0.487
52 week HV Low:	0.099
Current HV Percentile:	32%
Implied Volatility:	23.45%
VWAP:	117.538

Trade Analysis	Calls		Puts		Total	
Total Volume:	203,497		120,896		324,393	
Traded at BID or below:	94,078		49,949		144,027	
...% of total:	46%		41%		44%	
Traded at ASK or above:	74,422		52,275		126,697	
...% of total:	36%		43%		39%	
Between the Market:	34,997		18,672		53,669	
...% of total:	17%		15%		16%	
Delta Between						
0 ... 20	68,968	33%	44,656	36%	113,624	35%
21 ... 40	44,240	21%	31,928	26%	76,168	23%
41 ... 60	60,457	29%	30,237	25%	90,694	27%
61 ... 80	20,379	10%	9,739	8%	30,118	9%
81 ... 100	9,453	4%	4,336	3%	13,789	4%

Sizzle Index	1.116
Call Sizzle Index	1.049
Put Sizzle Index	1.25
Volatility Sizzle	0.992
Stock Sizzle	0.733
P/C Ratio	0.594

For illustration purposes only.

Another common volatility study used by many traders on their charts is the Bollinger Bands study. This study is described and illustrated within the next few pages.

Standard Deviation

Standard deviation values are often studied and used by traders to determine the statistical probability of price movement to a certain value. The standard deviation value is a derivative of the data points created by price volatility (or movements) over a given period of time. It is shown as both a percentage and a numeric value at the upper right-hand corner of every option chain. From this you can conclude that these values are meaningful since they are shown for every contract expiration date.

The probability of landing outside one standard deviation of an underlying price theoretically means the current stock price and its time to expiration will remain within ±1 standard deviation 68.2% of the time. Based on research conducted by the staff of tastytrade, stock prices actually remain within this range 73% of the time. This is why many option traders sell call options at +1 standard deviation if bearish and sell put options at −1 standard deviation when bullish. Conservative traders frequently use ±2 standard deviations for increased safety. They also sell calls and puts at these standard deviation levels when neutral, as neutrally biased traders do not believe the stock price will make a substantial move in either direction.

Standard deviation is used to compute the probability of a price reaching a certain level. As mentioned, many option traders use two standard deviations above or below the current price of the underlying for short out of the money (OTM) option trades. For example, if the current price is $75 and the standard deviation for the selected option contract that expires in 140 days is 31.55% (± 11.866), the trader might place a trade at the $50 strike price below, the $100 strike price above, or both. These strike prices are roughly two standard deviations out of the money, i.e., above and below the current at the money strike price.

A standard deviation bell curve is shown in figure 8–10. It shows ± 1, ±2, and ±3 standard deviations from the centerline. Volatility can move in either direction, that is, it can increase or decrease. You can think of implied volatility as a pendulum that swings high and low, but always returns to and often through the centerline to the other side of the bell. When volatility is extremely high or low, it always retreats toward the centerline, which acts like gravity. This process helps traders develop a bias. They look for exceptionally high volatility to sell options, as premium is highest when volatility is highest. During low volatility, premiums are low. This condition encourages option traders to look for buying opportunities. Both buyers and sellers look for a return to neutrality. In fact, they depend on it.

Figure 8–10. The Standard Deviation Bell Curve

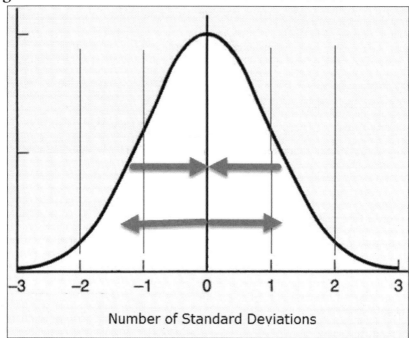

Number of Standard Deviations

Bollinger Bands

The Bollinger bands study draws a plotline above and below a 20-period simple moving average that represents two times the current standard deviation of the underlying. Hence, the Bollinger band "envelope" narrows and widens as current volatility compresses and expands. An example of the Bollinger band study is shown in figure 8–11.

Figure 8–11. The Bollinger Bands Volatility Study

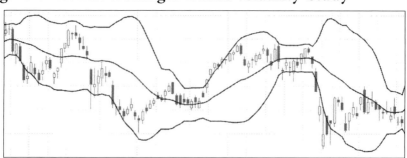

For illustration purposes only.

This is an excellent visual presentation of current volatility, because the standard deviation is a derivative of buying and selling activity. Notice how the bands collapse during periods of basing and widen during periods of buying or selling. Large price changes result from higher volatility — heavy buying and selling. Therefore, the distance of the bands from the central SMA(20) plot tracks current buying and selling activity quite accurately. Obviously, the bands do not reveal a directional bias. This is determined by looking at the SMA(20) plot, the opening and closing prices, and highs and lows represented by the candlesticks.

The Keltner Channel

Like the Bollinger bands, the Keltner channel is also a volatility study that resembles the Bollinger band study. The Keltner channel also uses the 20-period simple moving average as its centerline. But the exterior envelope lines are plotted using 1.5 times the 14-period average true price, or ATR(14). Therefore, the distance between the upper and lower plot is 3× the ATR(14). A price that extends above the upper channel is seen as a bullish event, while a price that drops below the bottom channel line is considered a bearish event. As you can see, the price always collapses back inside the exterior channels. When a price trend is moving sideways, candles that extend above the upper plot are considered an overbought signal; candles that extend below the lower plot are seen as an oversold signal. As with most studies, traders rarely draw a final conclusion from a single study. It's always preferable to see several studies that are in agreement with each other before settling on a final bias. The Keltner channel is shown on a chart in figure 8–12.

Figure 8–12. The Keltner Channel Volatility Study

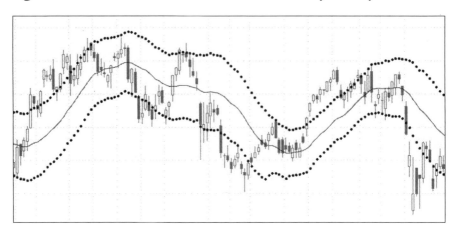

For illustration purposes only.

Trade-the-Market (TTM) Squeeze

Now that you've read about both Bollinger bands and the Keltner channel, the next study should be even more interesting. It is called the trade-the-market squeeze (abbreviated TTM_Squeeze). It is one of John Carter's studies. Mr. Carter also designed and introduced a few other studies including an interesting *TTM_ScalpAlert* used for "runaway markets." The scalp alert is designed to signal price pivot points following a series of three consecutive higher or lower closes. The TTM_ScalpAlert is designed for quick entries and exits on short interval charts.

The TTM_Squeeze study superimposes the Bollinger bands and Keltner channel studies on the same chart. A tick chart rather than a time interval chart is recommended for use with the TTM_Squeeze, because each candle represents a specified number of traders rather than simply the passage of time. You can choose to put these two studies on your chart, although the TTM_Squeeze study still works without their presence. Figure 8–13 provides an example of what this superimposition looks like when the studies are displayed. The exterior plots of the Keltner channels are represented by the dotted lines; the exterior Bollinger band plots are represented by the solid lines.

Figure 8–13. Bollinger Bands and Keltner Channel Squeezes

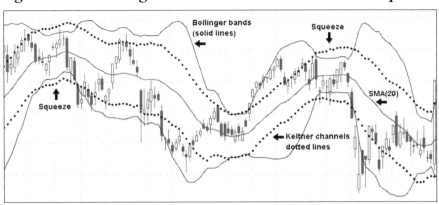

For illustration purposes only.

The purpose of overlaying the Keltner channel on the Bollinger band study is to find a price breakout. Price breakouts are sought by every serious trader. Finding the breakout maximizes profits. It's essentially getting in on the "ground floor" of a price move. This is much better than entering a trade somewhere in the middle or even worse, just before the price turns against your trade.

The reason this overlay signals a price breakout is that it compares volatility to the average price range. When the "squeeze is on," volatility, based on the standard deviation, has collapsed. If you recall from the standard deviation discussion, the pendulum always swings back toward the center of the bell like falling back from the "gravitational pull." So when volatility implodes, the likelihood of it swinging away from the centerline and back toward the exterior portion of the bell is highly probable. Also notice that the candles around the squeeze regions are either basing or quite small. Basing and small price candles are both indicative of low volatility. So a breakout is forming.

But in which direction will the price go? Enter the lower band of the TTM_Squeeze study. Notice in figure 8–14 how the TTM_ Squeeze study at the bottom of the chart actually predicts directional movement.

Figure 8–14. Breakout Signals from the TTM_Squeeze Study

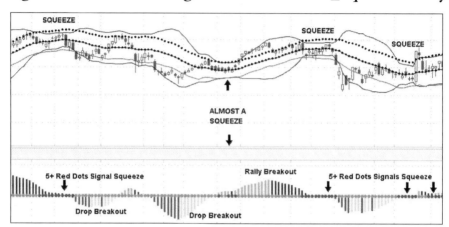

For illustration purposes only.

The rule for the TTM_Squeeze is to wait for a minimum of five red dots on the axis line of the study at the bottom portion of the chart. Looking at the Bollinger bands and Keltner channel above, you can see that the squeeze occurs when the Bollinger bands cross inside the Keltner channel plots. Next, look at the direction of the bars on the TTM_Squeeze study below. There, the study predicts the direction of the breakout — a rally or a drop. This is a powerful study and is used by many swing traders who are familiar with it.

Pivot Points

Although swing traders may never use the Pivot Points study, originally called *floor trader pivot points*, they are often used by futures traders who use shorter term time intervals from 15 minutes down to 1 minute in duration. Pivot points are in frequent use by futures and forex traders. Figure 8–15 illustrates the pivot points study with a pivot point (PP), two support levels (S1 and S2), and two resistance levels (R1 and R2). There are two more optional levels designated S3 and R3 that can be shown with this study.

Figure 8–15. The Floor Trader Pivot Points Study on a 5-Minute Chart

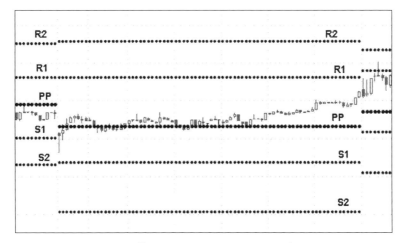

For illustration purposes only.

The pivot point study was introduced many years ago by exchange floor traders, primarily short-term day traders who worked on the futures exchange. Hence the name *floor trader pivots* is also used for this study. The study is based on observations of repetitive support and resistance levels. It uses the previous period's highs, lows, and closes to calculate the current period's support and resistance levels. The original theory purported the price of the underlying would remain between the S1 and R1 levels 70 percent of the time, and between the S2 and R2 lines 85 percent of the time. However, some sources strongly dispute this. The following values were prepared for use by forex traders, but it's difficult to validate this data without conducting a rigorous statistical analysis.

Pivot Line	*Probability of Closing Inside*	*Probability of Touching*
PP	N/A	76%
S1 or R1	56%	76%
S2 or R2	82%	33%
S3 or R3	94%	12%

The central pivot point (PP) and the support and resistance lines are calculated using the following simple formulas. The high, low, and close values are always based on the previous chart period.

Current Period	Previous Period's High, Low, and Close
Pivot point (PP)	(High + Low + Close)/3
Support 1 (S1)	(PP × 2) − High
Support 2 (S2)	PP − (High − Low)
Resistance 1 (R1)	(PP × 2) − Low
Resistance 2 (R2)	PP + (High − Low)

If an underlying price pierces the R1 or S1 lines, the consensus becomes bearish (R1) or bullish (S1). When a price rallies above R2, traders see this as an overbought signal. Similarly, a price drop below S2 signals an oversold condition. In concert with these signals, traders begin to look for candle shapes and patterns that are common to the formation of zones of supply or demand.

Fibonacci Retracements

The Fibonacci sequence was originated in the early 13th century by the Italian mathematician Leonardo Pisano Bigollo, also known as Leonardo Fibonacci. The sequence is constructed by adding each consecutive number to the previous number beginning with 0. The following series illustrates this process.

0+1=1, 1+1=2, 1+2=3, 2+3=5, 3+5=8, 5+8=13,
8+13=21, 13+21=34, 21+34=55, 34+55=89,
55+89=144, 89+144=233, 144+233=327, to ∞

The Fibonacci retracement lines put on price charts are ratios rather than actual Fibonacci numbers. For example, a Fib. number divided by the previous number provides many interesting outcomes: $21/13 = 1.6153$, $34/21 = 1.6190$, $55/34 = 1.6176$, $89/55 = 1.6181$, etc.

Fibonacci numbers divided by the next number in the sequence yields .6181 as follows:

34/55 =.6181, 55/89 = .6179, etc.

Numbers divided by another two places in the sequence approximate .3820 from:

13/34 = .382, 21/55 = .3818, 34/89 = .3820, 55/144 = .3819, etc.

The 1.618 value is called the "golden ratio." The inverse of 1.618 is .618. These ratios abound in both nature and human anatomy.

Charles Dow was one of the founders of the Dow Jones Industrial Average in addition to being the founder of the *Wall Street Journal.* Dow observed that stocks and other financial securities consistently experience pullbacks of ⅓, ½, and ⅔ of a previous rally. This happens across both long term and short term chart intervals. Dow also noticed that the set of Fibonacci based mathematical ratios found in nature and used by the Ancient Greeks — the 23.6%, 38.2%, 50.0%, 61.8%, and 78.6% — were closely correlated to the price retracement levels. This gave rise to the use of Fibonacci retracement lines on charts in addition to terms like *Fibonacci bounce.*

These Fibonacci retracement lines used on price charts are thought to be "magical." They are used to approximate high frequency price turning points. Therefore, Fibonacci retracement lines are often used for the placement of entry levels, protective stops, and profit targets. Figure 8–17 illustrates a price chart with Fibonacci retracement lines.

Some Fibonacci-centric traders remove the 23.6% and 78.6% retracement lines in addition to changing the 2.618 value to 200.0. The retracements are drawn on a chart by picking a low support level to the highest resistance level. Clicking at the support price near the bottom of the chart places the highest Fibonacci value at the first click. Sliding up and clicking on the top of the highest candle places 0.0% at the top.

Figure 8–16. A Typical Fibonacci Retracement Line Setup

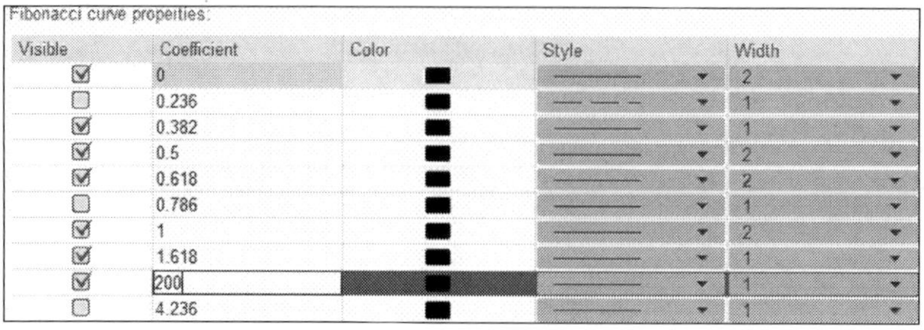

Fibonacci curve properties:				
Visible	Coefficient	Color	Style	Width
☑	0	■	────── ▾	2 ▾
☐	0.236	■	── ── ▾	1 ▾
☑	0.382	■	────── ▾	1 ▾
☑	0.5	■	────── ▾	2 ▾
☑	0.618	■	────── ▾	2 ▾
☐	0.786	■	────── ▾	1 ▾
☑	1	■	────── ▾	2 ▾
☑	1.618	■	────── ▾	1 ▾
☑	200	■	▾	1 ▾
☐	4.236	■	────── ▾	1 ▾

For illustration purposes only.

The dialog in figure 8–16 is a sample setup used by some, but certainly not all, Fibonacci traders.

A "Fibonacci bounce" often happens when a price drops to a Fibonacci retracement line and then reverses direction into a rally. An example would be when the price retreats from the 0.0% line to the 61.8% line where it hits a support level. Buyers enter the market and the price rallies back up beyond both the 50.0% and 23.6% retracement lines. The structure of this trade might resemble the following setup:

Limit Entry @ 50%
Protective Stop @ 78.6%
Profit Target @ 23.6%

A price chart with the Fibonacci retracements is shown in figure 8–17. Here, the retracements are drawn from the lowest point on the chart to the highest point. However, where you place the retracement lines must correspond to your trading strategy.

The chart in figure 8–17 includes an engulfed candle followed immediately by an engulfing candle. When located at a price reversal, or bounce, it is interpreted by some chart technicians as a support level. Many traders call this region a demand zone. This is followed by placing a limit entry at the top of the engulfed candle and a protective stop at its bottom.

Figure 8–17. Fibonacci Retracements on a Price Chart

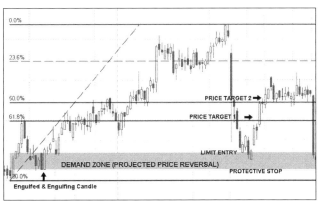

For illustration purposes only.

In this trade the 61.8% and the 50.0% Fibonacci retracements are used to set two profit target levels. Using two or more profit levels is a common practice, and is called *scaling out*. In the example, half the profit is taken at target 1 and the remainder at target 2.

The trader could also consider a *trailing stop* designed to follow the rally until the price reverses and drops by a specified amount — perhaps one dollar or more. The trader can use the average daily price range, i.e., the ATR(14), to help determine the trailing stop amount. The goal is to tolerate small reversals while protecting the current gains against a major reversal.

A bullish Fibonacci bounce setup finds a bounce off support followed by a bounce off resistance. The Fibonacci retracements are typically drawn up from support to resistance as shown. Figure 8–18 illustrates the general shape of the price drop-rally-drop-rally. The goal is to enter a trade at the 50% retracement following the first bounce off resistance, a stop at the 61.8% retracement, and a profit target at or above the 23.6% retracement. The retracements are created by dragging from support to resistance, i.e., from the bottom to the top.

Figure 8–18. Bullish Trade Setup Using Fibonacci Retracements

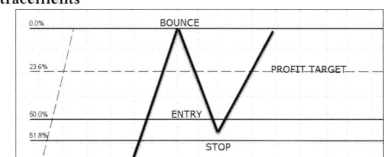

A bearish Fibonacci bounce setup is the exact opposite of the bullish bounce in both price movement and setup. When bearish, the bounce occurs off resistance followed by a drop to support and then another bounce. Figure 8–19 shows the bearish setup. Here, the retracement lines are dragged from top to bottom — the direction of drop. The line follows the candlesticks from a rally-drop-rally-drop.

Figure 8–19. Bearish Trade Setup Using Fibonacci Retracements

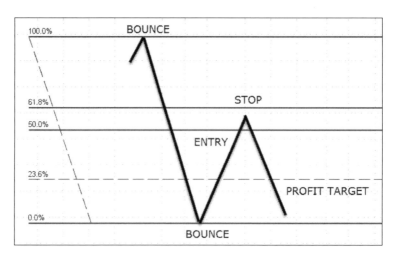

The Fibonacci retracements are regularly used by many of traders who depend on them to set their entry and exit levels. This is particularly true of both forex and futures traders who use short-term chart intervals. The Internet has an ample supply of websites that describe Fibonacci trading. However, as an option trader, you may find other studies that are more suitable for your analysis and trade setups. But never rule out any study until you've at least tested it.

Applying Studies

This chapter described roughly twenty chart studies that are in common use by experienced traders. As mentioned earlier, there are nearly 750 chart studies from which to choose. To describe the use, value, and underlying calculations performed by each of these would require a multivolume encyclopedia.

Your trading platform, whether it's thinkorswim®, TradeMonster, TradeStation, Trader Workstation, Options Express, ActiveTrader Pro®, or another, provides access to most of the popular chart studies with a few clicks of your mouse. The thinkorswim® platform has hundreds of chart studies — too many to count. It also includes online descriptions of each in its help documentation. In addition to providing these studies, the majority of the studies can be customized to suit a specific trading strategy. For example, you can change the number of periods used by a simple moving average, the colors and number of Fibonacci retracement lines, or the Keltner channel's default ATR(14) value of 1.5.

As these studies are applied to charts in the chapters that follow, some will be customized or combined to help in the analysis process. A flexible trading platform permits users to add so many studies to a chart that it becomes cluttered and difficult to read. Therefore, just use those studies you need, rather than looking at charts like the one shown in figure 8–20.

Figure 8–20. A Cluttered Candlestick Chart

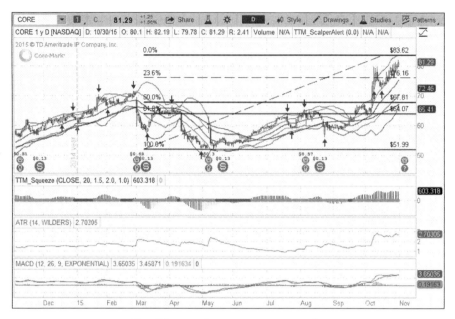

For illustration purposes only.

What did you learn in chapter 8?

1. Chart studies are also referred to as odds _____.

2. When shorting a stock, a protective stop is placed _____ the limit entry price.

3. _____ is the speed at which the market moves.

4. Volatility is a result of high _____ _____.

5. Comparing price momentum of a stock to its index is called _____ weighting.

6. Four momentum oscillators include the CCI, MACD, RSI, and _____ oscillator.

7. The exponential moving average places more weight on the most _____ price points.

8. MACD is an acronym for moving average _____-_____.

9. The _____ shows the average price range over the past 14 days.

10. Two volatility measures include _____ and _____ (or current) volatility.

11. Current volatility is an excellent measure of trader_____.

12. When IV is at 50%, it is halfway between the _____ and _____ of _____.

13. The acronym VWAP stands for _____-_____ _____ _____.

14. The VWAP is the average price at which most of the _____ has occurred.

15. One standard deviation is 68.2%. It is a measure of price _____ and trader sentiment.

16. Many option traders use the standard deviation as a _____ measure.

17. The Bollinger Band envelope is 2× the _____ _____above and below the SMA(20) centerline.

18. The envelope of the Keltner Channel study is 1.5× the _____ above and below the SMA(20) centerline.

19. The TTM_Squeeze signals a price breakout when _____ _____ _____appear on the axis line.

20. The Fibonacci value 1.616, which abounds in nature, is called the _____ _____.

9 ORDER TYPES AND DURATIONS

Introduction

This chapter examines types of trade entries and exits, including market and limit orders, protective stops, and trade closures. For example, you can enter orders and stops that expire at the end of the trading day, or that continue to work for days or even months until they are triggered by a preset value, such as piercing a particular price, a specified *Delta* value on the underlying option chain, or even the crossover of two simple moving average plots.

Of course, the complexity of your order and stop triggers depends entirely on the available features and capabilities offered by your trading platform. This may be one of the deciding factors in your choice of a brokerage.

Order Durations

When you send a stock order to your broker, it is most often received by the governing exchange as a day order. This happens unless you change the default DAY order to a GTC, EXT, or GTC_EXT order. Some brokerages offer even more choices, but the four order types listed here usually suffice. Following is a description of these four in addition to a few others.

For illustration purposes only.

Day

The day order is the most commonly used order style. It is most often used with limit orders when a "limit price" is specified. Once you've entered the number of shares (or option contracts) you wish to buy or sell and a price, your order is ready to send. Clicking the Send, Confirm and Send, or Submit Order button, regardless of the name used by your trading platform, sends a Day order unless you change the order type. Day orders continue to work for the entire day until filled or until the market closes at 4:00 EST. Hence the term *Day Order*.

Good Till Canceled (GTC)

A *good till canceled* order continues to work until you cancel it, or until it expires after a specified number of days. The duration is governed by the brokerage, and typically ranges from 60 to 90 days. Be sure to ask your brokerage about the duration of GTC trades. This is important if you have long-term "buy and hold" stock positions or LEAPS option contracts.

Most traders use the GTC style duration with protective stops. They want protective stops to remain in force for weeks or months at a time to prevent a loss from a sudden price reversal. Traders using bracketed trades often enter their buy orders as day trades accompanied by GTC protective stops and GTC limit sell orders. Examine the order bar in figure 9–1. This is a typical order bar with a $31 limit day order to buy stock SKX. It includes a GTC protective stop market order (MKT) $1.00 below and a GTC LIMIT order for profit $2.00 above.

Figure 9–1. Order Bar with a Bracketed Trade

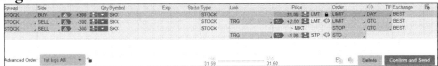

For illustration purposes only.

Also notice the "**1st trgs All**" in the **Advanced Order** drop-down box near the bottom left-hand corner of the Order dialog. This causes the GTC stop and the profit orders to begin working if and when the $31 buy order fills. However, if the limit buy order is never filled, all three legs of this order expire when the market closes at the end of the day.

Extended Trading Hours (EXT or Day+)

Equities can be traded outside normal trading hours by using EXT or Day+ (depending on the trading platform) on your order bar. When specifying extended trading hours, your orders continue to work for another 4 hours, or until 8:00 p.m. EST. You can also use this duration to enter trades beginning at 4:00 a.m. EST in the morning. Note that options trade only inside the normal trading day from 9:30 a.m. till 4:00 p.m. EST.

Good Till Canceled Extended (GTC EXT)

Just as the abbreviation implies, this good till canceled order includes extended trading hours. Therefore, your working orders are active for 60 to 90 days during both normal and extended market hours.

> **NOTE**   Not all trading platforms support all of the order duration types listed. You can check with your brokerage to determine which ones are available and which ones are not. However, it is possible to get along quite well using the four durations described above.

Good Till Date (GTD)

A *good till date* order continues to work until a specific date is reached. For example, if the trader wants to cancel the order after two days, a date two days later than the current date can be specified.

Immediate or Cancel (IOC)

The *immediate or cancel* style order must fill as soon as the order is submitted. Any unfilled portion of the order, which can include the entire order, is automatically canceled.

Fill or Kill (FOK)

This order style requires the entire order to be filled. If any portion of the order cannot be matched, the entire order is canceled.

Minute

A minute order expires if it remains unfilled for a specified number of minutes. You may wish to close a working order if it remains unfilled for five minutes. You can also specify shorter or longer time intervals, such as one or ten minutes.

Order Triggers

Figure 9–1 includes an order trigger that reads *1st trgs All* (in the bottom left-hand corner). This causes the good till canceled stop and limit orders to be placed if the first leg of the order, which is a DAY buy order, is filled. Hence, the protective stop and profit target become working orders — one for protection, the other for profit. Because these legs are styled as good till canceled (GTC), they remain as working orders until they either fill or expire. These orders automatically assume what traders call a *one cancels other* (OCO) condition. If the stop order fills, the target order is canceled. If the target order fills, then the stop order is canceled.

For illustration purposes only.

Single Order

The Single Order trigger sends the current order, which becomes a working order. This can be either a buy or a sell order, although this order style is most commonly used with sell orders. In the case of a market order, it typically fills within seconds. Limit orders must wait for a market maker to match a limit buy order with sell orders on the other side of the trade.

Blast All

This Blast All trigger simultaneously sends every leg of an order. In the case of a stock order with a protective stop, as soon as the order is submitted both the limit buy and the market sell orders become working orders.

1st trgs Seq (or OSO)

Some trading platforms call this an OSO style order, for "order sends order." It is designed to send each leg of a multilegged order one at a time. Each order is filled in sequence, that is, the first order must fill before the second order; the second order must fill before the third, and so on.

1st trgs All

This order style was described in the opening paragraph to order triggers. It was shown as the Advanced Order selection in figure 9–1. This trigger style combines *blast all* and *first triggers OCO* (described next). Therefore, you can use this trigger style to send a limit entry order to sell *n* shares of a stock with a market stop order, and one or more limit sell orders above for profits. Of course, in the case of *selling short*, the limit sell order is for entry, with a market stop above and one or more limit profit target(s) below. The 1st triggers all makes all legs of these trades working orders. The stop and limit order legs intended for profit are OCO (one cancels other). Hence, if the order fills, the protective stop and profit target legs remain in force until one or the other is triggered by a price move. When one order fills, the other is simultaneously canceled and "you're out."

One Cancels Other (OCO)

A one cancels other trigger simply cancels one working order based on the fulfillment of another. When a trader has two working orders, if one fills the other is automatically canceled. Think of a protective stop and a profit target in a long trade. (Recall that a *long* trade involves buying a stock or some other equity.) If the protective stop fills, the OCO trigger automatically cancels the companion profit leg. This takes the trader completely out of the trade, as all working legs are closed.

1st trgs OCO, 1st trgs 2 OCO, 1st trgs 3 OCO

As just mentioned, OCO means "one cancels other." If a profit target fills, the companion stop cancels, or *vice versa*. Note that multiple OCOs may exist if a trader puts on two or more buy or sell orders on the same stock at the same time. Each may be bracketed with stop loss and profit legs. The OCOs are intended to cancel the companion order of each leg.

You may wonder why there would be a need for two or more OCO triggers. Here, only a brief example is provided to help clarify the purpose and use of the 1st trgs 3 OCO trigger. A more detailed explanation with a setup example followed by a description of *scaling out* is included in the bracketed trades and scaling out sections included near the end of this chapter.

Many traders use *scaling*, which means they use two or three profit targets at different price levels. Each profit target requires a companion stop. The three stops may be at identical price levels, while the profit targets may be at levels $3, $4, and $5 above a single limit entry price. However, the stops must match the number of shares being sold at each of the three profit targets. For example, if a long 600-share order is filled, each of the three profit targets and stops become working orders. In this example, each profit target is set up to sell 200 shares of stock. If the first profit target triggers, the 200-share companion stop is canceled. This leaves 400 shares in the trader's account. If the price rallies to the second profit target, another 200 shares are sold for profit and again, the 200-share companion stop is canceled. Now only 200 shares remain in the traders account. One 200-share profit target and one companion 200-share stop remain. Hence, the need for the 1st trgs 3 OCO trigger.

Order Types

Limit and market orders have both been briefly described. Following is a closer look at these and several other order types.

Market Orders

Stocks and options both involve bid and ask prices. In stocks, a bid price is the purchase price at which market buy orders are filled. The ask price is the selling price. Highly liquid stocks typically have small differences between the bid and the ask price. The difference between the bid and ask prices for stocks with low trading volumes is much greater.

NOTE   As you will see in the hands-on activities contained in chapters 14 and 15, option traders use the bid to
sell and the ask to buy.

When buying and selling stock, long (buy) market orders are
filled at the ask price, while short (sell) market orders are filled at the
bid price. Therefore, traders pay the highest prices and receive the
lowest prices with market orders. In a fast moving, high-volatility
market, traders may be disappointed with the price paid or received
when using a market order. But the advantage to market orders is
that they fill much faster than limit orders.

The price paid or received from a market order depends on the
volume of orders currently in the queue and the difference between
the bid and the ask price. The market maker attempts to match and
fill buy and sell orders as quickly as possible. Market makers will even
take positions in these trades to expedite order fulfillment. (And, of
course, they make money doing this.) If you either buy or sell a large
number of shares, your market order will usually fill at several different prices as the shares sell incrementally until the order is complete.

An example would be a 3,000-share order that fills a few hundred shares at a time. Each share lot may fill at different prices.
Although the shares usually trade within pennies of each other,
the variation depends on the spread between the bid and the ask
price. When the difference between the bid and ask price is large,
the volume is lower. This results in a wider range of market prices
either received or paid by the trader. A narrow range between the
bid and ask price indicates a higher volume. Therefore, the market
order prices received by or paid to a trader may only vary by a few
cents. This is one reason to examine trading volume and the difference between the bid and ask price before entering a market order
in preference to a limit order, described next. Avoid low-volume
stocks. With more than 64,000 stock symbols, there are plenty of
good, high-volume stocks with narrow bid to ask price ranges to

consider. However, only a few hundred symbols have ample trading volumes and price ranges to consider.

Limit Orders

Most professional traders use limit orders. A limit order specifies the trader will only accept a price that is equal to or better than the limit price. Buy limit orders accept a price at or below the limit price; sell limit orders accept a price at or above the limit price.

A day limit order to buy a stock that remains below the market price of the stock will expire unfilled. Limit orders typically fill midway between the bid and the ask price. The precise market price depends on trading volume and the corresponding difference between the bid and the ask price. You may submit an order that never fills. Consider unfilled limit orders as "nothing ventured, nothing gained (or lost)." This underscores the importance of examining volume and open interest before setting up and entering a trade.

Stop Orders

A stop order can be structured to sell or buy at a certain price level. There are protective stops and profit target stops. First, the protective stop is described.

Protective Stops (Stop Market Orders)

A short (sell) stop order is typically used for protection against an unwanted price drop. But stop orders are also used to trigger a *buy to cover* order when a trader holds a short position (such as selling short to capitalize on a price drop).

Protective stops are used to sell a stock that has dropped in price in order to salvage what value may remain in a position. Protective stops are also used to exit short stock positions when the price rallies above the entry price. Unless otherwise specified, a protective stop issues a market order. These are for protection against a loss. Therefore, you want to exit NOW! So when the stock price hits a stop level, a market order is triggered and the position is closed in the least possible amount of time.

Be sure to use good till canceled (GTC) style stops to keep them active for the duration of each trade. For long-term buy-and-hold positions, be sure to periodically renew all GTC stops. Many traders issue all GTC stops on the same date and set reminders to renew all stops in a single session.

Stops Used to Take Profit (Stop Limit Orders)

Limit orders are used to sell a rallying stock for profit, or buy-to-cover a dropping stock in the case of a short sale. Day traders are heavy users of both market order stops for protection and limit order stops for profit. These traders use the same entry and exit strategies across all trading venues, i.e., stocks, futures, and forex. And to a lesser extent, stops are used with options too.

A stop limit order is triggered as soon as the price of the security pierces the limit price. Traders use the stop limit order to sell shares of stock, future contracts, or a currency pair for profit. As mentioned earlier, they may sell half of their stock at one target price and the remainder at a second, higher target price, i.e., *scale out*. Of course day traders constantly monitor their positions and often take their profits manually when satisfied with an exit price.

Consider the following long stock position.

1. Bob, who is a day trader, anticipates a strong rally off of a support level.
2. He buys 100 shares of a $40 stock, sets a $38 protective stop below (a market order), and a $45 target using a stop limit order.
3. The price moves to $42.50.
4. Bob "slides" his protective stop from $38 to $41.50 to prevent a loss. This also assures a profit.
5. The price rallies to $45; the stop limit order triggers and Bob receives $5 profit per share — a total of $500 less commissions.

Now consider an example of a short stock sale.

1. Sally notices a strong reversal following a poor earnings report.
2. She enters a short limit order by shorting (selling) 500 shares of stock at $50. She includes a $52 protective stop market order and a $46 stop limit order as her profit target.
3. The stock price quickly drops to $47. Sally slides her stop market order from $52 down to $48 to eliminate the possibility of a loss.
4. The price continues to drop. Sally moves the stop limit target from $46 to $44 and the stop market order from $48 to $47.
5. Three hours later the stock turns and rallies back and pierces the $47 level.
6. The stop market order triggers a buy to cover order. Sally receives an average of $46.90 per share — a profit of $1,550 less commissions.

Trailing Stops

Trailing stops are market orders that are used for either protection or to take profits. A trailing stop dynamically trails, or "follows," price movement either upward or downward, as specified by the trader. Trailing stops can be set at a dollar amount or as a percentage of the underlying price. For example, a $1.00 trailing stop triggers a market order if the price of the underlying reverses direction by $1.00. A 5% trailing stop triggers a market sell order if a stock rallies to $100 and then drops to $95. Trailing stops can be set as DAY or GTC orders.

Other Triggers

The above described stops are all triggered by a specified market price or pecentage. But several other triggers are available for use. Some trading platforms accommodate the use of other stop triggers with a special order dialog. These "order rules" permit traders to set up stops based on a bid or ask price or even a chart study. For example, if the price moves below or above a 20-period simple moving average, the SMA(20), an order can be triggered. The thinkorswim® trading platform provides an Order Rules dialog for this purpose.

Figure 9–2. Choosing an Alternate Order Trigger

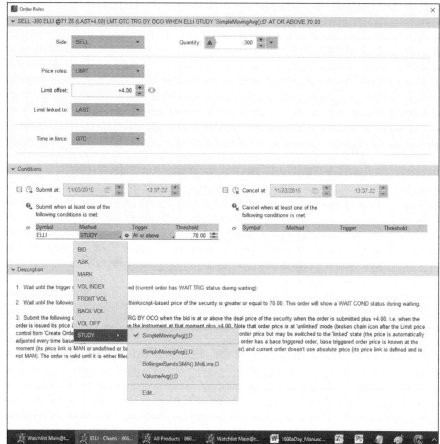

For illustration purposes only.

Figure 9–2 shows a variety of trigger choices including the bid, ask, or mark (the market price which is at the midpoint of the bid and the ask price). Notice that you can tie it to the front or back volatility, the volatility difference, or use a study. Studies can include plots, such as a simple moving average (SMA), the SMA or midline of the Bollinger bands, or a trading volume average. The Edit line permits users to change values. For example, a trader may wish to change the default 9-period simple moving average plot — the SMA(9) — to an SMA(20).

Front volatility represents the front month's volatility — the first 30-day period. Volatility is important to all traders. It is especially important to option traders. Volatility is tied directly to option premiums; high volatility increases premium values. Back volatility refers to the last 30 days of an option contract period. The difference in front and back is found by subtracting back volatility from front volatility. Traders who sell premium want high front volatility and low back volatility. Those who buy options or use certain spreads that benefit from an increase in volatility want the volatility to increase at the back end of these trades. It is common for back month options to have wider bid to ask spreads. This is called "slippage" and is something option writers (sellers) count on.

Buying Long and Selling Short

Although the terms long and short have been introduced as buying (long) and selling (short), they are used so often that it's important for these terms to become part of your everyday trading vocabulary. Being long in a stock or ETF means you own it. Shorting a stock or ETF means you're selling it. This is just as true with option contracts. A short call and a long put are interpreted as selling a call and buying a put. These terms will be used extensively throughout the remainder of this book.

You will also see trade notation that makes use of minus and plus signs. The notation for shorting ten $150 call contracts on Boeing Aircraft that expire on the third Friday of October 2017 is written:

−10 BA 150 Oct 17 CALLS

The 150 represents the *strike price* of the call.

The notation for five long $140 put contracts on Boeing Aircraft that expire on the third Friday of October 2017 is written:

+5 BA 140 Oct 17 PUTS.

The strike price for this long put is $140.

Recall that the third Friday of the month is called *expiration Friday*. So going long is buying and shorting is selling. Get used to these terms, as they are used by all experienced traders, and as a trader yourself, you will hear them and use them often.

Order Entry

Many new traders struggle with the steps involved in placing trades. Even after they examine their order setup, they may be reticent to send it. Even the simplest orders can be worrisome. To counter this, new traders should spend several days, if not weeks, in simulated trading. Consider practicing the following steps:

1. Scan several stock charts over decreasing time intervals until you find one that's near a support or resistance level.
2. Use an oversold/overbought study to determine the status.
3. Check the Bollinger bands to see the volatility.
4. Draw price levels on your chart including a limit entry, protective stop, and profit target.
5. Use a "trading ladder," such as the thinkorswim® Active Trader or the TradeStation ladder to structure your trade.
6. Submit the trade as a 1st trgs All and monitor the working order until it fills or expires unfilled.
7. Keep a record of each trade. Include the date, symbol, entry and stop levels, and final outcome, including cancels, fills, profits, and losses. (As mentioned earlier, you may want to capture the price chart and jot your trade information on it.)
8. Repeat your paper trading until you are confident in the scanning, trade setup, and order entry, and trade monitoring processes.

Bonus (Saving and Annotating Price Charts):

Many computer users are not familiar with the steps used to capture objects displayed on their computer monitors. Following is a quick tutorial on how to capture, annotate, and save the information displayed on your screen. Note that some trading platforms permit this by using a built-in menu. But you can also use the following steps. And if you'd rather not use Windows Paint, you can paste your captured illustrations directly into MS Word. This permits you to keep your records in a single Word file for each day, week, or month. Step 5 includes the key sequence used to capture either a full screen or a selected window.

1. Begin by finding the Paint accessory (or application) on your PC. Use the Windows Start button to display "All Apps." Then find the Paint app in the list of Windows Accessories.
2. Open Paint. Spend some time learning to use the drawing tools and the File menu.
3. Type text, draw lines, add and then erase objects, select and move drawn objects, and erase objects. Use **Ctrl+PgUp** and **Ctrl+PgDn** to zoom in and out.
4. Use **Save As**. Either choose an existing folder or create a new one for you trading files.
5. To capture a full screen, press **PrtSc** to save it to memory; to capture an active window, press **Alt+PrtSc**.
6. Once captured, open Paint and press **Ctrl+V** to paste the captured graphic to the drawing area.
7. Type the trading data in a convenient blank region of the chart graphic. (You may need to select a contrasting color for your text.)
8. Then use **Save As**. Select the economical GIF file format. (You'll want to use the JPEG or JPG format for high resolution photographs.)

With this practice behind you in addition to knowing how your trades are working, you will begin to see what works and what doesn't. You can use this experience as a basis for the development of a set of trading rules. Rules-based trading is discussed in chapter 10. Examples of rules can be found at the end of chapter 13.

Trading Ladders (Active Trader)

Both thinkorswim® and TradeStation, among others, provide trading ladders discussed earlier in both chapters 3 and 4. Trading ladders provide the ability to enter market and limit orders, and provide an interface for structuring OCO and bracketed trades. Figure 9–3 shows a typical trading ladder; figure 9–4 shows a bracketed trade setup. Note that the "–50" Qty Link is actually –500 shares (the last "0" is hidden in the text box). The system automatically splits the 1,000-share trade into two equal 500-share parts. Both include a protective stop $1.00 below the limit entry, and two 500-share profit targets. The bottom profit target is for 500 shares at $2.00 above the $39.12 entry, while the second 500-share target is for $3.00 in profit above the price of the limit entry.

Clicking a price level in the left-hand (green) ladder queues a buy order, while clicking on the red ladder queues a sell order. Notice how stop bubbles are displayed above and below. Also, you can see volume bars in the Volume column. The shaded bar in the price column shows the current price of the underlying at $39.13.

Figure 9–3. A Typical "Trading Ladder"

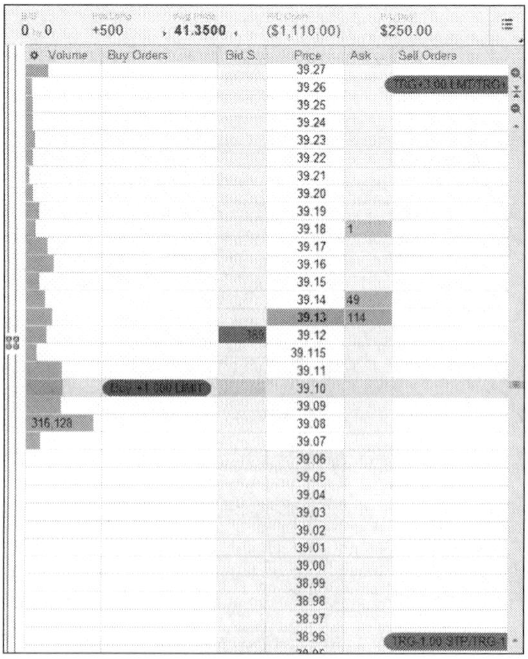

For illustration purposes only.

Figure 9–4. A 2-Bracket Trade

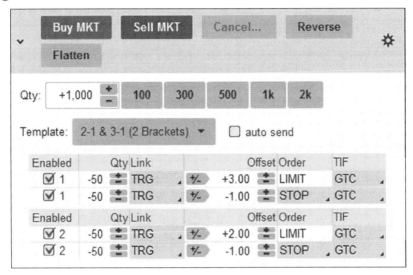

For illustration purposes only.

Once the trade is set up, clicking on a price bar displays an Order Confirmation dialog like the one shown in figure 9–5.

Figure 9–5. An Order Confirmation Dialog Showing a 2-Bracket Buy Order

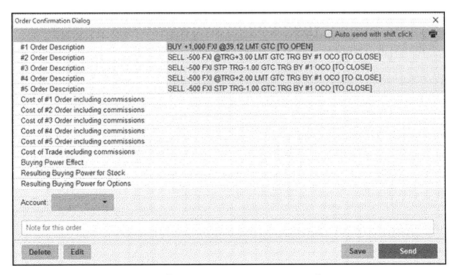

For illustration purposes only.

Figure 9–6. The Order Bar Showing the 2-Bracket Order

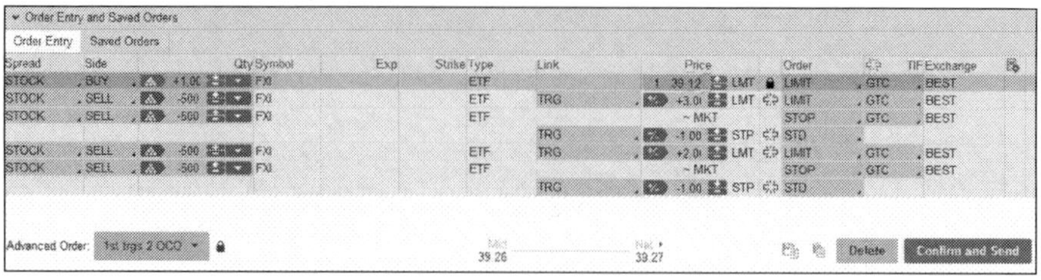

For illustration purposes only.

Clicking **Send** creates a working order. Notice that you can also delete the order if you change your mind, or click **Edit** to tweak the values on the order bar. The companion order bar for this bracketed order is shown in figure 9–6.

The Order Bar

The order bar is used to review a trade setup, edit quantities, prices, order styles, and durations. As previously mentioned, it is also used to modify stop triggers using the Order Rules dialog shown earlier in figure 9–2.

Bracketed Trades (The Risk-to-Reward Ratio)

Bracketed trades have been discussed and used throughout this book. But there are a few nuances that have not been discussed. These are introduced in the remaining portion of this chapter.

Entry–Stop–Target

Limit entries, protective market stop orders, and limit profit target stops have all been described. The difference from the entry price to the stop price depends on the amount of money in your account compared to the amount of money you're willing to put at risk. If you're willing to lose 1% of a $50,000 account, you would only put $500 at risk. If setting up a trade on a $30 stock, you must first determine where your protective stop will be set relative to the number of shares involved. The 200-share purchase of a $30 stock will cost $6,000 plus commission. If a stop that is 7%, or $2.10, below your entry level is triggered, you will lose $420.00, from .07 × $6,000). This is within your allowable loss (or *risk tolerance*). If the stock rallies off resistance to a profit target located at $35, you will realize a $1,000 profit. This is a 5:2.1 reward-to-risk ratio.

The purpose of this example is solely to point out the need for you to consider the size of your trade relative to your risk tolerance, and to set your stop positions based on what you can afford to risk. If the same trade levels involve 500 shares, your loss would exceed your 1% risk level, as you would lose $1,050. This amount would represent 2.1% of your account.

Entry Types

In addition to considering the location of support and resistance levels and your risk tolerance, you must also consider your entry level. The precise price at which you set your limit entry depends on several factors. These include your certainty that price support or resistance exists where you believe it does, which must be based on your chart analysis. And, of course, support and resistance levels have "slippage," that is, the price can reverse either above or below where you think it will. These seem like small considerations, but each has corresponding setup strategies that involve the entry types.

Consider figure 9–7. Notice the underlying is in an upward trend. You decide to set up a trade entry based on a recent pull-back and reversal that includes an engulfed candle. That candle also has a lower shadow extension that may be considered in your trade setup.

Figure 9–7. A Demand Zone: An Engulfed Candle at a Recent Price Reversal

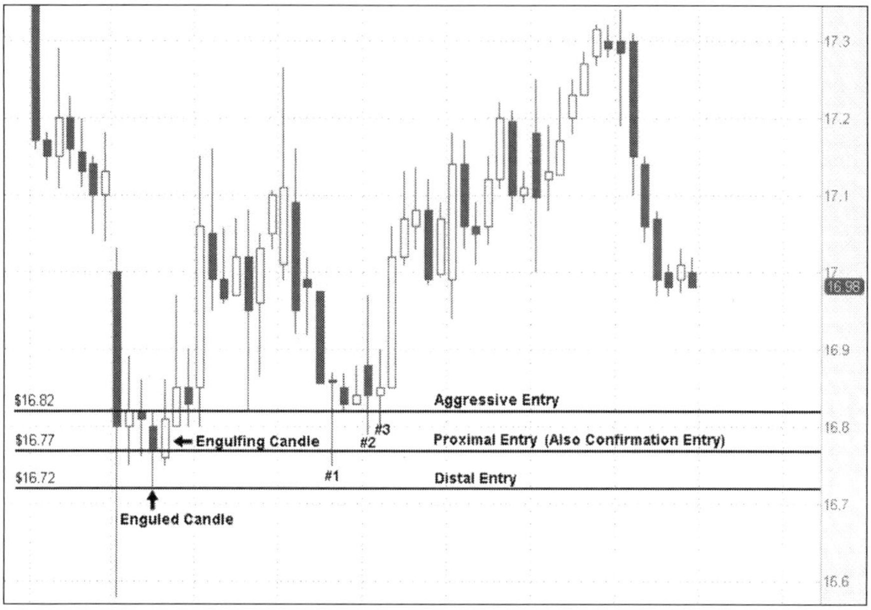

For illustration purposes only.

Aggressive Entry (Entry 1)

The aggressive entry is based on a line drawn from the high price of the engulfed candle body. Note that some traders use the opening price at the top of the engulfed candle body rather than the period high. In this case, the trader must believe the engulfed candle has marked a strong support level and is determined to fill a buy order at $16.82. The candle shadow extending from the bottom of #1 triggers the order. A protective GTC stop market order will also be placed with the entry about $1.20 (7%) below. The number of shares that accompany this order as well as the placement of the protective stop order depends on both account size and risk tolerance.

Proximal Entry

The proximal entry line is drawn at the bottom of the engulfed candle body at the $16.77 price level. Although this entry is more conservative than the aggressive entry, it still fills when the price pierces the $16.77 level to roughly $16.75. From there it turns and briefly rallies and closes in the mid-$16.80s. Although the price retreats toward support twice, marked by #2 and #3, the price never pierces either the proximal or distal entry levels. If a 7% protective stop is used, it would be placed near the $15.60 price level.

Distal Entry

The distal (or most distant) entry line is drawn at the bottom of the lower candle shadow. This is the most conservative entry level shown. As shown on figure 9–7, the price never reaches the $16.72 price level. Therefore, this order will expire upon market close of the current trading day.

Confirmation Entry

Both #2 and #3 can be considered confirmation entries. In #2 and #3 we see a price bounce off support. These entries are the safest, but not quite as profitable as the proximal entry, which has a wider price range. With entry at or near #3 with a 10-cent trailing stop as a profit target, the trailing stop would trigger on the first red candle to the right of #3 at about $17.00.

Sliding Stops

Still using figure 9–7, the trader could have used a fixed stop at around $17.30. Of course the trader can't predict when and where the price will turn. Many traders monitor their trades, either by watching their trading platform or by using a mobile trading app on their smartphone. They can also set alerts in which a text or e-mail message is sent to their smartphone. Therefore, when a trader sees an opportunity to take profits, he or she can manually close the trade for profit using either their primary trading platform or their mobile trading app.

Many active traders manually slide both protective stops and profit targets to minimize losses and maximize profits. Manually sliding profit targets is often referred to as "letting the profits run." So once you're in profit, it's advisable to slide your stops with the underlying's price movement. And whenever possible, move the protective stops beyond your entry price to insure against losses.

Protective Stop Do's and Don'ts

THE DON'T'S: There are many stories about traders who entered a bracketed trade that went against them. They were fully convinced that the price would eventually turn back toward profit. So they began to slide their stops ahead of the retreating price until they lost thousands of dollars in the trade. When they originally placed their trades, they calculated their risk tolerance and set their stops according to their rules. Violating their rules to give the underlying more "room" to turn resulted in "false hope" and financial loss. NEVER slide protective stops; if you do you're likely to achieve greater losses. Take your lumps while the trade remains within your risk tolerance. Otherwise, you may devastate your account holdings like so many have — by violating your rules and sliding stops farther and farther into despair.

It's only natural to want to maximize your profits when a trade is moving in your favor. Many experienced traders are pleased with 30% to 60% profits. They willingly close their positions at these levels. Others see these profit levels as good, then they convince themselves that there's still more to be made. But their greed often backfires. Many traders will tell you that they should have settled for the 30% to 60% profit, because their piggishness resulted in an unacceptable loss. There's a saying that bulls and bears make money while pigs get slaughtered. This is a good saying to remember.

THE DO'S: If your trade moves into 30% to 60% profit, jump on it. You can make more by "churning" 30% and 60% profits than waiting several more days for an additional ten to twenty percent.

Take your profit and trade again. Traders make more income by taking 30% three times than taking 60% once.

If your trade rallies (or drops) on the profitable side of your entry, always slide your protective stops to or above your entry level. But give your working trade some "room to work." While following the price into profit locks in profits and minimizes losses, when the trade is working in a highly volatile market, price transients spike up and then down in no apparent direction. Sliding your stop too close to the current price level will likely trigger the stop. It can be frustrating to get stopped out only to watch the price turn back toward profit. So watch the range and choppiness of the price movement and follow the trend, but not too close, or an instantaneous price transient can pierce your stop order and take you out of the trade in an instant.

Profit Target Stops Do's and Don'ts

As traders it's the human things that seem to defeat us. Our swagger sometimes makes us feel we can do no wrong, particularly if we just came off of a big win. This can cloud judgment and encourage irrational behavior, such as setting a profit target at an unachievable level. When the target is too far away, expect a loss. As mentioned several times, there's absolutely nothing wrong with a profit of 30%. If you think 30% is pathetic, then you shouldn't be a trader. So don't wait for the price of a trade to rally to impossible heights. If you do, you will be disappointed much of the time. Stick to your trading rules. Rules are typically developed over time and are tested through experience and successful trading results.

If and when a working trade achieves an acceptable level of profit, consider changing the limit stop order to a trailing stop order. If the price continues to move in your favor, when it does turn back you should realize profits. Some traders never use trailing stops. They don't want to lose a trade from a temporary reversal, only to see the price return to the dominant trend. The use of trailing stops may or may not fit your trading style. Their use is entirely up to you.

Scaling Out with Multiple Profit Targets

Many traders set multiple profit targets. As shown in the bracketed trade setup in figure 9–4, the trade is designed to take profit $2 above the entry — target 1 (or T1) and then $3 above the entry at a second profit target (T2). One thousand shares of the $39.12 stock has a cost of $39,120 plus commissions. If successful, the 1,000-share trade returns $1,000 at T1 and $1,500 at T2 for a total return of $2,500.

When scaling to two or more price targets, traders will slide the protective stop to the first profit target level labeled T1. If the price fails to reach the second price target, T2, and retreats to T1, another $1,000 profit is received when the stops triggers. Therefore, instead of a total of $2,500 profit the trade yields $2,000 in profit, less commissions and taxes, of course.

> **Note** The specific amount returned by market stop orders can vary based on the bid and ask price of the underlying and the difference between them. High volume stocks have small bid to ask variances. The price you receive from the sale of slow moving, low volume stocks may be substantially less than expected.

What did you learn in chapter 9?

1. A DAY order expires ____ _____`_____ ____ _____ _____ _____.

2. The GTC order stands for _____ _____ _____.

3. A _____ _____ is a GTC order that may execute during an after-hours trading session.

4. An _____ order is a day order that may execute during after-hours trading.

5. The 1st trgs All order is triggered when _____ _____is filled.

6. A Minute order type automatically _____ after a specified time interval.

7. An _____ order type closes all other working orders when one is filled.

8. The _____ _____ order immediately submits all orders to the market.

9. In a 1st trgs Seq order, the _____ order must fill before the second order is sent.

10. If a trader wants to fill an order immediately, a _____ order is used.

11. Limit orders will only fill at a price _____ ___ or _____ than that specified.

12. Protective stops should always use a _____ order type.

13. Going long or short means _____ or _____, respectively.

14. Selling ten Boeing 150 October 2017 call contracts is written: −10 BA

15. This option contract expires on the _____ of October 2017.

16. Buying five Boeing 140 October 2017 put contracts is written: +5 BA

17. The most conservative limit entry is called a _____ entry by some traders.

18. Traders often manage their working bracketed orders by _____ stops.
19. NEVER slide a _____ _____ for a greater loss.
20. If a bracketed trade moves into profit, slide your _____ _____ above the entry.

10 OPTIONS TERMINOLOGY

The Option Contract

Here we begin by briefly reexamining buyer and seller obligations. Option contracts are time-limited agreements between two parties, a seller and a buyer, to deliver and pay for a specified security if that security reaches an agreed upon price during the life of the option contract.

Summarizing Calls and Puts

Traders who are new to options often find the terminology confusing. Hearing about calls, puts, strikes, Delta, and Theta is like listening to a foreign language. In an attempt to clarify how call and put contracts work, several terms are presented and explained in this chapter. The next chapter expands these definitions with examples.

> **NOTE**   For convenience, the underlying optionable security will be referred to as stock. However, underlying optionable securities can be stocks, ETFs, futures, indexes, or e-mini futures contracts.

Recall that an in the money call is below the strike price of the option contract. When a call contract is in the money, the buyer has a contractual right to *exercise* the option by calling away the underlying stock from the seller. Of course the buyer is obligated to pay the seller for the stock at the contracted option price. So if the call option's strike price was $30 when traded, and the market price of the stock is $40, the option buyer must pay the option seller $30 per share. The option seller must deliver 100 shares per option contract now worth $40 per share. The buyer makes $10/share less the premium originally paid by the buyer when the $30 call option(s) were originally bought. If the seller doesn't own the stock, he/she must buy and deliver the $40 stock to the buyer — a loss of $10/share less the premium originally received when the call option(s) were sold.

Now consider a put option. When a put is in the money, it is above the option (or strike) price. In the case of a put option, the buyer can also exercise the put contract if the option price becomes in the money. In put options, the buyer of the put option contract has the right to "put the stock to the seller" at the contracted option price. Let's use the same stock as above. But now it's hit resistance and is about to suffer a price drop. With the stock now trading at $45/share, the option buyer pays $1.00/share to the seller for one $40 put contract. The seller is pleased to have the buyer's $100 in his/her account. But the stock bounces off resistance and drops straight down to $30/share. This places the $40 put options $10 in the money. (The seller says, "Ouch!" and the buyer says "Yeah!")

The option buyer exercises the $40 put contract by buying and delivering 100 shares of stock to the seller at a cost of $3,000 ($30/share). The seller of the $40 put pays the buyer $4,000 ($40/share) for the $30/share stock and takes delivery. The put buyer makes $1,000 in profit, while the put seller loses $1,000/share.

The following list includes four possible outcomes that correspond to option contracts — the entire universe of potential outcomes. Each outcome involves an option seller (writer) and an option buyer. Once you understand these and the data points displayed on every option chain that help you measure risk, you will be ready to begin testing option strategies.

1. Call contracts that expire out of the money — Contract expires worthless in seller's favor. Buyer loses cost of premium★.
2. Call contracts that become in the money prior to expiration — Buyer exercises option and calls stock away from seller. Buyer pays seller for the stock at the option price.
3. Put contracts that expire out of the money — Contract expires worthless in seller's favor. Buyer loses cost of premium★.
4. Put contracts that become in the money prior to expiration — Buyer puts stock to seller. Seller must pay Buyer for the stock at the option price

You now know the option price used by option buyers and sellers is the option's *strike price*. However, if the contract expires before the price of the underlying security reaches the agreed-upon strike price, the entire agreement becomes null and void and *expires worthless*.

In the money Call Contracts — If the strike price is exceeded by one cent, the buyer can exercise the option. When exercised, the seller is obligated to deliver the agreed upon number of shares *called away* by the buyer.

In the money Put Contracts — If the price of the security drops below the strike price of the put contract, the buyer can exercise the option and put the stock to the seller. The seller is obligated to pay the buyer for the contracted number of shares *put to* the seller at the *strike* price.

Exercising a Call Option:
1. Symbol BONG has been trending upward for several months with small $5 to $8 price reversals and consolidations, only to continue on its upward climb. It has recently pulled back to $50 per share.

★   The buyer may sell the option contracts prior to expiration to recover a portion of the premium originally paid. There must be enough time remaining and liquidity, i.e., trading volume, for the buyer's sell order to fill.

2. John analyzes the charts and concludes BONG is in a consolidation pattern. It will resume its upward trend within the next few weeks.

3. He buys two $52 call option contracts (100 shares/contract = 200 shares). The options cost $1.50/share for $300 in premium plus brokerage fees. The contract expires in six months.

4. Within 28 days, BONG rallies to $58.00. John exercises his $52 option contracts and "calls away" the BONG stock from the $52 option seller.

5. The option seller must deliver 200 shares of BONG stock to John.

6. John pays the option price of $52/share for 200 shares of BONG stock, a total of $10,400.

7. John sells the 200 shares of BONG's $58/share stock at market price for $11,600.

8. John's profit is $1,200 less the $300 in premium paid at entry, brokerage commissions, and option exchange fees.

Exercising a Put Option:

1. Symbol GRIT is trading at $39.50. It has recently rallied up from $32 to a historical resistance level of $40.

2. Sally studies GRIT's price charts. Her analysis reveals GRIT is overbought; all indicators point to a price drop in the coming weeks.

3. Sally buys two $38 put option contracts. She pays $1.50/share in premium for 200 shares for a total of $300 plus brokerage fees. Her option contracts expire in six months.

4. GRIT drops to $30. Sally exercises her $38 put options, pays $32/share for GRIT stock, and "puts" the 200 shares of GRIT stock to the seller.

5. The seller pays Sally $38/share for the 200 shares of stock now worth $32/share.

6. Sally profits $6.00 per share, or $1,200, less the $300 in premium she paid at entry plus about $30 in commissions and exchange fees.

With the preceding summary in place, this chapter examines many of the *moving parts* that comprise option contracts. These are all important to your option trading preparation. You MUST understand the "rules" of the game before you can play. An option chain was introduced in figure 2–1 of chapter 2. Callouts 1 through 14 that follow figure 2–1 describe the option chain.

Figure 10–1. The Option Chain

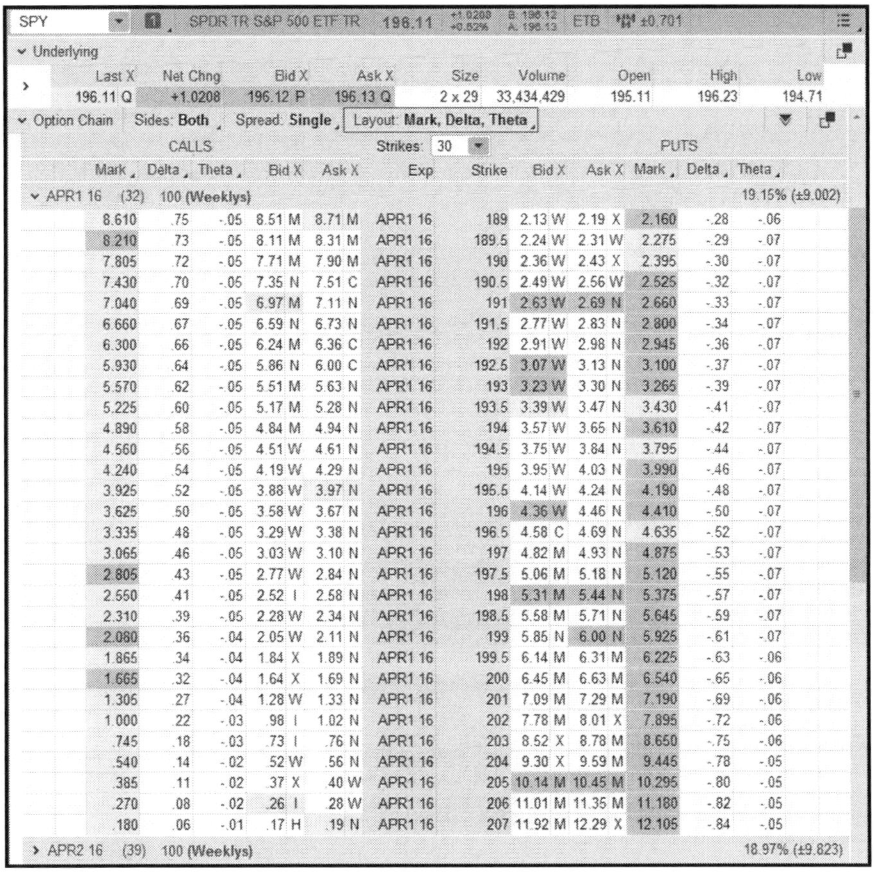

SPY | SPDR TR S&P 500 ETF TR 196.11 +1.0208 +0.52% B: 196.12 A: 196.13 ETB ±0.701

Underlying

Last X	Net Chng	Bid X	Ask X	Size	Volume	Open	High	Low
196.11 Q	+1.0208	196.12 P	196.13 Q	2 x 29	33,434,429	195.11	196.23	194.71

Option Chain Sides: Both Spread: Single Layout: Mark, Delta, Theta

CALLS Strikes: 30 PUTS

APR1 16 (32) 100 (Weeklys) 19.15% (±9.002)

Mark	Delta	Theta	Bid X	Ask X	Exp	Strike	Bid X	Ask X	Mark	Delta	Theta
8.610	.75	-.05	8.51 M	8.71 M	APR1 16	189	2.13 W	2.19 X	2.160	-.28	-.06
8.210	.73	-.05	8.11 M	8.31 M	APR1 16	189.5	2.24 W	2.31 W	2.275	-.29	-.07
7.805	.72	-.05	7.71 M	7.90 M	APR1 16	190	2.36 W	2.43 X	2.395	-.30	-.07
7.430	.70	-.05	7.35 N	7.51 C	APR1 16	190.5	2.49 W	2.56 W	2.525	-.32	-.07
7.040	.69	-.05	6.97 M	7.11 N	APR1 16	191	2.63 W	2.69 N	2.660	-.33	-.07
6.660	.67	-.05	6.59 N	6.73 N	APR1 16	191.5	2.77 W	2.83 N	2.800	-.34	-.07
6.300	.66	-.05	6.24 M	6.36 C	APR1 16	192	2.91 W	2.98 N	2.945	-.36	-.07
5.930	.64	-.05	5.86 N	6.00 C	APR1 16	192.5	3.07 W	3.13 N	3.100	-.37	-.07
5.570	.62	-.05	5.51 M	5.63 N	APR1 16	193	3.23 W	3.30 N	3.265	-.39	-.07
5.225	.60	-.05	5.17 M	5.28 N	APR1 16	193.5	3.39 W	3.47 N	3.430	-.41	-.07
4.890	.58	-.05	4.84 M	4.94 N	APR1 16	194	3.57 W	3.65 N	3.610	-.42	-.07
4.560	.56	-.05	4.51 W	4.61 N	APR1 16	194.5	3.75 W	3.84 N	3.795	-.44	-.07
4.240	.54	-.05	4.19 W	4.29 N	APR1 16	195	3.95 W	4.03 N	3.990	-.46	-.07
3.925	.52	-.05	3.88 W	3.97 N	APR1 16	195.5	4.14 W	4.24 N	4.190	-.48	-.07
3.625	.50	-.05	3.58 W	3.67 N	APR1 16	196	4.36 W	4.46 N	4.410	-.50	-.07
3.335	.48	-.05	3.29 W	3.38 N	APR1 16	196.5	4.58 C	4.69 N	4.635	-.52	-.07
3.065	.46	-.05	3.03 W	3.10 N	APR1 16	197	4.82 M	4.93 N	4.875	-.53	-.07
2.805	.43	-.05	2.77 W	2.84 N	APR1 16	197.5	5.06 M	5.18 N	5.120	-.55	-.07
2.550	.41	-.05	2.52 I	2.58 N	APR1 16	198	5.31 M	5.44 N	5.375	-.57	-.07
2.310	.39	-.05	2.28 W	2.34 N	APR1 16	198.5	5.58 M	5.71 N	5.645	-.59	-.07
2.080	.36	-.04	2.05 W	2.11 N	APR1 16	199	5.85 N	6.00 N	5.925	-.61	-.07
1.865	.34	-.04	1.84 X	1.89 N	APR1 16	199.5	6.14 M	6.31 M	6.225	-.63	-.06
1.665	.32	-.04	1.64 X	1.69 N	APR1 16	200	6.45 M	6.63 M	6.540	-.65	-.06
1.305	.27	-.04	1.28 W	1.33 N	APR1 16	201	7.09 M	7.29 M	7.190	-.69	-.06
1.000	.22	-.03	.98 I	1.02 N	APR1 16	202	7.78 M	8.01 X	7.895	-.72	-.06
.745	.18	-.03	.73 I	.76 N	APR1 16	203	8.52 X	8.78 M	8.650	-.75	-.06
.540	.14	-.02	.52 W	.56 N	APR1 16	204	9.30 X	9.59 M	9.445	-.78	-.05
.385	.11	-.02	.37 X	.40 W	APR1 16	205	10.14 M	10.45 M	10.295	-.80	-.05
.270	.08	-.02	.26 I	.28 W	APR1 16	206	11.01 M	11.35 M	11.180	-.82	-.05
.180	.06	-.01	.17 H	.19 N	APR1 16	207	11.92 M	12.29 X	12.105	-.84	-.05

APR2 16 (39) 100 (Weeklys) 18.97% (±9.823)

For illustration purposes only.

The underlying ETF SPY is currently trading at $196.11. Notice the shaded to white transitions halfway down the option chain. This is referred to as the *at the money* price level — the closest strike prices to SPY's market price of $196.11, which is between the $196 and $196.5 strike prices. Finally, notice the contract expiration date of **APR1 16 (32) 100 (Weeklys)**. This is the contract expiration date of the displayed option chain.

- The contracts expire on the first Friday of April 2016.
- The contracts expire in 32 days.
- Each contract represents 100 shares.
- The option contract is a weekly-expiration type contract.

The next available option expiration date is at the bottom of the option chain. The next contract expiration date is **APR2 16 (39) 100 (Weeklys)**. See if you can decipher the meanings of this annotation.

Expiration_____

Number of days remaining_____

Number of shares per option contract_____

Type of option contract (quarterly, monthly, etc.)_____

Contract style (American or European)_____

Now you know how the vertical column of prices below the word "strike" represents the available *strike prices*. You can choose a strike price based on your directional bias, available premium, and risk tolerance. But these are just a few things to consider. There's still a bit more to learn about the option chain.

Recall how the left-hand half of the option chain displays calls; the right-hand side displays puts. Again, notice the shaded and white backgrounds. The shaded values are "in the money," the white values are "out of the money." As you can see, in the money calls are below the price of the underlying, while out of the money calls are above the price of the underlying. The opposite is true on the put side. Out of the money puts are below the price of the underlying, while in the money puts are above the price of the underlying. (Confused yet? These will begin to make more sense as you continue.)

Now examine the shaded (in the money) values on the CALLS side of the option chain. Notice how the values in the Mark, Bid X, and Ask × columns increase as the call strike prices decrease. This is referred to as "getting deeper in the money." The value displayed in the Mark column is the current option premium value, expressed in dollars and cents. Mark (option premium) values increase as the Mark (or *market* value) moves deeper in the money.

At each strike price notice that the Mark price is halfway between the corresponding Bid X (sell) and Ask X (buy) prices. The same is true for the put options, but in reverse. In the money puts are above the current "at the money" market price of the underlying. Deeper in the money put values increase as the strike prices become higher. Look at the put Mark values to see how the premiums increase in concert with the rising strike prices of the puts.

Finally, let's consider another simple option trade. We will buy five $196.5 call contracts and sell five $199 call contracts. This option trade has two *legs* and is called a vertical spread — a long $196.5 call and a short $199 call (one above the other). Let's use the option chain to calculate the cost:

First, what is the Mark of the $196.5 call to be bought?
Second, what is the Mark of the $199 call to be sold?

The Mark of the $196.5 call is $3.335 per share; the Mark of the $199 call is $2.08. You expect to pay about $1.25 per share for this spread — a *debit* because we must pay money to enter this trade. You begin by holding down the Ctrl key. Then you click the Ask (buy) price on the call side of the $196.5 strike line and the Bid (sell) price on call side of the $199 strike.

You check the order bar and see your +5 $196.5 CALL and −5 $199 CALL contracts for symbol SPY. The price is a $1.25 per share debit — what you must pay per share. You verify the order is a LIMIT DAY order that will cost you $625. You submit the order. It will either fill or expire at the end of the trading day.

Let's consider a *credit* spread in which you sell five put option contracts for an immediate profit. You decide that you'd like to own 500 shares of the SPY ETF. But you don't want to pay the current market price of $196.11 per share. Perhaps you could get it for a little less — maybe something below $193. You study the option chain and notice the Mark of the 194 put is $3.61. You click in the Bid (sell) column on the put side of the 194 strike row. You enter −5 as the number of contracts to sell, verify the expiration date, the $3.60 credit (give or take a few cents), and LIMIT and DAY as the order type. You submit the order, which triggers. You receive $1,800 in premium less a brokerage commission and small 5-contract exchange fees.

If the price of SPY drops to $193.99 (one cent below your strike price), you may have 500 shares of SPY put to you for $194.00 per share (your option price). If this happens, you must pay $47,000 plus commissions. But if SPY's market price never reaches your $194 option price, your trade will expire worthless. As long as the premiums are worthwhile and the price is right, you can continue selling "out of the money" put contracts on SPY until 500 shares of the ETF is either put to you or you simply decide to stop selling put options. But over a period of several months, you may make several thousand dollars in option premium income.

These are simple examples of option trades. But there's much more to learn about options and how they work. This can be daunting to entry-level option traders. So the information that follows, especially in chapters 14 through 16, is intended to expand your knowledge of how options work by walking you through a number of popular option trades one step at a time.

Contract Obligations

Contractual obligations were introduced in the first paragraph of this chapter. As mentioned, every option contract includes buyer rights and seller obligations. You learned that option sellers are also called option *writers*. So when you see the term *writer*, you know it's synonymous with *seller*. Here, option contract styles are explained. These contract styles specify the rights of option contract buyers relative to when they can exercise their contractual rights. Next buyer and seller obligations as related to call and put contract are re-examined. These topics are essential to your understanding of how the option market works.

American and European Style Option Contracts

American and European style options cease trading at different times and are exercised differently. The exercise right of option buyers is the primary difference between the two contract styles. All optionable stocks and ETFs are based on American-style option contract rules. American style options can be exercised by option buyers whenever the price of the underlying pierces the contracted strike price — calls above and puts below by as little as one cent. In other words, the buyers of American-style option contracts can exercise the options they hold any time they become in the money (abbreviated ITM).

American-style options stop trading on the third Friday of the expiration month. As mentioned, this style of option contract can be exercised by a buyer whenever the price of the underlying exceeds (call options) or drops below (put options) the contracted strike price. These trades are typically *auto*-exercised. However, if the option buyer does not want to exercise his/her rights, the brokerage can be instructed to withhold exercise.

European style index options cease trading at the close of business on Thursdays prior to the third Friday of the month. In contrast to the American-style options, European-style options can only be exercised upon contract expiration if and only if the price of the underlying is ITM. Therefore, European-style option buyers cannot exercise their contract if the underlying price momentarily becomes ITM and then retreats from the contracted strike price.

While most broad-based financial index options are European execution style, such as the S&P 500 (SPX), NASDAQ (NDX), and Russell 2000 (RUT), a small number of smaller financial indices, such as the S&P 100 (OEX), are governed by American-style execution rules.

It's possible to suffer an unwanted surprise in the form of a financial loss by not understanding the underlying style of an option contract in which you are participating. Owners of American-style call options may believe that plenty of time remains for the underlying to retreat from the contract strike price only to see their stock called away.

Call Contracts

As you saw in the above examples, the option buyer of call contracts is obligated to pay the option seller a cash *premium* for the right to acquire an underlying security at a specified (strike) price. If the security reaches or exceeds the strike price of the call, the seller is obligated to deliver the contracted number of shares to the buyer for the agreed upon strike price. If the seller does not own the shares of stock, the seller must buy the stock at the current market price and deliver the shares of stock to the buyer. Also recall that when an option trade is not "covered" by shares of stock held in the seller's account, it is referred to as an *uncovered* or *naked* position.

Financial index options are "cash settled." You can't just own a few shares of each of 500 different stocks represented by the S&P 500. When one of the large financial indexes is exercised, such as the SPX (S&P 500), the seller is required to deliver cash to the buyer based on the market price of the index.

For example, if ten 100–share call contracts are traded at a strike price of $500 and the index price rallies to $525 at contract expiration, the buyer will exercise the option. This requires the seller to deliver $25,000 to the buyer — the difference between $525 and the original $500 strike price × 1,000 shares from:

$525/Share × 10 contracts × 100 shares/contract = $525,000
$500/Share × 10 contracts × 100 shares/contract = $500,000
$525,000 − $500,000 = $25,000. Ouch!

The buyer's obligation is controlled by the contracted strike price. Therefore, the seller receives $500.00 per share from the buyer for $525 per share in index value. To prevent this from happening, the seller must close the call option contract before the index price rallies beyond the $500 strike price. Closing requires the seller to buy back the call contract and pay the current option premium at the $500 strike price listed on the option chain. Although this is far less than $25 per share (the difference between $525 and $500, it can still amount to a substantial loss. And, of course, there must be enough market liquidity for the seller's order to fill. However, financial indexes usually have ample liquidity and fill quickly.

Put Contracts

The above put trade examples illustrated how put contracts work differently than call contracts relative to stock delivery. As with every active trade, there is always a seller and a buyer on either side. In the case of entering put contracts, buyers pay the premium listed at the selected strike. Sellers collect the premium from the buyers. If the market price of the underlying stock drops below the strike price of the put contract by one penny, the buyer can exercise the put contract and deliver the contracted number of shares to the seller. In exchange, the seller is contractually obligated to pay the buyer for the number of shares being delivered at the option's strike price.

An option trader sells ten $45 put contracts on a $50 stock and receives $0.40 per share from the buyer for a total of $400 in option premium. The price of the stock drops to $44.50. The buyer exercises the $45 option. The seller must pay the buyer $45/share × 1,000 shares (ten contracts) of stock. This amounts to $45,000 for 1,000 shares of stock having a current value of $44,500. The buyer "puts" the 1,000 shares of stock to the seller.

Cash-settled puts on a financial index work similarly, except the seller must deliver the difference of the strike price and the exercise price in cash to the buyer. There are only a few small financial indexes that use American-style options. And being American-style options, they can be exercised prior to contract expiration. Obviously, there's more risk associated with index options than with stock options. Stock can appreciate in value; cash only depreciates with inflation.

Number of Shares

Most option contracts include a specific number of shares. This is true for stocks, ETFs, and indices. Option contracts for e-mini futures do vary. The number of shares for each e-mini option contract is displayed on the order bars of their option chains. Fortunately, traders of most options only have to deal with two different contract quantities, and they are clearly labeled.

Standard Options

Call option contracts were first introduced in 1973 by the Chicago Board of Options Exchange (CBOE). The original structure included 100 shares of the underlying security per contract. This has been the standard since the inception of buying and selling these financial derivatives we call options. Standard option contracts continue to include 100 shares of the underlying security for each contract bought and sold. Each standard option contract you buy or sell represents the right to exchange 100 shares of the underlying security for the specified option price.

And, as you very well know by now, this contractual right and obligation can only be exercised if the price of the underlying security, such as stock, becomes in the money. Be aware that there is always a risk of being "called away" or "put to" prior to contract expiration if your option price becomes in the money. Fortunately, experienced option traders know how to use the statistical probabilities available on option chains to measure risk. These provide traders with the "mathematical odds" of one or more selected strike prices becoming in the money during the life of the option contracts.

Weekly Options

Weekly options were first introduced by the Chicago Board Options Exchange (CBOE) in October 2005. These contracts also involve 100 shares of the underlying security. The difference is expiration. Weekly options expire on the last trading day of the specified week, which is usually a Friday. The number following the month, such as DEC2, indicates the second Friday of December. When a holiday falls on a Friday, the number represents the last trading day of the week, which is probably a Thursday.

With the introduction of weekly expirations came a dramatic surge in trading volume. In early 2010 the trading volume of option contracts was below 30,000. By the end of August 2010, more than 300,000 weekly contracts were being traded. This volume has continued to grow ever since. The introduction of weekly options also provided an income windfall for the CBOE. And, of course, the introduction of "weeklys" also benefits active traders. Tens of thousands of educated option traders earn a steady income from buying and selling both monthly and weekly option contracts.

Mini Options

The CBOE introduced mini option contracts on March 18, 2013. The mini option contracts include 10 shares of the underlying, or the equivalent in the case of XSP. Mini option contracts are available on six stocks, ETFs, and a financial index including:

- Amazon (AMZN)
- Apple (AAPL)
- Google (Goog)
- SPDR Gold Trust (GLD)
- SPDR S&P 500 (SPY)
- S&P 500 Mini (XSP)

The last mini-option symbol, XSP, was introduced in 2006. This is a derivative of the S&P 500. The XSP value represents one-tenth of the current S&P 500 index value. Although the XSP includes 100 shares, its value is still equivalent to one-tenth of the S&P 500 index value, or 10 full shares of the S&P 500. Although this may sound confusing, it works out to having the same ten-share value of the other five mini options.

Mini-Option expirations occur on the third Friday of the expiration month. These are *American-Style* option contracts. This means they can be exercised at any time prior to contract expiration if they become in the money. Recall that *European-Style* option contracts are only exercised upon contract expiration. If you bought and currently own an American-style call or put contract that is in the money, your trading platform displays an **Exercise** link. This permits you to exercise your option contract at any time during normal trading hours prior to option contract expiration.

Expiration Dates

The option's expiration date you choose is one of the most important decisions made when entering an option contract. Once an option contract expiration date is past, the contact becomes invalid. Hence, a working short put contract that has not reached the contracted strike price and expires is said to *expire worthless*. Long-term option contracts introduce risk because the price of the underlying has more time to work — in both directions. You can look at the standard deviation figures on any option chain to see how the values increase with each successive contract expiration date. This demonstrates how the probability of having a wider move in the price of the underlying equity increases with the expansion of time.

There are monthly option contracts that stop trading and expire at the close of trading on the third Friday of each month. There are weekly option contracts that expire at market close on Friday of each week. There are also a few *quarterly* option contracts that expire on the last trading day of a calendar quarter.

Monthlies

Monthly option contracts stop trading at market close on the third Friday of the specified expiration month. Recall that we call the third Friday of the month *expiration Friday*. Although monthly options stop trading at Friday's market close, they are settled on the Saturday following expiration Friday.

Weeklys

Many weekly options begin trading on Thursdays of the week prior to expiration on Friday of the following week. Hence, they remain in force for 8 days, excluding holidays. The settlement time is a major difference between standard monthly options and weekly options. Weekly equity and ETF options are settled on Friday in the afternoon. Traders refer to these as being *p.m.-settled* options. These weekly option contracts continue to trade throughout the trading day on Friday until market close.

Index options are either a.m. or p.m. settled, depending on the specific index. The final trading day for a.m.-settled options is Thursday. The closing price is based on the opening price in effect on Friday morning. Hence, these are *a.m.-settled*, while others are p.m.-settled. The CBOE now offers weekly SPX options that expire on Tuesdays and Wednesdays,

LEAPS

Option contracts on Long-Term Equity Anticipation Securities (LEAPS) can have expiration dates up to three years in the future. These are ideal for buy-and-hold style investors who follow strong companies that offer stocks that consistently experience long-term rallies. Buying options is much less expensive than buying and holding the stocks. This gives investors more flexibility and diversity. Instead of depleting all the cash to buy several hundred shares of a single stock, you can use the same amount of money to control thousands of shares of multiple stocks by purchasing call contracts on a half-dozen different stocks.

Buying and holding either *in the money* or *at the money* call contracts, or contracts that are slightly above or below the current stock price, is a common practice. As the stock continues to rally, the option moves deeper into the money, and, as expected, the option premium also continues to increase in value. When the buyer is satisfied with the gain in premium value, the option contracts can be sold for a substantial gain.

Examples would be buying at- or near-the-money calls on GOOG, AMZN, PCLN, or BIDU and watching one or all rally by a hundred dollars. From this we realize that it's not necessary to own the stock to achieve large financial gains. We just have to choose strong, up-trending stocks with plenty of time to work in our favor. Or, we can buy puts on down-trending stocks.

The Option Chain

You were introduced to the option chain in chapter 2. Another option chain was included at the beginning of this chapter. Although some of the following information is repetitive, this is probably a good place for review and elaboration. You are getting close to examining, structuring, and managing some real option trades.

Calls and Puts

Recall how option premiums increase as the strike prices of calls decrease. Looking at the option chain in figure 10–1, examine the incremental Mark, Bid X, and Ask X columns on the call side of the figure. Then check these same values on the put side of the option chain. There's also a column with the heading *Delta*. This is a Greek letter that represents the English word *difference*.

Delta values are used to compute the change in premium values at each strike price based on a one-dollar change in the price of the underlying stock, ETF, index, future, etc. For years the value of Delta was used to compute the likelihood of the underlying to reach the strike price. Many traders still rely on the value of Delta for this purpose. For example, a 0.25 Delta is used by some to mean that the adjacent strike price has a 25% chance of becoming at the money (at the price of the underlying security) prior to the expiration of the option contract. All of the Greek values (Delta, Gamma, Theta, Vega, and Rho) that can be displayed on option chains are described in more detail in chapter 12.

Strike Prices

Now that you know where to find option strike prices (down the center vertical column of figure 10–1), you understand how option strike prices range from low at the top to high at the bottom. Most trading platforms permit the user to specify the number of strike prices to be displayed. For example, a value of 10 strikes displays five above and five below the current price of the underlying. There are some exceptionally low-volume stock option chains that only display four to six strike prices. Therefore, the more active stocks have more strike prices, contributing to much longer option chains. As a practical matter, most experienced traders only deal with three- to four-hundred symbols, in spite of there being more than 64,000. Most symbols are simply not worthwhile considering for a number of reasons. For example, trading volume, the market price, or option premiums may be too small, among other factors.

The strike price increments used within option chains vary with the price of the underlying security. The CBOE has guidelines to determine strike prices increments used on option chains.

CBOE Options Strike Price Increments

Original		More Recent	
Less than $25	2.50	Up to $20	$1
$25 to $200	$5.00	$20 – $50	$2.50
Greater than $200	$10		

Exceptions exist for highly active stocks in which $0.50 or $1.00 increments are sometimes used. As mentioned, the at the money strike price is the closest to the current price of the underlying. A strike price of $44.50 would be considered "at the money" if the underlying stock is trading at $45. Out of the money call strike prices are greater, while out of the money put strike prices are less.

Bid, Ask, Mark, Last (Premium)

You've been introduced to these terms. And as you've seen, they exist within an option chain's column headings. Bid is the option selling price and Ask is the buying price. The "X" is not significant. When selling to collect premium income, clicking Bid on the selected strike price row puts a sell order on the order bar. Clicking Ask puts a buy order on the order bar. The values on the order bar can be edited. The order bar displays the number of contracts, whether to sell (−) or buy (+), the expiration date, the strike price, the premium price, and the order type, i.e., LIMIT, MARKET, DAY, GTC, etc.

The Mark is interpreted as the *market* price. It is what an option trader expects to pay or receive in premium in dollars and cents for each share of stock within the option contract. A Mark value $0.30 would represent $30 per contract in option premium from 100 shares per contract multiplied by 30 cents per contract.

When used, the Last column represents the price of the most recent trade. The Mark may be $0.40, while the Last may be $0.55 — a 15-cent difference. Of course, the last could have traded several hours earlier. However, most traders will bump up the premium on a short (sell) trade by five or ten cents to see if it fills. If not, they can cancel and replace the working order if they are still interested in making the trade for less money. Similarly, buyers may offer less than the Mark value in an attempt to pay a little less when buying an option.

In both of the above situations, the trader's working orders may fill or be partially filled. If the trader gets too piggish, the order will probably expire at the end of the day unfilled. Of course this can depend on the current volatility of the underlying security. If the price is oscillating up and down, a small adjustment in price in the trader's favor often works. Too large an adjustment in premium value will likely fail.

Probabilities and Open Interest

Most option traders include several additional column headings on their option chains. This includes probability and open interest columns that can be used to evaluate different strike prices. For example, what's the likelihood of a particular strike price becoming at the money? As mentioned in the previous paragraph, the Delta value is often used for this purpose. But traders also use one of the following statistical probability values to evaluate the probability of different strike prices becoming in or at the money:

- Probability ITM — This is the statistical probability of the adjacent strike price becoming *in the money* during the term of the option contract.
- Probability OTM — This is the statistical probability of the adjacent strike price remaining *out of the money* during the term of the option contract. It is the opposite value of Probability ITM. Therefore, if Probability ITM is 95%, Probability OTM will be 5%.
- Probability Touching — This metric is slightly more conservative than the Probability ITM and OTM. By definition, this is the statistical probability of the adjacent strike price remaining out of the money (never "touching" the underlying) for the entire duration of the option contract.

Open interest is another important metric that all seasoned traders consider. Open interest is the number of option contracts that currently exist on the selected option chain. Open interest is shown at each strike price. It is a measure of *liquidity*. When open interest is low, traders abandon the current option chain and move on. When open interest is high, traders begin studying open interest levels, premium values, and the corresponding statistical probabilities at different strike prices. The corresponding price charts are also examined in order to determine support and resistance levels and to develop a bias relative to price outlook.

Greeks

Delta, briefly described above, is one of four *Greek* letters, in addition to *Vega*. These so-called *Greeks* are displayed on most option chains used by experienced option traders. Fortunately, all but one of the Greek letters represents an English word. The Greek values are described in detail in chapter 12. For the time being, they are listed for you here.

Delta — **D**ifference

Gamma — Measures the rate of change of Delta.

Theta — **T**ime

Vega — **V**olatility

Rho — **R**ate of interest (based on risk-free rate of return related to Treasury notes)

In, At, and Out of the money

These terms were illustrated on the option chain contained in figure 2–1. Each term is defined for both calls and puts in the following table.

Strike Price of a	*Underlying Price*	*In, At, or Out*
Call	Less than	In the money
Call	Greater than	Out of the money
Call	Equal to	At the money

Put	Less than	Out of the money
Put	Greater than	In the money
Put	Equal to	At the money

To Exercise or Not to Exercise

It's possible for an in the money position to remain unexercised for days, weeks, or even months. Option sellers have the right but not the obligation to exercise their options. If one or more buyers do not want to take delivery, they can instruct their brokerages not to exercise the contract upon contract expiration. There are instances in which the premium that must be paid to exercise an option contract exceeds the profit. Or option buyers might not want to deplete the cash reserves within their margin accounts. Regardless of the reason, if the strike price becomes deep in the money, option sellers should anticipate being exercised. They should take the necessary steps to minimize losses. Trade management strategies are presented in chapters 14 and 15 for each of the corresponding option strategies.

Picking the Expiration Date (Time = Risk)

Selecting a reasonable expiration date for the type of option trade being entered is extremely important. In fact, when trading rules are discussed, the time from the entry of your trade until contract expiration is always involved as part of your strategy rules. It has often been said that extended time is the buyer's friend and the seller's enemy. The following paragraphs explain why this is true.

Sell Inside 56 Days

When selling an option contract for premium income, your goal is to keep the premium. If your strike price is close to the price of the underlying, your risk is greater than it would be if your strike price is farther away. Giving the price more time to move against your position also introduces greater risk. Hence, most traders who sell options for premium income tend to sell put and/or call options at strike prices that are farther away from the price of the underlying, that is, farther out of the money using our options jargon.

In addition to selecting strike prices that are at "safe distances" out of the money, limiting the amount of time that the price of the underlying security has to work against you is also important. The probability of experiencing a losing trade increases with more time. When selling premium, your goal is to enter and exit the trade in the shortest possible time. Therefore, use weekly or quarterly option contracts that expire within a matter of weeks. The reverse logic is used when buying option contracts.

Buy 90 Days+

If you find an up-trending stock that is currently in a pull-back and poised for a break-out, you may be looking at a perfect candidate for a long call option. Now you should consider buying a long call at a strike price that is at or just out of the money. (Some traders look for a strike price having a Delta value around 0.30.) For example, you can buy $35 call contracts for $3.40/share in premium (the Mark value), or $40 call contracts for $1.20/share. You decide to buy 5 call contracts at the $40 strike for $6,000 plus commissions and option exchange fees. You are quite bullish and expect the stock to resume its upward trend. It's important to give the price of the stock plenty of time to rally in your favor. In the event of a price reversal, sufficient time is required for recovery and the resumption of the stock's upward trend.

As the stock price appreciates in value, the strike price of your long call moves deeper in the money and the premium increases in value. When the Mark (premium) of your $40 call contract reaches $2.40, the trade has achieved a profit of 50%. This is a good time to sell the five $40 calls. Premiums always begin to decline from *time decay* as option contracts approach the contract expiration dates. Time decay is measured by *Theta* — an important Greek metric that is available for use on every trader's option chain. With all other values remaining constant, a Theta value of −.02 means the premium value is dropping by 2 cents per share or $2.00 per contract each day.

The LEAPS

LEAPS (Long-Term Equity Anticipation Securities) were introduced earlier. Here, LEAPS are discussed relative to option contract expiration times. As you should know from the paragraph immediately following "Picking the Expiration Date," more time benefits option buyers. If you're bullish on one or more underlying stocks or ETFs, bullish style LEAPS option trades that expire in 18 to 36 months could certainly be of interest. Of course, this requires the trader to tie up premium dollars for 1–1/2 to 3 years. However, since you're using options rather than buying the stock, the amount of money involved is comparatively small. As you learned in chapter 2, options have a substantial amount of financial leverage. Using a LEAPS long call is a good example of the financial leverage offered by options.

Option Pricing

The premium values for options are derived using mathematical formulas. These formulas reside within a set of specialized market support software provided by the CBOE. The software programs simultaneously monitor millions of variables related to price levels, volume, volatility, interest rates, times remaining till expiration, bid and ask prices, and more. There is also the Greek value, Delta — controlled by a second variable called Gamma. And these are all tracked for thousands of underlying symbols at millions of strike prices.

Negotiations (Bid/Ask/Mark/Last)

Soon after the inception of call options by the CBOE, and before supercomputers and sophisticated software programs, traders manually negotiated the prices at which options were traded. They would squabble between the bid and ask prices and, if able to make a deal, would typically settle somewhere in between. Today, the mark represents the premium value — the so-called "negotiated price" that exists midway between the bid and the ask prices.

As discussed earlier, you don't have to settle at the mark. If the price shown in the last column is recent, you may try for a higher premium when selling or a lower premium when buying. In both of these cases, you are attempting to skew the trade price to your benefit. You can enter a trade price that is slightly in your favor to see if it fills. And it often will. If your working order doesn't fill within 15 to 30 minutes, cancel and change it to the current mark value to increase the odds for your working order to fill.

Bjerksun–Stensland, Binomial, Black-Scholes Formulas

Three different formulas that compute the prices of options are in use today. All three are briefly described to provide background and so you will recognize the names. However, you are not required to choose one formula over another, as this is the purview of your trading platform in concert with the CBOE.

The first mathematical formula used to compute option prices was published in a 1973 paper written and distributed by Fischer Black and Myron Scholes. The Black-Scholes formula calculated the values of European-style options, and essentially legitimatized option pricing used around the world. Robert Merton refined the model for which Merton and Black received the Nobel Memorial Prize in Economic Sciences.

Another mathematical formula that models option pricing is called the Binomial Options Pricing Model. This formula was introduced in 1979. It introduced what mathematicians refer to as a "discrete time" model. The model is designed to smooth varying prices over time. Some experts believe that the Binomial pricing model is superior to the others for its ability to accommodate a broader range of conditions throughout the durations of the underlying option contracts.

The Bjerksun-Stensland model is a third formula designed to compute option prices. This formula was developed to measure American-style option pricing.

Some option trading platforms incorporate all three formulas within their analytical tool sets, and are selectable to users. However, the outcomes are nearly identical. Using the default formula selected by your trading platform should be quite adequate.

The Chicago Board Options Exchange (cboe.com)

The Chicago Board Options Exchange (CBOE) introduced tradable call option contracts in April 1973. Since its beginning, CBOE continues to introduce numerous new product offerings. Some examples are the introduction of put options in 1977 and weekly options in 2005. The S&P 500 volatility index, symbol VIX, was also introduced in 2005. CBOE introduced tradable VIX options in 2006. The CBOE processes well over a billion option contract trades each year. More than 95% of these are traded electronically. The alternative, called *open outcry* trading and conducted on the exchange floors, is rapidly diminishing. CBOE became a publicly traded NASDAQ stock in 2010 under symbol CBOE.

If you have not visited the cboe.com website, you are encouraged to do so. Option traders can find a substantial amount of useful information there, including downloadable lists of weekly options, lists of exchange fees, a standard margin calculator designed to accommodate a variety of option strategies including both single option entries and multiple-leg option spreads. The CBOE also has online training webinars in addition to option education in the form of live seminars.

Trading Permissions (Approval Levels)

Option trading permissions are managed and assigned to investors by brokerages. Some brokerages use three levels, while others use five. Below are four option trading levels.

Option Trading Levels

Level	Description	Notation
1	Covered Call & Long Protective Puts	$+$Stock with $-$C / $+$P
2	Long Calls and Long Puts	$+$C or $+$P
3	Spreads and Straddles	$+$C & $-$C; $+$P & $-$C
4	Writing uncovered or naked options	$-$C / $-$P

Level 1 permits the covered calls and cash–covered puts.

Level 2 permits covered calls, cash–covered puts, the purchase of calls, and cash–covered puts.

Level 3 permits the simultaneous purchase and sale of calls (vertical spreads) and the purchase of puts and sale of calls.

Level 4 permits the sale of uncovered (or *naked*) calls and puts — the highest risk option spread.

Each level is cumulative, i.e., level 3 can do everything permitted for levels 1 and 2 in addition to selling spreads comprised of vertical call spreads. Some brokerages assign trading permission levels based on years of experience and educational coursework. Some even require clients to pass an option exam.

When you complete this book, you may wish to discuss option trading levels with your brokerage to determine what's required to qualify for the various levels. As a reminder, you cannot use strategies having unlimited risk in qualified retirement accounts, such as an IRA rollover. This prevents the writing (selling) of uncovered or naked positions that are permitted in level 4 accounts.

Trading Covered and Uncovered

Recall the mention of covered calls in the foreword and again in chapter 1. A covered option position describes one or more short (sold) option contracts that are collateralized by either stock or cash held within a trader's brokerage account.

Being Covered

Following is a description of a covered call.

1.   Stock XYZ is currently selling for $20.00 per share.
2.   The Mark (premium) of the $24 XYZ calls that expire in 8 days is $0.70.
3.   We choose Covered Stock and click Ask on the 24 call row to buy 1,000 shares of XYZ stock for $20,000 and simultaneously sell ten $24 calls contracts for a premium of $700. The net cost is $19,300 after subtracting the $700 from the $20,000.
4.   We examine the order bar for the above values; if correct, we submit the order.

The net cost of this trade is $19,300 ($20,000 − $700, less commissions). The trader holds onto the trade and the price of XYZ rallies to $24.25 within four days — prior to contract expiration. The $24 call is now *in the money*. The $24 call option buyer exercises the option (or *calls away* the $24.00 stock). As the option seller we are obligated to deliver the $24.25/share stock to the option buyer at the contracted strike price of $24. In exchange, the buyer is obligated to pay us $24 per share — our contracted strike price.

This was a profitable trade. We surrendered 1,000 shares of stock for $24 per share for which we originally paid $20,000 per share — a gain of $4.00 per share for a total of $4,000 in *intrinsic value*. We also received $700 in option premium in *extrinsic value*. Our total profit from this covered call is $4,700.

Being Uncovered (or *Naked*)

As described in the option trading levels table, traders must have the highest account level to trade naked options. Naked means that if the market goes against a trade, a substantial percentage of the underlying account could be lost. Therefore, traders must have a clear understanding of how naked trades work. If a naked trade becomes *in the money*, the trader can lose a lot of cash.

Recall the simple covered call in which the trader buys 100 shares of stock for every call contract sold. If the underlying price rallies one cent above the strike price of the covered call, the buyer can exercise the option contract and call the stock away from the seller.

In the case of a naked call, the buyer does not own the underlying stock. Therefore, the seller of the naked call must purchase the stock and deliver it to the buyer. The buyer must pay the seller for the stock at the original call contract's strike price, which may be much less than the current stock value. You should recall that in the case of a financial index, the seller must deliver the difference between the selling price and the current price of the index in cash. Following is another clarifying example.

> The S&P 500 index (SPX) is currently at $2,100; the Mark (premium) is $0.25/share for contracts that expire in 15 days. Janet sells 10 SPX 2125 CALLS and receives $250 in premium less fees.
>
> During the following week the SPX rallies to $2,130, $5 above Janet's $2,125 strike price.
>
> A buyer of the 2125 calls exercises the option contracts.
>
> Janet pays the buyers $5,000 in cash ($5.00 × 1,000 shares). She must also pay another $20 in transaction fees. This is the net difference between her selling 1,000 shares at a strike price of $2125 and the current $2130 price.

Now consider a naked put. If Janet had sold 20 $1800 naked SPX put contracts and the market crashed to $1500, Janet would owe the buyer of her uncovered puts $300 per share for 2,000 shares. This is an outflow of $600,000 from Janet's account.

Realistically, Janet would likely exit her position or add a long put one or two strikes below her short SPX put for "insurance" against an unsustainable loss.

Both of the above trades are examples of cash-settled option transactions.

TIP: As a practical matter, most option traders are more interested in transacting option trades for premium income rather than for stock ownership. Option buyers buy low and sell high; option writers sell high and buy low. It is always important to "do the math." Premium collection is usually more profitable than exercising an option for ownership of the underlying stock or ETF, unless the underlying security has made an exceptional price move.

What did you learn in chapter 10?

1. An option contract is a _____–_____ contract between two parties.

2. When a call or put option contract expires out of the money, it favors the _____.

3. The shaded portions of an option chain include strike prices that are _____ (abbrev.).

4. The midpoint between the Bid and Ask price is called the _____.

5. The trader pays premium when trading a _____ spread.

6. The trader receives premium when trading a _____ spread.

7. The two option contract styles are called the _____ and _____ style.

8. The _____ style option contract can be exercised prior to contract expiration.

9. The S&P 500 and NASDAQ financial index options are _____ style options.

10. Financial index options are _____ settled rather than stock settled.

11. Most option traders who trade LEAPS usually buy _____ _____.

12. Delta displays a decimal value at each strike price. Delta is used to calculate the change in premium value for a $_____ change in the price of the underlying security.

13. The Mark is interpreted as the _____ _____.

14. The most conservative probability metric is Probability _____.

15. Open Interest is important because it is a measure of _____.

16. Option sellers should sell inside _____ days.

17. Shorter times till expiration increase risk for option _____.

18. The first option premium calculation formula is known as the _____–_____ formula.

19. The Bjerksun–Stensland model was developed to calculate _____-Style options pricing.

20. Trading permissions are used to govern option trading levels and corresponding _____.

11 THE OPTION CHAIN — DIVING DEEPER

● ● ● ● ● ● ●

Accessing Option Chains

Option chains have become accessible on a variety of public websites. For example, you can go to nasdaq.com, marketwatch.com, or finance.yahoo.com — all open to anyone who wants to view an option chain for an underlying security of interest. Enter a valid symbol to display the underlying option chain. Then select an expiration date to see the details. Figure 11–1 is a screen shot of the Dec 15 CBOE stock options on the nasdaq.com website.

Active option traders make constant use of the option chains provided by their brokerages. Familiarity with a platform's functionality makes its use more efficient and contributes to trader confidence and accuracy.

Expiration Dates

Chapter 10 presented a substantial amount of information on types of options based on expirations. Here, a look at weekly and monthly expirations are viewed from a trading perspective.

Figure 11–1. An Option Chain on nasdaq.com

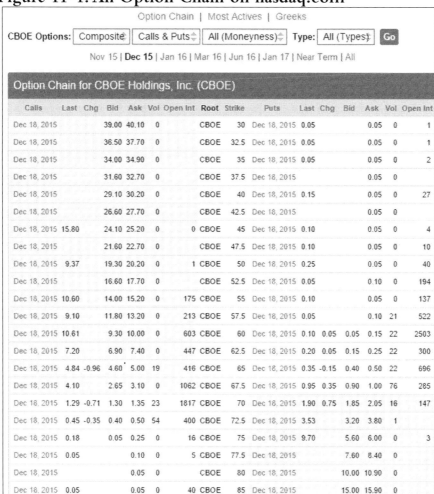

Weekly Expirations

Most weeklys, as they are often called, expire on Fridays of each week unless Friday happens to fall on a holiday. Many option traders specialize in short-term weekly option contracts that expire within 5 to 56 days. This is particularly true for option traders who specialize in *collecting premium*. They "churn" the market by selling several out of the money puts and/or calls week after week and pocket the proceeds. Some of these traders wait for their option contracts to expire. But many close their option contracts once they've achieved their profit goal, which is typically between 30% and 70%. Then they repeat the process. Doing this each and every week can result in a nice weekly income, especially if they adhere to a strict set of statistically proven trading rules. In 2016, the CBOE introduced S&P 500 index options that expire on Tuesdays and Wednesdays. Regardless of expiration, all options work much in the same way and are governed by price, time, volatility, and current interest rates. The hands-on trading activities in chapters 14 and 15 cover these variables in detail.

Monthly Expirations

Monthly expirations include contracts that expire on the third Friday of the month. There are also quarterly expirations; these also have third-Friday expirations. Option contract sellers, or *writers*, rarely sell option contracts for premium income having expiration dates longer than a few months. It's more likely to find option contract buyers or sellers whose outlooks and motives are different from the weekly "churners." One motive of a long-term call option seller is to transfer the underlying "covering" stock to a buyer on the other side of the trade. The goal is to profit from an increase in the price of the stock, in addition to the option premium received when the option was initially sold. And the buyer on the other side of this trade is likely bullish. The buyer of the call contract expects the price of the underlying security to rally. With enough time remaining, the buyer may profit by either selling the option contract for more premium than originally paid or exercising the call option(s) for profit.

In the case of a put, the seller must be willing to acquire the stock from the buyer of the put option at the option price. This type of trade may be entered every two months in hopes of either acquiring the stock at the contracted strike price, collecting premium, or both.

Another common motive for buying long-term put options is to create a hedge against a precipitous price drop. For example, the put buyer may want to set a loss limit by buying a put option contract at a specific strike price. You may wonder why the buyer doesn't simply enter a stop order. Stop orders are almost always market orders. The stop price could be substantially below the option strike price, depending on the bid to ask spread. However, the long put option "locks in" the selling price of the hedged stock at the strike price of the option contract. The equity collar option strategy, described in chapter 14, is an excellent hedging strategy. It is also less expensive than buying a slightly OTM put option because it includes a short OTM call which offsets the cost of the premium spent when buying the put option.

Strike Prices

The different strike (or option) prices displayed on an option chain correspond to the value of the underlying security (stock, ETF, financial index, or futures contract). The CBOE Strike Price Increments table in chapter 10 listed the most common increments used on option chains. You can also look at any option chain to see these increments, which often vary according to the trading volume of the underlying security.

Users can adjust the number of strike prices displayed within an option chain. This is done by entering a numerical value in a text box above the column of strike prices. Entering 40 displays 20 strike prices above and 20 below the at the money market price of the underlying security. Entering ALL displays all available strike prices for the underlying security. ALL is often too many strike prices on an actively traded stock or financial index. Some of these have as many as several hundred strike prices. This requires scrolling from the lowest price down to those strike prices that exist within a reasonable trading range. Therefore, you may want to set the number of strike prices to a value that eliminates the need to constantly scroll up and down the list.

Another issue with displaying too many strike prices is the amount of space it requires to view the entire option chain. Other features, such as access to option chains that expire at later dates and order bars, are often pushed down out of view, again, requiring excessive scrolling.

Premium

The Mark value was briefly introduced as option premium (or the current value) in chapter 2. And there it explained how the default Mark value, which can be thought of as the market value, is midway between the option's Bid (sell) and Ask (buy) price. The Mark value is different for each strike price and for every call and put within an option chain. Examining any option chain reveals how the Mark (or premium) values increase as calls and puts go deeper in the money and decrease as they move farther out of the money (away from the price of the underlying security).

The values in the following table are from the option chain shown in figure 10–1 of the previous chapter. Notice the call and put premium values at the $192, $196, and $200 strike prices in the following table.

Comparing Premium Values In, At, and Out of the money

Location	Calls	Premium	Puts	Premium
In the money (ITM)	$192 call	$6.300	$200 put	$6.540
At the money (ATM)	$196 call	$3.625	$196 put	$4.410
Out of the money (OTM)	$200 call	$2.080	$192 put	$2.945

This demonstrates something you will become quite familiar with as you gain experience as an option trader. Premiums increase as strike prices become deeper in the money. Premiums decrease as strike prices become farther out of the money. And at the money Delta hovers close to 0.50 (more about Delta later). This is true with both calls and puts as shown in the above table. Getting closer to the price of the underlying, i.e., the at the money strike price, increases the potential return. But it also increases the risk of the trade by a substantial amount. Unless option call sellers want stock to be called away, or put sellers want the stock put to them, they always sell option contracts that are several strike prices out of the money to reduce risk. And they also choose option chains with near-term expiration dates to reduce the time the price of the underlying has to work against their position (or "strike price").

Spreads

A *spread* is an option trading strategy involving two or more *legs*. For example, a vertical call spread, sometimes referred to as a *bull call spread*, includes buying a call at or near the money (the price of the underlying) and selling an out of the money call several strikes above (farther out of the money). Both legs usually expire at the same time so the same option chain is used for both legs. However, option traders often buy longer expiration options than those they sell.

This is a bullish strategy because the trader expects the price of the underlying to rally. The long (bought) $38 call is expected to appreciate in value as the stock price increases. The premium received from the short $41 call helps to finance the cost of the long $38 call. Notice the Mark values. The trader must pay $1.00 for the long $38 call and receives approximately $0.50 for the short call for a total cost of $0.50/share from $100 \times (\$1.00 - \$0.50) = \$50$. This would be a debit spread, as the trader pays more premium than is received.

Figure 11–2. Vertical (Bull Call) Spread Example

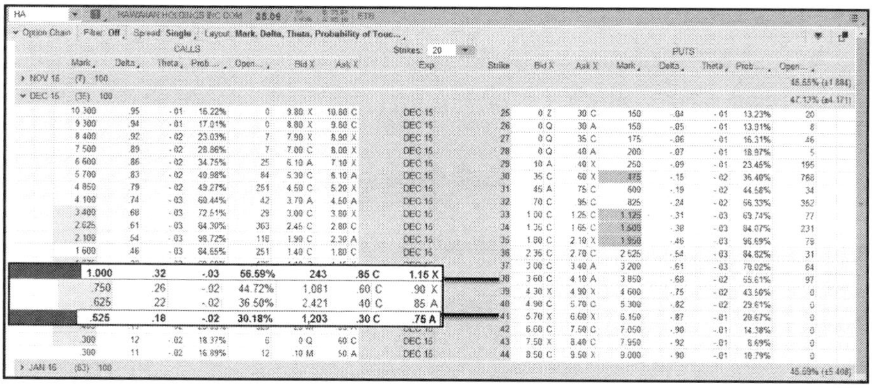

For illustration purposes only.

Figure 11–3. Profit/Loss Profile of a Bull-Call Spread

	A	B	C	D	E	F	G	H
1	Symbol	Current	Action	Contracts	Call/Put	Stk Price	Mark	Cost
2	HA	$35.09	Buy	1	Call	$ 38.00	$ 1.00	$ (100.00)
3	HA	$35.09	Sell	-1	Call	$ 41.00	$ 0.50	$ 50.00
4	Total Premium (debit spread)							$ (50.00)
5								
6	PRIOR TO EXPIRATION HA RALLIES TO $42; BOTH CALLS ARE EXERCISED:							
7	Trader's Profits and Losses:							
8	$41 short call option is exercised @ 100 shares/contract:							
9	Trader must buy and deliver $42 stock to buyer of his short $41 ca							$ (4,200.00)
10	Buyer must pay trader his $41/share strike price							$ 4,100.00
11	Our trader's profit/loss frin the Short Call:							$ (100.00)
12								
13	$38 Long Call option is exercised @ 100 shares/contract:							
14	Trader pays $38/share for the $42/share stock							$ (3,800.00)
15	Trader can now sell stock for $42/share							$ 4,200.00
16	Cost of original option trade							$ (50.00)
17	Our trader's profit/loss from the Long Call:							$ 350.00
18	Less approximately $40 in commissions							$ (40.00)
19	Net Profit/Loss							$ 210.00

If the trader owns sufficient shares of the underlying HA stock, the short $41 call is *covered* by the stock. Without ownership of the HA stock, the short $41 call is *naked* (uncovered). Therefore, if the price of HA exceeds the $41 strike price, the trader is aware of the buyer's exercise right to call the stock away. When exercised, the option seller is required to deliver the stock to the buyer at the strike price of $41 per share. The owner of the vertical spread would offset the cost of the short $41 call by exercising the long $38 call position. This results in a profitable trade. Figure 11-3 above illustrates the profit/loss profile for this bull call spread, assuming the price of HA rallies to $42 and is exercised prior to contract expiration.

In this example the trader's bullish bias was correct. Both option legs were exercised, our trader delivered the stock to the buyer of the $41 call, and received and immediately liquidated the stock received from the long $38 call. The entire exchange resulted in a $210 profit.

If the price of HA had suffered a major drop, the trader would have lost the $50 per share plus commissions on the spread, but not on the cost of the drop in shares of stock, which is how many covered call traders suffer losses — not from the options, but from a drop in the value of the underlying stock. With the proper trading level, the trader could possibly have sold the long $38 call position for whatever premium still remained prior to expiration. Of course this requires sufficient liquidity for the order to fill. But this would expose the short $41 call as a naked call, much too risky with time remaining and this close to the money. Unless the trader is approved to sell naked options, the brokerage would reject the attempt to sell the long call.

Bid and Ask Spread

You should recall that when we place option trades on an underlying option chain, we click the Bid price to sell and the Ask price to buy — the exact opposite of how Bid and Ask are used in buying and selling equities (stocks, ETFs, futures, and forex pairs). Because this book is about options, we'll stay with Bid (sell) and Ask (buy) as used with options.

So with options, clicking Ask places a buy order; clicking Bid places a sell order. However, as you already know, the Mark (midway between the Bid and Ask) is the price at which option trades usually settle.

In the previous material describing volatility and the difference (or the *spread*) between the Bid to Ask prices, high trading volume tends to reduce the spread between the Bid and Ask prices, especially with high trading volume stocks like AAPL or FB, with volumes in the millions and open interest in the thousands. And even on the same high-volume option chain, you can see how the bid to ask spreads widen as they move farther OTM with correspondingly lower open interest values. Low trading volume stocks and ETFs that trade less than a million shares per day have much wider spreads between the Bid and Ask prices. An example is the high-dividend ETF symbol HDV. This ETF has an average daily trading volume of about a half-million shares. There are much lower volumes than a half-million, but many of these do not even offer Bid and Ask values for more than one or two strike prices above or below the price of the underlying — the *at the money* (ATM) strike price.

Compare the spreads between AAPL and HDV in Figure 11–4. This illustrates the spread difference between high and low volume equities. At one call strike price out of the money, the bid to ask spread for AAPL is 3 cents, while the same spread for HDV is 80 cents.

When the spread between the Bid and Ask prices is extremely "wide," there's more "slop" in the trading price. It's possible to enter a trade only to find that you've lost twenty or thirty dollars per contract as soon as the trade fills. This is just one of the risks associated with trading low volume equities. The lack of open interest diminishes liquidity. This increases risk. Without liquidity, your entry and exit orders may never fill.

Figure 11–4. Bid and Ask Spread Example: AAPL & HDV

Calls		AAPL			Puts	
Bid X	Ask X	Exp		Strike	Bid X	Ask X
8.80 N	8.95 X	DEC 15		105	1.42 Z	1.47 C
5.15 T	5.25 W	DEC 15		110	2.75 B	2.81 W
2.52 M	2.55 W	DEC 15		115	5.05 X	5.20 X
.99 B	1.00 C	DEC 15		120	8.50 X	8.70 X

		HDV				
Bid X	Ask X	Exp		Strike	Bid X	Ask X
1.35 C	3.30 C	DEC 15		71	.30 C	1.20 C
1.15 C	1.95 C	DEC 15		72	.60 C	1.40 C
.55 C	1.35 C	DEC 15		73	.95 C	1.80 C
.05 C	.95 C	DEC 15		74	.85 C	2.60 C

For illustration purposes only.

Notice the letters M, W, and C next to the Bid and Ask values. These are the exchanges from which the Bid and Ask quotations are retrieved. Typically, your trading platform uses "Best" as the default Bid, Ask, and Mark prices. You are advised to simply let your trading platform do the work of picking an exchange based on the best price. Many wonder why a brokerage even bothers to display the exchange sources on option chains. Although showing a letter next to each price has little practical value, some suspect it's done just because the exchange information is readily available and easy to add, or it's an attempt to achieve full disclosure.

From the Underlying's Price

By now you know that at the money strike prices are the closest to the price of the underlying. And you've figured out that the statistical probability of being in the money and remaining out of the money is directly related to how close a strike price is to *the money* — the strike that's closest to the price of the underlying security. As you move farther from the money, the premiums decline in value. These values correspond to risk. The old adage "higher risk returns greater rewards" is quite true with options.

Selling for Premium Income

It goes without saying that making prudent trades is always advisable. When selling options for premium income, the option trader wants the premium income to be sufficiently high to justify the trade. The trader also wants to be far enough out of the money to minimize the risk of being exercised, i.e., becoming in the money. As you saw in the preceding Bull Call Spread example, the trader's short call was quite close to the money. And the price rallied above the price of the short $41 call. Taking a closer look at the $41 strike price within the option chain, a 30.18% Probability of Touching (see the Prob...column in figure 11–2) existed. From this, the trader determined the odds of HA's price reaching $41 was less than 69.8%

(one standard deviation). But because this covered call was a debit spread, it carried risk. First, the trader needed a rally in order to close both legs for an increase in the combined premium. This would require the trader to buy back the short call and sell the long call. To profit, the premium required to close both the long and short legs must exceed the $0.50 debit originally paid at entry plus the transaction fees. Most experienced traders would not make this trade, as there is simply not enough profit potential to make it worthwhile.

The standard deviation, which is displayed on every option chain, is another metric watched by option traders. The standard deviation is based on the underlying's most recent price volatility and the time remaining until contract expiration. With 35 days remaining, the standard deviation math suggests that the price can range ±$4.171. The option chain used in figure 11–2 shows the price of HA to be at $35.09. For the price to rally to $42 required an increase of $6.91 in less than 35 days. This is 65.66% beyond the $4.171 standard deviation value. If the trader had doubled the standard deviation value to 2 × 4.171 and added it to the underlying price of $35.09, a strike price of either $43 or $44 would have been considered. Of course the premium amount offered at these farther out of the money call strike prices must be acceptable to the trader.

If the Bull Call Spread trader had used the $43 strike price for the short call, that leg would have most likely expired worthless and wouldn't have been exercised. The trader would have exercised the long $38 call by paying $3,800 for $4,200 worth of HA stock — a profit of $400 less commissions, plus about $30 in premium originally collected for the sale of the $43 call contract upon entry.

Buying Option Contracts (Paying Premium)
When buying one or more option contracts, you must pay premium. Option premium is higher when expiration dates are farther away in time. You pay more for options that expire in six months than for

options that expire in one month. Looking at the option chain for symbol CRM, compare the 75 put and call ask prices for the JAN 16 (62 days remaining) and the JAN 17 (433 days remaining).

Figure 11–5. How Time Relates to Option Premiums

	CALLS						Strikes: 6				PUTS			
	Mark	Delta	Theta	Open	Bid X	Ask X	Exp	Strike	Bid X	Ask X	Mark	Delta	Theta	Open
▾ JAN 16	(62)	100												42.70% (±10.788)
	8.150	71	-.03	5.736	8.05 X	8.25 T	JAN 16	70	2.49 C	2.59 X	2.540	-.29	-.03	3.219
	6.575	63	-.04	2.346	6.50 C	6.65 M	JAN 16	72.5	3.35 C	3.50 C	3.425	-.37	-.04	826
	5.175	55	-.04	5.114	5.10 X	5.25 C	JAN 16	75	4.45 C	4.65 X	4.550	-.45	-.04	2.124
	3.975	47	-.04	1.898	3.90 C	4.05 C	JAN 16	77.5	5.75 C	5.95 X	5.850	-.53	-.04	1.623
	3.020	39	-.04	3.612	2.94 C	3.10 C	JAN 16	80	7.30 C	7.50 X	7.400	-.61	-.04	656
	2.250	32	-.03	2.627	2.18 C	2.32 C	JAN 16	82.5	9.05 T	9.20 X	9.125	-.66	-.03	124
▸ FEB 16	(97)	100												38.71% (±12.244)
▸ MAR 16	(125)	100												39.35% (±14.178)
▸ MAY 16	(188)	100												38.01% (±16.901)
▾ JAN 17	(433)	100												33.52% (±23.048)
	13.750	66	-.01	7.276	12.85 W	14.65 C	JAN 17	70	6.85 C	7.55 C	7.200	-.34	-.01	121
	12.400	62	-.01	3.637	11.55 C	13.25 C	JAN 17	72.5	7.90 C	8.65 C	8.275	-.38	-.01	153
	11.275	58	-.01	7.109	10.75 C	11.80 C	JAN 17	75	9.05 C	9.80 C	9.425	-.42	-.01	334
	10.025	55	-.01	155	9.55 C	10.50 C	JAN 17	77.5	10.30 C	11.15 C	10.725	-.46	-.01	30
	8.800	51	-.01	2.819	8.20 C	9.40 C	JAN 17	80	11.60 C	12.35 C	11.975	-.50	-.01	64
	7.750	47	-.01	37	7.15 C	8.35 C	JAN 17	82.5	13.05 C	13.80 C	13.425	-.55	-.01	220
▸ JAN 18	(797)	100												29.43% (±27.964)

For illustration purposes only.

The differences in the premium costs between the two expiration dates, which are slightly more than one year apart, are more than double. Buyers of option contracts should be reasonably confident in their bullish or bearish bias when investing in premium for a monetary return. When buying, always give yourself sufficient time for the trade to work in your favor. Most prudent traders buy option contracts with contract expiration dates of 90 days or more. A long time till expiration minimizes the daily price reduction from *time decay*. Notice the Theta columns in the option chain of figure 11–5. The fractional values indicate the amount of value in dollars and cents that is exiting the option's premium with each passing day. In the Jan 16 expiration chain the Theta is $–0.04 per share at the 72.5 thru the 80 strike prices. Owning ten option contracts represents 1,000 shares of the underlying stock. The 1,000 shares of CRM stock represented by the ten option contracts are losing 4 cents in premium value per day. This is a $40.00 per day loss, from $0.04 \times 1,000$.

In addition to buying options for income, there are other reasons for buying options. As previously mentioned, put options are often purchased as *hedges*.

> **DEFINITION OF A HEDGE**: A hedge is an investment that reduces the risk of an adverse price movement against an asset. Homeowner's insurance is a simple example of a hedge. You pay an insurance premium. Your house burns down and the insurance company offsets your loss with the dollar benefit you purchased. In the case of the ownership of a financial equity, such as a stock, ETF, or an option contract, a hedge consists of taking an offsetting position. If there were such a thing as a perfect hedge, it would reduce risk to zero, except for the cost of the hedge, itself.

Here are two examples of buying option contracts as hedges.

1. You own 1,000 shares of stock that have rallied by $20. The charts tell you that a drop is looming. To offset a loss from a drop in the price of the stock, you buy ten at the money put contracts that expire in 90 days. If the stock drops below the strike price of your put, you can exercise the put and recover from a major loss in the value of your stock. With 90 days until expiration, you have some time to see if the stock rallies back in your favor. Otherwise, you exercise prior to expiration and while there is still enough open interest to be filled.
2. You have shorted 1,000 shares of stock in anticipation of a drop in price. As insurance against a rally, you buy ten at the money call contracts as a hedge against a possible rally. If the stock rallies above the strike price of your long calls, you can exercise your option contracts to call away the stock from an option seller. This will offset the cost originally paid for the stock.

Calls and Puts

Calls and puts have been described in a variety of introductory trade examples. Now that you've examined several option chains, you know that data columns corresponding to calls are on the left-hand side of a conventional option chain. Data columns corresponding to puts are on the right-hand side. And, of course, you also know contract strike prices are listed in a central column that divides the call and put data. With the exception of figure 11–3, most illustrations of option chains within this book clearly show the location of both calls and puts.

As an option trader, it's vital to know the difference in how calls and puts work when initially traded and when exercised. Several of the previous option trade examples provided some insights to how long and short calls and puts work. This section takes a final look at the operation of each.

American and European Styles

Before getting into long and short calls and puts, let's review option contract styles — the American style and European style. The American style, which governs common stock and ETFs, can be exercised prior to contract expiration if an option contract breaches the option price (becomes in the money). The European style option contracts govern most large financial indexes including the S&P 500, NASDAQ, and Russell 2000. These can only be exercised following contract expiration when the option contract expires in the money. Option contracts that remain out of the money can still be bought and sold by their owners if enough time and sufficient liquidity remains, but they cannot be exercised.

Who Keeps the Premium?

Traders who successfully sell option contracts receive option premium from option buyers. The premium is immediately transferred into the option seller's account to consummate the transaction. The premium is the seller's to keep — forever! Of course the option trade may not work. In spite of what happens, the premium received is kept for all time by the option seller. If the option trade goes against the seller, the seller may be required to pay cash to the option buyer to settle the trade. But this has nothing to do with the amount of premium income originally received when the contract was initially transacted.

Long Call (Buying a Call)

Buying a call in anticipation of a price rally is a bullish strategy. When an in the money, at the money, or slightly out of the money call is purchased, the trader expects the price to rally. If the price of the underlying rallies and the strike price of the calls become deeper in the money, the trader can sell the option contracts and collect more premium than originally paid. The amount of the price increase, the volatility, and the amount of time that remains in the option contract governs the amount of premium the buyer may receive. And, of course, if the long call becomes in the money, the buyer can exercise the option and call the stock away from the seller, pay the option contract price for the underlying stock, and then sell the stock for profit.

Out of or at the Money at Expiration

If the strike price of a call remains out of the money, i.e., above the price of the underlying equity, the trader may be able to sell the option contracts to recover part of the premium originally paid for the call options. However, there must be enough time and open interest (liquidity) remaining for the order to fill. If the trader holds the position through contract expiration, the trade will expire worthless. When this happens, the trader suffers a 100% loss of the premium originally paid for the call options.

In the Money by 1 Cent Prior to Expiration

If the strike price of the call is in the money by one cent prior to expiration, the trader can either exercise the option and buy the stock at the optionable strike price, or simply sell the option for any premium that may remain. But before exercising the option, the trader will calculate the difference in profit between exercising the option and selling for premium income. With ample time remaining till expiration, it can be more profitable to sell for premium than to exercise the option for a stock that is only a few cents in the money.

Many option traders are not interested in holding stock or ETFs within their brokerage accounts. When given a choice, they prefer to restrict their activity to buying and selling option contracts rather than buying and selling stocks or ETFs, which are always susceptible to price drops during market pullbacks.

Short Call (Selling a Call)

Selling a call can be bullish, neutral, or bearish, depending on the trader's goal and the selected option strategy. If the trader believes the price of the underlying is moving sideways or dropping, the trader may sell out of the money calls to collect premium income. Without owning the underlying stock, this would be an uncovered call. Uncovered calls require the highest level of option trading permission. And uncovered calls carry unlimited risk. Without having the proper option trading permission, attempts to transact uncovered calls are automatically rejected by the brokerage.

Selling a naked call for premium is always a high–risk, low–reward strategy. (The only income is from the premium collected.) Sellers of out of the money calls select strike prices having low probabilities of becoming in the money throughout the duration of the option contract.

A trader is bullish when selling covered calls in which the trader owns shares of stock equivalent to those represented by the number of option contracts sold. The trader's goal is to collect premium with the possibility of having the stock called away for a nice profit compared to the original cost of the stock (what the trader paid when the stock was originally purchased). However, the trader might simply be interested in premium income, without intending to sell the stock. In fact, the trader can sell covered calls using the same stock multiple times without ever being called away. This requires the seller's call strike price to remain out of the money through expiration. Both of these situations are described in the following two paragraphs.

Out of or at the Money at Expiration

When a short call contract remains out of the money through contract expiration, it expires worthless. The option contract becomes null and void and can no longer be exercised.

In the Money by 1 Cent Prior to or at Expiration

If a short call becomes in the money by one cent or more prior to contract expiration, the buyer of the call has the right to exercise the option. When exercised, the buyer calls the stock away from the seller and pays the seller for the stock at the contracted strike price. For example, if the short call's strike price is $52 and the price rallies to $54, the buyer can exercise the option contract. The buyer must pay $52 per share for the stock; the seller must deliver stock worth $54 per share to the buyer.

If the stock was originally purchased for $45 per share, the seller realizes a gain in *intrinsic* value of $7 per share. The intrinsic value is based on the difference in the price of the stock when bought and when sold ($52 − $45 = $7). The seller also profits from the *extrinsic* (premium) value originally collected when the call was sold. Recall how the terms intrinsic and extrinsic are used by option traders. They were introduced earlier and are used again later in this chapter.

Long Put (Buying a Put)

Buying one or more put contracts is typically a bearish transaction. Buying a long put at a strike price close to or even in the money may be done in anticipation of a price drop. As discussed earlier, a long put becomes deeper in the money as the price of the underlying equity drops. The premium value of the in the money put increases. Given enough time, a large price drop can easily double or triple the premium originally paid by the buyer.

Buying puts as hedges was explained earlier. Using a long put as a hedging strategy can lock in accumulated profits. Even better, combining long puts with short OTM calls creates an *equity collar*, a popular hedging strategy that is treated in detail in chapter 14. Using a put as a hedge is best when the put's strike price is above the price originally paid for the subject stock. If the price of the under-lying drops below the price of the long put, the trader can exercise the option and put the stock to the seller on the other side of the trade. When exercised, the seller of the put contract is required to pay the buyer for the stock at the put option's strike price.

Out of or at the Money at Expiration

A long put expires worthless if it remains out of the-money through contract expiration. Remaining out of the money means the price of the underlying never dropped to the strike price of the put.

The trader may attempt to sell the put option to collect what premium may remain in the position. If sold, the trader recovers part of the original premium paid. As before, this requires enough remaining time and liquidity for the trade to fill. If the sell order remains unfilled, the option contract will expire worthless. The trader loses 100% of the premium originally paid.

In the Money by 1 Cent Prior to or at Expiration

A put becomes in the money when the price of the underlying drops below the option contract's strike price by 1 cent or more. The buyer has the right to exercise the option contract and put the stock to the seller. The seller must pay for the stock at the option's strike price.

Short Put (Selling a Put)

Many traders sell out of the money puts for premium income, where an out of the money put is several strike prices below the current at the money price of the underlying. These traders sim-ply want to collect premium. They have no interest in owning the underlying equity. It's common to choose strike prices that are far out of the-money, and that expire within a few weeks. Selling far out of the money and limiting the amount of time remaining in an option contract is a tradeoff. Choosing option contracts that expire within a matter of days to a few weeks with far out of the money strike prices reduces premium. Many traders are willing to forfeit higher premium income to reduce the risk of being exercised. Their highest priority is to remain far enough out of the money to either expire worthless or to close the trade for a 30% to 70% profit.

There are also traders who sell put options hoping to own the optionable stock. They see the premium as a "discount coupon" which offsets the full price of the stock. Here's an example:

- Stock XYZ pays a quarterly dividend of $0.50/share and is presently trading at $40.
- Gail likes XYZ's dividends; she sells a $39 put option for a $2.00/share premium.
- The price of XYZ momentarily falls to $39.
- The XYZ option buyer exercises the option and puts 100 shares of XYZ to Gail.
- Gail pays the option price of $39 per share for the XYZ stock.
- Subtracting the $2.00 in premium, Gail's net cost is $37/share for stock worth $39/share.
- Gail's is satisfied with the outcome. She owns 100 shares of XYZ which has an annual dividend yield of $2.00/share.

Out of or at the money at Expiration

If the short put remains out of the money (below the price of the underlying) through contract expiration, the contract expires worthless. The premium collected is profit. This is the most common goal for traders who make a steady income by regularly selling out of the money put options for premium.

In the money by 1 Cent at Expiration

As described in the short put (Selling a Put) paragraph, if the price of a stock or ETF falls below the strike price of the option contract by 1 cent or more, the option buyer can exercise the option and put the stock to the seller. The seller must pay the buyer for the number of shares represented by the option contract at the governing option price.

Following is an option contract *truth table*. The information within this table was summarized in the previous chapter. Although similar, this table examines trader obligations from both a buyer and seller perspective. It summarizes the obligations of option buyers and sellers relative to being out of the money or in the money. Bear in mind the applicable option contract style, i.e., American style or European style.

American–Style Option Contract Obligations

Option Type	*Premium*	*Expires Out of the money*	*★In the money*
Buy a Call (Long Call)	Buyer pays	Expires worthless Seller Profits	Buyer exercises option and calls shares away from Seller; pays Seller at the established strike price.
Sell a Call (Short Call)	Seller receives	Expires worthless Seller Profits	Buyer exercises option and calls shares away from Seller; pays Seller at the established strike price.
Buy a Put (Long Put)	Buyer pays	Expires worthless Seller Profits	Buyer exercises option and puts shares to Seller; Seller pays Buyer at the established strike price.
Sell a Put (Short Put)	Seller receives	Expires worthless Seller Profits	Buyer exercises option and puts shares to Seller. Seller pays Buyer at the established strike price.

★European-style options cannot be exercised prior to contract expiration. European-style options are settled immediately following contract expiration when the option's strike price expires in the money.

Bid (sell), Ask (buy), Mark, and Last (as related to options)

As you should recall, clicking in the Bid cell initiates a sell order and clicking in the Ask cell initiates a buy order at the selected strike price. The Mark represents the *market price* of the option, and is midway between the Bid and Ask values. You can think of the Mark value as the negotiated price between a seller and a buyer. Many traders "bump" the price that's given on the order bar in hopes of receiving better premium or, in the case of buyers, in hopes of paying a bit less. Orders with adjusted premiums often remain unfilled. Traders often watch these adjusted trades work for a period of time. If they remain unfilled and the trader is willing to settle for the current market price, the premium may be adjusted and resent in hopes of being filled.

Most options trade in 5-cent increments. However, there are also many *penny increment options*. These trade in one-cent increments. Instead of trading in 35 to 40 to 45 cent increments, these may trade in 36 to 37 to 38 cent increments. Traders often attempt to pick up or save a few cents by making minor adjustments to the premium price prior to entering their orders. If the trading activity is brisk, the trade is more likely to fill from normal price movement.

Short (Selling *Premium*)

You've already read about how traders collect premium income by selling puts and calls. Recall how option sellers select option contracts that expire within several days to a few weeks' time. And they choose strike prices that are safely out of the money. The farther out of the money the safer they become. Of course as the strike prices move farther away from the at the money strike price, premiums suffer substantial reductions in value. Check the rapid declines in the Ask prices of the calls and the puts of figure 11–1 as they move farther out of the money.

Another common strategy is to simultaneously sell out of the money calls and out of the money puts having the same expiration dates. This is strategy is called a *strangle*. Traders that use this strategy collect premium from both the call and the put legs of the strangle. The trader's bias should be neutral — that is, the price of the underlying should remain somewhere between the two strike prices throughout the duration of the option contract. The trader's goal is to pocket the premiums and for both of the option contract positions to expire out of the money and worthless. This strategy, among many others, is described in detail in chapter 14 where you are guided through numerous option trading activities.

Because selling options carries more risk than buying options, knowing how to determine the statistical probabilities that correspond to risk is important. Risk measurement metrics are introduced in the Statistical Probability Measures later in this chapter.

Long (Buying *Premium*)

When buying one or more option contracts, regardless of the strike price or whether a put or a call, the total amount of money at risk is the premium paid by the buyer. Recall how time is the buyer's friend and the seller's enemy. Then think about the effect of time decay — the closer to contract expiration, the lower the premium. Knowing that premium values depreciate as option contracts approach expiration encourages option sellers to sell, let the premium drop in value, and then buy back at a much lower price than originally paid.

Option buyers look for brief periods of low volatility when premiums are at their lowest levels. Once bought, option buyers are rewarded by an upturn in volatility, which increases premium values. And, as you already know, option buyers want plenty of time for their long trades to work in their favor. If a trader buys a call and the price of the underlying rallies, the call becomes deeper in the money. If plenty of time remains until expiration, the value of the premium may double or even triple. The buyer can then sell the options for a profit.

In the case of a long put, as the price of the underlying drops, the option premium appreciates in value. Just as in the long call, the buyer can sell the long put option for profit. Again, the put buyers want plenty of time for the market price underlying stock to drop in their favor.

In both long calls and puts, option contracts are bought in anticipation of selling the options for profit. Although options can be exercised, many option traders simply want to buy and sell the options. Many have no interest in ponying up the cash required to buy the underlying stock. Rather, high volume call and put buyers are more interested in exploiting the financial leverage offered by buying options low and then selling them high. And they repeat this process as often as possible.

Statistical Probability Measures (ITM, OTM, Touching)

Several measurement tools exist on full-featured option chains. Just like the many available chart studies, option traders prefer some measures over others. Here, some common statistical probability measures are discussed. These should be used in concert with other available data points including the effect of price change on premium values (*Delta*), open interest, time decay (*Theta*), and volatility (*Vega*). These Greek values are both useful and quite meaningful to option traders. Therefore, they are displayable within columns on most option chains. The "Greeks" are briefly discussed at the end of this chapter, and examined more closely in chapter 12.

The puts portion of an option chain is shown in figure 11–6. Among other option measurement data, figure 11–6 includes the three probability measures, i.e., Probability ITM (in the money), Probability OTM (out of the money), Probability Touching ("touching" the money).

Notice the Probability columns. The Probability ITM (in the money) is the inverse of Probability OTM (out of the money). A close examination of these at the 100 strike price row shows the Prob. ITM at 5.05% and the Prob. OTM is at 94.95%. Putting both of these on an option chain at the same time is redundant. While looking at these, notice how the Delta values are quite close to the Prob. ITM values. Moving across the 100 strike row a Delta value of .05 is displayed — nearly identical to the Prob. ITM value of 5.05%. As previously mentioned, Delta values were once universally used to measure a strike price's probability of becoming in the money.

Some trading platforms permit values to be displayed in as many as five decimal places. Although two to three decimal places are usually sufficient, having more gives traders a closer match to the Prob. ITM value. This can be particularly useful when trading options on e-mini futures (see chapter 15).

Figure 11–6. Probability ITM, OTM, and Touching

Strike	Bid X	Ask X	Mark	Delta	Open Int	Volume	Prob ITM	Prob OTM	Prob Touch 27.57% (±4.501)
90	.04 C	.05 W	.045	-.01	558	120	1.42%	98.56%	2.79%
91	.05 N	.06 H	.055	-.01	0	168	1.71%	98.29%	3.35%
92	.05 X	.07 X	.060	-.01	0	45	1.88%	98.12%	3.69%
93	.06 X	.08 M	.070	-.02	0	13	2.18%	97.82%	4.27%
94	.07 C	.09 X	.080	-.02	0	20	2.49%	97.51%	4.88%
95	.08 C	.10 W	.090	-.02	2,485	690	2.80%	97.20%	5.50%
96	.09 X	.11 A	.100	-.03	546	306	3.14%	96.86%	6.16%
97	.10 X	.12 N	.110	-.03	188	150	3.49%	96.51%	6.85%
98	.12 I	.13 Q	.125	-.03	567	205	3.98%	96.02%	7.82%
98.5	.13 H	.14 H	.135	-.04	266	111	4.29%	95.71%	8.43%
99	.13 X	.15 X	.140	-.04	990	7	4.50%	95.50%	8.84%
99.5	.14 X	.16 X	.150	-.04	209	22	4.83%	95.17%	9.48%
100	.15 C	.16 N	.155	-.04	4,742	54	5.05%	94.95%	9.92%
101	.17 C	.18 Q	.175	-.05	1,044	1	5.76%	94.24%	11.31%
102	.19 A	.21 M	.200	-.06	327	24	6.63%	93.37%	13.03%
103	.22 I	.23 Z	.225	-.07	577	54	7.57%	92.43%	14.87%
104	.25 C	.27 M	.260	-.08	606	83	8.82%	91.18%	17.32%
105	.30 Q	.31 Q	.305	-.09	1,143	2,516	10.36%	89.62%	20.39%
106	.35 I	.37 A	.360	-.11	874	416	12.29%	87.71%	24.13%
107	.42 C	.44 C	.430	-.13	1,878	406	14.66%	85.34%	28.79%
108	.52 N	.54 M	.530	-.16	1,325	3,436	17.81%	82.19%	34.95%
109	.65 M	.67 M	.660	-.20	1,633	395	21.72%	78.28%	42.60%
110	.82 M	.84 Z	.830	-.25	3,283	1,223	26.54%	73.46%	52.00%
111	1.05 Q	1.07 H	1.060	-.31	2,195	1,127	32.44%	67.56%	63.48%
112	1.34 Q	1.36 Q	1.360	-.38	2,114	945	39.26%	60.74%	76.71%
113	1.70 Q	1.71 Q	1.705	-.45	1,932	1,978	46.91%	53.09%	91.48%
114	2.14 Q	2.16 Z	2.150	-.53	1,288	457	55.21%	44.79%	91.92%
115	2.67 Z	2.69 Q	2.680	-.62	3,433	606	63.79%	36.21%	74.12%
116	3.25 X	3.35 X	3.300	-.71	1,674	242	72.23%	27.77%	56.70%
117	4.00 H	4.05 A	4.025	-.79	1,509	79	79.76%	20.24%	41.24%
118	4.75 X	4.85 X	4.800	-.86	1,213	81	86.82%	13.18%	26.80%
119	5.55 X	5.80 X	5.675	-.91	710	19	91.76%	8.24%	16.73%
120	6.45 X	6.70 X	6.575	-.96	2,648	38	96.30%	3.70%	7.50%
121	7.40 X	7.65 X	7.525	-.99	1,433	30	99.35%	0.65%	1.32%
122	8.40 X	8.65 X	8.525	-.99	532	14	99.41%	0.59%	1.19%
123	9.35 X	9.60 I	9.475	-1.00	624	0	100.00%	0.00%	0.00%
124	10.35 X	10.60 X	10.475	-1.00	286	5	100.00%	0.00%	0.00%
125	11.30 M	11.60 A	11.450	-1.00	383	10	100.00%	0.00%	0.00%
126	12.30 A	12.60 W	12.450	-1.00	32	0	100.00%	0.00%	0.00%
127	13.30 A	13.60 W	13.450	-1.00	4	0	100.00%	0.00%	0.00%
128	14.30 A	14.60 A	14.450	-1.00	0	0	100.00%	0.00%	0.00%
129	15.35 X	15.60 M	15.475	-1.00	0	0	100.00%	0.00%	0.00%

AAPL   APPLE INC COM   113.54   +1.29 +1.37%   B 113.55 113.56   ETB   NASDAQ   ±0.655   Company Profile

PUTS

For illustration purposes only.

Now notice the Prob.Touch column. Unlike thinkorswim®, most trading platforms are limited to the use of Delta or the Probability ITM/OTM values. In any case, the Probability of Touching value is more conservative than the Probability ITM. Again, looking at the 100 strike row, the Probability of Touching is 9.92% compared to a Probability ITM value of 5.05%. The difference is fairly straightforward. Probability of Touching indicates the probability of ever touching the at the money price throughout the life of the contract. In other words, it should remain out of the money for the full duration of the contract. This is particularly important for American-style option contracts, which apply to most stock, ETF, and small index options. Because options can be exercised when the underlying is in the money by even one penny, these Probability values are in frequent use. The ITM and OTM values indicate where the strike price is calculated to be at contract expiration. Unlike Probability of Touching, the math does not predict the strike price will never touch the ATM price of the option through expiration. It implies the underlying will unlikely be ITM at contract expiration.

This encourages American-style option traders to either use Probability Touching or select a lower Probability ITM value to remain safe. Although European-style option traders may feel secure in their use of the Probability ITM or OTM values, it would seem even safer to use the Probability of Touching values.

Open Interest and Volume

Figure 11–6 also includes the Open Interest and Volume columns. The Open Interest values tell traders the number of option contracts that currently exist for every call and put strike price. This is important to option traders, as it shows the current interest in the underlying security, and even lists open interest at each strike price. A cluster of strike prices that display Open Interest values of several hundred per strike price indicates a brisk level of trading activity.

This relates directly to liquidity. A fairly priced option order fills quickly when the corresponding open interest is high.

Trading volume is another value that can be examined. But volume is reset daily at market open. Therefore, a low volume in the early hours of trading may not be a reason to avoid the trade. The volume may become hundreds of thousands or even millions by midday. So you may use open interest to measure option liquidity instead.

Standard Deviations

The use of standard deviations, often represented by the symbol sigma (σ), was briefly mentioned as a value that many option traders use to manage risk. The standard deviation value of the current option chain is usually displayed on every option chain. It tells traders the mathematical probability for how much the price of the underlying will move for the duration of the option contract. In other words, it computes the number of price points using the time remaining until contract expiration. Many use one sigma for safety, while others double the standard deviation value and consider it statistically out of reach to an unwanted rally or drop in the price of the underlying equity. Of course this is a projection, and never an ironclad guaranty.

Although this is not a math book, it may be useful to know how standard deviations are derived. The computation requires several steps, summarized here.

1. Find the average (or *mean*) of a series of numbers (these are the prices of all trades over a specified period of time).
2. For each number in the series, subtract the mean and square the result.
3. Another mean value is calculated from the squared differences of each number in the series.
4. The above mean uses the constant N.
5. Finally the square root of N-1 produces the standard deviation of the original series of values.

Here's a simple derivation. The stock XYZ has been trading at the following prices:

$5 + 6 + 4 + 5 + 6 + 5 + 4 + 5 = 40$

$40/8 = 5$ (This is the mean value of the above series of eight numbers)

Now subtract the mean from each of the eight values and square the result. (Recall from junior high math that multiplying two negative values yields a positive value, i.e., $-2 \times -2 = 4$.)

$5 - 5 = 0^2 = 0 \quad 6 - 5 = 1^2 = 1 \quad 4 - 5 = -1^2 = 1 \quad 5 - 5 = 0^2 = 0$

$6 - 5 = 1^2 = 1 \quad 5 - 5 = 0^2 = 0 \quad 4 - 5 = -1^2 = 1 \quad 5 - 5 = 0^2 = 1$

Next, add the results of the above 8 computations and divide by 8

$0 + 1 + 1 + 0 + 1 + 0 + 1 + 1 = 5/8 = 0.625$

Use the preceding result of 0.625, called N, and subtract 1. $N-1 = 0.625 - 1 = .3750$.

Finally, derive the standard deviation of the original series of eight numbers with the square root of $N-1$. The square root of 0.3750 is 0.61237, the standard deviation of the original series of eight numbers. Isn't it nice to have computer software make these computations for you?

Introduction to the "Greeks"

Because this chapter describes option chains, it would be incomplete without a brief introduction to the use of those values referred to as the *Greeks*. Values that control the outlook for option premium are displayed in the columns of each option chain. These columns have Greek letter names, like Delta and Theta to name just two. The Greek values were originally used to designate mathematical constants and variables used within the Black-Scholes formula that was developed

to compute option premium values based on such variables as volatility, time remaining till expiration, current interest rates, and so on.

The data within these Greek-labeled columns are quite meaningful to experienced option traders. However, just the weirdness of
Greek letters is a turn-off for many fledgling option traders. They
simply wring their hands and go back to buying and selling stocks
and ETFs. Or they ignore the Greek values at their peril.

Don't be alarmed by the Greek letters, or the data within columns beneath them. The Greeks were mentioned in chapter 2 and
then listed in chapter 10. Here we expand a bit on the most common Greeks: Delta, Theta, and Vega. Then in chapter 12 the Greeks
Rho and Gamma are described and more information on Delta,
Theta, and Vega is also presented.

Before checking the effect of an individual Greek on option
premium values, the Greek values, themselves, are influenced by the
existing market sentiment. For example, the volatility Greek, Vega,
is the most influential of the Greek constants. It measures current
volatility, which is based on current market sentiment. A trading
frenzy can cause a substantial swing in the value of Vega. This results
in a change in option premium values. As a direct result of increased
volatility, which is reflected in the value of Vega, the values of both
Theta and Delta are influenced.

Delta

Delta measures a change in premium value relative to a $1.00 change
in the underlying stock. A Delta value that is close to .5 is usually
found adjacent to the at the money strike price. Notice Delta values
of −.45 and −.53 at the 113 and 114 strike prices of figure 11–6. This
indicates that a $1.00 increase in the underlying AAPL stock will
reduce the put premium of the 113 strike price from the current
$1.705 to $1.255. A Delta value of 0.25 would change the premium
price, either up or down depending whether a put or a call and the
trajectory of the underlying price, by $0.25.

Theta

Theta tells an option trader how much premium value is exiting with each passing day. Some option buyers refer to Theta as the "silent killer," as it is reducing the daily value of option premium. Option sellers are big fans of Theta. They like to "sell high and buy low" — contrary to the ever popular "buy low and sell high" statement we've always heard. Option sellers let Theta go to work on the premiums they sell. When they realize a profit north of 30% to 70%, they frequently enter a *buy to close* order to eliminate future risk. Then the traders sell again in hopes that Theta will work in their favor again.

The decay in premium is called *extrinsic* value. Regardless of what it's called, the Theta value describes the amount of money, in dollars and cents, that is being lost for each share of stock held in their option contracts. When holding one 100-share option contract, a Theta value of .04 suggests a loss of 4 cents per share per day, or a drop of $4.00 per day per contract. As the expiration date draws near, Theta may rise to .50. This is a $50 per 100-share contract reduction in premium value.

Vega

Vega is a measure of current implied volatility. Recall that implied volatility is compared to historical volatility. It compares current buying and selling activity to historical buying and selling activity. The Vega value of an option reflects a change in the value of the option premium for each 1% change in underlying volatility. Hence, premiums are typically higher when volatility is higher. An increase in volatility drives premium prices up. It follows that a decrease in volatility is reflected by a drop in premium values. Check this example:

- The Mark (premium) of a $50 call is currently at $2.00.
- The Vega of the $50 strike is 0.15 with a current volatility of 25%.

- The volatility increases from 25% to 26% — a 1% increase.
- The option premium rises to $2.15 from $2.00 + 0.15 = $2.15.
- If the volatility dropped by 2% from 25% to 23%, the option premium would also drop to $1.70 from $2 − (2 × 0.15) = $1.70.

Vega also loses extrinsic value with each passing day. Longer times to expiration result in substantially higher Vega values. Option contracts having six months to a year remaining until expiration also have higher Theta values. In fact, both Theta and Vega control most of the premium values.

Once you understand how Theta and Vega work, you will be able to see how each of these metrics influence premium values. You can evaluate volatility (Vega) and time (Theta) values in concert with open interest, probability values, and your chart studies. Then you can "trade what you see," or reject a trade and continue scanning until you find a trade setup that complies with your rules (See chapter 13 for rules.)

What did you learn in chapter 11?

1. Weekly options expire on Fridays of _____ _____ except for holidays.
2. Monthly and quarterly option contracts expire on the _____ _____ of the month.
3. Debit spreads require a trader to pay _____ upon entry.
4. Long-term options cost _____ than short-term options.
5. Buying a call in anticipation of a price rally is a _____ strategy.
6. When a call becomes ITM, the call buyer can either _____ or _____ the call contract.
7. Many option traders are not interested in holding _____ or _____ (abbrev.).
8. Stocks are more susceptible to _____ _____ in a bear market.
9. When selling a call, the trader's goal is to collect premium without being _____.
10. Selling a naked call requires the highest _____ _____ _____.
11. A short call expires _____ if it remains OTM through contract expiration.
12. Buying one or more put options is a _____ strategy.
13. Many traders sell OTM puts for _____ _____.
14. When buying premium, the total amount put at risk is the price _____.
15. Three probability values include ITM, OTM, and _____.
16. Probability values are especially important to _____ _____.
17. The column headed by Vega represents the effect of _____ on premium value.
18. The little-used Greek letter Rho represents rate of _____.

19. The effect of a $1.00 change on option premium is represented by _____.

20. The Greek letter Gamma controls the rate of change of _____.

12 MORE ABOUT THE GREEKS

●●●●●●●

Why Greek?

Mathematical equations frequently represent constant and variable values with Greek letters. The letter Σ is commonly used for summation, Δ is used for difference, and π is used for 3.14 (or pi), and so on. The Black-Scholes formula used Greek symbols Delta (difference), Theta (time value), Rho (rate of interest), and Gamma (the rate of change of Delta). They also used the term *Vega* as a measure of volatility. Although Vega isn't a Greek letter, you must admit it's a reasonable choice for "volatility." This chapter provides additional information about the Greeks. As you already know, Greek letters are used within mathematical formulas to derive the values of option premiums.

The previous chapter introduced the purpose of the most frequently used Greek values — Delta, Theta, and Vega. In addition to taking another look at these three most popular Greeks, this chapter also examines the more obscure Gamma and Rho. But obscurity may underestimate the importance of these Greeks, as they are both quite impactful on the value of option premiums.

Delta (Difference) and Gamma
(Delta's Rate of Change)

Delta measures the directional risk present in every option strategy. As you learned in chapter 11, Delta values at strike prices closest to the price of the underlying (the at the money strike price) is typically close to 0.5. The value of Gamma is the highest at this strike price. Figure 12–1 shows the Delta and Gamma values of near the money AAPL call options with 10 days remaining until expiration.

Figure 12–1. Delta-Gamma Values — Ten Days Remaining till Expiration

	Mark	Delta	Gamma	Theta	Vega	Open.Int	Prob.To	Bid X	Ask X	Strike
> NOV 15	(3) 100									
∨ NOV4 15	(10) 100 (Weeklys)									
	4.850	.80	.05	-.06	.06	1,507	42.82%	4.80 X	4.90 A	110
	4.000	.75	.06	-.07	.06	381	52.30%	3.95 C	4.05 X	111
	3.225	.69	.07	-.07	.07	668	64.60%	3.20 C	3.25 X	112
	2.515	.61	.08	-.08	.08	1,913	79.02%	2.50 M	2.53 X	113
	1.880	.53	.09	-.08	.08	1,673	95.33%	1.87 H	1.89 Z	114
	1.345	.44	.09	-.07	.08	2,709	86.00%	1.34 H	1.35 Z	115
	.910	.34	.09	-.07	.07	3,040	66.72%	.90 M	.92 M	116
	.580	.25	.08	-.06	.06	4,010	48.62%	.57 M	.59 Z	117
	.350	.17	.07	-.04	.05	4,161	33.22%	.34 X	.36 Z	118
	.205	.11	.05	-.03	.04	3,439	21.58%	.20 X	.21 Q	119
> DEC1 15	(17) 100 (Weeklys)									

For illustration purposes only.

Gamma values become higher as option contracts approach expiration. When Gamma is high, changes in the price of the underlying stock increases the effect on premium values. Therefore, high Gamma values increase a trader's risk or reward, depending on the directional bias of the corresponding option strategy in use.

Notice that Gamma is .09 near AAPL's at the money strike prices with ten days remaining until expiration. The Gamma values in two later option chains, one expiring in 17 days and the next in 24 days, are shown in figure 12–2. This illustrates the typical decline in the value of Gamma from .09 to .07 and then to .05.

Figure 12–2. Gamma Values with 10, 17, and 24 Days Remaining till Expiration

	Mark	Delta	Gamma	Strike
⌄ NOV4 15 (10) 100 (Weeklys)				
	4.700	.79	.05	110
	3.900	.73	.06	111
	3.100	.67	.08	112
	2.395	.60	.08	113
	1.780	.51	.09	114
	1.265	.42	.09	115
	.845	.32	.09	116
	.535	.24	.08	117
⌄ DEC1 15 (17) 100 (Weeklys)				
	5.200	.73	.05	110
	4.425	.69	.05	111
	3.700	.63	.06	112
	3.025	.58	.06	113
	2.430	.51	.07	114
	1.900	.44	.07	115
	1.455	.38	.07	116
	1.080	.31	.06	117
⌄ DEC2 15 (24) 100 (Weeklys)				
	5.575	.70	.04	110
	4.825	.66	.05	111
	4.150	.62	.05	112
	3.500	.57	.05	113
	2.920	.51	.05	114
	2.405	.46	.06	115
	1.940	.40	.05	116

(For illustration purposes only.)

This figure illustrates how the amount of time remaining until expiration influences the value of Gamma.

To further clarify the impact of Gamma, a Gamma value of .04 changes Delta's value by .04 for each one dollar move in AAPL. Because there are many factors that influence option pricing, calculations are interdependent. Changes in Vega and Theta also influence the value of Gamma and its Delta derivative.

Gamma values are positive and negative based on where they are found on an option chain. For example, long calls, puts, and debit spreads have positive Gamma values. Short calls, puts, and credit spreads have negative Gamma values.

An example of a Gamma-Delta-neutral option spread is provided in chapter 14. This spread uses both Delta and Gamma values to determine the number of long and short contracts required to set up a Delta-Gamma neutral spread. A third leg within this strategy involves shorting the underlying stock to achieve neutrality among the three legs of the spread. Each share of stock has a Delta value of 1.0 — a fact that is used in the Gamma-Delta-neutral spread. Strike prices of deep in the money puts can have Delta values of −1.0. Deep in the money calls can have Delta values of +1.0.

Vega (Volatility)

Of all the Greeks, Vega has the most impact on premium values. And this makes sense because it measures current volatility — a measure of trading volume. The value of Vega increases as volatility increases and declines as volatility decreases. Vega is tied directly to the current volatility of the underlying optionable security. Recall from the previous chapter how the Vega of an option is the measure of a 1% change in the volatility of the underlying security. Here's another example of how Vega influences premium values.

- At a certain strike price, the current premium value is $1.50 and Vega is .20.
- The volatility of the underlying security increases by 1%.
- The current .20 Vega is multiplied by $1.50 + 0.20 = $1.70.
- A 1% reduction in volatility would reduce the premium value from $1.50 − (1 × 0.2) = $1.30.

Recall how Vega values displayed on option chains are always positive. As mentioned above, certain spreads can produce net negative Vega values. One example is when a trader buys near-the-money option contracts with a 4.5 Vega and sells out of the money option contracts with an 8.5 Vega value. Summing the short 8.5 Vega with the long 4.5 Vega produces –4.0 Vegas.

Option traders look upon Vega as a measure of risk or reward resulting from changes in volatility. A trader's bias and the option strategy chosen are most often based on current volatility. Premiums are high when implied volatility is high — a good time to sell options for income. Options are cheaper when implied (current) volatility is unusually low — the best time to consider buying options at a discount.

Looking at several option chains quickly reveals how the value of Vega increases with the extension of time. More distant expiration dates have higher Vega values than short-term expiration dates. In addition, Vega is also highest at those strike prices closest to the money. Look at the Vega values in figure 12–3. Notice how the values of Vega increase relative to the location within each option chain and its time till expiration.

Figure 12–3. How Time and Position Influence the Values of Vega

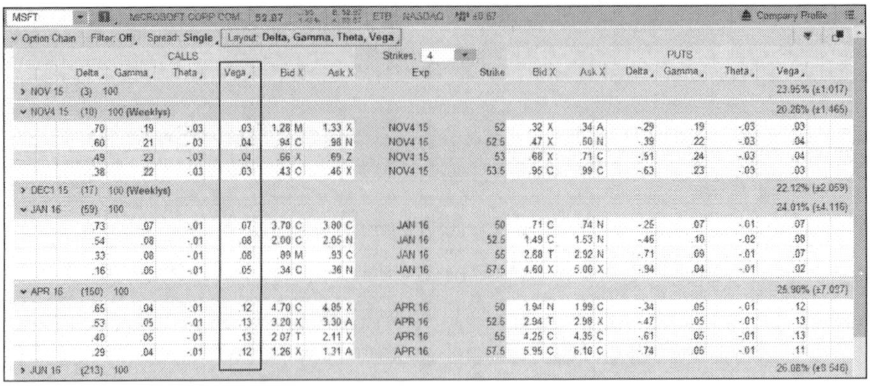

MSFT MICROSOFT CORP COM 52.87 ETB NASDAQ Company Profile

Option Chain Filter: Off, Spread: Single, Layout: Delta, Gamma, Theta, Vega

CALLS | Strikes: 4 | PUTS

	Delta	Gamma	Theta	Vega	Bid X	Ask X	Exp	Strike	Bid X	Ask X	Delta	Gamma	Theta	Vega
NOV 15 (3) 100														23.95% (±1.017)
NOV4 15 (10) 100 (Weeklys)														20.26% (±1.465)
	.70	.19	-.03	.03	1.28 M	1.33 X	NOV4 15	52	.32 X	.34 A	-.29	.19	-.03	.03
	.60	.21	-.03	.04	.94 C	.98 N	NOV4 15	52.5	.47 X	.50 N	-.39	.22	-.03	.04
	.49	.23	-.03	.04	.66 X	.69 Z	NOV4 15	53	.68 X	.71 C	-.51	.24	-.03	.04
	.38	.22	-.03	.03	.43 C	.46 X	NOV4 15	53.5	.95 C	.99 C	-.63	.23	-.03	.03
DEC1 15 (17) 100 (Weeklys)														22.12% (±2.059)
JAN 16 (59) 100														24.01% (±4.116)
	.73	.07	-.01	.07	3.70 C	3.80 C	JAN 16	50	.71 C	.74 N	-.25	.07	-.01	.07
	.54	.08	-.01	.08	2.00 C	2.05 N	JAN 16	52.5	1.49 C	1.53 N	-.46	.10	-.02	.08
	.33	.08	-.01	.08	.89 M	.93 C	JAN 16	55	2.88 T	2.92 N	-.71	.09	-.01	.07
	.16	.05	-.01	.05	.34 C	.36 N	JAN 16	57.5	4.60 X	5.00 X	-.94	.04	-.01	.02
APR 16 (150) 100														25.90% (±7.037)
	.65	.04	-.01	.12	4.70 C	4.85 X	APR 16	50	1.94 N	1.99 C	-.34	.05	-.01	.12
	.53	.05	-.01	.13	3.20 X	3.30 A	APR 16	52.5	2.94 T	2.98 X	-.47	.05	-.01	.13
	.40	.05	-.01	.13	2.07 T	2.11 X	APR 16	55	4.25 C	4.35 C	-.61	.05	-.01	.13
	.29	.04	-.01	.12	1.26 X	1.31 A	APR 16	57.5	5.95 C	6.10 C	-.74	.05	-.01	.11
JUN 16 (213) 100														26.08% (±8.546)

For illustration purposes only.

Figure 12–4. Premium Declining Over Time as Measured by Theta

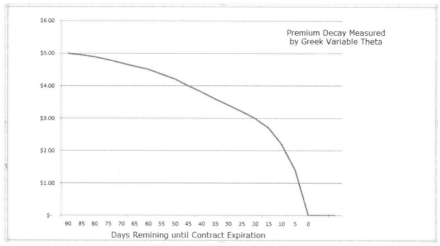

Theta (Time Value)

The Greek letter Theta on an option chain and the amount of time remaining in the underlying contract are tightly coupled. As explained in chapter 11, the value of Theta tells option traders how much premium value is exiting with the passage of each day. When Theta values are plotted on a graph with 90 days until expiration, the plot begins with an almost indistinguishable downward slope. When it reaches 30 days till expiration, the slope begins to turn downward quite rapidly. Figure 12–4 illustrates the slope of Theta from 90 days through expiration.

Notice how the value of Theta increases as the contract approaches expiration in figure 12–5. The value exiting each of the four option chains increases with the passage of time. With nine days remaining, Theta tells us how the premium value is exiting at a rate of $0.07 cents per share per day, or $7.00 per day for each 100-share contract. With 149 days remaining, Theta is only −.03 — the premium value is exiting at a rate of $3.00 per day per contract.

Figure 12–5. Theta Values at Four Different Contract Expiration Dates

		Mark	Delta	Gamma	Theta	Vega	Open.Int	Prob.To...	Bid X	Ask X
> NOV 15	(2) 100									
v NOV4 15	(9) 100 (Weeklys)									
		1.680	.55	.11	-.07	.08	4,564	90.60%	1.66 Q	1.70 X
		1.160	.44	.11	-.07	.08	5,448	87.50%	1.14 X	1.18 X
> DEC1 15	(16) 100 (Weeklys)									
v DEC2 15	(23) 100 (Weeklys)									
		2.860	.53	.06	-.05	.12	1,399	94.97%	2.82 M	2.90 C
		2.330	.47	.06	-.05	.12	1,503	93.04%	2.29 X	2.37 X
> DEC 15	(30) 100									
v DEC4 15	(36) 100 (Weeklys)									
		3.625	.53	.05	-.04	.15	819	96.18%	3.55 X	3.70 A
		3.075	.48	.05	-.04	.15	452	94.54%	3.00 X	3.15 A
> DEC5 15	(43) 100									
> JAN 16	(58) 100									
v JAN 16	(58) 10 (Mini)									
		6.000	.62	.03	-.03	.18	821	79.11%	3.50 X	8.50 X
		2.750	.41	.04	-.03	.18	313	78.52%	0 Z	5.50 Z
> FEB 16	(93) 100									
v APR 16	(149) 100									
		9.325	.57	.02	-.03	.29	21,760	92.06%	9.25 X	9.40 W
		6.775	.47	.02	-.03	.30	26,075	88.87%	6.70 X	6.85 A
> JUN 16	(212) 100									

AAPL — APPLE INC COM 117.29 +3.60 +3.17% B: 117.45 A: 117.48 ETB NASDAQ
Option Chain — Filter: Off, Spread: Single, Layout: Mark, Delta, Gamma, Theta, Vega, Open I...
CALLS

For illustration purposes only.

Theta is both useful and easy to read. Option buyers watch Theta carefully. When the daily depreciation begins to signal an unacceptable loss, a buyer will enter a sell to close order in an attempt to recover what premium may be left. Of course it's possible to wait too long to close a trade that's soured. When this happens, the only benefit may be a tax write-down.

The seller on the opposite side of the same contract appreciates the high Thetas as the contract approaches expiration. This gives the seller several choices:

1. Let the contract expire worthless and keep the original premium.
2. Buy to close by paying substantially less premium than originally received.

3. Wait a little longer for more premium to exit. Pay even less for increased profit.
4. Roll the position to a later expiration date for additional premium if the strike price is still far enough out of the money with an acceptable premium value.

Extrinsic (Time) Value

<u>Review</u>: Extrinsic (time) value is the reduction of premium value as an option contract draws closer to the contract expiration date. Buyers pay premium to sellers. As time passes option premiums decrease. Similarly, an option seller's goal is to collect premium for income. If the contract remains out of the money until contract expiration, the contract expires worthless. The option contract value at expiration is zero. The premium income retained by the seller is extrinsic value. If a buyer still holds the same option at expiration, the extrinsic value is zero, and worthless. Good for the seller, bad for the buyer.

Intrinsic Value

<u>Review</u>: Intrinsic value is calculated as the net difference between two strike prices, which usually involves the price of the underlying stock or ETF. A call option buyer may lose extrinsic (exiting premium) value resulting from the daily passage of time. If the strike price of a buyer's call option becomes in the money from a rally in the market value of the underlying stock, the buyer can exercise the option and call the stock away from the seller. An example could be buying a $25 call contract for $0.75 per share — a cost of $75 per contract. The underlying stock rallies to $28. The call buyer exercises the option and calls away the $28 stock from the seller. The buyer pays the seller the agreed upon $25 option price and immediately sells the stock for $28 per share. The call buyer pockets the $3.00 intrinsic value less the $0.75 premium (the extrinsic value) originally paid. The $3.00 intrinsic value less the $0.75 extrinsic value nets the buyer a profit of $2.25 per share, less transaction fees. Good for the buyer!

Buying and Immediately Selling an In the Money Call

Extrinsic and intrinsic values are good to know, as they help us understand how options work. So why can't we just buy a call that's in the money at something like a 0.70 Delta and then exercise the option and sell the stock immediately for a quick profit? Sounds easy, but unfortunately it doesn't work. If it did, all option traders would be multimillionaires. So why won't this work? The option premium paid added to the price of the underlying stock exceeds the price of buying the stock outright. Buying the stock for $50/share, paying $5/share in option premium, and then selling the stock for $50 doesn't work. (And, of course, the call option is lost when exercised.)

To make money on a long call, the price of the underlying must rally above the combined price of the strike price (intrinsic value) and the premium paid (extrinsic value). You can look at any option chain and use your calculator to do the arithmetic — an interesting learning exercise.

Rho (Rate of Interest)

The fifth and final Greek constant is labeled *Rho*, for rate of interest. Rho is a measure of the prevailing interest rate. Many option traders never consider Rho, as interest rates have been stable for the past several years. But when interest rates are moving, which was certainly the case during the Carter administration, Rho introduced a new source of risk. When interest rates rise, call premiums rise and put premiums fall. Naturally, the opposite is true — low interest rates keep call premiums low and put premiums high.

Why is this true? The cost of money corresponds directly to interest rates. When interest rates rise, call prices rise and put prices fall. And, of course, the reverse occurs when interest rates fall. Rho is used to determine how much corresponding call and put prices change from an increase or decrease in interest rates. The value of Rho rises more quickly for in the money options. Traders are more attracted to call options when interest rates are high because of the higher premium values. This is because it may be more prudent to earn interest at high rates than to invest in puts having lower premiums. Again, the cost of money can be an important factor during periods of high interest.

Like many of the Greeks, the value of Rho is higher for long-term option contracts compared to shorter term contracts. In particular, LEAPS options that expire nine months to a year or more are sensitive to high Rho values. Figure 12–6 shows Rho values across four option chains with increasingly longer expiration dates. Notice how call Rho values are positive while put Rho values are negative. Also, notice how Rho call values are typically higher at the money, while Rho put values become more negative as the put strike prices rise in value.

Figure 12–6. Rho Values at Four Different Contract Expiration Dates

MSFT ▾ 🔲 MICROSOFT C. 53.85 +.86 +1.69% B 53.85 A 54.25 ETB NASDAQ 🔔 ±0.46 Company Profile ≡

Option Chain Filter: Off, Spread: Single, Layout: Mark, Rho

| CALLS | | | | | Strikes: 4 ▾ | | PUTS | | |
Mark	Rho	Bid X	Ask X	Exp	Strike	Bid X	Ask X	Mark	Rho
✓ NOV4 15 (9) 100 (Weeklys)									18.51% (±1.284)
1.110	.01	1.06 X	1.16 M	NOV4 15	53	.27 X	.32 N	.295	.00
.780	.01	.75 X	.81 N	NOV4 15	53.5	.43 X	.50 X	.465	-.01
.510	.01	.48 X	.54 X	NOV4 15	54	.64 X	.70 X	.670	-.01
.300	.00	.27 X	.33 C	NOV4 15	54.5	.95 N	1.06 X	1.005	-.01
＞ DEC1 15 (16) 100 (Weeklys)									20.89% (±1.91)
✓ DEC2 15 (23) 100 (Weeklys)									20.71% (±2.261)
1.525	.02	1.48 X	1.57 X	DEC2 15	53	.64 X	.76 X	.700	-.01
1.205	.02	1.16 X	1.25 X	DEC2 15	53.5	.83 X	.94 X	.885	-.02
.935	.02	.90 X	.97 M	DEC2 15	54	1.06 C	1.19 X	1.125	-.02
.720	.01	.67 X	.77 X	DEC2 15	54.5	1.34 X	1.45 X	1.395	-.02
＞ DEC 15 (30) 100									22.04% (±2.742)
✓ DEC4 15 (36) 100 (Weeklys)									20.78% (±2.828)
1.830	.03	1.75 B	1.91 X	DEC4 15	53	.91 M	.99 M	.950	-.02
1.515	.03	1.45 B	1.58 X	DEC4 15	53.5	1.10 X	1.21 X	1.155	-.03
1.230	.02	1.20 X	1.26 N	DEC4 15	54	1.33 X	1.45 X	1.390	-.03
.995	.02	.96 X	1.03 X	DEC4 15	54.5	1.60 X	1.70 X	1.650	-.03
✓ JAN 17 (429) 100									25.71% (±12.299)
7.100	.24	7.00 C	7.20 X	JAN 17	50	3.85 X	4.05 X	3.950	-.28
5.700	.23	5.60 X	5.80 X	JAN 17	52.5	4.95 X	5.15 X	5.050	-.34
4.475	.21	4.40 X	4.55 X	JAN 17	55	6.25 X	6.45 X	6.350	-.41
3.475	.19	3.40 M	3.55 X	JAN 17	57.5	7.75 X	7.95 X	7.850	-.47
＞ JAN 18 (793) 100									25.86% (±17.2)

For illustration purposes only.

What did you learn in chapter 12?

1. Greek letters are commonly used in _____ _____.

2. The Greek letters used to calculate option _____ were first used in the Black–Scholes formula.

3. An English word that fits the meaning of Delta is _____.

4. A fitting Greek letter for Rate of Interest is _____.

5. Both *Vega* and _____ begin with the letter **V**.

6. The strike price closest to the money has a Delta value close to _____.

7. Delta values _____ as call strike prices become deeper ITM.

8. Vega values are _____ ATM.

9. Delta values become smaller as call strike prices move _____ _____ (abbrev.).

10. Delta values for ITM puts are _____.

11. Put Delta values increase as strike prices move _____ _____ (abbrev.).

12. Gamma values of calls are highest when _____ (abbrev.).

13. A negative Theta value shows the daily _____ in premium value at each _____ price.

14. Gamma values are higher when an option contract _____ _____.

15. Vega is the measure of a 1% change in the volatility of the _____ _____.

16. Vega values are always _____.

17. *Extrinsic* (time) value is the exiting of _____ with the passage of each _____.

18. *Intrinsic* value is calculated as the net difference in value between two _____ _____.

19. Rho is rarely considered by some _____ _____.

20. When interest rates are high, Rho can introduce a new source of _____.

13 RULES-BASED TRADING

Trading in the Casino

Trading rules are essential. They replace emotion with rational action. And they help us apply thoroughly tested processes. Without an understanding of chart analysis, the use of studies, how implied volatility influences premiums, or the use of statistical probabilities, most novice traders who consider themselves active traders are "trading in a casino." In fact, many actually use the term "playing the market."

The previous chapters provide basic information on chart analysis, probability statistics, and a smattering of risk management. The use of this information begins to transform trading from a game of random chance to a more rational and purpose-driven activity.

This chapter provides a broad list of suggestions that support the development of your own trading rules. Before getting into the rules of dos, following are some common don'ts, all of which involve trader emotion — the most influential driving force of price movement.

Emotion

Emotion is your enemy! It defeats rational thought. It encourages you to make trades based on what you feel, hear, hope, or think rather than what you see. And as you were told, *only trade what you see*. Following are some common errors that are based on actual trader practices. Even before you read about and employ a set of trading rules, you should be sensitive to these trading taboos. Many traders who know better and who usually abide by rules have fallen victim to these practices.

Sliding Stops

Bracketed stock trades were discussed in chapters 4 and 7 and again in chapter 9. Bracketed trades are commonly used by equity traders. Buy and hold-style stock and ETF traders often use stops to preserve profits or to prevent losses from sudden price reversals. Stops have a purpose. Stops are set to trigger when things go awry. But let's get emotional and defeat the stop. We "feel" like the price will stop dropping. Perhaps it will turn and rally back within just a few cents below the established stop. So let's slide the stop down another 50 cents to a dollar.

But the price just keeps dropping. Okay. Now we're sure the price will reverse its downward trend and rally back. Let's slide the stop down by another dollar. Darn! It just keeps dropping. We can't keep doing this! We've already lost a few thousand dollars. So let it go! And we finally put the mouse down and let it happen, all the while shaking our head and talking to ourselves. We just lost several thousand dollars. That was really dopey.

Rule 1 — Never slide a stop when a trade is going against you. You already calculated an acceptable loss, so let it work and take your medicine. Otherwise, you may contract a terminal illness called *myfundsaregone*. Losing a planned amount means your rules worked.

On the other side of your trade is your profit target in the form of a limit stop. You are encouraged to slide this to achieve more profit. And if the price of the underlying rallies above your entry, slide the protective stop up to lock in profit. Now if there's a reversal, you're prepared! But for the reasons described above, never slide your protective stops to incur a major loss.

Revenge Trading

This is a practice that is probably done by men more than women. And it's more common among men because they tend to be irrationally competitive. They abandon their business rules and return to the gaming tables. I bought MSFT and it triggered my stop. I'm going to grab another chunk of MSFT and teach it a lesson by getting my money back. So watch out, MSFT, because I'm fixin' to teach you a lesson!

The trader buys two MSFT covered calls that expire in 8 days. But the price keeps dropping. He keeps the $80 in premium from the OTM short calls, but loses $400 on the stock. Brilliant!

If the trader had spent the same amount of time scanning his watch lists and charts for a good trade, he might have made a few hundred dollars. NEVER try to get your money back by trading the same symbol for revenge. Symbols are letters on paper or a screen. Symbols don't care.

Pet Symbols

There are buy-and-hold market investors who hold about a dozen symbols within their portfolios to which they have strong attachments. An example is high-yield dividend stocks. These are primarily energy-related master limited partnerships (MLPs). There are also investment counselors who write articles and sell subscriptions to lists of these high-yield energy-related dividend stocks. So many people remain heavily invested in the same time-tested MLPs for years. And until 2014, most have been "well behaved." And to their credit MLPs have returned an impressive stream of dividend income. Occasionally MLP stocks can be sold for nice profits and then replaced with more shares of cheaper MLPs stocks having even higher dividend yields. This action provides an increase in dividend income and capital gains. Many MLP investors are aware of how this action can increase the value of their portfolios as well as increasing their monthly dividend income.

But we can become comfortable with our collection of familiar symbols. The thought of taking profit by making a few adjustments puts us into unfamiliar territory. Our familiarity with what often become *pet stocks* leads us to keep the ones that have been working so well over time. Even when stocks double or triple in value, we rarely consider adding a single protective stop. We don't want to risk the loss of an old friend that's always been well behaved and that continue to yield an excellent stream of dividend income. The goal of our portfolio in terms of a steady income has been working for many years. ("If it ain't broke, don't fix it.")

Unfortunately, the absence of protective stops can create substantial vulnerability. When the energy sector saw a dramatic decline, including exploration, drilling, refining, and pipeline stocks, the MLP investor's accounts suffered devastating losses. Many accounts lost more than fifty percent in value. Although much of the dividend income continues, many of the dividend distributions were either suspended or reduced.

Some of us have learned hard lessons from a lack of diversification, the absence of protective stops, and an odd love affair with certain symbols or market sectors. Of course the symbols were familiar. And we vetted the underlying companies behind these familiar stocks. They're familiar old friends. But the price we pay for our attachment to a short list of symbols can be costly. As mentioned, there are more than 64,000 stock symbols. With more than 300 good stock symbols to choose from, diversification is not difficult. As the old saw goes, "Don't put all your eggs in one basket."

Hot Tips and Rumors

Many people who are invested in the market watch programs with market commentators like Kramer on CNBC or the Fox Business Channel's *Bulls and Bears*. They are certainly entertaining. But their "stock tips" are usually based on fundamental analysis rather than technical analysis. Buying and holding stocks from companies with excellent fundamentals is certainly not unreasonable. But it may not match market timing. If you don't look at the charts for signals, like a bear flag or a double bottom with a morning star or kicker near a historical support level, you'll probably have a good chance of experiencing a loss on your trade right out of the "chute."

We also hear stock symbols touted by friends, family members, and neighbors. It's certainly okay to check them out on the charts. And you'll be glad you did. Having read the first twelve chapters of this book, you probably know more than the person who proposed a stock or ETF symbol to you. You now have an advantage, because you can check the charts and trade what you see, rather than what you hear, or for that matter, what somebody else thinks or hopes.

Being a Pig

This is something that most active traders, if not all, experience. As traders, we want our trading business to be profitable. So we want as much profit as we can get. Often traders look at a working trade that's already made between 30% and 60% in profit. It's only natural to want a little more. After all, that's why we're in the trading business. So let's wait for 80% profit and then close the order. This is piggish thinking. Disciplined traders are happy to take a profit of 30% to 70% "off the table." But it's only natural to think you're a "winner." (There's the casino-like game, again.) So let's let it run — maybe it'll hit 90%. Then we'll close the trade. By the end of the day or week, the trade turns against us and we've lost 25%.

That 20–20 hindsight can be punishing. The lesson learned is that pigs are much more vulnerable to price reversals than those who regularly exit earlier for reasonable profits.

Trading as a Business

As a trader, whether part time or full time, you are operating a business — a "trading business." In fact, your business is similar to a retail sales enterprise that buys at wholesale prices, sells at retail prices, and pockets the difference as income. The charter of your trading business must be underpinned by trading rules. Without discipline based on tested rules, you will not know what, why, or when to trade. And you may not understand your trading results.

Establishing a set of trading rules will simplify your life. As you scan possible trade setups, you'll be able to discard those that don't fit, and focus on those that do. This illustrates how rules speed up the scanning process. They increase the efficiency of your trading activities. Then, when setups meeting your criteria are found, they will "jump off the page." It's like panning for "color." If the dirt is junk, keep moving until you find a good spot. Find the right charts, option chains, and premiums. Then find the right strategy. You can enter it in simulation and check the risk profile. If, according to your rules, the trade has a high probability for success, use it.

If your rules indicate that the premium is too weak, too close to the money for safety, or lacks substantial open interest, retreat. Resume scanning for a trade that fits within the framework of your rules.

Many traders have two or three to perhaps a half dozen favorite trading strategies. Each strategy has a different structure based on factors like price trends and chart patterns, supply and demand zones, current volatility, open interest, ATR(14) values, premium amounts, standard deviation values, and statistical probabilities. Hence, you will likely have a different set of rules for each of your trading strategies. As you become a more active option trader, you will find setups that consistently work, work most of the time, work some of the time, and never seem to work. This is good to know! Now you can separate the "wheat from the chaff" and focus on your favorite, high-probability trades.

Developing and Following Rules

It's possible to have both general rules that apply to every trade and explicit rules that may only apply to one or two specific option strategies. Here is a partial list of information and tools traders consider when starting the trading day and eventually scanning for, entering, and/or managing their working trades:

- Trading hours
- Current market sentiment based on world, national, and economic news sources, international stock indexes (FTSE, DAX, CAC, NIKKEI, HSI, etc), U.S. indexes, index and commodity futures, etc.
- Acceptable minimum and maximum prices of stocks and ETFs
- Minimum acceptable trading volume versus price
- Acceptable option premium values
- Acceptable risk based on Probabilities, Delta, Gamma, Theta, and/or Vega values
- Reward to risk ratios, expressed in dollars or percentages
- Minimum Open Interest levels on option chains
- Acceptable implied volatility percentages related to long and short option strategies
- Allowable days till expiration for short options and for long options
- Acceptable profit or loss used to trigger trade closures
- Acceptable trading strategies based on price levels, volatility, and/or standard deviation
- Chart studies that correspond to different trading strategies
- Chart patterns that show dominant trend and signal price reversals or consolidation
- A record of each trade using a printed form or Excel worksheet

There are additional considerations found in fundamental analysis — the strength and financial stability of underlying companies. Fundamental analysts examine P/E ratios, market capitalizations, balance sheets, insider trading, corporate debt, quarterly and annual sales growth, etc. Some traders become so anal they "choke." But it's also possible to over simplify. In any event, most of the above entries are useful. Following are some things to consider in preparation to becoming an option trader. Many apply to all four trading venues — equities, options, futures, and forex.

Checking the News

The first thing that many traders do at the beginning of their trading day is to check the financial news. It's important to learn if there are any news events that might impact overall market sentiment. Many of the financial networks, including Fox Business, Bloomberg, and CNBC provide snapshots of the financial indexes, index futures, commodities, treasuries, different market sectors. There are also some informative Internet sites. For example, the www.cnbc.com/pre-markets/ website provides a snapshot of pre-markets including those listed in the second entry on the preceding page. Many traders also watch the streaming video on the tastytrades.com website. Not only do the tastytrades.com hosts and their guests discuss current market outlooks, they usually include some trading education and a few actual trade setups. Because the primary hosts, Tom Sosnoff and Tony Battista, are option gurus, tastytrades.com is beneficial to option traders.

It was Tom and Tony who collaborated on the development of the thinkorswim® trading platform that is now distributed free of charge to TD Ameritrade clients. It's interesting to watch Tom and Tony discuss and enter option trades. They also discuss their rationale and the supporting metrics including volatility, time, and Greek values such as Delta, Gamma, Theta, and Vega. The tastytrades.com webcast is on the air from 7 a.m. until 3 p.m. CST each weekday. Because the early morning segment begins an hour and a half before the market opens, it can be quite informative for traders across the market spectrum, i.e., options, equity, futures, and forex traders.

Trading Hours

Although the hours have been introduced, not all traders are active during the first and last trading hours of the day nor during the lunch hour "lull." There are other traders that actually like the first and last trading hours as the volatility sometimes picks up. This is particularly true during the first hour when overnight gaps may fill. Futures and commodity traders look for strong rallies below or strong drops above gaps for scalping. Recall how scalping is used extensively by day traders and futures traders, both intraday traders (in and out in the same day). Both look for and trade overnight gaps. These traders are typically in and out of a trade within several minutes to a few hours. Their goal is to take quick profits as the price gaps fill.

When the highest volatility is within the first trading hour of the day, between 9:30 and 10:30 a.m. EST, many option traders look for high opening implied volatility. This brings option premium sellers into the market. When the implied volatility is low, option buyers are looking for cheap premiums on oversold or overbought symbols.

Trade Analysis

Thorough trade analysis involves the selection of one or more symbols on a watchlist, analyzing the corresponding price charts and option chains. All three must meet your rules. Find the right trends and price levels on the chart; look at the price, volume, ATR(14), and IV% on the watch list; and check the Bid/Ask/Mark (premium), probability ITM, open interest, Theta, Delta, and Vega on the option chain. If the values fit one of your favorite trading strategies, set up and enter your trade.

Scanning for Qualified Trades (Watch Lists)

Many traders establish watch lists that are populated with symbols that meet a set of specified criteria. Following is the top portion of a NASDAQ 100 watch list arranged in alphabetical order by symbol.

Figure 13–1. A NASDAQ 100 Watch List with Default Column Headings

Symbol ▲		Last	Net Chng		Bid	Ask ✻
AAL		42.20	-.10	▥	42.11	44.35
AAPL		119.30	+.52	▥	110.20	121.50
ADBE	◉	91.81	+.05	▥	74.00	118.85
ADI	◉◎	59.42	-.35	▥	59.00	59.99
ADP	◉	87.29	+.90	▥	35.52	92.00
ADSK		60.55	-1.84	▥	59.91	60.75
AKAM		56.92	-2.29	▥	50.18	70.00
ALTR		52.72	+.03	▥	48.28	52.96
ALXN		173.59	-.89	▥	169.00	175.31
AMAT		18.18	-.02	▥	17.58	18.30
AMGN		159.91	+.42	▥	159.50	166.00
AMZN		668.45	+7.18	▥	666.01	671.00
ATVI		37.51	+.50	▥	37.41	37.98
AVGO	◉◎	126.40	+1.19	▥	126.01	129.10
BBBY		53.62	-.19	▥	49.05	57.22
BIDU		206.69	-1.11	▥	205.30	207.65
BIIB		290.16	+.72	▥	277.01	297.78
BRCM	◎	53.53	+.73	▥	53.33	53.72

Watchlist Main@thinkorswim [build 1880.13] — □ ✕

Watchlist NASDAQ 100

For illustration purposes only.

The above watch list illustration is a default public watchlist. You can also create your own personal watch list comprised of stocks that meet certain price and volume criteria. You should also customize your watch list by adding average daily volume (ADV), implied volatility, and other columns to help you find those symbols that fit within your rules, especially if they include average trading volume, ATR(14) and IV%. And you can sort on implied volatility or ADV to see the most or least active symbols. Finally, you can synchronize the symbols within your watch list with the corresponding charts and option chains to streamline the scanning process.

Chart Analysis

Once a symbol meets the price, implied volatility, and average volume criteria, the corresponding price charts are examined. You know how to do this by moving from long-term to shorter term interval charts. As you know, we always look for the price trend first. Once a consistent trend is found, zoom it to check the chart patterns. In particular, scan for levels of support and resistance and reversal and consolidation patterns. You're looking for either price turning points or breakouts. The chart patterns are reinforced by applying useful chart studies such as the MACD, Market Forecast, Bollinger bands, Keltner channel, TTM_Squeeze, or moving average crossover.

Figure 13–2 shows how four different day charts can simultaneously be displayed for scanning long watch lists of trade candidates. Each chart is a day chart that covers a 12-month period.

Figure 13–2. Simultaneously Scanning Four Day-Interval Charts

For illustration purposes only.

Figure 13–3. Zooming in on an Area of Interest

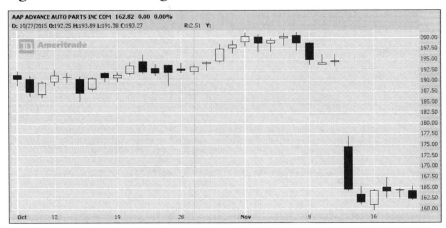

For illustration purposes only.

Scanning involves looking at price trends and chart patterns. Initially, a line chart may be used to maximize visibility. Charts that show interest can be displayed as candlestick charts and the right-most 30 to 60 days of candles enlarged to examine the patterns for signals. This process helps traders expedite their searches for possible price reversals or consolidations.

Notice the top left-hand line chart in figure 13–2. The AAP stock has been in an uptrend since mid May. It experienced a major pullback in November. It could be useful to examine the most recent news, including the latest earnings report, to understand what's happening. In any case, a closer examination of the latest candles are viewed in figure 13–3. Among the candles are a spinning top and a dragonfly — all signs of trader indecision.

Although the line chart may have enticed us to take a closer look, it would appear that AAP is presently moving sideways. Because a reasonable support level (demand zone) has not materialized, it's time to move on and resume the scanning process.

Examining Option Chains

Figure 7–2 introduced you to a trading platform configuration commonly used by option traders. It is comprised of a watch list, a chart window, and an option chain. When the watch list symbols are synchronized with charts and option chains, with the exception of breaking news, you are able to see enough to either reject the symbol or to take a closer look. Assuming the chart is signaling a price breakout, you may be ready to trade.

But price breakouts are not necessarily compatible with all option strategies, just as high implied volatility attracts option sellers while low implied volatility is favored by buyers. For example, with sufficient daily volume, there are also option strategies that are compatible with sideways price movement. An example would be to simultaneously sell short-term, out of the money puts and calls for premium income. As you should recall, this strategy is called a *strangle*. So in spite of the chart's sideways movement, the combined premiums of the put and the call may be sufficiently high and the strike prices both at safe distances from the market price of the underlying. In other words, we can consider a trade.

Here are some suggestions that can serve as a basis for rules once you begin trading option contracts. The more you trade, the more confident you will become in your setups, entries, and trade management.

Choosing an Expiration Date

The time to contract expiration has already been described several times. It's reiterated in the rules for consideration in the final paragraph of this chapter. As you should know by now, more time to contract expiration introduces risk to option sellers. The price of the option has more time to work against the seller of either puts or calls. And you also know if the price is given enough time to rally above the strike price of the seller of a call contract, the buyer has the right to call away the stock from the seller at the option price. On the put side, if the price drops below the seller's strike price, the buyer can exercise the option and put the stock to the seller. So here's a rule: NEVER sell premium using option contracts that expire in more than eight weeks (shorter is even better).

Option traders often enter calendar, diagonal, and to a lesser extent, double-diagonal spreads. These demonstrate the option trader's propensity to sell contracts that expire sooner than those they buy. The following four option contract order bars were examined in late November of 2015 with less than 45 days remaining till expiration for the short (sold) positions.

The negative (short) Qty values designate sell orders. The positive (long) Qty values designate buy orders. Notice how in all four of these trade examples, the option contracts sold expire prior to the option contracts bought. In fact, on the second order line, which is more realistic, the options sold expire six months earlier than the options bought. This greatly reduces the risk exposure of the short contracts. And, of course, it increases the likelihood of the short contracts to remain out of the money throughout the life of the contract. The long calls and puts have more time to work in the trader's favor, increasing the chance for the trader's long positions to become in the money. If and when that happens, the trader may choose to exercise the long options, or simply sell the options for profit.

Figure 13.4. Calendar and Diagonal Option Strategy Examples

Spread	Side		Qty	Symbol	Exp	Strike	Type	Link		Price		Order	
CALEND.	BUY		+10	CBOE	JAN 16	72.5	CALL			.55	LMT	LIMIT	DAY
	SELL		-10	CBOE	DEC 15	72.5	CALL			DEBIT			

Spread	Side		Qty	Symbol	Exp	Strike	Type	Link		Price		Order	
CALEND.	BUY		+10	CBOE	JUN 16	72.5	CALL			2.65	LMT	LIMIT	DAY
	SELL		-10	CBOE	DEC 15	72.5	CALL			DEBIT			

Spread	Side		Qty	Symbol	Exp	Strike	Type	Link		Price		Order	
DIAGONAL	BUY		+10	CBOE	MAR 16	80	CALL			26	LMT	LIMIT	DAY
	SELL		-10	CBOE	JAN 16	77.5	CALL			DEBIT			

Spread	Side		Qty	Symbol	Exp	Strike	Type	Link		Price		Order	
DBL DIAG	BUY		+10	CBOE	JAN 16	77.5	CALL			.75	LMT	LIMIT	DAY
	BUY		+10	CBOE	JAN 16	62.5	PUT			CREDIT			
	SELL		-10	CBOE	DEC 15	72.5	CALL						
	SELL		-10	CBOE	DEC 15	67.5	PUT						

For illustration purposes only.

Figure 13–5. Understanding What's on the Order Bar

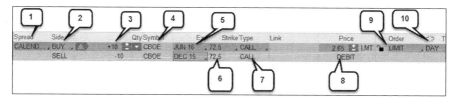

For illustration purposes only.

Now you can write down your contract duration rule: Buy ≥ 90 days, Sell ≤ 56 days. Before moving on, study the parts of the order bar. It is essential to carefully examine the information that corresponds to your orders prior to submitting them.

Legend:

1 Option Spread Name	6 The strike price of each leg
2 Buy or Sell the Option Contracts	7 The strike type, i.e., a CALL or a PUT
3 Quantity of contracts (+ = Buy, – = Sell)	8 The option price (premium); a debit or a credit
4 Symbol of underlying equity	9 Order Type (Limit, Market, Stop, etc.)
5 The expiration date of each leg	10 Time in Force (a Day or GTC order)

Current Trader Sentiment (Implied Volatility Percentage)

Option chains do not have to show every possible metric to be useful. You can add columns to your watch lists to include average trading volumes, implied volatility percentages, and the ATR(14). You can also add a flexible chart grid to view four or more time intervals at the same time as you move through your watch list scanning for trade setups. Figure 13–6 shows four charts for the same symbol in Week, Day, Hour, and 30-minute time intervals.

Figure 13–6. Viewing Four Different Charts on the Same Underlying

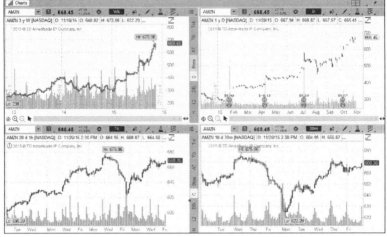

For illustration purposes only.

As you already know, the Implied Volatility Percentage is extremely important to the chosen option strategy. If you wish to sell premium, sort your watch list in descending order by IV%. If you want to buy premium while it's cheap, sort the watch list on the IV% column in ascending order.

Figure 13–7. Adding Imp Vol% and ATR(14) Columns to a Watch List

Watchlist Main@thinkorswim [build 1880.13]

Watchlist default

Symbol	Last	Net Chng	Impl Vol	Volume	ATR	Div	Div.Freq
$DJI	17823.81	+91.06	N/A	153,141,8...	182.81	N/A	--
VXN	17.03	-.91	N/A	0	1.67	N/A	--
/YM[Z5]	17805	+98.00	177.81%	103,435	218.0	N/A	--
VIX	15.47	-1.52	95.50%	0	2.14	N/A	--
VNR	5.47	-.35	86.87%	1,746,226	0.5	.1175	M
RVX	18.39	-.89	65.92%	0	1.63	N/A	--
/NQ[Z5]	4690.00	+30.00	64.64%	177,125	66.45	N/A	--
HLF	56.73	+.24	56.25%	1,082,669	2.13	N/A	--
HA	37.73	+.95	47.67%	825,012	1.31	N/A	--
TWTR	26.27	-.05	47.52%	10,835,292	1.11	N/A	--
SFL	16.96	-.12	46.13%	550,186	0.35	.44	Q

For illustration purposes only.

Open Interest

Experienced option traders always examine current open interest on their option chains. It's important because it tells them how many option contracts are currently working at each strike price. As a rule of thumb, look for a cumulative open interest value of 300 on both the put and call side of each strike price of interest. The sum of the open interest values for all calls and puts on the option chain being examined should be somewhere around 5,000. Even more open interest is better.

As you already know from previous discussion, high open interest values assure liquidity. A reasonable premium offer will be much more likely to fill. And you should be able to close your working orders for profit, or when necessary, to exit a losing position. If you see weak open interest, look elsewhere. When you find strong open interest, begin looking for an entry. Not only does strong open interest validate the trade for you, it tells you that a lot of other traders like the same trade. (Great minds work alike!)

Notice the option chain in figure 13–8. The open interest is in the tens of thousands, while the premiums are reasonably low. This might be a buying opportunity. However, there are other factors to consider. The day chart is choppy, showing trader indecision over the past 6 months. The 30-minute chart shows a $3/share pull back one trading day ago. GILD has an ATR(14) of $2.56 with a low IV% of 15.56%. These are buy signals, but they are not supported by the charts. The Market Forecast study is at 27.78. Therefore, we leave GILD and move on.

Figure 13–8. Strong Open Interest on an Options Chain

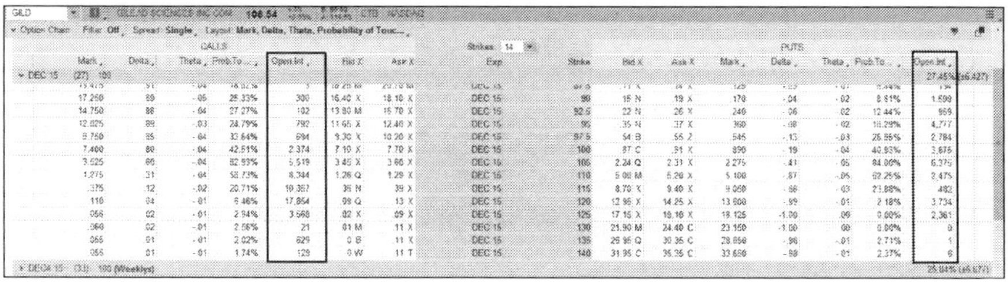
GILD 106.54 NASDAQ
Option Chain Filter: Off, Spread: Single, Layout: Mark, Delta, Theta, Probability of Touc...
Strikes: 14
DEC 15 (27) 100 — 27.45% (±6.427)

CALLS Mark	Delta	Theta	Prob.To...	Open.Int	Bid X	Ask X	Exp	Strike	PUTS Bid X	Ask X	Mark	Delta	Theta	Prob.To...	Open.Int
[illegible]	[illegible]	[illegible]	[illegible]	[illegible]	[illegible]	[illegible]	[illegible]	[illegible]	[illegible]	[illegible]	[illegible]	[illegible]	[illegible]	[illegible]	[illegible]
17.250	.89	-.05	25.33%	300	16.40 X	18.10 X	DEC 15	90	.15 N	.19 X	.170	-.04	-.02	8.61%	1,599
14.750	.88	-.04	27.27%	102	13.80 M	15.70 X	DEC 15	92.5	.22 N	.26 X	.240	-.06	-.02	12.44%	969
12.025	.88	-.03	28.79%	792	11.65 X	12.40 X	DEC 15	95	.35 N	.37 X	.360	-.08	-.02	18.29%	4,777
9.750	.85	-.04	33.64%	694	9.30 X	10.20 X	DEC 15	97.5	.54 B	.55 Z	.545	-.13	-.03	26.85%	2,784
7.400	.80	-.04	42.51%	2,374	7.10 X	7.70 X	DEC 15	100	.87 C	.91 X	.890	-.19	-.04	40.93%	3,676
3.525	.60	-.04	82.93%	5,519	3.45 X	3.60 X	DEC 15	105	2.24 Q	2.31 X	2.275	-.41	-.05	84.00%	6,375
1.275	.31	-.04	58.73%	8,344	1.26 Q	1.29 X	DEC 15	110	5.00 M	5.20 X	5.100	-.87	-.05	62.25%	2,475
.375	.12	-.02	20.71%	10,357	.36 N	.39 X	DEC 15	115	8.70 X	9.40 X	9.050	-.88	-.03	23.88%	482
.110	.04	-.01	6.46%	17,854	.09 Q	.13 X	DEC 15	120	12.95 X	14.25 X	13.600	-.99	-.01	2.18%	3,734
.056	.02	-.01	2.94%	3,568	.02 X	.09 X	DEC 15	125	17.15 X	19.10 X	18.125	-1.00	.00	0.00%	2,361
.060	.02	-.01	2.56%	21	.01 M	.11 X	DEC 15	130	21.90 M	24.40 C	23.150	-1.00	.00	0.00%	0
.055	.01	-.01	2.02%	629	0 B	.11 X	DEC 15	135	26.95 Q	30.35 C	28.650	-.98	-.01	2.71%	1
.055	.01	-.01	1.74%	129	0 W	.11 T	DEC 15	140	31.95 C	35.35 C	33.650	-.98	-.01	2.37%	6

DEC4 15 (33) 100 (Weeklys) — 25.84% (±6.677)

For illustration purposes only.

Standard Deviation and Probabilities

The option chain in figure 13–8 also includes standard deviation and the probability of touching values. If your trading platform doesn't include Probability of Touching values, use Probability ITM (*in the money*), which should be reasonably close, but slightly less conservative. A put strike price that is two standard deviations out of the money is usually reasonable when implied volatility is close to historical volatility levels. Using a probability of touching value below 30% indicates the odds of being at the money is less than 70%.

Also notice the standard deviation value of ±6.427 in the upper right-hand corner of the option chain. Standard deviation was discussed at length in chapter 11. As mentioned, some option sellers feel "safe" when one or more short entries are two standard deviations away from the at the money strike price. As you will see, these traders may be better off by going out two standard deviations, or 12.854, above or below the current price of the underlying than those who are using a 25% Probability of Touching. The option chain in figure 13.8 illustrates this point.

Notice the current strike price shown on figure 13–8 is 106.54. Subtracting two standard deviations from 106.54 is 93.686. The 95 put has a current Probability of Touching of 18.29%. This demonstrates how two standard deviations can be even safer than a Probability of Touching value in the mid 20's.

Notice how the probabilities of touching and the call premiums are only a few strike prices out of the money and drop much more rapidly than those on the put side. Statistically, the market drops faster than it rallies. You will find both risk and premiums are higher on put options than on call options.

When trading financial indexes, such as the SPX, NDX, and RUT, traders get even farther out of the money. Some use 5.0% or even lower Probability of Touching or Probability ITM values. This is especially true on the put side. Often, call premiums are not attractive enough to consider. As briefly discussed earlier, index options are traded naked and cash settled. They are among the most risky option trades undertaken by option traders. And they are carefully monitored to avoid major losses, which is always possible.

Checking the Greeks

Each of the option measures represented by Greek letters were described in chapter 12. You can add each of the five Greeks on an option chain along with the usual Bid and Ask columns. But this tends to crowd your option chains, not to mention the added space it occupies on your monitor. So you can omit Rho and even Gamma if you like. Both Theta and Delta are important, and you may wish to add Vega too. And be sure to add Mark and Open Interest as well.

The default column set found on option chains rarely display more than four to six columns. Figure 13–9 displays thinkorswim® platform's default columns.

Now consider customizing the option chain layout to include the columns shown in figure 13–10, which shows the CALLS portion of an option chain.

Figure 13–9. A Typical Option Chain with its Default Columns

	Last X	Net Chng	Bid X	Ask X	Exp	Strike	Bid X	Ask X	Last X	Net Chng
SPY		SPDR TR S&P 500 ETF TR	209.3108	+.7608 +0.35%	B: 207.75 A: 209.97	ETB				
Option Chain	Filter: Off	Spread: Single	Layout: Last X, Net Change							
	CALLS				Strikes: 14				PUTS	
DEC 15	(27) 100									
	6.82 M	+.41	6.83 M	6.95 M	DEC 15	204	1.77 X	1.82 Q	1.83 Z	-.47
	6.05 A	+.40	6.05 M	6.14 M	DEC 15	205	2.01 C	2.06 Q	2.08 Z	-.51
	5.29 Z	+.39	5.28 X	5.35 X	DEC 15	206	2.30 Z	2.33 N	2.34 M	-.65
	4.49 I	+.26	4.54 Q	4.60 M	DEC 15	207	2.58 M	2.64 X	2.64 I	-.71
	3.85 C	+.30	3.83 Q	3.89 X	DEC 15	208	2.92 M	2.99 X	3.00 Z	-.68
	3.18 B	+.21	3.17 Q	3.21 Z	DEC 15	209	3.35 Z	3.38 X	3.43 B	-.69
	2.57 I	+.15	2.56 Q	2.60 Z	DEC 15	210	3.78 Q	3.84 Q	3.80 B	-.87
	2.00 Z	+.11	2.00 Q	2.04 Z	DEC 15	211	4.27 M	4.36 M	4.32 W	-.98
	1.54 I	+.07	1.52 Z	1.55 Z	DEC 15	212	4.83 M	4.94 B	4.97 I	-.95
	1.09 Q	-.02	1.10 A	1.14 Z	DEC 15	213	5.40 M	5.62 X	5.66 I	-.89
	.78 B	-.02	.77 W	.80 Z	DEC 15	214	6.13 M	6.36 X	6.50 H	-.50
	.54 C	-.02	.52 W	.55 Z	DEC 15	215	6.89 X	7.16 X	7.34 X	-.84
	.34 B	-.05	.34 N	.35 M	DEC 15	216	7.74 M	8.03 C	8.04 I	-.81
DEC 15	(27) 10 (Mini)									

For illustration purposes only.

Figure 13–10. CALLS Portion of an Option Chain with a Modified Layout

Mark	Delta	Theta	Vega	Prob. Touch	Open Int	Bid X	Ask X	Exp
FEB 16 (10) 100								
4.225	.62	-.14	.07	80.00%	1,838	4.15 W	4.30 X	FEB 16
3.900	.60	-.14	.07	84.71%	6,372	3.80 X	4.00 X	FEB 16
3.625	.57	-.14	.07	89.69%	842	3.55 X	3.70 X	FEB 16
3.325	.54	-.14	.07	94.59%	1,355	3.25 C	3.40 W	FEB 16
3.035	.52	-.14	.07	99.60%	805	2.97 C	3.10 W	FEB 16
2.755	.49	-.14	.07	94.87%	18,252	2.69 X	2.82 E	FEB 16
2.280	.44	-.13	.07	83.75%	2,019	2.23 W	2.33 W	FEB 16
1.840	.38	-.13	.07	72.66%	2,329	1.79 X	1.89 W	FEB 16
1.475	.33	-.12	.06	62.11%	2,434	1.43 X	1.52 W	FEB 16
1.160	.28	-.11	.06	52.12%	5,224	1.13 X	1.19 Z	FEB 16

Underlying: FACEBOOK INC COM 99.54 ... ETB ±1.921

Last X 99.54 Q — Net Chng -.21 — Bid X 96.00 Q — Ask X 100.20 Q

Option Chain — Sides: Both, Spread: Single, Layout: Mark, Delta, Theta, Vega, Probability o... — Strikes: ALL

For illustration purposes only.

The column layout shown in figure 13–10 provides a substantial amount of information considered important to option traders. You may also wish to add Vega. However, if your watch list includes current Implied Volatility Percentages, you can use that value rather than adding yet another column to an already crowded option table. In either case, the current premiums are computed for you — a direct result of Vega, Theta, Delta, Gamma, and Rho — the five Greeks used for the derivation of option premium values. All option chain values are constantly being calculated and updated.

When trading an option contract, develop rules similar to the following for entry:

When buying option contracts during periods of low implied volatility:

- The underlying chart should signal a price rally from reversal or consolidation near a support level.
- Look for a bull flag, cup and handle, double bottoms, etc.
- Consider bullish strategies such as covered calls, bull call spreads, bull put spreads, collars, long straddles, long strangles, long calls, call butterflies, straps, etc.

- Use contract expiration dates ≥ 90 days for long options.
- Use call strike prices with Deltas ≥ .30; debit call spreads Deltas ≥ .45.

When selling option contracts for premium income during periods of high implied volatility:

- The underlying chart should be trending downward off of resistance; look for reversal/consolidation patterns such as a bear flag.
- Consider bearish strategies such as out of the money bear call spreads, bear put spreads, cash-covered puts, diagonal bear put spreads, short strangles, iron condors, put butterflies, etc.
- Require premiums to make trade entry worthwhile. Look for premiums ≥ $0.40 (adjust according to your own rules for minimum acceptable premium).
- Sell call contracts when the underlying price chart signals sideways or dropping price actions, and premiums are sufficiently high.
- Use contract expiration dates for your short legs that expire in less than seven weeks.
- Probability of Touching: Stocks/ETFs ≤ 25%; Financial index calls: ≤ 8.0%; Financial index puts ≤ 5.0%
- Delta: Put Deltas ≤ −0.05; Call Deltas ≤ .08
- Sell put contracts when the underlying price chart signals sideways or rallying price actions, and premiums are high (≥ $0.30).
- Delta: Put Deltas < −.15; Call Deltas ≥ 0.03

If you are confounded by some of the general rules listed above, you will see them again in several of the trades described in chapter 14. There, the rationale for choosing strategies, strike prices, and supporting option chain values is developed. The values and strategies presented in the preceding list of general guidelines will begin to make much more sense as you are stepped through actual trading examples.

Risk Management

Every active trader has stories to tell about losing trades. But by following a set of risk management rules, they minimize those losses to acceptable levels. So their rules work! They don't lose a penny more than they're willing to lose. In spite of the loss, the prudent use of an affordable trade size or exit strategy that work according to your rules are both acceptable.

Position Size

How much are you willing to lose? This is always something to consider when setting up a trade. If you buy 10 option contracts involving 1,000 shares and pay $0.50 in premium per share (plus your brokerage's transaction fees), you are putting $500 at risk. Can you afford to lose $500? If your risk tolerance is 1.0%, then your account size should be $50,000.

Look at your account and compute the amount of money you're willing to risk on each trade. If it's 1.0%, then trade accordingly. The actual amount you put at risk for each trade is displayed on the Order Confirmation dialog that's displayed just prior to submitting an order. If the amount shown exceeds your risk tolerance, reduce the number of contracts until if complies with your rules.

Stop Placement

When your option order includes a stop that's designed to either sell to close or buy to close a position that's turning against you, be sure to compute the maximum possible loss. For example, if your risk tolerance is $500 and you buy 10 option contracts for $1.00 per share in premium and pay $1,000 dollars, you can enter a good till canceled (GTC) Mark-triggered stop at or below $0.50 (recall that the Mark is the current premium value). Although Mark triggers usually work just fine, there are times when prices spike at market open. This is caused when large volumes of orders are waiting to be filled and are all triggered at the same time. This sometimes results in unwanted price transients that trigger Mark-based stop orders. For example, a $500 loss could occur even though the trade is quite safe. This is especially true for short puts.

To avoid being taken out of a perfectly good position, some traders use Delta-triggered stops. Delta is much less susceptible to instantaneous transients that occur at market open. Although Delta may not be exactly at the $0.50 Mark, you can estimate a Delta value that is close enough to keep you from losing trades that are working in your favor. This is done by looking at the Delta value closest to the desired Mark. Be sure to reevaluate the Delta-Mark relationship throughout the life of the trade and adjust the Delta-triggered stop value as necessary.

Alerts

Many of today's computer-based trading platforms take advantage of modern communications technologies including e-mail and text messaging. You can set and send e-mail and text messaging alerts to your mobile phone. These alerts notify traders when a trade or a stop order is filled. You can also send alerts when the price of a particular symbol reaches a specified value. Figure 13–11 is an example of a setup dialog that includes a variety of alerts.

Figure 13–11. An Alert Dialog

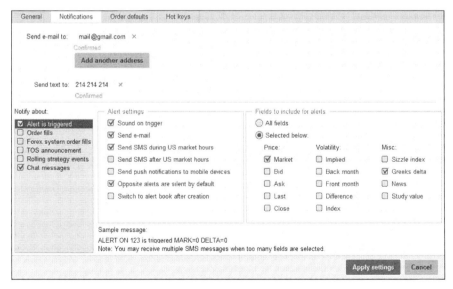

For illustration purposes only.

If you select too many alert triggers, you may receive a continuous stream of e-mails and text messages. This can be extremely annoying. Therefore, only use those alerts that signal you to take required actions. For example, set an alert when a trade is either being threatened or perhaps approaching a desired entry level. Because most traders now have mobile phones, consider downloading your brokerage's mobile app. You can use it for exits and entries. If your brokerage doesn't provide a free mobile app, find another brokerage that does. Otherwise, you may never be able to leave home without worrying about your active positions.

Buy and Hold Equity Investors

Buy and hold investors are not active traders. And they rarely know much about technical analysis. They may look at a price chart for trends and historical price levels, but having backgrounds in topics like support and resistance, price patterns, and candle shapes is rare. Buy and hold investors are concerned with fundamental analysis. They want to know all about the underlying company or series of companies that comprise a market sector held within an ETF.

They examine earnings releases, dividend yields, analyst reports, and even insider actions related to the purchase and sale of company stock.

News Releases and Analyst Reports

Both news releases about companies and upgrades or downgrades by market analysts often influence responses from investors. These responses can be measured by an increase in volatility. Good news and analyst upgrades drive prices up, while the opposite is true with bad news and downgrades. But this may only be a moment in time. Strong, cash-rich companies with good fundamentals like AAPL, Microsoft, AT&T, and Boeing usually weather short-term setbacks only to continue trending upward — these are the trends active traders are looking for.

Figure 13–12. Company Fundamentals Example (finance.yahoo.com)

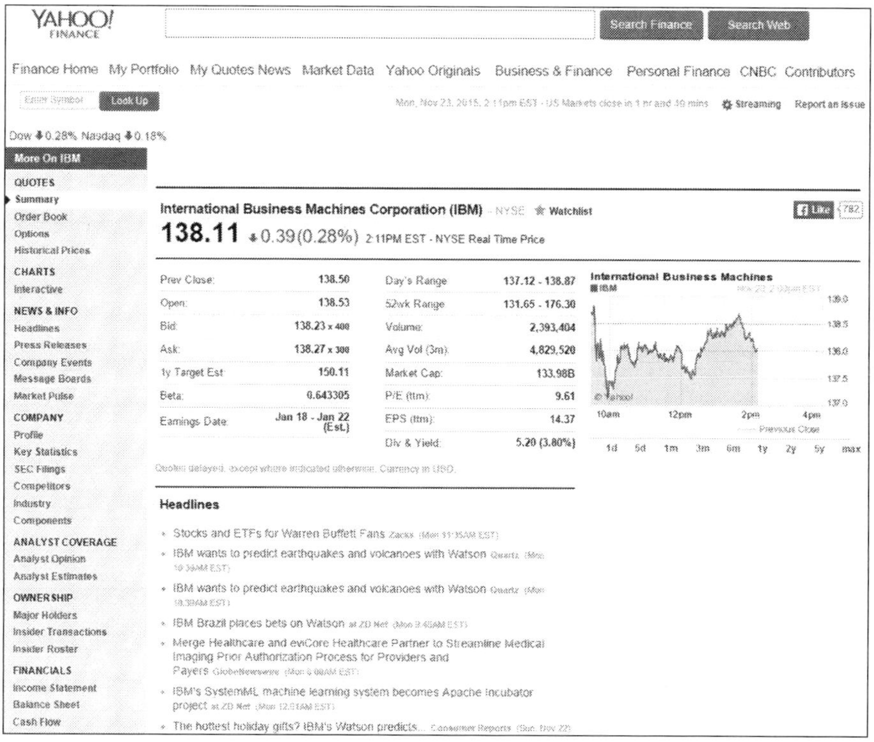

Excerpted from finance.yahoo.com

All publicly traded companies traded within the U.S. market must provide the SEC with financial statements. You can go to the SEC's website to find the public filings. Another private source of this kind of information is the finance.yahoo.com website. There, you can examine company fundamentals in order to be satisfied with the viability of a long-term investment.

Balance Sheets, Income Statements, and Cash Flow

Notice the column of links down the left-hand edge of figure 13–12. The balance sheets, income statements, and cash flow are all available for the underlying symbol — in this case, IBM. The type of financial data provided here is extremely important to buy-and-hold investors. This is especially true of Cash Flow. Many investors consider companies that "gush cash" like Apple, McDonalds, Amazon, Walmart, and Proctor and Gamble as long-term buy-and-hold candidates.

Insider Transactions

Figure 13–12 also includes a link to Insider Transactions. This shows ownership and the purchases and sales of corporate officers. When corporate officers, who are likely to have a reasonable understanding of a company's financial outlook, are buying shares of company stock, investors view this as a positive sign. In contrast, when two or more insiders are dumping shares of company stock, investors see this as a signal to either look elsewhere, or to sell shares of stock that they may currently hold.

Earnings Releases and Dividends

Earnings releases and dividend distributions often result in large price swings of a company's stock price.

Earnings Releases Earnings that exceed estimates usually result in price increases. Earnings reports that miss earnings estimates can decimate the price of the underlying stock. Knowing this, many traders check earnings release dates before they consider acquiring a stock.

But the obvious is not always true. It's interesting to note that on occasion even good earnings reports are followed by a drop in the price of the company's stock. Although this is not a common event, it happens. This is another reason to let prices settle before taking a long-term position.

Earnings reports can also affect other companies within the same market sector. If the earnings report from a company in the materials or transportation sectors is bad, it can degrade the prices of other companies within the same sectors, even when they are having good results. So in addition to evaluating individual companies, it's always prudent to evaluate the overall performance of the market sector to which they belong. There are charts, such as the Big Chart on the Investools website, that show traders which market sectors are in favor, neutral, and out of favor. The Big Chart also shows market sector trends toward or away from favorability.

A SPDRs website is available at www.sectorspdr.com/sector-spdr/tools/sector-tracker. As most traders are aware, SPDRs offers a number of sector-specific ETFs including:

SPDRs Market Sector Exchange Traded Funds

XLY — Consumer Discretionary	XLV — Health Care
XLP — Consumer Staples	XLI — Industrials
XLE — Energy	XL — Materials
XLFS — Financial Services	XLU — Utilities
XLF — Financials	

A sector overview from this site is shown in figure 13–13.

Figure 13–13. SPDRs Market Sector ETF Tracker

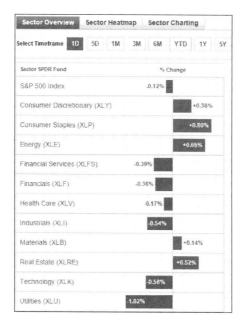

Figure 13–14. SPDRs Market Sector ETF Charting

The website also includes a Sector Heat Map and Sector Charting across different time periods. A chart of the technology sector, SPDR symbol XLK, is shown in figure 13–14.

Dividend Distributions The proximity to dividend distributions also impacts the price of a stock. For example, a company with a $40 stock price that distributes a $0.50 per share dividend typically suffers a 50 cent per share price drop. This is because the dividend distribution reduces the company's cash holdings by 50 cents per share. However, the price of stock usually recovers rapidly when the company is profitable and is able to recover its cash reserves.

Like earnings releases, many traders wait for shares to recover. Others who are willing to suffer a temporary setback in the price of the stock buy the stock in time to collect the dividend distribution. Note that dividend distributions include:

- An announcement date — when the amount and dividend distribution is announced

- An exercise date — when the funds for the dividend are set aside
- A record date — when the dividend is allocated on behalf of each shareholder
- A distribution date — when the dividend is transferred to the shareholder's account

Rules for Consideration

Following is a broad summary that provides a basis for establishing more detailed rules. Although the following rules are aimed at trading options, many are applicable to other trading venues.

The Trading Routine (Daily or Weekly)

Update and scan watch lists for trade setups.

Synchronize your watch list symbols with your charts and option chains.

Examine your watch lists, charts, and option chains.

Only enter trades that comply with your rules.

Record your trades (see record keeping at the end of this chapter.)

Monitor each of your filled trades to make sure they are performing according to plan.

Do whatever is necessary to close a losing trade and to maximize winning trades.

Review and update your rules based on trading outcomes.

Watch Lists

Stocks and ETFs with prices greater than $20 per share and less than $200

Stocks and/or options with trading volumes of one million shares per day

Optionable stocks and ETFs

Stocks with upward price trends making higher highs and higher lows

Charts — What to Look For

Definite upward or downward trend

Clear reversal or consolidation signal from a recognizable chart pattern

Confirming candles, i.e, dojis, spinning tops, morning stars, white clouds, etc.

Price near historical support level (near demand) or historical resistance level (near supply)

Once a trade candidate is found, examine the charts from long to short time intervals.

Risk Management

- Initially, never risk more than 0.5% to 1% of your account value.
- After multiple proven successes, consider but do not exceed 1.5% to 2% in risk.
- Buy long-term option contracts when volatility is low.
- Buy longer-term option contracts that expire in more than 90 days when volatility is low.
- Sell short-term option contracts that expire inside eight weeks when volatility is high.
- Never pay more premium or buy more contracts than you can afford.
- Never sell more premium or sell more contracts than you can afford to deliver if exercised.
- If buying stock, use bracketed trades, i.e., limit entry, protective stop, profit target(s).
- The largest losses in covered call option contracts are from a drop in the stock price.

When to Exit a Trade

Remember, option buyers are not obligated to exercise, while option sellers are obligated to deliver either stock (calls) or cash (puts) when exercised.

When possible, option buyers should consider exiting with a sell to close order to avoid losing more than 50% of the premium paid.

Option sellers should be willing to exit option position with 30% to 70% in profit.

Option sellers typically make more premium income by "churning." Churning is high-frequency trading by selling, closing, and selling again time after time.

Whenever possible, attempt to close or roll short option positions that are moving against you before they are exercised. (Exception: covered calls profit from the sale of the underlying stock.)

Record Keeping

Keeping trade records is useful for determining which option strategies work best and which are marginal or poor. Consider setting up an Excel worksheet or printing a form that includes most, if not all, of the following information. The form example accommodates option strategies with up to four legs such as iron condors and butterflies.

Symbol_____ Date-Time: Entry____/____/____ |___:____ Exit____/____/____ |___:____

--------------------------------CHART ANALYSIS--------------------------------

Trend(s):	Wk.	Day	Hr.	30m	Chart Pattern:	Studies:
Up	☐	☐	☐	☐	☐ Reversal	☐ IV% _____%
Slightly Up	☐	☐	☐	☐	☐ Consolidation	☐ SMA(___) ATR(14) $____.___
Neutral	☐	☐	☐	☐	☐ At Support	☐ _____
Slightly Down	☐	☐	☐	☐	☐ At Resistance	☐ _____
Down	☐	☐	☐	☐	☐ Signal:_____	☐ _____

Bias: ☐ Bullish ☐ Bearish ☐ Neutral ☐ Other:_____

Option Strategy:_____ Price of Underlying: $_____
☐ Buy Call: Strike:$_____Premium Paid: $_____ Exp. Date: _____Days:_____
Probability ITM____% | Open Int.: @ Strike:_____ Total:_____ | Theta:_____ Delta:_____

☐ Sell Call: Strike:$_____Premium Rcvd: $_____ Exp. Date: _____Days:____
Probability ITM____% | Open Int.: @ Strike:_____ Total:_____ | Theta:_____ Delta:_____

☐ Buy Put: Strike:$_____Premium Paid: $_____ Exp. Date: _____Days:_____
Probability ITM____% | Open Int.: @ Strike:_____ Total:_____ | Theta:_____ Delta:_____

☐ Sell Put: Strike:$_____Premium Rcvd: $_____ Exp. Date: _____Days:____
Probability ITM____% | Open Int.: @ Strike:_____ Total:_____ | Theta:_____ Delta:_____

Contracts:_____ Price: $_____ ☐ Debit ☐ Credit Fees:$_____ Total:$_____
Results: Exit Type(s): ☐ Sell to Close ☐ Buy to Close Cost:$_____ Fees:
Profit/Loss: $_____ | **Comments:** _____

What did you learn in chapter 13?

1. _____ can be a trader's enemy.
2. Never slide a stop when a trade is _____ _____ _____.
3. Your rules work when you lose a _____ _____.
4. Pet _____ are also among the taboos traders engage in.
5. Those hot tips you get from the so-called "gurus" on TV are _____.
6. Instead of taking the advice of friends and family, trade what you _____.
7. Being a _____ often happens when a trader is unwilling to settle for a 60% profit.
8. Trading should be run like a _____.
9. The charter of a trading business should be underpinned by a set of _____ _____.
10. Rules make your scanning and trading processes more _____.
11. Different strategies usually have different _____ _____.
12. Write ten or more topics to include in your trading rules:
    a. Trading
    b. Market
    c. Acceptable price
    d. Acceptable trading
    e. Acceptable option
    f. Acceptable _____ based on probabilities and Greek values
    g. Reward-to-_____ _____ (for bracketed entries)
    h. Minimum _____ Interest levels on option chains
    i. Acceptable IV% for each
    j. Acceptable times till _____ for long and short option trades

    k. Acceptable _____ level for exiting a position

    l. Acceptable option strategy based on price charts, IV%, _____, and bias

    m. Maintain _____ _____ with chart bias, entry, exit, and P/L data

13. The highest market volatility is usually during the _____ and _____ trading hours of the day.

14. Option traders sell _____-_____ contracts and buy _____-_____ contracts.

15. Add IV%, ATR(14) and Volume columns to your _____ _____.

16. Option traders check statistical _____ and/or _____ _____ values.

17. Position size is a major part of _____ _____.

18. _____ can send e-mail or text messages to smartphones.

19. Some trading strategies avoid _____ _____ and _____ dates while some use them.

20. Many option sellers can make more premium income by _____ rather than holding till expiration.

14 Let's Trade Options!

●●●●●●●

Finding Your Trading Style

Even if you only set aside a few days each week to trade, when you open a brokerage account and begin trading options, you will find yourself checking the market each morning. This is often done using our smartphones, because it's both easy and readily available. It's only natural to want to stay in touch. In fact, it's necessary. We must know how the market is affecting our working trades. We want to know what it's doing to the securities we're holding within our brokerage accounts. And even if it's not a trading day, we may find ourselves walking to our computer and launching our trading platform. Perhaps we only intended to make a few minor adjustments or check a few symbols out of curiosity. But before we know it, it's lunch time. If you get "sucked in," perhaps it would have been better not to look.

Really? Perhaps we should trade each and every morning for a few hours and then quit after we've done the work. And by doing this we can plan our day in advance, put on some trades, take some profits, and shut down after a few short hours. Being reactive shows a lack of planning, and can foster emotional responses and a sense of panic. It's much better to be proactive — being proactive fosters planning, and planning leads to success. So think about how you want to trade, and plan your mornings! Develop a proactive trading style. Follow a well-thought-out, rational script and stick to it. A well-planned trading session that follows your scanning, trade entry, and trade management rules will work much better than a series of knee-jerk reactions.

If you've got an 8:00 to 5:00 job, scan for and set up your trading ideas the night before. Use a pocket-sized notebook or your smart-phone's notepad to jot down your trading ideas. Include the symbols, prices, expiration dates, strike prices, premiums, probabilities, and exit dates — all based on your rules. Get to work a half-hour early and use your smartphone to enter and monitor your trades. This should take only a matter of minutes if you planned well.

When we first began trading, none of us had a trading style. Trading styles are unique to each person based on our family, work, and trading environment. We just can't know our trading style until we've traded for a while. But our styles do evolve over time. So begin. Try the morning routine, or do your setups the night before. Then manage your trading like a disciplined business, because it is.

Trading Levels and Permissions Reminder

Recall from chapter 10 that risk-based trading levels and corresponding trade strategies exist for different experience levels. If unsure, check with your brokerage to determine what strategies are available to your level. Also remember that you cannot use strategies that have unlimited risk within a qualified retirement account such as an IRA Rollover Account. This is prohibited by the U.S. Securities and Exchange Commission (SEC).

Account Size and Growth

Growing the size of your account by not losing money is "rule number 1." Rule number 2 is "Obey rule number 1." The size of your account corresponds to how many contracts you can trade. Unless confronted by a dire emergency, avoid withdrawals, transfers to a brokerage money market account, or ACH transfers to your checking account. Retain your profits for reinvestment. Follow your risk management rules. And, of course, reinvest your profits in high probability trades. Avoid questionable trades based on tips, hope, or a "gut feel."

It takes money to make money. It should be obvious that the more money you have, the more money you can make. "The rich get richer." This is especially true for rich traders. As your account grows, you'll be able to trade both bigger and safer. By trading more contracts, you can settle for lower premiums much farther out of the money to minimize your exposure to risk. Selling 10 contracts for $0.30 premium at a 15% Probability ITM is considerably better than selling 5 contracts for $0.40 premium at a 30% Probability ITM.

Risk Management (Preserve and Grow Your Capital)

Traders often see clear winning trade opportunities only to be rejected by their risk management rules. But risk management — especially for beginning traders with small accounts — is part of "rule number 1." Be sure to compute the maximum downside of each trade before entry. If you have to reduce the number of contracts or buy or sell cheaper options, do it. Otherwise, a few bad trades can put you out of the trading business.

Risk information is provided for each of the trades covered within this chapter. The risk associated with an option is determined by an option strategy's structure. The high risk strategies include the sale of calls and puts. These short option positions are always vulnerable to being exercised. If the strike price of a short option becomes in the money, the option can be exercised at the buyer's discretion. When exercised, call sellers must deliver stock; put sellers must pay for stock "put to them."

Because option buyers have a right but not an obligation to exercise an option contract, the maximum risk is the price of entry. Even when the premium paid may be in the thousands of dollars, the strategy is still dubbed "a limited risk strategy." This is because option buyers understand the maximum cost when they buy call and/or put options.

Option buyers are also said to have high reward, unlimited profit trades. This is because option buyers benefit from a rally or drop in the price of the underlying security. For example, buying a long at the money call on a stock that experiences a strong rally is considered an "unlimited reward" strategy. Similarly, buying a long put on a stock that experiences a precipitous drop is also an unlimited reward option strategy. The option premium increases in value and can be sold for a profit. Or, the option contract can be exercised for stock (calls) or cash (puts).

Using Margin: Standard Margin and Portfolio Margin

Brokerages provide account margin based on the equity in your account. An example of the use of margin was provided to show its importance. Margin is required to back new trade entries while waiting for recent trades to settle. Without margin, many active traders would not be active. They would have to wait several days for each trade to settle before another one could be placed.

Standard margin typically uses 50% of a trader's account equity as collateral. The equity must include large exchange stocks and ETFs. Penny (pink sheet) stocks do not qualify in the calculation of equity. Experienced option traders rarely buy and hold penny stocks.

Portfolio margin is granted by brokerages in accordance with SEC rules. Brokerages require minimum account balances before portfolio margin is granted. These balances typically begin at $100,000 and upward. Examples are Interactive Brokers which requires $100,000; TD Ameritrade requires a minimum balance of $125,000. Comparing the portfolio margin rules of Interactive Brokers and TD Ameritrade, Interactive Brokers grants portfolio margin based on years of option trading experience. TD Ameritrade grants portfolio margin based on experience, options education, and requires clients to pass a 20-question multiple-choice options test.

Portfolio margin increases borrowing power. Portfolio margined accounts collateralize 85% of account equity compared to 50% of the account equity held within a standard margin account. Almost all experienced, active traders with sufficient account sizes apply for portfolio margin. Brokerage rules requiring years of option trading experience, options education, and/or testing are intended to protect inexperienced traders from entering risky trades that may deplete their account.

A naked trade — such as selling a call on the NASDAQ financial index, can be extremely dangerous. Only option traders with the highest permission levels and who understand the risks are permitted to trade uncovered. A trader can potentially lose millions of dollars on a single short call if the market rockets through the trader's strike price. If this happens, the trader could lose his or her entire brokerage account in addition to being indebted to the brokerage. This is why option traders must know what they're doing, in addition to showing their option trading competency to the brokerage.

If you study the information in this book, you should be able to pass an options test. So study it. Understand how the Greeks affect premium. Try out the CBOE margin calculator. And pay particular attention to how option strategies work, including the synthetic option strategies.

Scanning for Trades

The scanning process begins with the development of a watch list. The watch list should include only those symbols that match a certain criterion, such as daily trading volume, implied volatility, average daily price range, etc. You may also want to look at symbols that are within one or more market sectors that are currently in favor.

You will use option strategies that involve buying premium when volatility is low. This reduces the amount of premium paid for entry. Option buyers also like longer times till contract expiration to give their strategies time to work in their favor without losing value from an increase in Theta. Conversely, option strategies that involve selling premium are used when implied volatility is high. Premium is at its highest during periods of high implied volatility. Premium sellers select options that expire in a matter of days or weeks. Theta is their friend. The short time to expiration reduces premium values. An option premium seller may sell for $1.00/share and buy back for $0.25 — a $0.75/share profit.

Now all you have to do is decide whether you're a seller, a buyer, or both. Of course the pros do both. More money can be made buying options on stocks that are in the midst of a strong price breakout than selling premium for a few cents per share. But, of course, the buyer's chart analysis must be correct, because a breakout is needed in the right direction.

Limited risk is another benefit of option buying. The maximum loss is usually limited to the premium paid at entry. Premium sellers are willing to settle for the premium received when they enter a trade. And thousands of option traders do quite well just selling premium.

Once you've studied the strategies described in this chapter and the next, try the ones that you like on "paper." You may find two, three, or more that you like, and that seem reasonable — perhaps even easy. These should be strategies that are the most understand-able and suit your personality relative to the amount of risk and reward they offer. Develop rules for each. The rules should include a clear understanding of your bias based on the price charts. Also establish strategy parameters based on days till expiration, accept-able implied volatility percentages (and Vega), premium amounts, Probability ITM (or touching), Open Interest (liquidity), and Delta and Theta values.

Then create watch lists that include symbols that fit one or more of your strategies. For example, you may want to buy options close to earnings release dates. Or perhaps build a list of longtime up-trending stocks and look for reversals and breakout opportunities. There is no right or wrong strategy in itself. It is only wrong if you do not understand how it works, what can happen, and/or how to manage it.

A watch list, price chart, and option chain combination was illustrated in figure 7–2. Also recall the efficiency created by synchronizing the symbols on a watch list to both the charts and option chains. Set up your trading platform so it mimics the figure. Then work your way through the different trading strategies described in this chapter and chapter 15. Of course you will choose different symbols, strike prices, and expiration dates. But be sure to test each strategy and examine the corresponding risk profiles to learn how they work.

Using Watch Lists

The first step in scanning is to compile a watch list. These are used in combination with price charts and option chains. Most brokerages provide public watch lists comprised of publically traded companies within the S&P 500, NASDAQ, Russell 2000, Dow Jones Industrial, etc. There are also lists of dividend stocks, symbols nearing earnings releases, lists of weekly options, and many others.

You can also create personal watch lists based on a number of parameters including but certainly not limited to such things as price, volume, market sector, and/or chart studies. Some traders use built-in scanners provided within their trading platforms to create and save lists of stocks that meet certain parameters. These parameters can include (but are not limited to) price levels, daily trading volumes, moving average crossovers, and more. Recall that you can even create a list of stocks that feature *penny increment options*. These are options that trade in penny increments rather than 5-cent premium increments.

You can also download lists of stocks from financial websites hosted by financial publishers such as *Investors Business Daily*. Once downloaded, the list must be opened in Excel, stripped of everything except the symbols, which should be in column A. These lists are easily imported into most trading platforms using a series of import dialogs designed specifically for importing and exporting watch lists.

The CBOE lists approximately 440 stocks, ETFs and financial indexes having weekly options. Most expire on Friday of each week, barring holidays. A new list of weekly options becomes available each Thursday morning of the week.

Following are the steps used to download the CBOE weeklys and then to import them into a working watch list. Note that this can be done every week of the year.

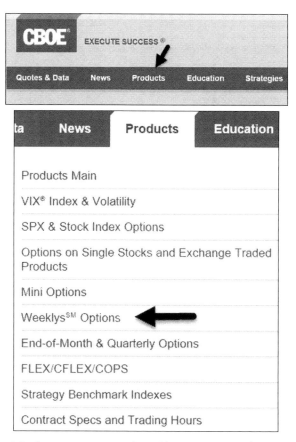

Provided as a courtesy by Chicago Board Options Exchange, Incorporated.

1. Open your web browser and type **www.cboe.com** and press **Enter** to display the CBOE home page.
2. Click **Products** to open the Products webpage.
3. Notice the Products page is displayed. Now click **Weeklys[SM] Options** as shown in the Products list to the right.
4. Find and click the **Available Weeklys** at the left-hand side of the page. Then click the blue link labeled **Click Here to download a Spreadsheet of Available Weeklys**.
5. An Excel-compatible worksheet with the filename weeklysmf.xls is downloaded to the Download folder of your PC.
6. Find the file and open it in Excel.
7. The Excel file resembles the one contained in figure 14–1.

NOTE The symbols in column A will be broken up into four equal comma-separated value files for importing to four new Weekly-A through Weekly-D watch lists.

Figure 14–1. List of CBOE Weekly Options in Excel

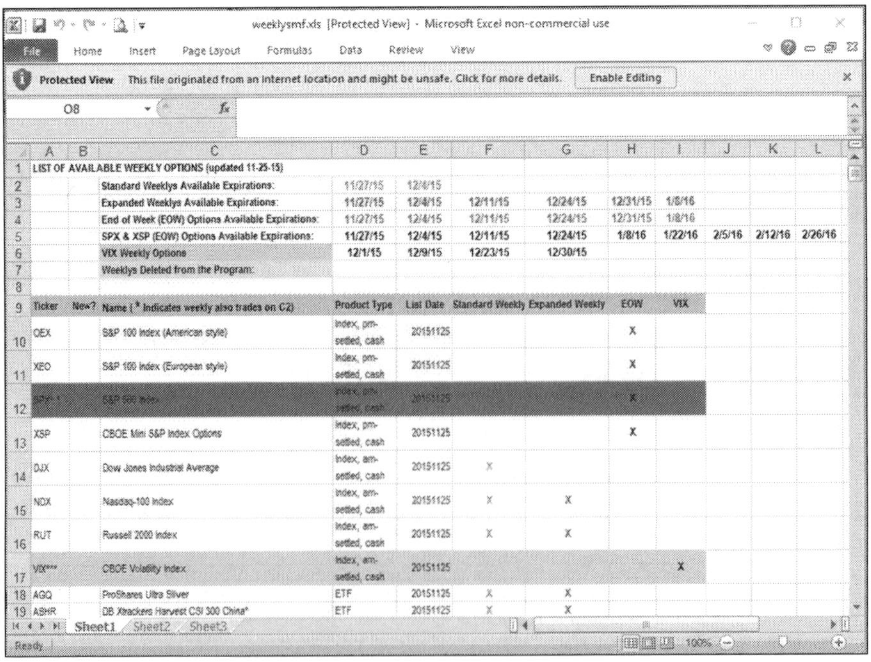

	A	B	C	D	E	F	G	H	I	J	K	L
1	LIST OF AVAILABLE WEEKLY OPTIONS (updated 11-25-15)											
2			Standard Weeklys Available Expirations:	11/27/15	12/4/15							
3			Expanded Weeklys Available Expirations:	11/27/15	12/4/15	12/11/15	12/24/15	12/31/15	1/8/16			
4			End of Week (EOW) Options Available Expirations:	11/27/15	12/4/15	12/11/15	12/24/15	12/31/15	1/8/16			
5			SPX & XSP (EOW) Options Available Expirations:	11/27/15	12/4/15	12/11/15	12/24/15	1/8/16	1/22/16	2/5/16	2/12/16	2/26/16
6			VIX Weekly Options	12/1/15	12/9/15	12/23/15	12/30/15					
7			Weeklys Deleted from the Program:									
8												
9	Ticker	New?	Name (* Indicates weekly also trades on C2)	Product Type	List Date	Standard Weekly	Expanded Weekly	EOW	VIX			
10	OEX		S&P 100 Index (American style)	Index, pm-settled, cash	20151125			X				
11	XEO		S&P 100 Index (European style)	Index, pm-settled, cash	20151125			X				
12	SPX* *		S&P 500 Index	Index, pm-settled, cash	20151125			X				
13	XSP		CBOE Mini S&P Index Options	Index, pm-settled, cash	20151125			X				
14	DJX		Dow Jones Industrial Average	Index, am-settled, cash	20151125	X						
15	NDX		Nasdaq-100 Index	Index, am-settled, cash	20151125	X	X					
16	RUT		Russell 2000 Index	Index, am-settled, cash	20151125	X	X					
17	VIX***		CBOE Volatility Index	Index, am-settled, cash	20151125				X			
18	AGQ		ProShares Ultra Silver	ETF	20151125	X	X					
19	ASHR		DB Xtrackers Harvest CSI 300 China*	ETF	20151125	X	X					

Provided as a courtesy by Chicago Board Options Exchange, Incorporated.

8. Click the **Enable Editing** button at the top of the worksheet. Then select row numbers **1** through **8**. Right-click to display the Excel shortcut menu and click **Delete** to remove rows 1 through 8.

9. Click on column heading **B**. Hold down the **Shift** key and click column heading **Z** to highlight columns B through Z.

10. Right-click to display the Excel shortcut menu and click **Delete** to remove columns B through Z. All that remains is the list of symbols in column A.

11. Go to Row 425 and click on the row number to the left of the first blank row.

12. Hold down **Ctrl+Shift** and press **End** to highlight all rows below.

13. Press **Del** to remove the highlighted rows from the worksheet.

14. Sort the symbol list in ascending order using Excel's Data A→Z sort feature. Then locate and delete the asterisks to the right of the SPX and VIX symbols.

15. Click **File** and then **Save As**. Choose **CSV (ms–dos) (*.CSV)** from the **Save as** type drop-down. Click **Save** and continue responding to the prompts to save the file in csv format (clean comma-separated-value format).

16. Use Excel to break the list into four portions. Save rows 1 to 85 with filename Weeklys-A.csv, rows 86 to 170 as Weeklys-B. csv, rows 171 through 256 as Weeklys-C.csv, and the remaining symbols as Weeklys-D.csv. You now have four separate csv files ready to import as watch lists. Note that four smaller watch lists are more manageable than one large watch list.

17. Use your trading platform to create a new watch list; name it Weeklys-A and import the Weeklys-A.csv file.

18. Repeat step 17 to create Weeklys-B through Weeklys-D watch lists.

19. Add IV_Percentile, ATR, and VolumeAvg to each of the Weekly watch lists and remove unwanted columns until all three watch lists contain the column headings shown in fig-ure 14–2.

Figure 14–2. Weeklys — A, B, C and D Watch Lists

Symbol ▲		Last	⇕ Net Chng	IV_Percentile	ATR	Volume... ⚙
AAL	☺	41.31	+.08	7.25	1.13	4153098.0
AAPL	☺	118.03	-.85	11.04	2.42	2.13233...
ABBV	☺	60.29	-.84	22.15	1.78	4861015.0
ACN	☺☺	107.10	-.25	41.94	1.37	1789282.0
ADM		36.47	+.43	39.45	1.07	5281827.0
AET		103.95	-2.13	50.42	3.64	2271036.0
AGNC	⑤	17.84	-.23	45.08	0.24	1741054.0
AGU		97.12	-.38	22.44	2.21	427944.0
AIG	⑤	63.15	+.03	13.55	1.06	6068159.0
AKAM		57.68	+1.06	29.43	1.73	1422810.0
ALTR		52.81	-.01	30.79	0.2	1420659.0
AMBA	☺☺	58.27	+1.95	43.42	3.56	1855305.0
AMT		99.09	-.17	24.2	1.54	965920.0
ANF	⑤☺	26.72	+.45	19.15	1.34	3634842.0
ANTM	⑤	131.00	-.63	45.34	3.79	1641139.0
APA		50.35	-.56	44.33	2.2	2455821.0
APC	⑤	61.13	-.89	44.83	2.69	2780714.0
ASHR		37.85	+.34	18.71	0.74	813742.0
ATVI		37.23	+.39	34.27	1.15	4218148.0
AVGO	☺☺	128.39	+.05	56.43	4.07	2139595.0
AXP		71.69	+.06	16.49	1.03	4391278.0

Watchlist — WEEKLYS_A — ☰

For illustration purposes only.

NOTE The four weeklys watch lists can be used in most of the following hands-on activities. (Of course you can use public or personal watch lists if you prefer.) When using the CBOE weeklys, be sure you've created, saved, and imported all four. Once they are imported, you can delete unwanted symbol rows with prices below $20 and volumes less than one million.

20. If supported by your trading platform, put the weekly watch list, charts, and option chain in separate windows.

21. Synchronize the weekly watch lists with your charts and option chains (some trading platforms do this automatically). You may be required to type symbols into the chart and option chain windows that correspond to each symbol within your watch list.

Chart Analysis Over Different Time Intervals

Chapters 11 and 12 discussed the use of charts across several time intervals. Because of its importance, this practice is a dominant theme throughout this book.

Using the charts in concert with both historical and current implied volatility percentage is helpful. Tying volatility to chart trends, patterns, and supporting studies quickly qualify or reject each symbol linked to your watch list. And you will find many charts and option chains that do not qualify. You may find many trade setups that happened within the past few weeks and wonder why you didn't find them earlier. Never obsess. It's important to reduce the time required to scan for your trade entries. So make the scanning process as efficient as possible to save valuable time. If an underlying chart doesn't signal a current trading opportunity, move on quickly until you find a trade candidate. Remember, there are plenty of symbols to examine. That's why we use several small watch lists. Keep looking until you find that perfect chart pattern.

Your ultimate goal is to work your way through the watch list and charts quickly so you can spend time examining a corresponding option chain. As you know, many experienced option traders begin their analysis and set up work well before the market opens. This frees them to do a final check and then enter their trades without having to waste precious time during market hours scanning, selecting high probability strategies, and finally entering their trades.

Of course the first thing they do is check their charts, update their watch lists or create new ones based on their initial scans.

Figure 14–3a illustrates a chart with trendlines, support and resistance levels, a bull flag, and a cup and handle. This chart encourages a bullish trading strategy. A closer look reveals promising candle shapes that signal possible price reversals. Of course these must be caught in real time. But the historical moves can be quite instructive.

Figure 14–3a. Finding Trends and Signals on Charts (Bullish)

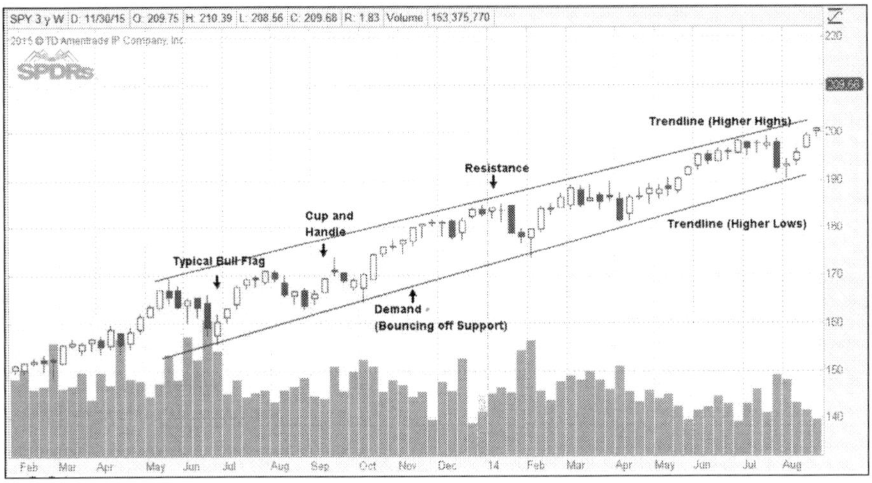

For illustration purposes only.

Figure 14–3b illustrates a down-trending chart with a bearish engulfed candle. The setup shows a 3:1 reward-to-risk setup for the underlying stock. Bearish setups for stock trades are also useful for option trades. For example, the chart example shown in figure 14–3b is ideal for option strategies such as a long at the money put, a strip, or a synthetic short stock among others. These strategies and many more are described within this chapter. Both of these and other bearish strategies should expire in roughly 90 to 120 days depending on premiums.

Figure 14–3b. Finding Trends and Signals on Charts (Bearish)

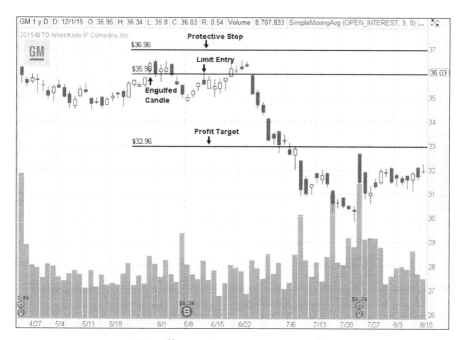

For illustration purposes only.

Checking the Option Chains: Premium and Probability

Option chains and terminology are described in substantial depth in chapters 10 through 12. Chapter 10 describes buyer and seller obligations. It explains what can happen when an option position becomes in the money. Chapter 11 explores the data displayed within option chains and how that information is used by option traders. Chapter 12 continues that discussion by describing the use and meaning of the Greek values Delta, Gamma, Theta, Vega, and Rho. All of these can be added to option chains to enhance analysis. But too many columns can create clutter. Restrict the columns to those that are most useful — Mark, Probability ITM or Touching, Open Interest, Delta, and Theta. All option chains automatically include Strike, Bid, and Ask columns.

In spite of all the useful metrics found on option chains, they may be disappointing. Premium values (Bid, Ask, Mark) or Open Interest values may be too low. The number of available strike prices may be too restrictive. When this happens, and it will, move back to the watch list and continue scanning by choosing the next symbol.

However, if you find the premium values, open interest, probability levels, and Delta and Theta values that fit your trading rules, and the contract expiration date is suitable, select an option strategy and enter a trade using one of the option strategies that follow.

Using Risk Profiles

Every good option trading platform provides access to risk profiles, sometimes called *risk graphs*. These graphs are used to analyze the effect of time and price changes on profits and losses of an underlying option trade. Risk profiles show all possible outcomes that correspond to different prices of the underlying stock and different calendar days within the contract period. Calendars permit traders to walk through each day between entry and contract expiration. Traders can also slide across the chart to different prices of the underlying to determine the profit or loss status at each price point. Therefore, both time and the market price of the underlying are used to show all possible outcomes of the corresponding option trade.

There's also a table of price slices that can be set to see how the values of the Greeks are affected over time and at different stock prices. Risk profiles also permit traders to view shaded areas that represent standard deviation values using 1σ, 2σ, or 3σ (1x through 3x standard deviations).

Of course there is never 100% certainty relative to what the price of the underlying will do from one day to the next. An earnings report could cause the price of an underlying stock to drop or rally. An overall market downturn could drag down the entire universe of stocks.

But having a bias is useful. It permits traders to look at all possibilities based on time and price. These risk profiles provide an excellent way to "check the wind" before you "set sail." And when the conditions are right, plan on a "calm day at sea."

NOTE   Although options are financial derivatives of stocks, ETFs, financial indexes, and futures, the term *stock* is used throughout the following procedures unless otherwise specified.

Risk Profile Example

The Adobe stock, symbol ADBE, is currently trading at $91.77. The option chain is shown in figure 14–4a; a corresponding risk profile is shown in figure 14–4b. The shaded area within a risk profile encompasses where the trade is likely to be on the date shown in the risk graph calendar.

The data, including the shaded area, is based on the price of the underlying option. If left unchanged, the shaded area usually represents one standard deviation (68.27%) either side of the current price. Of course it doesn't tell us the direction of the price, but it does tell us the probable price range over time (excluding current volatility). Examine the short call vertical spread entry in figure 14–4a. The strike price and number of contracts shown on the order bar are:

Setup Parameters
- −10 ADBE JAN 16 $100 CALLS with a Mark of $0.705
- +10 ADBE JAN 16 $105 CALLS with a Mark of $0.205
- This is a $0.50/share in premium difference.
- This trade produces a credit of $500 in premium income.

Figure 14–4a. Vertical CALL Credit Spread

ADBE		ADOBE SYSTEMS INC COM	91.775	+1.865 +2.07%	@ 91.77 A 91.73	ETB NASDAQ	±4.56			Company Profile

Underlying

	Last X	Net Chng	Bid X	Ask X	Size	Volume	Open	High	Low
>	91.775 D	+1.865	91.77 Q	91.78 Z	5 x 2	969,949	90.13	92.03	90.13

Option Chain Filter: Off, Spread: Single, Layout: Mark, Delta, Theta, Probability of Touc...,

	CALLS					Strikes: 14			PUTS				

Mark, De..., Th..., Pr..., O...,	Bid X	Ask X	Exp	Strike	Bid X	Ask X	Mark, De..., Th..., Pr..., O...,

JAN 16 (42) 100 — 30.03% (±7.564)

Mark	De	Th	Pr	O	Bid X	Ask X	Exp	Strike	Bid X	Ask X	Mark	De	Th	Pr	O
		-.03	30.1...	1,31	10.13 X	10.50 X	JAN 16	82.5	.04 X	.07 X	.035	-.13	-.03	33.2...	100
8.125	.78	-.03	49.4...	1,755	8.05 X	8.20 X	JAN 16	85	1.24 Q	1.28 X	1.260	-.22	-.03	48.3...	771
6.175	.70	-.04	65.2...	787	6.10 X	6.25 X	JAN 16	87.5	1.81 Q	1.88 X	1.845	-.30	-.04	64.9...	727
4.525	.60	-.04	84.9...	1,380	4.45 X	4.60 X	JAN 16	90	2.66 N	2.70 N	2.680	-.40	-.04	84.7...	718
3.125	.49	-.04	93.0...	848	3.05 X	3.20 X	JAN 16	92.5	3.75 M	3.85 X	3.800	-.51	-.04	92.9...	312

Mark	De...	Th...	Pr...	O...	Bid X	Ask X	Exp	Strike			
									5.250	-.63	-.04	69.5...	146
									6.950	-.74	-.03	48.3...	81
.705	.17	-.02	30.8...	810	.67 C	.74 X	JAN 16	100	8.900	-.83	-.02	30.9...	127
.205	.06	-.01	10.7...	1,141	.18 X	.23 C	JAN 16	105	13.450	-.91	-.01	13.3...	26
.065	.02	.00	3.65%	100	.01 C	.12 M	JAN 16	110	17.95 A	18.80 X	18.375	-.92	-.02	9.91%	2

Positions and Simulated Trades

ADBE										
STK			0 ADBE		STOCK	.00	32.30%	.00	
VERTICAL	SELL	-10 ADBE	JAN 16	100	CALL	50	25.21%	-109.67	- x
	BUY	+10 ADBE	JAN 16	105	CALL	CREDIT	24.84%		

For illustration purposes only.

Notice the probability of touching (Pr...) of the short $100 CALL is 30.8%. This is slightly more than one standard deviation away from the current market price of ADBE.

Although Probability ITM or the more conservative Probability of Touching (not available on all trading platforms) are more commonly used, a trader might double ADBE's current ATR(14) value of $1.67 displayed in the watch list. This results in values of +$3.34 and −$.3.34 for the top and bottom price slices. The center price slice is set to ADBE's current price represented by $0 in the Price Slices section of the Risk Profile. Notice the shaded standard deviation region of ±68.27%. The 2 × ATR(14) is represented by the vertical dashed lines shown on either side of the current price of ADBE. One standard deviation is well within the 2x ±ATR(14) range manually entered as the top and bottom price slices. With the chart calendar set to the expiration date, this trade has a high probability of earning $488.00 in premium as shown in the P/L Day and P/L Open columns of the Price Slices section. This figure is derived from the $500 in premium less $12 in commissions. The effect of commissions can be added to the risk profile or ignored with an INCLUDE/EXCLUDE setting. (Notice INCLUDE immediately below the Risk Profile button.)

Finally, you can slide your mouse cursor across the risk profile chart and click to draw a vertical dashed line at different price levels along the horizontal price axis. When you click at different prices, the corresponding P/L and Greek values change to reflect the selected price points.

Most seasoned option traders use statistical probabilities when selecting an option strike price. In fact, the ATR(14) study is rarely used for this purpose, and shown here for comparison purposes only. Furthermore, closing a trade when it achieves a profit of 50% to 70% (a typical profit goal) substantially increases the probability for success by shortening the duration of the trade. Immediately reinvesting the proceeds into one or more following trades multiplies the trader's income. Therefore, it's always good to have premium-based profit goal and a plan to either roll the current trade to a new, high probability position or to find a new trade setup.

Figure 14–4b. Vertical CALL Credit Spread Risk Profile

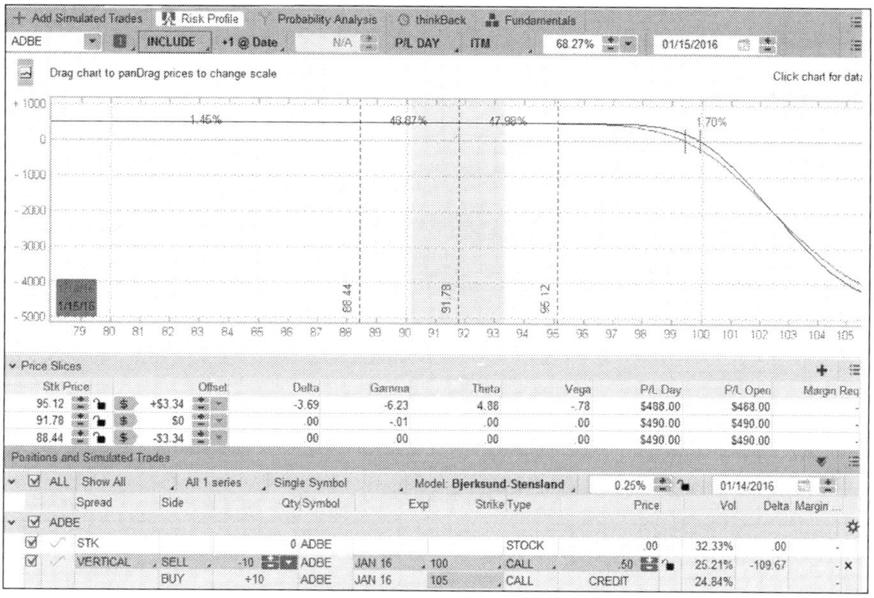

For illustration purposes only.

The risk profile includes black and red plot lines. The red line is the P/L of this vertical credit spread. The black line plots the current value of ADBE. This is referred to as the *live value*. Both lines track the dates entered on the risk profile's calendar. As time passes the two plot lines may diverge as the plot of the live value increases or decreases relative to the plot represented by the vertical spread's profit or loss.

In the example the Saturday following expiration Friday is selected on the top calendar. Another calendar exists below the Price Slices. Incrementing the calendar dates show the probabilities of being in the money at expiration. This is the primary objective of using risk profiles to understand the probability of success and the possible risks.

Price Slices can be added or removed to view other possible outcomes. The example shows dollar values based on 2x the ATR(14) above and below the current price of ADBE stock. But as mentioned above, statistical probability percentage values are typically used. Using 2x the standard deviation would also be a reasonable value to examine in this example.

The computed break-even price of the underlying stock and the vertical spread is shown. This is where the plot lines cross the $0 horizontal axis. Be sure to set the date to the corresponding expiration Friday on the calendar to see where this occurs.

Notice the **ITM** to the right of **P/L Day**. The risk profile is set to Probability ITM. This can be set to **OTM** or **Touching**, which redraws the graph based on these selections.

NOTE   While Probability Touching is supported by think-orswim®, not all trading platforms include this feature. Many traders use either Probability ITM or Delta values. As mentioned, Probability Touching is slightly more conservative than Probability ITM.

Some applications permit the addition of multiple day steps. This adds colored lines that correspond to each day step added to the risk profile. The thinkorswim® trading application also permits traders to view projected values for each of the Greek values over time. The values are based on the current probability statistics. If you are using a full-featured platform that provides these features, be sure to try out the different settings to see how they work.

Of course you could spend many hours drilling down into all the features available with risk profiles. If you do this with every trade, by the time you finish examining every possibility you will likely miss the trade. Use the basic information provided to understand probable outcomes and risks. Look at where the trade is at expiration. Establish a premium goal. Then find an exit point in time in which the profit is adequate. This is a basic use of a risk profile.

About the Hands-On Activities

Each of the option strategies described in the remainder of this chapter and in chapter 15 are accompanied by *Hands-On Activities*. These are hands-on, step-by-step procedures designed to guide you through the scanning, set up, trade entry, and trade management processes required for each the following option strategies. Be sure to use the *Setup Parameters* as a basis for selecting suitable trade candidates. Having a few good watch lists and synchronizing them to your charts and option chains will expedite your scanning process.

Actual option chains and risk profiles are provided as trade samples. Use them as models for your own selections and entries. Immediately following each trade entry are suggestions for trade management and a list of the most likely outcomes.

BE SURE to use simulation or "paper trading" until you are confident in how to scan, enter, and manage each option strategy. Be sure to use the risk profiles; these show you where the price of the underlying must be for the selected option strategy to return profit. When you find two or more option strategies that consistently provide profitable returns on paper, consider taking them live.

And **TAKE YOUR PROFIT!** Always watch the profit and loss (P/L) of each trade. Take profit when a trade achieves 30% to 70%. Over time, high volume turnover at wholesale is more profitable than low volume turnover at retail. We call this *churning*.

The Short Call

Structure

−1 OTM CALL

Expiration ≤ 56 days. (Shorter time to expiration reduces risk!)

NOTE   This is an uncovered (or *naked*) credit option strategy intended to collect premium. Only traders having the highest option trading permission can use this strategy.

WHY BEGIN WITH A SHORT CALL? Many who do not understand how options work avoid this strategy because they believe it to be extremely dangerous. And they would be right. Perhaps another reason is due to the SEC's requirement for brokerages to post disclaimers warning investors about the risks associated with options. Brokerages require clients to have three or four years of option trading experience. And as you know, some brokerages require their clients to pass options tests before they are granted portfolio margin and permitted to trade uncovered options. So this chapter begins with the highest risk option position — the *naked short call* — the *Venus Fly Trap* of option strategies. You can literally "blow out your account" with a naked short call. So option traders must know how this is possible. Consider the following example.

Gene is convinced the price of Billabong Pharmaceutical stock, symbol BONG, which is presently trading at $180/share is poised for a large drop due to a poor earnings report. BONG has spent a fortune in R&D on a dopamine pump implant for Parkinson's disease patients. Billabong Pharmaceutical's income statement and balance sheet are bleeding red. Many respected market analysts have downgraded BONG's stock from hold to sell. The $185 short call premiums are presently $5 per share. Although Gene doesn't own BONG stock, he's certain BONG is about to crash.

1. Gene sells ten $185 call contracts (1,000 shares) that expire in just eight days, and happily collects $5,000 in premium income.
2. He uses the premium he received to buy +10 BONG 175 puts. When the BONG stock drops, Gene's ten long puts will be deep in the money (ITM) for a huge profit.
3. Before the end of the day, Billabong Pharmaceutical announces FDA approval and the release of their long awaited dopamine pump to the market with billions in sales backlog.
4. The stock shoots up to $390/share in a matter of minutes.
5. Gene's short call is exercised (and his long put is worthless).
6. Gene must buy 1,000 shares of BONG for $390/share and deliver it to the option buyer.
7. The option buyer gladly pays the $185,000 call strike price for $390,000 worth of stock.
8. Gene reluctantly buys and delivers $390,000 in stock for which he receives $185,000.
9. Gene loses $205,000, the difference between $390,000 paid and $185,000 received, plus the debit paid for the 10 long 175 puts.

A net loss of $205,000 in a matter of hours is a hard way to learn. In addition to the amount of money that can be lost with this strategy, it has a limited profit potential compared to the downside risk. Even with the highest option trading permission, all experienced option traders are sensitive to the risk that accompanies naked short calls. Until you are willing to suffer the risk, cover your short calls with either stock ownership, as in a covered call, or a long call at a slightly higher strike price for "insurance." If strongly bearish, near the money puts could be bought in anticipation of a strong price drop. All of these strategies are detailed in this chapter.

Description and Goals

The short call is a limited reward, **unlimited risk,** bearish to neutral strategy intended to collect option premium income. The strategy requires the highest level of option trading permission. Unlike the short put described next, a strong price rally in the underlying stock can result in an unlimited loss. However, because the stock price involved in a short cash-covered put can only drop to zero, and depending on your trading permissions, the cash-covered short put is permitted when sufficient account equity exists.

In spite of the limited reward and high risk, many experienced traders use short calls on a regular basis. They scan for stocks having values close to the following within the option chain:

Setup Parameters

- Goal: Premium collection
- Bias: Bearish to neutral (based on chart trend and pattern)
- Debit/Credit: Credit
- Chart Trend: Neutral to downward
- Momentum Oscillator: Overbought near historical resistance level
- Keltner Channel: Extended ATR(14) envelope in anticipation of a reduction.
- Implied Volatility ≥ 70%; Seller wants high current IV% for high premium in anticipation of an IV% reversal and a drop in premium.
- Greeks: Delta ≤ .25; Theta negative; Vega positive
- Days till Expiry: ≤ 56 Days (Shorter is better to minimize risk.)
- Premium (Mark): ≥ $0.40 (Considering the risk, higher premium is better.)

- Probability ITM: ≤ 25% (Low Probability ITM important.)
- Open Interest at Strike Price: ≈ 300; Total open interest @ all strikes > 5,000
- Risk Amount ≈ 1.0% of account equity (governed by number of contracts traded)

GENERAL NOTES

(These general notes apply to all hands-on trading activities in chapters 14 and 15.)

1. For brevity the acronyms for out of the money (OTM), in the money (ITM), and at the money (ATM) are used throughout the remainder of this book.
2. All working trades should be monitored.
3. Learn how to enter GTC Mark- or Delta-triggered stops. Stops are often used to either take profits or to avoid excessive losses.
4. While reasonable, the above setup parameters are approximate; use values based on your experiential rules for Probability ITM, Mark (premium value), Open Interest, Theta, and Delta.
5. When summing a long call Delta and a short call Delta, the short call Delta is subtracted. This is also true for the other Greeks, i.e., Theta, Gamma, Vega, and Rho.
6. Consider placing the Keltner channel study on your charts. The centerline of this study uses the SMA(20); the envelope plots above and below the central SMA(20) are $1.5 \times$ ATR(14). Some traders increase $1.5 \times$ ATR(14) to $2.0 \times$ ATR(14). This study works well on Daily interval charts.
7. Bias is based on price chart trend, patterns, and proximity to support or resistance.
8. Option sellers want current high IV% in anticipation of a reversal toward historical volatility.
9. Sellers choose option contracts that expire within days to several weeks, but rarely more than two months.
10. Sellers look for premium amounts that justify the risk of closing early for a loss. Being exercised is NOT an option with the

exception of strategies specifically designed to be exercised such as short puts for stock ownership and vertical debit spreads.)

11. ALWAYS ensure adequate open interest before entry.

How the Strategy Works

Sell one OTM call and collect the premium less commissions and exchange fees. Hold onto the trade until your P/L Open statement shows a 30% to 70% profit, as shown on your position statement. Although taking your profit and entering another trade is recommended, you may also let this trade expire worthless if the strike price of the short call option remains safely OTM.

Hands-On Activity

Scanning for a Trade

1. Choose a contract date that expires within 20 days or less.
2. Look at the option chain in figure 14–5.
3. Select a call strike price having values close to these:
   a. Mark ≥ $1.00 (Price in example = $1.185)
   b. Prob. ITM ≤ 25% (In this setup the 100 strike with Prob. ITM of 24.54% is used.)

Figure 14–5a. Short Call Option Chain

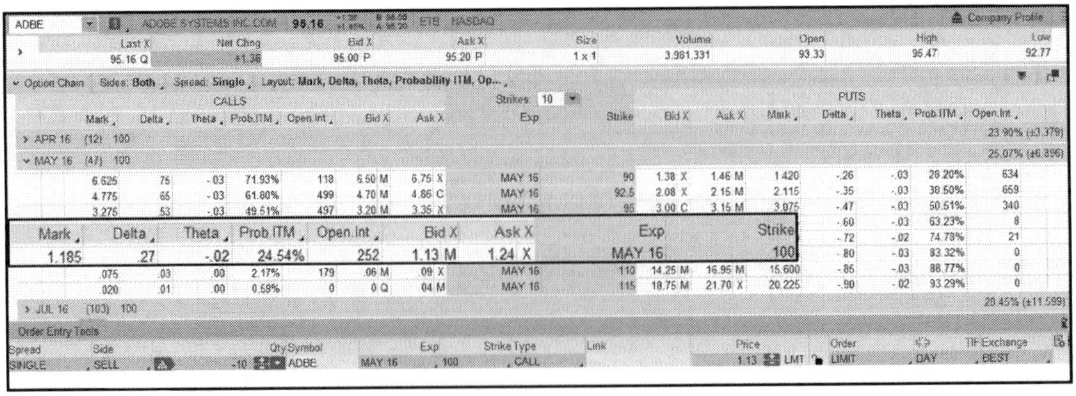

For illustration purposes only.

NOTE The 100 strike price is slightly below our 25% Probability ITM rule. To be even safer, and with sufficient premium, the trader might consider the $105 strike price. Never let greed for a few more dollars replace safety. Although the 24.54% is within the trader's probability rule, safer is always better. Seasoned option traders often settle for a little less premium to increase their safety margin. This is particularly true in the case of a naked short call, which many traders would avoid entirely. Although the 100 strike price of the call has an open interest of 252, all nearby strike prices exceed 300 contracts for acceptable liquidity.

    c.   Open Interest at strike price ≥ 300; overall ≥ 5,000 (Example = 252; overall > 5,000).

4.   Notice the risk profile plot in figure 14–5b. The strategy's profit of $1,113 remains constant as long as the price of ADBE remains below the $100 strike price. If the price of ADBE breaches the $100 strike price, this trade begins to accrue a major loss.

Figure 14–5b. Short Call Risk Profile

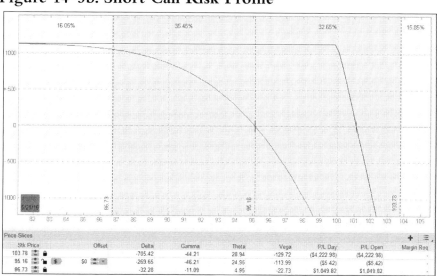

For illustration purposes only.

Entry

1. Choose the option contract date (in this example, MAY 16 (47) is selected).
2. Ensure the Open Interest provides sufficient liquidity.
3. Click the CALLS **Bid** column at the 100 strike price with a 24.54% Prob. ITM.)
4. Check the order bar to verify it contains entries similar to these:
SINGLE SELL -10 ADBE MAY 16 100 CALL 1.13 LMT LIMIT DAY
5. If the order bar values are correct, click **Confirm and Send.**
6. Evaluate the Order Confirmation information. If satisfactory, click **Send**.
7. If filled, seller collects $1,113 in premium less commissions and exchange fees.

Risks

The risk profile for this trade begins at the left-hand axis $1,113 above the $0 horizontal P/L axis. If the strike price of the short call becomes ITM by one cent, it may be exercised. This requires the seller to deliver 100 shares of stock to the buyer for each of the ten call contracts sold. However, being exercised usually happens when a trade is within a few days of expiration.

This order has 10 contracts or 1,000 shares. If the stock reaches $102/share and is exercised, the seller must buy and deliver $1,000 shares of stock to the buyer at a cost of $100,000. The buyer must pay the seller the option price per share, which is $100,000. The seller loses $2,000 in intrinsic value less the $1,113 in premium received when traded. The total loss amounts to $887 less the roundtrip transaction fees.

Trade Management

Monitor the trade. If threatened, buy to close (#4 below) or roll (#5 below). You could also place a working GTC buy to close order having a Mark value of 50% of the premium originally received at entry. If the trade begins to suffer a loss, close it and walk away.

Possible Outcomes

1. The price of the stock remains far below $100 and the option contract expires worthless. The option seller makes $1,310 less commissions — the trader's goal.
2. The decrease in premium presents an opportunity for the trader to buy to close the short call position for 50% profit of approximately $650. The GTC buy to close order mentioned in Trade Management could be used to achieve this outcome.
3. The trader rolls the trade for net premium credit with a buy to close and a companion sell to open order at a later expiration date. Before finalizing the roll, the trader opens and examines the option chain of the new position to ensure the new position complies with his or her trading rules.
4. The price of the stock rallies and threatens the short call option. The trader enters a buy to close order for a loss. The loss amount depends on current premium when closed.
5. The price of the stock threatens the option strike price; the trader rolls the trade with a buy to close and a simultaneous sell to open order at a farther OTM strike price and at later expiration date.
6. The price of the stock is rallying rapidly. The trader buys a protective long call one or two strike prices above the short call as insurance. This only works if the price remains below the original strike price of the short call or if it rallies above the strike price of the long "protective" call. The worst case is if the price of the stock expires at a price between the short and long calls and the short call is exercised. The seller of the call must deliver the underlying stock to the buyer in addition to having paid extra premium for the unused long call leg.
7. The trader hasn't been paying attention to his short call. To the trader's surprise, the short call becomes ITM and is exercised; the option

seller must buy and deliver stock to the option buyer, who pays the seller for the stock at the strike price of the option. The option seller suffers an unplanned loss that exceeds a few thousand dollars.

8. To defend against being exercised for a loss, the trader could buy the stock at the option price of the short call to preempt being exercised for a loss if the price of the stock continues to rally. Hence, the stock could be delivered to the buyer at the strike price of the short call.

Cash-Covered Short Put

Structure

−1 OTM PUT

This is a credit option strategy; expiration ≤ 56 days. The selected strike price depends on whether the trader:

1. Wants to collect more premium closer to the money and own the underlying stock, or
2. Collect less premium farther OTM and avoid ownership of the underlying stock.

Description and Goals

This is a limited reward, high-risk neutral to bullish strategy used to collect option premium income from the sale of one or more put options. The seller must have sufficient cash to pay for the underlying stock if the short put option becomes ITM and is exercised. When this happens, the buyer puts the stock to the seller, who must pay for the stock at the option price.

Of course the option seller can also buy to close the option for a profit. This is typically done when the original premium value drops to 30% or more.

Cash-covered short puts are also used to acquire stock that a put option seller is interested in owning. When this is the seller's goal and the option is exercised by the buyer, the premium originally collected by option seller offsets the cost of buying the stock (having the stock put to the seller).

Consider an example. A put seller wants to own a $32 stock; a $30 put option is sold for $2.00 in premium per share. The price drops to $29.00 and the buyer on the other side of the trade exercises the $30 option and puts the stock to the seller. The seller receives the $29.00/share stock and pays $30/share for it. Because the put seller originally received $2.00 in premium, the total cost for the $29.0 stock is $28.00 plus transaction fees.

Some traders sell cash-covered puts on the same stock multiple times until the strike price of the short put is finally ITM and exercised. When a series of cash-covered short puts is sold over a long period of time, it is possible for the seller to collect a substantial amount of premium income before either having the short put exercised or ceasing to sell the short puts due to a change in market conditions.

Setup Parameters

- Goal: Premium collection; the strike price of the short put should remain OTM through either expiration or when bought to close for a 30% to 70% profit.
- Bias: Neutral to bullish (based on chart trend and pattern)
- Debit/Credit: Credit
- Chart Trend: Moving into an uptrend
- Momentum Oscillator: Oversold near historical support level
- Keltner Channel: Narrow ATR(14) envelope in anticipation of an expansion
- Implied Volatility ≥ 70%; Seller wants high current IV% for high premium income and anticipation of an IV% reversal.
- Greeks: Delta ≤ −0.20; Theta positive; Vega negative
- Days till Expiry: ≤ 56 Days (Shorter is better to minimize risk with good premium.)

- Premium (Mark): ≥ $0.40
- Probability ITM: ≤ 25%
- Open Interest at Strike Price: ≈ 300; Total open interest @ all strikes > 3,000
- Risk Amount ≈1.0% of account equity (governed by contracts traded)

How the Strategy Works

Sell one OTM put and collect the premium less commissions and exchange fees. If the strike price of the short becomes ITM and is exercised, the seller must take delivery of the stock and pay the buyer at the option price per share.

Hands-On Activity

Scanning for a Trade

1. Synchronize your watch list with the charts and option chain.
2. Look for an oversold, up-trending stock near support.
3. Verify high implied volatility at or above 80% on the watch list for high premium.
4. On the option chain choose a contract date that expires within 56 days or less.
5. Check for plenty of open interest and ample premium at a safe OTM strike price with a probability ITM ≤ 25% (see the option chain in figure 14–6a).
6. Notice the risk profile in figure 14–6b; HLF must drop below $41.47 for this trade to lose money. Selling 10 put contracts for 1.02/share will return $1,020. Since the Mark is $1.11, the trade will likely return a few dollars more.
7. You can use the risk profile to perform "what if's" by adding and changing the price slice values and dates to determine different trade outcomes.

Figure 14–6a. Short Put Option Chain

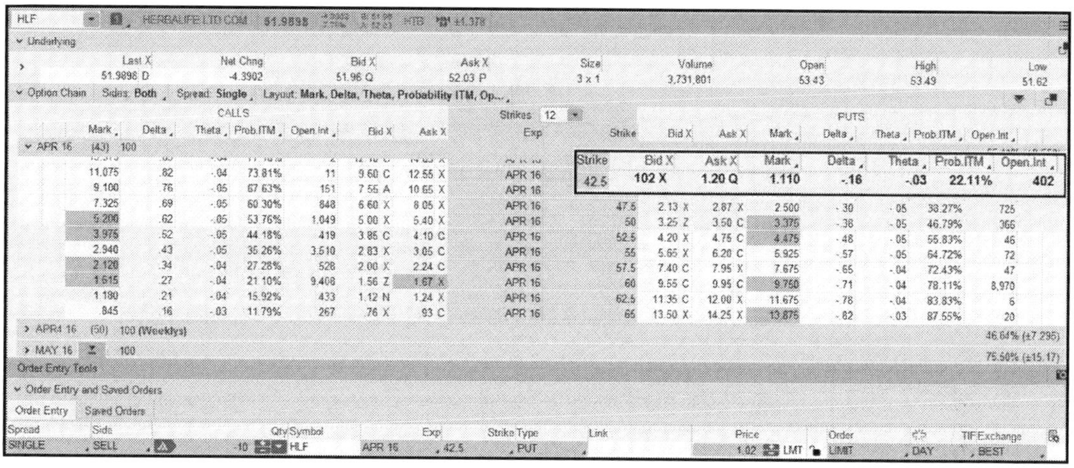

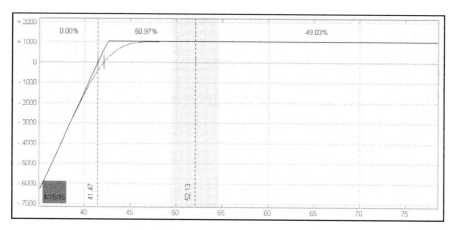

For illustration purposes only.

Figure 14–6b. Short Put Risk Profile

For illustration purposes only.

8. Select a put strike price having values close to these:
    a. Mark ≥ $1.00 (Actual = 1.02 × 1,000 = $1,020)
    b. Prob. ITM ≤ 30% (Actual = 22.11%)
    c. Open Interest at strike price ≥ 300; overall ≥ 5,000 (Actual = 402, total > 15,000)

Entry

1. Choose the option contract date (in this example, MAR 16 is selected).
2. Ensure the Open Interest provides sufficient liquidity.
3. Click the PUTS **Bid** column at the 55 strike price.
4. Check the order bar to verify it contains entries similar to these:

SINGLE SELL -10 HLF APR 16 42.5 PUT 1.02 LMT LIMIT DAY

5. If the order bar values are correct, click **Confirm and Send**.
6. Evaluate the Order Confirmation information. If satisfactory, click **Send**.
7. If filled, seller collects $1,020 in premium less commissions and exchange fees.

Risks

If the strike price of the short put becomes ITM by one cent, it may be exercised. This requires the seller to buy 100 shares of stock from the buyer for each of the ten put contracts sold (This order has 10 contracts or 1,000 shares.) The stock will cost $50,000. Of course it can be sold to recover most of the loss, retained in anticipation of a price recovery, or used with covered call options.

Trade Management

Monitor the trade. If threatened, buy to close (#4 below) or roll (#5 below). If the underlying stock begins a precipitous drop, consider buying a put (#6 below) one strike below the short put for "insurance."

Possible Outcomes

1. The option contract expires worthless — the trader's goal.
2. The decrease in premium presents an opportunity for the trader to buy to close the short put position for profit.
3. The trader rolls the trade for net premium credit with a buy to close and a companion sell to open order at a later expiration date.

4. The price of the underlying threatens the position; the trader buys to close for a loss.

5. The price of the underlying threatens the position; the trader rolls the trade with a buy to close and a simultaneous sell to open order at a lower strike price and at either the same or a later expiration date, depending on what is found within the option chains.

6. The price of the underlying is dropping rapidly. The trader buys a protective long put one or two strike prices below the current short put for insurance against a substantial loss. This only works if the price remains higher than the original strike price of the short put or drops below the strike price of the long "protective" put. The worst case is if the price of the underlying expires at a price between the short and long puts and the short put is exercised. The seller must pay for the underlying stock in addition to having paid extra premium for the unused long put leg.

7. The position is ITM and exercised. The buyer delivers the stock to the seller who must pay for the stock at the strike price of the option.

8. The seller might consider shorting the HLF stock as a hedge.

The Long Call

Structure

+1 slightly OTM, ATM, or ITM CALL (depends on bullish bias and time till expiration)

Very bullish debit strategy; expiration ≥ 90 days

Description and Goals

This is an unlimited reward, limited risk, very bullish strategy in which a trader buys one or more near or ATM option contracts in anticipation of a strong rally. The premium paid for the long call is the maximum possible loss. An increase in the underlying will drive the strike price of the long call deeper ITM, resulting in an increase in premium value. Although costlier, giving this trade plenty of time to work, perhaps even using a LEAPS option is common.

Once the buyer is satisfied with the amount of available profit, the buyer can sell the option contracts for a profit in premium. However, this is not a common event. Theta typically reduces premium faster than it rises from a price increase in the stock. Many active traders are quite satisfied with 30% to 70% profit, as shown in the P/L Open column of their brokerage statement.

The buyer may decide to exercise the option contract and pay for the underlying stock at the option price, especially if the price of the stock has experienced a strong rally above the original option price at entry. Once it is exercised, the buyer can sell the stock for a substantial profit.

Setup Parameters

- Goal: An increase in the market price of the underlying. If the option becomes ITM or the premium reaches the trader's target price, the option is either sold or exercised for a profit.
- Bias: Very Bullish (based on chart trend and pattern)
- Debit/Credit: Debit
- Chart Trend: Up on weekly chart; presently basing near support
- Momentum Oscillator: Oversold near historical support level
- Keltner Channel: Narrow ATR(14) envelope in anticipation of an expansion
- Implied Volatility ≤ 20%; Buyer wants low current IV% in anticipation of a substantial increase in IV%.
- Greeks: Delta ≥ 0.35; Theta negative; Vega positive
- Days till Expiry: > 90 Days (Give the stock plenty of time to rally in your favor.)
- Premium (Mark): Begin with contracts × premium ≤ 1.0% of account value.

- Probability ITM: ≥ 40% and ≤ 60% (Adjust for premium and allowable risk.)
- Open Interest at Strike Price: ≈ 500; Total open interest @ all strikes ≥ 10,000
- Risk Amount ≈ 1.0% of account equity (governed by number of contracts purchased)

Hands-On Activity

How the Strategy Works

Buy one ATM call and pay the premium plus commissions and exchange fees. Provide enough time for a sustained price rally to move the long call strike price deep ITM. Then sell the option for profit, or exercise the option for the stock. Your choice depends on acquiring the most profit.

Scanning for a Trade

1. Find an oversold stock near support that is presently forming a reversal and breakout pattern. This could include a bull flag, cup and handle, or double bottom.
2. Ensure low current implied volatility is at or below 20% for reduced premium.
3. Choose a contract date that expires in 90 days or more.
4. Look at the option chain in figure 14–7a.

NOTE   The following option contract expires in 97 days. However, if affordable, consider using even more time till expiration, which is well within your trading rules. This gives the trade more time to work in your favor. The downside is the cost of premium, which is always higher within longer term option contracts.

Figure 14–7a. Long Call Option Chain

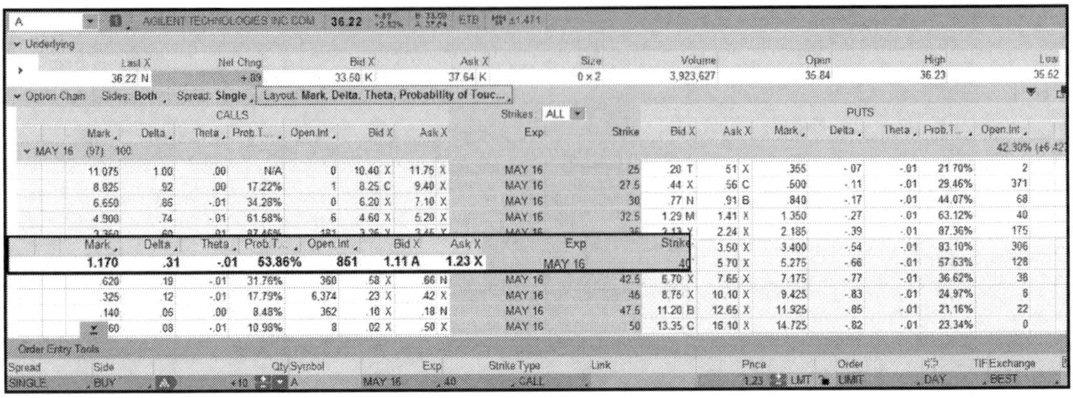

For illustration purposes only.

5. Select a call strike price having values close to these:
   a. Mark ≈ $1.00
   b. Prob. Touching ≥ 50%
   c. Open Interest at strike price ≈ 300; overall ≥ 8,000

Entry

1. Choose the option contract that expires in ≥ 90 days. (The MAY 16 contract is selected with 97 days remaining.)
2. Ensure the Open Interest provides sufficient liquidity.
   NOTE Notice this symbol has thousands of open interest transactions. Open interest increases as an option contract moves within a few weeks of its expiration date. Open interest begins to decline as options are exited prior to expiration.
3. Click the CALLS **Ask** column at the $40 strike price. (Notice a Delta value of .31.)
4. Check the order bar to verify it contains entries similar to these:
   SINGLE BUY +10 A MAY 16 40 CALL 1.23 LMT LIMIT DAY
5. Check the risk profile in figure 14–7b. The stock price must rally to $42.31 to achieve breakeven.
6. If the order bar values are correct, click **Confirm and Send.**
7. Evaluate the Order Confirmation information. If satisfactory, click **Send.**

Figure 14–7b. Long Call Risk Profile

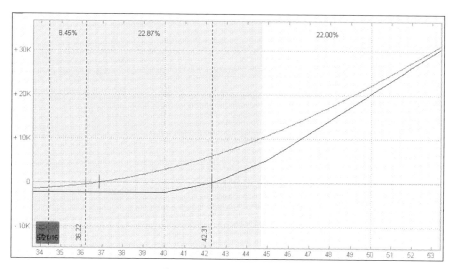

For illustration purposes only.

8. If filled, you own 10 A (Agilent Technology) 40 MAY 16 CALLS
    for $1.23/share for a total cost of $1,230 plus commissions and
    exchange fees. (This is a limit order, so it's entirely possible that
    your order may fill for less than the $1.23, perhaps at the $1.17
    Mark price for a cost of $1,170 plus transaction fees.)

Risks
Buyers have rights, but not obligations. The buyer's primary risk is
the amount of money paid in premium upon entry. In this example,
if the order fills as entered, the maximum risk is the $1,230 plus the
transaction fees originally paid for the option contracts.

Trade Management
Monitor the trade. You chose the underlying stock because it was
in an upward trend with a bullish chart pattern near support. If the
price performs in accordance with your analysis, it should resume
its rally. If you are willing to settle for 30% profit, be ready to sell the
options if the the premium rises from $1.23 to $1.59 or more. You

can also enter a GTC Mark-triggered stop order designed to issue a sell to close order if the Mark achieves a 50% to 70% profit. Another possibility would be to exercise the call option if the underlying stock rallies to $3.00 or more per share. The stock could be sold for a reasonable profit in intrinsic value. However, the ITM premiums could well deliver more than $3.00 per share, so it is incumbent on the option trader to do the math.

> **NOTE** Both protective and profit-target stops are commonly used by option traders. For example, you can place a GTC stop order if the Mark (premium) of the underlying option reaches a predetermined value, such as a 70% increase or a $25% decrease in the original premium paid. A Mark value of $2.09, from 1.7 x $1.23, would provide a profit of 70%. A Mark value of 90 cents could be used for protection. Delta-triggered stops are also used. For example, an ITM GTC Delta stop trigger at a Delta value of around .65 would return a reasonable profit. Of course, with ample time remaining prior to contract expiration, the underlying stock must rally sufficiently to put the $40 strike price fairly deep ITM.

Possible Outcomes

1. The price of the stock rallies according to plan and the strike price of the option contract becomes deep ITM. The buyer sells the option contract for $1.50/share more than originally paid and achieves a nice profit.
2. The price of the stock rallies according to plan and the strike price of the option contract becomes deep ITM. The buyer exercises the option and buys the stock from the option seller for several dollars below market price. The buyer immediately sells the stock for a substantial profit, or retains the stock in anticipation of a continuing price rally.

3. The option contract expires worthless. Without taking action, the buyer loses the entire premium originally paid.

4. The price rally either stalls or reverses and the premium begins to decrease in value. The buyer can place a sell to close order in an attempt to salvage some of the premium originally paid at entry.

5. The price of the stock remains in the low $40's. With ample time remaining, the trader sells ten $45 short call contracts and collects $500 in premium. This results in a "bull call spread." Within 30 days, the buyer rolls the $45 short call into another $45 call for another $300 in premium. Finally, the trader buys back the short $45 call and sells the long $40 call for $700. The trader recovered $1,500 in premium, but lost $1,000 dollars because the stock never rallied according to plan.

6. After studying the charts, the trader rolls the trade by combining a sell to close order with a buy to open order at a later contract expiration date. The trader may also choose a different strike price based on chart analysis. This may be "throwing good money after bad," unless there is a compelling reason to use what little premium may remain to help finance the new position when rolling. (Many traders will more than likely close the trade and move on. But with enough time remaining, selling short OTM calls will help recover some of the original premium paid when the 40 long call was initially entered.)

The Long Put

Structure

+1 OTM PUT

Expiration $\geq$ 90 days; this is a very bearish debit option strategy.

The strike price can be ATM to slightly OTM based on premium required and risk tolerance.

Description and Goals

This is another limited risk, unlimited reward strong bearish strategy in which one or more put options are bought. This strategy profits substantially from a drop in the price of the underlying stock as the long put's selected strike price either nears or becomes ITM. If the strike price of the long put becomes deep ITM, the buyer can sell the option for more premium than originally paid at entry. The buyer may prefer to exercise the option if more profit is available.

Long puts can also be used as hedges against a drop in the price of an underlying stock held within a trader's account. The cost of the long put can be reduced using what is called the collar strategy. The collar strategy combines a short call with the long put. The premium received from the sale of the short call offsets the cost of the long put, which can be substantial. The collar strategy is included in this chapter.

Because the long put benefits from a substantial drop in the underlying stock price, the buyer of the long put can buy the stock at a lower market price and then put the stock to an option seller on the other side of the trade. The seller on the other side of this trade is required to pay the buyer for the stock at the buyer's original option price. This transaction makes the long put extremely profitable. Here's an example:

1. A trader buys an ATM $50 put option for $2.00/share in premium.
2. The underlying stock drops to $45.
3. The put buyer exercises the option contract and receives $50/share for stock worth $45/share (the current market price).
4. Subtracting the $2.00/share option premium originally paid, the put buyer nets $3/share in profit less transaction fees.

If the buyer uses the put as "insurance" against a large price drop in an underlying stock that's held within the buyer's account, the long put protects the put buyer against a major loss. This is an example of using the long put as a stop-loss to guard against a strong price drop below the strike price of the long put.

Setup Parameters

- Goal: A substantial drop in the market price of the underlying. If the option becomes ITM, sell or exercise for profit.
- Bias: Very bearish, based on an overbought stock near resistance on the price chart
- Debit/Credit: Debit
- Chart Trend: Basing near resistance; pulling back from recent high
- Momentum Oscillator: Overbought near resistance
- Keltner Channel: Reduced ATR(14) envelope in anticipation of increased selling
- Implied Volatility $\leq$ 20%; Low IV% is used because the buyer wants to minimize the premium cost at entry. It also provides potential for an increase in IV% and premium.
- Greeks: Delta $\leq$ −0.25; Theta negative; Vega positive
- Days till Expiry: $\geq$ 90 Days (More gives the price additional time to work for the buyer.)
- Premium (Mark): Contracts × Premium should be $\leq$ 1.0% of account value.
- Probability of Touching or ITM: $\geq$ 50%
- Open Interest at Strike Price: $\approx$ 300; Total open interest @ all strikes $\geq$ 5,000
- Risk Amount $\approx$ 1.0% of account equity (governed by number of contracts traded)

How the Strategy Works

Buy one OTM put and pay the premium plus commissions and exchange fees. Wait for the premium to increase as a result of the anticipated drop in the market price of the underlying stock. Either sell the options for a profit in the premium or exercise the option by buying and putting the stock to the seller at the higher option price for profit.

Hands-On Activity

Scanning for a Trade

1. Locate a chart in which the price is trending downward in a current reversal pattern near resistance (see figure 14–8a).

   NOTE   The chart in figure 14–8a was captured several days prior to the option chain shown in figure 14–8b. The chart illustrates a downward-trending stock that traders look for when considering either shoring a stock or buying a long put option contract.

2. Choose an option contract date that expires in 90 days or more such as the one shown in figure 14–8b.

Figure 14–8a. Finding a Downward Trending Price at a Resistance Level

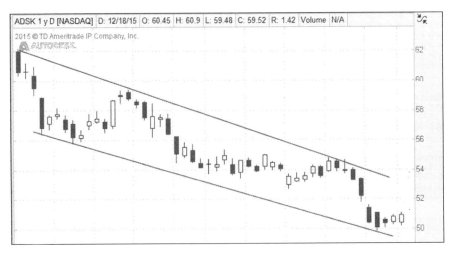

For illustration purposes only.

3. Select a put strike price having values close to these:

Figure 14–8b. Long Put Option Chain

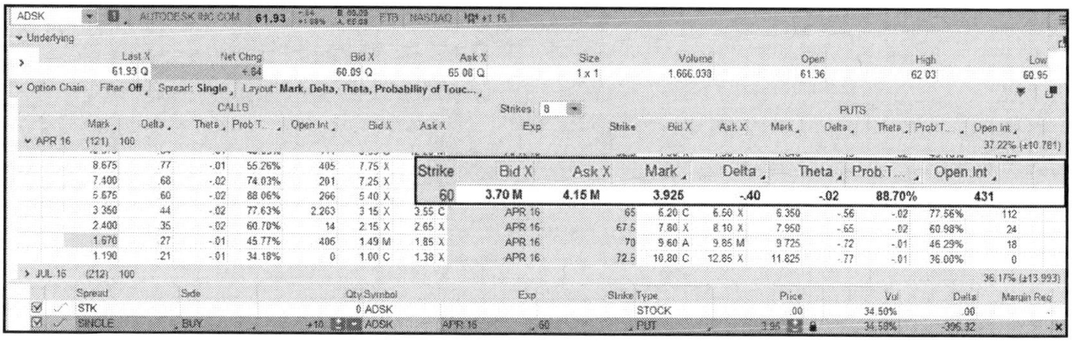

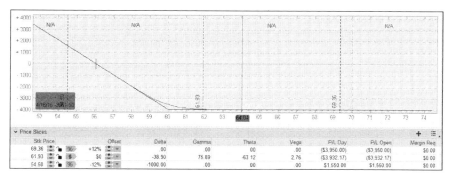

For illustration purposes only.

a. Mark > $3.00 at a Delta of approximately ≥.–40. (The selected strike price depends upon the price of the underlying, the premium value, current IV%, and risk tolerance.)
b. Prob. Touching > 80%
c. Open Interest at strike price ≥ 300; overall ≥ 3,000 (Actual = 431; overall > 8,000)

4. Examine the risk profile in figure 14–8c. Notice the maximum loss is the premium paid. The potential profit for a 12% drop in price is $1,550. More profit is available if the ADSK stock drops even farther.

Figure 14–8c. Long Put Risk Profile

For illustration purposes only.

Entry

1. Choose the option contract date (in this example, APR 16 is selected).
2. Ensure the Open Interest provides sufficient liquidity.
3. Click the PUTS **Ask** column at the 60.00 strike price.
4. Check the order bar to verify it contains entries similar to these:

SINGLE BUY +10 ADSK APR 16 60 PUT 3.95 LMT LIMIT DAY
DEBIT

5. If the order bar values are correct, click **Confirm and Send**.
6. Evaluate the Order Confirmation information. If satisfactory, click **Send**.
7. If filled, you own 10 ADSK (Autodesk, Inc.) 60.00 APR 16 PUTS for $61.93/Share for a total cost of $3,950 plus commissions and exchange fees. (This is a limit order. It's entirely possible that your order may fill closer to the current Mark of $3,925.)

Risks

Because option buyers have rights rather than obligations, the primary risk is the amount of money paid in premium upon entry. In this example the maximum risk is the $395 per contract plus the transaction fees.

Trade Management

Monitor the trade. If you bought the put with the intention of selling it for more premium than you paid, be prepared to enter a sell to close order when the premium increases by 30% to $5.14. You can also enter a Mark-triggered stop order designed to issue a sell to close order if the Mark becomes at or greater than $5.14. However, most longtime, experienced traders watch their trades and exit manually.

If you bought the $60 put as a hedge and the price of the stock drops below your $60 strike price, consider exercising the option and putting the stock to the seller.

If the price drop stalls, and ADSK begins to rally, consider entering a sell to close order to salvage as much of your premium as possible. However, always give your trade ample time to work in your favor before retreating, particularly if your original trade analysis was valid. Refrain from panicking when a temporary reversal occurs, especially when there's still plenty of time remaining until expiration.

Possible Outcomes

1. The option contract expires worthless. Without taking action the buyer will lose all premium, commissions, and exchange fees originally paid.

2. The price of the stock reverses direction and begins to rally. The buyer enters a sell to close order to recover as much premium as possible.

3. The price of the stock drops below the strike price of the put option. The buyer enters a sell to close order and receives more premium than originally paid.

4. If the stock price drops substantially below the option price; the buyer may exercise the option and put the stock to the seller. The buyer can profit by putting the stock to the seller who must pay the buyer the higher option strike price for the stock.

5. If additional analysis shows the stock at support with rising demand, the buyer may retain the stock until it can be sold to recover the option premium paid.

6. The price rally either stalls or reverses. The premium begins to decrease in value. The buyer can place a sell to close order in an attempt to salvage some of the premium originally paid at entry.

7. After studying the charts, the trader rolls the trade by combining a sell to close order with a buy to open order at a later contract expiration date. The trader may also choose a different strike price based on chart analysis. As in a previous example, this may be "throwing good money after bad" unless there is a compelling reason to use what little premium may remain to help finance the new position within the rolling order. (Most experienced traders will more than likely just close the trade and move on.)

The Covered Call or Covered Stock

Structure

+100 Shares, −1 OTM CALL

    Expiration date ≤ 60 days

NOTE   This is a debit option strategy when the trader simultaneously buys the stock and sells an OTM call. It is a credit strategy if the stock is already owned by the trader when the OTM call is sold. The strike price of the OTM call depends on whether the trader wants to:

1. Collect more premium in the future and keep the underlying stock, or
2. Keep the current premium in addition to having the underlying stock called away.

Description and Goals

The covered call strategy has been mentioned several times and the term *covered* was briefly described in chapter 10. The strategy involves the ownership of 100 shares of stock for each OTM call option sold. Although considered a limited reward strategy from the premium collected, substantial risk can exist from a possible drop in the price of the covering stock.

As just mentioned, the covered call involves selling an OTM call option that is collateralized by stock held within the option trader's brokerage account. The stock ownership underwrites the risk involved in the OTM short call option contract. If the short call becomes ITM and is exercised, the trader can deliver the stock already owned.

As you now know, when a short call is exercised by a buyer, the seller of the short call option must deliver the stock to the buyer. The option buyer must pay the seller for the stock at the short call option's strike price. Having the stock called away at a price higher than originally paid for the stock is part of the covered call strategy.

It is common for covered call options to be sold on stock already held within the option seller's brokerage account. For example, a trader who owns 1,000 shares of AAPL might sell ten OTM covered call options at a strike price that is $4 or more higher than current stock price. Of course the selected strike depends on available premium.

If the price of AAPL rallies and the shares are called away, the seller of the covered call options must deliver the shares of AAPL to the buyer at the option price. In this case, the seller profits from both the original option premium received in addition to the $4.00 increase in the price of the AAPL stock. The combination of several dollars in profit from the gain in intrinsic (stock) value and the higher premium originally received by being just a few dollars OTM is much more profitable than simply collecting $0.50 to $1.00/share in premium by trading farther OTM in an attempt to be "safe." Income from the increase in stock value is a desirable feature of the covered call strategy.

Traders who want to keep the underlying stock — their "pet stock" — will typically settle for much less premium income by going farther OTM. So these traders' initial goal is to collect a small amount of option premium and repeat the strategy several times throughout the following months or even years. But if the goal is to maximize profit, then the trader will sell premium at a strike price much closer to the current price of the underlying stock. These option traders are quite willing to have the stock called away at a higher price than originally paid. Therefore, the premium collected plus the profit received from the stock sale provides an even greater reward.

If the trader wants the stock back for another round of covered calls, a slightly OTM put can be sold. Again, if the strike price is close enough to the money, the premium will be high. This can be repeated until the option is exercised and the stock is put back to the trader. Then the trader can resume selling covered calls. Of course for this strategy to be satisfactory over the long haul, the underlying stock should be trending upward or moving sideways within a narrow band of support and resistance. But this condition coexists with low volatility. So it can be difficult to find sideways stocks with good premiums. It may be necessary to select a strike price at a higher Delta that is either ATM or even ITM for higher premium.

Covered calls often include the simultaneous purchase of stock and sale of short call options for a single commission. Trading platforms typically refer to the covered call strategy as a *Covered Stock*. Again, the goal is to collect premium in addition to potentially collecting income from an increase in the market price of the underlying stock.

As previously mentioned in the cash-covered put strategy, traders who want to own a stock often use cash-covered puts to acquire stocks at a discount. The premium received from the cash-covered put is used to reduce the purchase price of the targeted stock. For example, if a $50 stock is purchased in concert with a short put that pays $2.50/share in premium, the trader pays $47.50/share for the stock.

Although covered calls can be quite profitable from upward trending stocks, the ownership of the underlying stock can punish this strategy when the price of the stock suffers a drop in price. While the trader collects option premium, the drop in the stock price quickly defeats the gain in premium collected from this strategy. This is discussed in more detail in the following trade management section.

The Poor Man's Covered Call

This strategy is a variant of the traditional covered call. It involves buying a long-term (LEAP) slightly ITM call option contract that expires in 9 to 24 months (depending on premium and risk tolerance). This minimizes the effect of Theta (premium erosion from time). It also reduces the cost of the trade because you are buying an option rather than the underlying stock used to cover your short OTM call.

So the setup for a $50 stock might be to buy an ITM or ATM call for say $5.00/share that expires in about 12 months and sell an OTM call that expires inside 56 days. If the short call expires worthless or is bought back for profit, you can repeat the trade a few more times before closing the long "covering" call. Of course the price of the stock might breach the strike price of the short call at which time you exercise the long call and deliver the stock to the buyer at the strike price of the short call. The profit is comprised of the original premium plus the difference between the strike prices of the long and short calls.

The major problem with this strategy is in a possible lack in liquidity for the long-call option. Without it, you may not be able to fill the long-call's sell to close order. Without being filled, you would be required to pay cash for the stock that must be delivered to the buyer of the short call. The hard lesson learned here is to ALWAYS require ample liquidity before entering an option trade that must be closed quickly at some point in the future.

Setup Parameters

- Goal: An increase in the market price of the underlying. If the option becomes ITM, sell or exercise for profit. If the option remains OTM, repeat for another round of option income.
- Bias: Bullish (based on chart trend and pattern)
- Debit/Credit: Credit (excluding the cost of the stock)
- Chart Trend: Weekly and daily charts show consistent uptrends; presently basing.
- Momentum Oscillator: Oversold near recent support level
- Keltner Channel: Narrow ATR(14) envelope in anticipation of expansion
- Implied Volatility $\geq$ 80%; Covered call trader wants good IV% for good premium plus a strong potential for a price rally in the underlying stock.
- Greeks: Delta $\geq$ −0.25; Theta positive; Vega negative

- Days till Expiry: ≤ 60 Days
- Premium (Mark): ≥ $1.00 (when willing to sell the stock; less if you want to keep the stock)
- Probability ITM: ≈ 50% (more for higher premiums and to increase the opportunity to sell the stock for profit)
- Open Interest at Strike Price: ≥ 500; Total open interest @ all strikes > 10,000.
- Risk Amount ≈ 1.0% of account equity (governed by number of contracts traded)

How the Strategy Works

A traditional covered call strategy works by selling one OTM call contract for each 100 shares of stock either owned or bought in a covered stock transaction. If the underlying stock is not currently owned, simultaneously buy 100 shares of stock for each short call option contract sold. When simultaneously buying the stock and selling the short call options, the option premium collected is deducted from the price of the stock. You will pay a single commission for this trade plus an exchange fee for each option contract sold. If the option contract expires worthless, repeat until the stock is called away for profit.

Hands-On Activity

Scanning for a Trade

1. Scan for an up-trending stock that is presently oversold and near historical support.
2. Look for high current implied volatility at or above 80%.
3. Choose a contract date that expires in less than 60 days (the example in figure 14–9a expires in 36 days).
4. Look at the option chains in figure 14–9a. The top chain is set to **Spread: Single**.

Figure 14–9a. Covered Call Option Chain

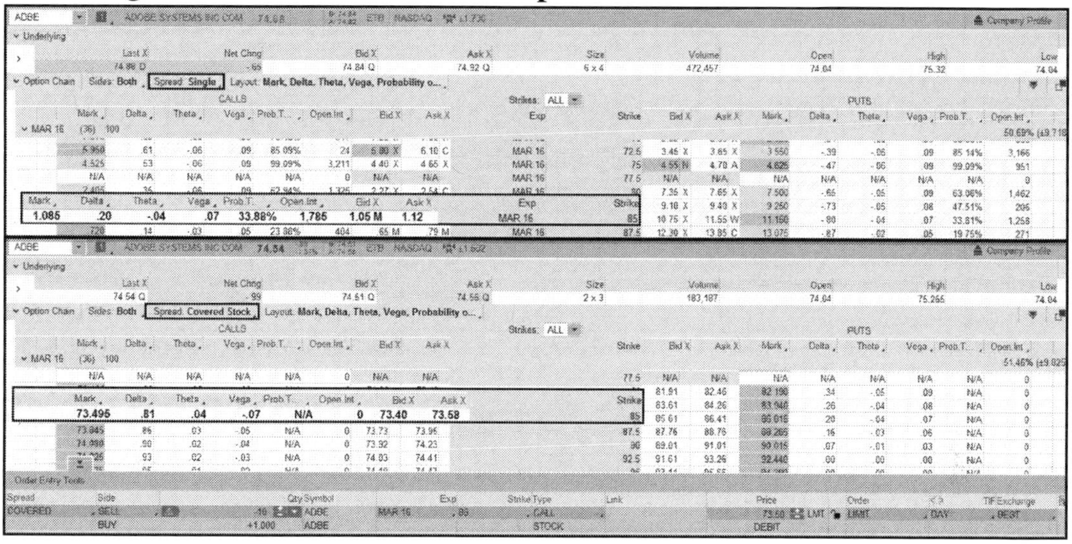

For illustration purposes only.

NOTE Always use Spread **Single** to evaluate option chain values including open interest, premiums, probabilities, etc. at each strike price before changing the Spread type to **Covered Stock** (both spread types are outlined in the figure).

5. Buy 1,000 shares of symbol ADBE (Adobe Systems) and simultaneously sell 10 MAR 16 $85 CALLS that expire in 36 days as described in the following entry paragraph.

Figure 14–9b. Covered Call Risk Profile

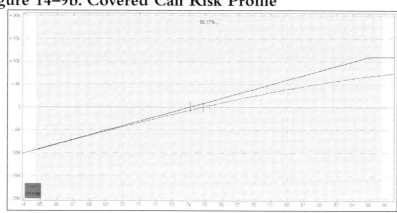

For illustration purposes only.

Entry

1. Choose the option contract date (in this example, MAR 16 is selected).
2. Ensure the Open Interest provides sufficient liquidity (use Spread: Single to check Open Interest values).
3. Click on **Single.** Examine the Spread drop-down list. Click **Covered Stock**.
4. Notice the values change. The Ask opposite the 85 CALLS strike price is now 73.58 (the stock price less the premium credit).
5. Click on the CALLS **Ask** column (the 73.58) at the $85 Strike. **NOTE** Clicking **Ask** buys the stock and sells the option when **Covered Stock** is selected as the *Spread* (see both of the Spread types, i.e., Single and Covered Stock in figure 14–9a above).
6. Review the order bar at the bottom of figure 14–9a. You are selling –10 85 call contracts and buying +1,000 shares of ADBE. You will pay (DEBIT) $73.50 for stock currently trading at $75.54. (The stock price is reduced by the premium received from the short 85 call.)
7. Check the order bar to verify it contains entries similar to these:

COVERED   SELL   -10   ADBE   MAR 16   85   CALL 73.50   LMT   LIMIT   DAY
            BUY   +1,000   ADBE   STOCK   DEBIT

8. If the order bar values are correct, click **Confirm and Send.**
9. Evaluate the Order Confirmation information. If satisfactory, click **Send**. (If filled, seller pays $73,500 for 1,000 shares of stock worth $74, 880 plus commissions and exchange fees. One contract would cost $7,350 plus fees.)

Risks

If the strike price of the short call becomes ITM by one cent, it may be exercised. The buyer must pay the seller $85.00/share for the stock. And of course the seller has already received the original premium of approximately ($1.05/share or $105 per contract sold).

The greatest risk in the covered call strategy is a drop in the price of the stock. When this happens the stock may have to be sold for a loss. Of course the trader retains the original $1,050 premium ($105 per option contract) received when traded. This is why it's important to carefully analyze the current stock price level on the charts to find a stock near a historical support level where buyer demand occurs.

Trade Management

Carefully monitor the price of the stock. If it begins to drop, you may be required to sell the stock before suffering a substantial loss. Selling the stock may require you to buy back your option to prevent the threat of holding a short call. In fact, without the highest option trading level, your brokerage will require you to exit the remaining naked short call. If the loss is due to an analyst downgrade or a poor earnings report, consider buying a put as a hedge against a substantial loss in the stock value.

With your short call intact, the long protective put creates what option traders call a collar. The collar option strategy consists of ownership of stock plus a long put and a short call. The collar strategy is described in detail later in this chapter. If you exercise the long put, you would simultaneously buy back your short call to prevent exposure to the naked call. If you happen to be eligible to trade naked options, you may still want to close the uncovered call, depending on volatility and the short call's Probability ITM.

But what about a simple protective stop a few dollars below the current price of ADBE? Some might think putting on an ADBE protective stop would be better — certainly cheaper, because protective stops are free until they fill. But we must think this through. If a protective stop is triggered, there's that naked short call again. For this reason, your brokerage's trading software would probably reject an attempt to enter a protective stop. So the collar (buying a long put) would be the most prudent stock hedging strategy, and the short call would be closed if and when you decide to exercise the long put.

An alternative is to simply retain the stock and sell more covered calls against it. At some point, a stock like ADBE will likely reverse its pullback and resume its upward trend. If your original analysis was rational and based upon proven trading rules, don't be hard on yourself. Nobody is correct 100% of the time relative to what the market is likely to do.

Possible Outcomes

1. The option contract expires worthless and the stock price moves either sideways or is slightly above the original purchase price — one of the trader's original goals. This outcome permits the trader to sell another covered call on the underlying stock.

2. The price of the stock has rallied to the option's strike price; the buyer exercises the option and pays the seller $85/share for stock originally bought in the mid $70's.

3. The stock price rallies above $80 and the short call remains OTM at expiration. The trader sells the stock for a profit and begins scanning other symbols for trade opportunities.

4. The stock price remains where it is. The passage of time (Theta) erodes the premium to $0.40 per share. The trader enters a buy to close order on the short $85 call for a 60% profit. The trader likes the stock and keeps it for future covered calls and/or an increase in the stock price.

5. The option's strike price remains OTM, but the contract has not expired. The trader rolls the ten $85 MAR 16 option contracts into $85 APR 16 options for additional premium with a buy to close order on the $85 option contract and a companion $85 sell to open option contract.

6. The price of the stock rallies to $85.25 (25 cents ITM). The trader is bullish on the stock and decides to roll the option

contract with a buy to close order on the $85 option contract and simultaneously sells a $90 APR 16 option contract for additional premium income.

7.   The price of the stock is rallying rapidly. The trader buys an ATM long call in anticipation of a continued strong rally. The trader also decides to let the stock be called away at the $85/share strike price. The stock is called away for $85/share. The trader's long call moves deeper ITM and is sold for profit.

8.   The option seller has the highest option trading permission and has a $72 protective stop on the stock. He assumes that if the $72 stop triggers, his $85 short call is quite safe. The price of the stock drops and the $72 protective stop triggers. The option seller loses $2.50/share from the drop in the price of the stock. This is offset by the $1.00 in premium originally collected when the covered stock was sold.

Bull Call Spread

Structure
+1 ATM, ITM, or slightly OTM CALL and −1 OTM CALL
   Same expiration dates ≥ 90 days; this is a debit option strategy.

Description and Goals
As implied by its name, the bull call spread is a popular bullish option strategy that offers both limited risk and reward. This strategy is usually a debit spread because the premium paid for the long call is almost always higher than that received from the sale of the short, farther OTM call. When the bullish bias proves to be correct and the long call becomes ITM, the premium of the long call can increase and be sold for more than originally paid.

This spread also belongs to the *vertical spread* family of option strategies. Vertical spreads are made up of two legs: one above the other on the same side of an option chain. In other words, vertical spreads include two calls or two puts at different strike prices. One leg is long and the other is short.

The bull call spread is used when a trader sees an up-trending stock with a price pattern signaling a rally off support, i.e., an increase in demand for the stock. The goal is for the long call to increase in value as the underlying stock price rallies. If the price of the underlying stock causes the short call to become ITM, the trade remains profitable as the long call is more valuable than the short call. More income is derived from exercising the long call option than is lost if the short call option is exercised and called away.

Barring exercise, the entire strategy can be closed for profit if the premium of the long call is equal to or slightly higher than the premium originally paid when this spread was initially traded. However, this must be done before Theta begins to erode the premium value of the long call beyond repair. Hence, bull call spreads most often use option contracts that expire in 90+ days. The longer time frame gives the underlying stock more time to work in the trader's favor.

Setup Parameters

- Goal: An increase in the market price of the underlying. If the long option becomes deep ITM, sell or exercise for profit. If both legs remain OTM, consider repeating for another round of income if market conditions still comply with your trading rules.
- Bias: Strong Bullish (based on chart trend and pattern)
- Debit/Credit: Debit
- Chart Trend: Weekly and daily charts show consistent uptrends; presently basing.
- Momentum Oscillator: Oversold near recent support level
- Keltner Channel: Narrow ATR(14) envelope in anticipation of expansion.
- Implied Volatility > 20% and < 40%; buyer wants low current IV% in anticipation of an IV% increase; this also reduces the premium cost of the long call leg.

- Greeks: Long leg Delta ≥ 0.30; Short leg Delta ≤ .30, Theta negative; Vega positive (both legs of the bull call spread can be ITM or OTM depending on the premium to be paid. See the debit call spread later in this chapter, which is another example of a bull call spread.)
- Days till Expiry: ≥ 90 days to give the trade time to work in trader's favor
- Net Premium (±Marks): ≥ −$1.00 (This can vary widely depending on your account balance and the distance between the long call and short call strike prices.)
- Probability ITM: +CALL > 70%; −CALL ≤ 30% (about one standard deviation OTM)
- Open Interest at Strike Price: ≈ 300; total open interest @ all strikes > 8,000
- Risk Amount ≈1.0% of account equity (governed by number of contracts traded)

  NOTE   The *bear put spread* strategy uses put options in the same way that the bull call spread uses call options. The bear put spread is bearish and favors a drop in the price of the underlying stock for profit. The bear put spread has the following structure:

  +1 ATM PUT and −1 OTM PUT

After studying the bull call spread, see if you can construct a bear put spread on an option chain. Select an overbought stock or ETF near a resistance level.

How the Strategy Works

The bull call spread is similar to the covered call, except a long call is used to "cover" the farther OTM short call. Buy one ATM or slightly OTM call (around a Delta .35 to .45) and sell one OTM call having the same expiration date for a net debit in premium.

The premium received from the short call offsets part of the cost of the long call. This trade is much cheaper than a covered call as it does not involve the cost of the underlying stock. The price of the underlying stock must rally to offset the original cost of the premium paid. And of course, Theta is also doing its work of eroding daily premiums. This depreciates the value of the long call and increases the value of the short call. The goal is for the stock to rally high enough to be able to sell the long call for more premium than originally paid, while the premium value of the short call decreases and can be bought for less premium than originally received. More profit may be available if the trader chooses to exercise the long call, it's possible for the stock to be sold at a price that is higher than the option price of the short call.

Hands-On Activity

Scanning for a Trade

1. Find an up-trending, oversold stock signaling a breakout from support, as shown in figure 14–10a.

   NOTE Figure 14–10a shows the SPY ETF price breaking through the bottom band of the Keltner channel. The bands have been extended from the default value of 1.5 to 2.0 ATR(14) on either side of the 20-period simple moving average, i.e., the SMA(20).

2. Choose a contract date that expires in 90 or more days.

3. Look at the option chain in figure 14–10b. The long call premium at the 202 strike for the underlying SPY SPDR ETF is $6.53. The short call premium at the $207 strike price is $3.89. The sum of the long and short call premiums comes to a $2.59 debit as shown on the order bar.

4. Study the bull call spread setup on the option chain in figure 14–10b. Then examine the risk profile in figure 14–10c.

Figure 14–10a. Finding a Bull Call Spread Candidate on a Chart

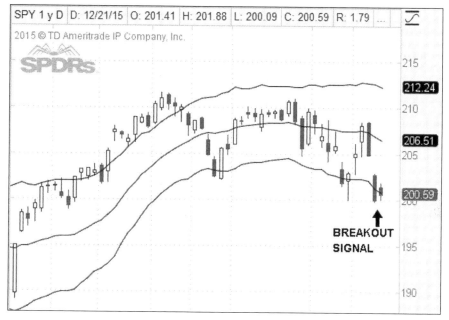

For illustration purposes only.

Figure 14–10b. Bull Call Spread Option Profile

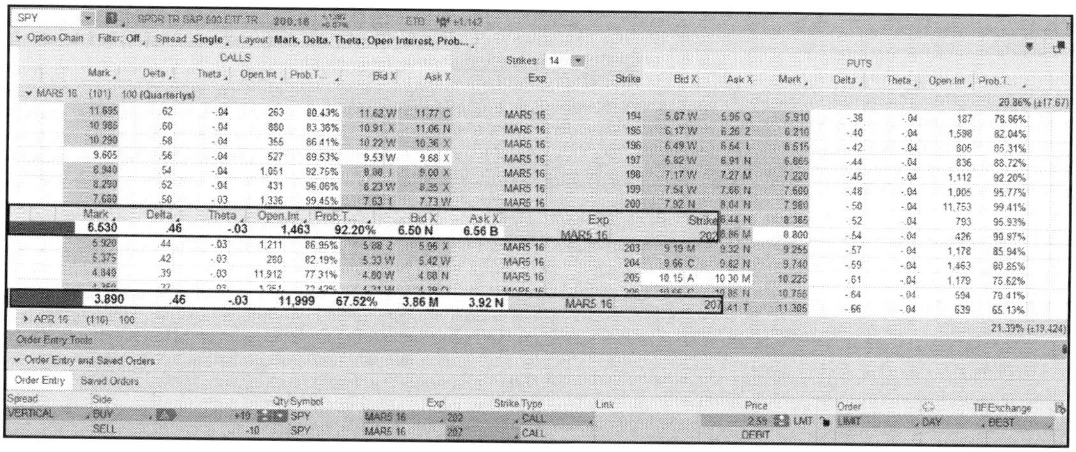

For illustration purposes only.

Figure 14–10c. Bull Call Spread Risk Profile

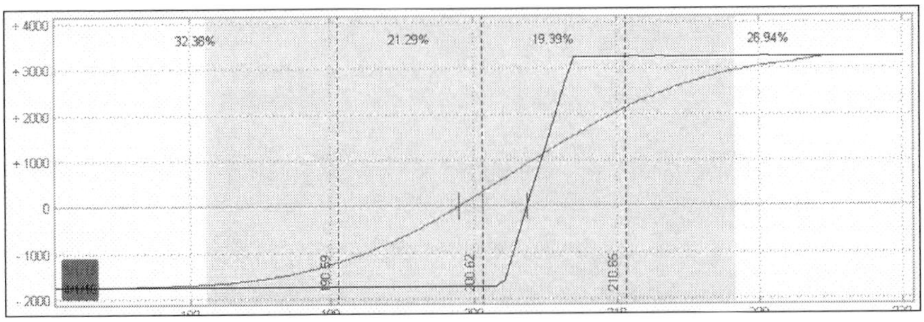

For illustration purposes only.

The risk profile begins at the initial cost of the trade on day one. You can use the calendars to "walk" the trade through time. The top calendar can be set to the Saturday following contract expiration. The line graph plots profits and losses for each price of the underlying. Profits and losses, in dollars, are displayed on the vertical Y axis. The P/L values correspond to possible price points of the underlying shown on the X axis at the bottom of the graph. You can adjust the dates throughout the life of the trade using the two calendars — one above the risk profile and the other immediately below the P/L Open column of the Price Slices section. You can add more price slices to see profits and losses based on other possible price levels of the underlying security.

If the price of the SPY SPDR ETF reaches $207 or more, your long call can be exercised for $5.00/share in profit less the original $2,590 cost of the trade. The short call can be called away if ITM by at least $207.01 per share. If both legs are exercised, your final gross profit is roughly $5,000 — the difference between 1,000 × (207 − 202). Subtracting the $2,590 originally paid, your net profit is $2,410 from $5,000 − $2,590 = $2,410. Other possible outcomes are provided in the Possible Outcomes section for this trade. Follow the steps described in the following entry procedure.

Entry

1. Choose the option contract date (in this example, MAY 16 is selected).
2. Ensure the Open Interest provides sufficient liquidity.
3. Click the CALLS **Ask** column at the 202 strike price to add the $202 calls order bar.
4. Press and hold the **Ctrl** key and click the CALLS **Bid** column at the 207 strike price to add the $207 calls to the order bar.
5. Check the order bar to verify it contains entries similar to these:

VERTICAL	BUY	+10	SPY	MAR 16	202	CALL	2.59		LMT	LIMIT	DAY
	SELL	-10	SPY	MAR5 16	207	CALL	DEBIT				

6. If the order bar values are correct, click **Confirm and Send.**
7. Evaluate the Order Confirmation information. The cost of this order is $2.59 per share or $2,590 plus fees.
8. If satisfactory, click **Send**.
9. If filled, you own 10 SPY MAY 16 $202 CALLS and sold 10 SPY MAY 16 $207 CALLS for a total cost of $2,590 plus commissions and exchange fees.

Risks

The major risk associated with a bull call spread is the total premium initially spent at entry. Even if the price of the underlying stock suffers a substantial price drop, the trade does not lose additional value. (Of course, the long call option loses premium value with time.) Delta tells you how much premium is exiting for each $1.00 loss in the stock price. Theta tells you how much premium value is exiting with the passage of each day. Because of the lengthy amount of time remaining till expiration, Theta is still only $0.03/share. The underlying premium of the long call declines faster than that of the short calls. This is because Delta is higher nearer the money.

Trade Management

If the stock continues to rally as expected at entry, let the profits run. The premium value of the $202 long call will appreciate rapidly. The $202 Delta will increase as the strike price becomes deeper ITM. Monitor the trade. If time begins to erode the premium, close both legs of the trade for profit before Theta begins to accelerate the reduction of the long call premium.

Also consider exercising the long call option and simultaneously buying to close the short call. Then you can sell the stock for a profit.

If the price of the underlying breaches the strike price of the short call, you can exercise the long call for something above $5.00 per share. If (and when) the short call is exercised, the buyer of the short call must pay $207/share. You are required to deliver 1,000 shares of stock at something above $207/share — the option price of your short call leg. The long call cannot be sold for profit without simultaneously closing the short call. Of course the short call would become an uncovered short call without the presence of the long call.

Possible Outcomes

1. The stock remains below $202 and the option contracts expire worthless. Without taking action, the buyer loses the premium originally paid for the long $202 call less the premium received from the short $207 call.

2. The price of the stock rallies and breaches the price of the $207 short call according to plan. The trader exercises the $202 long call and pays $202/share for stock now worth something north of $207/share. The buyer on the other side of the $207 short call also exercises the option and pays $207/share for SPY. The bull call spread earns $5,000 less the original $2,590 debit less transaction fees.

3. The price of the long call rallies to $206 with only 10 days remaining till contract expiration. The trader enters a buy to close order for the $207 short call which fills for $0.50 in premium cost.

Next, the trader exercises the $202 option and immediately sells the SPY ETF for $206/share — a profit of $4.00/share.

4. The price of the long call rallies to $206 with only 10 days remaining till contract expiration. The trader enters a buy to close order for the $207 short call which fills for $0.50 in premium cost. The premium of the long call has risen as the long call goes deeper ITM. The option contract has ample liquidity (open interest) and can be sold for a $4.50/share, or $4,500 in total premium. Once both legs of the trade are closed, the trader realizes a profit from the sale of the long call option less the original cost and the premium paid to close the $207 short call as follows:

    ● Premium received when selling the ITM $202 long call: $4,500
    ● Original premium paid for the spread: $2,590
    ● Premium paid to close the OTM $207 short call: $500
    ● Total Profit: $4,500 − $3,090 = $1,410 (less transaction fees)

5. The anticipated price rally stalls and then reverses direction. The premium value of the $202 long call begins to decrease. The trader decides to recover as much premium as possible to minimize the loss. The trader places a buy to close order for the $207 short call for slightly less premium than originally paid and a sell to close order for the long $202 long call to recover the premium that remains. The trade loses several hundred dollars in premium.

6. After studying the charts, the trader rolls the trade by combining a sell to close order with a buy to open order at a later contract expiration date. The trader may also choose different strike prices based on chart analysis and a new support level. This may be "throwing good money after bad," unless there is a compelling reason to use what little premium may remain to help finance the new position within the rolling order. (As previously mentioned, most experienced traders will more than likely just close the trade and move on, rather than creating a rolling order.)

Bull Put Spread

Structure

+1 OTM PUT, −1 ATM or slightly OTM PUT

Same expiration dates; typically ≤ 60 days, but can be longer

Description and Goals

As the name implies traders who use the bull-put spread expect the price of the underlying stock to rally. It is a limited risk, limited reward strategy, and is popular in spite of its limited profit potential comprised of the net credit received when the short put is sold for more premium than the cost of the long put located at an OTM strike price below. Hence, the primary goal of this strategy is to collect a net premium that is calculated by subtracting the cost (debit) of the long put from the credit received from the sale of the short put. And, of course, a rally in the price of the stock moves the short ATM put away from the prospect of being exercised.

Finding an underlying symbol to be used with this strategy requires scanning for an up-trending stock with a chart pattern that signals a price rally off of a historical support level. The scanning process also includes the evaluation of option premium to ensure the net premium received is worth the risk associated with this trade.

The long OTM put also adds "insurance" to this strategy by limiting the amount that can be lost. If the underlying price should drop below the long OTM put before the short ITM put is exercised, the trader may close both legs and recover some premium from the long leg. If the short ITM put is exercised, the trader may exercise the long put to offset the loss.

Setup Parameters

- Goal: Premium collection and an increase in the market price of the underlying.

- Bias: Strong Bullish (based on chart trend and a consolidation or reversal pattern)
- Debit/Credit: Credit
- Chart Trend: Weekly and daily charts show consistent down-trends; presently basing
- Momentum Oscillator: Oversold near historical resistance level
- Keltner Channel: Narrow ATR (14) envelope in anticipation of expansion
- Implied Volatility % ≥ 60% and ≤ 80%; Buyer wants moderate current IV% for reasonable premium, as this strategy buys one or more puts and sells an equal number of puts above.
- Greeks: Delta ≥ 0.30 (or a Delta spread width ≈.20); net Theta positive; net Vega negative
- Days till Expiry: ≤ 45 days (Minimize the risk associated with the short put.)
- Net Premium (±Marks): ≥ $0.75 (governed by account balance if unsuccessful)
- Probability ITM: +PUT ≤ 80%; −PUT ≤ 90% (at or slightly ITM)
- Open Interest at Strike Price: ≈ 300; Total open interest @ all strikes > 8,000
- Risk Amount ≈1.0% of account equity (governed by number of contracts traded)

How the Strategy Works

Buy one OTM put and sell one ATM put having the same expiration date for a net income of $1.00 or more per share in premium. The spread between the long put and short put may have to be "widened" by one or two strike prices to increase premium income. This action depends entirely on the separation between strike prices. Too much separation between the short and long puts can defeat the protection provided by the long put.

As the price of the underlying stock rallies, the short put and long put go farther OTM. The premium values decline and the spread can be sold for a profit of 30% or more.

If the price suffers a large drop, the long put serves as "insurance" against a major loss.

Hands-On Activity

Scanning for a Trade

1. Choose a contract date that expires in less than 60 days.
2. Look at the option chain in figure 14–11a. The price of the underlying CRM stock is $78.18. The short put premium at the 77.5 strike price is $2.37; the long put premium at the 75 strike price is $1,485. The combination nets approximately $0.90 per share in premium income.
3. Check the option chain in figure 14–11a and the risk profile in figure 14–11b. The risk profile shows vertical lines at ±2 standard deviations either side of the current stock price.

    NOTE The risk profile's price slices are quite flexible. You can use standard deviations, percentages, or dollar values above and below the current stock price. You can also add price slices if you wish to evaluate two or even more potential values.

Figure 14–11a. Bull Put Spread Option Chain

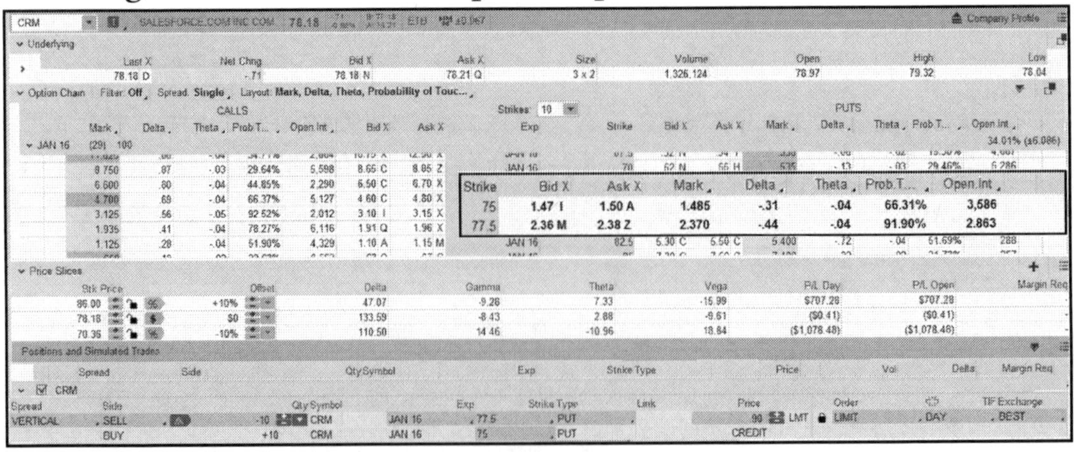

For illustration purposes only.

Figure 14–11b. The Bull Put Spread Risk Profile (±2 Standard Deviations Shown)

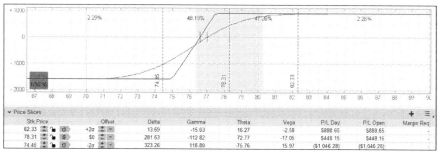

For illustration purposes only.

Entry

1. Choose the option contract date (in this example, JAN 16 is selected).
2. Ensure the Open Interest provides sufficient liquidity.
3. Click the PUTS **Bid** column at the 77.5 strike price to add the 77.5 puts order bar.
4. Press and hold the **Ctrl** key and click the PUTS **Ask** column at the 75 strike price to add the long 75 puts order bar. This creates the bull put spread strategy.
5. Verify the two legs of the debit call spread on the order bar in figure 14–11a. The values should be similar to these.

VERTICAL	SELL	-10	CRM	JAN 16	77.5	PUT	.90		LMT	LIMIT	DAY
	BUY	+10	CRM	JAN 16	75	PUT	CREDIT				

6. If the order bar values are correct, click **Confirm and Send**.
7. Evaluate the Order Confirmation information. If satisfactory, click **Send**.

Risks

The primary risk associated with the bull put spread is when an unwanted drop in the price of the underlying stock occurs. A price drop penalizes the trader if the short put becomes deeper ITM and is exercised prior to or upon contract expiration. When the contract is exercised, the buyer puts the stock to the seller who must pay the buyer at the short put's option price. For example, if the option price of the short put is $60 and the stock drops to $56, the seller must pay $60 per share for stock valued at $56. This is a loss of $400 per option contract.

If the option price of the long put is at $58, our trader could exercise the long put to offset the loss from the short option by $200 per contract and then sell the stock on the open market. Of course the trader could also hold the stock in hopes of a price reversal and rally.

Trade Management

If the price of the stock rallies as expected, the trader can wait for the contract to expire worthless. If enough liquidity and high enough premium exists to sell to close the long put, the trader may decide to enter an order to close the long put. However, the trader must be confident that the price of the underlying stock will not reverse direction and drop back to the strike price of the short put.

As mentioned in the preceding Risks paragraph, if the price of the underlying drops below the strike price of the short put, the short put may be exercised for a substantial loss. That loss might be offset if the long put becomes ITM as mentioned in the Risks paragraph. The worst case is when the stock price settles somewhere between the strike prices of the short put and the long put. (This is one of the outcomes described below.)

Possible Outcomes

1. The underlying stock price rallies according to plan and the market price is greater than the strike price of the short put at expiration. Both put contracts expire worthless. The trader retains the original premium collected upon entry.

2. The underlying stock price rallies according to plan. CRM's market price rallies several dollars above the strike price of the

short put a week prior to contract expiration. The short put's probability of becoming ITM drops below 15%. The long put is sold to recover residual premium; the remaining short is retained and expires worthless upon contract expiration. The trader retains 100% of the original premium collected when this trade was entered in addition to the premium collected from the sale of the long OTM put. (Increasing premium income by selling a long option is a common option strategy; in fact, it is at the core of the butterfly spread described later in this chapter.)

3. The price of the underlying drops to $72 — below the $75 strike price of the long put. The short put is exercised and the trader pays $77.50/share for the $72/share CRM stock. The trader exercises the long $75 put and receives $75/share for the $72 stock. The trader loses $2.50/share. This loss is offset by the $0.90 in premium originally collected at entry. The net loss is $1.60/share for ten contracts (or 1,000 shares) from:
    ● Short put: pay $77.50/share × 1,000 = $77,500
    ● Long put: receive $75/share × 1,000 = $75,000
    ● Loss: $2.50/share from $77.50 − $75.00
    ● Add back the $0.90/share premium received at entry: $2.50 − $0.90 = $1.60
    ● Total Loss: $1.60/share × 1,000 = $1,600

    NOTE   As long as the price of CRM stock is below the strike price of the long put, it can be exercised for $75/share anytime prior to contract expiration, as an American style option contract governs the option trader's exercise rights. Regardless of how far the price of the long put drops, the long $75 put restricts the amount that can be lost. (This same dynamic is used in the popular *iron condor* strategy, also described later in this chapter.)

4. The price of the underlying is at $76/share (between the strike price of the short and long puts). The short put is exercised and the stock is put to the seller who must pay $77.50/share for the

CRM stock. Our trader loses $1.50/share ($77.50 − $76.00) which is offset somewhat by the original $0.90/share premium received upon entry. This results in a total loss of $0.60/share, a total loss of $600 for ten contracts. The long put either expires worthless or the trader may attempt to sell it for what little premium may remain.

4. Once the trader is in possession of the CRM stock, it may either be sold for the $600 loss plus transaction fees or retained in anticipation of a rally. Of course, any expected rally should be based upon a careful evaluation of the underlying price charts.

ITM Vertical Call Spread

Structure

+1 ITM CALL, −1 ITM CALL higher strike

Same expiration dates (typically ≤ 60 days, but can be longer)

Important: Avoid earnings releases for the duration of the option contract.

Description and Goals

This option strategy is actually another bull call spread except it is an ITM bull call spread. Although it has the identical structure to the popular bull call spread strategy, both the long and short call strike prices are both placed ITM. The difference between the long and short ITM calls is usually two or more strike prices. The strategy is a debit spread. It is a controlled risk, limited reward strategy. The higher strike price of the long call is usually several dollars more than the premium received from the sale of the short call. The maximum risk is the debit paid upon entry. The maximum profit is limited by the strike price of the short call.

This strategy is used with up-trending stocks in which the trader must have a strong bullish bias. Therefore, the trader expects the price of the underlying stock to experience a strong rally within the next 60 to 80 days. Stocks that have been experiencing steady upward price trends over a long period of time are selected when a strong pullback is observed. Common signals include a bull flag, cup and handle, a double or triple bottom, or a previously encompassed candle near a historical support level. Oversold studies off recent historical lows may signal an imbalance in equilibrium. Seek a price drop to a historical support level where demand causes the stock price to reverse and resume its upward trend.

This spread is recommended by trader Chuck Hughes. Mr. Hughes uses a modified Keltner Channel on a day-interval chart to locate pullbacks that pierce the bottom Keltner Channel band. The normal $1.5 \times ATR(14)$ is modified to $2.0 \times ATR(14)$ above and below the default 20-period simple moving average. The charts of longtime up-trending stocks are searched for pull-backs that resemble the bull flag or cup and handle pattern mentioned above. Both of these patterns are described in chapter 7.

As outlined in the structure, the ITM long call leg and an ITM or ATM short call leg are separated by two to four strikes, or roughly a $10 to $20 spread. Both legs of this spread use the same expiration date. As the name implies, this is an ITM debit spread. Of course the position of the short call helps to finance the total cost of this strategy.

It's important to avoid earnings releases for the duration of this strategy to avoid unwanted price transients from a negative earnings report. The 60-day duration gives this strategy time to resume its normal upward price trend from the low point when traded. Because a long ITM position is included, look for reasonably low implied volatility.

Setup Parameters

- Goal: A strong price rally off support. This strategy profits from an increase in premium as the ITM calls become deeper ITM.

The short ITM call is closed and the long ITM call is closed for profit. The maximum loss is the premium debit paid at entry.

- Bias: Strong Bullish (see Keltner Channel below)
- Debit/Credit: Debit
- Chart Trend: Weekly and daily charts show consistent uptrends; presently basing
- Momentum Oscillator: Oversold near recent support level
- Keltner Channel: Dropping candles breaking through bottom $2.0 \times$ ATR(14) envelope and basing in anticipation of a return to the dominant upward trend
- Implied Volatility % $\geq$ 40%; buyer wants moderate current IV% for low long call premium at entry. This trade requires a rally to follow to succeed.
- Greeks: Delta positive; Theta positive; Vega positive
- Days till Expiry: $\approx$ 60 days (Require enough time to resume upward trend.)
- Net Premium ($\pm$Marks): $\geq$ −\$3.00 to −\$15.00 (governed by account balance and risk rules)
- Probability ITM: Both the +CALL and −CALL are ITM when traded; Deltas are > 0.60.
- Open Interest at Strike Prices: $\approx$ 500; Total open interest @ all strikes > 8,000
- Risk Amount $\approx$1.0% of account equity (governed by premium and number of contracts)

How the Strategy Works

Choose an upward trending stock in which the price has temporarily pierced the bottom 2.0 ATR(14) envelope. Figure 14–12a illustrates a long-term upward trending stock in which a breakout opportunity exists. The signal is valid and provides an opportunity for a successful trade.

Figure 14–12a. ITM Vertical Call Spread Price Chart with Modified Keltner Channel

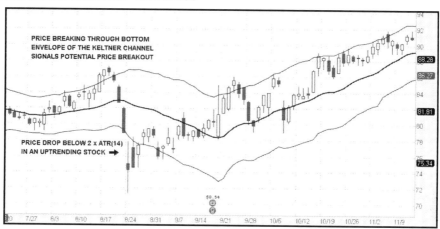

For illustration purposes only.

The preceding chart shows a drop below the ATR(14), signaling a price reversal and possible entry for a resumption in the trend. But this drop should not occur within 60 days prior to an earnings release. Unfortunately, this chart illustrates a price drops that is too close to an earnings release, so you would pass and continue scanning for a similar setup. The combined premium plus transaction costs for this strategy is the maximum amount put at risk when entering the trade. Because trade entry requires a high debit, use your risk management rules to govern the number of contracts and corresponding money put at risk.

The potential rally from the bottom wick of the lowest candle (the low for the chart interval) is in the neighborhood of $72. Approximately one month later the price breaks above the ATR(14)'s top envelope at $86 — a strong rally of $14.00 as predicted.

Hands-On Activity

Scanning for a Trade

1. Choose a contract date that expires in approximately 60 days.
2. Ensure that the contract period does not include an earnings release event.

3. Examine the option chain in figure 14–12b and the risk profile in figure 14–12c.

4. The price of the underlying ADBE stock is $86.11. The long call premium at the 75 strike price is $12.20; the short call premium at the 85 strike price is $4.45. The debit paid is $12.20 − $4.45 = $7.75.

5. Examine the risk profile in figure 14–12c to see what price is required for this strategy to return a profit. The strategy becomes profitable when ADBE rallies above $82.71.

Entry

1. Choose the option contract date (in this example, APR 16 is selected).

2. Ensure the Open Interest provides sufficient liquidity. (Both legs are above 300.)

3. Click the CALLS **Ask** column at the 75 strike price to add $75 calls to the order bar.

4. Press and hold the **Ctrl** key and click the CALLS **Bid** column at the 85 strike price to add the $85 short calls to the order bar.

5. Your option chain and order bar should resemble the one shown in figure 14–12b.

Figure 14–12b. ITM Vertical Call Spread Option Chain

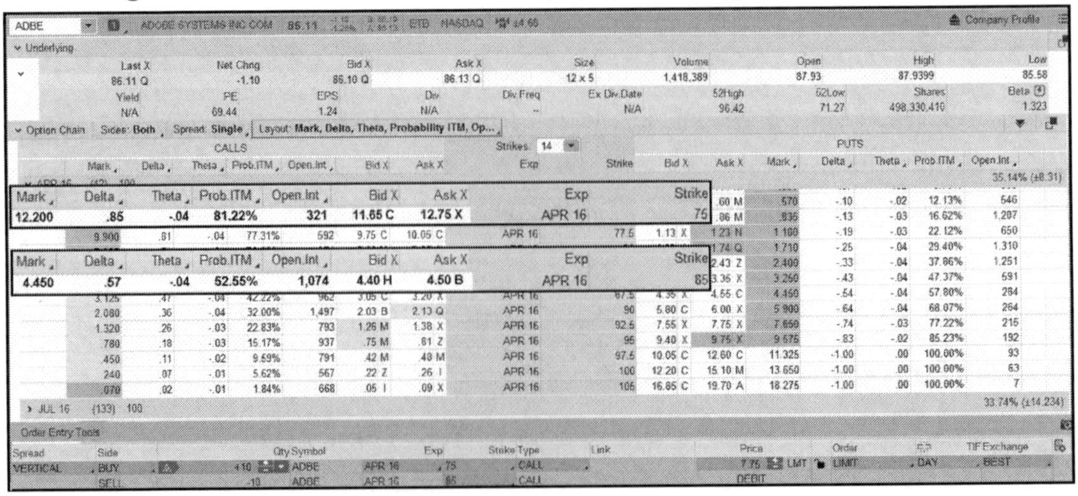

For illustration purposes only.

Figure 14–12c. ITM Verical Call Spread Risk Profile

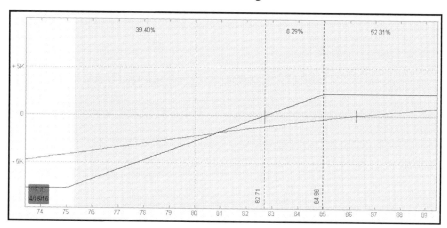

For illustration purposes only.

6. Verify the two legs of the debit call spread on the order bar, including the number of contracts, are similar to these:

VERTICAL	BUY	+10	ADBE	APR 16	75	CALL	7.75		LMT	LIMIT	DAY
	SELL	-10	ADBE	FEB 16	85	CALL	DEBIT				

7. If your order bar values are reasonable, click **Confirm and Send.**

8. Evaluate the Order Confirmation information. If satisfactory, click **Send**.

9. If filled, you own 10 ADBE 16 $75 CALLS and sold 10 ADBE APR 16 $85 CALLS for a total cost of $7,750 plus commissions and exchange fees. This is the maximum amount of money at risk. (When trading a small account, trade fewer option contracts.)

Risks

If the price of ADBE fails to resume its upward trend or drops within the contract period, the debit paid at entry is the maximum amount at risk. If the short call can be closed you may be able to sell what premium remains in the long call to salvage part of the premium originally paid.

Trade Management

If the underlying stock price rallies as planned, the trader can buy to close the short call and sell to close the long call for a profit. The trader can also exercise the long call at the original option price and then sell the stock for profit. If the price of the stock moves sideways or drops, consider closing both legs of this trade to recover some of the premium originally paid.

Possible Outcomes

1. The price of the underlying drops below the strike price of the long call option and expires worthless. Without taking action, the buyer loses the premium originally paid for the long 75 call less the premium received from the short $85 call.

2. The price of the stock rallies and breaches the $85 short call price according to plan. The buyer on the other side of the short $85 call exercises the option for $85/share. Our trader exercises the $75 option by paying $75.00/share and delivers the stock to the buyer of the short $85 call. A gross profit of $10.00/share is received less transaction fees. If the price of the ADBE stock rallies even higher than $85, the profit from this trade increases accordingly.

3. The price of the long call rallies to $90. The trader exercises the 75 option contract and pays $75/share for the $90/share stock — a gain of $15/share. If the $85 short call contracts have not been exercised, the trader closes the options with a buy to close order and pays the required premium.

4. After studying the charts, the trader rolls the trade by combining a sell to close order with a buy to open order, both at a later contract expiration date. The trader may also choose different strike prices based on chart analysis and a new support level. This may be a case of "throwing good money after bad" unless there is a compelling reason to use what little premium may remain to help finance the new position within the rolling order. The fact that the price breaks the lower Keltner channel $2.0 \times ATR(14)$ band is

a short event that signals a price reversal. If the reversal and break-out fails, the price may continue downward or sideways. When this trade doesn't work, retreat and look for other opportunities. (As previously mentioned, when the breakout signals prove false, experienced traders will close the trade and move on.)

Iron Condors, Jade Lizards, and Twisted Sisters (Hedged Strategies)

Structure

Iron Condor:

−1 OTM PUT, +1 farther OTM PUT, and −1 OTM CALL, +1 farther OTM CALL

The variations:

Jade Lizard: −1 OTM PUT (unprotected), −1 OTM CALL, +1 farther OTM CALL

Twisted Sister: −1 OTM PUT, +1 farther OTM PUT, −1 OTM CALL (unprotected)

All contracts in these option strategies have same expiration date, typically ≤ 56 days.

Description and Goals

The iron condor is a neu-tral strategy that includes a short call and a short put bracketed by a long call and a long put one or two strikes farther OTM as shown in the adjacent diagram.

The goal of the iron condor is to collect more premium from short put and call than is paid for the long put and call. The long put and call are typically one or more strikes farther OTM. These long legs are used for "insurance" to minimize a loss from an unexpected strong rally or drop in the price of the underlying.

Before the iron condor is entered, there must be both substantial liquidity and premium to make this strategy worth considering. This is required to offset the cost of the exchange fees that must be paid for four different option contract legs. For example, a ten-contract iron condor includes 40 option contracts (4 legs of 10 contracts each). If you are paying an exchange fee of $1.00 for each of the ten option contracts, you must pay $40 at entry and another $40 at exit for a roundtrip cost of $80 in exchange fees plus your brokerage commissions. Of course you can let the contracts expire worthless to avoid the exit fees. However, this restriction may not be possible if one of your vertical spreads is threatened by a price move of the underlying stock or if you wish to take what small amount of profit is offered prior to expiration. Therefore, when using an iron condor, ensure sufficient premium exists to justify the cost of the exchange fees and brokerage commissions.

The account margin used by iron condors is reduced by the long call and put legs. The ability to trade a greater number of contracts for less margin expense is a major advantage of this strategy. But as mentioned in the preceding paragraph, the fact that the iron condor used four separate option legs increases the overhead. So it is important to ensure the premium credit is sufficiently high to offset the cost of the exchange fees.

Creating the iron condor requires the trader to move the long insurance legs far enough above the short call and below the put to receive sufficient premium. Because premiums are typically higher for puts than for calls, the distance between the two strikes of the put legs may be narrower than that of the calls. For example, the short and long puts may be separated by a single strike while the short and long calls may be separated by two or three strikes for increased premium.

There are two variations to the iron condor. When only a short call leg is used (omitting the long call insurance leg), the trade is called a *twisted sister*. Traders who use twisted sisters are confident that the price of the underlying will not rally to the strike price of the short call, which is actually the dreaded short call. Recall how an unprotected short call is an uncovered option trade (and only permitted for traders with the highest option trading permission).

The other variation is called a *jade lizard*. Traders who use jade lizards omit the protective long put below the short put leg. This results in a cash-covered put and a short call that is backed by a long call above for insurance.

Knowing these two iron condor variations exist should suffice. Obviously, not paying the premium required for one of the long option legs increases the net premium received. But before you enter either of these unprotected variations, be sure of your bias is based on the underlying price charts. The small amount of premium and exchange fees saved by omitting one of the long protective option legs may not be worth the risk of being exercised.

Setup Parameters

- Goals: Collect the difference in premiums between the short and farther OTM long put and the short call and farther OTM long call. Sell the long call, put, or both for more income when safe to do so. Adhere to your rules before "uncovering" either of the short legs.
- Bias: Neutral to slightly bearish (An ideal price should have well-defined support and resistance levels; this strategy is not well-suited to a bullish bias.)
- Debit/Credit: Credit
- Chart Trend: Weekly and daily charts show long-term neutral price movement within a narrow support and resistance range.
- Momentum Oscillator: Neutral to slightly overbought
- Keltner Channel: ATR(14) envelope mildly narrow
- Implied Volatility % ≥ 20% and ≤ 40%; buyer wants moderate IV% for moderate premium; however excessive volatility may result in an excessive price drop or rally.
- Greeks: Delta ±0 (offsetting); Theta negative; Vega negative
- Days till Expiry: < 45 days; The goal is premium collection; Theta is the iron condor's ally.

- Net Premium (±Marks): ≥ $0.40;Sufficient premium is required to afford the involved risk.
- Probability ITM: All legs should be far OTM with Deltas at or below ±0.20. The −call leg should have a lower Probability ITM and Delta value than the −PUT leg, i.e., less ≤ 0.15.
- Open Interest at Strike Prices: ≥ 500; total open interest @ all strikes > 10,000
- Bid to Ask spread (the difference between the Bid and Ask prices) should be quite small;something ≤ $0.04 is acceptable for many actively traded stocks with prices below $100.The spread increases substantially with higher prices of the underlying.
- Risk Amount ≈1.0% of account equity (governed by premium and number of contracts)

How the Iron Condor Strategy Works

Choose iron condor candidate stocks based on price charts with well-defined support and resistance levels as shown on the QQQ price chart shown in figure 14–13a.

Figure 14–13a. Finding an Iron Condor Trade on the QQQ Price Chart

For illustration purposes only.

Figure 14–13b. Setting up the Iron Condor Option Chain

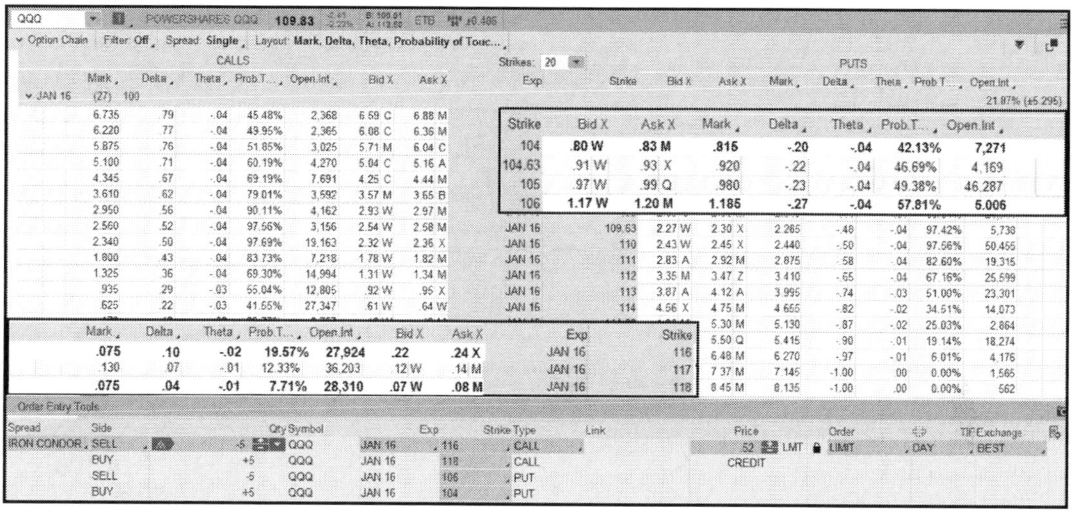

For illustration purposes only.

Once an iron condor candidate is found on the price chart, examine the corresponding option chain. The QQQ option chain is shown in figure 14–13b. Notice the highlighted put and call strike prices. These indicate all four of the OTM iron condor legs comprised of a short and long put and a short and long call. The selected option chain includes contracts that expire in 27 days.

As you can see from the option chain in figure 14–13b, enough premium should exist to justify the cost of the trade. The iron condor shown on the order bar provides $0.52/share. The five contracts × four legs result in a total of 20 option contracts, or roughly $20 in exchange fees. Assuming a brokerage fee of between $5 and $10, the transaction costs come to $30. The premium collected amounts to $260. This nets $230 in premium income after trading fees.

Before entering the order, the iron condor risk profile is examined. The risk profile for this trade is shown in figure 14–13c.

Figure 14–13c. Examining an Iron Condor Risk Profile

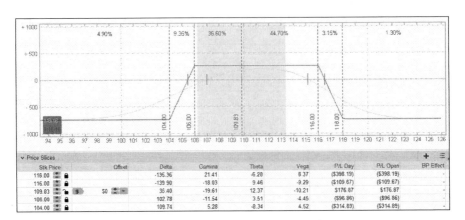

For illustration purposes only.

As long as the price of the underlying stock remains between support and resistance levels and the short call and put legs, the trade will provide the intended premium income. It will either expire worthless or you can close it when a satisfactory level of profit is returned.

The call side of the iron condor is the most vulnerable, as the price could settle between the short and long call legs and be exercised. This situation would require you to deliver the optioned stock to the buyer on the other side of your short call leg. And, the protective long leg would essentially be "baggage." Because of this prospect, carefully monitor the short call and be prepared to close it as necessary. If the price rallies past the long protective leg and both call options are exercised, the loss is restricted to the difference between the cost and income generated by the two call legs.

The short and long put legs of this strategy have the same construct as a bull put spread. The short put becomes a cash-covered put (explained earlier) and the long put below limits a possible loss to its strike price. This makes the put legs of the iron condor more conservative and less risky than that of the call legs.

Because the iron condor variations were alluded to above, the jade lizard is briefly described. The jade lizard is a safer strategy than its twisted sister cousin, which includes the more vulnerable short call option. Also notice how the jade lizard's put options offer superior premium when compared to the premium offered by the more vulnerable call options of the twisted sister.

Figure 14–13d includes a QQQ jade lizard setup on an option chain; figure 14–13e presents a corresponding jade lizard risk profile. Although similar, it's apparent that the put side of this strategy is missing its long protective put leg. This is reflected by the continuation of the downward angular loss plot at the left-hand side of the graph.

Also notice the premium has increased from \$0.52/share to \$1.34/share for a total of \$670 in premium income. This is a 2.58% increase in income — a considerably richer option strategy for a small increase in the amount of risk.

Figure 14–13d. Setting up the Jade Lizard Option Chain

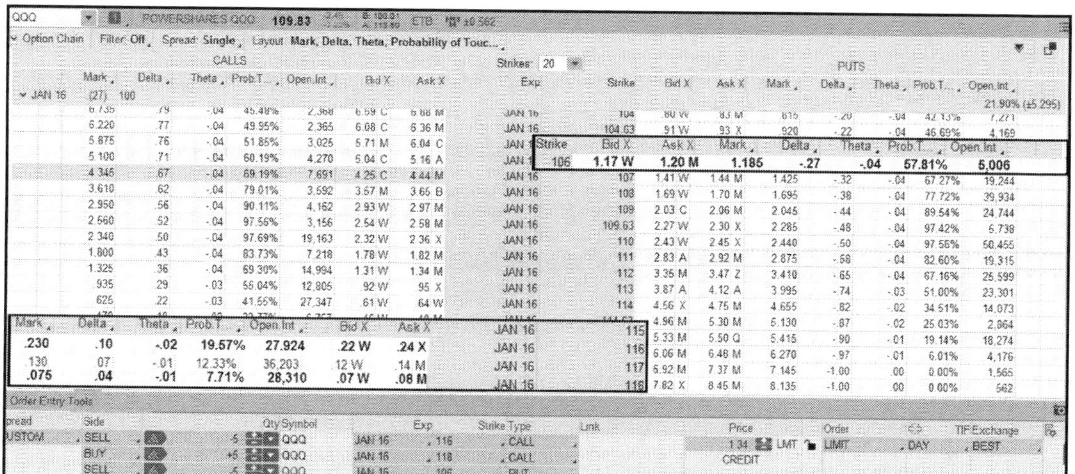

For illustration purposes only.

Figure 14–13e. Examining a Jade Lizard Risk Profile

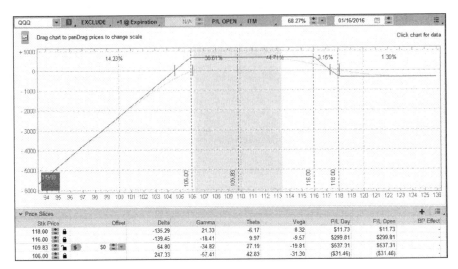

For illustration purposes only.

Hands-On Activity

Scanning for a Trade

When scanning for an iron condor trade, look for charts similar to the one shown in figure 14–13a.

1. Watch for well-defined support and resistance levels and neutral (sideways) price movements.
2. The option chain should include strike prices that are far enough OTM to be reasonably safe, especially on the call side of this spread.
3. Ensure there is adequate premium to warrant the risk and transaction fees.
4. Look for sufficiently high open interest to assure plenty of liquidity. This is also reflected in the amount of separation between the Bid and Ask prices — typically less than $0.04 to $0.05 cents.
5. Stay away from earnings release dates for the duration of the option contract.

6. Examine the risk profile to find the acceptable price levels; your goal is for the stock price to remain between the strike prices of the short call and short put.

Entry

Most trading platforms provide several option strategy settings that permit you to put all required legs on the order bar in a single click. The iron condor strategy is usually among them. This displays four legs in the strike column. Clicking on one of the chosen strike prices puts four iron condor legs on the order bar at the same time. On the order bar, edit the strike price values, the Buy/Sell (±) indicators, and number of contracts, as needed, for each leg of the strategy until they correspond to your intentions. CAREFULLY check each line before submitting the order. If preferred, you may leave the option chain spread setting at Single. Add each of the four iron condor legs individually. A common method is to click the appropriate Bid (sell) and Ask (buy) cell while holding down the Ctrl key. Repeat this process for each of the four legs until all are located on the order bar.

1. Choose the option contract date (in this example, JAN 16 is selected).
2. Ensure the Open Interest provides sufficient liquidity.
3. Set the number of Strikes **ALL** to provide access to all CALLS and PUTS strike prices.
4. Examine the strike prices of your short call and short put to make sure they are sufficiently OTM to be reasonably safe by checking the corresponding Delta and Probability ITM values.
5. Press and hold the **Ctrl** key while clicking the CALLS 116 **Bid** and the CALLS 118 **Ask**. Ensure both calls are added to the order bar with each click.
6. Press and hold the **Ctrl** key while clicking the PUTS 106 **Bid** and the PUTS 104 **Ask**. Ensure the two puts are added to the order bar with each click.

7. Check for sufficient premium to ensure the trade is worth the risk.
8. Verify each of the four legs of the iron condor on the order bar, including the number of contracts, are similar to these:

CUSTOM	SELL	-5	QQQ	JAN 16	116	CALL	.52		LMT	LIMIT	DAY
	BUY	+5	QQQ	JAN 16	118	CALL	CREDIT				
	SELL	-5	QQQ	JAN 16	106	PUT					
	SELL	+5	QQQ	JAN 16	104	PUT					

9. If ready, click **Confirm and Send**.
10. Evaluate the Order Confirmation information. If satisfactory, click **Send**.

Risks

The iron condor strategy is considered by many traders to be a reasonably safe and conservative strategy. This is because it has protective long call and long put legs outside the short call and short put legs. As long as the price of the underlying stock remains between the strike prices of the short put and short call, the trade remains profitable. If and when the price of the underlying breaches the long put or long call, the loss is minimized by the presence of the long positions. Recall how the long put within the bull put spread strategy protects the short put against a potential for a loss beyond that of the long protective put.

As mentioned near the beginning of the iron condor discussion, the most dangerous leg in this four-leg strategy is the short call. If the price of the underlying breaches the short call's strike price and is exercised without reaching the strike price of the protective long call, the short call loses the benefit of the protective long call leg. Stock must be delivered to the exercising call buyer. The potential for this to happen increases as the number of strikes between the short and long calls' increase.

You may wonder why a trader would add this level of risk to the call side of the iron condor. Increasing the number of strikes between the short and long call can be the result of a desire for more premium income. It may also be done from ignorance of the risks involved within the iron condor strategy. Granted, if structured correctly at safe OTM strike prices, most iron condors perform as expected. But they are not iron clad, as "iron condor" may imply. That said, be sure to keep your strikes reasonably tight and far OTM. And more importantly, closely monitor your trades.

As previously mentioned, the short put is much safer. It is essentially a cash-covered put that's protected by a long put one or more strikes below. The width between your put strikes can be a bit wider depending on your risk tolerance. If your short put is exercised and the stock is put to you, it is not the end of the world. Go ahead and pay for it. Then wait for the stock recover and/or use it with a covered call or perhaps a covered strangle, also described in this chapter. However, this is not possible when trading iron condors on financial indexes, as they are cash settled rather than stock settled.

Trade Management

Iron condors are typically in and out of the market in a relatively short time. Most iron condors are traded on option chains that expire within 20 to 40 days. These shorter time frames reduce risk, and Theta punishes option buyers by eroding what little premium remains. Because the iron condor is a neutral to slightly bearish bias strategy, the primary concern is an upward price swing toward the strike price of the short call. Regardless of the price direction, the main concern is with the threatened side of this trade — the puts when the underlying stock price is dropping; the calls when it is rallying.

Like most option strategies designed to collect premium, the iron condor may be closed when Theta has reduced the premium by 30% to 70% of the original value. When a long call or put becomes exceptionally safe, consider a sell to close order for additional premium income. But be sure the companion short position is secure according to your trading rules. Of course traders can also wait for their iron condors to expire worthless. Although any of these actions are acceptable, by selling the farthest OTM long put or call leg, it's possible to add even more income to the trade.

Regardless of the trader's initial plan, he/she should NEVER leave an iron condor unattended. When traveling the trader can set an alert and manage the trade with his or her smartphone or laptop computer. If completely off the grid, the trader should consider setting a Delta- or Mark-triggered stop (see Index Options in chapter 15). In any event, it's important to have a maintenance plan. The last thing traders want is to be blindsided by an ugly surprise — especially an expensive one when a working short call is exercised. If the stock price threatens the short call, close both calls immediately! If the short put is threatened, the trader may consider letting it become exercised if the stock is desirable. Obtaining stock at the market price less premium is usually acceptable if the price of the stock is still close to the short put's option price. However, if the trader's account balance requires stock to be sold to finance the purchase of the underlying iron condor stock, the trader may decide to enter a buy to close order on the short put to close it before it can be exercised.

If forced to close a threatened leg, keep the other legs and let them work. You may close the safe OTM call for the premium that may remain. Then monitor the remaining short option (if approved to trade uncovered calls). Sell it when it reaches an acceptable profit level. But never let an uncovered short call get close to the money.

NOTE   Because there are four individual legs within an iron condor, the open interest must be sufficiently high for the iron condor's working order to fill. Each leg is filled independently by multiple traders, not in a "bundle" to a single trader. It's more difficult to fill multiple-leg option strategies than it is one- or two-leg strategies. Traders quickly discover this fact when many of their multiple-leg orders expire at the end of the trading day without being filled. This is often caused when one of the sell to open legs within the strategy becomes too expensive to buy or one of the open-to-buy orders becomes too far below the market price to fill.

Possible Outcomes

1. The price of the underlying remains between the strike prices of the short put and the short call as expected and the options expire worthless.

2. The price of the underlying remains between the strike prices of the short put and the short call as expected. One or both long positions are sold for the remaining premium. (The long call must be retained without naked call writing permission.)

3. The strike price of the short call is getting dangerously close to the money. It is closed with a buy to close order. The three legs that remain are retained until it is safe to sell the remaining long call and put.

4. The strike price of the short call is getting dangerously close to the money. Both the short and long calls are closed for less premium than originally paid. The long put is also sold for a small amount of premium. In this outcome the iron condor returned a small amount of profit in spite of having to pay premium for the short call's buy to close order.

5. The price of the underlying drops and pierces the strike prices of both the short put and the long put. The short put is exercised and the stock is put to the iron condor trader. The trader exercises the long put to reduce the loss. The total loss amounts to the difference between the strike price of the short put and the strike price of the long put, which is $106 − $104 = $2.00 in the above example. As in the bull put spread, the loss is calculated by multiplying $2.00 by the number of contracts (500) multiplied by 100 shares per contract. This would be a loss of $1,000 from: $2.00 between strikes × 500 shares = $1,000. This loss is reduced by the original premium received when the trade

was originally filled. On the call side of the iron condor, both the short and long calls expire worthless.

Short Strangle

Structure

−1 OTM PUT, −1 OTM CALL
Same expiration dates; ≤ 56 days

Description and Goals

By definition a *strangle* is the simultaneous purchase or sale of a call and a put at different strike prices. A long strangle is the purchase of an OTM call and put. A trader would use a long strangle — a debit spread — to benefit from a strong move in the price of the underlying in either direction. The short strangle, described here, is a premium collection strategy, and therefore a credit spread. The short strangle is a neutral to mildly bearish premium collection strategy. It is a high risk limited reward strategy. As with all credit spreads, the risk exists from the possibility of having the short put or call become ITM.

The conventional short strangle employs the same expiration date for the short put and the short call. The strike prices selected for each leg should be far enough OTM to minimize the probability of being exercised. The option contract's expiration dates should be inside two months. Many traders limit the risk of short strangles by leveraging the effect of Theta and choosing contracts expiring within two or three weeks. The fact that premium sellers see time as an enemy and Theta as an ally is especially true in the case of a short strangle.

The short strangle is popular with traders who specialize in premium collection strategies because premium is collected from two short legs rather than just one, as in a cash-covered put. But the risk involved in this strategy is high. And the naked short call involved in this strategy requires short strangle trader to hold the highest option trading level, i.e., permission to trade uncovered options.

There are also long and short straddles. Like strangles, straddles buy or sell One or more puts and calls. The difference is that straddles always use identical strike prices for both the call and the put options. For example, a long straddle might buy a $50 call and a $50 put, while a short straddle would sell a $50 call and a $50 put. On the other hand, strangles buy one or more calls or puts at different strike prices. You learn how to construct, enter, and manage both the long strangle and long and short straddles in hands-on activities provided later in this chapter. Here, we walk through the entry and management of a short strangle.

Setup Parameters

- Goals: Select and collect premium from a far OTM short call and short put strike that are safely OTM. Be willing to settle for less premium to be safe.
- Bias: Neutral to slightly bearish; price level should have well-defined support and resistance levels; this strategy is not well-suited to a bullish bias because of the naked short call leg.
- Debit/Credit: Credit
- Chart Trend: Daily and hourly charts do not reveal any radical price breakouts; price remains within moderate support and resistance levels.
- Momentum Oscillator: Midrange to mildly oversold
- Keltner Channel: Flat ATR (14) envelope indicates price stability
- Implied Volatility % ≥ 80%; buyer wants high IV% for high premium followed by a decline in volatility
- Greeks: Delta ±0 (offsetting); Theta positive; Vega negative
- Days till Expiry: ≤ 56 days; The goal is premium collection and an increase in Theta and a reduction in Vega.
- Net Premium (both Marks): ≥ $0.50; Sufficient premium is required to afford the involved risk.

- Probability ITM: Both legs should be far OTM. The short call leg should have a lower Probability ITM value than the short put leg, i.e., less ≤ 0.15%. (If trading a financial index such as the SPX or NDX, consider a Probability ITM ≤ 5.0%.)
- Open Interest at Strike Prices: ≥ 500 (more is better); total open interest @ all strikes > 10,000
- Bid-to-Ask spread: The difference between the Bid and Ask prices should be quite small; something ≤ $0.04 is acceptable. This spread is substantially wider within the financial indexes. But the higher open interest (liquidity) makes this acceptable. Short strangles and short puts are used extensively on the financial indexes. The Bid-to-Ask spreads on the indexes are frequently in dollar amounts.
- Risk Amount ≈1.0% of account equity (governed by premium and number of contracts)

How the Strategy Works

Simultaneously sell a far OTM put and a far OTM call above and below historical resistance and support levels. Select option contracts that expire within about 45 days. The premium collected is the total amount of profit delivered by this strategy. Monitor the trade and close it when you've earned 30% to 70% in profit as shown on your P/L Open statement. Then do it again.

Churn with frequent selling, closing, and selling over and over. If you can make 50% profit from three trades in the same amount of time it takes for a short strangle to expire worthless, you earn 50% more income by being an active trader.

Hands-On Activity

Scanning for a Trade

1. Choose a contract date that expires in less than 56 days (less is usually better when enough premium is available).

2. Although this may not be as important as in the above debit call strategy, consider choosing a contract period that does not include an earnings release event.

3. Look at the option chain in figure 14–14a.

4. The price of the underlying CRM stock is $78.19. The short call premium at the 95 strike price is $0.165; the short put premium at the 62.5 strike price is $0.335. The credit received is $0.50 — the sum of the put and call Marks.

5. Examine the risk profile in figure 14–14b. The $500 premium is shown at the top of the plot. Although there are never guarantees, the plot within the risk profile shows this trade to have limited risk.

Figure 14–14a. The Short Strangle Option Chain

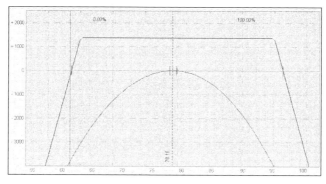

For illustration purposes only.

Figure 14–14b. The Risk Profile for the Short Strangle

For illustration purposes only.

Entry

1. Choose a CRM contract date that expires within 56 days (shorter is even better if enough premium exists). You may want to determine if the contract period includes an earnings release event.

2. Set the number of Strikes to **ALL** so you can see all CALL and PUT strike prices.

3. Look at the option chain in figure 14–14a.

4. Notice the price of the underlying CRM stock is $78.19.

5. Examine the strike prices and premiums offered by the short calls and short puts. Find strike prices sufficiently OTM to be reasonably safe by checking the corresponding Delta and Probability ITM values.

6. Find an OTM call strike price with a Probability ITM that is less than 25% and a short put strike price with a Probability ITM that is less than 25%.

   CAUTION! When trading a short strangle on a financial index, such as the SPX, NDX, or RUT, your Probability ITM should be at or below 2.5% for safety. (Even two standard deviations OTM can carry too much risk for comfort.) If the premium of the short call is unacceptably low, abandon it. Or, if willing to take a risk, slide a few strikes closer to the money and back the short call with a long call for insurance. This also reduces margin stress.

7. The short call premium at the 95 strike price is $0.165; the short put premium at the 62.5 strike price is $0.335. The credit received is $0.165 + $0.335 = $0.50.

8. Examine the risk profile in figure 14–14b to see the price range plot within which this short strangle is shown to be safe.

9. Click the **62.5** PUTS **Bid** to add the 62.5 puts to the order bar.

10. Press and hold the **Ctrl** key and click the **95** CALLS **Bid** to add the 95 calls.

11. Ensure the order bar includes both the short put and the short call and the desired premium credit of $0.50.
12. Check the order bar to verify it contains entries similar to these:

STRANGLE   SELL   –10   CRM   FEB 16   95   CALL   .50   LMT   LIMIT   DAY
            SELL   –10   CRM   FEB 16   62.5   PUT   CREDIT

13. If all values are reasonable, click **Confirm and Send**.
14. Evaluate the Order Confirmation information. If satisfactory, click **Send**.

Risks

The short strangle is vulnerable to a strong price change in either direction. If either of the short legs becomes ITM, they can be exercised. Of course the naked short call is the most vulnerable in which the underlying stock must be purchased and delivered to the buyer when exercised. Be ready to close the threatened position as necessary.

If the short put becomes ITM and is exercised, the trader must pay for the stock at the short put's option price and take delivery of the stock. If the price of the acquired stock stops its decline and begins to rally, the trader may recover and even profit over time from what has become a cash-covered put.

Trade Management

Because the short strangle is a premium collection option strategy, many traders simply close the option for profit. This is achieved by paying less premium to close the short strangle than originally received when the trade was entered.

The short strangle should be carefully monitored to ensure both short legs remain well OTM. If the short call is threatened, enter a buy to close order to close it before it is vulnerable to being exercised.

Of course rolling either up (to a farther OTM strike price, same expiration) or rolling out (to a farther OTM strike price that expires at a later date) can be examined. When rolling, consider both the added cost and the security of the position.

If the price is experiencing a strong rally, the trader could buy a long call one strike above the threatened short call leg as insurance (like the call legs of an iron condor). This can limit the loss to the difference between the short and long call legs if the price of the underlying rallies above the protective long-call's strike price.

The short call can also be rolled to a higher strike price at a later expiration date. This action alleviates the current risk by moving the strike price farther OTM to a safer position. Rolling might also garner a small amount of additional premium, although it could also cost a few cents depending on current volatility and premium values.

Possible Outcomes

1. The price of the underlying remains between the strike prices of the short call and the short put as expected, and the options expire worthless.
2. The price of the underlying remains between the strike prices of the short call and the short put. Both of these legs are closed for a 50% profit a few weeks prior to expiration.
3. The short call and short put are both rolled to a later expiration date for additional premium income.
4. The strike price of the short call is getting dangerously close to the money. It is closed with a buy to close order. The short put remains and is even farther OTM. The trader lets it expires worthless.
5. The strike price of the short call is getting dangerously close to the money. The trader buys a long call one strike above the short call for protection. But the short call still carries risk in spite of the introduction of the long call.
6. The strike price of the short call is getting dangerously close to the money. The trader rolls the short call a few strikes farther

OTM to a later expiration for a small amount of premium (or the trader is willing to pay a few cents in premium to mitigate the threat of being exercised).

7. The short put is threatened by a strong drop in the price of the CRM stock. The trader decides to enter a buy to close order to eliminate the prospect of being exercised.

8. The short put is threatened by a strong drop in the price of the CRM stock. The trader likes the CRM stock and decides to retain the short put in the event it is exercised. The trader can now enter a buy to close order on the short call for profit or let it expire worthless.

Covered Short Strangle

Structure

+100 Shares, –1 OTM CALL, –1 OTM PUT
Same expiration dates; ≤ 56 days

Description and Goals

This strategy is similar to the short strangle, but it is supplemented by ownership of the underlying stock. So this strategy essentially combines a covered call and a short put. The short put creates a short strangle — both described earlier within this chapter. Recall how the short strangle is an unlimited risk strategy, while the covered call is a limited risk, limited reward strategy (unless, as previously mentioned, the market price of the covering stock suffers a radical drop).

The covered strangle returns more premium than a covered call from the addition of the premium received from the short put leg. A greater upside potential also exists if the price of the underlying stock rallies to and breaches the strike price of the OTM short call. Like the covered call, the covering stock can be delivered to the buyer of the short call for a price higher than that originally paid (just as in the covered call). Meanwhile, the short put becomes safer by becoming farther OTM.

Recall how the biggest risk associated with the covered call strategy is a possible drop in the price of the underlying stock. A price decline in the stock of just a dollar or two can quickly turn the covered short strangle into a loser. As with all trades, it's quite important to study the price charts to determine the likelihood of the price remaining between the support and resistance levels. If the stock price rallies toward the short call, the trader can either let the covered short put expire worthless or buy to close it for profit. Once out, the trader can enter another covered short strangle for another round of premium income. This is an excellent use of stock held within a trader's account. But the trader must be willing to own more shares of stock in the event the short put is exercised.

If the short call is breached and exercised, the trader of the covered short strangle can deliver the stock owned at the option price of the short call for a profit in intrinsic (stock) value. The premium originally received from the sale of the short put and short call (the extrinsic value) supplements the total profit provided by this strategy.

If the stock price remains between the strike prices of the short put and call, the profit is restricted to the premium collected at entry. Once the profit has reached a satisfactory level, the covered strangle can either be closed or rolled for another round of option income.

Setup Parameters

- Goals: Collect premium from a short call and a short put. The call is covered by the ownership of the underlying stock. The put is cash covered.
- Bias: Neutral to slightly bullish; price level should have well-defined support and resistance levels; this strategy is well-suited to a bullish bias because of the ownership of the underlying stock.
- Debit/Credit: Credit (excluding the price of the covering stock)

- Chart Trend: Daily and hourly charts do not reveal any radical price breakouts; price remains within moderate support and resistance levels.
- Momentum Oscillator: Midrange to mildly oversold
- Keltner Channel: Flat ATR (14) envelope indicates price stability.
- Implied Volatility % ≥ 80%; buyer wants high IV% for high premium followed by a decline in volatility.
- Greeks: Delta ±0 (offsetting; stock has a Delta value of 1.0); Theta positive; Vega negative
- Days till Expiry: ≤ 60 days; The goal is premium collection and an increase in the price of the stock.
- Net Premium (both Marks): ≥ $0.50; Sufficient premium is required to afford the involved risk of the uncovered put leg.
- Probability ITM: Both legs should be far OTM with Deltas at or below ±0.25. The −call leg should have a lower Probability ITM and Delta value than the −put leg, i.e., less ≤ 0.15. (If trading a financial index such as the SPX or NDX, consider a Probability ITM ≤ 5.0%.)
- Open Interest at Strike Prices: ≥ 500 (more is better); total open interest @ all strikes > 10,000
- Bid-to-Ask spread (the difference between the Bid and Ask prices) should be tighter than usual to reflect the higher than normal trading volatility.
- Risk Amount ≈1.0% of account equity (governed by premium and number of contracts)

How the Strategy Works

As mentioned in the preceding paragraph, a trader may already own the covering stock or may buy it at the same time the short strangle is traded. This would require the purchase of a *covered stock* followed by the sale of the short put leg. (As described above, the short strangle is comprised of stock ownership that covers a short call; the short put is cash covered.)

If the underlying stock price drops sufficiently to cause the short put to become ITM, it may be exercised and put to the trader at the short put's option price. This would certainly happen if the short put is ITM at expiration.

Hands-On Activity

Scanning for a Trade

1. If not already within your account, buy 100 shares of the covering stock for each option contract you plan to sell. In this example, HLF stock is selected based on the charts.

2. Choose a contract date that expires within 60 days.

3. Look at the option chain in figure 14–15a.

4. The price of the underlying HLF stock is $55.23. The short call premium at the 65 strike price is $0.84; the short put premium at the 40.0 strike price is $0.565. The credit received is $1.40 — the sum of the Marks rounded down to the nearest penny.

5. Examine the risk profile in figure 14–15b. The $1,400 premium for 10 contracts is shown at the top of the plot. Although there is never 100% certainty, the plot within the risk profile shows this trade to have limited risk. If the price of HLF rallies to $65, the risk graph would limit the maximum risk to the $65 strike price of the short call.

Figure 14–15a. Covered Short Strangle Option Chain

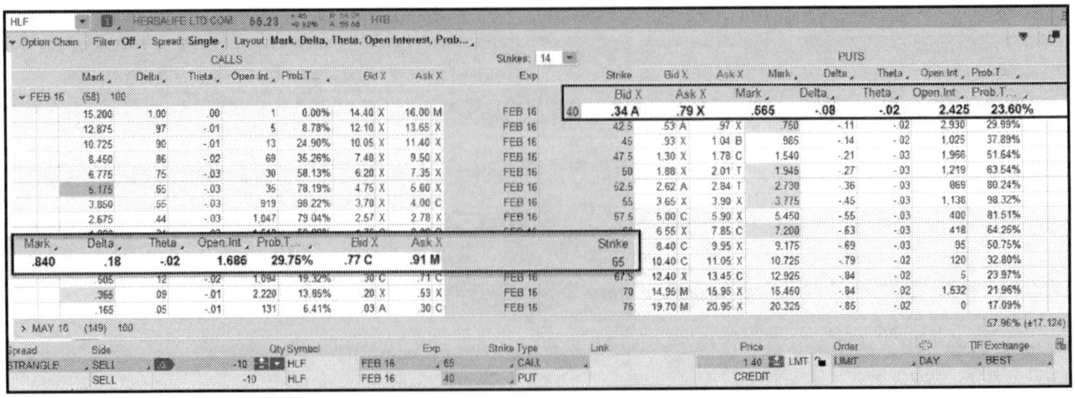

For illustration purposes only.

Figure 14–15b. Covered Short Strangle Risk Profile (Only Plots Options)

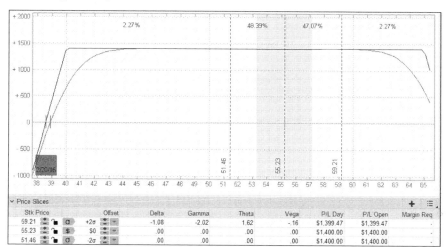

Stk Price				Offset	Delta	Gamma	Theta	Vega	P/L Day	P/L Open	Margin Req
59.21				+2σ	-1.08	-2.02	1.62	-.16	$1,399.47	$1,399.47	-
55.23				$0	.00	.00	.00	.00	$1,400.00	$1,400.00	-
51.46				-2σ	.00	.00	.00	.00	$1,400.00	$1,400.00	-

For illustration purposes only.

Entry

1. Choose an HLF option chain with a contract date that expires within 56 days (shorter is even better if enough premium exists). You may want to determine if the contract period includes an earnings release event.
2. Set the number of Strikes to **ALL** so you can see all CALLS and PUTS strike prices.
3. Look at the option chain in figure 14–15a.
4. Notice the price of the underlying HLF stock is $59.23.
5. Examine the strike prices and premiums offered by the short calls and short puts. Find strike prices sufficiently OTM to be reasonably safe by checking the corresponding Delta and Probability ITM values.
6. Find an OTM call strike price with a Probability ITM that is less than 30% and a short put strike price with a Probability ITM that is less than 25%.

7. The short call premium at the 65 strike price is $0.84; the short put premium at the 40 strike price is $0.565. The credit received is $0.84 + $0.565 = $1.40.

8. Examine the risk profile in figure 14–15b to see the price range plot within which this short strangle is shown to be safe (Note that the profile only plots the options and not the stock).

9. Click the PUTS **40 Bid** cell to add the short 40 PUT to the order bar.

10. Press and hold the **Ctrl** key and click the CALLS **65 Bid** to add the short 65 CALL to the order bar.

11. Ensure the order bar includes both the short put and the short call and the desired premium credit of $1.40.

12. Check the order bar to verify it contains entries similar to these:

STRANGLE	SELL	−10	HLF	FEB 16	65	CALL	1.40	LMT	LIMIT	DAY
	SELL	−10	HLF	FEB 16	40	PUT	CREDIT			

13. If ready, click **Confirm and Send**.

14. Evaluate the Order Confirmation information. If satisfactory, click **Send**.

Risks

The covered short strangle is vulnerable to a strong price drop. If the short put leg is ITM by one penny at expiration, it can be exercised. If it is substantially ITM prior to expiration, it may be exercised. When exercised, the stock is delivered to the option seller at the strike price of the short put.

The short call is covered by the underlying stock. If the 65 strike is pierced by a strong rally in the stock and the short call is exercised, the covered short strangle trader can deliver the stock he bought for $55.23/share to the buyer who must pay $65/share for the HLF stock. This is a nice profit in intrinsic value amounting to $9.72 per HLF share called away by the buyer of the short call. The covered short strangle trader also received the $0.56 premium from the short put when the trade was originally entered.

If the short put becomes ITM and is exercised, the seller of the covered short strangle must pay for the stock at the short put's option price and take delivery. This would constitute a $15.23 loss in the value of the HLF stock already owned by the trader — by far the largest risk within this trade.

Trade Management

Because the covered short strangle is a premium collection option strategy, many traders simply close the option for profit and repeat the trade at a later expiration date. This is achieved by paying less premium to close the short strangle than collected when originally sold.

The covered short strangle should be monitored. In this strategy the short put becomes the most vulnerable from a strong drop in the price of HLF.

If the price is experiencing a strong rally that pierces the short call's strike price, the covered short strangle seller may be able to profit by selling the stock to the buyer of the short call when exercised.

The short call can also be rolled to a higher strike price at a later expiration date. This action is designed to alleviate the current risk by moving the strike price farther OTM to a safer strike price. Rolling might also garner a small amount of additional premium, although it could also cost a small amount depending on the amount of time remaining, the current volatility, and ultimately, the remaining premium.

Possible Outcomes

1. The price of the underlying remains between the strike prices of the short call and the short put as expected and the options expire worthless.
2. The price of the underlying remains between the strike prices of the short put and the short call. The short call and short put are closed for a 70% profit a few weeks prior to expiration.

3. The short call and short put are both rolled to a later expiration date for additional premium income.

4. The strike price of the short call becomes ITM and is exercised. The seller delivers the HLF stock to the short call's buyer for a $9.72 profit. The short put remains and is even farther OTM. The trader lets it expires worthless or closes it for a profit prior to expiration.

5. The strike price of the short call is approaching the money. The seller of the covered short strangle watches the trade work and is not concerned about having the HLF stock called away for the reason described in possible outcome number 4 above.

6. The strike price of the short put, which now resembles a cash-covered put, is getting dangerously close to the money. The trader rolls the short put farther OTM to a later expiration date for a small amount of premium (or the trader is willing to pay a few cents in premium to mitigate the threat of being exercised).

7. The short put is threated by a strong drop in the price of the HLF stock. The trader decides to enter a buy to close order to eliminate the prospect of being exercised, which requires paying for 1,000 more shares of HLF stock.

Long Strangle

Structure

+1 OTM CALL, +1 OTM PUT
Same expiration dates; ≥ 90 days

Description and Goals

As the name implies, the long strangle includes a long call and a long put at slightly OTM strike prices with identical expiration dates. Being long, it is a debit spread. It is used when a trader anticipates a strong price move in the underlying stock. It is considered a limited risk, unlimited reward strategy if the underlying stock reacts with a substantial price rally or drop, which is the primary goal of this strategy. Although many option texts represent the long strangle as being a neutral bias strategy, in reality, it is anything but neutral. It would be better called a "non-directional" strategy. But, of course, either a strong bullish or bearish bias will suffice nicely.

But neutrality defeats this strategy and implies sideways price movement. If this happens, the long strangle trader can lose the premium paid upon entry. Of course buying the long call and long put option contracts make the long strangle a debit spread. It is more costly when the strike prices of the long call and put are close to the money.

Some of the previous strategies tried in this chapter cautioned traders to stay clear of earnings releases, especially in directional strategies like the debit call spread, that depend on the price of the underlying to return to the prevailing upward trend. But the long strangle is not directional. It relies on sudden volatility and a corresponding price rally or drop. The worst condition is price neutrality over an extended period of time, which renders the long strangle strategy worthless.

The market often reacts to earnings releases with unusually high trading volume. Companies that miss their earnings forecast see sell-offs, and of course, those that exceed their forecasts see an increase in buying. Although this is not always the case, it is a common market reaction.

The long strangle trader wants an increase in volatility to push up premiums. And because the long strangle is nondirectional and based on increased volatility, either good or bad news is desirable. When the price of the underlying stock reacts with a large move in one direction, the trader can sell the unwanted leg and keep the leg that's rallying in his or her favor. Once the stock has completed its run and is near market equilibrium, the remaining long option contract can be sold for a profit in premium.

Of course the trader could also exercise the remaining option contracts. The call options would be exercised and the stock sold for a profit. The put options would be exercised and the stock would be put to the seller who would be required to pay the higher option price for the depressed stock. See the possible outcomes paragraph at the end of this section for more information on these transactions.

Setup Parameters

- Goal: This trade anticipates a strong price move of the underlying stock in either direction.
- Bias: Looking for a strong rally or drop resulting from a company event such as an earnings release. Look for companies in either highly favorable or unfavorable market sectors.
- Debit/Credit: Debit
- Implied Volatility % ≤ 20%; buyer wants low IV% for low premium at entry followed by a strong increase in volatility.
- Chart Trend: Daily and hourly charts reveal substantial price swings within a matter of weeks to a few months.
- Momentum Oscillator: Presently midrange between previous overbought/oversold conditions
- Keltner Channel: The ATR(14) envelope is currently narrow; the envelope historically experiences frequent expansion and compression.
- Greeks: Delta ±0 (offsetting); Theta negative; Vega positive
- Days till Expiry: ≥ 90 days; Give this strategy plenty of time to work in your favor. The goal is a strong change in the price of the underlying stock without a large increase in the value of Theta (time decay). It's always possible that overall market sentiment can impact the underlying stock. Refrain from exiting this strategy prematurely.
- Net Premium (both Marks): ≤ $10.00; The premium is the amount put at risk. It should be based on your account size, i.e., what you are willing to lose.
- Probability ITM: ≥ 85%; Both legs should be slightly OTM, based on premium and the width between strike prices.

- Open Interest at Strike Prices: ≥ 500 (more is better); Total open interest @ all strikes ≥ 10,000. Liquidity is required to fill both the initial trade and sell to close orders that may follow.
- Bid to Ask spread (the difference between the Bid and Ask prices) should be slightly wider than usual as an indication of the current low volatility.
- Risk Amount ≈1.0% of account equity (governed by premium and number of contracts)

How the Strategy Works

Simultaneously buy a slightly OTM call and a slightly OTM put that both expire at the same time some 90 or more days in the future. A good time to trade a long strangle is just prior to a company event, such as an earnings release, in anticipation of a strong price move in the underlying stock in addition to an increase in current volatility. Because the trader owns one or more long puts and calls, the price move can be in either direction to achieve a profit in premium from the affected side, i.e., either the call or the put side.

The side opposite the beneficial price move can be sold to recover part of the premium originally paid. In fact, with enough volatility, the premium may be close to the amount originally paid.

The surviving leg of this trade can either be exercised for profit or the option can be sold for the increase in premium. This requires the trader to do the math to determine which action returns the most profit.

Finally, if the event has little effect on the stock price, the trader has several choices:

- Either or both the call and put options can be sold to salvage part of the premium originally paid.
- One of the option contracts can be sold and the other retained, based on the dominant price trend.

- One of the option contracts can be sold and the remaining leg can be used as part of a bull put spread or a bull call spread. You stepped through both of these spreads earlier in this chapter. The remaining leg can also be incorporated into a diagonal or calendar spread. Hands-on activities are provided for both of these spreads later in this chapter.

Hands-On Activity

Scanning for a Trade

1. Develop a watch of companies having upcoming earnings releases. You may find such a list on your trading platform, as some brokerages provide a list of symbols with pending earnings announcements. Many trading platforms display symbols representing company events, including earnings releases, on price charts, watch lists, or both.

2. Ensure the stock prices (Last) column are within the desired range. This depends on your account size. An example might be stocks having prices from $30 to $100.

3. Add an Implied Volatility column to your watch list. Then sort on implied volatility percentage in ascending order (lowest to highest IV%).

4. Synchronize the watch list to the charts and option chains so you can see all three windows at the same time or be able to quickly switch between them.

5. ATR(14): Look for a relatively low price range that accompanies low implied volatility for a reduction in the premium that must be paid.

6. Examine option chains with expiration dates greater than 90 days. Look for earnings releases occurring within the next few weeks. (Some traders prefer shorter-term, less expensive trade entries that encompass earnings releases.

This is especially true when a major price movement is expected.)

7. Look for affordable premiums according to your personal risk tolerance. These should have low implied volatility and reasonably low premiums. Look for basing patterns on the underlying price charts.

8. Symbol QIHU has current low IV% and an earnings release inside 30 days. It is currently trading at $73.00 and has experienced radical price swings in the neighborhood of $30/share.

9. The option contracts within the option chain shown in figure 14–16a expire in 176 days — well above the recommended 90+ day expiration.

10. The $72.5 long put and $77.5 long call option contracts can be bought for $2.40 per share of each. This is a total of $2,400 in premium that must be paid for ten contracts of each.

11. The risk profile for this trade is shown in figure 14–16b. Notice how this trade moves into profit if the price of the underlying moves below $68.50 or above $78.50 per share. The risk profile will change substantially if one side of this trade is sold to recover a portion of the premium paid at entry.

Figure 14–16a. A Long Strangle Option Chain

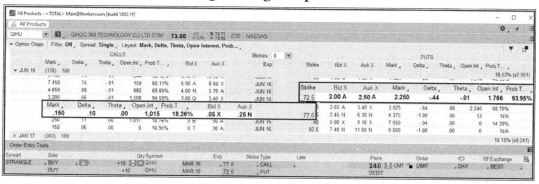

For illustration purposes only.

Figure 14–16b. Long Strangle Risk Profile

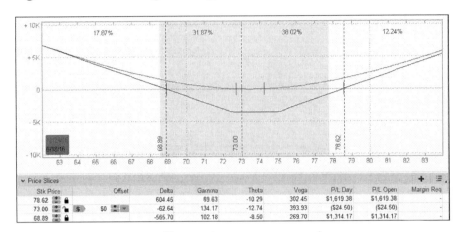

For illustration purposes only.

Entry

1. The next earnings release for QIHU occurs within 30 days. You've examined several option chains and settled on the JUN 16 option chain which expires in 176 days.

2. The charts show how QIHU consistently experiences substantial price swings.

3. The risk profile shows a profit if QIHU rallies beyond $78.62 or drops below $68.89. QIHU appears to be ideal for the long strangle strategy. (It would also work for a long straddle, but let's do the long strangle to reduce the premium expense.)

4. Set the number of Strikes to be displayed to **8** since you plan to use strike prices that are only one to three strikes OTM.

5. After careful examination click the PUTS **72.5 Ask** cell to add the 72.5 long put to the order bar.

6. Press and hold the **Ctrl** key and click the CALLS **77.5 Ask** cell to add the 77.5 long call to the order bar.

7. Ensure the order bar includes **+10** contracts for both the 72.5 PUT and the 77.5 CALL for a $2.40 DEBIT.

8. Check the order bar to verify it contains entries similar to these:

STRANGLE	BUY	+10	QIHU	JUN 16	72.5	CALL	2.40	LMT	LIMIT DAY
	BUY	+10	QIHU	JUN 16	75	PUT	DEBIT		

9. When ready click **Confirm and Send**.

10. Evaluate the Order Confirmation information. If satisfactory, click **Send**.

Risks

Your maximum risk is the $2.40/share you've spent to enter this trade. The risk profile indicates that QIHU must rally past $78.62 or drop below $68.89 for this long strangle to become profitable. However, once price movement either upward or downward is established, you can sell the opposite side of this trade to recover part of the premium originally paid for that leg.

Of course you must be confident that the long-term price trend will be sustained based on your chart analysis and company or market sector news. Because you are aware of the radical price movement of QIHU (see figure 14–16c), you are confident that you have given your long strangle ample time to be a winning trade.

Figure 14–16c. QIHU Price Range

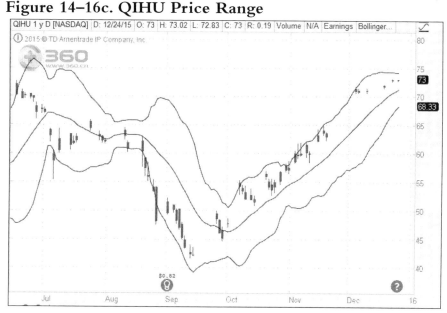

For illustration purposes only.

Trade Management

The primary concern with this option strategy is a continuous sideways movement of the price of QIHU (Qihoo 360 Technology Company, LTD). As mentioned in the description, a strong price change in either direction is required for the long strangle to return a profit. Therefore, if the stock remains within a narrow price range, consider selling both the put and the call to recover some of your premium. However, do not be too hasty, because there should be plenty of time for this trade to reward you. Early exit is a trading flaw common to many inexperienced traders. It is more emotional than rational. Of course if the sideways move exists too long, Theta will eventually erode the premium before the trade can be closed. Although unlikely, waiting too long can prevent recovery of enough premium value to pay the small amount of money spent on exchange and brokerage fees.

If the price of the underlying makes a strong move, sell the opposite side and ride the move until it's ready to reverse direction. You can also establish an e-mail or smartphone alert to notify you when the Mark and/or Delta of either leg reaches a predetermined value.

If the profitable side of this trade becomes deep ITM, consider exercising the option contract. Otherwise, sell the option itself for the increased premium, which can be substantial. Whichever of these two actions you decide upon, do not wait too long as Theta will begin to erode the remaining premium. This may force you to exercise the call option and sell the stock. Or, in the case of the put option, buy and deliver the stock and then sell the stock for profit, which can also be substantial. Of course each transaction carries the overhead of transaction fees. Before making a final decision, do the math to determine the most profitable course of action.

Possible Outcomes

1. If the price of the underlying stock of your long strangle begins to drop, determine if a downward trend is forming. If so, let

it run downward as the strike price of the long put becomes deeper ITM. When the P/L Open value on your account statement for this trade becomes profitable by at least 30% to 70%, consider selling the put option to collect the profit in addition to selling the long call option.

2. This strategy can return unlimited profit. If a substantial amount of time remains until contract expiration, it may be premature to either sell or exercise the profitable long put option too soon. However, you can enter a sell to close order on the opposite side to salvage the available premium that remains. Once the price of the profitable option begins to reverse direction, sell the option for more premium than originally paid.

3. Assuming the conditions described in outcome 2 above, calculate the profit in premium versus the profit collected by exercising the option and then selling the stock. Exercising the option may be substantially more profitable than selling the option, in spite of having to pay two brokerage commissions — one to exercise and a second to sell the stock. (Be sure to calculate the return between selling the premium and exercising the stock.)

4. If the underlying stock begins to rally and your analysis indicates an upward trend is forming, sell the long put and retain the long call. Follow the stock upward until the trade is profitable by 70%. Once the P/L Open on your account statement shows an acceptable profit, either enter a sell to close order or exercise the option. Before choosing, do the math to see which choice provides the most profit after paying all commissions and exchange fees. If the rally has momentum, let the profits run until you detect a reversal.

5. DON'T GIVE UP! If the price of the underlying stock moves sideways and remains between the strike prices of your long call and long put for a month or more, your account statement will display a loss in both the P/L Open and P/L Day columns. However, a lot can happen in the months that remain, and it

probably will. Because the QIHU stock typically experiences strong price fluctuations, it is unlikely that the price will remain between the narrow strike prices of this long strangle. Based on the price chart in figure 14–16c, it is apparent that the price of QIHU is quite unstable. Because this trade has several months remaining until expiration, the trader should let it continue to work as a breakout is quite likely.

Long Straddle

Structure

+1 ATM CALL, +1 ATM PUT
The put and call legs of straddles are always at the same strike price; expiration ≥ 90 days.

Description and Goals

The long straddle is similar to the long strangle strategy. It is a limited risk and unlimited reward strategy. The long straddle includes a long call and a long put either ATM or very close to the price of the underlying stock. Both legs use the same expiration date, which is typically more than 90 days from the entry date.

Like the long strangle, the premium paid is the maximum risk associated with this strategy. Because the selected strike price is either ATM or as close to the money as possible, the premium paid for the long straddle is higher than that paid for the long strangle, which uses different strike prices for the long put and for the long call that are typically one to three strike prices OTM.

Like the long strangle, the long straddle also requires the price of the underlying stock to make a strong move in either direction to become profitable. For this strategy to work, current volatility must be low to reduce the premium paid at entry. For success, this strategy also requires an upswing in implied volatility with the usual increase in premium. Because the selected option contracts expire in three or more months, this trade provides ample time for the underlying volatility and price to move in the trader's favor.

An uptick in premium may be sufficient to sell the option contracts back to the market for profit. Of course once the price movement of the underlying becomes directional, such as making a move upward, the long put can be sold. The remaining long call can be followed until the price stalls. When this happens, the call option is either sold for a profit or exercised. If exercised, the trader would normally acquire the underlying stock at the option's original strike price and then sell the stock at the current market price for the difference, which constitutes the trader's profit.

This strategy can expire worthless if the underlying stock price fails to make a strong move. Like the long strangle, the long straddle should be used near a company event, such as an earnings release, a stock split, or immediately following a strong overnight price gap followed by a major reduction in implied volatility.

Setup Parameters

- Goal: Like the long strangle, the long straddle also requires a strong price move of the underlying stock in either direction.
- Bias: Looking for a strong rally or drop resulting from a company event such as an earnings release. Look for companies in either highly favorable or unfavorable market sectors.
- Debit/Credit: Debit
- Chart Trend: Daily and hourly charts reveal substantial price swings within a matter of weeks to a few months.
- Momentum Oscillator: Presently midrange between previous overbought/oversold conditions
- Keltner Channel: The ATR(14) envelope is currently narrow; the envelope historically experiences frequent expansion and compression.
- Implied Volatility % $\leq$ 20%; buyer wants low IV% for low premium at entry followed by a strong increase in volatility.

- Greeks: Delta ±0 (offsetting); Theta negative; Vega positive
- Days till Expiry: ≥ 90 days; Give this strategy plenty of time to work in your favor. The goal is a strong change in the price of the underlying stock without a large increase in the value of Theta (time decay). It's always possible that overall market sentiment can impact the underlying stock. Refrain from exiting this strategy prematurely.
- Net Premium (both Marks): ≤ $10.00; The premium is the amount put at risk. It should be based on your account size, i.e., what you are willing to lose. (Long straddle premiums are higher than long strangle premiums because they are ATM rather than slightly OTM.)
- Probability ITM: ≥ 94%; Both legs are as close to the price of the underlying as possible.
- Open Interest at Strike Prices: ≥ 500 (more is better); total open interest @ all strikes ≥ 10,000. Liquidity is required to fill both the initial trade and sell to close orders that may follow.
- Bid to Ask spread (the difference between the Bid and Ask prices) should be slightly wider than usual to reflect the presence of current low volatility.
- Risk Amount ≈1.0% of account equity (governed by premium and number of contracts)

How the Strategy Works

NOTE The difference between the long straddle and long strangle is the placement of the strike prices. The long call and long put legs both have identical expiration dates in these strategies. The long and short straddle use identical call and put strike prices, while the long strangle uses different strike prices—both slightly OTM.

Simultaneously buy the same number of ATM calls and ATM puts at the same strike price having the same expiration dates. The contracts should expire in 90 days or more to give this strategy time to work in the trader's favor. The long straddle is traded just prior to a company event, such as an earnings release, in anticipation of a strong price move in the underlying stock in addition to an increase in current volatility. Because the trader owns one or more puts and calls, the move can be in either direction to achieve a strong increase in the premium of the affected side (the call or the put side).

The side opposite the beneficial price move can be sold to recover part of the premium originally paid. In fact, with enough volatility, the premium may actually increase above the amount originally paid.

The surviving leg of this trade can either be exercised at the option's strike price for profit or the option contract can be sold for the increased premium. This requires the trader to do the math to determine which action returns the most profit.

Finally, if the event has little effect on the stock price, the trader has several choices:

- Both the call and put options can be sold to salvage part of the premium originally paid.
- One of the option contracts can be sold and the other retained, based on the dominant trend.
- One of the option contracts can be sold and the remaining leg can be used as part of a bull put spread or a bull call spread. The remaining leg could also be incorporated into a diagonal or calendar spread, both described later in this chapter.

Hands-On Activity

Scanning for a Trade
1. As with the long strangle, develop a watch list of companies having upcoming earnings releases. You may find such a list on

your trading platform, as some brokerages provide a list of symbols with pending earnings announcements. You can also see earnings release symbols on price charts, watch lists, or both.

2. Ensure the stock prices (Last) column are within the desired range. This depends on your account size. An example might be stocks having prices from $30 to $100.

3. Add an Implied Volatility column to your watch list. Then sort on implied volatility percentage in ascending order (lowest to highest IV%).

4. Synchronize the watch list to the charts and option chains so you can see all three windows at the same time or be able to quickly switch between them.

5. ATR(14): As with the preceding long call and long put strategies, look for a relatively low price range that accompanies low implied volatility for a reduction in the premium that must be paid.

6. Examine option chains with expiration dates greater than 90 days. Look for earnings releases occurring within the next 15 to 30 days.

7. Look for affordable premiums according to your personal risk tolerance. These should have low implied volatility and lower than normal premium values.

8. Because the long straddle and long strangle are quite similar, symbol QIHU is ideal for either of these strategies. QIHU has current low IV% and an earnings release inside 30 days. It is currently trading at $73.00 and has experienced radical price swings of $30/share as shown in figure 14–16c above.

9. The option contracts within the option chain shown in figure 14–17a expire in 175 days—well above the recommended 90+ day expiration.

10. The $72.5 long put and long call option contracts are closest to the money. They are bought for $5.45 for each long call and

long put pair for a total of $5,450 in combined premiums for ten contracts of each.

11. The risk profile for this trade is shown in figure 14–17b. Notice how this trade becomes profitable if the price of the underlying moves below $67.04 per share or above $77.95 per share. The risk profile will change substantially if one side of this trade is sold to recover some of the premium originally paid upon entry.

Figure 14–17a. Long Straddle Option Chain

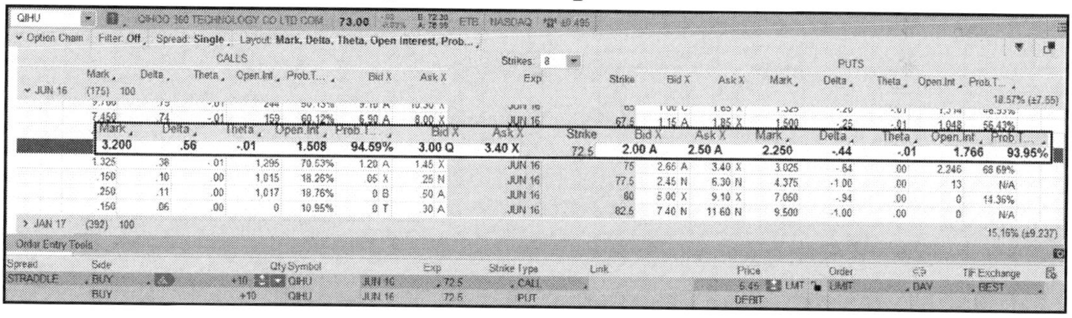

For illustration purposes only.

Figure 14–17b. Long Straddle Risk Profile

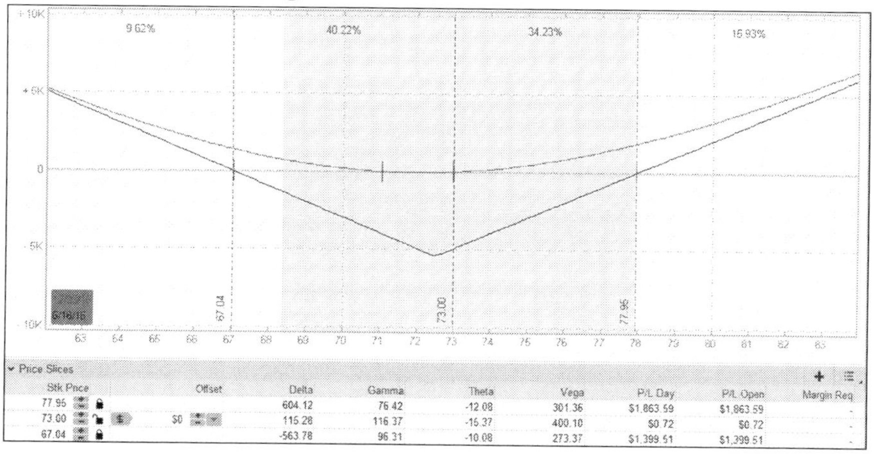

For illustration purposes only.

Entry

1. The next earnings release for QIHU occurs within 30 days. You've examined several option chains and settled on the JUN 16 option chain which expires in 175 days.

2. An analysis of the QIHU charts show how its price is in constant fluctuation. The risk profile shows a profit if QIHU rallies beyond 77.95 or drops below $67.04. QIHU is ideal for the long straddle strategy.

3. Set the number of Strikes to **8** since you need only see strike prices that are ATM.

4. After careful examination click the PUTS **72.5 Ask** cell to add the 72.5 long PUT to the order bar.

5. Press and hold the **Ctrl** key and click the CALLS **72.5 Ask** cell to add the 72.5 long CALL to the order bar.

6. Ensure the order bar includes +**10** contracts for both the 72.5 PUT and the 72.5 CALL for a $5.45 DEBIT.

7. Check the order bar to verify it contains entries similar to these:

STRADDLE   BUY   +10 QIHU   JUN 16   72.5   CALL 5.45   LMT   LIMIT   DAY
             BUY   +10 QIHU   JUN 16   72.5   PUT   DEBIT

8. When ready click **Confirm and Send**.

9. Evaluate the Order Confirmation information. If satisfactory, click **Send**.

Risks

Your maximum risk is the $5,450 paid for the long straddle at entry. The risk profile indicated that the QIHU stock price must rally above $77.95 or drop below $67.04 for this long straddle to be profitable. However, once price movement either upward or downward is established, sell the opposite side of this trade to recover part of the premium originally paid.

Of course you must be confident in the long-term price direction based on your chart analysis and company or market sector news. Because you are aware of the radical price fluctuations that are typical to QIHU (see figure 14–16c), you are confident that this will be a winning trade.

Trade Management

The primary concern with this option strategy is a continuous sideways movement of the price of QIHU (Qihoo 360 Technology Company, LTD). As you know, both the long strangle and long straddle require a strong price move to be profitable. A sustained sideways price trend is the worst possible outcome for either of these long strategies.

If the underlying stock remains within a narrow price range, consider selling both the put and the call to recover some premium. But don't be premature in your exit, especially if several months remain until expiration. Your biggest concern is a rise in Theta and the erosion of your premium. Theta is the death knell of all long option strategies and announces the arrival of contract expiration. Waiting too long to exit may prevent recovery of some of the premium you originally paid when you entered the trade.

If the price of the underlying makes a strong move, sell the opposite side and monitor your P/L Open until you are satisfied with the profit. Consider establishing an e-mail or smartphone alert to notify you when the Mark and/or Delta of either leg reaches a predetermined value.

If the profitable side of this trade becomes deep ITM, consider exercising the option contract. Otherwise, sell the option back to the market for the profit in increased premium.

Whichever of these two actions you decide upon (exercise or sell to close), do not wait too long as Theta will begin to erode the remaining premium. This may force your hand, causing you to sell for all remaining premium in a single transaction. Exercising the option requires two distinct transactions. Each requires commissions plus the exchange fees. Before making a final decision, do the math to determine the most profitable outcome.

Possible Outcomes

1. If the price of the underlying stock of your long strangle begins to drop, determine if a downward trend is forming. If so, let it run downward as the strike price of the long put becomes deeper ITM. When the P/L Open value on your account statement for this trade becomes profitable by at least 30% to 70%, consider selling both the put and call options to collect the available premium.

2. Because the long straddle can return unlimited profit if a substantial amount of time remains until contract expiration, it may be premature to either sell or exercise the profitable long put option too soon. However, you can enter a sell to close order on the opposite side of the straddle to salvage what premium may still remain. Once the price of the profitable side of this option begins to reverse direction, sell it for more premium than originally paid.

3. Assuming the conditions described in outcome 2 above, calculate the profit in premium versus the profit collected by exercising the option and then selling the stock. Exercising the option may be substantially more profitable than selling the option, in spite of having to pay two brokerage commissions — one to exercise and a second to sell the stock.

4. If the underlying stock begins to rally and your analysis indicates an upward trend is forming, sell the long put and retain the long call. Follow the stock upward until the trade is profitable. Once the P/L Open on your account statement shows an acceptable profit, either enter a sell to close order or exercise the option. As in number 3 above, do the math to see which action is most profitable.

5. DON'T GIVE UP! If the price of the underlying stock moves sideways and remains close to the strike price for a month or more, your account statement will display a loss in both the P/L Open and P/L Day columns. However, a lot can happen

in the months that remain, and it probably will. Because the QIHU stock typically experiences strong price fluctuations, it is unlikely that the price will remain at the strike price of your straddle. Based on the price chart in figure 14–16c, it is apparent that the price of QIHU is quite volatile. Because this trade has several months remaining until expiration, and based on the price history shown on the chart, the trader should let it continue to work as a breakout is likely to occur.

Strip

Structure

+1 ATM CALL, +2 ATM PUTS
Same expiration date; ≥ 90 days

Description and Goals

The strip is an unbalanced bearish strategy with limited risk and unlimited reward. Some consider it a neutral strategy, but because its structure includes two long puts and only one long call, it favors a drop in the price of the underlying stock. The preferred goal of this strategy is a substantial price drop in the underlying stock to increase the value of the two long puts as they move deeper ITM. A secondary goal is a strong rally in the price of the underlying stock.

As shown in the above trade structure, the strip is a debit strategy because it is constructed with two ATM long puts and one ATM long call. An example of a strip might be the purchase of +5 ATM calls and +10 ATM puts. For this strategy achieve the most profit, the price of the underlying stock must drop. Therefore, consider the strip strategy as a bearish version of the long straddle just described. A drop in the price of the underlying stock drives the long put deeper ITM. It can then be exercised or sold for more premium than originally paid.

If the price of the underlying stock rallies, the long call becomes profitable. The trader can sell the long puts and then let the long call work for profit.

Just as with long strangles and long straddles, the strip strategy is dependent on a strong price move. Although the strip favors a drop in the price of the underlying, it can also be profitable if the price of the underlying stock experiences an exceptionally strong rally, making the long call profitable. Some may think of the long call as a hedge against being wrong in the trader's initial bias. And so it is.

Setup Parameters

- Goals: A strong downward price move in the underlying increases the premium of the two ATM puts. If wrong and the price of the underlying rallies, the ATM puts can be sold and the ATM call increases in value as it moves deeper ITM.
- Bias: Bearish bias and looking for a strong drop resulting from a company event such as a poor earnings release. Look at price charts of stock moving into unfavorable market sectors.
- Debit/Credit: Debit
- Chart Trend: Daily and hourly charts reveal substantial price swings within a matter of weeks to a few months. The dominant long-term price trend is downward.
- Momentum Oscillator: Presently midrange between previous overbought/oversold conditions
- Keltner Channel: The ATR(14) envelope is currently narrow; the envelope historically experiences frequent expansion and compression.
- Implied Volatility % $\leq$ 20%; buyer wants low IV% for low premium at entry followed by a strong increase in volatility.
- Greeks: Delta negative; Theta negative; Vega positive
- Days till Expiry: $\geq$ 90 days; Give this strategy plenty of time to work in your favor. The goal is a strong drop in the price of the underlying stock without a large increase in the value of Theta

(time decay). It's always possible that overall market sentiment can impact the underlying stock. Refrain from exiting this strategy prematurely.

- Net Premium (both Marks): ≤ $10.00; the premium is the total amount being risked. It should be based on your account size, i.e., what you are willing to lose. (When more than one long put contract is bought, the strip premiums are less than that paid for the long straddle because there are only half as many long call premiums as there are long put premiums.)
- Probability ITM: ≥ 94%; Both legs are placed as close to the current price of the underlying as possible.
- Open Interest at Strike Prices: ≥ 500 (more is better); total open interest @ all strikes ≥ 10,000. Liquidity is required to fill both the initial trade and sell to close orders that may follow.
- Bid to Ask spread: Like the long strangle and straddle, the Bid to Ask spread (the difference between the Bid and Ask prices) should be slightly wider than usual to reflect the presence of current low volatility.
- Risk Amount ≈ 1.0% of account equity (governed by premium and number of contracts)

How the Strategy Works

This strategy works in the same way as the long straddle. Of course it favors a price drop rather than a rally. As with the long straddle, a strong price movement, especially a drop, is needed for this strategy to be profitable. Otherwise, it works identically to the long straddle.

Hands-On Activity

Scanning for a Trade

1. As with the long straddle, develop a watch list of companies having upcoming earnings releases. You may find such a list on your trading platform, as some brokerages provide a list of

symbols with pending earnings announcements. You can also see earnings release symbols on price charts, watch lists, or both.

2. Ensure the stock prices (Last) column are within the desired price range. This will depend on your account size. An example might be stocks having prices from $30 to $100.

3. Add an ImpVol% column to your watch list. Then sort on implied volatility percentage in ascending order (lowest to highest IV%).

4. Synchronize the watch list to the charts and option chains so you can see all three windows at the same time or be able to quickly switch between them.

5. ATR(14): As with the preceding long call and long put strategies, look for a relatively low price range that accompanies low implied volatility for a reduction in the cost of premium at entry. Be sure to examine the ATR(14) on a daily chart.

6. Examine option chains with expiration dates greater than 90 days. Look for earnings releases occurring within the next 15 to 30 days.

7. Find overbought stocks with prices near resistance that appear poised for a likely drop.

8. Look for affordable premiums according to your personal risk tolerance. These should have low implied volatility and reasonably low premiums.

9. Because the long straddle and long strangle are quite similar, symbol QIHU is ideal for the strip strategy as well as the strap strategy that is described next. QIHU has current low IV% and an earnings release inside 30 days. It is currently trading at $73.00 and has experienced radical price swings of $30/ share as shown in the chart contained in figure 14–16c above.

10. The option contracts within the option chain shown in figure 14–18a expire in 175 days. This is well above the recommended 90+ days till expiration.

11. The ten $72.5 long puts and the five long call option contracts are closest to the money. The trader pays $2.25 per share for ten 72.50 puts and $3.20 per share for five 72.50 calls for a total of $7,700 in combined premiums for fifteen contracts.

12. The risk profile for this trade is shown in figure 14–18b. Notice how this trade becomes profitable if the price of the underlying QIHU stock drops by $4.45 to $68.65 or rallies by $7.20 to $80.20. This is a good illustration of how the strip strategy is so much more bearish than bullish. It also illustrates the need for QIHU to make a strong move in either direction. As shown in the risk profile, a price drop is much more rewarding than a price rally.

Figure 14–18a. Strip Option Chain

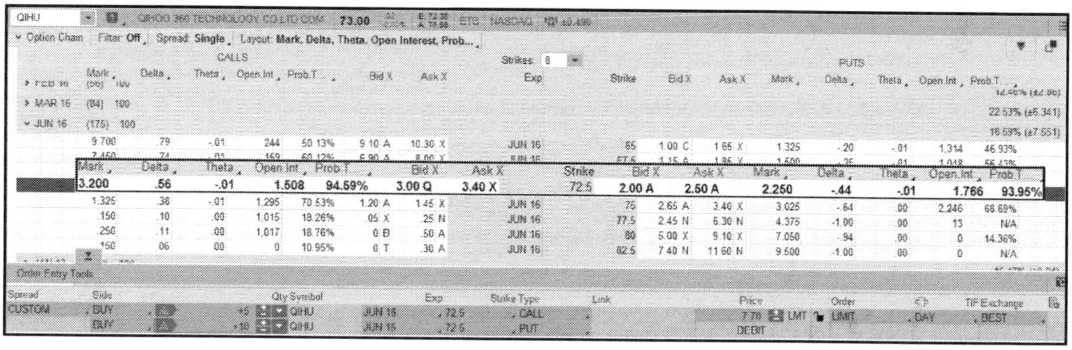

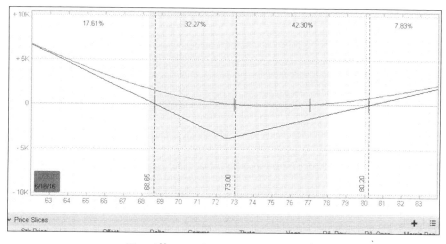

For illustration purposes only.

Figure 14–18b. Strip Risk Profile

For illustration purposes only.

Entry

1. The next earnings release for QIHU occurs within 30 days. You've examined several option chains and settled on the JUN 16 option chain which expires in 175 days.
2. The charts show how QIHU consistently experiences a substantial amount of price movement. The risk profile shows a profit if QIHU rallies beyond $80.20 or drops below $68.65. QIHU appears to be an ideal candidate for the strip option strategy.
3. Set the number of Strikes to **8** to display those strike prices that are close to the money. Using the strip requires only access to the ATM strike prices.
4. After careful examination click the PUTS **72.5 Ask** cell to add the 72.5 long puts to the order bar.
5. Press and hold the **Ctrl** key and click the CALLS **72.5 Ask** cell to add the 72.5 long calls to the order bar.
6. Change the Spread from STRADDLE to CUSTOM. This permits you to change the Qty values independently.
7. Change the CALL Qty value to +5 and the PUT Qty value to +10 as shown in figure 14–18a.
8. Notice the DEBIT price of $7.70 for 5 72.5 CALL contracts and 10 72.5 PUT contracts.
9. Check the order bar to verify it contains entries similar to these:

CUSTOM BUY +5 QIHU JUN 16 72.5 CALL 7.70   LMT   LIMIT   DAY
         BUY +10 QIHU JUN 16 72.5 PUT   DEBIT

10. When ready click **Confirm and Send**.
11. Evaluate the Order Confirmation information. If satisfactory, click **Send**.

Risks

Your maximum risk is the $7,700 paid for the strip at entry. The risk profile indicated that the QIHU stock price must rally above $80.20 or drop below $68.65 for this strip strategy to be profitable.

However, once price movement either upward or downward is established, sell the opposite side of this trade to recover part of the premium originally paid.

Of course you should be reasonably confident in strong price drop off resistance based on your chart analysis. This might be bolstered by poor earnings or a lack of confidence in QIHU's market sector or region of the world. You are also encouraged by the radical price fluctuations that are typical to QIHU, as you saw in figure 14–16c.

Trade Management

The primary concern with this option strategy is a continuous sideways movement of the price of QIHU (Qihoo 360 Technology Company, LTD). Like the long strangle and long straddle, the strip also requires a strong price move in the underlying to be profitable. A sustained sideways price trend is the worst possible outcome for all of these long strategies.

If the underlying stock remains within a narrow price range, consider selling both the put and the call to recover some premium. But don't be premature in your exit, especially if several months remain until expiration. Your biggest concern is a rise in Theta and the erosion of your premium. As mentioned above, Theta is the death knell of all long option strategies and announces the arrival of contract expiration. Waiting too long to exit can prevent recovery of the premium you originally paid when you entered the trade.

If the price of the underlying makes a strong move (especially a price drop), sell the opposite side and monitor your P/L Open until you are satisfied with the profit. As with most working trades, consider establishing an e-mail or smartphone alert to notify you when the Mark and/or Delta of either leg reaches a predetermined value.

If the long puts become deep ITM, consider exercising the strip option contract. Otherwise, sell the option back to the market for the profit in increased premium.

Whichever of these two actions you decide upon (exercise or sell to close), do not wait too long as Theta will begin to erode the remaining premium. This may force you to exit the trade by selling the remaining premium. You may also exercise the option and then sell the stock for a profit. Exercising and then selling are two transactions with two commissions plus the exchange fees. As you should know by now, before making a final decision, calculate the most profitable action, i.e., whether to sell for premium (close) or exercise.

Possible Outcomes

1. If the price of the underlying stock of your strip strategy begins to drop, determine if a downward trend is forming. If so, let it run downward to let the strike price of the long put travel deeper ITM. When the P/L Open value on your account statement for this trade becomes profitable by at least 30% to 70%, consider selling both the put and call options to collect the available premium.

2. Because the strip can return unlimited profit if a substantial amount of time remains until contract expiration, it may be premature to either sell or exercise the profitable strip option too soon. However, you can enter a sell to close order on the opposite side of the strip to salvage what premium may still remain. Once the price of the profitable side of this option begins to reverse direction, sell it for more premium than originally paid.

3. You may decide to *scale* out. This involves taking part of the profit and letting the remaining options work. For example, you may be able to close 4 ATM puts and 2 ATM calls to recover part or all of the initial premium paid. The remaining 6 ATM puts and 3 ATM calls can continue to work for more profit. If they stall, you must decide if there's still time to regain the downward slide. If not, then it's probably time to close or exercise the trade.

4. Assuming the conditions described in outcome 2 above, calculate the profit in premium versus the profit collected by

exercising the option and then selling the stock. Exercising the option may be substantially more profitable than selling the option for premium in spite of having to pay more in brokerage and exchange fees for multiple transactions.

5. If the underlying stock begins to rally and your analysis indicates an upward trend is forming, sell the long puts. Retain the long calls until you've established a bias. Follow the stock upward until the trade is profitable. Once the P/L Open on your account statement shows an acceptable profit, either enter a sell to close order or exercise the option. As with all long option strategies, calculate the outcomes to determine which provides the best yield.

6. DON'T GIVE UP! If the price of the underlying stock moves sideways and remains within a dollar of the 72.5 strike price for a month or more, your account statement will display a loss in both the P/L Open and P/L Day columns. However, much can happen in the months that remain, and it probably will. Because the QIHU stock typically experiences strong price fluctuations, it is unlikely that the price will remain ATM. Based on the price chart in figure 14–16c, it is apparent that the price of QIHU is quite volatile. Because this trade has several months remaining until expiration, let the trade continue to work as a breakout is quite likely.

Strap

Structure
+2 ATM CALLS, +1 ATM PUT
Same expiration dates; ≥ 90 days

Description and Goals
The strap is an unbalanced bullish strategy with limited risk and unlimited reward. The strap's construction is a *mirror image* of the strip described above. In other words, it is the exact opposite in the number

of calls and puts. The strap includes two ATM long calls for each ATM long put. And, as you can see, it's quite evident that the strap is a bullish strategy. The preferred goal of this strategy is a strong rally in the market price of the underlying stock. This increases the value of the two long call legs as they move deeper ITM. A secondary goal would be a substantial price drop in the underlying stock to move the long put deeper ITM. Of course this is less desirable because it returns half of the income provided by the two long calls on the other side of this trade.

Like the strip described above, the strap is also a debit spread. An example of a strap is the purchase of +5 ATM puts and +10 ATM calls. As mentioned, this strategy achieves the most profit when the price of the underlying stock rallies. Therefore, consider the strap strategy as an unbalanced bullish version of the long straddle option strategy.

Because a rally in the price of the underlying stock drives the long call deeper ITM, it can either be exercised or sold for more premium than originally paid. If the price of the underlying stock drops, the long put becomes profitable. The trader can sell the long calls and then follow the long put deeper into profit.

Just as with long strangles, long straddles, and the strip, the strap strategy is also dependent on a strong directional price move. Although the strap favors a rally in price, it can also be profitable if the price of the underlying stock experiences an exceptionally strong drop, making the long put more profitable than the cost of entry. However, the long put also serves as a hedge against a drop in the price of the underlying.

Setup Parameters

- Goals: A strong upward price move in the underlying increases the premium of the two ATM calls. If wrong and the price of the underlying drops, the ATM calls can be sold and the ATM put increases in value as it becomes deeper ITM.
- Bias: Bullish bias and looking for a strong rally resulting from a company event such as an earnings release. Examine the price charts of stocks moving into favorable market sectors.

- Debit/Credit: Debit
- Chart Trend: Daily and hourly charts reveal substantial price swings within a matter of weeks to a few months. The dominant long-term price trend is upward.
- Momentum Oscillator: Presently midrange between previous overbought/oversold conditions
- Keltner Channel: The ATR(14) envelope is currently narrow; the envelope historically experiences frequent expansion and compression.
- Implied Volatility % ≤ 20%; buyer wants low IV% for low premium at entry followed by a strong increase in volatility.
- Greeks: Delta positive; Theta negative; Vega positive
- Days till Expiry: ≥ 90 days; Give this strategy plenty of time to work in your favor. The goal is a strong rally in the price of the underlying stock without a large increase in the value of Theta (time decay). Prevailing market sentiment can impact the underlying stock. Refrain from exiting this strategy prematurely.
- Net Premium (both Marks): ≤ $10.00; the premium is the total amount at risk. It should be based on your account size, i.e., what you are willing to lose. (When more than one long call contract is bought, the strap premiums are less than that paid for the long straddle because there are only half as many long put premiums as there are long call premiums.)
- Probability ITM: ≥ 90%; Both legs are placed as close to the current price of the underlying as possible.
- Open Interest at Strike Prices: ≥ 500 (more is better); total open interest @ all strikes ≥ 10,000. Liquidity is required to fill both the initial trade and sell to close orders that may follow.
- Bid to Ask spread (the difference between the Bid and Ask prices) should be a bit wider than normal due to the lower volatility.
- Risk Amount ≈1.0% of account equity (governed by premium and number of contracts)

How the Strategy Works

This strategy works in the same way as the long straddle. Of course it favors a price rally rather than a drop. As with the long straddle, a strong price movement, especially a rally, is needed for this strategy to be profitable. In all other respects, it works identically to the long straddle.

Hands-On Activity

Scanning for a Trade

1. As with the long straddle, long strangle, and strip, develop a watch list of companies having upcoming earnings releases. You may find such a list on your trading platform, as some brokerages provide a list of symbols with pending earnings announcements. You can also see earnings release symbols on price charts, watch lists, or both.

2. Ensure the stock prices (Last) column are within the desired range. This depends on your account size. An example might be stocks having prices from $30 to $100.

3. Add an Implied Volatility column to your watch list and the ATR(14) study to your charts. Then sort on implied volatility percentage in ascending order (lowest to highest IV%).

4. Synchronize the watch list to the charts and option chains so you can see all three windows at the same time or be able to quickly switch between them.

5. ATR(14): Using a daily chart, look for a relatively low price range that accompanies low implied volatility for a reduction in the premium that must be paid.

6. Examine option chains with expiration dates greater than 90 days. Look for earnings releases occurring within the next 15 to 30 days.

7. Find overbought stocks with prices near resistance that appear poised for a likely drop.

8. Look for affordable premiums according to your personal risk tolerance. These should have low implied volatility and reasonably low premiums.

9. Because the long straddle and long strangle are quite similar, symbol QIHU is ideal for the strip strategy as it was for the strap strategy described above. QIHU has current low IV% and an earnings release inside 30 days. It is currently trading at $73.00 and has experienced radical price swings of $30/share as shown in the chart contained in figure 14–16c above.

10. The option contracts within the option chain shown in figure 14–19a expire in 174 days — well above the recommended 90+ day expiration.

11. The ten $72.5 long call and the five $72.5 long put option contracts are closest to the money. The trader pays $2.25 per share for five 72.50 puts and $3.20 per share for ten 72.50 calls for a total of $8,650 in combined premiums for fifteen contracts.

12. The risk profile for this trade is shown in figure 14–19b. Notice how this trade becomes profitable if the price of the underlying QIHU stock rallies to $76.82, an increase of $3.82, or drops by $9.15 to $63.85. This illustrates why the strap strategy is more bullish than bearish. It also shows how a reasonable QIHU price move in either direction is necessary for this strategy to succeed.

Figure 14–19a. Strap Option Chain

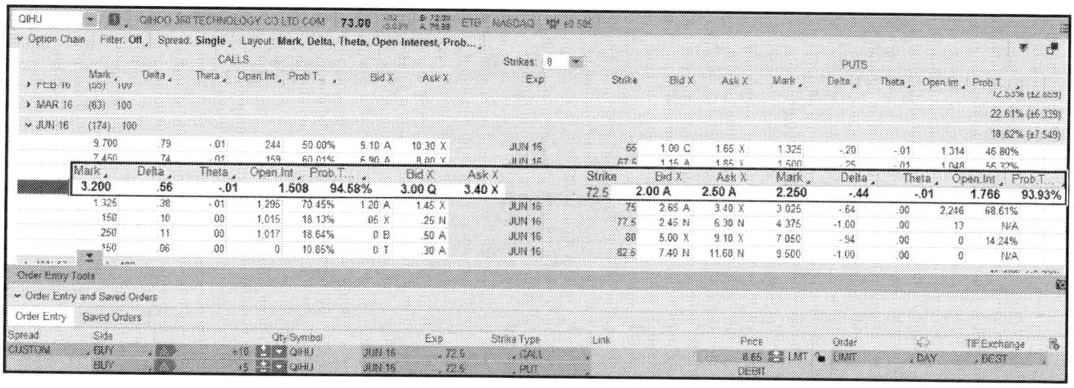

For illustration purposes only.

Figure 14–19b. Strap Risk Profile

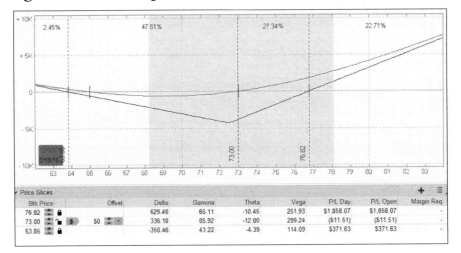

For illustration purposes only.

Entry

1. The next earnings release for QIHU occurs within 30 days. You've examined several option chains and settled on the JUN 16 option chain which expires in 174 days.

2. The charts show how QIHU consistently experiences a substantial amount of price movement. The risk profile shows a profit if QIHU rallies beyond $76.82 or drops below $63.85. QIHU appears to be ideal for the strap option strategy.

3. Set the number of Strikes to **8** since you only need to see strike prices that are ATM.

4. After careful examination click the PUTS **72.5 Ask** cell to add the 72.5 long PUT to the order bar.

5. Press and hold the **Ctrl** key and click the CALLS **72.5 Ask** cell to add the 72.5 long CALL to the order bar.

6. Change the Spread from STRADDLE to CUSTOM. This permits you to change the Qty values independently.

7. Change the CALL Qty value to +10 and the PUT Qty value to +5 as shown in figure 14–19a.

8. Notice the DEBIT price of $8.65 for 10 72.5 CALL contracts and 5 72.5 PUT contracts.
9. Check the order bar to verify it contains entries similar to these:

CUSTOM BUY +10 QIHU JUN 16 72.5 CALL 8.65 LMT LIMIT DAY
         BUY +5 QIHU JUN 16 72.5 PUT DEBIT

10. When ready click **Confirm and Send**.
11. Evaluate the Order Confirmation information. If satisfactory, click **Send**.

Risks

Your maximum risk is the $8,650 paid for the strap at entry. The risk profile indicated that the QIHU stock price must rally above $76.82 or drop below $63.85 for this strap to be profitable. However, once price movement either upward or downward is established, sell the opposite side of this trade to recover part of the premium originally paid.

Of course you should be reasonably confident in strong price rally off of historical support based on your chart analysis. This might be bolstered by good earnings or increased confidence in QIHU's market sector or region of the world. You are also encouraged by the radical price fluctuations that are typical to QIHU as shown in figure 14–16c.

Trade Management

The primary concern with any of these long straddle-like strategies, including the long strangle, the strip, and the strap is a continuous sideways movement of the price of QIHU (Qihoo 360 Technology Company, LTD). Like all of these strategies, the strap requires a strong price move in the underlying to be profitable. A sustained sideways price trend is the worst possible outcome for any of these long ATM or near the money strategies.

If the underlying stock remains within a narrow price range, consider selling both the puts and the calls to recover some premium.

But don't be premature in your exit when ample time remains until expiration. Your biggest concern is a rise in Theta and the erosion of your premium. Theta is the enemy of all long option strategies, and heralds the arrival of contract expiration. Of course, waiting too long to exit can prevent recovery of sufficient premium to pay the exchange and brokerage fees.

If the price of the underlying makes a strong move (especially a price rally), sell the opposite side and monitor your P/L Open until you are satisfied with the profit. As with most working trades, consider establishing an e-mail or smartphone alert to notify you when the Mark and/or Delta of either leg reaches a predetermined value.

If the long calls become deep ITM, consider exercising the strap option contract. Otherwise, sell the option back to the market for a nice profit in increased premium.

Whichever of these two actions you decide upon (exercise or sell to close), do not wait too long as Theta will begin to erode the remaining premium. This may force you to exit the trade by selling what premium may remain. You may also exercise the option and then sell the stock for a profit. Exercising and then selling are two transactions with two commissions plus the exchange fees. Before making a final decision, calculate the most profitable action, i.e., sell to close or exercise your option and then sell the stock.

Possible Outcomes

1. If the price of the underlying stock of your strap strategy begins to rally, determine if an upward trend is forming. If so, let it run as the strike price of the long call becomes deeper ITM. When the P/L Open value on your account statement for this trade becomes profitable by at least 30% to 70%, consider selling both the put and call options to collect the available premium.

2. Because the strap can return unlimited profit if a substantial amount of time remains until contract expiration, it may be premature to either sell or exercise the profitable strap option too soon. However, you can enter a sell to close order on the opposite, rapidly fading side of the strap to salvage what premium remains. Once the price of the profitable side of this option begins to reverse direction, sell it for more premium than originally paid.

3. Assuming the conditions described in outcome 2 above, calculate the profit in premium versus the profit collected by exercising the option and then selling the stock. Exercising the option may be substantially more profitable than selling the option for the increase in premium, in spite of having to pay two brokerage commissions — one to exercise and a second to sell the stock.

4. If the underlying stock begins to rally and your analysis indicates an upward trend is forming, sell the long puts and retain the long calls. Follow the stock upward until the trade is profitable. Once the P/L Open on your account statement shows an acceptable profit, either enter a sell to close order or exercise the option. As in number 3 above, do the math to determine which course of action to take.

5. DON'T GIVE UP! If the price of the underlying stock moves sideways and remains within a dollar of the 72.5 strike price for a month or more, your account statement will display a loss in both the P/L Open and P/L Day columns. However, a lot can happen in the months that remain, and it probably will. Because the QIHU stock typically experiences strong price fluctuations, it is unlikely that the price will remain ATM. Based on the price chart in figure 14–16c, it is apparent that the price of QIHU is quite volatile. Because this trade has several months remaining until expiration, let the trade continue to work as a breakout is quite likely.

Ratio Spreads and Diagonal Ratio Spreads

Structure:

+1 ATM or slightly OTM CALL

−2 far OTM CALLS

(both ≤ 60 days)

or

+1 ATM or slightly OTM PUT

−2 far OTM PUTS

(both ≤ 60 days)

Diagonal Call Ratio Spread (preferred)

+1 ATM or slightly OTM CALL (≥ 90 days)

−2 far OTM CALLS (≤ 45 days)

Diagonal Put Ratio Spread (preferred)

+1 ATM or slightly OTM PUT (≥ 90 days)

−2 far OTM PUTS (≤ 45 days)

Description and Goals

With your background in how long and short puts and calls work, you will likely understand the constructs and possible outcomes associated with call and put ratio spreads. Both call and put ratio spreads are debit spreads. And the short puts or calls expose these strategies to unlimited risk with limited reward in premium income. Because of the risk, ratio spreads must be carefully managed.

But don't let the high risk scare you away. Ratio spreads can return a substantial amount of income by doubling up on the number of contracts being sold. And if the long calls or puts move deeper ITM and are sold, so much the better. Of course the trader's directional bias and the placement of the OTM strike price must both be right.

It's evident why these strategies are called *ratio spreads*. They are unbalanced. The bullish call ratio spread typically includes +1 ATM or slightly OTM call and −2 farther OTM calls. The bearish put ratio spread includes +1 ATM or slightly OTM put and −2 farther OTM puts. Both involve a 2:1 ratio, although some traders may use 3:1 or even more relying on their certainty of having their short calls or short puts far enough OTM to prevent their becoming ITM.

Choosing a nearer expiration date for the short leg than for the long leg is referred to as a *ratio put diagonal spread* or a *ratio call diagonal spread*. The diagonal ratio spread is superior. This construct permits the trader to exit the short options sooner — perhaps before it is threatened. The trader retains the long options, which may require additional time to become profitable. And because the long option has more time to work, it retains its value longer.

Call ratio spreads are bullish in anticipation of a moderate rally in the price of the underlying stock. As expected, put ratio spreads are bearish in anticipation of a moderate drop in the price of the underlying. The term moderate is used because a strong price rally or drop can place the short legs of a ratio spread in jeopardy.

The goal of the call and put ratio spreads is for the price of the underlying stock to move toward, but remain inside, the short call or put legs throughout the life of the option contracts. You may wonder why traders would even consider a ratio spread. If the short legs of this strategy become ITM, this strategy can suffer a substantial loss. This is especially true of the call ratio spread in which the trader must purchase and deliver stock to the buyers of multiple short calls — ouch!

Obviously, experienced traders never expect their short calls or puts to become ITM. And the experienced option traders rarely choose the same expiration dates for both the long and short legs of their ratio spreads. Their plan is to eventually sell the long calls or puts. This, in combination with the premium income from the

OTM short options, can return a profit. If the price rallies in favor of the long call or put, the entire trade can be closed for profit. If the underlying moves sideways or away from a long leg, the trader can sell the long leg and let the multiple short legs expire worthless.

Hence, the cost of entry is minimized by the sale of multiple OTM puts or calls. And by moving a safe distance OTM and choosing options that expire in a matter of several days to a few weeks reduces the probability of having the short leg becoming ITM prior to expiration.

Now consider diagonal ratio spreads. Recall how the bull call spread uses the same number of long and short call contracts rather than a 2:1 ratio. And the bear put spread buys ATM or slightly OTM puts and sells farther OTM puts. The main differences are the 2:1 ratios. The standard call ratio spread (the strategy using the same expiration dates for both legs) carries the most risk because of the exposed uncovered call. For this reason some traders avoid it. But this is limiting when a stock is trending upward. In any case, the hands-on activity uses the safest variant of the ratio spread. The diagonal put ratio spread is used to illustrate the operation of this strategy. The activity employs one ATM long put ≥ 90 days (the *back* contract) two far OTM short puts ≤ 45 days (the *front* contracts).

Setup Parameters

- Goals: A moderate drop in the price of the underlying stock puts the long ATM put deeper ITM to increase its value; the OTM short puts must remain safely OTM.
- Bias: Bearish; look for a moderate price drop based on a recent rally approaching resistance.
- Debit/Credit: Debit (more premium paid for the ATM long put than received from the OTM short puts)
- Chart Trend: Daily and hourly charts reveal a reasonably stable price range between established support and resistance. The

dominant price trend has been mildly downward for nearly a year.

- Momentum Oscillator: Slightly overbought near resistance
- Keltner Channel: The ATR(14) envelope is currently mid-range; the envelope is characterized by mild expansions and contractions.
- Implied Volatility % ≥ 60% and ≤ 90%; high IV% is desirable in anticipation of a drop IV% and in the premium of the short puts. A small drop in the price of the underlying moves the long put ITM as desired; the short puts must remain safely OTM.
- Greeks: Delta < −.25; Theta negative; Vega positive
- Days till Expiry: Short puts ≤ 45 (less is better); Long put ≥ 90 days (more is better); exit the short puts while OTM; give the long put plenty of time to work in your favor. Refrain from exiting this strategy prematurely. If ample time remains on the long put, sell more OTM puts.
- Net Premium (both Marks): ≤ $5.00; the premium paid should be offset by the premium received from the sale of the multiple OTM short puts.
- Probability ITM: Long put ≥ 80%; short put ≤ 25%. Keep the short puts safely OTM and the long put either close to or ATM.
- Open Interest at Strike Prices: ≥ 500 (more is better); total open interest @ all strikes ≥ 10,000. Liquidity is required to fill both the long put's sell to close order and the short put's buy to close orders.
- Bid to Ask spread (the difference between the Bid and Ask prices) A reasonably narrow Bid to Ask spread is desirable to reflect good trading volume and acceptable open interest.
- Risk Amount ≈1.0% of account equity (governed by premium and number of contracts)

How the Strategy Works

This diagonal put ratio spread is used with symbol ELLI which has a current price of $64.67. As shown on the option chain of figure

14–20a, the spread is constructed by buying +5 60 PUTS expiring in 111 days and selling −10 50 PUTS expiring in 20 days. The total debit shown for this ratio spread is $4.80. The total cost for entry is $2,400 for 5 long puts (500 × $5.65) and 10 short puts (1,000 × −$0.425) plus commissions and exchange fees.

As shown on the risk profile in figure 14–20b, this trade becomes neutral at around $64. If the ELLI's price drops to $50, the P/L Open on the risk profile shows a $3,761.03 profit less transaction fees. It's important for the price of ELLI to remain above $50 for the following 50 days. If the short puts are sold for a 60% profit and the long puts remain viable, it's possible to sell another ten short puts for additional premium income.

But if the price of ELLI begins to rally, the long puts are sold for profit, or it can be exercised when more profit is available.

Hands-On Activity

Scanning for a Trade

1. Develop a watch list of stocks with low IV% and with prices nearing historical resistance levels in anticipation of a price reversal and drop.
2. Ensure the stock prices (Last) column are within the desired range. This depends on your account size. The example being used is to list stocks having prices from $30 to $100.
3. ATR(14): Using a daily chart, look for a moderately strong average price range that accompanies high implied volatility for an increase in the premium received from the short options. (If several short options are sold while the long option is retained, the eventual return in premium income makes this diagonal ratio spread quite profitable.)
4. Synchronize the watch list to the charts and option chains so you can see all three windows at the same time or be able to quickly switch between them.

5. Examine a series of option chains. Display two expiration dates: one expiring within 45 days for ten short puts and another expiring in 90 days or more for five long puts.

6. Avoid earnings releases occurring within the short put's expiration date.

7. Find overbought stocks with prices near resistance that are presently overbought and poised for a drop.

8. Look for affordable premiums according to your personal risk tolerance. Implied volatility should be reasonably high and expected to return toward neutral IV%.

9. ELLI appears to be a good candidate, as it fits a bearish bias, has a high IV%, and has ample open interest for liquidity.

10. Use the option chains similar to those shown in figure 14–20a. One expires in 111 days and will work nicely for the long puts; the other expires in 20 days and is ideal for the short puts.

11. Five 60 long puts and ten 50 short puts are reasonable for this diagonal ratio put spread.

12. The risk profile for this trade shown in figure 14–20b plots an increase in profit as the ELLI's price drops toward the short puts.

Figure 14–20a. Diagonal Put Ratio Spread Option Chain

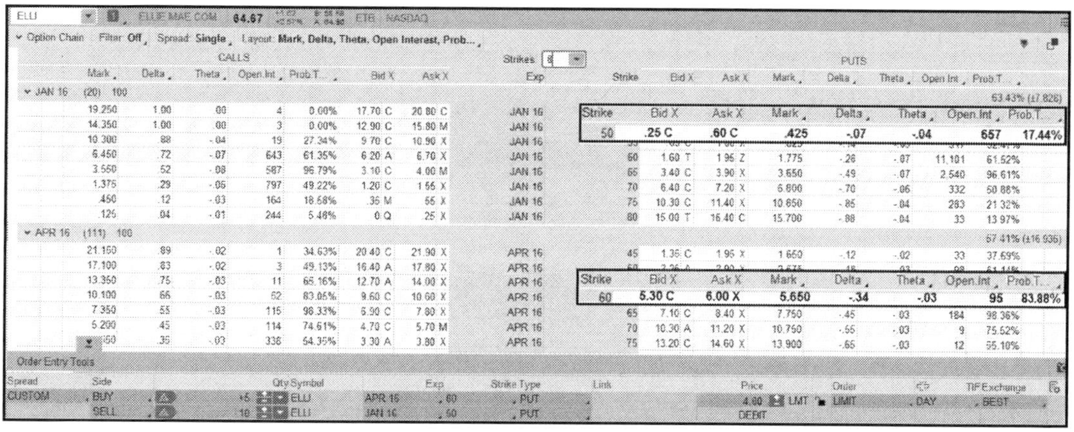

For illustration purposes only.

Figure 14–20b. Diagonal Put Ratio Spread Risk Profile

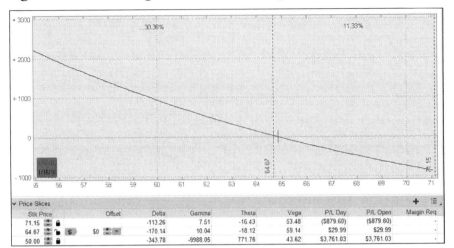

For illustration purposes only.

Entry

1. The earnings release for ELLI is not scheduled until well after the expiration of the short puts.

2. The current IV% is near 65%. This is enough to consider a diagonal put ratio spread.

3. After examining several option chains, the Jan 16 (20) and APR 16 (111) option chains are selected and simultaneously displayed.

4. The charts show ELLI to be overbought near resistance and poised for a drop in price. The institutional sellers are likely to begin dumping ELLI based on the charts.

5. You decide to buy +5 APR 16 60 PUTS and sell –10 JAN 16 PUTS.

6. Set the number of Strikes to **14** so you can see all involved strikes for this spread.

7. After careful examination, click the APR 16 PUTS **60 Ask** cell to add the 60 long PUT to the order bar.

8. Press and hold the **Ctrl** key and click the JAN 16 CALLS **50 Bid** cell to add the 50 short CALL to the order bar.

9. Change the order bar Spread from STRADDLE to CUSTOM. (This permits you to change the Qty values independently.)
10. Change the 60 PUT Qty value to +**5** and the 50 PUT Qty value to −10 as shown in figure 14–20a.
11. Notice the DEBIT price of $4.80 for −10 50 PUT contracts and +5 60 PUT contracts.
12. Check the order bar to verify it contains entries similar to these:

CUSTOM	BUY	+5	ELLI	APR 16	60	PUT	4.80	LMT	LIMIT	DAY
	BUY	−10	ELLI	JAN 16	50	PUT	DEBIT			

13. When ready click **Confirm and Send**.
14. Evaluate the Order Confirmation information. If satisfactory, click **Send**.

Risks

As with all short options, the short OTM puts pose the most risk in this diagonal put ratio spread. And, as always, the only risk associated with the five long $60 puts is the possible loss of the premium paid when entering this diagonal ratio spread. Of course, if the ten short puts are exercised, our trader must take delivery of 1,000 shares of ELLI stock and pay the $50/share option price totaling $50,000.

If the short $50 puts are ITM, then the five $60 long put options are even deeper ITM. Our ratio spread trader will deliver 500 shares of ELLI to the $60 put option seller, who must pay $60/share for 500 shares, or $30,000. Now our trader has a $20,000 cash deficit. But our ratio spread trader still holds 500 shares of ELLI stock. Assuming the market price of ELLI is now $48/share, our ratio spread trader can sell the 500 shares of ELLI for $24,000. Now our trader has recovered a total of $54,000 in cash. Confused? Let's break this down to see the final outcome.

Trade Entry (Debit):..<$4,800>

10 contracts (1,000 shares) of the $50 short put exercised:......<$50,000>

5 contracts (500 shares) of the $60 long put exercised...........$30,000

Sell remaining 500 shares of ELLI @ ≈ $48/share: $24,000

Profit/Loss: ....<$800>

Of course our trader can hold on to the ELLI stock in anticipation of a bounce off support followed by a rally. This is where our trader must rely on technical analysis skills in addition to the impact that stock versus cash has on his or her margin balance.

Trade Management

As mentioned in the above risk paragraph, the primary concern is with the short put options becoming ITM. As long as the short puts are sufficiently far OTM and scheduled to expire within a matter of days to a few weeks, they should remain well OTM. If, however, the short puts are threatened, consider either rolling them to a lower, farther OTM strike price or enter a buy to close order.

When the short puts are threatened, the long puts would be deep ITM. The long puts can either be sold for a nice profit, especially if plenty of time remains, or the long puts can be exercised for ownership and resale of the underlying stock.

If the underlying stock begins to rally, the short puts are safe and the premium collected is secure. But the long puts begin to lose premium value. If ELLI stock continues to rally, the long put should be sold for any premium that remains to either break even or at least minimize losses before they become even worse.

As with most working trades, consider establishing an e-mail or smartphone alert to notify you when the Mark and/or Delta of either the long put or short put reaches a predetermined value.

And, of course, you can enter a Mark-triggered stop. The stop would automatically close the long puts if and when they become at or below a specified premium value.

Possible Outcomes

1. The diagonal put ratio has a limited number of outcomes. First, the trade may work as intended. The short puts expire worthless or can be closed for pennies while the long puts begin to move ITM — also for profit. Of course this requires ELLI's price to drop according to the trader's bearish bias.

2. The price of the underlying stock may remain neutral or begin to rally in opposition to the trader's bias. This causes the long put to drop in value. Although there may still be several months remaining till expiration, it may be time to recover as much premium as possible and move on. And, in fact, the trader can sell the premium that remains in the long put. Added to the premium received from the short puts, the trade may return a small profit or be close to breakeven.

3. The price of ELLI drops to around $58. The long put is now ITM, and the short puts are about to expire. Close or roll the short puts for profit. Keep the long puts and use them again with another diagonal put ratio spread.

4. The price of ELLI drops according to plan. The short puts are about to expire, and the long puts are deep ITM. Let the short puts expire worthless and sell the long put options for profit.

5. The price of ELLI drops according to plan. The short puts are about to expire, and the long puts are ITM. Let the short puts expire worthless, exercise the long put, and sell the stock for a substantial profit.

6. The P/L Open is at 50% to 70% in profit. Let the short puts expire worthless and sell to close the long puts. You're out!

Long Guts Strangle

Structure

+1 ITM CALL, +1 ITM PUT
Same expiration ≥ 90 days

Description and Goals

The long guts strangle is a debit spread and is essentially a long strangle. As shown in the above structure, the strike prices are ITM instead of OTM. And, of course, choosing long ITM strike prices makes entry more expensive than that of an OTM long strangle. Both are said to have a neutral bias, limited risk, unlimited reward strategy. But *au contraire*, a big price move is essential for this strategy to return a profit. So why spend the extra money to go ITM? Option traders know how Gamma and Delta values have the most impact on ATM premiums. But being ITM gets option traders closer to Delta values of 1.0 for calls and −1.0 for puts. If the option price reaches one of these values, option premiums increase by $1.00 for each $1.00 change in the price of the underlying stock. But because the higher cost of entry increases risk, some option traders consider long guts irrational.

In spite of this thinking, the long guts strategy can be a high reward strategy when a substantial price move in the underlying occurs. Because ITM call and put premiums are more expensive than the traditional long strangle, this strategy is appropriately called "long guts." It takes courage to invest in high priced ITM premiums in anticipation of a major price breakout. And because this strategy is nondirectional, it would seem that the trader is uncertain about whether to expect a rally or a drop in the price of the underlying stock. This signals indecisiveness — and is almost casino-like. It resembles "betting on red" in a game of roulette.

But the trader may be smarter than the casino gambler if the setup is correct, because the trader can win on either red or black. At entry the trader wants low implied volatility to reduce the amount of premium paid. And the trader wants plenty of time for this trade to work to minimize the effect of Theta. Extended time gives the underlying price plenty of time to move in one direction or the other. In addition, the trader wants to enter this trade near an event — probably just prior to an earnings release. And finally, the trader will choose an underlying stock with a history of strong volatility, those stocks that are constantly rallying and dropping on the price charts, with high ATR(14) values to validate strong trading volumes. All these factors are needed for this "gutsy" trade, and move it from the casino to a much more rational trading strategy.

Setup Parameters

- Goals: This strategy requires a substantial investment in premium, and therefore requires a strong price rally or drop in the underlying. Give it plenty of time to work in your favor.
- Bias: Strongly bearish or bullish; requires a strong price move in either direction based on historical price volatility of the underlying.
- Debit/Credit: Debit (The price chart should be basing near either a support or resistance level. Check the TTM_Squeeze in search of a potential price breakout. If unavailable, superimpose the Bollinger bands and Keltner channel studies as shown in chapter 8.)
- Chart Trend: Daily and hourly charts reveal a series of strong price swings over time.
- Momentum Oscillator: Presently midrange between periods of strong overbought and oversold conditions
- Keltner Channel: The ATR(14) envelope is currently compressed after a series of strong expansions and contractions.
- Implied Volatility % $\leq$ 20%; low IV% is desirable for low current premium paid followed by a rise in IV% and an accompanying price move.
- Greeks: Delta ± 0 (neutral); Theta negative; Vega positive
- Days till Expiry: $\geq$ 90 days (more is better); give these long options plenty of time to work in your favor. Refrain from exiting this strategy prematurely.

- Net Premium (both Marks): ≤ $20.00; this is an expensive strategy and requires a substantial investment and a strong price move for success.
- Probability ITM: Both call and put legs are ITM when purchased.
- Open Interest at Strike Prices: ≥ 500 (more is better); total open interest @ all strikes ≥ 10,000. Good liquidity is required to fill both long legs of this spread especially when one or both legs are exited.
- Bid to Ask spread should be wider than usual at entry and then narrow with a corresponding increase in trading volume.
- Risk Amount ≈1.0% of account equity (governed by premium and number of contracts)

How the Strategy Works

The long guts strangle requires a substantial investment in premium at entry. Therefore, this strategy also requires a strong price move to return a profit. When a price breakout forms, be ready to sell the losing side and retain the profitable side.

For example, if the price of the underlying stock makes a strong upward move, prepare to sell the long put to recover premium. Keep the call as it moves deeper ITM. Exercise or sell the long call for profit.

If the price of the underlying stock drops, let the short put become even deeper ITM. Be ready to sell the call and either exercise or sell the put for profit.

If trading volume remains low and the price of the underlying stock flounders, consider selling both legs to recover a portion of the original premium paid at entry.

Hands-On Activity

Scanning for a Trade

1. Develop a watch list of stocks nearing earnings releases. Synchronize the watch list with the option chains and price charts.

2. Ensure the stock prices (Last) column are within the desired price range. This depends on your account size. The example being used is to list stocks having prices from $30 to $100.

3. Add an Imp Vol% column to your watch list. Then sort on implied volatility percentage in ascending order (lowest to highest IV%).

4. Keltner Channel: Using a daily chart, locate stocks in which the Keltner channel's external envelopes are presently in a squeeze. This reflects light trading volume in a stock that is typically much higher. (You may want to add the Bollinger bands study to your charts.)

5. Synchronize the watch list to the charts and option chains so you can see all three windows at the same time or be able to quickly switch between them.

6. Scan the corresponding charts for stocks having substantial price swings throughout the year and with low current IV% as shown on your watch list.

7. Begin examining the option chains that expire in more than 90 days. Even longer is okay.

8. Evaluate the premiums for ITM puts and calls. (Also consider the call and put premiums of ATM strikes.)

9. Look for affordable premiums according to your personal risk tolerance. Implied volatility should be less than 20% and expected to rise at earnings.

10. V (Visa) appears to be a good candidate. It is a low IV%, strong open interest (liquidity), and price swings that regularly move up and down by $20. V's price chart, which is dropping off resistance, is shown in figure 14–21a. The option chain is in figure 14–21b.

11. Buying two ITM/ATM calls and puts produces the risk profile shown in figure 14–21c.

Figure 14–21a. Price Chart for a Long Guts Strangle

For illustration purposes only.

Figure 14–21b. Long Guts Strangle Option Chain

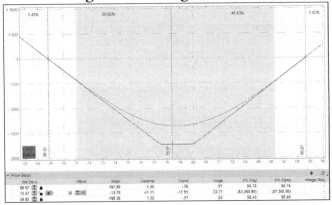

For illustration purposes only.

Figure 14–21c. Long Guts Strangle Risk Profile

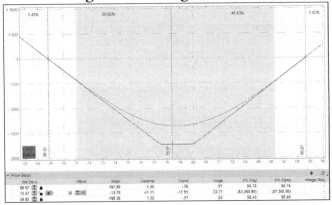

For illustration purposes only.

Entry

1. The earnings release for V is scheduled within the next few weeks.
2. The current IV% is near 18%. This is low enough to qualify for a long guts strangle spread.
3. After examining several option chains, the JUN 16 (172) option chain is selected.
4. The charts show the price of V currently basing; trading volume is low.
5. You decide to buy +2 JUN 16 77.5 CALLS and buy +2 JUN 16 80 PUTS.
6. Set the number of Strikes to **6** to make it easier to see the strikes for this spread.
7. After careful examination click the PUTS **80 Ask** cell to add the 80 long PUT to the order bar.
8. Press and hold the **Ctrl** key and click the CALLS **77.5 Ask** cell to add the 77.5 long CALL to the order bar.
9. Notice the Spread label on the order bar displays STRANGLE.
10. Notice the DEBIT price of $11.20 for +2 80 PUT contracts and +2 77.5 CALL contracts.
11. Check the order bar to verify it contains entries similar to these:

STRANGLE BUY +2 V JUN 16 77.5 CALL 11.20 LMT LIMIT DAY
          BUY +2 V JAN5 16 80 PUT DEBIT

12. When ready click **Confirm and Send**.
13. Evaluate the Order Confirmation information. If satisfactory, click **Send**.

Risks

This trade includes two call and two put contracts for a total cost of $2,240 plus transaction fees. The number of contracts was kept small due to the high cost of entry.

The risk profile in figure 14–21c shows how the stock price must rally from $78.37 to $88.67 or drop to $68.83 before this trade is profitable. With 172 days remaining until expiration, this is quite likely. If a dominant trend is revealed, the losing side should be sold and the profitable side retained as it moves deeper ITM. This substantially increases the profit potential.

The shaded area within the risk profile represents two standard deviations either side of the current price at the date of expiration. This tells us that the price of the underlying must move beyond two standard deviations to approach profit. Upon examination of the risk profile, the trader may be reticent to enter this trade unless the market, or market segment to which Visa belongs, is making a major move.

In spite of this example, the long guts strangle strategy can work quite well under the right circumstances. These include finding stocks with extreme price movements and low current IV%. And, of course, a pending earnings release can be helpful. So don't discount this strategy as being too costly for the possible return on investment. Your job is to find the conditions that contribute to narrower crossovers into the profit zone on the risk profile graph — perhaps just a $5 move rather than the $10 price move of this Visa trade.

Trade Management

This trade should be watched for a price breakout in either direction. However, if a substantial increase in implied volatility occurs within a short time after entry, and the strike prices remain ATM, it may be possible to sell the options for slightly more than originally paid.

Of course the goal is for a strong change in the underlying price to occur. If a definite trend is established, sell the side that is moving farther OTM and follow the side that is moving deeper ITM. Then take off the trade when it's profitable. If the price turns and begins to reduce your premium, consider closing the trade.

Possible Outcomes

1. Within three months the price of V has rallied to $95. The long put is sold for $2.75 per share in premium for a total of $550. The long $77.5 call is exercised for a profit of $17.50/share for $3,500. The trade returns a gross profit of $3,700 less the $2,240 cost of entry for a net profit of $2,010, from $550 + $3,700 −$2,240 = $2,010.

2. Within three months the price of V has dropped to $60. The long call is sold for $2.75 per share in premium to recover $550. The $80 long put is exercised for a profit of $20.00/share for a profit of $4,000. The trade returns a gross profit of $4,550 less the $2,240 cost of entry for a net profit of $2,310.

3. The price of V remains between $68.83 and $88.67 for 90 days, and has moved back to $78.50. The trader is able to sell the ATM long call and long put for $5.00. Based on 200 shares of each, the trader recovers $1,000. The trade loses $1,230 plus transaction fees.

Obviously, the outcome examples illustrate a limited number of price examples. In spite of just three examples, they represent possible outcomes of the long guts strangle strategy.

The Collar Spread (or Equity Collar)

Structure

−1 OTM CALLS, +1 OTM PUTS, +100 SHARES
Same expiration; typically ≥ 60 days and ≤ 120 days

Description and Goals

The collar spread is a neutral bias, low risk, low reward strategy that is most frequently used for hedging a stock presently held within a trader's account. This is particularly true for traders who have a large number of shares of stock and are concerned with downside risk caused by a major drop in the market price of the stock.

As explained in the long put strategy narrative, long puts are sometimes purchased as a hedge against a loss in the corresponding stock. But paying $2 to perhaps as much as $3 in premium for each share of stock held in one's account for insurance against a possible drop is expensive. Putting on a working protective stop on the stock is free. However, stops are market orders. So stops can be exercised several dollars below the intended stop price, particularly when a price is in rapid decline. Put options do have the advantage of locking in the hedge at the option price of the long put.

Enter the collar spread! To offset the cost of the long put (that $2 or $3 mentioned above), an OTM call can be simultaneously sold. The premium received from the short call helps to finance the cost of the long put. This produces an equity collar and provides a substantial reduction in the cost of the hedge.

Ownership of the stock in concert with the OTM short call also introduces a covered call. For example, if the trader owns 1,000 shares of stock that's trading at $50/share and sells ten OTM $55 calls, a covered call exists on the call side of the collar spread. If the stock rallies past the $55 strike price of the short call and is exercised, the trader delivers the stock for $55/share, $5.00 more per share than when the collar was entered. And the trader would simultaneously sell the long put to recover a portion of the premium originally paid.

If a long $48 protective put was bought and the stock drops to $43, the long put can be exercised. The put writer must pay $48/share for stock that is now worth $43/share. So the equity collar offers two goals: 1) inexpensive protection against a drop in the price of the stock, and 2) profit from a rally in the price of the stock that puts the strike price of the short call ITM.

It's possible to use a diagonal equity collar in which the long put expires much later than the short call. This permits rolling the short call several times to increase premium income.

Setup Parameters

- Goals: To hedge against a drop in the price of the stock. A secondary goal is to profit from a rally in the price of the underlying stock.
- Bias: Neutral to bullish; a rally is preferred to a drop in the price of the underlying stock held in the trader's account.
- Debit/Credit: Debit
- Chart Trend: Daily and hourly charts reveal price stability within a moderate to narrow support and resistance range.
- Momentum Oscillator: Presently midrange; rarely indicates historical oversold/overbought strength
- Keltner Channel: The ATR(14) external envelope is reasonably level with only mild expansions and contractions.
- Implied Volatility % $\geq$ 40% and $\leq$ 60% to maintain price and premium neutrality
- Greeks: Delta slightly negative excluding long stock; Theta negative; Vega positive
- Days till Expiry: $\geq$ 90 days (more is better); retain the protective equity collar for several months. It is intended as insurance; the profit motive is subordinate to insurance against a drop in the price of the underlying stock.
- Net Premium (both Marks): $\leq$ \$1.00 if possible; use OTM strike prices having similar premium values.
- Probability ITM: $\geq$ 60% for the long put leg, $\leq$ 33% for short call leg
- Open Interest at Strike Prices: $\geq$ 300 (more is better); total open interest @ all strikes $\geq$ 10,000
- Bid to Ask spread: The spread should be at a reasonably normal range, current volatility should be near historical volatility.
- Risk Amount $\approx$1.0% of account equity (governed by premium and number of contracts)

How the Strategy Works

An investor has accumulated 1,000 shares of BONG now trading at $44.75. The trader is familiar with protective puts but they are expensive. BONG's 10-month $40 put option has a cost of $1.80 per share. This will cost $1,800 plus transaction fees.

The trader decides to reduce the cost of protection by selling 10 OTM $50 calls at the same time for premium income of $1.40 per share to offset the cost of the long $40 put contracts.

The investor's 10-month $40-$55 equity collar is summarized here:

Presently owns 1,000 shares of BONG stock priced at $44.75
+10 40 PUTS @ $1.80
−10 55 CALLS @ $1.40
Total cost for ten months of insurance is $0.40/share = $400.00

Hands-On Activity

Scanning for a Trade

1. Because this strategy is tied to the ownership of stock, scanning only involves looking at several different option chains that correspond to the underlying stock.
2. The trader owns 1,000 shares of Apple stock, symbol AAPL, which is presently trading at $106.82. AAPL has been declining over the past month, and the trader wants to "stop the bleeding."
3. The trader examines the JUN 16 AAPL option chain expiring in 172 days.
4. The trader decides to buy +10 JUN 16 95 PUTs and sell −10 JUN 16 125 CALLs to help offset the cost of the long 95 protective PUTs (see figure 14–22a).
5. The trade is put on the order bar; the collar will cost $1,870.
6. The risk profile in figure 14–22b reveals that AAPL must rally above $112 for this collar spread to achieve breakeven, and higher to be profitable.

7. Figure 14–22b also shows a drop in the price of AAPL to the price of the $95 long put suffers a loss of nearly $12,000.
    NOTE Most option traders are well aware of how losses from stock ownership usually exceed those losses experienced from carefully constructed and timed option trades. This collar spread serves as a protective stop and is not intended as a money-making option strategy.

Figure 14–22a. Collar Spread Option Chain

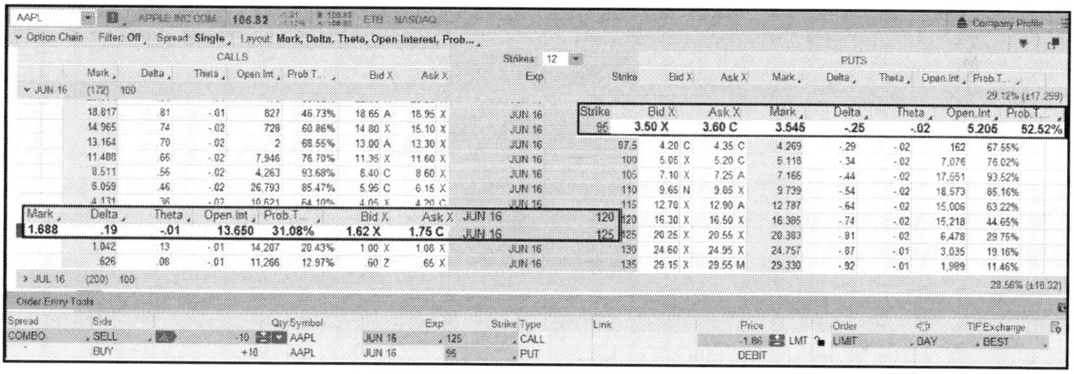

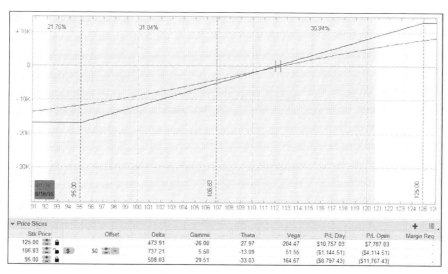

For illustration purposes only.

Figure 14–22b. Collar Spread Risk Profile

For illustration purposes only.

Entry

1. After examining several AAPL option chains, the JUN 16 (172) option chain is selected.
2. Because you own 1,000 shares of AAPL, your collar spread must include 10 long puts and 10 short calls.
3. You choose the 95 long PUT to limit losses in the AAPL stock to $95/share. You choose the $125 call for enough premium to offset the cost of the long put to less than $2,000. Set the number of Strikes to **12** so you can see all involved strikes for this spread.
4. Click the PUTS **95 Ask** cell to add the 95 long PUT to the order bar.
5. Press and hold the **Ctrl** key and click the CALLS **125 Bid** cell to add the 125 short CALL to the order bar.
6. Check the order bar to verify it contains entries similar to these:

COMBO SELL –10 AAPL JUN 16 125   CALL 1.86   LMT   LIMIT   DAY
  BUY +10 AAPL JUN 16 95   PUT   DEBIT

7. Verify your setup. Then click **Confirm and Send**.
8. Evaluate the Order Confirmation information. If satisfactory, click **Send**.

Risks

The largest risk associated with this collar spread is the ownership of the AAPL stock, which is declining in value. If the price of AAPL continues to drop to one cent below the $95 price of your long put, you can exercise the option and exit.

If AAPL's price remains between $95 and $125, your loss will consist of the $1,860 in premium paid upon entry. The $11.86/share drop in the price of AAPL from 106.82 to $95 will cause the trader to lose another $11,820 in stock value. Any additional drop in the price of AAPL is hedged by the $95 long put.

If AAPL rallies above $112/share, the spread becomes profitable as shown on the risk profile. It's even possible to recover losses in the AAPL stock, depending on what was paid when AAPL was originally purchased.

Trade Management

Keep an eye on this collar as it works. If AAPL begins to rally, consider selling the long put to recover some of the premium paid at entry. But be confident that AAPL is underbought and appears to be in sustained upward trend.

Also watch the price of AAPL as it relates to the short $125 call. If the AAPL stock rallies above $125, it may be exercised for $125/share. Depending on the purchase price of the AAPL stock, this could provide a sizable profit.

If you had entered a diagonal collar with a long-term long put option and a shorter-term short call option, you could roll the short call several times to recover much if not all of the premium paid for the long put.

Possible Outcomes

1. AAPL pierces the $125 strike of the short call. Close both options and sell the stock for profit.
2. AAPL closes below the $95 strike long put option and continues to drop in price. Exercise the long put for $95/share and buy to close the short OTM call.
3. AAPL remains between $95 and $125. With less than 60 days remaining until expiration, and depending on what premium remains in the working collar spread, consider rolling the OTM short calls and long puts to a later expiration date. This should be less expensive than starting over from scratch.
4. AAPL remains between $95 and $125. If a diagonal equity collar is used, roll the short calls several times to receive additional premium throughout the life of this trade.

Butterfly Spreads

Structure

Long Call Butterfly Spread: +1 ITM CALL, –2 ATM CALLS, +1 OTM CALL

Long Put Butterfly Spread: +1 ITM PUT, –2 ATM PUTS, +1 OTM PUT

Same expiration dates ≤ 56 days, or different expirations, i.e., long calls ≥ 90 days

May also be balanced or unbalanced depending on symmetry of OTM strike prices

Description and Goals

Both the long call and long put butterfly spreads are neutral spreads having limited risk and limited reward. Because both work in exactly the same way, only in opposite directions, this section focuses on the more bullish long call butterfly spread. Butterfly spreads use less margin value as a result of built-in hedges (the long legs on either side of the short ATM legs). This provides a reduction in the use of margin.

Although ultimately a credit spread in which you collect more premium than paid, the butterfly is a debit spread at entry. The total cost of the two long legs is always more than the premium received from the two ATM short legs. However, as time reduces the value of the options, your P/L statement begins to reveal a profit. Once the trade achieves a profit approaching 50% to 60%, exit the trade. The exterior legs are sold for considerably more than the amount required to buy back the interior legs. Of course this makes the butterfly strategy one that must be monitored throughout its life.

There are also long and short iron butterflies, broken wing butterflies, and unbalanced butterflies. The structures of these butterfly spreads are included in the appendix.

The balanced call and put butterfly spreads are the most common. For example, two ATM short call or put options are bracketed by single long OTM and ITM long call or put options. In the balanced butterfly spread, the two exterior long legs are equidistant above and below the ATM legs. For example, if two short ATM call

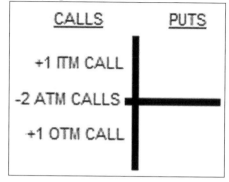

legs are at $45, then one long call might be placed at $40 and the other at $50—both $5.00 away. The credit collected when closed is the maximum income. As soon as a butterfly is traded, time begins to reduce the premium values. Butterfly spreads are typically closed for profit within a matter of several days to a few weeks.

A broken wing butterfly eliminates one of the exterior long legs. If the ITM long call or put leg is eliminated, the trade may return a credit at entry. But this increases risk due to the unprotected side. If the short options that were originally ATM at entry go deep ITM, the trade will be punishing, especially in the case of call butterflies.

Setup Parameters

- Goals: To exit when the premium value exceeds the cost of premium at entry.
- Bias: Neutral to slightly bearish. A price rally to a point slightly above the strike price of the OTM call or a drop to a price at or slightly below the ITM call prevents this spread from earning a profit. Partial recovery is possible from the unaffected long option, but it will be insignificant.
- Debit/Credit: Debit
- Chart Trend: Daily and hourly charts reveal price stability within a moderate to narrow support and resistance range.

- Momentum Oscillator: Presently midrange; rarely indicates historical oversold/overbought strength
- Keltner Channel: The ATR(14) envelope is reasonably level with only mild expansions and contractions.
- Implied Volatility % ≥ 40% and ≤ 60% to maintain price neutrality
- Greeks: Delta negative; Theta slightly positive; Vega ≈ 0
- Days till Expiry: ≤ 21 days
- Net Premium (3 Marks): ≤ $2.00; the example's three strike prices have a net cost of $4.90.
- Probability ITM: ≥ 75%; Includes an ITM call, an ATM call, and a slightly OTM call
- Open Interest at all three strike prices: ≥ 500; total open interest @ all strikes ≥ 10,000
- Bid to Ask spread: The spread should be within a normal range, as it is desirable to enter this trade when current volatility is near historical volatility.
- Risk Amount ≈1.0% of account equity (governed by premium and number of contracts)

How the Strategy Works

The long call butterfly spread depends on price stability for profit. This strategy depends on the effect of Theta to erode the premium of the short options. Large price rallies and drops quickly defeat this strategy. If the price of the underlying stock drops by a few dollars, enter buy to close orders on both of the long calls.

If the strike price of the short calls remains close to the market price of the underlying, enter a buy to close order when an acceptable profit becomes available. Remember, a butterfly spread is limited risk, limited reward strategy. It is a debit spread at entry and a credit spread at closure.

Hands-On Activity

Scanning for a Trade

1. Having the price of the underlying remain within a fairly narrow range is the most important attribute of stocks used with butterfly spreads.
2. ATR(14) should be near historical levels to match a neutral implied volatility level.
3. Avoid stocks having large price swings or approaching an earnings release or dividend distribution.
4. The trader examines the FEB 16 KR option chain expiring in 22 days.
5. KR is currently trading at $37.52. The trader decides to use three consecutive strike prices including the $35, $37.5, and $40.
6. The Spread dropdown list is used to change **Single** to **Butterfly**. Clicking the CALLS 37.5 Ask puts all three legs of the BUTTERFLY spread on the order bar for a DEBIT of $0.98 as a LIMIT DAY order as follows:
   BUY +5 KR FEB 16 35 CALL
   SELL −10 KR FEB 16 37.5 CALL
   BUY +5KR FEB 16 40 CALL
7. The entry cost of this long call butterfly spread is $490 plus transaction fees. The maximum possible profit would be $875 less transaction fees.
8. See the order bars in figure 14–23a; the risk profile is shown in figure 14–23b.
9. The risk profile tells the trader that the price of KR must remain between $36 and $39 to either succeed or achieve breakeven.
   NOTE The exterior long calls of this butterfly spread would most likely be widened a few dollars to give the price of KR more room to work in favor of the trade. This would be done on the order bar. For example, setting the long calls

at \$32.50 and \$42.50 might be done to give the price more latitude. The order bar would resemble the following illustration. The cost of entry would be increased to \$1,490 plus transaction fees.

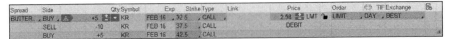

For illustration purposes only.

Figure 14–23a. Long Call Butterfly Spread Option Chain

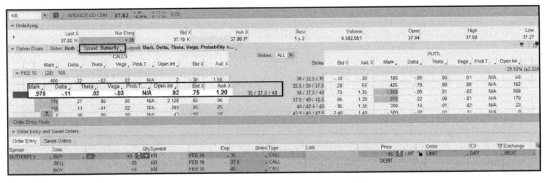

For illustration purposes only.

Figure 14–23b. Long Call Butterfly Spread Risk Profile

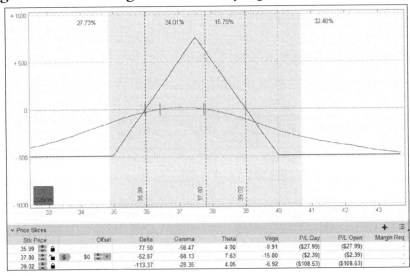

For illustration purposes only.

Entry

1. After examining several KR option chains, the FEB 16 (22) option chain is selected. It meets the setup parameters including good open interest.

2. Check the risk profile and step it through the calendar. The peak profit of $760 makes this trade reasonable. With a cost of $490, the maximum return on investment is 64.4%.

3. Look at the strike price premiums closest to the current $37.82 price of KR. These will be used in this long call butterfly spread.

4. Click the **Spread** drop down list and then click **Butterfly** as the Spread type.

5. Notice how the strike prices are assembled in consecutive groups of three.

6. Click the CALLS **Ask** cell at the **35/37.5/40** strikes.

7. Check the order bar for the label "BUTTERFLY." Verify the values on the three order bars contain entries similar to these:

BUTTERFLY   BUY   +5   KR   FEB 16   35   CALL .98   LMT   LIMIT   DAY

SELL   –10   KR   FEB 16   37.5   CALL   DEBIT

BUY   +5   KR   FEB 16   40   CALL

8. Check the .98 DEBIT Price. If filled, this spread will cost $490 plus transaction fees.

9. Verify your setup. Then click **Confirm and Send**.

10. Evaluate the Order Confirmation information. If satisfactory, click **Send**.

11. Watch your P/L Open values; when this trade returns 50% or more in profit, close it.

Risks

The greatest risk in this trade is the $490 plus fees paid at entry. If the price of KR falls below $35 or rises above $40, as shown in figure 14–23b, the trade will lose money. The exchange fees and commissions must also be considered in this spread. If the trader pays $1.00 per contract in exchange fees, a round-trip costs a whopping

$40.00 plus commissions. If paying the maximum rate of $10.00 in brokerage commissions, the round trip overhead becomes $60. If you are an active trader, these charges should encourage you to discuss rates more suitable to your trading volume.

Returning to the long call butterfly spread, the −10 short calls could wind up deep ITM. Fortunately, one of the two protective long calls of this spread is also deep ITM because these long legs are only one strike price above and below the short calls. This off-sets the cost associated with the two short calls if they are exercised before they are closed.

Trade Management

The long butterfly spread is typically managed by watching price movement of the underlying and the P/L Open value on your brokerage's position statement. If the spread achieves 30% to 60% in profit, close the trade and take profit. You may also consider closing one of the long legs that is moving farther OTM. However, be aware that this makes the trade vulnerable to a price reversal back toward that leg.

If the market price of the underlying stock begins to trend in either direction, check the price charts to determine what may be happening. It can be an overall market shift, or you may detect institutional trading actions that are often telegraphed by unusually long, directional candles on a short-interval or a tick price chart. If the underlying stock is currently oversold or overbought, it should return to equilibrium. If enough time remains for recovery, let the trade work a few days longer. However, if the trade is approaching contract expiration, Theta will be punishing premiums. Exit the trade and try to recover some of the remaining long call premium value.

Possible Outcomes

1. Time passes and the price of KR remains between $35 and $40. The P/L Open value indicates a reasonable profit. Close all three legs of the trade for profit.

2. Time passes and the price of KR remains between $35 and $40. The P/L Open value indicates a reasonable profit. Close the trade for profit. Although the short call legs may remain well OTM through expiration, the risk is too high to leave them exposed. Never leave the short legs unprotected. Always exit all three legs at the same time.

3. Only 10 days remain till expiration. The price of KR has dropped and all three legs are OTM. Close all three legs of the butterfly spread with sell to close orders for the long $35 and $40 calls and a buy to close order for the short $37.50 calls.

4. Only 10 days remain till expiration. The price of KR has rallied to $42 and all three legs become ITM. Buy to close the −10 $37.50 legs before they are exercised. With both of the $35 and $40 legs ITM, exercise the $35 leg and sell the stock for $7/share profit. Sell the $40 option for remaining premium.

5. Only 10 days remain till expiration. The price of KR has rallied to $42. All three legs are ITM. The −10 $37.50 legs are exercised requiring delivery of 1,000 shares worth of $42 per share stock, for which you receive $37,500 — a loss of $4,500. You exercise the +5 $35 calls and collect $7.00/share totaling $3,500. You can also collect $2.00 per share for the +5 $40 calls for another $1,000. (Check the premium first; it may be better.) The $3,500 and $1,000 collected offsets the $4,500 loss from the −10 37.50 calls. The total expense is approximately $100 is transaction fees.

CALLS EXERCISED @ $42.00

+5 $35 Calls: Buy for $35 and sell for $42 ($7 × 500 = $3,500

−10 $37.50 Calls: Buy 1,000 shares of KR for $42/share and sell for $37.50 = <$4,500>

+5 $40 Calls: Buy for $40 and sell for $42 ($2 × 500 = $1,000)

OUTCOME: $3,500 + $1,000 − $4,500 = $0.00 (Less transaction fees)

---

6. The price of KR has suffered a substantial drop in price. The trader attempts to sell the 10 long option contracts for remaining premium. The −10 37.5 CALL contracts expire worthless.

Calendar Spread

Structure

+1 ATM or OTM PUT (≥ 90 days), −1 ATM or OTM PUT (≤ 56 days, same strike)

or

+1 ATM or OTM CALL (≥ 90 days), −1 ATM or OTM CALL (≤ 56 days, same strike)

Description and Goals

Both put and call calendar spreads are considered limited risk, limited reward neutral bias spreads. The calendar spreads shown above are debit spreads because the cost of the long legs are more expensive than the premium received from the short legs. But calendar spreads are easily constructed as credit spreads by buying front month options and selling the back month options. By now you know that back month, longer-term option premiums are costlier than front month premiums. Consider the following example of a credit calendar spread:

+1 ATM PUT (≤ 56 days), −1 ATM PUT (≥ 90 days, same strike)

As a practical matter, most option traders prefer to sell options expiring inside 60 days or less. Many who focus on selling premium prefer 56 days (8 weeks) or reduce the risk associated with time. Therefore, the example trade stays with this convention by using the first structure shown above — a debit put calendar spread.

Calendar spreads are also called *horizontal spreads* and *time spreads*. These names are used because the same strike prices on the same side of the option chain have different expiration dates. If using a debit calendar spread, a trader can retain the long back month option while rolling the short front month option two or three times to collect more premium income. Rolling, i.e., buying to close and reselling to open the front month option at a slightly later expiration date, takes advantage of time decay in the front month's premium values.

Although the two above structures are both debit spreads, rolling the front month option contracts two or more times can quickly changes this strategy into a credit spread. Because the short and long legs are both ATM (the same strike price), if they move ITM, both legs can be exercised to neutralize losses except for the usual transaction fees.

The put calendar spread is usually more desirable than the call calendar spread because potential ITM exercise costs exist at lower strike prices. And, of course, while puts can only drop to zero, calls can rally to infinity.

If slightly bullish, the trader is more likely to choose a put calendar spread to avoid the hassle of exercising and being exercised. Being exercised also cuts off the opportunity to sell more front month short options for additional premium income.

If the price of the underlying stock rallies according to plan, the short put moves farther OTM. When the short leg is far enough OTM, the trader can roll the front month OTM short option for additional premium to increase profit. If the options move deeper ITM, the short leg can be closed before it is exercised. Then, if the back month ITM option is ITM by several dollars, the trader can either exercise the long option or sell it for the available premium, which can be substantial if enough time remains till expiration.

Setup Parameters

- Goals: Hold the back month long option and roll the front month short option multiple times.

- Bias: Neutral to slightly bearish or bullish. A small OTM price move is most desirable to permit the trader to roll the short leg once or twice for increased premium income.
- Debit/Credit: Debit (when front month option is sold and back month option is bought)
- Chart Trend: Daily and hourly charts reveal price stability within a moderate to narrow support and resistance range.
- Momentum Oscillator: Presently midrange; rarely indicates historical oversold/overbought strength
- Keltner Channel: The ATR(14) envelope is reasonably level with only mild expansions and contractions.
- Implied Volatility % ≥ 20% and ≤ 30% to maintain price neutrality
- Greeks: Delta negative; Theta positive; Vega positive
- Days till Expiry: Short leg ≤ 45 days; Long leg ≥ 90 days (more is better)
- Net Premium (±2 Marks): ≤ −$1.00
- Probability ITM: ≥ 85%; (both legs are ATM)
- Open Interest: ≥ 300; Total open interest @ all strikes ≥ 8,000
- Bid to Ask spread should be slightly wider than normal as is the case with lower than normal trading volume.
- Risk Amount ≈1.0% of account equity (governed by premium and number of contracts)

How the Strategy Works

Although the call and put calendar spreads work identically, the slightly less expensive put calendar spread is examined. The trader is slightly bullish on Billabong Pharmaceutical's stock, symbol BONG. It is presently trading at $55.66. Two $55 JAN 16 (29) puts are sold for a premium of $1.58/share and two $55 JUN 16 (169) puts are bought for a premium of −$3.52. This calendar spread costs the trader $1.94/share, or a total cost of $388 plus a commissions and four exchange fees. (The order bar in the sample trade computes a total debit of $1.98/share.)

The risk profile indicates this trade has a profit potential as long as BONG's price remains above $51.60. It may be possible to roll the short $55 put three to four times for approximately $150 to $200 in income per roll before the long $55 put approaches its JUN 16 expiration. About 30 to 40 days prior to expiration, Theta will begin to erode the premium that remains in the long $55 JUN 16 put. But by rolling the short put several times before mid-May, this trade has a potential of earning more than $700 in profit before a sell to close order is finally entered on the long put for a bit more premium income.

Of course BONG could suffer a price drop. If the $55 strikes become ITM, it will force the trader's hand into:

1. Closing the short leg and selling the long leg, or
2. Exercising and being exercised for a loss in commissions and exchange fees.

Hands-On Activity

Scanning for a Trade

1. Scan price charts for prices that are neutral to slightly bullish. Avoid stocks near earnings releases or dividends and subject to large price swings.
2. Ensure the ATR(14) and IV% columns are on your watch list. Find symbols having IV% values near 25%.
3. Examine two option chains for your setup: The short ATM put should expire within about 40 days; the long ATM put should expire in more than 90 days.
4. The trader examines the MSFT JAN 16 (29) and the JUN 16 (169) option chain.
5. MSFT is currently trading at $55.48. The trader decides to sell −3 JAN 16 55 PUTS and buy +3 JUN 16 55 PUTS.
6. Set up this put calendar spread by performing the steps in the following Entry procedure.

Entry

1. Set the MSFT option chain to **6** strikes.
2. Expand the JAN5 (29) and the JUN 26 (169) option chains and scroll until you can see the 55 ATM strikes for both contract expiration dates.
3. Click the **MSFT JAN5 16 (29) PUTS Bid** cell at the **55** strike price.
4. Press and hold the **Ctrl** key and click the **MSFT JUN16 (169) Ask** cell at the **55** strike price.
5. Compare your option chain to the one shown in figure 14–24a.
6. If required, change the **Qty** value of each order bar to **3**. Then check the order bar to ensure that it contains entries similar to these:

CALENDAR	BUY	+3	MSFT	JUN 16 55	PUT	1.95 LMT	LIMIT DAY
	SELL	–3	MSFT	JAN5 16 55	PUT	DEBIT	

7. Check the risk profile in figure 14–24b. The risk profile only plots the trade through the expiration of the short leg. Your profit potential can be much better when trading additional front calendar $55 short puts with retention of the back JUN16 long put.

   NOTE The risk profile shows a reasonable profit if MSFT returns to the original $55 price at which this calendar spread was initially traded and as the short put nears expiration.
8. Verify your setup. Then click **Confirm and Send**.
9. Evaluate the Order Confirmation information. If satisfactory, click **Send**.
10. Watch your P/L Open values; when the short put is near expiration, roll into another $55 short put that expires inside 30 to 40 days (depending on premium collection).

Figure 14–24a. Calendar Spread Option Chain

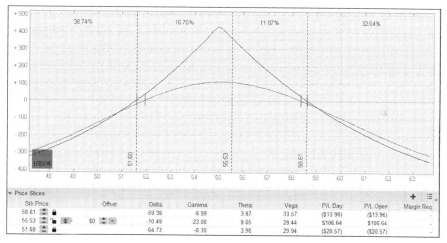

For illustration purposes only.

Figure 14–24b. Calendar Spread Risk Profile

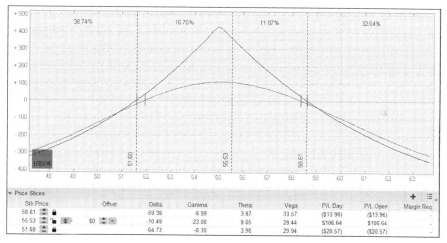

For illustration purposes only.

Risks

The greatest risk in this trade is the loss of the original premium paid at entry in addition to the commissions and exchange fees. The loss becomes greater in commissions and exchange fees if the short and long puts move ITM and are exercised. As mentioned in the preceding description and goals paragraph, simultaneously buying and selling the MSFT stock is an offsetting transaction. However, there can be an additional $75 in transaction fees, depending on your fee structure, if the price of MSFT becomes ITM and is exercised.

Trade Management

The calendar spread is reasonably easy to manage. Because losses are limited to the cost of entry and the overhead costs associated with exercising, check your P/L Open values to see how the trade is trending.

If the original strike price remains OTM, be sure to evaluate the premium remaining in the short call. Be sure to examine the amount of premiums available At the original strike prices on option chains that expire at later dates.

If MSFT experiences a substantial drop in price, it's possible to convert your calendar spread into a diagonal bear spread (explained next) by selling a farther OTM short put at a safer strike price.

Of course, moving farther OTM reduces the premium collected when rolling a calendar spread into a diagonal calendar spread, i.e., retaining the long put and rolling the short put to a farther OTM strike price expiring inside 56 days.

Possible Outcomes

1. Time passes and the price of MSFT remains between $52 and $58. The premium value of the short put decreases and the long put declines only slightly as the short put approaches expiration. The long put is retained and the short put is rolled out to a later expiration date for more premium income.

2. Within a week the price of MSFT rallies to $60. Both the short put and the long put are farther OTM. The trade is retained until the short put can be safely rolled. The short put is carefully monitored in case the price of MSFT begins to drop.

3. Within a few weeks the price of MSFT rallies to $60. The trader closes both legs in an attempt to recover as much premium as possible.

4. The MSFT stock price drops to $48. The short put is rolled to a later expiration date at a lower strike price. The long put is sold for profit.
5. The MSFT stock price drops to $48. The long put is exercised for profit by acquiring the stock for $48 and putting the stock to the seller of the long put for $55 (the option price). The trader pays the necessary premium to close the short put before it is exercised.
6. The MSFT stock price drops to $48. The long $55 put is exercised for profit by acquiring the stock for $48. The short $55 put is also exercised. The trader delivers the $48/share MSFT stock to the buyer of the $55 short put for a small loss.

Diagonal Spreads

Structure

−1 OTM CALL (≤ 56 days), +1 OTM, ATM, or ITM CALL (≥ 90 days, different strike)

or

−1 OTM PUT (≤ 56 days), +1 OTM, ATM or ITM PUT (≥ 90 days, different strike)

Description and Goals

A diagonal spread is another *time spread* that combines two call or two put legs at different strike prices and expiration dates. Diagonal spreads are limited risk, limited reward option strategies. When structured as a debit spread the risk corresponds to the net cost of the premium upon entry. Like the calendar spread, the diagonal spread can be structured as either a credit or a debit spread depending on whether the front month option is bought or sold.

A diagonal spread can resemble either a bull call or a bear put spread. The diagonal spread is superior due to the longer time till expiration of the long leg, compared to the shorter (and safer) time till expiration of the short leg. Like the bull call and bear put spreads, if the short OTM options become ITM and are exercised, the trade becomes profitable. If the long call remains near the money, the short leg can be rolled for additional premium income. Therefore, there are at least three possible goals:

1. Roll the short leg for premium (more profit).
2. Exercise the long leg if ITM; if the short leg remains, close it (more profit).
3. Sell to close the long leg and buy to close the short leg (more profit).

Number 1 above is similar to one of the calendar spread goals in rolling the short OTM leg two or more times to collect additional premium. Goal numbers 2 and 3 are the same as those for the bull call and bear put spreads. Either exercise the long options or sell premium for profit — both desirable.

A diagonal credit spread buys the front month option and sells the back month option. More premium is collected for the short back month option than is paid for the long front month option. The strike prices can be identical to those used for debit version. However, Theta begins to attack the value of the front month long call upon entry. In spite of receiving a credit, and unless the diagonal credit spread is exercised, the ability to roll the short, back month option is unlikely if not impossible. And, as the front month long option nears expiration, the entire trade should be exited to avoid ownership of a single naked short leg. Naked short puts or calls are always vulnerable to becoming ITM and being exercised.

Setup Parameters

- Goals: Premium collection by selling front month short options two or more times
- Bias: Neutral to bearish (put version) or bullish (call version). The debit spread is preferred to the credit spread for the reasons given in the above description and goals paragraph.
- Debit/Credit: Debit when short leg uses front month and long leg uses back month

- Chart Trend: Daily and hourly charts reveal price stability within a moderate to narrow support and resistance range. Calls favor a slight downward trend over the past six to nine months; puts favor a slight upward trend over the same time period.
- Momentum Oscillator: Presently midrange; rarely indicates historical strong oversold/overbought conditions
- Keltner Channel: The ATR(14) envelope is reasonably level with only mild expansions and contractions over the past four to six months.
- Implied Volatility % ≤ 20% to avoid a strong price rally or drop
- Greeks: Delta negative; Theta positive; Vega positive
- Days till Expiry

  Debit spread: Short leg ≤ 56 days; Long leg ≥ 90 days (more is better)

  Credit spread: Long leg ≤ 56 days; Short leg ≤ 90 days (The credit spread's back month expiration should be approximately 30 days later.)
- Net Premium (±2 Marks): ≤ −$1.00
- Probability ITM: Long strike: ≥ 75%; Short strike: ≤ 30%
- Open Interest: ≥ 250 at both strike prices; total open interest @ all strikes ≥ 8,000
- Bid to Ask spread: Wider than normal due to lower trading volume and IV%
- Risk Amount ≈1.0% of account equity (governed by premium and number of contracts)

How the Strategy Works

Consider either the diagonal put debit spread or the diagonal call debit spread. In each an ATM or slightly OTM long option is purchased that expires in 90 or more days. An OTM short option is sold that expires inside 56 days.

If the short leg remains OTM, it may be rolled once or twice for more premium income. If the OTM short leg becomes ITM and is exercised, the long ITM leg is also exercised for a profitable outcome.

- The call diagonal spread fails when the market price of the underlying stock drops and the spread becomes OTM.
- The put diagonal spread fails with the market price of the underlying stock rallies and the spread becomes OTM.

Hands-On Activity

Scanning for a Trade

1. Scan price charts for prices that are neutral to slightly bullish or bearish. Avoid stocks that are approaching an earnings release and subject to large price swings.
2. Check the ATR(14) study on the day interval chart and the IV% value on the watch list to ensure a below normal price range and an implied volatility value near 20%.
3. Examine two option chains for your setup: The short OTM put should expire inside 45 days; the long ATM or slightly OTM put should expire in more than 90 days.
4. The trader examines the MSFT JAN 16 (28) and the JUN 16 (168) option chain.
5. MSFT is currently trading at $55.48. The trader decides to sell −3 JAN 16 50 PUTS and buy +3 JUN 16 55 PUTS, a debit of $3.20/share for a cost of $960 plus transaction fees.
6. Trade this diagonal put spread by performing the steps in the following Entry procedure.

Entry

1. Open the MSFT option chain and enter **22** in the **Strikes** text box.
2. Be sure the Spreads **Single** is selected. Then expand the JAN5 (28) and the JUN 26 (168) option chains and scroll until you can see the 50 strike in the top option chain and the 55 strike in the bottom option chain.
3. Click the **MSFT JAN5 16 PUTS Bid** cell at the **50** strike price.

4. Press and hold the **Ctrl** key and click the **MSFT JUN16 PUTS Ask** cell at the **55** strike price.

5. Compare your option chain to the one shown in figure 14–25a.

6. If required, change the **Qty** value of each order bar to **3**. Now check the order bar to verify it contains entries similar to these:

DIAGONAL   BUY   +3   MSFT   JUN 16   55   PUT   3.20 LMT   LIMIT   DAY

SELL   –3   MSFT   JAN5 16 50   PUT   DEBIT

7. Check the risk profile in figure 14–25b. Of course the risk profile only shows the current legs. Your profit potential can increase by rolling into more $55 short puts and retaining the JUN16 long put. This spread can return a nice profit if the price of MSFT drops to $50 (see the $50.00 price slice).

8. Verify your setup. Then click **Confirm and Send**.

9. Evaluate the Order Confirmation information. If satisfactory, click **Send**.

10. Watch your P/L Open values. When profitable, close both legs for even more profit. If the long put is still OTM or ITM, sell more OTM puts for more premium.

Figure 14–25a. Diagonal Put Spread Option Chain

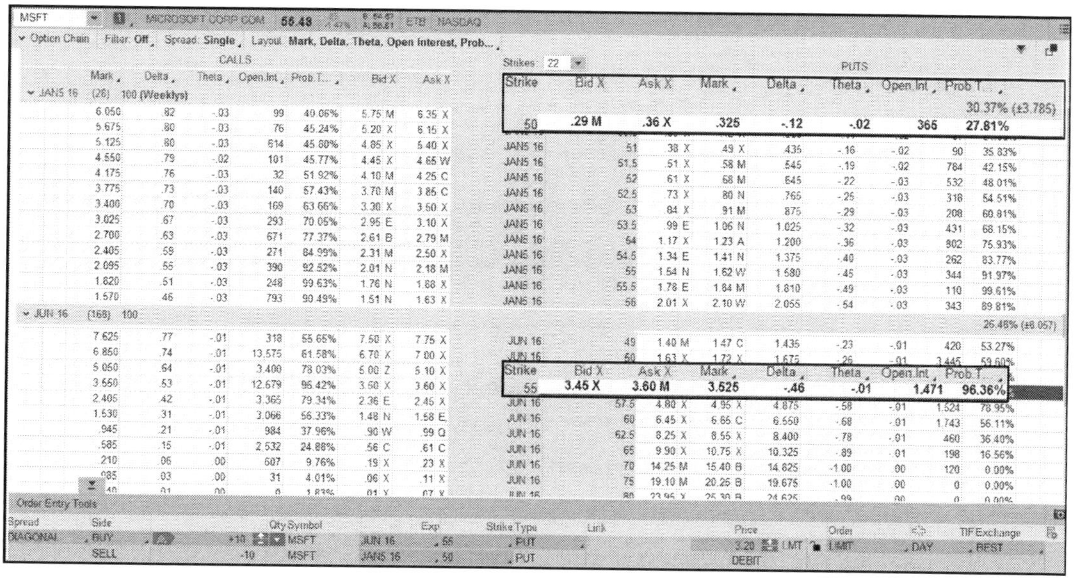

For illustration purposes only.

Figure 14–25b. Diagonal Put Spread Risk Profile

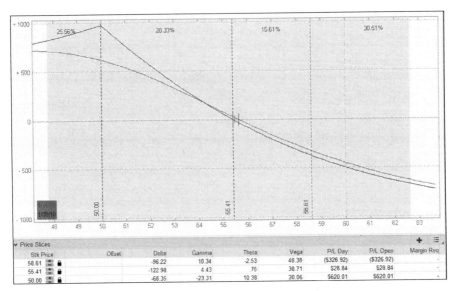

For illustration purposes only.

Risks

The major risk involved with the debit diagonal put spread is a rally in the price of the underlying stock. This abandons your position and diminishes the probability for profits. Of course you can still sell more puts for premium, but if too far OTM, the premium may be negligible.

Trade Management

This is an easy trade to manage unless the price of the underlying stock experiences a strong rally. A rally reduces the premium of both the long and short puts as they move farther OTM. Consider selling the long put. Temporarily hold the short put as the premium declines. Either buy it back or let it expire worthless. These actions should recover a good portion of the original debit spent at entry.

If the price of MSFT remains within a few dollars of the original price when this trade was entered, roll out to more OTM puts for additional premium. However, if the MSFT stock drops a few cents below the strike price of the short put, close the short put or roll out to a farther OTM short put. You may also decide to sell the long put for profit. If sufficient intrinsic value is available, you may want to exercise the long put for more profit.

Possible Outcomes

1. The price of MSFT remains between $55 and $51 throughout the life of the long put contract. Roll the $50 short put as many times as possible for additional premium income.

2. The price of MSFT begins to rally above the original price of $55.48 when the diagonal spread was originally traded. Close the long option contract to recover as much premium as possible. Hold the short option, which is now farther OTM with a lower Probability ITM. If enough time remains, consider holding the short put through expiration.

3. The price of MSFT falls to $49. Close the short $50 put and exercise the long $55 put for a $6.00/share profit in MSFT stock less transaction fees.

4. The price of MSFT falls to $50. Close the short $50 put and sell the long $55 put for a profit in premium. This choice requires the trader to calculate the best outcome, i.e., exercise the option or collect more premium than paid.

Synthetic Options

Synthetics Explained

A synthetic strategy is created when financial derivatives are combined to simulate another financial instrument or transaction. Whether an option strategy or futures strategy, the financial derivative is created artificially. A synthetic strategy simulates another instrument by combining the features of a collection of other assets. Options can be used to create a synthetic stock. For example, simultaneously buying an ATM call and selling an ATM put creates a synthetic long stock. A synthetic short stock is created by buying an

ATM put and selling an ATM call. Both of these synthetic option strategies have the same capital-gain potential as either buying or selling the underlying stock.

CAUTION! Only two of the synthetics are considered reasonable for beginning option traders. These include the synthetic long stock (strongly bullish) and the synthetic short call (strongly bearish). Both of these are described in the following two strategy sections. The synthetic long call and long put might also be considered. Both have built-in hedges to partially offset a potential loss in stock value if the price moves against the trade. The synthetic short stock includes a naked short call and is not recommended for use by new option traders. The synthetic short stock and synthetic short put are not included in the following strategies, although you may wish to test them both in simulation to see how they work. Their structures are included in the following table.

Synthetics Summary

Option Name	Structure	Risk
Synthetic Long Stock:	+1 ATM CALL, −1 ATM PUT	Strong upside protection from long call, downside is a cash-covered put (**Bullish bias must be correct!**)
Synthetic Short Call:	−1 ATM PUT, −100 Shares	Unlimited upside risk to both the short put and the short stock (**Bearish bias must be correct!**)

Synthetic Short Put:	−1 ATM CALL, +100 Shares	Similar to a covered call; stock covers upside risk of the short call.
Synthetic Long Call:	+1 ATM PUT, +100 Shares	Downside protection from long put offset by drop in long stock value (**Proceed with caution.**)
Synthetic Long Put:	+1 CALL, −100 Shares	Upside protection from long call offset by drop in short stock value (**Proceed with caution.**)
Synthetic Short Stock:	+1 ATM PUT, − ATM CALL	Unlimited downside profit potential, unlimited upside risk from naked short call (**Not recommended!**)

Synthetic Long Stock

Structure
+1 ATM CALL, −1 ATM PUT (Same expiration, ≈40 to 60 days)

Description and Goals
The Synthetic long stock includes both unlimited risk and unlimited reward. The short put creates the risk of this strategy. However, the risk may be acceptable if the trader would like to own the underlying stock. For the strategy to work properly, the trader's strong bullish bias must be correct. If the price of the underlying stock rallies according to plan, the ATM call moves deeper ITM and increases

in value. It can be exercised or the higher premium can be sold for a profit. Meanwhile, the short ATM put, which provided premium used to supplement the cost of the long ATM call, moves farther OTM and into safety. This leg can be either closed for profit or retained until it expires worthless.

If the trader is wrong and the underlying stock drops in price, the long ATM call quickly decreases in value. The short put becomes ITM and can be exercised for a loss.

Setup Parameters

- Goal: Strong rally in the underlying stock to move the short put OTM and the long call deep ITM for profit
- Bias: Extremely bullish
- Debit/Credit: Usually a small debit
- Chart Trend: Daily and hourly charts reveal a price near a historical resistance level and basing to form a price breakout into a strong rally.
- Momentum Oscillator: An oversold condition should exist at entry.
- Keltner Channel: The ATR(14) envelope should be compressed and in the early stages of expansion when this trade is entered.
- Implied Volatility % is not critical as the long and short positions offset each other.
- Greeks: Delta: Slightly Positive; Theta: Not Critical; Vega Not Critical
- Days till Expiry: Typically less than two months
- Net Premium (±2 Marks): ≤ −$1.00
- Probability ITM: Long and short strikes: ≥ 75%
- Open Interest: ≥ 500 at the ATM strike price; total open interest @ all strikes ≥ 10,000
- Bid to Ask spread should be within the normal range to reflect low to midrange implied volatility.

- Risk Amount ≈1.0% of account equity (governed by premium and number of contracts)

How the Strategy Works

Buying the ATM call and selling the ATM put reduces the cost of entry, as the put premium received offsets much of the premium paid for the long call. The difference in premium is typically a small debit. If the stock rallies according to plan, the long call option can either be sold or exercised for profit. If the short put moves farther OTM, it may expire worthless or be closed. The choice depends on the likelihood of the short put becoming ITM.

If the price of the underlying drops, the long call loses value, while the short put becomes ITM. If the short put is exercised, this synthetic long stock strategy results in a moderate loss. Ultimately, the outcome depends somewhat on the ability of the underlying stock to recover value.

Hands-On Activity

Scanning for a Trade

1. Scan price charts for uptrending, bullish stocks. Avoid stocks approaching earnings releases or dividend distributions and subject to unpredictable price swings. This is especially true if you expect the possibility of a drop in price.
2. Add an IV% column to your watch list and sort the column is ascending order and scroll down to find stocks with midrange implied volatilities near 50%.
3. Consider using the TTM_Squeeze or perhaps the Keltner Channel to find an uptrending stock with a recent pullback near support. Your chart analysis should indicate the formation of a strong price breakout from an increase in demand.
4. Examine an option chain that expires inside 60 days.

5. Look at the ATM call and put premiums and estimate the cost of the trade. The ATM short put premium should be close to the premium value of the ATM long call.

6. The trader chooses the MSFT JAN 16 (28) option chain. However, a longer time till expiration could be considered to give the trade more time to work in the trader's favor.

7. MSFT is currently trading at $55.48. The trader decides to sell 5 JAN 16 55 PUTS and buy +5 JAN 16 55 CALLS, a debit of $0.52/share for a total cost of $260 plus transaction fees.

8. Trade this synthetic long stock by performing the steps in the following Entry procedure.

Entry

1. Open the MSFT option chain and enter **8** in the **Strikes** text box so you can see the ATM strike prices without excessive clutter.

2. Be sure the Spreads **Single** is selected. Then expand the JAN5 16 (28) option chain.

3. Click the **MSFT JAN5 16 PUTS Bid** cell at the **55** strike price.

4. Press and hold the **Ctrl** key and click the **MSFT JAN5 16 CALLS Ask** cell at the **55** strike price.

5. Compare your option chain to the one shown in figure 14–26a.

6. If required, change the **Qty** value of each order bar to **5**. Then check the remaining values on the order bar to verify it contains entries similar to these:

```
COMBO  BUY   +5  MSFT   JAN5 16   55 CALL    .52      LMT    LIMIT   DAY
             SELL  –5  MSFT   JAN5 16   55 PUT       DEBIT
```

7. Check the risk profile in figure 14–26b. The risk profile shows how this strategy begins to return profit as the price of MSFT rallies above $55.52. As long as the bullish bias is correct, the synthetic long stock strategy returns a substantial profit.

8. Verify the setup. Then click **Confirm and Send**.

9. Evaluate the Order Confirmation information. If satisfactory, click **Send**.

Figure 14–26a. Synthetic Long Stock Option Chain

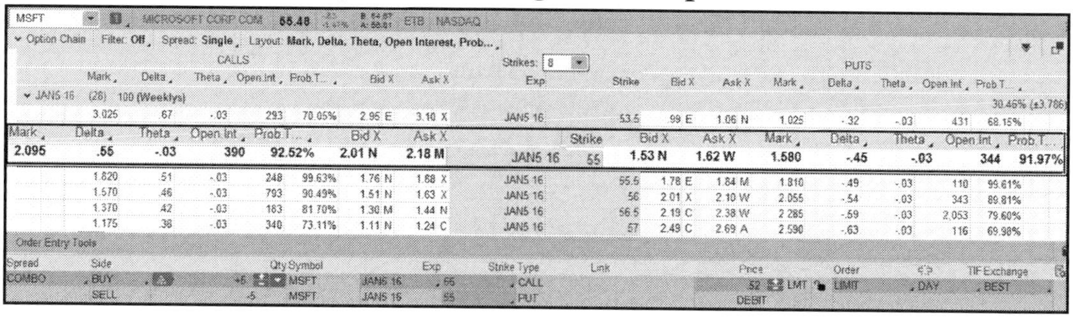

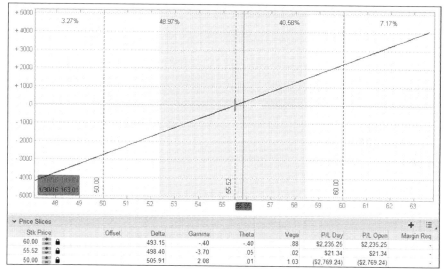

For illustration purposes only.

Figure 14–26b. Synthetic Long Stock Risk Profile

For illustration purposes only.

Risks

The obvious risk associated with the synthetic long stock strategy is an unexpected drop in the price of the underlying stock. Of course the underlying stock could also remain within a dollar above the entry price through expiration. This prevents this trade from being profitable, as the premium of the long call exits more rapidly as the options near expiration.

The short put leg carries the most risk within this trade. If it becomes ITM, the trader would be compelled to buy back the put unless the trader wants to own 500 shares of MSFT. This may be acceptable if the trader considered this outcome when the trade was entered.

Trade Management

As long as the price of the underlying stock rallies as expected, monitor the trade to ensure that it works in your favor. If the P/L Open indicates a 30% to 70% profit, prepare to close the trade by selling to close the long call and buying to close the short put. However, when ample time remains and the stock continues to rally, consider letting the profit run until the price of the stock approaches resistance and becomes oversold. Then sell to close the long call leg for the remaining premium. If the short leg is far enough OTM to be reasonably safe, consider letting it expire worthless. Otherwise, spend the few dollars it takes to buy to close the short put before it becomes deeper ITM and is exercised.

Possible Outcomes

1. The price of MSFT rallies to $59.00. The trader closes the short puts and sells the long calls for profit, which are now ITM.
2. The price of MSFT rallies to $59.00. The trader exercises the long ITM calls for a $4.00/share profit less transaction fees. The short puts are retained as Theta continues to reduce the premium value that remains. The short puts provide additional profit.
3. The price of MSFT drops below $50. The short put is exercised. The trader must pay $55/share for 500 shares of MSFT stock to the buyer of the short puts. The buyer pays the option price of $50/share for the short stock. The trade loses $5.00 per share for 500 shares of MSFT. This is a $2,500 loss for the stock plus the original $260 cost of trade and the transaction fees required to exit the trade.

Synthetic Short Stock

Structure

+1 ATM PUT, −1 ATM CALL (Same expiration, ≤ 56 days)

Description and Goals

Due to the uncovered short call, this strategy requires the trader to have the highest option permissions. Just like the synthetic long stock, the Synthetic short stock includes both unlimited risk and unlimited reward. In fact, the risk is even higher than that of the synthetic long stock. This trade can quickly experience a major loss if the trader's strong bearish bias is incorrect.

But if the price of the underlying stock drops according to plan, the long ATM put moves deeper ITM and increases in value. It can be exercised or the corresponding increase in premium value can be sold for profit. Meanwhile, the short ATM call, which provided premium used to finance the cost of the long ATM put, moves farther OTM into safety.

If the trader is wrong and the price of the underlying stock rallies, the long ATM put quickly declines in value. The uncovered short call becomes ITM and can be exercised for a large loss.

Setup Parameters

- Goal: Strong drop in the underlying stock to move the short call farther OTM and the long put deep ITM for profit
- Bias: Extremely bearish
- Debit/Credit: Small debit or credit
- Chart Trend: Daily and hourly charts reveal a recent price rally and basing near a historical resistance level. The stock is overbought and poised for a drop in price.
- Momentum Oscillator: Presently beginning to reverse from a strong overbought condition

- Keltner Channel: The ATR (14) envelope presently narrow following a previous expansion from selling volume. It is beginning to expand from new selling volume.
- Implied Volatility % ≈ 50%
- Greeks: Delta: Slightly Negative; Theta: Not Critical; Vega: Not Critical
- Days till Expiry: ≤ 56 days
- Net Premium (±2 Marks): ≤ −$1.00
- Probability ITM: Short and long strikes: ≥ 75%
- Open Interest: ≥ 500 at the ATM strike price; total open interest @ all strikes ≥ 10,000
- Bid to Ask spread should be within its normal range.
- Risk Amount ≈1.0% of account equity (governed by premium and number of contracts)

How the Strategy Works

Buying the ATM put and selling the ATM call reduces the cost of entry, as the call premium received offsets the put premium paid resulting in a small credit spread. If the price of the underlying stock drops and the long put becomes ITM, the option can either be sold or exercised for profit. If the price of the underlying stock rallies against the trade and the short call is exercised, the trader must buy and deliver the stock to the seller and suffer a loss in the difference between the higher market price and the original ATM call's option price. Hence, an unexpected price rally places the naked short call ITM and the trade suffers a hefty loss.

Hands-On Activity

Scanning for a Trade

1. Scan price charts for down-trending, bearish stocks. Avoid stocks near price earnings and subject to unpredictable price swings, especially if you expect the possibility of a rally in price. You may also want to look for overbought stocks approaching

historical resistance levels near dividend dates. This is especially true when historical price drops occur near dividend dates.

2. Add an IV% column to your watch list and sort the column in ascending order; scroll down to find stocks with midrange implied volatilities near 50%.

3. Consider using the TTM_Squeeze study or perhaps the Keltner Channel to find an overbought stock near historical resistance. The chart analysis should indicate the formation of pullback resulting from a drop in demand that signals a pending supply.

4. Examine an option chain that expires inside 60 days.

5. Look at the ATM call and put premiums and estimate the cost of the trade. The ATM long put premium should be slightly less than the premium value of the ATM short call.

6. The trader chooses the CRM FEB 16 (48) option chain.

7. CRM is currently trading at $78.40. The trader decides to buy +5 FEB 16 80 PUTS and sell –5 FEB 16 80 CALLS, a debit of $1.49/share for a cost of $745 plus transaction fees.

8. Trade this synthetic short stock by performing the steps in the following Entry procedure.

Entry

1. Open the CRM option chain and enter **8** in the **Strikes** text box so you can see the ATM strike prices without excessive clutter.

2. Be sure the Spreads **Single** is selected. Then expand the FEB 16 (48) option chain.

3. Click the **CRM FEB 16 PUTS Ask** cell at the **80** strike price.

4. Press and hold the **Ctrl** key and click the **CRM FEB 16 CALLS Bid** cell at the **80** strike price.

5. Compare your option chain to the one shown in figure 14–27a.

6. If required, change the **Qty** value of each order bar to **5**. Now check the rest of the values on the order bar for entries similar to these:

COMBO	BUY	+5	CRM	FEB 16	80	PUT	1.49	LMT	LIMIT	DAY
	SELL	–5	CRM	FEB 16	80	CALL	DEBIT			

7. Check the risk profile in figure 14–27b. The risk profile shows how this strategy begins to return profit when the price of CRM drops below $78.40. As long as the bearish bias is correct, the synthetic short stock strategy returns a substantial profit.

8. Verify the setup. Then click **Confirm and Send**.

9. Evaluate the **Order Confirmation** information. If satisfactory, click **Send**.

Figure 14–27a. Synthetic Short Stock Option Chain

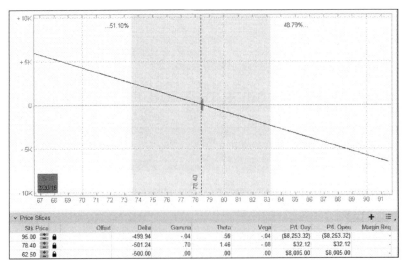

For illustration purposes only.

Figure 14–27b. Synthetic Short Stock Risk Profile

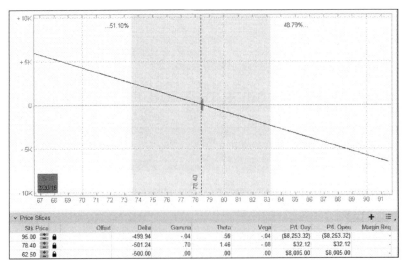

For illustration purposes only.

Risks

The obvious risk associated with the synthetic short stock strategy is an unwanted rally in the price of the underlying stock. Of course the underlying stock could also remain within a few dollars below the entry price through expiration. This would prevent this trade from being profitable, as Theta begins to erode the premium value of the long put as the trade nears expiration. The short call must remain OTM for this trade to succeed.

As mentioned, the uncovered short call can be menacing if the price of the underlying stock experiences a substantial rally. This makes this trade extremely dangerous. If the trader happens to own shares of the underlying stock, the trade would resemble an equity collar rather than a synthetic short strangle. But because the trader has a strong bearish bias, ownership of the stock is unlikely. If the price of the underlying rallies above the strike price of the short call, the trader will be compelled to close the short call immediately.

Trade Management

As long as the price of the underlying stock drops as expected, let the trade continue to work. If the P/L Open indicates 30% to 60% in profit, prepare to close both legs of this trade. However, if the contract still has several weeks till expiration and the stock continues to drop, consider letting the profit run until the price of the stock approaches resistance and shows signs of reversing direction. Then either sell the long put leg for the premium or exercise it. If the short call is far enough OTM to be reasonably safe, consider letting it expire worthless. Otherwise, spend the few dollars it takes to eliminate the threat posed by the short call.

If the price of the underlying stock begins to rally, buy to close the short call. Be prepared to pay whatever is required to prevent it from being exercised.

Possible Outcomes

1. The price of CRM drops to $75. The trader closes the short call and either sells or exercises the ITM long put for profit.
2. The price of CRM rallies to $86. The trader's bias was obviously wrong. The short call is closed before it is exercised. The trader attempts to sell the OTM long put for what premium may remain.
3. The price of CRM rallies to $86 and the short naked call is ITM by $6.00 and exercised. The trader sells the long put for $0.50/share (a total of $125 in premium less fees). The trader simultaneously delivers 500 shares of $86 stock to the buyer of the call options and receives $80/share for the stock for a loss of $3,000. The trader is glad only five short call contracts were transacted.

The Gamma–Delta Neutral Spread

Structure

$+x$ ATM CALLS, $-y$ OTM CALLS, $-z$ Shares
(Same expiration ≤ 7 trading days.)

Description and Goals

This vertical "ratio" spread is a medium risk, high reward, neutral strategy. The goal is for the price of the underlying stock to be reasonably stable from entry through contract expiration. The combined premium collected from the short calls and the sale of the long calls deliver profit. The shorted stock provides a hedge against a possible drop in the price of the stock. The strategy avoids excessive risk because it expires within a matter of a few days to perhaps one week. The structure resembles a ratio spread, as more short options are sold than long options are bought. Perhaps most of the risk resides in the price of the shorted stock.

Because this spread uses a large number of option contracts it is important to use a discount brokerage to reduce the cost of exchange fees. As you will see in the hands-on activity, this strategy typically buys and sells a few dozen option contracts.

As you've learned, most premium collection spreads rely on Theta for a rapid drop in premium value. In for a dollar and out for a dime — these can be rewarding premium collection, high risk strategies. You are also aware of how risk and reward are directly linked. The short strangle is one example of a high risk premium collection strategy that can provide a substantial amount of income, especially when current volatility is high and the expiration date is a few months away.

More conservative low risk, low reward spreads exist at the other end of the option strategy universe. Examples of these include covered calls, bull call spreads, bear put spreads, iron condors, and butterfly spreads. While conservative, their profit expectations can be somewhat limiting. In spite of their limitations, many option traders make good livings regularly employing two or three of these conservative strategies.

The Gamma–Delta neutral spread hedges the net Gamma and net Delta of each position to maintain directional neutrality. The strategy is quite interesting because it makes direct use of Greek values. This trade illustrates how the Greek values can interact to maintain neutrality.

When setting up this trade, the values of Gamma are used to calculate the number of long and short calls required to achieve neutral Gamma. Then the Delta values of both legs are summed to determine how many shares of the underlying stock must be shorted to achieve a neutral Delta value, where each share of stock has a Delta value of 1.0.

The ratio of Gamma is calculated using the Gamma values found at the strike prices of the long ATM call and the farther OTM short call. Assume you wish to buy ATM or slightly OTM TWTR long calls and sell farther OTM TWTR short calls.

Neutralizing Gamma

We examine the Gamma value at the 22 strike price expiring on Friday of the following week — 9 days till expiration. Then take the Gamma value at the 24.00 strike price on the same option chain. Here are some actual values, using three decimal places on the underlying option chain:

TWTR price at $21.33

Call Strikes	Mark	Gamma	Delta	Theta	×100
$22 (Long)	.52	.209	.408	−.036	10.5
$24.00 (Short)	.14	.105	.138	*.023	20.9

★Shorting Theta provides a positive value from −1 × −1 = +1.

Multiply the Gamma value at each strike by 100 to obtain the number of 100-share contracts required for the opposite legs. You can use a lower multiplier if required to reduce the number of contracts. Regardless of the multiplier, it must be the same to achieve neutral Gamma. Using 100 as shown in the table, neutral Gamma is achieved with −21 short calls at the 24 strike price (rounding 20.9 up) and +10 long calls at the 22 strike price (rounding 10.5 down).

Neutralizing Delta

Delta is offset by shorting shares of stock. Finding the number of shares required to achieve neutral Deltas is computed by summing the Delta values within the long and short call legs. Summing Delta produces a positive result. This requires shorting n shares of TWTR to achieve neutral Delta. The fact that each share of stock has a Delta value of 1.0 makes this easy.

Using the Delta values on the option chain, Delta at the 22 strike is .487 and .142 at the 24 strike. Because there are 100 shares per contract, the number of contracts is multiplied by 100 in the following values:

$+1000 \times .408 = 408$
$-2100 \times .138 = -290$
Sum -290 and $408 = 118$ Delta
Shorting 118 shares of TWTR neutralizes Delta

Using the TWTR option chain expiring on Friday of the following week:

Buy 10 22 TWTR calls
Sell 21 24 TWTR calls
Short 118 shares of TWTR stock

The Gamma-Delta neutral spread exploits Theta. Because of the short time till expiration, Theta immediately benefits the short OTM call contracts to move this leg into profit. Summing the daily Theta values of both legs provides each day's profit or loss.

1000 shares $\times -.036 = -\$36.00$
2100 shares $\times .023 = +\$46.00$
Daily P/L $= 46 - 36 = \$10.00$ gain on day one.

This spread shows a limited return of $10.00 on the first day. All things being equal, the return will increase as it approaches expiration. And there are always other stock candidates to consider. As mentioned above, the number of contracts results in a substantial overhead cost in option exchange fees. And, of course, the added risk of shorting the stock and the inclusion of naked short calls can also be worrisome to some. Because of the cost, this strategy requires a sizeable account and your brokerage's highest option trading level.

The best approach is to test this trade on paper, or back trade it using historical market data. Don't use this strategy until you're confident that it works in your favor. There are option traders who favor and regularly use this strategy. Try several simulated trades to become familiar with the setup. Check the outcomes. If successful (and affordable), you may want to include the Gamma-Delta neutral spread within your repertoire of trading strategies. The desire to use this strategy in addition to being able to trade short strangles and short put options on the financial indexes may encourage you to apply to your brokerage for permission to trade higher level option strategies.

Setup Parameters

- Goal: Premium collection; the time from entry to exit should be within a matter of days.
- Bias: Neutral (A premium collection strategy that shorts stock to achieve a neutral Delta)
- Debit/Credit: Debit at entry, credit at exit
- Chart Trend: Daily and hourly charts reveal a stable price range within a narrow support and resistance channel.
- Momentum Oscillator: Presently exists at a long-term neutral value
- Keltner Channel: The ATR(14) envelope presently level with only minor historical expansion and contraction activity
- Implied Volatility % $\geq 20\% \leq 40\%$
- Greeks: Delta: Neutral; Theta: Positive; Vega: Slightly Positive
- Days till Expiry: 5 to 7 Days
- Net Premium Cost: ±2 Marks: $\leq -\$5.00$ (less is better)
- Probability ITM: Long ATM calls $\geq 35\%$, short OTM call strikes $\leq 25\%$

- Open Interest: ≥ 300 at each strike price; total open interest @ all strikes ≥ 8,000
- Bid to Ask spread: The bid-to-ask spread should be close to historical levels.
- Risk Amount ≈1.0% of account equity (governed by premium and number of contracts)

How the Strategy Works

Select an option contract expiring within one week. Pick an ATM long call and an OTM short call strike price. The short OTM call should have a high probability of remaining OTM through expiration.

Next, use the Gamma values of each strike price multiplied by the same number, such as either 100 or 1,000, to determine the number of contracts to buy/sell for the other leg of this spread. Use the long Gamma × 100 to find the number of short call contracts to sell. Then use the short Gamma × 1000 to find the number of long calls to buy. Next, sum the Delta values of the long and short call legs. The Delta value of each option leg corresponds to the number of shares being traded at each strike price. (Reminder: the Delta value of a short call is negative.) Use the sum of the Deltas to determine the number of shares of stock to short. (Recall that each share of stock has a Delta value of 1.0).

Once all values are known, proceed by first shorting the shares of stock. You may wish to use a bracketed trade with a stop loss above and a target below — a customary stock trading practice. Then trade the computed number of long and short call contracts. This is a Single CUSTOM spread. The CUSTOM spread type is required to simultaneously enter a different number of long and short call contracts.

Take 30% to 70% profit when available (use the P/L Open value on your position statement). DO NOT let the short OTM calls become ITM. If necessary, close the number of short call contracts exceeding the number of long call contracts. For example, if you have 20 short calls and 10 long calls, close 10 short calls. The remaining 10 long call and 10 short call contracts form a bull call spread. The bull call spread hands-on activity is provided earlier in this chapter.

Hands-On Activity

Scanning for a Trade

1. Setup your option chain to display the Greek values Gamma, Delta, and Theta to three decimal places.
2. Scan price charts for neutral or slightly bearish stocks. Avoid stocks near price earnings and subject to unpredictable price swings, especially if you see the potential for a strong price rally.
3. Search for stocks with moderately low ATR(14) values that trade a few million shares in daily volume.
4. Look for adequate open interest at the call strike prices.
5. Sort the IV% column to your watch list in ascending order; scroll down to find stocks with midrange implied volatilities between 20% and 40%.
6. Consider using the Keltner Channel study to find a stock that remains near the SMA(20) and between the upper and lower 1.5 × ATR(14) bands.
7. Examine option chains that expire inside a week. If the stock's price chart pattern and studies display the behavior you are seeking, check the corresponding option chains for available premium.
8. Look at the ATM and OTM call premiums and estimate the cost of the trade. The OTM short call premium should offset much of the cost of the ATM long call premium.
9. The trader chooses the TWTR JAN 16 (9) option chain.
10. TWTR is currently trading at $21.39. The trader tentatively decides to buy 22 calls and sell 24 calls based on available premium, Probability ITM, and reasonable Theta values shown in the option chain of figure 14–28a. But the number of contracts must be computed.

Figure 14–28a. Gamma-Delta Neutral Spread Option Chain

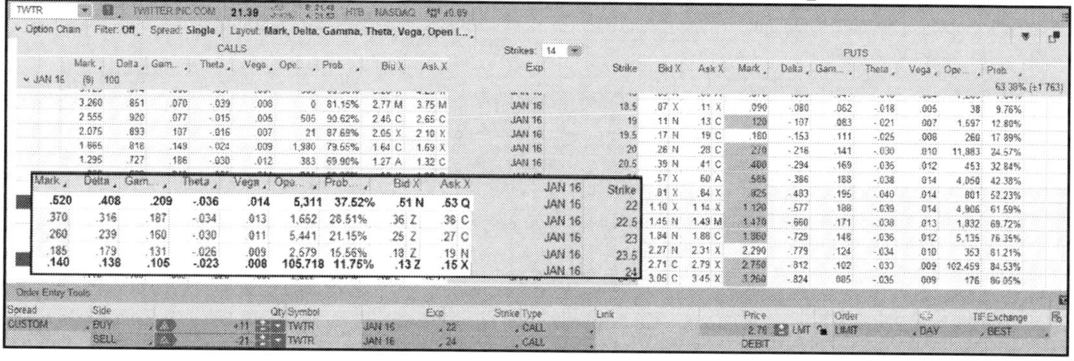

For illustration purposes only.

11. Using a calculator and a notepad, the trader multiplies 1,000 × the Gamma values of the short and long legs to determine the number of contracts required to neutralize Gamma.

12. Next the net Delta value is computed for the combined number of contracts in this spread. This tells the trader how many shares of stock to short.

13. The trader examines the Risk Profile shown in figure 14–28b.
    NOTE The risk profile does not show the profit or loss from shorting the stock used to neutralize Delta. The P/L from a change in the price of the underlying stock can be seen. Notice breakeven and peak profit is displayed on the plot. One concern is the vulnerability of the shorted stock to a strong price rally.

14. The notepad includes the following entries:

---

22 call Gamma = .209 × 1000 = 21 Short Calls at the 24 strike price

24 call Gamma = .105 × 1000 = 10 Long Calls at the 22 strike price.

22 call Delta = 1,000 × .408 = −408

24 call Delta = −2100 × −.138 = 290

Delta summed = 118 (Neutralize Delta by shorting 118 shares of TWTR)

Figure 14–28b. Gamma–Delta Neutral Spread Risk Profile (Options Only)

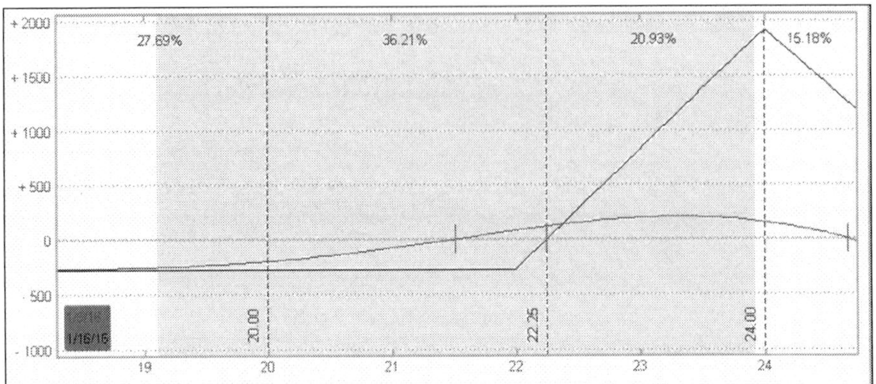

Stk Price	Offset	Delta	Gamma	Theta	Vega	P/L Day	P/L Open	Margin Req
24.00		-148.865	-240.007	71.494	-23.365	$155.32	$155.32	-
22.25		142.281	-69.738	27.616	-7.625	$116.33	$116.33	-
20.00		86.220	64.828	-6.130	3.053	($198.57)	($198.57)	-

For illustration purposes only.

15. Trade this Gamma–Delta neutral spread using your notes and by performing the steps in the following Entry procedure.

Entry

1. Start your trading platform's simulation mode, i.e., paper trading.
2. Scan the price charts for a neutral stock using the Keltner Channel study. The current price should be between the upper and lower ATR(14) envelope near the SMA(20) plot line.
3. Check the chart for corporate events. In particular, avoid upcoming earnings releases during the short life of this trade.
4. Look at the stock on your watch list and check the IV%. It should be between 20% and 40%.
5. Open the underlying's option chain (similar to the one shown in figure 14–28a) that expires within five days to a week.
6. Use your trading platform's setup dialog to display three decimal places on your option chains.
7. Be sure the Spread **Single** is selected. Then expand the option chain.

8. Jot down the Greek and premium values of strike prices with acceptable open interest, Probability ITM, and Greek values.

9. Use Gamma to calculate the number of call contracts required to achieve Gamma neutrality at each strike price. (Use a multiplier such as 100, 500, or 1,000 to obtain the number of contracts that fits your account size and risk tolerance.)

10. Sum the Delta values to calculate the number of stock shares to short in order to achieve Delta neutrality.

11. Short the required number of shares of the underlying stock. Consider including a protective stop a dollar or two above the price of your short stock position. This is "free protection" against a strong rally.

12. Click the CALLS **Ask** cell to put the long call on the order bar.

13. Press and hold **Ctrl** and then click the CALLS **Bid** cell to put the short call on the order bar.

14. Change the order bar **Spread** from VERTICAL to CUSTOM. Then increment the **Qty** values to agree with the number of long and short contracts required for Gamma neutrality.

15. Examine all values on the order bar. The trade will be a DEBIT spread with roughly twice as many OTM short calls as ATM or slightly OTM long calls.

16. Check the risk profile to determine how this spread responds to changes in the price of the underlying stock.

17. Finally, verify the setup on the order bar to ensure they are similar to these values:

CUSTOM   BUY   +11 TWTR   JAN 16   22   CALL   2.78   LMT LIMIT   DAY
           SELL   −21 TWTR   JAN 16   24   CALL   DEBIT

18. If the order bar is satisfactory, click **Confirm and Send**.

19. Evaluate the Order Confirmation information. The net cost of the option contracts is $278. If satisfactory, click **Send**.

20. Watch your P/L Open values. Although you may wish to close the trade when profitable by 30% to 70%, it may be more rewarding to let the short leg expire worthless. If the price of

the underlying stock has dropped, consider closing it for profit with a buy to cover stock order.

Risks

Because contract expiration is only a matter of days away, the trade is a major benefactor of Theta. In spite of minimizing risk by using short times till expiry, be careful not to pay more for entry than you can earn from this trade. You may have to move the strike price of the short call closer to that of the long call to reduce the cost of entry. Of course this introduces additional risk of having the short calls become ATM and exercised. This will also reduce the value of Delta and the corresponding number of shares of stock to be shorted.

As with most option trades that involve stock, the stock often carries the most risk. With a Delta value of 1.0 per share, a $1.00 change has more impact than on the premium. Because the ATM call options with a Delta value of roughly .50, a $1.00 change in the stock price causes a 50-cent change in the premium. Hence, this trade would lose value from a price increase in the shorted stock. Fortunately, the number of shares of stock required to achieve neutral Delta is small relative to the number of short call options. But this introduces a new concern. You must watch your short calls because of the uncovered contracts. As mentioned, you can buy to close the uncovered short calls and let the remaining ones work as you would a bull call spread.

Trade Management

As long as the underlying stock remains within a reasonable price range, as indicated by your chart and the Keltner Channel study, this trade is likely to return a reasonable profit. As with all option strategies, the price of the underlying stock dictates the outcome. The Gamma-Delta neutral strategy works well when the underlying remains within a narrow price range. Even a small rise in the price of the TWTR stock is more than offset by the long $22 call options.

For example, if the shorted 118 shares of TWTR stock experience a loss of $1.00/share, the increase in premium value of the eleven long $22 calls more than offsets this loss. Assuming the long call becomes ATM with a Delta of .50, even if the premium of the long call has declined from $0.52/share to $0.30/share, the long call premium value will have risen to $330. This more than offsets the $118 loss in stock value. The 21 short $24 calls returned a premium of $294 at entry. This is retained as long as the short call remains OTM. So even with a $1.00 decrease in short stock value from the $1.00 rally, the trade earns $506. Subtract the original cost of $278 at entry and the trade earns $228 in profit, a return of 182% profit in a matter of a few days.

If the 118 shares of TWTR stock drops by $1.00, the stock earns $118 dollars in profit. The premium value of the 11 long $22 calls will have declined to approximately $0.18/share, a residual value of $198. Add this to the $294 short call premium income, and the trade earns $610 from $198 + $294 + 118. Subtract the original cost of $278 when entered, and the trade returns a $332 profit, a return of 219.4%.

Possible Outcomes

1. The price of the underlying stock remains within a narrow range through contract expiration. The P/L statement shows a daily and cumulative profit through expiration. The trader closes all positions for profit.
2. The price of the underlying stock rallies above the long call but remains below the strike price of the OTM short call. The price of the short stock triggers its protective stop and the stock position is closed. With only a few days remaining and sufficient liquidity (open interest), the long ITM call can be sold and a buy to close order is entered to liquidate the short call options

for less than originally paid. The premium collected from the sale of the long call option offsets part if not all of the loss from the short stock.

3. The price of the underlying stock drops by several dollars. The trader enters a buy to cover order on the long stock for profit. The long call is sold for a few hundred dollars in premium. The OTM short calls expire worthless. The trade returns a profit.

4. The price of the underlying stock experiences a breakout and rallies above the strike price of the short OTM calls, which are exercised. The shorted stock is stopped out and closed for a small loss of a few hundred dollars. The long ITM call is exercised for profit to offset part of the cost of buying and delivering stock to the buyer of the short OTM call contacts. The trade suffers a substantial loss.

5. The price of the underlying stock experiences a breakout and rallies above the strike price of the long calls. It continues toward the strike price of the short OTM calls. The protective stop on the short stock is automatically triggered to minimize loss from the short stock's unwanted rally. Before the short OTM calls are exercised, the trader enters a buy to close order and exits in the "nick of time." The premium paid to close the short call options is slightly more than that received when the trade was entered. The trader then exercises the remaining long ITM calls and sells the stock at market price to recover a portion of the loss. The trade suffers a loss.

6. Number 5 above was poorly managed. The trader should have closed the short calls and either sold or exercised the ITM long calls for profit, depending on relative returns.

Naked Puts, Calls, and Strangles on the Financial Indexes

$-n$ OTM PUTS (Expiration ≤ 56 days)

$-n$ OTM CALLS (Expiration ≤ 56 days)

$-n$ OTM PUTS, $-n$ OTM CALLS (Same expiration, ≤ 56 days)

Who Can Trade Naked?

These strategies are among the author's personal favorites, as thousands of dollars per month in option income is possible. But because the three trades described here are uncovered (or *naked*), all require the highest option trading permission. Therefore, be advised to tread carefully when selling uncovered options, even if you are a high-level option trader having several years of trading experience.

The highest number of trades occurs on the following three indexes:

- S&P 500 (symbol SPX)
- NASDAQ (symbol NDX)
- Russell 2000 (symbol RUT)

Other indexes that offer option contracts include the S&P 100 (OEX), the VIX, and RVX. Options can also be traded on the financial index futures (called the e-minis). An introduction to futures and a hands-on option trading activity on the S&P 500 e-mini future is provided in chapter 15.

Definition and Risks

Selling uncovered option contracts introduces a substantial amount of risk. This was demonstrated in the lead-up to the short call strategy near the beginning of this chapter. Recall the Billabong Pharmaceuticals example. It unexpectedly rallied putting the strike price of a trader's short call deep ITM. The results were devastating. There's a true story about an option trader who lost everything when the underlying pharmaceutical stock of his naked short call rallied some 1600% in a matter of a few short hours. That event ended a trading career in bankruptcy.

Although the cash-covered short put is somewhat safer than a short call, it can also pose danger. For example, the strike price of the underlying, such as the RUT, SPX, and NDX, range from $800 to more than $5,000. Having 10 or more contracts one to three strikes ITM can lead to losses in the tens of thousands of dollars.

Cash Settled

You should also recall how the index options are cash settled. This was alluded to in chapter 3. If an OTM call is exercised, the seller must deliver cash to the seller at current market price. In exchange, the option buyer pays the seller in cash at the seller's strike price. The difference can be in the thousands of dollars, depending on the underlying index and the difference between the original option price and the market price when exercised.

Volatility Indexes

The CBOE tracks the trading volatility of each financial index. Volatility information is available online at https://www.cboe.com/micro/volatility/introduction.aspx. Use this web link to display a table like the one shown here. As shown, the table includes several volatility indexes. Two of the listed volatility indexes, the VIX and RVX, offer options.

Ticker	Index	Sym	Last	Pt. Change
VIX®	CBOE Volatility Index	VIX	16.80	0.30
VXN℠	CBOE NASDAQ Volatility Index	VXN	19.42	-0.23
VXO℠	CBOE S&P 100 Volatility Index	VXO	16.76	-0.50
VXD℠	CBOE DJIA Volatility Index	VXD	15.85	-0.52
RVX℠	CBOE Russell 2000 Volatility Index	RVX	19.99	-0.26
VXST℠	CBOE Short-Term Volatility Index	VXST	15.83	0.63
VXV℠	CBOE 3-Month Volatility Index	VXV	19.34	-0.13
VXMT℠	CBOE Mid-Term Volatility Index	VXMT	21.10	-0.20

Provided as a courtesy by Chicago Board Options Exchange, Incorporated.

Manual and Automated Protective Stops

Although most traders manage option trades on financial indexes manually, some set protective stops. These are similar to those used with bracketed stock trades. Once they set a GTC working stop, they walk away confident that their position is protected from danger. And, if the trader knows what he or she is doing, the trade may indeed be protected. However, most active traders monitor their trades. If threatened, they interact by closing, rolling, or adding a protective long leg. Losses are sometimes partially or fully offset. For example, traders can sell on the opposite side (closing a put and selling a call), selling a farther OTM put, buying a farther OTM protective leg to reduce risk and/or margin stress, converting a single short leg to a short strangle, rolling up, rolling out, etc. This is a major advantage of options; you have many choices.

Stock Symbols and Option Codes

Stock symbols must be used to transact stock and ETF trades. And index symbols exist for the same reason. These index symbols are used to display the corresponding option chains. In fact, your favorite trading platform likely permits you to trigger a buy to close order based on the market price, or Mark, of the underlying stock. For example, if the stock drops within a few strikes of the option price, you may trigger a GTC buy to close order. But what is the current premium? There's really no way to tell, because Vega (volatility) can create havoc with option premiums.

So instead of using the stock symbol that corresponds to a working option contract, a unique option code can be used instead. Look at the following option code:

.SPXW160122P1600

This unique option code is for the S&P 500 index. Breaking down the symbol, it represents the following:

SPX — S&P 500 Index Symbol
W — Weekly option
160122 — Expires on 01/22/2016

P — Put option
1600 — 1600 Strike Price

An option code can be used to establish a stop that is triggered by the Mark value. In fact, you can choose the Mark, Bid, Ask, or even the Delta value of one or more working option contracts. And your triggers can be based on one of the following conditions:

- At or below
- At or above
- Trail stop
- Below
- Above

When the option code is used to convey the details of the underlying option contract(s), you can set stops based on these option values, all available on the underlying option chain:

- Mark (the option's premium, or Mark value)
- Bid (the option's Bid price)
- Ask (the option's Ask price)
- Delta (the option's Delta value)
- Study (a chart study, such as an SMA(20) price crossover)

Mark-Triggered versus Delta-Triggered Stops
The value of Delta is considerably more stable than the value of the Mark. It's possible for there to be a million or more orders waiting to be filled when the market opens. When this happens, the value of the Mark can experience an instantaneous price spike. This price transient can reach a waiting Mark-triggered stop. This can trigger the Mark-based stop and prematurely close a working trade. This can result in an unwanted loss or a premature exit.

As mentioned, this usually happens at the beginning of a trading day. Hence, many traders prefer Delta-triggered stops. When using a

Delta-triggered stop on a far OTM short put, consider a Delta trigger value **At or below −.10.** Of course this depends entirely on your strike price. Delta-triggered stops on far OTM short calls might use trigger values like **At or above +.30.** Whichever is used, be sure to look at the option chain, the Delta values, and the Probability ITM% before deciding on a safe Delta trigger value. Note that these values are affected by current volatility, time remaining till expiration, Gamma, and even Rho.

If the value of Delta does trigger your stop, your trade will suffer a loss. That loss may be five times the value of the original premium collected when the trade was entered. But losing five times is better than losing everything. This should be part of your risk management rules. And when your rules limit a loss, they're working! Without them, you could lose everything.

Although stop-loss triggers are available for working options, most experienced traders prefer to manage their working trades in person. They may use alerts to notify them when a position is approaching trouble, but they prefer to intervene in manually. There are just too many alternatives that can be used to turn around a bad situation.

Margin Calls, Stress Tests, and Reg. T Calls

Margin calls are something experienced traders always do their best to avoid. Margin calls are issued by brokerages to alert traders when the equity in their accounts falls short of the equity required to collateralize working orders. This can happen when the price of one or more securities drops below the amount required to finance the trader's margined securities. It can also happen when the position of one or more naked option contracts are exposed to unusually high market volatility.

When a margin call is received, the trader must respond by either adding funds to the account or closing one or more positions to alleviate the overage. Each brokerage uses a formula to compute a margin deficiency. A notice similar to the following is sent to traders whose margin accounts are out of compliance.

> We are writing to inform you that your account ****86245 has been set to closing only. Your portfolio, when beta weighted to the SPX and stressed down 20%, represents a theoretical loss of more than 2 times your current account value; our parameters allow for risk of no more than 2 times on the downside and 3 times on the upside. Given this increased risk we may require you to reduce your position to limit the total exposure. If the downside risk exceeds 3 times equity, it must be brought under 2 times equity by the end of the day.

Brokerages accounts are continuously and automatically stress tested to determine the likelihood of the account equity becoming deficient. Accounts become stressed when the underlying volatility indexes, such as the VIX or VXN, experience sharp increases. This can exceed allowable stress on uncovered short puts or calls, especially on one of the financial indexes.

You can read about margin risk on the Options Clearing Corporation's website at http://www.optionsclearing.com/risk-management/margins/. There, you'll see that the OCC monitors the effect of volatility on margin using their *System for Theoretical Analysis and Numerical Simulations* (STANS).

The most severe violations in account deficiencies trigger what are called Regulation T Filings. These are submitted to investors who have not promptly paid for a securities transaction according to Federal Reserve Board's Regulation T and SEC Rule 15c3–3. The Reg. T call applies primarily to short stock sales and uncovered short options. The rule requires the broker-dealer to either liquidate an unfulfilled position or acquire an extension from the examining regulatory authority. Without being granted an extension, if a sold security is not delivered to the buyer within ten business days following the settlement date, the broker-dealer must stand good for the transaction. This is a strong incentive for your broker to monitor your account.

With this background in margin deficiencies in place, be sure to always watch your margin levels. Triggering a margin call, or Reg. T call, or both can be expensive. Even when a working short put or call on an index appears far enough OTM to expire worthless, a sudden increase in volatility or a drop in the value of several stocks within the underlying brokerage account can result in your receipt of a margin call notice.

Always know in advance how you'll handle a sudden margin call. Some things you can do include:

- Close some or all working short option contracts to return within margin compliance.
- Buy an equivalent number of option contracts one or two strikes farther OTM.
- Or, as a last resort, sell stock, transfer more shares of stock into your account, or transfer additional cash into your brokerage account to offset the margin deficiency.

Selling SPX Puts

Structure

$-n$ far OTM PUTS (*naked* puts expiring $\leq$ 45 days)

Description and Goals

This is considered a low reward, high risk strategy because profit is limited to premium income. Although it is quite popular, those traders who use this strategy should have substantial experience. In particular, they must know what can happen if the price of the SPX begins to approach the strike price of a short put. But if this strategy is regularly used throughout the year on any of the *big three* financial indexes (SPX, NDX, RUT), and it can be extremely profitable. Many traders make thousands of dollars each month selling far OTM puts and calls for premium on these indexes. This is precisely the kind of trades in use by many high-income option traders.

> **NOTE** Although the option strategies focus on the S&P 500 index, symbol SPX, the same strategies are used with other financial indexes including the NDX (NASDAQ), RUT (Russell 2000), and even the OEX (S&P 100 index). Also consider the exchange traded funds, such as the QQQ, SPY, and IWM. These ETFs can be considered if enough premium exists to make the risk worthwhile. And as you will see in chapter 15, options can also be traded on the e-mini financial index futures in essentially the same way as the financial indexes, themselves. While all track changes in the underlying indexes they're tied to, the ETFs are much more affordable. And they are "share settled" rather than cash settled, which reduces risk.

The primary goal of selling far OTM puts on a financial index, such as the SPX, RUT, or NDX, is to collect weekly, bi-weekly, or monthly premium income. Selling OTM puts requires the trader to have a neutral to bullish bias. In other words, the trader wants to remain OTM throughout the duration of the selected option contract. Of course these trades can be closed for substantial profits as the underlying option positions approach their expiration dates. Consider an example of how a short put might be used for regular income.

1. A trader has a neutral bias.
2. The SPX is currently at $2,000 and the VIX (volatility index) is near 18.

3. The trader sells 20 1700 put contracts expiring within 28 days and collects $0.50 per share, or $1,000 in premium less transaction fees.

4. The VIX remains between 15 and 20. Theta begins its work of reducing premium value.

5. Within 14 days the Mark (premium) value at the 1700 put has dropped to 25 cents.

6. The trader rolls the 20 contracts to the next expiration date.

7. When the contracts are rolled, the trader keeps $500 profit from the initial trade (originally sold 20 contracts for $0.50/share, closed for $0.25/share).

8. The trader rolls the 20 contracts another 28 days out in time for another $0.50/share in premium. The roll collects an additional $1,000 in premium. The cumulative premium collected is now $1,500 less the $500 required to roll the first trade.

9. The SPX remains near or slightly higher than $2,000; the trader continues to roll short SPX put contracts from the original 1700 strike to higher strikes.

10. Although the trader must change strike prices to correspond to SPX price actions, the premiums range between 35 and 60 cents and accumulate over time. By the end of the calendar year, the trader will have accrued a five-figure income in SPX premiums.

    NOTE Presently (when this book was written) sixty percent of premium income received from financial index options was treated as a capital gain. The remaining forty percent is taxed as ordinary income.

Although the above trading regimen sounds quite easy, the short call MUST remain far OTM to avoid the possibility of being exercised. Each trade must use a strike having a Probability ITM well below 5%. This will give each trade excellent odds for success until rolled or finally closed. You've read and understand how churning works, i.e., constantly trading and rolling for additional profit. And you understand how churning increases cumulative income over time. A previous example explained how churning involves making 50% profit three times in the same time it takes to make 100% one time. Churning returns 150% versus holding a trade until expiration to make 100%. To appreciate the difference, think about doing this all year long, perhaps 36 times, rather than just 12 or 14 times.

Recall the second advantage: rolling is a single transaction with one brokerage fee; selling and then buying a new position requires two commissions. Although there are no commissions or exchange fees when option contracts expire worthless, these fees are small when compared to the overall profit returned by churning.

Setup Parameters

- Goal: Collect premium by selling a far OTM put with an extremely low probability of becoming ITM. Plan to churn these trades for increased income.
- Bias: Neutral to bullish (a premium-collection strategy that shorts far OTM puts)
- Debit/Credit: Credit
- Chart Trend: Neutral to slight rally
- Momentum Oscillator: Slightly oversold near a historical support level
- Keltner Channel: An extended ATR(14) envelope exists signifying high premium.
- Implied Volatility % $\geq$ 40% (Higher is better for increased premium.)
- VIX value: Best when close to 20; below 15 reduces available premiums; higher introduces risk requiring the strike price to be farther OTM.
- Margin: Ensure sufficient account equity exists to avoid a margin call.
- Greeks: Delta: Negative; Theta: Negative; Vega: Positive

- Days till Expiry: ≤ 56 Days (Shorter is better providing sufficient premium.)
- Net Premium Income: ≥ $0.40 (Even more is often possible based on the value of the VIX.)
- Probability ITM: < 5.00% (Essential to remain OTM; always choose a safe OTM strike price, perhaps even ≤ 2.5%. Probability Touching should be ≤ 5.00%.)
- Open Interest: ≥ 600 at selected strike price; total open interest @ all strikes > 50,000. (The financial indexes are characterized by excellent liquidity from high levels of open interest.)
- Bid to Ask spread on financial indexes are typically quite wide and often ignored by index traders who are primarily concerned with selecting a safe, far OTM strike price. However, a wide spread encourages many traders to attempt entry prices at more favorable premiums.
- Risk Amount: This is a high risk strategy that requires careful management. Be ready to close this trade; never risk more than 1.5% of account equity on any single trade.

How the Strategy Works

For a highly profitable option strategy, the structure of a single short SPX put is quite simple. The trader's goal is to sell one or more put options located at a strike price that is unlikely to become ATM throughout the life of the selected contract. Under normal circumstances, and when the VIX volatility index is at 20 or less, this strategy usually works quite well.

Because the S&P 500 averages the stock prices of 500 large companies like Facebook, Netflix, Apple, Amazon, etc., the value of the index is typically slower to move than its individual constituent stocks. While some stock prices rally, others decline. This tends to stabilize the index price and mitigates risk. Of course there are times when the entire market trends downward or upward. These are times when it's best to wait for the market to stabilize and for the value of the VIX to return to between 15 and 20.

Most traders are only too aware of the fact that the market typically falls much faster than it rises. This adds more risk to puts than to calls. You can verify this by looking at practically any option chain. Go to the same number of strikes OTM and compare the put and call premiums. The put premiums are higher than the call premiums. This is another reason why most traders prefer short puts over short calls. They are able to choose strike prices that are much farther OTM for better premium. Following the SPX short put activity, the short call strategy is examined. There, our discussion compares risk between a short put and a short call in more detail.

Hands-On Activity

Scanning for a Trade

1. Scan the SPX price charts to determine the current trend. Your goal is to develop a neutral to bullish directional bias.
2. Put the VIX on your current watch list and check the value. Look for a neutral value of between 15 and 20. A high VIX value can add substantial stress to a short SPX put and result in a margin call.
3. Select an option chain that expires inside 45 days. Shorter is even better because it's safer. (The example SPX option chain in figure 14–29 expires in 13 days. The premium is unusually high, as a VIX value of 27 existed when this screen was captured.)
4. Study the premium (Mark) values at strike prices having a Probability Touching at or below 5%. Consider being even farther OTM with increased times till expiration. (Looking at the SPX 1620 put strike in the option chain pictured in figure 14–29, notice how the Prob. ITM value is roughly 50% lower than the Prob. Touch value. If using Prob. ITM rather than Prob. Touch, select strike prices with a Prob. ITM value at or below 2.5%.)

Figure 14–29. SPX Short Put Option Chain

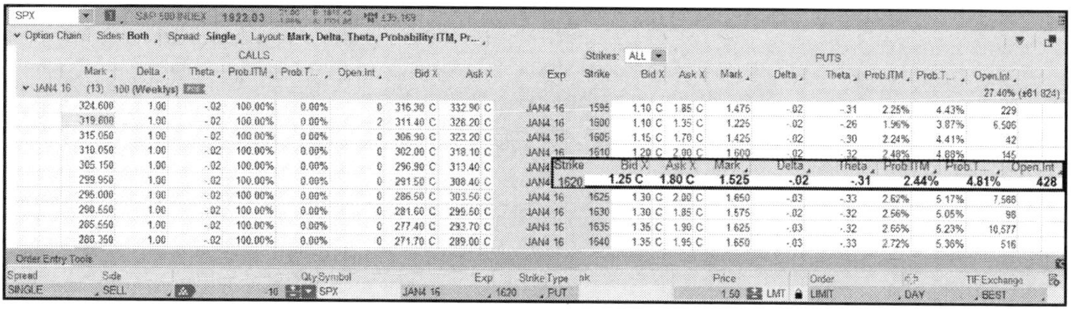

SPX · S&P 500 INDEX 1922.03

Option Chain · Sides: **Both** · Spread: **Single** · Layout: **Mark, Delta, Theta, Probability ITM, Pr...** · Strikes: ALL

JAN4 16 (13) 100 (Weeklys) · 27.40% (±61.824)

CALLS Mark	Delta	Theta	Prob.ITM	Prob.T...	Open.Int	Bid X	Ask X	Exp	Strike	PUTS Bid X	Ask X	Mark	Delta	Theta	Prob.ITM	Prob.T...	Open.Int
324.600	1.00	-.02	100.00%	0.00%	0	316.30 C	332.90 C	JAN4 16	1595	1.10 C	1.85 C	1.475	-.02	-.31	2.25%	4.43%	229
319.800	1.00	-.02	100.00%	0.00%	2	311.40 C	328.20 C	JAN4 16	1600	1.10 C	1.35 C	1.225	-.02	-.26	1.56%	3.87%	6,506
315.050	1.00	-.02	100.00%	0.00%	0	306.90 C	323.20 C	JAN4 16	1605	1.15 C	1.70 C	1.425	-.02	-.30	2.24%	4.41%	42
310.050	1.00	-.02	100.00%	0.00%	0	302.00 C	318.10 C	JAN4 16	1610	1.20 C	2.00 C	1.600	-.02	-.32	2.48%	4.88%	145
305.150	1.00	-.02	100.00%	0.00%	0	296.90 C	313.40 C	JAN4	Strike	Bid X	Ask X	Mark	Delta	Theta	Prob.ITM	Prob.T...	Open.Int
299.950	1.00	-.02	100.00%	0.00%	0	291.50 C	308.40 C	JAN4	**1620**	**1.25 C**	**1.80 C**	**1.525**	**-.02**	**-.31**	**2.44%**	**4.81%**	**428**
295.000	1.00	-.02	100.00%	0.00%	0	286.50 C	303.50 C	JAN4 16	1625	1.30 C	2.00 C	1.650	-.03	-.33	2.62%	5.17%	7,566
290.550	1.00	-.02	100.00%	0.00%	0	281.60 C	299.50 C	JAN4 16	1630	1.30 C	1.85 C	1.575	-.02	-.32	2.56%	5.05%	96
285.550	1.00	-.02	100.00%	0.00%	0	277.40 C	293.70 C	JAN4 16	1635	1.35 C	1.90 C	1.625	-.03	-.32	2.65%	5.23%	10,577
280.350	1.00	-.02	100.00%	0.00%	0	271.70 C	289.00 C	JAN4 16	1640	1.35 C	1.95 C	1.650	-.03	-.33	2.72%	5.36%	516

Order Entry Tools

Spread	Side	Qty	Symbol	Exp	Strike	Type	Price	Order	TIF	Exchange
SINGLE	SELL	10	SPX	JAN4 16	1620	PUT	1.50 LMT	LIMIT	DAY	BEST

For illustrative purposes only.

5. With the SPX currently at 1922.03, the trader decides upon the 1620 put with an exceptional premium of $1.50 per share. (The Bid to Ask spread is $0.55.)
6. The trader can easily determine the profit of this trade without a risk profile. The trade remains profitable by $3,000 as long as the SPX stays above the 1620 strike price. At $150 per contract in premium (100 shares × $1.50), 20 contracts collect $3,000. The trader knows quite well that as long as the SPX index remains above 1620 strike price, the option contract will expire worthless, may be exited for profit with a buy to close order, or rolled into a new short SPX put option expiring at a later date. All of these would be considered when the premium drops below $0.75 — a profit of $1,500 within a matter of several days to perhaps a week.
7. Trade this short SPX put by performing the steps in the following Entry procedure.

Entry

1. Open the SPX option chain that expires within a few weeks. The JAN4 16 is selected.
2. Be sure the Spread **Single** is selected. Then expand the JAN 16 (13) option chain.
3. Click the **PUTS Bid** cell at the **1620** strike price. (See figure 14–29.) Of course the trader is quite aware of how a drop in price to 1619.99 or below can cause this trade to fail.

4. Check the order bar to verify it contains entries similar to these:

SINGLE SELL –10 SPX JAN4 16 1620 PUT 1.50 LMT LIMIT DAY

5. Verify the setup. Then click **Confirm and Send**.
6. Evaluate the Order Confirmation information. If satisfactory, click **Send**.
7. Watch your P/L Open values and the price of the SPX. When the trade returns a profit of 60% or more close or roll the trade.
8. Continue selling far OTM (safe) SPX puts throughout the year.
9. Consider the churning strategy by rolling or closing and then trading again.

Remember that a roll charges a single brokerage commission, while closing and opening in two transactions require two commissions. However, option exchange fees are based on the number of contracts traded (both one way and round trip). Also recall how neither brokerage commissions nor exchange fees are charged when an option contract expires worthless.

Risks

Two possible risks exist with the short SPX put trade. The first is becoming ITM by one cent. But if the SPX drops far below 1620, the cash required to settle this trade will be substantial. In this respect, this is a low reward, high risk trade. When a short SPX put is working, the trader must pay close attention to both the trade and account margin to ensure that sufficient funds exist to prevent a margin call. Never enter an uncovered short put or call on any of the financial indexes and simply walk away assuming the trade is safe. And always watch available account margin. The high premiums can tempt traders to sell too many contracts too close to the money only to see their margin evaporate followed by a margin call.

Trade Management

1. This trade must be closely monitored once it is filled. If the price of the SPX remains within a narrow range or trends upward, your working trade remains safe. The trade's P/L Open value tells you when it's time to roll into another trade for more premium.

2. If the price of the SPX remains within a narrow range or trends upward, your working trade remains safe. If you have more short SPX puts working simultaneously, you may let the first one expire worthless as long as it remains safely OTM.

3. Set an alert based on the price (Mark) of the SPX index. If the SPX begins to drop toward the strike price of your working short put, consider:

   a. Closing the trade and "taking your lumps."
   b. Buying an equal number of puts one or two strikes below to serve as insurance, and to reduce margin stress. (If the index price reverses direction, you may be able to sell the long insurance leg for a profit.)
   c. Close the trade and offset some of the loss by selling OTM SPX call contracts.
   d. Close the trade and sell farther OTM SPX puts to offset some of the loss.
   e. Do both c and d above.

4. Enter a GTC Delta triggered stop. If Delta becomes "At or below -.10" as viewed on the option chain, a buy to close order will trigger. (You can also enter a GTC Mark-triggered stop based on a Mark value of $\leq$ $0.75, which would produce a 50% profit.)

Possible Outcomes

1. This simple strategy has a limited number of outcomes. First, letting the far OTM SPX short put expire worthless is one possibility. This returns the intended $1,500 in profit.

2. The OTM SPX short put remains well below the SPX ATM strike price. When the trade gains 30% to 70% in profit, the trader rolls the 1620 short put into another short SPX put which expires on a later expiration date for additional premium. By churning, the trader retains a profit of $750 from the first trade and collects another $1,500 in premium income when rolled ($3,000 − $750 to buy to close the first contract). By churning, the trader makes $2,250 in roughly one week. This is half the time of what would be required to let the first trade expire worthless in approximately two weeks.

3. The price of the SPX drops. The short put becomes within a 30% Probability ITM. The trader enters a buy to close order to exit the position. Then the trader begins to look for OTM short calls and farther OTM (safer) short puts to recover some of the money used to close the original short put.

4. The trader rolls the short put to the next expiration date and farther OTM to a much safer OTM strike price. By rolling, the trader recovers some of the money used to close the original SPX short put.

5. The trader combines 3 and 4 above. Both the SPX short calls and puts are placed at safe OTM strike prices with low probabilities of becoming ITM.

6. The price of the SPX drops. The VIX rises above 30, and the current 1620 put is stressed. The brokerage issues a margin call to the trader. The trader examines the current margin and determines the current position, although still far OTM, is indeed stressed by the uptick in volatility. A decision is made to close 10 contracts to bring the trade back into compliance. (This outcome shows the importance of monitoring your account margin to remain within SEC Rule 15c3–3 compliance to avoid the receipt of a margin call.)

Selling SPX Calls

Structure

$-n$ OTM CALLS ($\leq$ 45 Days)

Description and Goals

Like the short SPX put, this is another popular high risk, low reward option strategy intended to collect premium. In fact, it is often riskier than the short SPX put because acceptable premiums are almost always much closer to the SPX's ATM strike price. When using short calls the trader's bias must be neutral or bearish. A strong rally threatens this position. This causes premium to increase above the level at which the option was originally sold. That loss is immediately reflected in the P/L Open and P/L Day columns of the trader's brokerage account statement.

Like the short SPX put, the probability of becoming ITM is carefully chosen. But balancing premium with risk is more difficult on the call side of the option chain. As initially mentioned, a suitable strike price is almost always closer to the money to collect enough premium to justify the risk. The trader knows a strong rally can quickly defeat this trade, forcing the position to be closed to prevent a substantial loss. However, if the short call succeeds, it can be rolled into a later expiration date and perhaps a different call strike price for additional profit. So the churning strategy can be used with short SPX calls in the same way they are used with short SPX puts. But, always exercise caution when using either short SPX puts or calls.

Like the short SPX put, the short SPX call must be actively managed. And when the value of the VIX (*volatility index*) increases, the position may become stressed and require trader intervention to either avoid or respond to a margin call. Although closing a threatened short SPX call can be quite costly, it's much less expensive than being exercised. Settling an exercised call can easily reduce a trader's entire account to zero. This is why many traders find it difficult to justify short SPX calls. They are closer to the ATM price of the SPX for less premium income than that of a short SPX put.

Setup Parameters

- Goal: Collect premium by selling a far OTM call. The selected strike price must have an exceptionally low probability of becoming ITM. Consider churning this trade if another safe OTM strike price that offers sufficient premium is available.
- Bias: Neutral to bearish (A price rally threatens the success of this trade.)
- Debit/Credit: Credit
- Chart Trend: Daily and hourly charts reveal basing near a historical resistance level with the possible formation of a downturn in the index price.
- Momentum Oscillator: Presently beginning to reverse from a previous overbought condition
- Keltner Channel: The ATR(14) envelope presently narrow following an expansion in buying volume. The envelope is beginning to expand from fresh selling volume.
- Implied Volatility % ≥ 20% (Higher IV% increases premium. It is also an indicator of a possible move in the value of SPX index.)
- VIX value: Most short SPX sellers prefer the VIX value to be close to 20; below 15 reduces available premiums; high volatility values introduce risk requiring the strike price to be moved even farther OTM.
- Greeks: Delta: Negative; Theta: Positive; Vega: Negative
- Days till Expiry: ≤ 45 Days (Although the premiums can be substantially higher, farther OTM strike prices and shorter times till expiration are selected for increased safety.)
- Net Premium Income: ≥ $0.40 (Even more is often possible based on the value of the VIX.)

- Probability ITM: ≤ 2.50% (Low Probability value is essential to remain OTM; always choose a safe OTM strike price. Probability Touching should be ≤ 5.00%.)
- Open Interest: ≥ 300 at selected strike price; total open interest @ all strikes > 50,000. Open interest is typically higher for SPX puts than for SPX calls. The financial indexes are characterized by excellent liquidity from high levels of open interest. Open interest diminishes with longer times till contract expiration and increases as the contract approaches expiration.
- Bid to Ask spread: The value of the bid to ask spread on index options is normally wide. This provides a broader range of acceptable entry prices. Traders often adjust the Mark by several cents in their favor to improve the entry price of their trades.
- Risk Amount ≈1.0% of account equity (governed by premium and number of contracts)

How the Strategy Works

Like the short put, one or more short SPX call contracts are sold at the same OTM strike price. It can be entered on the order bar with a single mouse click. The trader's goal is to sell long SPX calls at a strike price that is unlikely to become ITM throughout the life of the selected option contract. Under normal circumstances, and when the VIX volatility index is at 20 or less, this strategy can work quite well.

And, of course, this is the S&P 500 index and less volatile than an individual stock. But to reiterate, there are times when the entire market experiences a strong move — usually downward. It's best to wait for the market to normalize before selling naked calls. Because the short calls are usually closer to the ATM strike price of the SPX, it's best to wait for the VIX to retreat to a value below 20.

As mentioned in the description and goals paragraph, the short call is often avoided because of the risk associated with being closer to the money than that of the short put. And, of course, there's a matter of the higher penalty associated with the higher strike price of the call as compared to much lower strike prices of far OTM puts.

Hands-On Activity

Scanning for a Trade

1. Scan the SPX price charts to determine the current trend. Your goal is to develop a neutral to bearish directional bias.

2. Put the VIX on your current watch list and check the value. Look for a neutral value of between 15 and 20. A high VIX value can add stress to a short SPX call just as it can the short SPX put and result in a margin call.

3. Select an option chain that expires inside 45 days. Shorter is even better for short calls to reduce risk. More time is the short option trader's enemy. (The example SPX option chain in figure 14–30 expires in 13 days. The premium is unusually high, as a VIX value of 27 existed when this screen was captured.)

Figure 14–30. SPX Short Call Option Chain

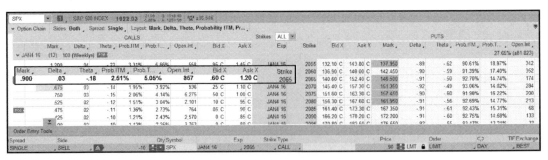

For illustrative purposes only.

4. Study the premium (Mark) values at strike prices having a Probability Touching at or below 5%. Consider the SPX 2065 call strike in the option chain pictured in figure 14–30. Notice how the Prob. ITM value is close to 2.5%.

5. The SPX option chain in figure 14–30 shows the current value of the SPX at 1922.03. The trader looks at the Open Interest

and the Probability ITM and Probability Touching of the call strike price of 2065. With only 13 days until expiration, a premium (Mark) value of 90 cents, a Bid to Ask spread of 60 cents, all indicators give the trader a "green light."

6. The trader can easily determine the profit of this trade without a risk profile. Ten contracts collect $900 of premium in 13 days, with an opportunity to potentially roll this position within a week.

7. Trade this short SPX put by performing the steps in the following Entry procedure.

Entry

1. Open the SPX option chain that expires within a few weeks. The JAN4 16 is selected.

2. Enter **ALL** in the Strikes text box in order to see the strike prices of far OTM calls.

3. Be sure the Spread **Single** is selected.

4. Scroll down to see the option chain values corresponding to the 2065 call strike price.

5. Click the **CALLS Bid** cell at the **2065** strike price. (See figure 14–30.) The trader knows how a rally in price to 2065 or above causes this trade to fail.

6. Check the order bar to verify it contains the entries similar to these:

SINGLE   SELL   –10   SPX   JAN4 16   2065   CALL   .90   LMT   LIMIT   DAY

7. Verify the setup. Then click **Confirm and Send**.

8. Evaluate the Order Confirmation information. If satisfactory, click **Send**.

9. Watch your P/L Open values and the price of the SPX. When the trade returns a profit of 30% to 60% or more close or roll the trade.

10. Continue selling far OTM (safe) SPX puts throughout the year. Consider the churning strategy by rolling or closing and then

trading again. (Remember that a roll charges a single brokerage commission, while closing and opening in two transactions require two commissions.) However, option exchange fees are based on the number of contracts traded (both one way and round trip). Recall how neither brokerage commissions nor exchange fees are charged when an option contract expires worthless.

Risks

The same risks exist with the short SPX call as with the short SPX put. First, a rally in the price of the SPX can threaten the strike price. This gives the trader a "gut check" and requires the position to be reduced or sold. In the case of a 10-contract short call, it's possible to buy to close half of the contracts to bring the account back into margin compliance. But simply holding on in hopes of a reversal can increase the cost to close the trade. The original 90-cent premium may exceed $5.00 in a matter of minutes and result in a 5:1 loss. When the trade begins to suffer from insufficient account margin, a margin call is sure to follow.

When a short SPX call is working, it must be carefully monitored. Never let it get away from you, as the penalty can be severe. But, if you are far enough OTM and watch it, you stand a good chance of making a substantial profit if the Probability ITM or Touching indicators prove to be correct.

Trade Management

1. This trade must be closely monitored once it is filled. If the price of the SPX remains within a narrow range or trends downward, your working trade remains safe. The trade's P/L Open value tells you when it's time to roll into another trade for more premium.

2. If the price of the SPX remains within a narrow range or trends downward, your working trade remains safe. If you have two or

more additional short SPX calls working simultaneously, you may let the first one expire worthless as long as it remains safely OTM.

3. Set an alert based on the price (Mark) of the SPX index. If the SPX begins to rally toward the strike price of your working short call, consider:

   a. Closing the trade and "taking your lumps."

   b. Buying an equal number of calls one or two strikes above to serve as insurance and to reduce margin stress.

   c. Close the trade and offset some of the loss by selling OTM SPX put contracts.

   d. Close the trade and sell farther OTM SPX calls to offset some of the loss.

   e. Do both c and d above.

4. Enter a GTC (good till canceled) Delta triggered stop. If Delta becomes "At or above .15" as viewed on the option chain, a buy to close order will trigger. (You can also enter a GTC Mark-triggered stop based on a Mark value of $\leq$ \$0.45.)

Possible Outcomes

1. This simple strategy has a limited number of outcomes. First, letting the far OTM SPX short call expire worthless is one possibility. This returns the intended \$900 in profit.

2. The OTM SPX short call remains well above the SPX ATM strike price. When the trade gains 30% to 60% in profit, the trader rolls the 2065 short call into another short SPX call which expires on a later expiration date for additional premium. By churning, the trader retains a profit of \$450 from the first trade and collects another \$900 in premium income when rolled (\$900 − \$450 to buy to close the first contract). By churning, the trader makes \$1,350 in roughly one week. This is half the time of what would be required to let the first trade expire worthless in approximately two weeks.

3. The price of the SPX rallies. The short call becomes within a 30% Probability ITM. The trader enters a buy to close order and exits the position. Then the trader begins to look for OTM short puts and farther OTM (safer) short calls to recover some of the money used to close the original short call.

4. The trader rolls the short call to the next expiration date and farther OTM to a much safer OTM strike price. By rolling, the trader recovers some of the money paid to close the original SPX short call.

5. The trader combines 3 and 4 above. Both the SPX short calls and puts are placed at safe OTM strike prices with even lower probabilities of becoming ATM. The price of the SPX rallies. The VIX rises above 30, and the current 2065 call is stressed. The brokerage issues a margin call to the trader. The trader examines the current margin and determines the current position, although still far OTM, is indeed stressed. A decision is made to close six contracts to bring the trade back into compliance. (As with the SPX put example, this outcome shows the importance of monitoring account margin to remain within SEC Rule 15c3–3 compliance and avoid the receipt of a margin call.)

Selling SPX Strangles

Structure
−*n* OTM CALLS, −*n* OTM PUTS (≤ 45 Days)

Description and Goals
This option strategy is a popular high risk, low reward premium selling spread. It combines the two strategies just described: selling SPX puts and selling SPX calls. Although low reward by definition (selling premium is considered low reward), thousands of dollars can be made on a single trade when the trader has a large brokerage account that permits selling 20 to even 100 contracts at a time.

When combined into a single spread, the two OTM short options each provide premium income. Summing both can be substantial. For example, collecting a $0.40 premium and a $0.30 premium returns $0.70 per share in total premium. Fifty contracts (5,000 shares) each earns $3,500 less transaction fees.

The SPX strangle permits traders to select farther OTM strike prices to decrease the risk of each leg. For example, moving several strikes farther OTM on the short put below and the short call above reduces the individual risk of each leg while collecting a reasonable amount in premium income. (You may also wish to consider a diagonal short strangle in which shorter term call options and longer term put options are used.)

In the event the value of the SPX begins to rise or drop, steps are taken to reduce the risk. As with the short OTM put or call, the threatened leg can be closed and the safe one retained. The individual legs are dealt with in the same way as an individual short put or short call.

While one leg may need attention, the opposite leg becomes even farther OTM and safer. For example, while closing, rolling, or perhaps buying a farther OTM call for insurance, the short put becomes safer and continues to work in the trader's favor. Of course the premium of the call leg may become more expensive than the combined premium received when the trade was originally entered. This is not an uncommon event, as any experienced option trader will tell you.

Setup Parameters

- Goal: Collect premium by selling far OTM puts and calls.
- Bias: Mostly neutral to slightly bullish or bearish (a premium collection strategy that shorts far OTM calls and puts)
- Debit/Credit: Substantial Credit
- Implied Volatility % ≥ 20% (Higher IV% increases premium. It is also an indicator of a possible move in the value of SPX index.)

- Chart Trend: Daily and hourly charts reveal a neutral to slight downtrend over the past few weeks.
- Momentum Oscillator: Oscillator values are within a neutral to a mildly overbought range.
- Keltner Channel: The ATR (14) envelope has been fairly flat for the past two weeks without any strong expansions or contractions from abnormally high trading volumes.
- Implied Volatility %: Between ≥ 20% and ≤ 50% (Higher IV% increases premium. It is also an indicator of a possible move in the value of SPX index.)
- VIX value: Most short SPX sellers prefer the VIX value to be close to 20; below 15 reduces available premiums; high volatility values introduce risk requiring the strike price to be moved to a strike price substantially farther OTM.
- Greeks (summing both sides): Delta: Slightly Positive; Theta: Positive; Vega: Negative
- Days till Expiry: ≤ 45 Days (Shorter is better providing sufficient premium. Longer expirations increase risk. Some traders use option contracts expiring in 56 days. Although the premiums can be substantially higher, farther OTM strike prices are selected for increased safety when using longer contract periods.)
- Net Premium Income (combined): ≥ $.80 (Even more is often possible based on the value of the VIX.)
- Probability ITM: ≤ 2.50% (Low Probability value is essential to remain OTM; always choose a safe OTM strike price. Probability Touching should be ≤ 3.00%.)
- Open Interest: ≥ 300 at selected strike price; total open interest @ all strikes > 50,000. (The financial indexes are characterized by excellent liquidity from high levels of open interest. Open interest is less with later times till expiration. Open interest increases as the time remaining until expiration draws nearer.)

- Bid to Ask spread: The value of the bid to ask spread on index options is normally wide. This provides a broader range of acceptable entry prices. Traders often adjust the Mark by several cents in their favor to improve the entry price of their trades.
- Risk Amount ≈1.0% of account equity (governed by premium and number of contracts)

How the Strategy Works

This is the most profitable premium collection strategy in use. The index premiums are among the best. Selling for premium income is a simple strategy and is quite easy to monitor. The range of ATM SPX strike prices can remain in a reasonably wide band above the short put and below the short call and still be acceptable. The trader's goal is for Theta to erode the premium as fast as possible while the SPX remains within the acceptable range of strike prices.

As the trade approaches the contract expiration date and the trade has garnered 30% to 70% in profit, the trade achieves success. Either a buy to close order is placed or one or both legs of the trade are rolled into a calendar spread profit. This requires the trader to buy to close the near term contracts and sell to open contracts that expire on the next expiration date for additional profit.

If the trade is threatened by a sudden price move, the threatened leg is dealt with while the opposite leg remains profitable and is even safer than when the trade was initially entered.

Hands-On Activity

Scanning for a Trade

1. Scan the SPX price charts to determine the current trend. Your goal is to develop a neutral to slightly bearish or bullish bias.
2. Put the VIX on your current watch list and check the value. Look for a neutral value of between 15 and 20. A high VIX value can add stress to short SPX puts and calls. This requires the

trader to select farther OTM strike prices for safety. Being too close invites trouble, including the possibility of a margin call. It may also influence the use of contracts having shorter expiration dates with higher values of Theta.

3. Select an option chain that expires inside 45 days. Shorter is even better to reduce risk, as more time gives the trade time to work against one of the short legs. (The example SPX option chain in figure 14–31 expires in 11 days. The premium is unusually high, as a VIX value of 27 existed when this option chain was captured.)

4. Study the premium (Mark) values at strike prices having a Probability Touching at or below 2.5%. Consider the SPX 1600 put strike and the SPX 2045 call strike in the option chain pictured in figure 14–31. Notice how the Prob. ITM values are both below 2.5%.

5. The SPX option chain in figure 14–31 shows the value of the SPX at 1916.71. The trader also examines the Open Interest to ensure there is sufficient liquidity. With only 11 days until expiration, a combined premium of $1.40 per share and narrow Bid to Ask spreads are well within the necessary trading parameters.

6. The trader can easily determine the profit of this trade without a risk profile. Ten contracts collect $1,400 of premium in 11 days, with an opportunity to potentially roll one or both positions in less than a week.

7. Trade this short SPX strangle by performing the steps in the following Entry procedure.

Entry
1. Open the SPX option chain that expires within a few weeks. The JAN4 16 is selected with eleven days till expiration.
2. Enter **ALL** in the Strikes text box in order to see the strike prices of both far OTM puts and calls.
3. Be sure the Spread **Single** is selected.

4. Scroll down to see the option chain values corresponding to the 2045 call strike price.

5. Click the **CALLS Bid** cell at the **2045** strike price. (See figure 14–31.) The trader knows how a rally in price to 2045 or above can cause this leg of the short strangle to fail.

6. Scroll up to see the option chain values corresponding to the 1600 put strike price.

7. Press and hold the **Ctrl** key and click the **PUTS Bid** cell at the **1600** strike price to add the second leg of the short strangle. (See figure 14–31.) The trader knows how a drop in price to 1600 or below can cause this leg of the short strangle to fail.

8. Check the order bar to verify it contains entries similar to these:

STRANGLE SELL –10 SPX JAN4 16 2045 CALL 1.40 LMT LIMIT DAY

STRANGLE SELL –10 SPX JAN4 16 1600 PUT CREDIT

9. Verify the setup. Then click **Confirm and Send**.

Figure 14–31. SPX Short Strangle Option Chain

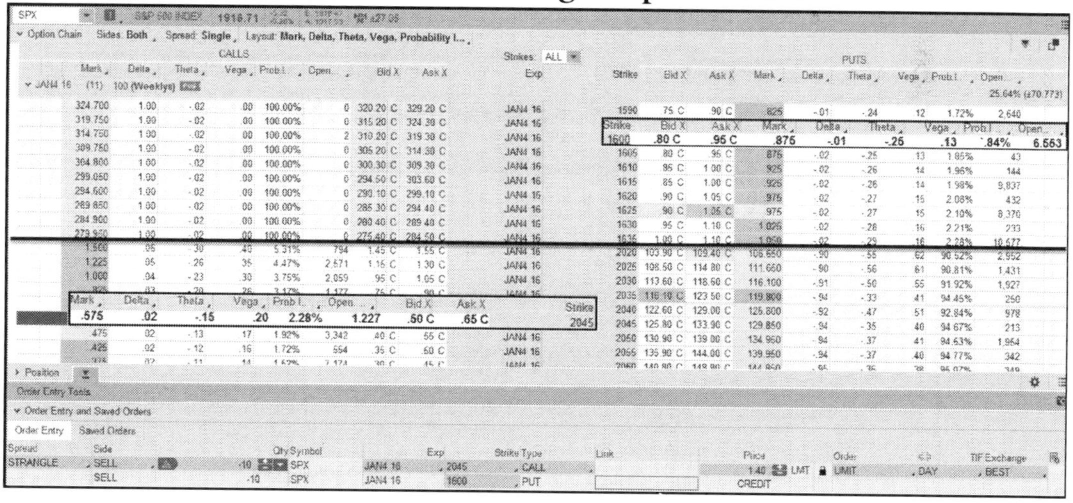

For illustrative purposes only.

10. Evaluate the Order Confirmation information. If satisfactory, click **Send**.

11. Watch your P/L Open values and the price of the SPX. When the trade returns a profit of 50% or more close or roll one or both legs of the trade for profit.

12. Continue selling far OTM (safe) SPX puts (and calls when safe) throughout the year. Consider the churning strategy by rolling or closing and then trading again. (Remember that a roll charges a single brokerage commission, while closing and opening in two transactions require two commissions. However, option exchange fees are based on the number of contracts traded (both one way and round trip). Recall how neither brokerage commissions nor exchange fees are charged when an option contract expires worthless.

Risks

It should be obvious that this trade carries risks identical to those described for the short SPX put and the short SPX call. Both require the strike prices to remain well OTM and between the two strike prices to avoid a margin call or, worse yet, being exercised. If the SPX index approaches either leg of this trade, and with moderate to high volatility (a VIX value at or considerably above 25), the premium required to close the short SPX call or put can reach several dollars. Due to this substantial expense, be sure to study and use the trade management techniques suggested in the next paragraph.

Trade Management

The short SPX strangle is a strategy that requires careful monitoring. Consider setting alerts based on the Mark, strike prices located some distance above the short put and below the short call, or Delta values that signal the probability of one or both of the strike prices becoming ITM. This is particularly important if you are required to be away from your computer.

Make it priority to install your brokerage's mobile app on your smartphone. Then spend the time required to learn how to use it. In particular, this trade in addition to the single short put and short call trades, require periodic attention. If nothing else, look in on them to ensure both short legs remain well OTM. If you detect an unwanted move in the value of the SPX toward a working short leg, have a plan to cope with that move.

Be ready to do one of the following:

- Close the threatened leg
- Roll the threatened leg up, i.e., farther OTM, within the same expiration date. Doing this can be costly since the threatened position is closer to the money with higher premiums.
- Roll it into a calendar spread at a farther OTM, safer strike price
- Buy an insurance leg one or two strikes farther OTM
- Sweat it out and hope the contract will not expire ITM or trigger a margin call. (Really? This is where you must take charge. Remember to trade what you see and never what you hope, feel, think, or hear.)

Possible Outcomes

1. This is also a reasonably simple strategy with a limited number of outcomes. First, letting the far OTM SPX short put and call expire worthless is one possibility. This returns the intended $1,400 in profit in eleven days.

2. Both the OTM SPX short call and put remain well OTM, with the SPX ATM strike price halfway between. When the trade gains 50% to 60% in profit, the trader rolls both legs into another short SPX strangle which expires on a later expiration date for additional premium. By churning, the trader retains a profit of $700 from the first trade and collects more premium income when rolled. By churning, the trader increases the amount of premium collected by making many more trades within the same amount of time.

3. The price of the SPX rallies. The strike price of the short call moves to within a 30% Probability ITM. The trader enters a buy to close order to exit the position. Then the trader begins to look for another OTM short put to recover some of the money used to close the short call. Meanwhile, the initial short put remains profitable.

4. The trader rolls the short call to the next expiration date and farther OTM to a much safer OTM strike price. By rolling, the trader may collect some premium from selling the longer term, farther OTM short call. The trader may also sell another short OTM put for additional premium income.

5. The price of the SPX drops. The short put becomes within a 30% Probability ITM. The trader enters a buy to close order to exit the position. Then the trader begins to look for another OTM short call to recover some of the money used to close the short put. Meanwhile, the initial short call is profitable.

6. The trader rolls the short put to the next expiration date and farther OTM to a much safer OTM strike price. By rolling, the trader recovers some of the money used to close the original SPX short put. The trader may also sell another short OTM call for additional premium income.

7. The trader combines 5 and 6 above. Both the SPX short puts and calls are placed at safe OTM strike prices with even lower probabilities of becoming ATM. The price of the SPX rallies. The VIX rises above 30, and the current 2045 call is stressed. The brokerage issues a margin call to the trader. The trader examines the current margin and determines that the current position, although still far OTM, is indeed stressed. A decision is made to close all or a portion of the short calls to bring the margin back into compliance. (To reiterate from the previous short call discussion, this outcome shows the importance of monitoring account margin to remain within SEC Rule 15c3–3 compliance to avoid the receipt of a margin call.)

Buying SPX Calls

Structure

+*n* OTM CALLS (≥ 90 days)

Description and Goals

As you should know by now, buying options always carries less risk than selling them. And the goal of entering a long option position is to buy low and sell high. When a trader's analysis and resulting bullish bias is correct, the long SPX call is highly profitable. And, as with all long options, buying a long SPX call is considered a low-risk strategy because the money spent buying premium is the entire amount put at risk.

When buying, the trader has no obligations beyond paying the premium required to enter the trade. Of course, buying premium is always directional, one of the downsides of long options. But the total premium paid is the entire risk. As you can see, SPX premiums are quite pricey, especially when selecting a strike price that's close to the SPX's ATM strike within a contract that expires in 90 or more days in the future.

If the SPX buyer's bias is correct and the SPX index increases by 5%, the long call can become either ATM or ITM. This depends on the strike chosen. When the call options are sold for more than originally paid, the trade can become quite profitable. Of course long options can also be exercised when ITM — the deeper the better for the option buyer.

Using a 100-point rally, which is quite achievable for a 2,000 point or higher index, the trader may pay $25/share or $2,500 per contract. With the SPX at 2,000, a 5%, 100-point rally could easily increase the underlying premium to $50/share for a 200% increase. Two contracts would return 200 × $50/share less the $10/share paid upon entry. This returns a net profit of $10,000. The value of Delta increases as the buyer's strike price moves closer to the money. This increases the premium value, so even more profit is likely.

If the buyer is wrong, the premium spent can be lost. Of course the buyer can recover some of the original premium spent by selling the option contracts prior to expiration. But the trader should not act prematurely, as there may still be enough time for the value of the SPX to reverse direction.

Many traders concentrate on credit spreads that sell premium. But some traders are quite successful using long LEAPS options. These trades work for a year or more in anticipation of a substantial increase in the price of the underlying. Option traders who bought long call LEAPS on stocks like NFLX, TESLA or AMZN made hundreds of thousands in profit. So buying calls can be quite rewarding, and LEAPS option contracts that do not expire for three years are readily available on the SPX, RUT, and NDX financial indexes.

Setup Parameters

- Goal. Buy a call that will become deep ITM and either sell it or exercise it for a profit.
- Bias: Extremely bullish (a premium buying strategy in anticipation of a strong rally in the value of the SPX index)
- Debit/Credit: Debit (May be expensive; the trader's bias must be correct to profit. The alternative is the loss of the premium spent at entry, which can be substantial.
- Chart Trend: Daily and hourly charts reveal basing near a historical support level with the possible formation of a price breakout into a rally.
- Momentum Oscillator: Presently beginning to reverse from a previous oversold condition
- Keltner Channel: The ATR(14) envelope presently narrow to reflect basing. The envelope appears to be expanding from fresh buying volume.

- Implied Volatility %: ≥ 20% ≤ 40% (Higher IV% increases premium. It is also an indicator of a possible move in the value of SPX index.)
- Implied Volatility % ≤ 20% (Lower IV% decreases the premium paid at entry. It is also an indicator of a possible breakout in the value of SPX index, as low IV% typically reverses direction and increases premium values.)
- VIX value: Most buyers of SPX calls prefer the VIX value to be between 11 and 13 to reduce the cost of premiums when the trade is entered.
- Greeks: Delta: Positive (≤ 20); Theta: Negative; Vega: Positive
- Days till Expiry: ≥ 90 Days (Even longer is better providing affordable premium. Longer expiration gives the trade longer to work; the effect of Theta is greatly reduced during the early months of this trade. Although longer times till expiration increase the cost of entry, the expectation is for the selected strike price of the long call to move either ATM or ITM.
- Net Premium Cost: ≥ $8.00 (Based on current VIX value; an increase in the VIX increases premiums.)
- Probability ITM: ≥ 10% (Low Probability value reduces cost of entry; because of the high cost of entry, this trade could remain OTM through expiration; select the lowest affordable call strike price to increase the probability of a successful outcome.)
- Open Interest: ≥ 300 at selected strike price; total open interest @ all strikes > 50,000. (The financial indexes are characterized by excellent liquidity from high levels of open interest. Open interest is less with later times till expiration. Open interest increases as the time remaining until expiration draws nearer.)
- Bid to Ask spread: The value of the bid-to-ask spread on index options is normally wide. This provides a broader range of acceptable entry prices. Traders often adjust the Mark by several cents in their favor to improve the entry price of their trades.
- Risk Amount ≈1.0% of account equity (governed by premium and number of contracts)

How the Strategy Works

This trade requires the trader to select an option chain that expires in more than 90 days. Even a longer time till expiry is better if the premium is affordable. This gives the long SPX call more time to work in the trader's favor. As suggested above, the trader must have a strong bullish bias. And, for the trade to return its potential in strong profit, the SPX must rally. Once the strike price of the call is either ATM or ITM, the trader can either sell the premium for a profit or exercise the option contract for additional income.

The strategy fails if the SPX drops in value. However, because the position continues to work for a long period of time, it is likely for this trade to succeed. If the SPX continues to move sideways until Theta begins to erode the value of the trader's position, the long call options may be sold to recover a portion of the premium that remains.

Hands-On Activity

Scanning for a Trade

1. Scan the SPX price charts to determine the current trend. Your goal is to develop a bias. If the SPX is oversold and ready to break out from a historical support level, you become bullish and expect the SPX to experience a rally.

2. Put the VIX on your current watch list and check the value. Look for a value of between 15 and 20. An unusually high VIX value increases the cost of entry, as volatility drives up the cost of premiums.

3. Select an option chain that expires in 90 or more days. This reduces the effect of Theta during the first few months of your working long call. Just as important, it gives your trade more time to work in your favor while maintaining most of the premium value. (The example SPX option chain in figure 14–32b expires in 108 days. The premium is slightly higher than normal with a VIX value of 25 when this option chain was captured.)

4. Study the premium (Mark) values at strike prices above the current ATM strike prices. Be sure they are affordable and fit your risk tolerance.

5. Consider the SPX 2075 call strike in the option chain pictured in figure 14–32b; the Mark displays a premium value of $15.10. There is ample Open Interest.

6. The trader decides to buy one contract (100 shares) at a cost of $1,510 plus transaction fees, which fits within the trader's risk tolerance.

7. Trade this long SPX call by performing the steps in the following entry procedure.

   CAUTION In spite of the fact that the SPX is usually stable, large price moves do happen. Figure 14–32a is an example of a 231 point move in just 30 days. Keep this in mind when selecting an OTM strike price.

Figure 14–32a. SPX Rallies $231.28 in 30 Days with VIX at 22.5

For illustrative purposes only.

Entry

1. Open the SPX option chain that expires in more than 90 days. The APR5 16 is selected with 108 days till expiration. 2.

   Enter **16** to **30** in the Strikes text box in order to see the ATM and slightly OTM call strike prices.

2. Be sure the Spread **Single** is selected.

3. Examine the premium values (Marks) and find one that fits within your budget. Choose the 2075 call with a premium value of $15.10.

4. Click the **CALLS Ask** cell at the **2075** strike price. (See figure 14–32b.) The trader knows how a rally in price to 2075 or above can cause this leg of the long call to deliver a substantial profit.

5. Edit the order bar to buy one contract. Then examine it to verify entries similar to these:

SINGLE   BUY   +1   SPX   APR5 16   2075   CALL   15.10   LMT   LIMIT   DAY

Figure 14–32b. Long SPX Call Option Chain

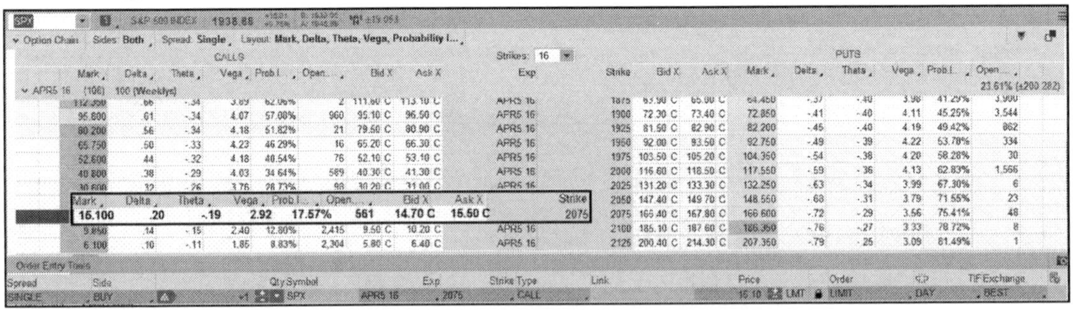

For illustrative purposes only.

7. Once verified, click **Confirm and Send**.

8. Evaluate the Order Confirmation information. If satisfactory, click **Send**.

Risks

The primary risk associated with long option contracts is the money spent when entered. The amount of money invested in premiums should always be within the trader's risk tolerance. And that tolerance should be based on a set of established trading rules. When buying options, those same trading rules require the use of long-term contracts. These should always be expiration dates of 90 days or more. However, there are cases when even 90 days may be short. Of course, prudent traders balance time and the cost of premium. As shown in this trade example, the premiums increased substantially with corresponding increases in the amount of time to expiration.

Trade Management

Watch P/L Open values an d the price of the SPX. If the SPX rallies according to plan:

- Close the trade when it returns a profit of 30% to 70% (70% of $1,510 returns a $1,057 profit).
- Exercise the option and collect the cash difference between the option strike price and the current SPX value. For example, if the SPX rallies to $2,100, your profit is $25 per share for 100 shares, or $2,500 less the original $1,510 premium totaling $990 less transaction fees.

If the SPX begins to drop in value contrary to your bias and you're within a few months of contract expiration, consider selling the 2075 call to recover some of the premium spent at entry (before Theta begins taking its toll).

To recover, examine some of the far OTM puts and calls. Consider selling SPX puts and/or calls for premium income. If successful, these trades can offset the initial cost of your long SPX 2075 call option.

Possible Outcomes

1. This simple, limited-risk strategy can be extremely successful when the trader's bias is correct. If a price rally ensues shortly after the long SPX call is sold, a 70% profit return around $1,100 is quite possible.

2. This trade can be discouraging when a trader must wait several months for the long 2075 call to become ITM. And, if the SPX remains below 2075, the trader may find it necessary to sell the 2075 call for slightly less than originally paid.

3. If the 2075 call becomes deep ITM, the wait becomes worthwhile. It is possible for this trade to return several thousand dollars if the 2075 call becomes deep ITM and is exercised.

4. If the trader is wrong about a pending breakout to the upside, and the SPX begins to drop, the maximum loss is the $1,510 plus the transaction fees spent at entry. An attribute of a long option contract is that there are rarely any surprises because option buyers do not have obligations.

5. The trader could use the remaining premium to roll the current 2075 position into a calendar spread at a later expiration date and a different strike price. This increases the cost of the second trade by adding more premium to the amount already spent. But, if the trader is confident in a strong rally to follow, using the remaining premium does offset the cost of moving the trade to another position. As mentioned in earlier descriptions, this action requires serious thought, as it may be another example of throwing good money after bad. It might also fit the ill-advised and abhorrent act of "revenge trading."

Buying SPX Puts

Structure

+n OTM PUTS ($\geq$ 90 days)

Description and Goals

Buying far OTM puts can be extremely expensive. Even when premiums are moderate, with a VIX value around 12 or 13, the strike price of the OTM long put may be a few hundred points below the current ATM strike price of the SPX. With an exceptionally strong bearish bias, a trader may be disappointed when examining the SPX option chains expiring in 90 or more days. The premiums are often well above $15 per share. And even worse, the value of Delta is somewhere between −.10 and −.15. This tells the trader how a 1-point drop in the SPX only increases the premium value by 10 to 15 cents.

Strike	Bid X	Ask X	Mark	Delta	Theta	Vega	Prob.I.	Open.Int

SPX — S&P 500 INDEX 1921.21 +30.93 +1.64% B 1920.30 A 1921.21 ±8.379
Option Chain   Sides: Both   Spread: Single   Layout: Mark, Delta, Theta, Vega, Probability I...

PUTS

Strike	Bid X	Ask X	Mark	Delta	Theta	Vega	Prob.I.	Open.Int
APR 16	(91)	100						23.70% (±183.025)
1600	14.90 C	15.80 C	15.350	-.10	-.28	1.72	13.22%	9,346
1610	15.70 C	16.60 C	16.150	-.11	-.29	1.78	13.82%	0
1620	16.60 C	17.50 C	17.050	-.11	-.30	1.85	14.47%	0
1625	17.00 C	18.00 C	17.500	-.12	-.30	1.88	14.80%	1,778
1630	17.50 C	18.30 C	17.900	-.12	-.31	1.91	15.11%	0
1640	18.40 C	19.40 C	18.900	-.13	-.32	1.99	15.83%	0
1650	19.40 C	20.40 C	19.900	-.13	-.32	2.06	16.55%	8,021
1660	20.40 C	21.50 C	20.950	-.14	-.33	2.13	17.30%	0
1670	21.60 C	22.60 C	22.100	-.15	-.34	2.20	18.10%	1
1675	22.10 C	23.20 C	22.650	-.15	-.34	2.24	18.50%	337
1680	22.70 C	23.70 C	23.200	-.15	-.35	2.28	18.89%	417
1690	24.00 C	25.00 C	24.500	-.16	-.35	2.36	19.78%	601
1700	25.30 C	26.30 C	25.800	-.17	-.36	2.43	20.67%	5,029
1710	26.70 C	27.70 C	27.200	-.18	-.37	2.51	21.61%	519

For illustrative purposes only.

SPX PUTS expiring in 91 days are shown in the preceding option chain. Notice the premium is nearly $20/share and the value of Delta is a meager −.13.

Of course the trader may sell a put and then buy a second put one or two strikes farther OTM. This finances the cost of the long put and in fact turns the trade into a credit spread.

But the trader is confident in his bearish bias. So what can be done with his/her strong bearish bias with SPX puts when they are much too expensive? This is where creativity may be called upon. Think about these possibilities:

1. Compare the premium values of the 1640 and 1650 strike prices — a $1.00 difference.
2. Buy option contracts on a more affordable SPX derivative such as the SPY ETF.

Number 1 is too obvious to ignore. The trader can buy a 1640 put and sell a 1650 put to receive a $1.00/share credit. Our trader decides to put on 50 contracts of each (5,000 shares). When filled, $5,000 is immediately deposited in the trader's account. Recognize the bottom half of an iron condor? Of course the trader can also look at far OTM calls for even more premium. This is an example of using an iron condor on a financial index. And because of the bearish bias, the trader might also sell OTM calls without buying the protective leg. However, because of the exposure to time and margin stress, settling for a traditional iron condor is more conservative.

Recall how complex trades having multiple legs are more difficult to fill. Adding the short and long calls to this trade adds complexity, making it more difficult to fill. Some traders become impatient and modify the trade by lowering the credit amount of their working orders. They are willing to give away dollars to get filled. Others reduce the complexity of the iron condor by breaking it down into two separate orders — one for the puts and the other for the calls. But don't give up on your working order prematurely. When properly priced and with sufficient liquidity (open interest and volume), the trade is likely to fill.

Whenever unfilled orders exist, be sure to check on them in the "Working Orders" section of your trading platform. If the market price changes, you can either adjust your price to the market price or cancel the order if you are not satisfied with the new market price.

Number 2 requires the trader to examine SPY option chains. Because it is a derivative of the S&P 500 index, its behavior will be similar but not identical. Trading activity on the SPX and the SPY is different because each has a different universe of traders. Of course there is a loose linkage between the behaviors of each. Both move in tandem, but the value of the SPY is approximately one tenth of the value of the S&P financial index.

Buying an SPY put closely resembles shorting stock in anticipation of a substantial price decline. The sample price chart in figure 14–33a illustrates how fast a financial index can drop in spite of the fact that it is comprised of 500 different stocks. But as you know, the market is driven by emotion. And emotion is often irrational. The SPX price chart shown in figure 14–33a illustrates the fact that the market can rally as fast as it falls. In five days the SPX dropped nearly $297, or more than fourteen percent. This example teaches traders to be cautious. Being greedy for more premium often pushes traders to the brink. It's always possible to suffer a substantial loss in a matter of minutes by getting too close to the money.

Ignoring long puts is similar to ignoring shorts on stocks. This is a common mistake made by novice traders. Most novices only go long on both stocks and options. They assume that trading means buying low and selling high. But buying puts and shorting stocks is just as profitable — perhaps more so because downward momentum is usually stronger and much faster. Remember, most novice traders have never shorted a stock and rarely use protective stops or targets. These are the people you want on the other side of your trades.

Setup Parameters

- Goal: Buy one or more SPX puts; sell for profit once the SPX drops in price.
- Bias: Extremely bearish (a premium-buying strategy in anticipation of a strong drop in the value of the SPX index)
- Debit/Credit: Substantial debit at entry
- Chart Trend: Daily and hourly charts reveal basing near a historical resistance level with the possible formation of a downward price breakout.
- Momentum Oscillator: Presently beginning to reverse from a previous overbought condition

- Keltner Channel: The ATR (14) envelope is presently narrow to reflect basing. The envelope begins to expand from fresh selling volume.
- Implied Volatility % ≥ 20% (Higher IV% increases premium. It is also an indicator of a possible move in the value of SPX index.)
- Implied Volatility % ≤ 20% (Lower IV% decreases the premium paid at entry. It is also an indicator of a possible selloff and drop in the value of SPX index. Low IV% typically reverses direction and increases premium values.)
- VIX value: Most buyers of SPX puts prefer the VIX value to be between 11 and 13 to reduce the cost of premiums when the trade is entered.
- Greeks: Delta: Negative; Theta: Negative; Vega: Positive
- Days till Expiry: ≥ 90 Days (Even longer is better providing affordable premium.) Longer expiration gives the trade longer to work in the buyer's favor; the effect of Theta is greatly diminished during the early months of this trade. Although longer times till expiration increase the cost of entry, the expectation is for the selected strike price of the long put to move much closer to the ATM strike price.
- Net Premium Cost: ≥ $8.00 (Based on current VIX value; an increase in the VIX increases premiums.)
- Probability ITM: ≥ 10% (Low Probability value reduces cost of entry, because of the high cost of entry, this trade can remain OTM through expiration. Select the highest affordable put strike price to increase the probability of a successful outcome.)
- Open Interest: ≥ 300 at selected strike price; total open interest @ all strikes > 20,000. (The financial indexes are characterized by excellent liquidity from high levels of open interest. Open interest is less with later times till expiration. Open interest increases as the time remaining until expiration draws nearer.)
- Bid to Ask spread: The value of the bid to ask spread on index options is normally wide. This provides a broader range of

acceptable entry prices. Traders often adjust the Mark by several cents in their favor to improve the entry price of their trades.

- Risk Amount ≈1.0% of account equity (governed by premium and number of contracts)

How the Strategy Works

For the purchase of put option contracts to return a profit, the price of the underlying equity must incur a substantial drop in price. An examination of the Delta value at the selected strike price shown in figure 14–33b tells the trader a long SPY 188 put costs $6.00 per share. With a Delta of −.41, a $1.00 drop in the value of the SPY increases the premium of the 188 put by $0.41 cents. As the price of the SPY drops, Delta's value at the 188 strike increases. A fast $2 to $3 drop increases the premium. Once the trader is satisfied with an increase of 30% to 70% in premium, the option can be sold. Of course the long SPY put can also be exercised, depending on the relative profits.

If the value of the SPX index increases during the life of this option contract, the remaining premium of the long 188 SPY put can be sold in order to recover some of the premium originally paid. This should be done within a month to six weeks prior to the April expiration date.

Hands-On Activity

Scanning for a Trade

1. Scan and compare the SPX and SPY price charts to determine the current trend. Your goal is to develop a bias. If the charts indicate a strong overbought condition that signals an imminent price reversal, especially when the prices are near a historical resistance level, you become bearish. You expect a strong price drop in the SPX index.

2. Put the VIX on your current watch list and check the value. Look for a value of between 15 and 20. An unusually high VIX value increases the cost of entry, as volatility drives up the cost of premiums.

3. Select an option chain that expires in 90 or more days. This reduces the effect of Theta during the first few months of your working long put. Just as important, it gives your trade more time to work in your favor while maintaining most of the $6.50 in premium value. (The SPY option chain in figure 14–33b expires in 92 days. The premium is slightly higher than normal with a VIX value of 24 when this option chain was captured.)

4. The trader decides to buy three contracts (300 shares) at a cost of $1,950 plus transaction fees. This amount fits within the trader's risk tolerance.

5. Trade this long SPY put by performing the steps in the following entry procedure.

Figure 14–33a. SPX Drops $296.94 in 5 Trading Days with VIX at 22.5

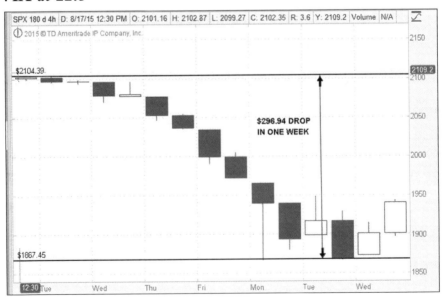

For illustrative purposes only.

Entry

1. Open the SPY option chain that expires in more than 90 days. The APR 16 (92) is selected with 92 days till expiration.
2. Be sure the Spread **Single** is selected.
3. Put **12** in the Strikes text box in order to see strike prices close to the money. Examine the 188 strike price row on the PUTS side of the option chain.
4. Notice the premium value (Mark) of 6.52. Determine the number of contracts to use to fit within your budget. Consider 3 contracts for a cost of $1,956 plus transaction costs.
5. Click the **PUTS Ask** cell at the **188** strike price as shown on figure 14–33b. The trader expects the SPY price to drop to 184 or less for an increase above the premium paid.
6. Edit the order bar to sell three contracts. Then examine it to verify entries similar to these:

SINGLE   BUY   +3   SPY   APR 16   188   PUT   6.50   LMT   LIMIT   DAY

Figure 14–33b. SPY Long Put Option Chain

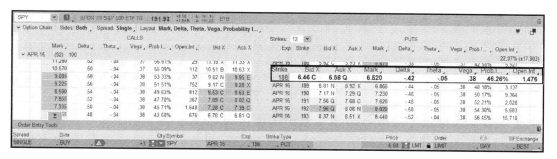

For illustrative purposes only.

7. Once verified, click **Confirm and Send**.
8. Evaluate the Order Confirmation information. If satisfactory, click **Send**.

Risks

The primary risk associated with long option contracts is the loss of the money spent on premium when the trade is entered. The amount of money invested in premiums should always be within the trader's risk tolerance. And that tolerance should be based on a set of established trading rules. When buying options, those same trading rules require the use of long-term option contracts. These should always expire in at least 90 days or more. However, there are cases when even 90 days may be short. Prudent traders balance time and the cost of premium. Premium increases markedly with a corresponding increase in the amount of time remaining until expiration.

Trade Management

Watch P/L Open values and the price of the SPY. If the value of the SPX index drops according to plan:

- Close the trade when it returns a profit of 50% or more (60% of $1,956 is $1,174), or
- Exercise the option and collect the cash difference between the option strike price and the current SPY value. For example, if the SPY drops to $180, your profit should approach $2,000 above your initial investment.

If the SPY begins to rally in value contrary to your bias and you're within a few months of contract expiration, consider selling the 188 put contracts to recover some of the premium spent at entry (before Theta begins increasing its toll on the remaining premium).

To recover, examine some of the far OTM puts and calls. Consider selling SPY puts and/or calls for premium income. If successful, these trades can more than offset the initial cost of your long SPY 188 put options.

Possible Outcomes

1. The desired outcome of this trade is for the trader's bias to be rewarded by a price decline in the SPY. If the SPY moves several dollars below the long 188 put, it should be sold.

2. If the SPY drops $10 or more below 188, exercise the option for a $10/share profit (minimum). A $10 drop returns $3,000 in SPY ETF share value less the original $1,956 spent at entry.

3. The SPY stalls and begins to rally. The underlying premium of the 188 strike declines in value. Sell to close the position to recover the remaining premium.

4. If number 3 above occurs, consider buying ATM or slightly OTM call options, but only if your analysis indicates a sustained rally. Otherwise, walk away and look for other trade opportunities.

What did you learn in chapter 14?

1. You must have the highest option trading _____ to enter uncovered trades.

2. Try the strategies presented in chapter 14 on _____. Find and use those strategies that work best.

3. The first step in scanning is to compile a _____ _____.

4. A _____ _____ shows possible profits or losses based on an option setup at different prices of the underlying stock for all days between trade entry and expiration.

5. The short call is a high-risk, _____ option trade. It includes the sale of an OTM call.

6. The cash-covered short put is a _____ option strategy.

7. A long call option trader is _____ and buys an ATM or slightly OTM call in anticipation of a price rally. The risk is the amount paid for the option contract(s).

8. A long put option trader is _____ and buys an ATM or slightly OTM put in anticipation of a price drop. The risk is the _____ _____ for the option contract(s).

9. A covered call is a _____ strategy in which the trader buys an _____ _____ and sells a farther OTM call in anticipation of a price _____.

10. The bull call spread is also called a _____ _____ or a call spread. It buys a call and sells a farther OTM call.

11. The bull put spread buys an OTM put and sells an ATM put in anticipation of a price _____.

12. The debit spread trader must have a strong _____ bias. The maximum loss is the cost of _____. The goal is for both call legs to become deep _____ (abbrev.).

13. An iron condor is a _____ _____ strategy. It includes a short put and a short call and a farther OTM long put and long call.

14. A _____ _____ includes one naked short put, one naked short call, and one long call.

15. The short strangle is a high _____, limited _____ premium collection strategy.

16. A covered short strangle includes the ownership of_____.

17. A long strangle anticipates a strong _____ _____ in either direction.

18. A long straddle is similar to a long strangle but it uses _____ put and call strike prices.

19. The strip is an unbalanced bearish strategy because it buys a _____ _____ more puts than calls.

20. The strap is a mirror image of the _____ strategy. More calls make it a _____ strategy.

21. A ratio spread uses a different _____ of either put or call contracts at two different strike prices.

22. Diagonal ratio spreads use different _____ _____.

23. The long guts option strategy buys an ITM put and an _____ call. Due to the high entry cost, this strategy requires a strong price breakout to be profitable.

24. The equity collar spread is often used as a _____ _____ strategy.

25. Butterfly spreads include four option contracts and are limited _____ and _____ strategies.

26. The calendar spreads are limited risk, limited reward,_____ bias strategies.

27. The diagonal spread is another _____ _____ that combines a long and a short call or a long and a short put. The long legs use _____ _____ option contracts than do the short legs.

28. A long ATM call and a short ATM put is an example of a _____ _____ stock.

29. A short ATM put and shorting 100 shares of stock is a _____ _____ _____.

30. A short ATM Put and long 100 shares of stock is a _____ _____ _____.

31. A long call and shorting 100 shares of stock is a _____ _____ _____.

32. The Gamma–Delta neutral spread is similar to a _____ _____ that includes shorting a stock to neutralize _____.

33. Three of the financial index symbols commonly shorted: _____, _____, and _____.

34. The _____ volatility index is used with the S&P 500 financial index.

35. If exercised, a financial index option contract must be settled in _____.

36. SPX strangles involve the sale of SPX _____ and an SPX _____.

37. The market falls _____ than it rises; put premiums are _____ than call premiums..

38. For a trader to buy SPX calls, the trader must have a strong _____ bias.

39. Instead of buying SPX puts, a trader may prefer to buy _____ puts due to the high cost of SPX options.

40. The trader may finance a long SPX put by _____ an SPX put.

15 TRADING OPTIONS ON FUTURES

Introduction to Futures

Futures were initially introduced in the market venues section of chapter 3. A partial list of commodity futures symbols are included in a table there. And there are many traders who specialize in buying and selling commodity futures on a daily basis. Many are speculators who make up about 20% of the futures trading volume. The other 80 percent are traded by producers and processors, sometimes called dealer/processors, involved in agricultural production, energy, precious metals, and currencies.

Futures have been in use for more than 2,000 years to create and maintain orderly markets in what would otherwise be unpredictable chaos. Without knowing what a crop or metal will be worth, farmers, miners, cereal makers, and smelters cannot plan their business.

If you are familiar with the cyclical nature of other futures markets, then you may want to consider one or more of these:

Grain Markets	Currencies
Metals	10-Year Treasuries
Oil and Gas	30-Year Bonds

Of course there are many other futures to consider. For example, options on gold futures, symbol GC, and light sweet crude oil, symbol CL, are just two of many futures that offer option contracts. Both of these include 100 shares per option contract. Although agricultural, energy, metals, and financial futures are interesting, this chapter uses the financial index futures, or e-minis, to illustrate how a futures option is traded. It also compares S&P 500 (SPX) index option chains to S&P 500 e-mini option chains. And you may find S&P e-mini futures options more suited to your budget and risk tolerance than trading directly on the SPX index, itself. This is because the e-mini futures contracts are smaller versions of standard futures contracts and are cheaper than trading the SPX, NDX, or RUT. While e-mini futures options provide excellent financial leverage, potential losses can also be greater when an underlying e-mini moves against a position.

As with all options, buyers have exercise rights, but not obligations. A buyer can buy or sell an e-mini option contract at the underlying price within the life of the option contract.

Because the cost of e-mini futures options is comparatively cheap, they are sometimes used as hedges. This is done to protect against potential losses on a position that is vulnerable to a major price change. A futures option can be used to offset the loss. For example, one or more long put options can hedge against a price drop. A long call option can hedge a rally against a short position. Both gain value while the hedged positions decline in value. The number of futures options held reduces the loss. Although rarely done, the hedge could actually return an overall profit, but of course, this would require a major investment in the hedging futures option.

Option chains available on any reasonable trading platform can be used to compare available premiums between the SPX and the ES. Having financial indexes and equivalent futures option chains presents traders with choices.

Before moving to an ES trading example, more information about underlying futures contracts is provided. Like option contracts, every futures contract has a fixed expiration date. A table of expiration months and their corresponding symbols is included in chapter 3. Because this chapter describes options on the e-mini futures, it's important to know that e-mini futures options expire quarterly. For convenience, the letters used as suffixes to indicate the contract expiration months for e-mini futures contracts are:

March = H	June = M	September = U	December = Z

Option contracts on the e-mini futures expire at the close of market on the Thursday prior to the third Friday of the above listed months.

The number of shares in e-mini option contracts varies. Instead of the usual 100 shares per option contract, an ES option contract includes 50 shares; the NQ is 30 shares, and the YM is only 5 shares. These fractional share quantities are usually shown on the corresponding order bar. For example, the ES order bar includes a 1/50 notation to indicate 50 shares per option contract. This reduces the premium per contract that is paid for entry. It also encourages more option spreads at lower costs.

NOTE Trading platforms use a variety of prefixes to designate index and future symbols. Among these are slash signs (/) and dollar signs ($). This book uses /ES to designate the S&P 500 e-mini future.

It is not necessary to add the month's expiration suffix unless the current futures contracts are approaching their quarterly expiration. Unless within two weeks of the futures expiration date, it is usually sufficient to enter the basic two-letter futures symbol without the suffix.

Of course trading platforms vary. Different symbols, such as $ES, are used to differentiate e-minis from other security symbols. The same is true for the contract expiration suffixes. The thinkorswim® platform uses the slash sign as its prefix as in /ES. To specify an expiration month, the symbol is followed by a dash and the month designator. /TF-H designates the Russell 2000 March e-mini contracts. Although the trading example used in this chapter uses the S&P 500 index e-mini, symbol ES, you can also enter identical trades using any of the valid e-mini symbols.

As discussed earlier in chapter 3, each e-mini uses *points* divided by *tics* to represent values in dollars and cents. For reader convenience, the point and tic values are listed again here:

Contract	e-mini Symbol	Point Value	Tics/Point	Tic Value
S&P 500	ES	$50	4	$12.50
NASDAQ	NQ	$20	4	$5
DJIA	YM	$5	1	N/A
Russell 2K	TF	$100	10	$10
S&P 400	EMD	$10	10	$1

As shown in the above table, four tics exist within each ES point. An ES point has a value of $50; each of the four ES tics have a value of $12.50. As you can see, a 2-tic change in the ES e-mini future is worth $25. If looking for a less expensive entry or risk, consider trading options on the YM, NQ, or perhaps the EMD (the S&P 400 Mid Cap) as premiums are typically less costly for these lower priced e-minis.

Because American-style option contracts can be exercised at any time prior to expiration, this feature bodes well for trading options on futures. Within a straightforward futures contract, the buyer and seller are both obligated to complete the transaction on the specified date at the price set in the contract. Trading options on futures puts this requirement at arms-length. The buyer of an option is not obligated to comply with the requirements of a futures contract. But the seller is obligated to respond with cash to settle the option contract in the same way index options are settled.

Most futures speculators buy and sell futures contracts much like shares of stock are bought and sold. Bracketed trades with limit entries, protective stops and profit targets are common. Futures trader accounts are settled at the end of each trading day to reflect the day's transactions. But if a futures buyer allows a futures contract date to slip by without exiting, title to the underlying asset is acquired at the prevailing market price. The futures buyer may wind up renting a truck and driving it to a rail siding to take delivery of a cattle car full of livestock. According to one active futures trader, this actually happens.

Although e-mini contracts typically expire on different dates from those of option contracts, people who trade options on futures need only be concerned with the option contract expiration date. The trader is either buying or selling option premium based on the same price charts and using similar analytics and technical studies used with both stocks and ordinary stock options.

When setting up an option trade on an e-mini future, examine the values within the e-mini option chains. Look at Open interest, Delta, Vega, Theta, and Probability ITM/Touching. These are all available and work in the same way as they do with stock and financial index options.

However, do not assume the value of an e-mini future and the corresponding financial index that represents that e-mini is identical. To determine the current values of each, put both the financial index and the e-mini future symbols on the same watch list. An example that compares index to e-mini futures values is shown in figure 15–1.

Figure 15–1. Index to e-mini Value Comparisons

Symbol ▾		Last	Net Chng	ATR	Impl Vol ⚙
VXN		29.13	+3.17	3.08	N/A
VXD		25.57	+3.07	3.55	N/A ⊟
VIX		27.02	+3.07	3.33	117.06%
SPX		1880.33	-41.51	36.15	26.94%
RVX		29.65	+2.75	2.54	97.72%
RUT		1007.72478	-17.94178	23.02	29.66%
NDX		4141.0822	-131.8848	96.72	29.17%
/YM-Z		15916.17	-344.06	339.35	50.33%
/YM-U		N/A	N/A	loading	N/A
/YM-M		15899.12	-344.24	339.45	36.92%
/YM-H		15900.01	-342.32	339.5	41.03%
/YM[H6]	⏱	15937	-344.00	338.0	26.13%
/TF-Z		987.47	-12.26	27.76	54.54%
/TF-U		N/A	N/A	loading	N/A
/TF-M		970.42	-12.44	27.97	41.13%
/TF-H		971.31	-10.52	28.03	45.24%
/TF[H6]	⏱	1008.3	-12.20	26.8	34.55%
/NQ[H6]	⏱	4145.75	-111.75	109.56	29.01%
/ES-Z		1855.67	-38.06	42.9	50.03%
/ES-U		N/A	N/A	loading	N/A
/ES-M		1838.62	-38.24	43.11	36.61%
/ES-H		1839.51	-36.32	43.16	40.73%
/ES[H6]	⏱	1876.50	-38.00	41.89	25.53%
$DJI		15988.08	-390.97	295.22	N/A

For illustrative purposes only.

This chart was captured during a substantial market selloff. This is reflected by the declines in the values of all indexes and underlying e-mini contracts. As expected, the four corresponding volatility indexes (VXN, VXD, VIX and RVX) all reflect increases in value. Unusually strong selling occurred with the DOW dropping by 400 points during the day.

Having the e-mini values on a watch list provides an early snapshot of trading sentiment. Although this is not always an accurate indicator of how the market will proceed during normal trading hours, it does signal the sentiment of futures traders. However, as trading volumes ramp up during normal trading sessions, particularly when several large institutional orders are waiting overnight to fill, early morning futures trends may reverse direction when the market opens.

This can cause a substantial shift in the direction of the market. Although close, the e-mini values typically lead or lag the index values by several points. At night, the SPX and RUT remain constant, while the e-minis may see significant price fluctuations from strong overnight trading activity.

Trading Options on ES e-mini Futures

The e-mini futures options are quite similar to financial index options. The most commonly traded e-mini future is the ES (S&P 500 index future). Weekly option contracts are the most popular because of the lower risk. (As you know by now, less time minimizes risk.) There are several benefits to trading weekly options on ES e-mini futures. These include:

- The short duration of weekly options reduces risk.
- Trading options on futures does not require a trader to open a futures account.
- Pattern day trader minimums do not apply to trade options on e-mini futures.

Of course some drawbacks also exist. These are:

- The shorter times till expiration limit premiums.
- It is more difficult to find high return trades that meet your risk tolerance.
- It can be more difficult to have a limit order filled due to intense competition.

Setting up to trade an option on the ES e-mini requires shorter interval charts. Often you may enter and exit within the same day, although most option traders use swing trades by entering on day one and exiting a few days to a few weeks later when planned profits become available. But many intraday trades are made on futures options, especially the ES.

Begin by evaluating price charts starting with the 30-minute interval and progressing to a 1-minute chart. When examining an e-mini future on a trading ladder, the trading activity is usually quite volatile. In short, futures are more active than their underlying financial indexes. This results in the e-mini futures prices being more volatile than their corresponding financial indexes.

Many traders consider the futures market to be "casino-like." This is because many of those who regularly trade e-mini futures contracts are day traders. Both e-mini futures traders and day traders who work with stocks and ETFs are constantly scanning for scalping opportunities. Scalps are sought to provide a series of incremental profits by jumping in and out of dozens of trades over the course of a few hours. Day traders constantly buy long and sell short. Their entries usually depend on the price fluctuations shown on short-interval charts.

Day traders often have several trades working simultaneously on stocks, ETFs, and/or one or two e-mini future contracts. Most day traders suppress the order confirmation dialog. This dispatches their orders to their brokers as soon as they click their trading ladder with a sell or buy order. As mentioned, most use limit orders bracketed by stops and profit targets. Many day traders watch two to four charts at the same time with their hands on their mouse buttons, moving from one symbol to another, poised to enter a bracketed limit order, slide a working stop or limit entry a few tics up or down, or exit when the market moves either in favor of or against one of their working positions. While this resembles a chaotic juggling act, many e-mini futures traders adapt to the chaos and become talented jugglers.

Why Trade Futures?

When a futures contract is bought by a speculator, the speculator's bias is bullish. The goal, of course, is to buy a futures contract and then sell it for more than originally paid. When bearish, the speculator's goal is to sell one or more futures contracts and then buy them back for less than originally paid. Either works quite nicely. But there are some substantial differences between buying and selling stocks or options and trading futures.

Like options, futures also have excellent financial leverage. And they can be either bought or sold using limit or market orders. As mentioned earlier in this chapter, futures traders use bracketed trades with protective GTC stops and targets. For roughly 5% to 10% in account margin, a futures trader can control 100% of one or more futures contracts. For example, a futures trader can control $1,200 worth of gold for roughly $60 in account margin. This means gold worth $60,000 can be controlled by $3,000. A small 2% change in price (short or long) can return the trader $1,200 — a 40% profit. The fact that futures points are divided fractionally into tics, the trader can trade in smaller increments. (Even better, the number of shares bought and sold when trading options on futures are smaller yet.)

Unlike stock traders who must use account margin to short a stock, futures traders do not require additional margin when shorting (selling) futures contracts. This eliminates that pesky interest on margin unlike that required when shorting stocks. However, because of the amount of financial leverage available to futures traders, substantially more account margin is used in the futures realm than that of options traders.

But be aware that futures transaction fees are higher than that of stock or index options. You will pay roughly $2.00/contract when entering and again when exiting a futures option trade. Due to the higher overhead, some conservative traders prefer to let futures option contracts expire worthless to avoid the overhead of a round-trip transaction. Therefore, be sure to trade enough contracts to reduce the overhead as a percentage of the overall profit collected.

Futures account margin insures the broker or clearinghouse against losses from a trader's open futures position. When volatility increases,

Figure 15–2. e-mini Index Futures Margins

Contract	Symbol	Exchange	Full Margin	Day Margin
E-Mini NASDAQ	NQ	CME	$4840	$400*
E-Mini S&P	ES	CME	$5060	$400*
E-mini S&P MIDCAP 400	EMD	CME	$7370	$500
Mini Dow	YM	CME	$4290	$400*
Mini Russell 2000	TF	ICE	$5610	$500*

the futures trader's account may become stressed in the same way an SPX option contract position can stress a trader's account by an increase in the value of the VIX. This makes careless futures traders susceptible to margin calls. To see current margin requirements, you can view the CME/Chicago Board of Trade/NYMEX Company's website using the link: www.cmegroup.com/clearing/margins/. This link shows the impressive breadth of futures. A much more useful source for just e-mini index futures is found at http://www.globalfutures.com/accounts/margins.asp. A list of optionable e-minis is shown in figure 15–2.

Trading Option Contracts on an e-mini Future

Structures
+/–n PUTS, +/–n CALLS (≤ 45 days)

Description and Goals

Options are traded on the e-minis listed in figure 15–2 in precisely the same way as they are traded on stocks and ETFs. Option traders who use option strategies to collect premium use the identical strategies as on stocks and index options. Bullish traders can use bull call or bull put spread options on e-mini futures. And, of course, bearish traders may sell bear put spreads or short calls. When e-mini premiums are high, iron condors may also be used. The primary limitation to trading option contracts on futures is the same as trading options on financial indexes. This includes the trader's account size and the corresponding amount of available account margin.

Before trading options on futures, a pair of option chains is examined. The SPX option chain shown in figure 15–3a expires in 30 days, while the ES option chain in figure 15–3b expires in 31 days. Notice the differences in premium values. Also compare the Theta, Vega, and Probability of Touching values.

The spread between the Bid and Ask values at the 1200 PUTS rows is greater on the ES option chain. The Mark of the ES offers 33.3% more premium than that of the SPX. The Open Interest at the ES's 1200 put is roughly 40% of the SPX's Open Interest. But at 6,125, the liquidity of the 1200 ES contracts are certainly well within the tolerance of our trading rules. Looking at the ES's Probability of Touching, it is only 1/100th higher than that of the SPX. This is insignificant.

Figure 15–3a. The SPX (S&P 500 Index) Option Chain (30-Day Contract)

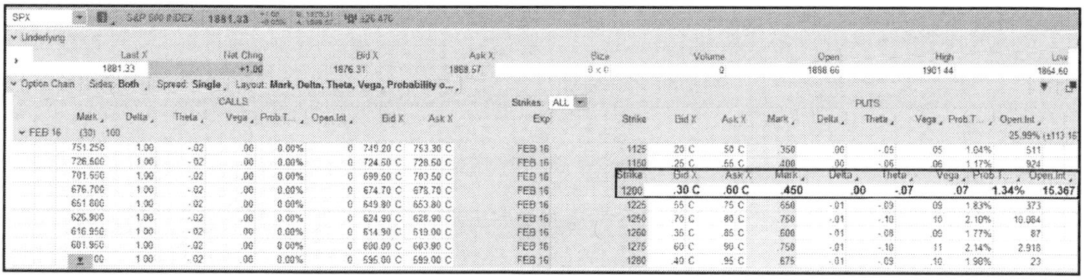

SPX | S&P 500 INDEX 1881.33

Underlying

Last X	Net Chng	Bid X	Ask X	Size	Volume	Open	High	Low
1881.33	+1.00	1876.31	1888.57	0 x 0	0	1888.66	1901.44	1864.60

Option Chain Sides: Both, Spread: Single, Layout: Mark, Delta, Theta, Vega, Probability o...

Strikes: ALL

CALLS Mark	Delta	Theta	Vega	Prob.T...	Open.Int	Bid X	Ask X	Exp	PUTS Strike	Bid X	Ask X	Mark	Delta	Theta	Vega	Prob.T...	Open.Int
FEB 16 (30) 100																	25.99% (±113.16
751.250	1.00	-.02	.00	0.00%	0	749.20 C	753.30 C	FEB 16	1125	.20 C	.50 C	.350	.00	-.05	.05	1.04%	511
726.600	1.00	-.02	.00	0.00%	0	724.50 C	728.50 C	FEB 16	1150	.25 C	.55 C	.400	.00	-.06	.06	1.17%	924
701.550	1.00	-.02	.00	0.00%	0	699.60 C	703.50 C	FEB 16	Strike	Bid X	Ask X	Mark	Delta	Theta	Vega	Prob.T...	Open.Int
676.700	1.00	-.02	.00	0.00%	0	674.70 C	678.70 C	FEB 16	**1200**	**.30 C**	**.60 C**	**.450**	**.00**	**-.07**	**.07**	**1.34%**	**15,367**
651.800	1.00	-.02	.00	0.00%	0	649.80 C	653.80 C	FEB 16	1225	.55 C	.75 C	.650	-.01	-.09	.09	1.83%	373
626.900	1.00	-.02	.00	0.00%	0	624.90 C	628.90 C	FEB 16	1250	.70 C	.80 C	.750	-.01	-.10	.10	2.10%	10,084
616.950	1.00	-.02	.00	0.00%	0	614.90 C	619.00 C	FEB 16	1260	.35 C	.85 C	.600	-.01	-.08	.09	1.77%	87
601.950	1.00	-.02	.00	0.00%	0	600.00 C	603.90 C	FEB 16	1275	.60 C	.90 C	.750	-.01	-.10	.11	2.14%	2,918
.00	1.00	-.02	.00	0.00%	0	595.00 C	599.00 C	FEB 16	1280	.40 C	.95 C	.675	-.01	-.09	.10	1.98%	23

For illustrative purposes only.

Figure 15–3b. ES (S&P 500 e-mini Future) Option Chain (31-Day Contract)

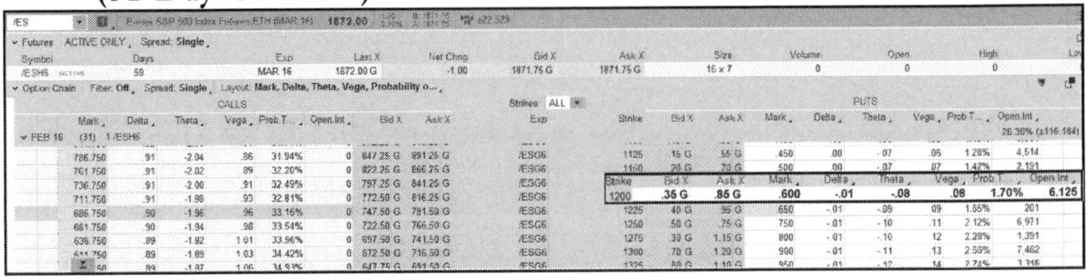

For illustrative purposes only.

The e-mini futures are always more volatile than the underlying index to which they belong. As mentioned, this is because a huge number of day traders spend the entire day scalping the e-mini futures contracts. In contrast, mostly swing traders buy and sell options on the financial indexes. These traders hold their positions for days, weeks, and even months. This greatly reduces the relative volatility between the two instruments.

Setup Parameters

- Goal: Sell for premium income; either close the trade upon acceptable earnings, or let it expire worthless to avoid transaction fees. Then trade again.
- Bias: Neutral to bullish (a premium-collection strategy that shorts far OTM puts)
- Debit/Credit: Credit
- Chart Trend: Neutral to a slight uptrend
- Momentum Oscillator: Slightly oversold near a historical support level
- Keltner Channel: An expansion in the ATR(14) envelope to reflect an increase in buying volume
- Implied Volatility % ≥ 20% (Higher is even better for increased premium income.)
- VIX value: Best when close to 20; below 15 reduces available premiums; higher introduces risk requiring the strike price to be farther OTM.

- Greeks: Delta: Negative; Theta: Negative; Vega: Positive
- Days till Expiry: ≤ 20 Days (Short times are better providing sufficient premium.) As you will see in figure 15–3c, the last / ES weekly option expires on the last day of the month, designated by (EOM).
- Net Premium Income: ≥ $0.40 (More is possible based on the value of the VIX.)
- Probability ITM: ≤ 4.00% (Essential to remain OTM; always choose a safe OTM strike price, perhaps even ≤ 2.5%. Probability Touching should be ≤ 5.00%.)
- Open Interest: ≥ 300 at selected strike price; total open interest @ all strikes > 20,000. (The financial index futures are characterized by excellent liquidity as indicated by high levels of open interest.)
- Bid to Ask spread: The value of the bid to ask spread on index options is normally wide. This provides a broader range of acceptable entry prices. Traders often adjust the Mark by several cents in their favor to improve the entry price of their trades.
- Risk Amount ≈1.0% of account equity (governed by premium and number of contracts)

How the Strategy Works

For a highly profitable options strategy, the structure of a single short ES put is quite simple. The trader's goal is to sell a single put located at a strike price that is unlikely to become ATM throughout the life of the selected option contract. This is why short times till expiration are used with this strategy. Under normal circumstances, and when the VIX volatility index is close to 20, this strategy usually works quite well.

Because the ES's underlying S&P 500 index averages the stock prices of 500 large companies like Facebook, Netflix, Amazon, etc., the value of the index is slower to move than most individual stocks. But as mentioned above, the ES moves faster than the SPX because the ES futures traders are constantly scalping the ES for small profits.

Still, while some of the underlying stock prices rally, others decline to maintain stability and to mitigate risk. And as every trader knows, the entire market sometimes sees significant downward or upward movement. These are times when it's best to wait for the market to normalize, when the value of the VIX returns to 15 or 20.

Most traders are only too aware of the fact that the market typically falls much faster than it rises. This adds more risk to puts than to calls. You can verify this by looking at practically any option chain. Go the same number of strikes OTM and compare the put and call premiums. The put premiums are higher than the call premiums. This is why many traders prefer short puts over short calls. They are able to choose strike prices that are much farther OTM for better premium that have adequate premiums.

Hands-On Activity

Scanning for a Trade

1. Scan both the SPX and ES price charts to determine the current trend. Your goal is to develop a neutral to bullish directional bias. Be sure to use chart intervals ranging from a day to 5 minutes. If you have more than one monitor, also look at a 1-minute chart.

2. Put the VIX on your current watch list and check the value. Look for a neutral value of between 15 and 20. A high VIX value can add substantial stress to a short ES put in the same way as it can with an SPX put. However, the short ES's are not as susceptible to stress as the SPX because of the smaller positions. But being too aggressive can result in a margin call. This is especially true if your ES strike price is too close to the current value of the S&P 500 index.

3. Select an option chain that expires inside 20 days. Shorter is even better because it's safer. (The example ES option chain in figure 15–3c expires in 9 days. The premium is unusually high, as a VIX value of 27.59 existed when this screen was captured.)

4. Study the premium (Mark) values at strike prices having a Probability ITM at or below 3%. Consider being even farther OTM if using longer times till expiration. Looking at the ES 1460 put strike in the option chain pictured in figure 15–3c, notice the Prob. Touching value is 2.01%. Of course even lower Prob. Touch value is always safer. (If using Prob. ITM rather than Prob. Touch, select strike prices with Prob. ITM values below 2.0%.)

5. With the ES currently at 1853.50, the trader decides upon the 1460 put with an attractive premium of $0.55 per share. (The Bid to Ask spread is quite good at only $0.15.)

6. The trader can easily determine the profit of this trade without a risk profile. Remember there are 50 shares per contract as shown by 1/50 on the option chain. Also, this trade expires at the end of month, designated by (EOM).

7. Ten ES option contracts returns a profit of $250 from 50 × 10 × $0.50. As long as the ES stays above the 1460 strike price, the trade remains profitable.

8. The trader will either close the trade when the premium drops to $0.25 or let it expire worthless if other trades are working at the same time. Of course the trader may decide to roll the trade into a calendar spread that includes a short ES put option expiring at a later date. All of these might be considered when the premium drops below $0.25.

9. Trade this short ES put by performing the steps in the following Entry procedure.

Entry

1. Open the ES option chain that expires within two weeks. The JAN 16 (9) is selected. This contract expires in 9 days at the end of the month (EOM).

2. Be sure the Spread **Single** is selected. Then expand the JAN 16 (9) option chain.

3. Click the **PUTS Bid** cell at the **1460** strike price. (See figure 15–3c.) Of course the trader knows how a drop in price to 1459.99 or below may cause this trade to fail.

4. Check the order bar to verify it includes entries similar to these:

SINGLE   SELL   –10   /ESH6 1/50   JAN4 16 (EOM)   1460   PUT   .55   LMT   LIMIT   DAY

Figure 15–3c. Selling 10 ES e-mini (S&P 500 Index) 1460 PUT Options

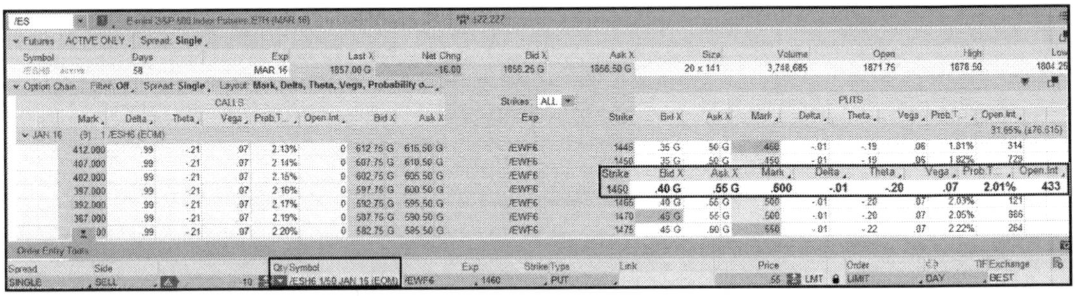

For illustrative purposes only.

5. Verify the setup. Then click **Confirm and Send**.

6. Evaluate the Order Confirmation information. If satisfactory, click **Send**.

7. Watch your P/L Open values and the price of the SPX. When the trade returns a profit of 30% to 70% or more close or roll the trade.

8. Continue selling far OTM (safe) ES puts throughout the year. Consider the churning strategy by rolling or closing and then trading again. (Remember that a roll charges a single brokerage commission, while closing and opening in two transactions require two commissions. However, option exchange fees are based on the number of contracts traded (both one way and round trip). Recall how neither brokerage commissions nor exchange fees are charged when an option contract expires worthless.

Risks

Two possible risks exist with the short ES put trade. The first is becoming ITM by one cent. But if the ES drops far below 1460, the cash required to settle the trade could be substantial. In this respect, this is a low reward, high risk trade. But it is not as risky as trading directly on the SPX due to the lower cost of entry and premium values.

In any case, when a short ES put is working, the trader must pay close attention to the trade and the margin used to ensure that sufficient account margin exists to prevent a margin call. Unlike a short put on the SPX, margin requirements are considerably smaller. In any case, always stay in touch with any uncovered option trade, regardless of the underlying security. And periodically check on your available account margin. Finally, high premiums often tempt traders to be "piggish." They sell too many contracts, get too close to the ATM strike price for more premium, or both. This is an excellent way to see account margin evaporate followed up by a margin call.

Trade Management

1.   This trade must be closely monitored once it is filled. If the price of the ES remains within a narrow range or trends upward, your working trade remains safe. The trade's P/L Open value tells you when it's time to roll into another trade for more premium income.

2.   If the price of the ES remains within a narrow range or trends upward, your working trade remains safe. If you have more short ES puts working simultaneously, you may let the first one expire worthless as long as it remains safely OTM. But don't pass up an opportunity to roll that trade into a new contract for more premium income.

3.   Set an alert based on the price (Mark) of the ES index. If the ES begins to drop toward your strike price, consider one of the following:

a. Close the trade and "take your lumps."

b. Buy an equal n umber of puts one or two strikes below to serve as insurance, and to reduce margin stress.

c. Close the trade and offset some of the loss by selling OTM ES call contracts.

d. Close the trade and sell farther OTM ES puts to offset some of the loss. e.Do both c and d above.

4. Enter a GTC (good till canceled) Delta-triggered stop. If Delta becomes "At or above −.15" as viewed on the option chain, trigger a "buy to close" order. (Depending on your trading platform, you may be required to reset the trigger price offset to 0.0.)

Possible Outcomes

1. This simple strategy has a limited number of outcomes. First, letting the far OTM ES short put expire worthless is one. This returns the intended $500 in profit.

2. The OTM ES short put remains well below the ES ATM strike price. When the trade gains 60% in profit, the trader rolls the 1460 short put into another short ES put which expires on a later expiration date. The trader collects another round of premium. By churning, the trader retains a profit of $300 from the first trade, pays $200 to close it, and collects another $500 in premium income when rolled. Churning earns $700 in roughly one week. This is half the time of what would otherwise be required to let the first trade expire worthless in approximately 9 trading days (almost two weeks).

3. The price of the ES drops, and the short put becomes within a 30% Probability ITM (near a Delta −.25 to −.30). The trader enters a buy to close order to exit the position. The trade suffers a loss.

4. The trader studies OTM short ES puts that exist farther OTM (safer) at later expiration dates. The trader's goal is to recover

some of the money that must be used to buy back the original short ES put. Based on the trader's findings, the short put is rolled into the next expiration date and farther OTM to a safer strike price. By rolling the trader recovers enough money to offset the cost of closing the original ES short put position.

5. The price of the ES drops. The VIX rises above 30 and the current 1460 put is stressed. The brokerage issues a margin call to the trader. The trader examines the current margin and determines the current position, although still far OTM, is indeed stressed. A decision is made to close 5 contracts to bring the trade back into compliance. (This outcome shows the importance of monitoring your account margin to remain within SEC Rule 15c3–3 compliance to avoid the receipt of a margin call.)

6. The price of the ES drops by some 25 points 1856 to 1825. The VIX rises above 30. The trader is aware that the 1460 put is about to become stressed. Before the brokerage issues a margin call and withdraws trading permission, the trader studies the current position. Although the 1460 put is still far OTM and unlikely to ever become ITM, the trader decides to buy ten 1450 put contracts two strikes below. This reduces margin stress and brings the trade back into SEC Rule 15c3–3 compliance.

What did you learn in chapter 15?

1. Futures have been in use for more than _____ years.
2. Many traders buy and sell _____ _____ on a daily basis.
3. Excluding speculators, futures contracts are traded between producers and _____.
4. Financial index futures are called the _____ futures.
5. Options on futures are _____ _____ than options on the underlying indexes.
6. Options on futures are sometimes used as a _____ to offset loss.
7. Long put e-mini options are used to hedge against a drop in the price of the corresponding _____ _____.
8. Hedges _____ _____ as the hedged security loses value.
9. The symbol for the SPX futures contracts is _____.
10. The e-mini future contracts expire in March, June, _____, and _____.
11. Future contracts use alphabetical _____ to represent contract expiration months.
12. The e-mini futures contracts are _____ style.
13. The symbol NQ-M represents the _____ e-mini futures contract that expires in _____.
14. The symbol for the S&P 400 mid-cap futures contracts is _____.
15. Most futures speculators buy and sell futures contracts much like shares of _____.
16. There are _____ shares per ES option contract.
17. The short duration of weekly options reduces _____.
18. Pattern day trader minimums _____ _____ apply to trade e-mini options.
19. Trading a short put on the ES e-mini future is similar to trading a short put on the SPX _____.
20. The market price of the SPX and the underlying ES e-mini future may be _____.

16 Trading Options on Small Accounts

● ● ● ● ● ● ●

Background

This chapter was suggested by an active options trader who regularly trades options on five- and six-figure brokerage and retirement accounts. To comply with risk management rules, the trades were initially limited to one or perhaps three or four option contracts. In spite of using smaller trades, the strategies and trading frequency are providing impressive returns on investment. It's only a matter of time until these small accounts will support the ability to trade more contracts for increased income. Eventually, the trader's patience and consistency may lead to financial independence.

There are a number of option traders who earn seven figures in income each and every year. Karen Supertrader and Chuck Hughes, both mentioned in the preface and chapter 1, are only two such traders. In fact, several high-income option traders collaborated with the author of this book. But according to most, they started with small accounts. It took them several years of study, high-frequency trading, churning, rolling, and conservation to grow their accounts to seven figures. One trader mentioned how he began with a basket of high-yield dividend stocks. These were used to collateralize option trades. He called it "double-dipping," i.e., using the same collateral to generate two sources of income. But regardless of what he called it, it obviously worked quite well.

In this final chapter we examine eight option strategies that are often used with smaller accounts. Several of these strategies, especially the covered call, short put, iron condor, and butterfly, were used by my friend. All the strategies included here are described in extensive detail within the hands-on activities of chapter 14. Although the long LEAP call didn't receive separate, stand-alone treatment, it was discussed in the Buying SPX Calls activity.

The goal of this chapter is to introduce strategies well suited to account growth. Growth requires the traders to husband their resources in a conservative and risk-averse manner. It will also require high-volume trading, a strategic mindset, trading tactics, patient discipline, and conservation.

Following is a list of eight option strategies that may be used with a small account balance and mid-level option trading permissions.

- Short OTM Put
- Covered Short Strangle
- Covered Call
- Bull Call Spread
- Iron Condor
- Butterfly Spread
- Long LEAP Call (with an optional short put)
- Long Strangle or Long Straddle

The Option Strategies

First, be sure you know how each strategy works and how to manage it. All eight option strategies are detailed in the hands-on activities provided in chapter 14 with the exception of the Long LEAP call. While the LEAP call is discussed in the Buying SPX Calls activity, the optional short put described in this chapter is not mentioned there. Be sure to check the setup parameters for each of the following eight strategies as provided in chapter 14.

Short OTM Put

(−1 OTM Put ≤ 56 Days)

This is a premium collection strategy that should only be used with a stock or ETF that you are willing to own within your brokerage account. The premium you collect discounts the price of the stock in the event the option is exercised and put to you. Because you don't mind owning the stock, holding it in your account provides a resource for other option strategies like the covered short strangle and covered call described below.

1. Check highly liquid stocks and ETFs with trading volumes in the millions of shares/day. Examples are stocks and ETFs like SPY, QQQ, IWM, AAPL, ADBE, etc.
2. Find OTM short puts with good premium of about ≥ $1.00/share on an up-trending stock that you wouldn't mind owning. (If you become ITM, the stock will be put to you.)
3. Ensure you can afford to pay for 100 shares.
4. Look for a premium ≈ $1.00/share as suggested in number 2 above.
5. Sell one or two short OTM (cash-covered) puts on the SPY, QQQ, IWM, and other ETFs that have high volume, strong open interest, high current IV% (≥ 50%), and < 30% probability ITM. I throttle back to 25% probability ITM when IV is ≥ 80%.
6. Enter a GTC buy to close order designed to trigger when the Mark is ≤ 45 cents.
7. Do it again! (Churn it!)

    NOTE Consider owning a high yield dividend stock such as a Master Limited Partnership (MLP). A few symbols to examine are EEP, ETE, NS, OKE, PAA, TCP, etc. You can Google MLP to find lists of symbols. Then check the underlying option chains to ensure reasonable premium values are available. While many MLPs have limited option volume and OTM strike prices, there are exceptions. Also, if owned within a qualified retirement account, MLP earnings must be included in your tax return. Otherwise, the tax deferral status of the retirement account may be revoked.

Covered Short Strangle

(−1 OTM Put, −1 OTM Call, +100 Shares, ≤ 56 Days)

In the event 100 or more shares of stock were put to you as a result of the short OTM put strategy described above, or you already own a stock, consider using it to cover one of the following trades. Of course the option metrics that correspond to the stock must qualify. If so, proceed as follows:

1. Your stock must be trading at a few million shares/day.
2. Find an OTM short put at a strike price with a Probability ITM < 30% and a premium ≥ $0.40.
3. Find an OTM short call at a strike price $5.00 OTM with a premium ≥ $0.30. (If the stock is called away, you make $5.00/ share plus the premium received at entry.)
4. If you already own the stock, sell the strangle. If you must buy the rallying stock, trade a covered stock that includes +100 shares for each short call sold. Then sell the put options to complete the trade.
5. Wait for a 50% profit in premium. If all setup parameters are still valid, roll into a later expiration date. Otherwise, close the trade and enter new positions that comply with the premium, probabilities, and strike price values described in number 2 and 3 above.
6. Keep churning until the underlying stock is called away.

NOTE If you become concerned about a drop in the price of the covering stock, consider an equity collar created by buying and holding a slightly OTM long put that expires > 90 days.

Covered Call

(−1 OTM Call, +100 Shares, ≤ 56 Days)

As with the above covered short strangle strategy, you should already own 100 shares of stock for each OTM call option to be sold. You may also buy the stock (as a "covered stock") when this trade is entered. However, covered calls are most vulnerable to a drop in the price of the covering stock. Be sure you have vetted the underlying stock using your price charts. It's essential that the stock price is oversold near support in anticipation of a rally.

1. Your stock must be trading at a few million shares/day.
2. Find an OTM short call at a strike price $5.00 OTM with a premium ≥ $0.30. (If the stock is called away, you make a $5.00/share plus the premium received at entry.
3. If you already own the stock, sell a strangle by selling the short call and an OTM short put. If you must buy the rallying stock, trade a covered stock that includes +100 shares for each short call. Then sell the put to complete the position.
4. Wait for a 50% profit in premium. If all setup parameters are still valid, roll into a later expiration date. Otherwise, close the trade and enter new positions that comply with the premium, probabilities, and strike price values described in number 2 and 3 above.
5. Keep churning until the underlying stock is called away.

Bull Call Spread or Calendar Bull Call Spread

(−1 OTM Call, ≤ 45 Days; +1 ATM or Slightly OTM Call, ≥ 90 Days)

Instead of owning stock to cover the OTM short call, a long call is used to provide the needed cover. This also eliminates the risk of a drop in the price of the stock. But, as with all trades, your bullish bias must be correct because this is a debit spread. The premium paid for the long call is always greater than the premium received from the sale of the farther OTM short call.

Your goal is for the price of the stock to rally above the strike price of the long call. If it rallies all the way to the strike price of the short call, which should be about $5 above the long call's strike price, all the better. The trade rewards you in the $5 intrinsic value plus the original short call premium less the debit paid at entry. If the price of the underlying stock drops, the trade loses the debit paid at entry.

1. The underlying stock must be trading at a few million shares/day.
2. Because this is a debit spread, find a stock with a current IV% between 20% and 40%.
3. Locate an affordable slightly OTM long call.
4. Check the strike price premiums $5.00 farther OTM for placement of your short call.
5. Although this varies with the price of the stock, try to limit the debit amount to something below $3.00/share.
6. Enter the trade and monitor the premium.
7. If the underlying stock or ETF rallies, be ready to close the short call for a 30% to 60% profit margin. Consider keeping the long call and selling another short call farther OTM for additional premium income.
8. If the stock experiences a strong rally that exceeds the $5.00 spread, close the short call and exercise the long call for a $5.00/share profit (less the original debit paid, of course).
9. If the uptrend in the underlying stock stalls and begins to reverse, consider closing the trade to recover a portion of the original premium spent. (But don't be too hasty. This may be a normal price consolidation.)

10. If number 7 occurs, keep churning your short OTM calls for more profit.

Iron Condor

(−1 OTM Call, +1 farther OTM Call,−1 OTM Put, +1 farther OTM Put) ≤ 56 Days

The iron condor is an excellent premium collection strategy. You should recall how the iron condor strategy has other permutations called the jade lizard and twisted sister. These were discussed in chapter 14. But here we look at the vanilla flavored iron condor with OTM call and put positions. However, feel free to take off either the call or put positions based on your analysis. In other words, if the underlying stock is experiencing a strong rally, trade the puts. And of course, if it's dropping, trade the calls.

But remember, options provide excellent flexibility. This is one of the reasons they are so popular among experienced traders. If the stock is experiencing a strong rally, perhaps a long ATM call could be added to the short and long OTM puts for a three legged custom strategy. This would use the premium collected from the OTM short and long put to finance the long call.

This derivative strategy reiterates the flexibility offered by options. Always look for the possibilities, because there may be a great trade waiting in the wings to be discovered.

When trading a traditional iron condor, we must find a stock or ETF with high trading volume and that is presently neutral to slightly bearish. Being strongly bullish is not desirable, as the price of the underlying would be moving toward the OTM short and long calls. The last thing we want is for our short call to become ITM. However, if this is the case and adequate premium exists on the put side of this trade, abandon the calls and focus on the puts.

1. As with the previous option strategies, select a stock or ETF that trades several million shares each day.

2. The income from this spread is the difference (or "width") in the premium received from the short legs and that paid for the long legs. Therefore, it may be necessary to buy two or three strikes farther OTM (above and below) the short call and put legs. An example could be to sell a $70 put and buy a $66 put with a premium spread (the difference in Marks) of $0.80 to $1.00/share. (You will want your strikes to be closer on the call side of this trade.) The put options should provide an $80 to $100 return per contract. Assuming a $40 return on the call side, each quartile of contracts returns $140. Selling three each returns $420. (Do this every three or four weeks and the annual income can amount to something in the neighborhood of $5,500 from just one strategy among several.)

3. Enter the trade and monitor the price of the underlying and the corresponding option premiums.

4. If the underlying stock or ETF rallies, be ready to close the short call and buy back the long call for any premium that remains.

5. If the stock drops, be prepared to close the short put and sell the long put.

6. Close for a 50% profit and do it again. Churning the iron condor throughout the year will help you build the amount of cash in your brokerage account and provide the equity required for larger trades and even stronger returns.

Butterfly Spread

(+1 OTM Call, −2 ATM Calls, +1 ITM Call) ≤ 30 Days
Or
(+1 OTM Put, −2 ATM Puts, +1 ITM Put) ≤ 30 Days

As you can see, you have choices. Both of the above butterfly spreads are balanced. And, as you may recall from chapter 14, there are also unbalanced and broken wing butterfly spreads. Here, we'll explore the balanced call version. The trader's goal is premium collection and safety. Although a debit spread when entered, the butterfly spread quickly responds to both Theta and a move in the price of the underlying — in either direction. Theta erodes the value of the two short calls making them cheaper to close when bought back. The price movement increases the value of one of the long call legs. This returns a profit when that leg is sold. The third leg is sold for whatever premium may remain. These actions are typically done in a matter of days following entry. Although the returns are moderate, they are nevertheless reasonable. The hedges provided by the long legs also contribute to the benefits of this strategy.

1. Select a stock or ETF that trades several million shares each day with good premiums.
2. The income from this spread is the decline in premium value of the two short calls and an increase in premium value of one of the long calls from a corresponding rally or a drop in the price of the underlying stock or ETF.
3. Monitor the P/L Open. When the profit achieves 30% to 50%, close the trade for profit.
4. Churning the butterfly spread throughout the year will contribute to the equity within your brokerage account.
   NOTE You can also enter a GTC close order based on the Mark value of this spread. Once it hits your target, the necessary buy-to-close and sell-to-close orders will be filled.

LEAP Call (with an optional short put)

(+1 slightly OTM or ATM Call, ≥ 1 year)
Optional:
(−1 OTM Put, ≤ 56 Days)

LEAPS are long-term option investments that use option contracts that expire in one to three years from the time of entry. LEAPs can be extremely profitable when your bullish or bearish bias is correct. You can exercise an option contract for a fraction of the current cost of the stock and sell it for much more than you originally paid using the leverage offered by options.

The downside of a LEAP is that the money you spend on the long-term call contracts will be tied up for many months to perhaps a few years. So it is important to be right relative to your expectations for the price of the underlying stock or ETF to make a strong move in the right direction.

Buying the LEAP can be expensive, particularly if buying an option on a high-priced stock. Be sure the IV is low at entry. And consider selling an OTM short put to help finance the cost of the long call leg. This makes it even more important to be right about your bullish bias. Having to spend money to close the short put will add to the expense of this strategy. And, of course, a drop in the price of the underlying means you may have been wrong in your analysis and bullish bias. If your short OTM puts produce cash, you may wish to sell more from time to time for additional option premium income. But selling the puts is secondary to your primary goal, which is achieving a major profit of several thousand dollars from the long call option, i.e., your LEAP.

The following steps walk you through the entry and exit of a successful LEAP option. As you will see, this is an extremely simple strategy. The work is in the analysis. It's always important to conduct a careful analysis prior to every trade; it's particularly important when entering a long-term LEAP option. So spend whatever time is necessary to be confident in the outcome of your evaluation. Consider each of the following steps.

1. As always, select a stock or ETF that trades several million shares each day with good premiums.

2. Find a strong, rallying stock of a solid growth company with excellent financials, lots of cash, and little to no debt. Quarterly sales growth should be evident. (This is a situation in which you want to do both fundamental and technical analysis.)

3. Examine option chains that expire in 12 to 24 months. Ensure above average open interest exists. With current IV% below 40%, evaluate the premium at a strike price between Delta .20 and .35.

4. Ensure the premium you must pay to buy this long call is both affordable and sustainable; the product of the number of option contracts × premium should be no more than 2% of your account value.

5. Buy the option contract(s) that are within your risk tolerance.

6. Check the position each time you use your trading platform to monitor its progress. If you financed entry by selling put options, determine if you can roll them. Ensure they remain safely OTM.

7. If the long call becomes deep ITM according to plan, you must now decide whether to sell it or keep it longer. Do another analysis to determine if the fundamentals and technical analyses are still working in your favor. If so, consider keeping the trade a bit longer. Even if Theta begins to reduce the premium of your long call, you are no longer concerned with premium. Now you are concerned with liquidity in the underlying stock. Because you are deep ITM, you will exercise the option for thousands of dollars in profit.

8. Finally, when satisfied with your results, exercise the premium and watch your account increase in value.

9. This is a one-time transaction; it will not be churned. However, if satisfied with this experience, you may be encouraged to find more LEAP opportunities.

Long Strangle or Long Straddle

Long Straddle: (+1 ATM Call, +1 ATM Put, ≥ 90 Days)

Or:

Long Strangle: (+1 OTM Call, +1 OTM Put, ≥ 90 Days)

As you may recall from chapter 14, the long straddle and long strangle are both debit strategies in which an equal number of calls and puts are purchased. As such, these strategies rely on strong moves in the price of the underlying stock or ETF to return the intended profit. Because ETFs are typically more stable than individual stocks, it's best to buy stock options when using either of these strategies.

Two other strategies that include long call and put legs are the strip and the strap. These are unbalanced and require a definite bullish (strap) or bearish (strip) bias. The strip includes two ATM puts for each ATM call, making it more bearish. The strap includes two ATM calls for each ATM put, which makes the strap more bullish.

Entering a long straddle is costlier than entering a long strangle, because the straddle buys more expensive ATM calls and puts while the long strangle buys OTM calls and puts. In our example, we'll follow the long strangle just because it's a bit cheaper. But this doesn't make it better. If you are trading the same stock, the straddle may return more profit with the same strong move in the market price of the underlying stock. This is particularly true if the "withering" leg is sold within a matter of several days to weeks following entry. Let's follow a long strangle to see what can happen.

1. Select a stock that has a history of volatility, with large price swings over a year's time.
2. Examine option chains that expire in more than 90 days; even longer is better if premiums are within your risk tolerance.

3. Verify ample open interest for liquidity, as you plan to sell one of the legs and keep the other for profit.

4. Wait for a period of basing on the price charts and low IV% before placing your trade.

5. Buy one or more slightly OTM put and call options that expire in roughly 100 to 150 days. Be sure the cost complies with your risk management rules.

6. Monitor the trade; you are looking for a strong move that is a common trait of the selected stock.

7. When the stock makes a decided move, either up or down, sell the opposite leg. For example, if the price begins to rally, sell the long put. If it begins to drop, sell the long call.

8. Check the price of the underlying stock and the long option each time you use your trading platform.

9. When the remaining long option becomes deep ITM, either sell it or exercise it based on the most profitable outcome.

10. If the trade worked, consider using the strategy again.

What did you learn in chapter 16?

1. A trader's patience and consistency can lead to _____ _____.

2. Most traders start with _____ _____.

3. Growth requires traders to husband their _____ in a conservative manner.

4. Check the setup _____ in chapter 14 before entering a trade.

5. The short OTM put is a _____ _____ strategy.

6. Use the short OTM put with a stock or ETF that you are willing to _____.

7. This strategy should be used with highly _____ stocks and ETFs.

8. Premium is higher when IV% is high; Probability ITM should be less than _____%.

9. The covered short strangle requires the ownership of_____.

10. The short strangle includes a short put and a _____ _____.

11. Trading the same strategy over and over is called _____.

12. The most vulnerable part of a covered call is the ownership of the _____.

13. Keep churning a covered call until the _____ is called away.

14. The primary goal of the iron condor strategy is to collect _____.

15. The iron condor includes _____ separate option legs.

16. Butterfly spreads can be balanced, _____, and broken_____.

17. A LEAP option contract may expire in one to _____ _____from the time of entry.

18. The long strangle buys one OTM call and one _____ _____.

19. The long straddle buys one _____ call and one _____
    _____.

20. Long straddles and strangles depend on a strong movement in
    the _____ of the underlying.

APPENDICES

Terms and Definitions

Alert — A trader established notification based on a preset value sent to inform the trader by e-mail and/or text messaging when a specified condition occurs. For example, if the price of the underlying security pierces an established price, the trader receives an alert for either information or in order to take action.

Ask Price — The buying price, or option premium, in dollars and cents, to be paid for each share of the underlying optionable security within an option contract (most often 100 shares per option contract). (When trading shares of stock, ask is used to sell and bid is used to buy.)

At the money (**ATM**) — An option strike price (or *exercise* price) that is closest to the current price of the underlying optionable security.

Backwardation (or Normal Backwardation) — See *Contango*.

Base or Basing — A term used to describe a sideways movement on a price chart. A rally, base, drop describes a sequence of upward, sideways, and downward price moves.

Bearish — A negative bias held by a trader who expects a security or market to decline in value.

Bearish Spread — An option spread designed to be profitable if the underlying security declines in price. A common bearish spread consists of buying an in the money put and selling an out of the money put. This is called a *bear put spread*.

Beta — A measure of how closely the movement of the market price of a stock corresponds to the movement of the financial index to which it belongs. For example, the beta value of AAPL stock is a comparison to its market price volatility to that of the S&P 500 financial index.

Bid Price — Option sell orders are initiated using the Bid cell on the selected strike price row of an option chain. The default price is the Mark, which is midway between the Bid and Ask prices.

Bid to Ask Spread — The difference in price between the Bid and Ask values on an option chain. An option chain's Mark value is midway between the Bid and Ask values.

Bracketed Trade — A trade that includes a limit entry, a protective stop, and a profit target. Typically used when buying shares of stock or ETFs.

Breakout — As applied to market price, a breakout refers to a strong price rally or drop. Traders look for entry opportunities when their analysis signals a possible price breakout.

Brokerage Account — An account held by the client of a brokerage firm that includes securities and cash. The value of the account may be used as collateral (or *margin*) to finance the purchase of stocks, options, futures contracts, and other marketable securities.

Bullish — A positive bias held by a trader who expects a security or market to increase in value.

Bullish Spread — An option spread designed to be profitable if the underlying security rises in price. A common bullish spread consists of buying an at the money call and selling an out of the money call. This spread is called a *bull call spread*.

Buy to Close Order — A buy order placed by an option trader who originally sold one or more option contracts. The buy to close order requires the option trader to pay premium to close an active position.

Calendar (or Time Spread) — An option spread created by selling one option and buying another on the same security. The option sold expires sooner than the option bought. This spread is named *calendar spread* because the two contracts have different expiration dates. The goal of a calendar spread is to receive more income from the sold option compared to the option that is purchased. If sufficient time remains in the option bought, another option may be sold for additional premium income.

Call — A call option contract entitles the buyer to acquire (or "call away") 100 shares per contract of the underlying security from the seller, who is contractually obligated to deliver the stock to the buyer. Of course this transaction must occur prior to contract expiration.

Called Away — The buyer of a call option may call the optioned security away from the seller if the option becomes ITM by one cent. (See *in the money*.) The seller must deliver the stock to the buyer, who must pay the seller the option price. If the seller does not own the called stock, he/she must purchase and deliver the stock to the buyer for a loss.

Candlestick Chart — A price chart that uses red and green rectangles that resemble the bodies of candles. The candles have lines above and below, called *shadows* or *wicks*. The bottom and top of each candle body represents the opening and closing price for the selected time interval, i.e., week, day, hour, etc. A green candle body represents a rally (a higher closing price than that of the opening price). Red candle bodies represent a drop candle, i.e., a lower closing price than that of the opening price.

Cash Settlement Option — Option contracts on financial indexes are cash settled rather than stock settled. In the case of either a call or a put, the seller must pay the buyer the difference between the option price and the current ITM price.

Chart Interval — Any of several chart time intervals used on price charts. Examples are weekly, daily, hourly, and minute charts. Most traders look across several time intervals to determine the characteristics of price movements across time. Experienced chart analysts use candlestick charts beginning with weekly intervals and working their way to shorter time intervals to develop an understanding of price characteristics. Chart studies are often applied to enhance a trader's expectation relative to future price movements.

Chart Study — A mathematical indicator used on security price charts to show price averages, overbought/oversold conditions, trading volume, average price movements, and much more.

Chicago Board of Exchange (CBOE) — The company responsible for providing live options data used by client brokerages throughout the world.

Closeout Date — A predetermined date upon which a contract should be closed to preserve the value that remains within an option position.

Closing Price — The final price at which a security traded at the end of the trading day. When applied to an option contract, this is the premium paid or received when a buy to close or sell to close transaction is processed.

Closing Purchase — A buy to close transaction conducted by the holder of a short option (the option writer) to liquidate an option position.

Closing Sale — A sell to close transaction conducted by the holder of a long option (the option buyer) to liquidate an option position.

Contango — This is a term related to a comparison between the spot price of a future and the current contract price. Some option traders borrow and misapply the term, in spite of the fact that options do not have *spot prices*. When the price of an option or futures contract is either rising or falling in value, it is said to be either contango or in normal backwardation. Contango is when the contract price exceeds the expected future spot price. In options, contango implies the current premium at the strike price of a short position has lost value, profiting the holder of a short option. Normal backwardation relates to the loss in the premium value of a long option.

Contract (or **Option Contract**) — An agreement to relinquish an underlying security if the agreed upon option price either exceeds the contracted call price by one cent or falls below the contracted put price by one cent. Contracts are managed by The Options Clearing Corporation.

Covered Option — A call option position that is collateralized by a security, such as shares of stock, or a put option contract that is collateralized by cash. When a covered call option contract is exercised by the option buyer, the seller must deliver the optioned securities to the buyer at the agreed upon option price.

Crossovers — On price charts, a crossover is the point at which one element or line crosses another. This can be the crossover of two moving average plots, a crossover of two study envelope lines, as when a Bollinger band envelope crosses inside the Keltner channel envelope, or when one or more price plots cross a standard moving average plotline.

Day Order — A limit or protective stop order that automatically expires at the end of the trading day. (See *good till canceled* order).

Delta — A mathematical value that determines the change in option premium value resulting from a $1.00 change in the market price of the underlying option security, such as a stock or ETF. Call Delta values are positive and increase from 0.0 to 1.0 as calls drop deeper in the money. Put Deltas are negative and range from 0.0 to −1.0. Put Deltas move closer to −1.0 as the put strike prices increase.

Discount Brokerage — A brokerage that offers unusually low commission and exchange fees.

Distal — A line drawn on a price chart at the bottom of a demand zone near support or the top of a supply zone near resistance to represent the location of a protective stop. Distal lines are the most distant from the current price.

Diversification — An investing strategy that spreads risk across a variety of companies, industry sectors, or both to reduce exposure to a single industry.

Drawing Tools — A toolset contained on most trading platforms that permits the user to draw trendlines, price lines, symbols, text, and other marks on the price chart.

Drop — A term used to describe a downward price movement.

E-mini Future — A futures derivative of a financial index such as the S&P 500 index. The e-mini futures are traded directly in the futures market or indirectly through options on futures. The e-mini financial index symbols are: S&P 500 = ES, NASDAQ = NQ, DJIA = YM, Russell 2000 = TF, and S&P 400 = EMD.

Electronic Communication Exchange Networks (ECNs) — ECNs are also called alternative trading networks. The ECNs support stock and currency trading outside the traditional stock exchanges. They are computer-driven networks designed to match limit orders.

Exchange Fees — An options exchange originated fee charged by an option exchange for each option contract bought or sold.

Exchange Traded Fund (ETF) - A security comprised of several stocks or a market index. ETFs are frequently made up of stocks belonging to the same market sector or geographical region. For example, an ETF may bundle several Asia-Pacific or European stocks.

Execution — The completion of a buy or sell order. This is transacted by market makers or to a lesser extent, on the floor of a stock exchange.

Exercise — Option buyers may execute (or "exercise") their contractual rights when the price of the underlying pierces an option price prior to contract expiration. Call buyers pay the option price for receipt of the optioned security (calls stock away from the seller). Put buyers put stock to the option seller. The underlying optioned securities and cash are transferred between buyer and seller accounts.

Exercise (or Strike) Price —The agreed upon option price (or strike price) per share of the underlying security. The call buyer pays the call seller, and the put seller pays the put buyer. The underlying optionable security and cash are transferred between buyer and seller accounts.

Expiration Day (or **Maturity Date**) —The final day of an option contract. Once an option contract expires, the option contract is null and void. The goal of an option seller is to have the option contract expire worthless at which time the option can no longer be exercised.

Foreign Currency Exchange (Forex) — The forex market is the largest security market in the world, trading in the trillions of dollars each day. Traders speculate on the increase and decrease of one currency, such as the dollar, against another currency, such as the British pound or Euro. They buy currency pairs comprised of a base and a quote currency. Forex buyers buy a base currency against the quote currency if the buyer expects the base currency to increase against the quote currency. If correct, the buyer sells the pair for a profit once the base currency has rallied to his/her satisfaction.

Full-Service Broker — A brokerage firm that provides a full array of products and services. This may include banking, market research, investment counseling, and a variety of investment quality securities. Full service brokerages usually charge higher transaction fees to cover the higher cost of their services.

Futures Contracts — A contract between a producer and a processor for the production and delivery of a product by the producer to the processor at an agreed upon contract price. The processor pays the processor in advance of delivery. Each futures contract has an expiration date and must be fulfilled prior to expiration. Futures speculators buy and sell futures contracts with an expectation of making profit margins from the difference between the buying and selling prices.

Gamma — Gamma values control the sensitivity of Delta to a price change in the market price of the underlying optionable security. A 0.15 change in Gamma causes the value of Delta to change by 0.15 with a $1.00 change in the underlying. Although ignored by many traders, Gamma is the Greek that controls premium. Hedging options rely on low Gamma to neutralize Delta, which in turn stabilizes premium value.

Good Till Canceled (GTC) Order — A limit or a stop order that remains in force for a sustained period of time. The amount of time a GTC order continues to work depends on the brokerage. Some limit GTC order to 60 or 90 days. Others allow their clients to specify GTC expiration dates.

Greeks — Greek letters used on several of the option chain column headings. The Greeks are found in the formulas used to compute option premium values. Some represent English-language words such as Delta (difference), Rho (rate of interest), Theta (time value), Vega (volatility). The Greek letter Gamma is used to determine the rate of change in Delta. (Although Vega is not a Greek letter, it was adopted to represent volatility.)

Hedge — A financial position designed to offset losses suffered by the failure of a secondary investment. It can be thought of as insurance against an unlimited loss. A perfect hedge returns 100 percent of the value of a secondary investment in the event it fails to produce the intended results.

Index Option An option whose underlying security is a stock index. Three popular index option symbols are the SPX (S&P 500), NDX (NASDAQ), the RUT (Russell 2000), all of which are heavily traded.

In the Money (ITM) — A call option is ITM when the market price of the underlying security is greater than the option's strike (exercise) price. A put option is ITM when the market price of the underlying security is less than the put option's strike (exercise) price.

Intrinsic Value — The difference between the current market value of the underlying security that is ITM and an option's strike price. A call that is $5 ITM has an intrinsic value of $5. Intrinsic value applies to the value of the underlying security. *Extrinsic* value applies to option premium values.

Inverted — Most often used as a maintenance technique to either offset a loss or receive a limited profit when one leg of a short strangle is jeopardized by becoming in the money. Becoming inverted occurs when a trader either buys a put above a short call or buys a call below a short put. The trader's goal is to minimize loss, and in some cases, the inversion may return a small profit. (A short strangle is constructed by selling the same number of option contracts of out of the money calls and out of the money puts that both expire on the same date.

Last Sale Price — The final price of an equity security (stock, ETF, option, etc.) when last sold or purchased. (Last is available on option chains to show the last premium amount paid at the strike prices of all call and put options.)

LEAPS — The acronym used for **L**ong-term **E**quity **A**ntici**P**ation **S**ecurities. LEAPS are typically used with call option contracts in anticipation of a strong price rally over one to three years. Many option contracts have expiration dates as far out as three years.

Leverage, Financial — An investment instrument that provides a higher rate of return using a smaller amount of money.

Limit Order — An order to purchase or sell at a specified price. When buying, the limit order requires the price of the underlying security to be at or below the limit price. When selling, the price of the underlying security must be at or above the specified price. Limit orders are transacted as either DAY or GTC orders.

Limited Risk — A risk management strategy. An example is buying an option contract in which the maximum risk is the premium paid at entry.

Liquid (or Liquidity) —The speed in which a security can be traded. In options, a high level of open interest signifies an acceptable level of liquidity.

Listed Options — Actively traded options that are listed on an options exchange, such as the CBOE.

Long Order— Buying a security is said to be taking a long position in that security.

Longer Term Options — Option contracts with long-term expiration dates, typically those contracts that expire in more than 90 days. Some longer-term options are classified as **L**ong-**T**erm **E**quity **A**ntici**P**ation **S**ecurities (LEAPS). These expire in one year or more. Some option contracts remain active for up to three years.

Liquidity and Liquidity Risk — Market liquidity is required for trades to execute in a reasonable amount of time. A low liquidity level indicates a lack of interest on the part of market traders. An illiquid security can languish unbought and unsold for months and years. Traders are advised to avoid entry into low liquidity securities. Funding liquidity is a concern of corporate treasurers who must find sufficient funds to keep the company afloat, i.e., pay bills and make payroll to sustain normal business operations.

Market Depth — The resistance to price change based on trading volume. Market depth is a measure of the trading volume required to move the price of the underlying security. A 100-share trade is not sufficient to impact the price when market depth is high. A trade of one million shares typically exceeds the market depth and moves the market price of the underlying security.

Market Order — An order to purchase or sell a security at the current listed market price. The price is established by an authorized *market maker* who represents the security exchange responsible for the selected security. Market orders are executed immediately and have priority over limit orders. Market orders are used with protective stops.

Market Sector — A market category that includes a specific type of business. Categories include basic materials, capital goods, consumer discretionary, consumer staples, energy, financial, health care, technology, telecommunications, transportation and utilities.

Maturity Date — Also called *contract expiration date*, the maturity date is the final trading day of an option contract. Upon contract expiration, all open positions cease to exist.

Moving Average — A mathematical average of data points over a specified period of time. Moving averages are used on financial price charts to show the average price over a selected interval of time. Examples are the SMA(9), SMA(20), SMA(50) or SMA(200) referring to 9-, 20-, 50-, or 200-period simple moving averages. Other types of moving averages also exist, such an exponential moving average (EMA) and triangular moving averages (TMA). The EMA places more emphasis on the most recent data points. The TMA places more emphasis on the center data points of the specified range, i.e., 9, 20, 50, 200, etc.

Naked Writing (or *Uncovered Short Puts or Calls*) — Selling an uncollateralized call option or a *cash covered* put option. The naked call or put seller does not have a position in the underlying security nor is it *covered* by a long option position as in a bull put spread strategy, which "covers" a farther OTM short call.

Neutral Option Strategy — An option strategy, such as the Gamma-Delta-Neutral spread, used to profit from a small fluctuation in the market price of the underlying stock. Neutral spreads are typically *ratio spreads*. An example is when a number of call option contacts are bought at one strike price and a greater number of call contracts are sold at a higher strike price to achieve Gamma neutrality. The sum of Deltas is used to determine how many shares of the underlying stock must be shorted, where each share of stock has a Delta value of 1.0.

Neutral Spread — An option spread in which the trader believes the price of the underlying security will move sideways, without either a strong price rally or drop. A common neutral spread consists of simultaneously selling an OTM call and an OTM put to collect premium. This spread is called a *short strangle*. The trader believes the market price of the underlying security will remain between the strike prices of the call and put through contract expiration.

Novice Trader — An amateur trader who is both uneducated and inexperienced in the dynamics of financial markets. Typically buys high and sells low. Novice traders are rarely familiar with account management or risk management strategies.

Odds Enhancer — Any one of hundreds of mathematical studies used by traders to enhance the statistical probability of their trading success. Odds enhancers are used on charts and tables to indicate such metrics as trader sentiment, trading volume, price breakouts or reductions, etc.

Open Interest — The number of working option contracts at each *strike price* listed on an option chain.

Opening Price — The first price at which a security or option is traded when the market initially opens.

Option — A derivative of a security that conveys a term-limited contract between a buyer and a seller. The buyer of a call option pays a contract premium for the right to buy call shares of the underlying security from a call seller, i.e., to call away shares at the option price. The buyer of a put option pays a contract premium for the right to put shares of the underlying security to the put seller, i.e., to put shares to the seller at the option price. However, the option contract can only be exercised by the option buyer if the market price of the underlying security exceeds the option price by at least one cent. This is called being in the money (ITM). If the option contract expires before the price of the underlying security becomes ITM, the option contract *expires worthless* and all contract obligations terminate.

Option Chain — A financial table used by option traders to buy and sell call and/or put option contracts at *strike prices* above, at, and below the current market price of the underlying security. Each option chain has a specific contract expiration date. Columns include essential information such as the Bid (sell) and Ask (buy) prices, current Open Interest, mathematical probabilities, time values, implied volatility, etc.

Options Clearing — An issuer of tradable option contracts. Examples include the Chicago Board of Exchange, American Stock Exchange, Pacific Stock Exchange, Philadelphia Stock Exchange, International Securities Exchange, etc.

Options Exchange — A for-profit company that transacts options trades. Examples include the Chicago Board Options Exchange, American Stock Exchange, and International Securities Exchange.

Option Selling (or Option Writing) — Clicking the Bid cell of a selected strike price row within an option chain is used to sell (or *write*) one or more option contracts. Most option contracts represent 100 of an underlying security. (See *covered writing, naked writing*).

Option Spread — An option trading strategy that includes two or more *legs* on the same security at different strike prices. A spread may simultaneously buy a call and sell a farther out of the money call (a *bull call spread*). Some option strategies, such as *butterfly* and *iron condor* spreads include two puts and two calls at different strike prices.

Option Strategy — Any one of many option strategies for buying, selling, or buying and selling option call and/or put contracts.

Order — An offer to buy or sell a financial security, including equities, option or future contracts, or foreign exchange currency pairs. Orders are transmitted by traders to brokerage companies who submit orders to one or more governing securities exchanges. Once received, buy and sell orders are matched by a market maker. Option market makers are contracted by exchanges to fulfill option buy and sell orders. Once orders are matched, electronic records of the order fulfillment are returned to the originating brokerages, who in turn notify the trader. Option orders include call and/or put option contracts at one or more strike prices. Some option spreads may also include the purchase of underlying shares of stock.

Order Bar — A horizontal row containing order information including buy and/or sell instructions, number of contracts, option price(s), option expiration date(s), order duration, order type (limit, market, stop, etc.).

One Cancels Other (OCO) — A bracketed order that includes one or more stops. When one stop triggers, all orders that may remain are automatically canceled. For example, when a protective stop is executed the companion profit target order is simultaneously canceled.

Order Confirmation Dialog — A dialog containing an order description and pricing information on a queued order ready for submission.

Order Duration — Order durations vary with the type of trade required to accomplish the trader's goal. There are DAY (expires at the close of normal trading hours), GTC (good until canceled orders), EXT (remains open during the day's extended trading hours), and GTC_EXT (an extended hours order that is good till canceled).

Order Rules Dialog — A dialog used to establish automated order triggers based on a price, an *option chain* value, or a chart study.

Out of the Money (OTM) — A call option strike price that is higher than the market price of the underlying optionable security. A put option strike price is lower than the market price of the underlying optionable security. The value of an OTM option contract is the available premium at the option strike price(s). The premium value, i.e., the Mark, is typically midway between an option's Bid and Ask price.

Portfolio Margin — A margin account originally promulgated by the SEC. A portfolio margin account grants additional credit to brokerage clients based on a minimum account balance (typically between $100,000 and $125,000) and the client's trading experience. While standard margin accounts are typically granted the use of 50% of their account equity, portfolio margin account holders may collateralize up to 85% of their account equity. This extends the ability of portfolio margin account holders to extend their trading activity.

Position — The position of a working trade is the number of shares, or option contracts, that is either bought or sold in anticipation of a profit. Option contracts often include two or more *legs* (or *spreads*) comprised of simultaneous buy (long) and sell (short) orders.

Premium — The value of each optioned share of an underlying security at the specified strike price. The premium value is typically midway between the Bid (sell) and Ask (buy) price, and is called the Mark (market price). Premium is highest when an option is initially traded. Premium values erode as the underlying option contract approaches the contract expiration date.

Professional Trader — A knowledgeable, experienced trader who makes a full-time living buying and selling securities listed on one or more financial markets is considered a professional trader.

Proximal — A line drawn on a price chart at the top of a demand zone near support or the bottom of a supply zone near resistance to represent a location near the entry point of a trade. Proximal lines are the closest to the current price.

Put — A put option entitles the buyer to *put* the optioned shares of the underlying security to the seller of the *put* option contract if the option price falls below the contract's strike price and becomes ITM. Each option contract typically includes 100 shares of stock. The exceptions are a handful of mini option contracts that include 10 shares per contract.

Rally — A term used to describe an upward move in price.

Return if Called — The amount of income received by a covered call writer, expressed as a percentage. The return includes the original premium received when traded, the appreciation in the value of the underlying stock, and any dividends paid prior exercise.

Rho — Rho measures the sensitivity to option premium caused by changes in the prevailing rate of interest. A Rho value of .050 causes a decrease in the value of option premiums by .050 if interest rates rise by 1.0.

Risk/Reward Management (also Trade Management) — The management of a working trade. May be closed for profit or rolled into another option position. The goal of trade management is to either avoid or minimize a financial loss.

Rolling Out — Simultaneously closing a working option position and opening a new position expiring at a later date.

Rolling Up — Closing an option and opening another that expires on the same date, but at a higher strike price when rolling up calls, or at a lower strike price when rolling up puts.

Scalp — The action of taking small profits from a small price increase in a long trade or a small decrease in a short trade. For example, a pattern day trader may buy 100 shares of a stock for $25/share and then sell it several minutes later for $25.20/share for a $20 profit. This requires scalping day traders to use low-commission, discount brokerages.

Sell to Close Order — A sell order placed by an option trader who originally bought one or more option contracts. If the sell to close order is filled, the option trader will receive option premium.

Sentiment (or Market Sentiment) — The current prevailing aggressiveness or timidity of buyers and/or sellers toward one or more securities or the financial market as a whole.

Simulated (Paper) Trading — A feature provided on many trading platforms that permits traders to practice their trading skills or to test new trading strategies.

Short Position — Selling a security, such as a stock, option, or future, is said to be shorting that position. Shorting a stock happens when a *bearish* trader sells a stock in anticipation of a drop in the market price of that stock. A *buy to cover* order is placed to close the position and take profit from the loss.

Short-Life Option — A short-life option contract expires within 60 days or less. Many weekly options that expire within days to a few weeks are traded.

Stock Capitalization Categories — Stock categories are divided by *market capitalization*. Large cap stocks are greater than ten billion dollars. Mid cap stocks range from one to ten billion dollars. Small cap stocks are less than one billion dollars.

Stock Scanner — A computer-based tool used to establish specific parameters, such as price ranges, volumes, current volatilities, moving average crossovers, etc. These parameters are used to find and list stocks meeting the established scan criteria.

Straddle — The straddle is an option strategy designed to profit from a strong price move in the underlying security in either direction. Strong trading volatility is desirable. A long straddle includes the simultaneous purchase of a put and a call on the same security having the same strike price and expiration date. A short straddle incudes the simultaneous sale of a put and a call at the same strike price and expiration date. Many straddles are traded at the current ATM (at the money) strike price.

Strangle — The short strangle is a neutral trade strategy that profits from the sale of an equivalent number of put and call option contracts on the same underlying security and with the same expiration dates. The strike prices are far OTM to avoid exercise throughout the option contract life. The goal of the short strangle is to collect premium by selling one or more put and call contracts. The long strangle buys put and call contracts at different strike prices and that expire on the same contract date. The buyer of a long strangle seeks a strong movement in the price of the underlying security.

With a substantial move in the underlying, the profitable position can be sold for more premium than originally spent on both legs of the strangle option.

Strike Price — Strike prices are in a column at the center of an option chain. An at the money (ATM) strike price is closest to the market value of the underlying security. Out of the money (OTM) call strike prices are greater than the ATM strike price; OTM put strike prices are lower that the ATM strike price. Option traders evaluate premium, open interest, and other values at different strike prices when constructing an option strategy. An option's strike price is also referred to as *the exercise price*.

Target Exit Point — A predetermined price to close a working order. The trader 1) buys an option contract for less than paid at entry, or 2) sells an option contract for more than paid at entry. (Buy for a dime and sell to close for a dollar, or sell for a dollar and buy to close for a dime.)

Time Premium — The reduction of an option's premium value, measured by the Greek Theta, caused by the passage of time. The decay of time premium is also referred to as *extrinsic value*. Premium value declines more rapidly as an option contract approaches the contract expiration date.

Time Spread — An option spread consisting of the purchase of an option and the simultaneous sale of a *different* option on the *same* security with a *nearer* expiration date. The purpose of a time spread is to profit from the accelerated loss in time value of the option that is written, relative to the option that is purchased. Time spreading is often a *neutral* strategy, but it can also be bullish or bearish, depending upon the options involved (more often referred to as a *calendar spread*).

Trading Days — There are 252 trading days in the year. (Also see trading hours.)

Trading Floor — The main floor of a stock or options exchange where market makers fill sell and buy orders. Most trading floor activity is being replaced by automated, computer-based trading.

Trading Hours — Normal trading hours begin at 9:30 a.m. and close at 4:00 p.m. EST. Morning extended trading hours are from 4:00 a.m. till 9:30 a.m. EST. Evening extended trading hours are from 4:00 p.m. through 8:00 p.m. EST.

Trading Ladder — A trading interface on a computer with vertical green and red bars that look like ladders. Each bar represents a price point of the underlying security. Clicking a green bar is used to buy a security at the selected price; clicking a red bar is used to sell a security at the selected price. Multiple OCO-style orders with a limit buy order, a protective stop, and a profit target (a *bracketed order*) are often structured and sent on trading ladders. Trading ladders are popular for use by pattern day traders and futures speculators.

Trading Platform — A trading platform is a computer-based trading application, either installed directly on a brokerage client's computer or accessible through the Internet. Trading platforms provide an interface between a brokerage client and the brokerage for round trip order entry, processing, and confirmation.

Transaction Fees (Commissions and Exchange Fees) — The cost of buying or selling a security. Commissions and exchange fees are charged by brokerage firms. The commissions paid are typically governed by a brokerage schedule. They can be a fixed fee per equity trade, such as $6.99 or $9.99 per trade or a per-share fee, such as $0.005 per share. Exchange fees originate at the options exchange, such as the CBOE. An exchange fee is charged for each option contract traded, and can range from $0.50 per contract to $1.50 per contract. Financial index option exchange fees are among the highest exchange fee charged to brokerages, which pass exchange fees through to their client transactions. Exchange fees are paid round trip, i.e., upon both trade entry and exit.

Trendline (*also* Trend Line) — Trendlines are used on price charts to show price direction. An upward trendline is called a *rally*, a downward trendline is called a *drop*. A sideways trendline is said to be *basing*. If a price is making a series of higher highs and higher lows, the price is said to be in an uptrend. If making a series of lower lows and lower highs, it is said to be in a downtrend.

Truncated Risk — Risk can be *truncated* (or hedged) by entering a stop-loss or buying/selling a position to limit possible losses of a working position. When an option contract is purchased, it has limited risk and unlimited reward. The risk is the money originally spent on option premium. Unlimited reward is based on a movement in the underlying in the trader's favor. For example, buying a call that moves deep in the money (ITM) can produce a profit that is many times greater than the original premium paid when the trade was entered.

Underlying — A stock, ETF, financial index, or futures contract. Option contracts are financial derivatives of an *underlying* security. This term is commonly used by traders who buy and sell equities, futures, and forex pairs.

Vega — Vega reflects a change in an option's price resulting from a change in the underlying security's *implied volatility*. Vega causes a change in premium value for every 1% change in implied volatility. A Vega value of 0.10 causes a premium change of $0.10 for each 1% change in implied volatility.

Vertical Spread — An option strategy comprised of two call or two put positions, one above the other, i.e., arranged vertically. A *bull call spread* is an example that includes buying a call and selling a call above, i.e., at a higher strike price. A *bear put spread* includes buying a put and selling a put below, i.e., at a lower strike price.

Volatility — A measure of the frequency at which trading is occurring; also a measure of trader sentiment. High current volatility indicates higher than usual trading activity. Historical volatility for a specific security is the average number of daily trades conducted over the past twelve months. Implied volatility compares current trading volume to historical volatility. Options traders make extensive use of implied volatility data. Volatility can have the most impact on the time value of option premium. High volatility causes greater price fluctuation, increasing risk and corresponding option premiums, and most noticeable for at the money options.

Volume — For options, the number of contracts that have been traded within a specific time period, usually a day or a week. For equity securities, futures, and forex, the volume represents the number of trades, typically in the millions, that are traded during each trading day.

VWAP — VWAP stands for *volume-weighted average price*. The VWAP is a measure of the underlying's price based upon the number of shares or contracts traded at different prices. It is the weighted average price at which most of the trading has occurred.

Watch List — A table that lists tradable securities of interest to a trader, usually stocks, ETFs, and futures. Many traders have multiple watch lists that fall into different categories or market sectors.

OPTION STRATEGY QUICK REFERENCE

Bullish Strategies

Bull Call Spread

(debit spread)

Structure: Buy 1 ITM, ATM, or
   slightly OTM Call, Sell 1 farther OTM Call (≤ 60 Days)

Potential: High Reward, Low
   Risk (looking for a strong
   rally)

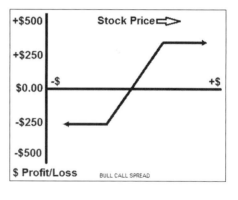

Max profit = Strike price of
   short call − Strike price of
long call − (Net premium paid + Transaction fees)

Max loss = Net premium paid + Transaction fees

Bull Calendar Spread

(debit spread)

Structure: Buy 1 slightly
   OTM Call (≥ 90 days),
Sell 1 OTM farther Call (≤
   60 days)

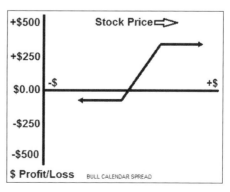

Potential: High Reward, Low Risk

(looking for a strong rally)

Max loss = Net premium paid + Transaction fees

Bull Put Spread

(credit spread)

Structure: Buy 1 OTM Put,
 Sell 1 ITM, ATM, or
 slightly OTM Put (≤ 60
 Days)

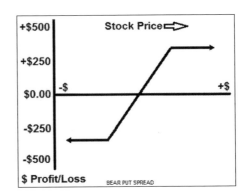

Potential: Low upside profit
 (premium collection)

High risk if short put becomes
 deep ITM

 Max profit achieved if stock price ≥ Strike price of short put

 Max profit = Net premium received −Transaction fees paid

Call Backspread

(debit spread)

Structure: Sell 1 ITM Call, Buy
 2 OTM Calls

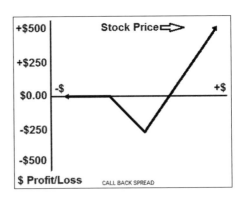

Potential: High Profit; Low
 Risk

Max loss = Strike price of long
 call − (Strike price of short
 call ±Net premium paid/
 received + Transaction fees)

Max loss occurs if stock price drops below the strike price of the
 short call.

Equity Collar Strategy

(debit spread)

Structure: Long 100 Shares (already owned),

Sell 1 OTM Call (≤ 60 Days),

Buy 1 ATM or slightly OTM Put (≤ 60 Days or ≥ 90 Days)

Potential: Low Profit; Low Risk

(Use to hedge against a drop in the price of the stock.)

Max profit = Strike price of short call − (Purchase price of stock + Net premium received − Transaction fees paid)

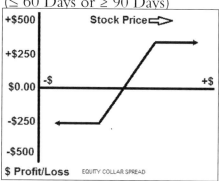

Max loss occurs when market price of underlying stock ≤ strike price of long put.

NOTE A collar is an excellent hedging strategy used with stock already held within the trader's account. It is intended to offset a drop in the market price of the stock.

Costless Collar

(neutral; debit if stock purchased at entry)

Structure: Long 100 Shares, Sell 1 OTM LEAPS Call, Buy 1 ATM LEAPS Put

Potential: Low Risk, Low Reward

(Primary risk in the cost of stock)

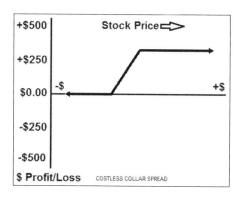

Max profit = Strike price of short call − (Purchase price of stock + Transaction fees)

Max profit is achieved when price of stock ≥ Strike price of short call.

Covered Call (OTM)

(debit spread when stock purchased **at** entry;
credit if stock already owned)
Structure: Long 100 Shares, Sell
 1 OTM Call ($\leq$ 60 Days)
Potential: Low Risk, Low
 Reward

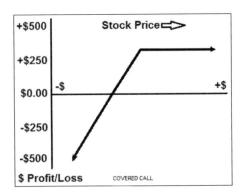

Max profit = Premium
 received − (Price of stock purchase + Strike price of short call
 − Transaction fees)

Covered Call (ITM)

(debit spread; similar to OTM
 covered call with more pre-
 mium paid at entry)
(Identical Risk Profile as OTM
 Covered Call)
Structure: Long 100 Shares, Sell
 1 ITM Call ($\leq$ 60 days)
Potential: Low Reward, Low
 Risk on Stock

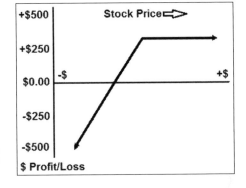

Max profit = Premium received − (Purchase price of stock + Strike
 price of short call − Transaction fees)
Consider churning this trade by continually closing for profit and
 selling another OTM call(s).

Covered Short Straddle

(credit spread; debit with purchase of stock)
Structure: Long 100 Shares, Sell
 1 ATM Call ($\leq$ 60 days),
 Sell 1 ATM Put ($\leq$ 60 days)

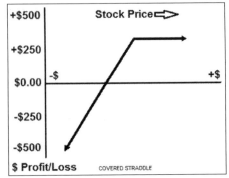

Potential: High Risk, Low Reward

Max profit = Strike price of short call − (Purchase price of stock − net premium received + Transaction fees)

Max loss = Short put or call being exercised; drop in market price of underlying stock

Diagonal Bull Call Spread

(debit spread)

Structure: Buy 1 ITM Call (≥ 90 days), Sell 1 OTM Call (≤ 60 days)

Potential: Low Reward, Low Risk

(Risk limited to premium paid upon entry)

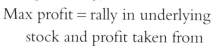
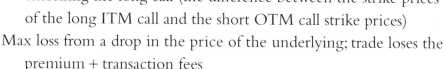

Max profit = rally in underlying stock and profit taken from exercising the long call (the difference between the strike prices of the long ITM call and the short OTM call strike prices)

Max loss from a drop in the price of the underlying; trade loses the premium + transaction fees

Long Call

(debit spread)

Structure: Buy 1 ATM Call (≥ 90 days or perhaps even a LEAP if a long-term bullish bias)

Potential: High Reward, Low Risk

Max loss = Debit + Transaction fees paid upon entry

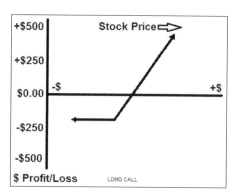

Max reward when long call becomes ITM from a price rally in the underlying

Married Put

(debit spread)

Structure: Long 100 Shares,
  Buy 1 ATM Put (≥ 90 days)

Potential: High Reward, Low
  Risk

Max profit received when price
  of stock > Purchase price of
  stock − (Premium paid for
  long put + Transaction fees)

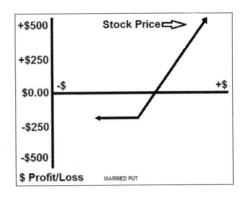

Protective Put

(debit)

Structure: Long 100 Shares,
  Buy 1 ATM Put (≥ 90 days)

Potential: High Reward, Low
  Risk

(excluding a drop in the price
  of the stock)

Max profit when Price of stock
  > (Purchase price of stock +
  Premium paid + Transaction fees)

Max loss = Neutral to drop in stock price − (Premium Paid +
  Purchase price of stock + Transaction fees)

Consider an Equity Collar spread as a less expensive alternative to
  hedging a drop in the
  market price of stock currently owned.

Uncovered Put Write

(credit)

(Also known as a cash-covered
  put or naked put)

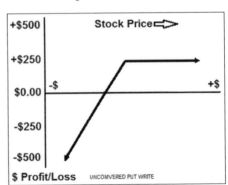

Structure: Sell 1 ATM Put (≤ 60 days)

Potential: High Risk, Low Reward limited to the premium received when entering the trade

Max profit = Premium received – Transaction fees

Max profit is achieved when price of stock > (Strike price of the short put – Transaction fees)

Covered Short Strangle or Covered Combination

(credit spread, excluding cost of stock)

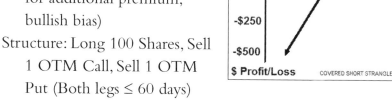

(Similar to a covered call with the addition of a short put for additional premium; bullish bias)

Structure: Long 100 Shares, Sell 1 OTM Call, Sell 1 OTM Put (Both legs ≤ 60 days)

Potential: Low Reward, Limited Risk

The short cash-covered put presents the most risk.

Max profit achieved when price of stock ≥ Strike price of short call (resembled a covered call)

Max profit = Strike price of short call – (Purchase price of stock + Premium received – Transaction fees)

Stock Repair Strategy

(Although difficult to achieve, this can be a credit spread if the long call premium is less than the premiums of the two OTM short calls.)

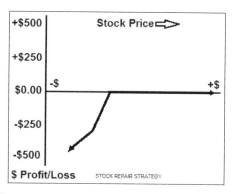

Structure: Buy 1 ATM Call (≥ 90 days),

Sell 2 OTM Calls (≤ 60 days)

Potential: Low Risk, Low Reward (only works when the stock price reverses into a strong rally)

Potential: Used to recover from a loss after stock has experienced a price drop. The options resemble a call ratio spread to reduce the cost of entry and to reduce the price of the stock required to achieve breakeven. Obviously, the stock must rally back to its original price for this strategy to work. Substantial drops in stock prices make recovery difficult if not impossible.

Bearish Strategies

Bear Call Spread

(credit spread; also known as a bear call credit spread)

Structure: Buy 1 OTM Call (≥ 90 days),

Sell 1 ITM Call (≤ 60 days)

Potential: Low Downside Reward, Low Upside Risk

(This strategy profits from the credit received from the short call.)

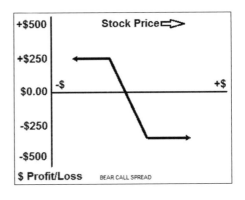

Max profit achieved when price of underlying ≤ Strike price of short call.

Max profit = Net premium received − Transaction fees

Max loss occurs when price of stock ≥ Strike price of long call

Max loss = Strike price of long call − (Strike price of short call − Net premium received + Transaction fees)

Bear Put Spread

(debit spread)

Structure: Buy 1 ITM Put, Sell 1 OTM Put

Potential: Low Reward, Low Risk

Max profit occurs when stock
price ≤ Strike price of short
put (i.e., the price of the
stock drops and the long
and short puts both become
ITM)

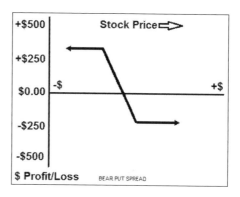

Max profit = Strike price of
long put − (Strike price of
short put + Net premium
paid + Transaction fees)

Max loss occurs when price of stock ≥ Strike price of long put
(the stock price rallies and both the long and short puts
become OTM).

Max loss = Net premium paid + Transaction fees

Covered Put

(credit spread with short stock)

Structure: Short 100 Shares,
Sell 1 ATM Put (≤ 60 days)

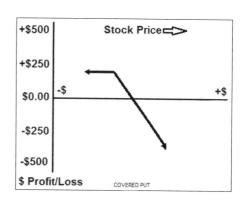

Potential: Low Reward; no
downside risk (except for a
stock rally against the short
stock)

Max profit achieved when
price of stock ≤ Strike price
of short put

Max profit = Premium received − Commission

Diagonal Bear Put Spread

(debit spread)

Structure: Buy 1 ITM Put (≥ 90 days),
Sell 1 OTM Put (≤ 60 days)

Potential: Low Upside Reward, Low Upside Risk

Maximum loss is the premium paid to enter the trade; if the stock price rallies, the trader may also suffer a loss from his/her stock position.

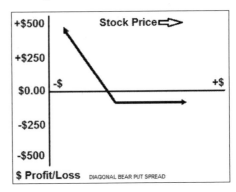

Long Put

(credit)

Structure: Buy 1 ATM Put

Potential: High Reward, Low Risk

(Bearish bias must be correct for reward.)

Maximum profit achieved when the price of the stock drops to zero

Profit = (Strike price of long put − Premium paid − Transaction fees)

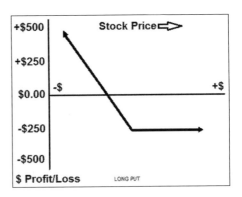

Out of the Money Naked Call

(credit) **High Risk — Not Recommended!**

Potential: Extremely Risky, Low Reward

Structure: Sell 1 OTM Call (without owning the stock)

Potential: Collect premium as long as call options remain OTM and expire worthless; repeat if market conditions

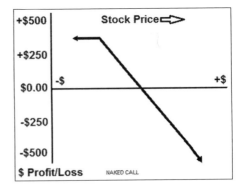

remain unchanged, and it is highly unlikely that option price becomes ITM.

Max loss can be punishing. If exercised, the option writer must buy and deliver the stock to the buyer, who must pay the seller for the stock at the lower option price.

Put Backspread

(debit spread) Also known as a Reverse Put Ratio Spread. The short put is cash-covered.)

Structure: Sell 1 ITM or ATM Put (≤ 60 days),

Buy 2 OTM Puts (≥ 90 days)

Potential: High reward, Low risk

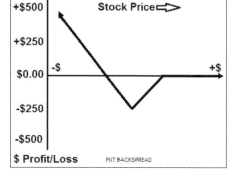

The 2:1 backspread sells puts at a higher strike price and buys twice as many puts at a lower strike price.

To profit, this strategy requires the market price of the underlying stock to drop just below the price of the long puts. This makes this strategy more unlikely to succeed.

Profit achieved when stock price < 2X the strike price of the long puts − Strike price of short put + Net premium received − Transaction fees

Profit = Strike price of long puts − Price of underlying − Strike price of the short put)

Max loss occurs when price of underlying = Strike price of long put.

Max loss = Strike price of short put − Strike price of Long puts − (Net premium received + Transaction fees)

Protective Call

(debit)

Structure: Short 100 Shares,
Buy 1 ATM Call (≥ 90 days)

Potential: Minimum Risk,
Maximum Reward

Profit achieved when price of
stock < Sale price of stock
– Premium paid

Profit = Stock sale price –
Stock price – Premium
paid

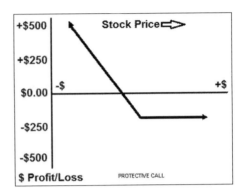

NOTE The protective long ATM call is a hedging strategy intended to offset a loss from an unwanted rally in the price of the short stock. (A GTC protective stop above the price of the short stock should also be considered to prevent high loss in the value of the stock.)

Neutral Strategies

Butterfly Spreads or Long Call Butterfly Spread

(debit entry, credit exit)
Butterfly spread risk profiles
are similar.

Structure: Buy 1 ITM Call, Sell
2 ATM Calls, Buy 1 OTM
Call (all ≤ 45 days)

Potential: Low Profit; Low Risk

Butterfly spreads are typically
balanced, i.e., the long calls
are the same number of

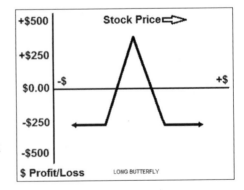

strikes away from the short ATM options. But several variations also exist, including a:

- Diagonal butterfly spread when long options expire ≥ 90 days
- Balanced or unbalanced based on the distance between the ATM strike and the long OTM strike prices chosen
- Bullish when using calls, or bearish when using puts
- Broken winged when one of the OTM call legs is omitted

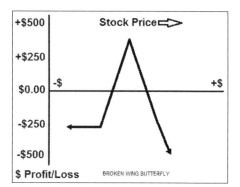

Max profit achieved when price of stock = Strike price of short calls

Max profit = Retention of premium collected from the short calls + Premium recovered from the sale of a deeper ITM call + Premium recovered from the OTM long call − Transaction fees

Max loss occurs when the price of the underlying breaches either of the long option legs.

Long Put Butterfly Spread

(debit entry, credit exit)

Structure: Buy 1 OTM Put, Sell 2 ATM Puts, Buy 1 ITM Put (all ≤ 45 days)

Potential: Low profit, Low risk

Max profit achieved when price of stock = Strike price of short put

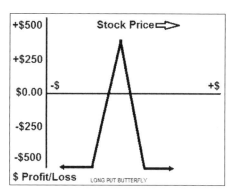

Max profit = Strike price of higher strike long put − Strike price of short put − Net premium paid − Transaction fees

Max loss occurs when stock price ≤ Strike price of lower strike long put OR stock price ≥ Strike price of higher strike long put.

Max loss = Net premium paid + Transaction fees

Breakeven:

Upper BE point = Strike price of highest strike long put − net premium paid

Lower BE point = Strike price of lowest strike long put + net premium paid

Short Put Butterfly Spread

(credit spread)

Structure: Sell 1 ITM Put, Buy 2 ATM Puts, Sell 1 OTM Put (≤ 45 Days)

Potential: Low Reward, Low Risk Strategy

Max loss occurs when stock price = Strike price of the two long puts

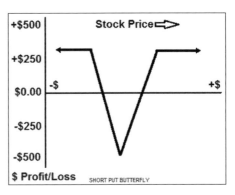

Max loss = Strike price of higher strike short put − Strike price of long put − Net premium received + Transaction fees

Iron Butterfly

(credit spread)

Structure: Buy 1 OTM Put, Sell 1 ATM Put, Sell 1 ATM Call, Buy 1 OTM Call (≤ 45 Days)

Potential: Low Risk, Low Reward (Price must remain neutral to succeed)

Max profit achieved when stock price = Strike price of short call/ put

Max profit = (Net premi um received − Transaction fees)

Calendar Straddle

(debit)

Structure: Sell Straddle (≤ 60
days), Buy second Straddle
(≥ 90 days)

Potential: Low Reward, Low
Risk strategy

Used with stocks having low
current volatility

Max profit when a large price
breakout occurs

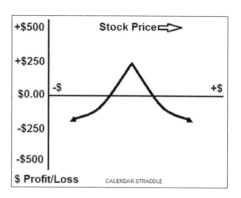

Condor

(debit spread)

Structure: Sell 1 ITM Call, Buy
1 ITM Call (lower strike),
Sell 1 OTM Call, Buy 1
OTM Call (higher strike)
(≤ 45 Days)

Potential: Low Reward, Low
Risk strategy

Max profit achieved when
price of stock is between
the strike prices of the 2 short calls

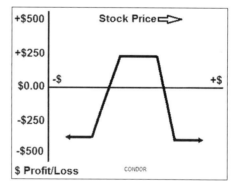

Max profit = Strike price of lower strike short call − (Strike price
of lower strike long call − net premium paid − Transaction fees)

Iron Condor

(credit spread; combines a call and a put vertical spread)

Structure: Sell 1 OTM Put, Buy 1 OTM Put (lower strike),
Sell 1 OTM Call, Buy 1 OTM Call (higher strike) (≤ 45 Days)

Potential: Low Reward, Low Risk strategy (collects net premium credits
provided by the differences
between long and short
options)

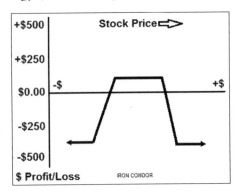

Max profit achieved when market price of stock remains
between strike prices of
short put and short call

Max profit = Net premium
received – Transaction fees

Long Straddle or Buy Straddle

(debit)

Risk profile resembles that of the
long strangle, except buying
OTM calls and puts rather
than ATM calls and puts.

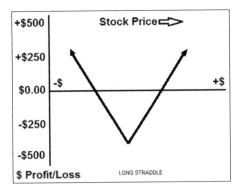

Structure: Buy 1 ATM Call, Buy
1 ATM Put (≥ 90 Days)

Potential: High Reward, Low
Risk (Risk = Premium paid
upon entry)

Profit achieved when stock price > Strike price of long call – –
net premium paid

OR

Stock price < Strike price of
long put – net premium paid

Max risk limited to premiums
paid

Long Strangle

(debit)

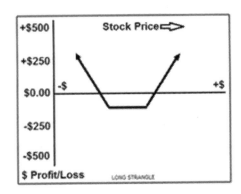

Structure: Buy 1 OTM Call, Buy 1 OTM Put (≥ 90 Days)

Potential: High profit potential; Low risk

Profit achieved when stock price > Strike price of long call – net premium paid

Max risk limited to premiums paid

Neutral Calendar Spread

(debit spread)

Structure: Sell 1 Near–Term ATM Call (≤ 60 days), Buy 1 Long–Term ATM Call (≥ 90 days)

Potential: Low Risk, Low Return

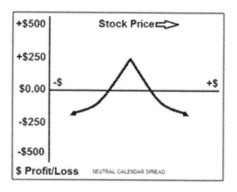

The maximum possible profit for the neutral calendar spread is limited to the premiums collected from the sale of the near month options minus any time decay of the longer term options. This happens if the underlying stock price remains unchanged on expiration of the near month options. Maximum profit obtained by selling multiple short-term ATM calls.

Put Ratio Spread

(neutral spread)

Structure: Buy 1 ITM Put, Sell 2 OTM Puts (≤ 60 Days)

Potential: High Risk, Low Reward (High downside loss, Limited profit potential (little or no upside risk)

Loss occurs when stock price < Strike price of short puts

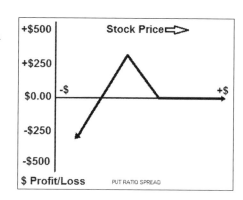

– (Strike price of long put – Strike price of short put + Net premium received)/No. of uncovered puts)

Ratio Call Write

(credit if stock owned; debit if stock purchased at entry)
Structure: Long 100 Shares, Sell 2 ATM Calls (≤ 60 Days)

Potential: High Risk, Low Reward (may be required to deliver 100 more shares of stock)

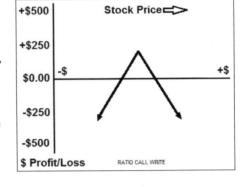

Max profit = Net premium received – Transaction fees

Loss = Stock price – Strike price of short call – Net premium received

OR

Cost of stock – Price of stock – Net premium received + Transaction fees

Ratio Put Write

(credit if stock owned; debit if stock purchased at entry)

Risk profile resembles that of the ratio call write, except selling 2 ATM puts rather than ATM calls.

Structure: Short 100 Shares, Sell 2 ATM Puts (≤ 60 Days)

Potential: Inferior strategy with high loss and limited profit potentials

Call Ratio Spread

(neutral spread)

Structure: Buy 1 ITM Call, Sell 2 OTM Calls (≤ 60 Days)

Potential: Low profit potential; High upside risk, little or no downside risk

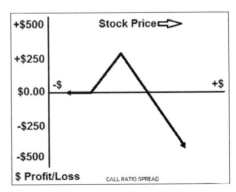

Max profit = Strike price of short call − Strike price of long call + Net premium received − Transaction fees

Short Butterfly

(credit spread)

Structure: Sell 1 ITM Call, Buy 2 ATM Calls, Sell 1 OTM Call

Potential: Low Reward, Low Risk

Max profit achieved when stock price ≤ Strike price of lower strike short call OR

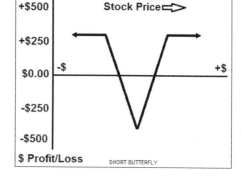

Stock price ≥ Strike price of higher strike short call

Max profit = Net premium received − Transaction fees

Short Condor

(debit spread)

Structure: Buy 1 ITM Call, Sell 1 ITM Call (lower strike), Buy 1 OTM Call, Sell 1 OTM Call (higher strike) (≤ 60 days)

Potential: Low Reward, Low Risk

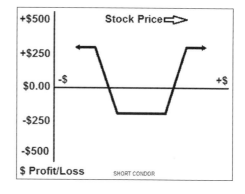

Max profit = Net premium received − Transaction fees

Max profit achieved when stock price ≤ Strike price of lower strike short call OR Stock price ≥ Strike price of higher strike short call

Short Straddle

(credit spread)

Structure: Sell 1 ATM Call, Sell 1 ATM Put (≤ 45 Days)

Potential: High Risk, Low Reward

Max profit = Premium received – Transaction fees

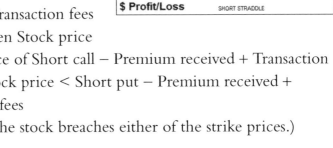

Loss occurs when Stock price > Strike price of Short call – Premium received + Transaction fees OR Stock price < Short put – Premium received + Transaction fees

(Loss occurs if the stock breaches either of the strike prices.)

Short Strangle

(credit spread)

Structure: Sell 1 OTM Call, Sell 1 OTM Put (≤ 60 Days)

Potential: High Risk, Low Reward (sell at least 1 standard deviation or more OTM)

Max profit = Premium received – Transaction fees

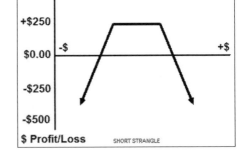

(As in the short straddle, loss occurs if the stock price breaks through either of the strike prices.)

Variable Ratio Write

(credit spread from options, debit if buying stock upon entry)

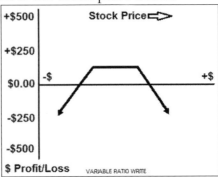

Structure: Long 100 Shares, Sell 1 ITM Call, Sell 1 OTM Call (≤ 60 Days)

Potential: High Risk, Low Reward

Max profit achieved when stock price is between the strike prices of the short calls

Max profit = Premium received + Strike price of lower strike short call − Stock price − Transaction fees

Reverse Iron Condor

(debit spread)

Structure: Buy 1 OTM Put, Sell 1 OTM Put (Lower Strike), Buy 1 OTM Call, Sell 1 OTM Call (Higher Strike)

Potential: Low Reward, Low Risk (risks premium paid upon entry)

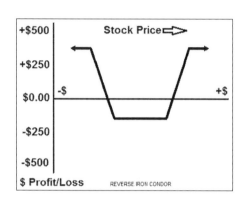

Max profit achieved when stock price < Strike price of short put OR Stock price > Strike price of short call

Max loss is limited to the net debit taken when entering the order.

Max loss = Premium paid + Transaction fees

Reverse Iron Butterfly

(credit spread)

Structure: Sell 1 OTM Put, Buy 1 ATM Put, Buy 1 ATM Call, Sell 1 OTM Call

Potential: Low Risk, Low Reward

Max profit achieve when stock price ≤ Strike price of short put OR Stock price ≥ Strike price of short call

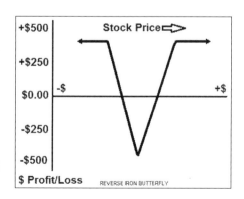

Long Guts

(debit spread; could also be called a long strangle)

Structure: Buy 1 ITM Call, Buy 1 ITM Put

Potential: High Reward, Low Risk (requires strong price move in either direction)

Max profit attained when the stock price makes a very strong move in either direction prior to expiration.

Risk is limited to the premiums and Transaction fees paid.

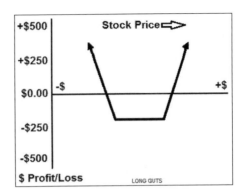

Short Guts

(credit spread)

Structure: Sell 1 ITM Call, Sell 1 ITM Put

Potential: Low Reward, High Risk

The stock price must reside between the strike prices of the short positions to be profitable.

Substantial loss may occur if market price of underlying stock puts either the put or the call deep ITM and is either bought back for a loss or exercised.

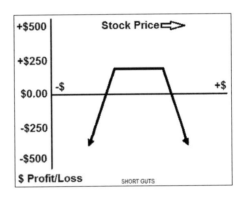

Long Call Ladder

(credit spread unless ITM Call premium higher than combined ATM and OTM Call premiums)

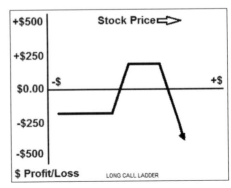

Structure: Buy 1 ITM Call, Sell 1 ATM Call, Sell 1 OTM Call

Potential: Low Reward; Low Downside risk; High Upside Risk

Max profit occurs when the stock price remains between strike prices of the call options sold.

Breakeven: Upper BE = Total strike prices of short calls − Strike price of long call − Premium paid − Transaction fees

Lower BE = Strike price of long call + Premium paid − Transaction fees

Short Call Ladder

(credit spread unless ITM Call premium higher than combined ATM and OTM Call premiums)

Structure: Sell 1 ITM Call, Buy 1 ATM Call, Buy 1 OTM Call

Potential: High Upside Reward; Low Downside Reward

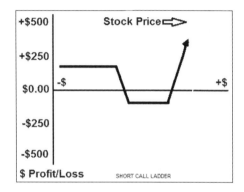

Profit achieved when stock price > Total strike prices of long calls − Strike price of short call + Net premium received

Max loss occurs when stock price is between the strike prices of the 2 long calls

Max loss = Strike price of lower strike long call − Strike price of short call − Net premium received + Transaction fees

Long Put Ladder

(credit spread unless ITM Put premium higher than combined ATM and OTM Put premiums)

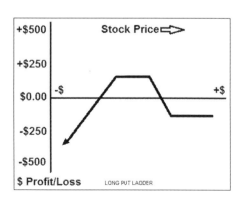

Structure: Buy 1 ITM Put, Sell 1 ATM Put, Sell 1 OTM Put (≤ 60 Days)

Potential: Low Reward, High Downside Risk; Low Upside Risk

Max profit achieved when stock price is between the strike prices of the 2 short puts

Loss occurs when stock price < Total strike prices of short puts − Strike price of long put + Net premium paid + Transaction fees.

Breakeven:

Upper BE = Strike price of long put − Net premium paid − Transaction fees

Lower BE = Total strike prices of short Puts − Strike p rice of long Put + Net premium paid − Transaction fees

Short Put Ladder

Also called a Bull Put Ladder (credit unless ITM Put premium higher than combined ATM and OTM Put premiums)

Structure: Sell 1 ITM Put, Buy 1 ATM Put, Buy 1 OTM Put (≤ 60 Days)

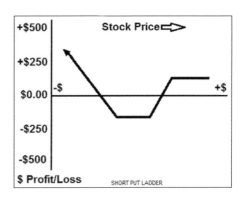

Potential: High Downside Reward; Low Upside Reward

(Used with significant near-term volatility)

Profit achieved when stock price < Total strike prices of long puts − Strike price of short put + Net premium received − Transaction fees

Profit = Lower breakeven − Stock price

Max loss occurs when stock price is between the strike prices of the 2 long puts

Max loss = Strike price of Short put − Strike price of higher strike long put − Net premium received + Transaction fees

Breakeven:

Upper BE = Strike price of short Put − Net premium received

Lower BE = total strike prices of long Puts − Strike price of short put + Net premium received

Strip

(debit spread; a modified, more bearish version of a straddle)

Structure: Buy 1 ATM Call, Buy 2 ATM Puts (≤ 60 Days)

Potential: High Reward, Low Risk

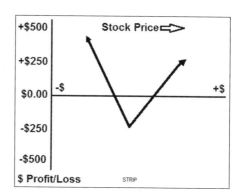

Profit achieved when stock price > Strike price of calls/puts + Net premium paid

OR

Stock price < Strike price of calls/puts − (Net premium paid/2)

Risk is limited to the net premium paid.

Max loss = Premium paid + Transaction fees

Strap

(debit spread; a modified, more bullish version of a straddle)

Structure: Buy 2 ATM Calls, Buy 1 ATM Put (≥ 90 Days)

Potential: High Reward; Low Risk

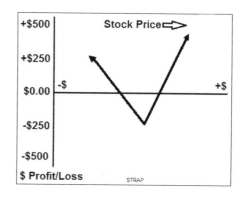

Profit achieved when stock price > strike price of calls/puts + (Net premium paid/1)

OR

Stock price < Strike price of calls/puts − Net Premium paid

Max loss = Premium paid + Transaction fees

Synthetic Strategies

Definition of "Synthetic" A synthetic strategy uses a financial instrument that is created artificially by simulating another instrument with the combined features of a collection of other assets. For example, you can create a synthetic stock by purchasing a call option and simultaneously selling a put option on the same stock. The synthetic stock would have the same capital-gain potential as the underlying stock.

> **NOTE** Unless otherwise noted, strategies use same expiration dates.

Synthetic Long Call

(debit strategy)

(Married put and Protective put strategies are examples of synthetic long calls.)

Structure: Long 100 Shares, Buy 1 ATM Put (≥ 90 Days)

Potential: High Reward, Low Risk (Unless market price of stock drops)

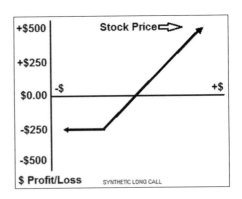

Profit achieved when price of stock > (purchase price of stock + premium paid)

Profit = price of stock − (purchase price of stock + premium paid + Transaction fees)

Synthetic Long Put

(debit strategy)

Structure: Short 100 Shares, Buy 1 ATM Call (≥ 90 Days)

Potential: High Reward, Low Risk (Unless market price of stock rallies)

Profit achieved when price of stock < (sale price of stock − premium paid)

Profit = Sale price of stock − (stock price + premium paid + Transaction fees)

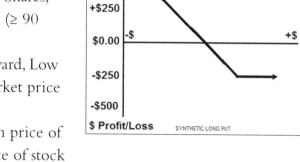

Synthetic Long Stock (Split Strikes)

(debit to neutral spread)

Structure: Buy 1 slightly OTM Call, Sell 1 slightly OTM Put (≤ 60 Days)

Potential: Strong price rally required to achieve a profit

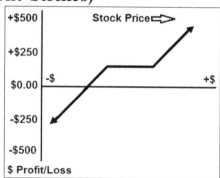

Synthetic Long Stock

(neutral spread)

Structure: Buy 1 ATM Call, Sell 1 ATM Put (≤ 60 Days)

Potential: High Reward; High Risk

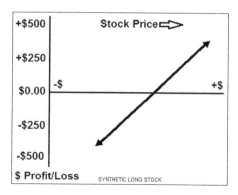

Synthetic Short Call

(credit strategy excluding cost of stock)

Structure: Short 100 shares; Sell 1 ATM Put (≤ 60 Days)

Potential: Low reward potential (Shorted stock also introduces a measure of risk.)

Maximum profit = Premium received − Transaction fees paid

Maximum profit achieved when price of stock $\leq$ strike price of short put

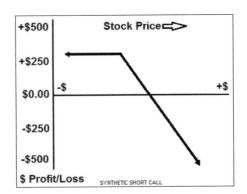

Synthetic Short Put

(credit strategy excluding cost of stock)

Structure: Long 100 shares; Sell 1 ATM Call (≤ 60 Days)

Potential: Low reward potential

Maximum profit = Premium Received − Transaction fees paid

Max Profit: Price of stock $\geq$ Strike price of short call

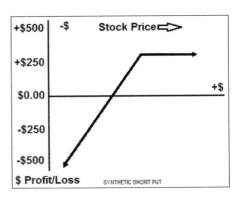

Synthetic Short Stock (Split Strikes)

(debit spread; typically a small debit is paid)

Structure: Sell 1 slightly OTM Call; Buy 1 slightly OTM Put (≤ 60 Days)

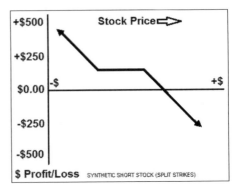

Potential: Split strike offers some upside protection.

Strong downward move produces profit. If stock price rises slightly, trade will not suffer any loss.

Synthetic Short Stock

(small debit; bearish on underlying stock)

Structure: Buy 1 ATM Put; Sell
1 ATM Call (≤ 60 Days)

Potential: High profit, High
risk

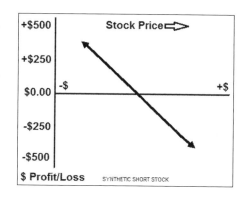

Long Call Synthetic Straddle

(debit strategy)

Structure: Buy 2 ATM Calls,
Short 100 shares

Potential: High Reward, Low
Risk (a synthetic of a long
call straddle)

Buying enough ATM calls
to cover twice the shares
shorted, i.e., buy 2 calls for
each 100 shares shorted

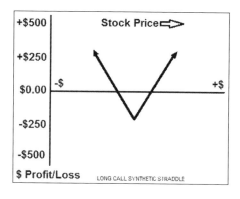

Long Put Synthetic Straddle

(debit)

Structure: Buy 2 ATM Puts;
Long 100 Shares (≥ 90
Days)

Potential: High profit, Low
risk

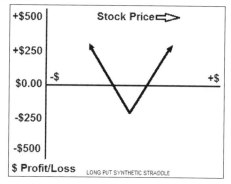

Used in anticipation of near-term high volatility; buy 2 ATM puts for each 100 long shares

Short Call Synthetic Straddle

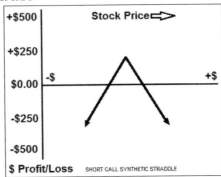

(credit strategy)

(Should have a strong bullish bias on the stock)

Structure: Sell 2 ATM Calls; Long 100 shares (≤ 60 Days)

Potential: Low Reward, High Risk

Only use this strategy when minimal volatility is expected.

Short Put Synthetic Straddle

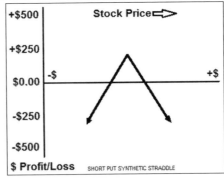

(credit strategy; **NOT RECOMMENDED!**)

(Should have a strong bearish bias on the stock)

Structure: Sell 2 ATM Puts; Short 100 Shares (≤ 60 Days)

Potential: Low Reward, High Risk

Like the Short Call Synthetic Straddle, use this strategy in anticipation of low volatility.

Summary of Synthetics Table

Spread Name	Long Call	Long Put	Short Call	Short Put	Long Stock	Short Stock	Comments
Synthetic Long Stock	●			●			Unlimited Risk/Reward BE = Strike +/− Premium
Synthetic Short Stock		●	●				Unlimited Risk/Reward BE = Strike +/− Premium
Synthetic Long Call		●			●		Unlimited Reward/Limited Risk; BE = Stock Price + Put Cost
Synthetic Short Call				●		●	Unlimited Risk/ Limited Reward BE = Stock Sale + Premium Received
Synthetic Long Put	●					●	Unlimited Reward/ Limited Risk BE = Stock Sale − Premium Paid
Synthetic Short Put			●		●		Unlimited Risk/Limited Reward BE = Stock Price − Premium Received

NOTES

1. BE = Breakeven
2. Transaction fees must also be deducted.
3. All puts and calls are ATM, i.e., 1 ATM Long Call, 1 ATM Short Put, etc.
4. All stock purchases/sales are 100 shares per option contract

THE CBOE MARGIN CALCULATOR

The CBOE margin calculator makes computing standard account margin an easy, straightforward process. While margin requirement corresponding to an options strategy, including most common spreads, can be calculated using basic arithmetic, the CBOE calculator speeds up the process. Of course you can also create your own margin calculator using an Excel worksheet.

Provided as a courtesy by Chicago Board Options Exchange, Incorporated.

But when you have a complex option strategy with multiple put and/or call legs at different strike prices, the CBOE's online margin calculator may do the job. This calculator is available at: http://www.cboe.com/tradtool/mcalc/.

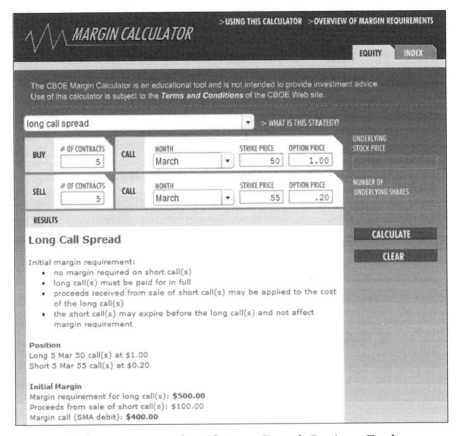

Provided as a courtesy by Chicago Board Options Exchange, Incorporated.

When the calculator loads, it provides a drop-down list of option strategies. It also permits the entry of the price of the underlying stock for strategies such as stock covered calls. The following margin calculation example is that of a long call spread, which is commonly called a bull call spread.

Notice how the margin requirements are displayed near the bottom of the above margin calculator illustration. As you can see, the margin requirement for the long call is $500 which must be paid when the trade is entered. The proceeds for the sale of the five short calls is $100. The total margin required for this trade is $400.

Now examine the following short strangle example on a $50/share stock. The strike prices of the short put and short call are $25 and $75, respectively. The premium values are entered in the Option Price boxes. This option computation expires in roughly 30 days (the calculation was made on January 21st with a third Friday February option contract expiration). With this setup, the CBOE margin calculator produces the indicated results:

NOTE Margin for long and short stock positions are easily calculated if you know your brokerage's margin percentage rate.

Long stock margin is calculated by multiplying the number of shares × the share price × the margin rate.

100 shares × $25 × 50% = $1,250

Short stock margin is calculated by using the identical formula plus the addition of the value of the shorted shares of stock. (150% is a shortcut to include the cost of the stock).

100 shares × $25 × 150% $3,750

Margin requirement for options are substantially different. Go to CBOE Margin Requirement Examples for Sample Options-based Positions to see actual examples.

Provided as a courtesy by Chicago Board Options Exchange, Incorporated.

One more calculation is made on an index. The index price is 2000, which would be similar the S&P 500 financial index, symbol SPX. As shown in the calculator illustration, five puts are sold 200 points below the price of the hypothetical SPX index, and five calls are sold 100 points above. Put premiums of $0.50 and call premiums of $0.25 are shown. The CBOE margin calculator produces the results shown in the next illustration.

Provided as a courtesy by Chicago Board Options Exchange, Incorporated.

As you can see, the CBOE calculator is quite easy to use. This is *standard* account margin. This typically uses 50% of the value of *big board* stocks held in your account. Traders having portfolio margin receive 85% credit of their account value. This margin calculator does NOT compute portfolio margin.

TEST YOUR OPTIONS KNOWLEDGE!

See how many of the following questions you can answer. An answer key is included following the chapter 16 *What Did You Learn* answer key.

1. The _____ value is midway between the Bid and the Ask values.
2. We trade options because they provide financial _____ and _____ when compared to trading stocks.
3. The at the money value of _____ is close to 0.5 for call options.
4. Gamma dictates the rate of change of _____.
5. Gamma's value is _____ when ATM.
6. We pay _____ when we buy a put or a call option.
7. We like to buy options when the IV% is _____.
8. We like to sell options when the IV% is _____.
9. Traders usually sell option contracts that expire within ____ (or ____) days.
10. Traders usually buy option contracts that expire in ____ or more days.
11. Name the five Greeks in alphabetical order: _____, _____, _____, _____, and _____.

12. A change in the value of _____ has the most effect on the price of option premium.

13. _____measures the decay in premium resulting from the passage of each day.

14. An option contract can only be exercised when the option price becomes _____ (abbrev.).

15. The seller of a _____ option must pay for the stock if the seller's option contract is exercised.

16. The seller of a _____ option must deliver stock to the option buyer if exercised.

17. An option contract is said to expire _____ if the strike price remains OTM for the duration of the contract.

18. An active American style option contract can be _____ if the underlying becomes ITM prior to contract expiration.

19. A European style option cannot be exercised prior to contract _____.

20. The call and put options are both bought ATM when trading buying a long _____.

21. The strip option strategy buys two ATM puts and _____ _____ call.

22. A bull call spread includes one or more ATM or slightly OTM long calls and an equal number of _____ _____.

23. The trader of a bull call spread expects the price of the underlying to _____ (or_____).

24. The candle that resembles a plus sign is called a _____.

25. The "shooting star" candle resembles an inverted _____.

26. A bracketed trade includes a limit entry, a _____stop, and a limit _____.

27. The acronym GTC stands for _____ _____ _____.

28. Financial index trades are _____ settled.

29. Mathematical studies used on price charts are called odds _____.

30. The acronym ATR, as in the ATR (14) study stands for _____ _____ _____.

31. The acronym MACD stands for moving average _____, _____.

32. The outer bands of the Keltner Channel are 1.5 × the _____ above and below the SMA(20).

33. The outer Bollinger bands measure increases and decreases in _____.

34. The acronym SMA stands for _____ _____ _____.

35. An uncovered short call is considered an extremely _____ option position.

36. The collar strategy is constructed from 100 shares of stock for each short call and _____ _____.

37. A common reversal pattern found with an up-trending stock is called a _____ flag.

38. The double top, triple top, and head and shoulders patterns are all considered bearish _____ patterns.

39. The cup and _____ is a popular bullish consolidation pattern.

40. The ES e-mini option contract includes _____ shares of stock per contract.

41. The ES e-mini futures contract includes four quarterly expiration date suffixes H-M-U-Z. The suffix U represents expiration in the month of _____.

42. Futures values are calculated using points and tics. The ES uses four tics per _____. Each ES tic has a value of $_____.

43. Forex pairs use a quote value and a _____ value. The EUR/USD pair represents the following currencies: _____/_____.

44. When away from your computer, you can use your _____ to monitor and manage trades.

45. Every trader should have a _____ system in case of a power outage.

46. Brokerages will often reduce commissions for an _____ trader.

47. An exchange fee must be paid for each _____ _____ either bought or sold.

48. Most traders develop _____ _____ of stock symbols that they frequently trade.

49. Holding a long list of different stocks in one's portfolio is not considered _____.

50. When a brokerage account becomes stressed, the trader may receive a _____ _____.

51. A margin account is used to expedite _____ rather than waiting for a trade to settle.

52. The highest option trading level permits option traders to use _____ trade strategies.

53. Another word for a naked call is an _____ call.

54. The short put and the short strangle are both _____ collection strategies.

55. Option buyers are not _____ to exercise an ITM position.

56. Option sellers have more _____ than option buyers.

57. 68.27% is one _____ _____ OTM.

58. When prices are rallying, basing, and dropping, trading volume is the lowest when the prices are _____.

59. The weighted average price at which most trading has occurred is referred to by the acronym _____.

60. The Open Interest values on option chains measure liquidity. When liquidity is low, submitted trades may not be _____.

61. Rolling a short call _____ the current position and _____ another position farther out in time.

62. A _____ spread is similar to a calendar spread.

63. There are balanced, unbalanced, and broken wing versions of the _____ spread.

64. Option traders can obtain a discount on the price of a stock by selling an OTM _____.

65. Trade what you _____ and not what you feel, hear, hope, or think.

66. The market opens in the morning at _____ EST and closes in the afternoon at _____ EST.

67. You can trade stocks during _____ hours using either _____ or _____ _____.

68. _____ is a technique used by day traders to regularly take small profits.

69. Many traders draw _____ retracements on their charts to find likely entry and exit levels.

70. Momentum _____ are used by many traders to determine overbought/oversold conditions.

71. Stock prices frequently rally off established _____ levels and drop from established _____ levels.

72. A _____ zone is a historical price turning point where demand becomes greater than supply.

73. The acronym OCO stands for _____ _____ _____.

74. Day traders most often use a trading _____ to enter and exit trades.

75. Most day traders use _____ trades with stops and profit targets.

76. Novice traders typically lack experience and trading _____.

77. Delta-triggered stops are more stable than _____-triggered stops.

78. Stocks and ETFs with a narrow Bid to Ask spread usually have high volume and high _____.

79. The _____ _____ is the resistance to price change based on trading volume.

80. A _____ spread sells more OTM options than the number of ATM options bought.

81. A _____ spread purchases a back-month option and sells a front-month option of the same underlying.

82. A midcap company is said to have a market capitalization value of between _____ _____ dollars and _____ _____ dollars.

83. A trader must have a _____ account to short a stock.

84. Simulated trading is also referred to as _____ trading.

85. Traders close long option positions using _____ to _____ orders.

86. Traders close short option positions using _____ to _____ orders.

87. Traders who short stocks make a profit when the price of the stock _____.

88. Option writers are the _____ of option contracts.

89. Market _____ match and fill buy and sell orders.

90. _____ exchanges, such as the CBOE, are for-profit companies that transact options trades.

91. The acronym ECN stands for _____ _____ _____.

92. A _____ spread is used when traders believe the price of the underlying will move sideways.

93. Traders are said to be _____ when they believe the price of the underlying will rally.

94. Traders often avoid company events, such as _____ _____, when they want to avoid a sudden price breakout.

95. The _____ moving average (EMA) places more emphasis on the most recent data points.

96. _____ orders fill faster than limit orders.

97. An order that requires the price of the underlying to be at, above, or below a specified price is a _____ order.

98. Financial _____ provides a higher rate of return using a smaller amount of money.

99. Long-term Equity Anticipation Security (LEAPS) options are typically used with _____ _____ options in anticipation of a price rally.

100. The value from a change in the underlying security is referred to as _____ value; the time value that remains in option premium is referred to as _____ value.

WHAT DID YOU LEARN ANSWER KEYS

Chapter 1 Answer Key

1. Is it possible to earn $1,000/day trading options? ☑ Yes ☐ NO.
2. How many trading days are in a calendar year? <u>252</u> .
3. Traders who enter 4 or more trades within 5 business days are <u>pattern</u> <u>day</u> traders, and must maintain a minimum margin account balance of <u>$25,000</u>.
4. Every trade involves the transfer of money from one trader's <u>account</u> to another's.
5. Every trade includes a buy and sell order between a <u>willing</u> <u>buyer</u> and <u>willing</u> <u>seller</u>.
6. In option trading, Bid = <u>sell</u> and Ask = <u>buy</u>.
7. A trader is said to *scalp* working trades for short-term <u>profits</u>.
8. Professional traders make their living by taking money from <u>novice</u> <u>traders.</u>
9. Professional traders develop and then use time-tested <u>rules</u>.
10. Novice traders typically buy when prices are <u>high</u> and sell when prices are <u>low</u>.
11. Floyd made $1,000 per day trading <u>covered</u> <u>call</u> options on a list of stocks.
12. Karen made <u>$41</u> <u>million</u> on index options in three years.

13. Chuck won world international trading championships <u>7</u> times by trading options.
14. It takes <u>money</u> to make money.
15. <u>Risk</u> <u>management</u> is always a top trading priority.
16. Trading involves <u>risk</u>.
17. Who is responsible for the outcome of trades? <u>The</u> <u>trader</u>.
18. Develop a fact-based <u>bias</u> before trading.
19. Most brokerages provide <u>education</u> and platform training.
20. To find option education, do a web search on the words <u>option</u> <u>education.</u>

Chapter 2 Answer Key

1. Financial leverage provides a bigger <u>return</u> with a smaller amount of <u>money</u>.
2. Options are financial <u>derivatives</u> of other equities and indexes.
3. Option traders buy and sell option contracts by paying and collecting <u>premium.</u>
4. <u>Option</u> <u>chains</u> are financial tables used to enter and exit option contracts.
5. Every option contract has an <u>expiration</u> date.
6. The left-hand side of an option chain lists <u>calls</u> and the right-hand side lists <u>puts</u>.
7. The closest option price to the market price of the underlying security is said to be <u>at</u> <u>the money.</u>
8. Abbreviations: ITM = <u>in</u> <u>the</u> <u>money</u> ATM = <u>at</u> <u>the</u> <u>money,</u> OTM = <u>out</u> <u>of</u> <u>the</u> <u>money.</u>
9. Example 1 in chapter 2 compares a stock trade to an option trade. The stock trade returned 8% on the investment while the option trade returned <u>100</u>%.
10. Options offer both financial leverage and <u>flexibility.</u>
11. What is a spread as applied to options? An option trade having two or more <u>legs</u>.
12. Time decay causes the price of option premiums to <u>decline.</u>

13. Simultaneously buying–to–close an option and selling to open a new position is referred to as <u>rolling.</u>

14. Rolls are used to increase profit. They can also be used for trade <u>maintenance.</u>

15. Taking a long position means to <u>buy</u> a stock or an option contract.

16. Standard day trading hours begin at <u>9:30</u> a.m. and end at <u>4:00</u> p.m. Eastern Time.

17. Standard option contracts include 100 shares; mini option contract include <u>10</u> shares.

18. Open Interest is the current number of <u>working orders.</u>

19. Probability ITM is the statistical probability of an option price becoming <u>in the money</u> through contract expiration.

20. The value of <u>Theta</u> is a measure of premium exiting an option with each passing day.

Chapter 3 Answer Key

1. Options are financial <u>derivatives</u> of equities.

2. In addition to a primary trading computer, traders should also have one or more <u>backup</u> systems.

3. Every trader should have a set of <u>trading</u> rules.

4. People who anticipate market growth are said to have a <u>bullish</u> bias.

5. The terms long and short mean <u>buy</u> and <u>sell</u>.

6. Bar charts were replaced with Japanese <u>candlestick</u> charts in the 1990s.

7. Institutional traders often buy or sell a few <u>million shares</u> at a time.

8. Three terms used to describe price dynamics include rally, <u>base,</u> and <u>drop.</u>

9. Standard deviation tracks the average number of data points produced by <u>trading activity</u>.

10. Call premium increases as the price of the underlying <u>rallies</u>.

11. The number of shares required to move the price of a security is called <u>market</u> <u>depth.</u>
12. When market liquidity is high, trades execute more <u>quickly.</u>
13. There are both physical securities exchanges and <u>electronic</u> securities exchanges.
14. A market maker is a dealer who matches <u>buy</u> and <u>sell</u> orders.
15. ECNs support trading outside traditional stock exchanges and are designed to match <u>limit</u> orders.
16. Holding a dozen or more stocks is not <u>diversification.</u>
17. Within each market sector are <u>industries.</u>
18. Most experienced traders study economic <u>data</u> and <u>reports.</u>
19. Penny stocks are also called <u>pink</u> sheet and <u>over</u> <u>the</u> counter stocks, are not regulated, and are considered risky.
20. Not all financial securities are <u>optionable.</u>

Chapter 4 Answer Key

1. Not all brokerages offer all trading <u>venues.</u>
2. Full-service brokerages typically charge <u>higher</u> transaction fees than discount brokerages.
3. Develop a <u>checklist</u> for evaluating your brokerage.
4. The <u>SIPC</u> protects brokerage accounts much like the FDIC protects bank accounts.
5. SEC reforms on <u>liquidity</u> ensure that broker–dealers maintain suitable reserves.
6. Active traders may be granted lower brokerage <u>commissions</u> and <u>fees.</u>
7. When buying or selling option contracts, two charges exist: a <u>commission</u> and <u>exchange</u> fees.
8. The <u>OCC</u> oversees options and futures trading.
9. A <u>margin</u> account allows investors to borrow money from the broker.
10. Brokerage margin accounts <u>eliminate</u> the time required for a trade to settle.

11. Penny stocks cannot be used as collateral for <u>margin</u>.

12. Experienced traders with high–dollar accounts may apply for <u>portfolio</u> margin.

13. A stock or option <u>scanner</u> lists stocks that meet one or more established criteria.

14. A <u>back</u> <u>trade</u> uses historical market data.

15. A table of stocks used by traders to scan for trades is called a <u>watch</u> <u>list</u>.

16. A <u>dynamic</u> watch list (sometimes called *radar*) automatically adds and removes symbols according to the scan criteria.

17. The <u>candlestick</u> chart type is the most popular in use today.

18. A <u>bracketed</u> trade includes a limit entry, a protective stop, and a profit target.

19. What is chart trading? Sliding and moving <u>stops</u> and <u>targets</u> directly on a price <u>chart</u>.

20. Some traders use <u>smartphones</u> to enter, manage, and exit trades.

Chapter 5 Answer Key

1. Trading is a <u>business</u> .

2. Trading is not a <u>casual</u> <u>hobby</u>.

3. Your trading equipment MUST be <u>reliable</u>.

4. Ensure you have fast access to your <u>brokerage</u>.

5. Do your market analysis and find potential trades before the <u>market</u> <u>opens</u>.

6. Quit trading at a <u>regular</u> <u>time</u>.

7. During your simulated trading experience, find out which trades <u>work</u> <u>best</u>.

8. Establish <u>rules</u> for each trading strategy. (See setup parameters in chapters 14 and 15.)

9. Find and trade in your <u>comfort</u> <u>zone</u>.

10. Traders blow out their accounts by ignoring their <u>risk</u> <u>manage-ment</u> rules.

11. Revenge <u>trading</u> is irrational.

12. Find the trades that work. Then <u>use them</u> for a steady stream of incremental returns.

13. Separate multiple displays are <u>not necessary.</u>

14. Microsoft Excel is useful for <u>downloading</u> and <u>uploading</u> watch lists and trading data.

15. You should have a <u>reliable</u> connection to your brokerage.

16. You should have a <u>backup plan</u>.

17. If your Internet service is intermittent, find another <u>service provider</u>.

18. Be sure to download the <u>smartphone trading application</u>.

19. Put your brokerage's <u>phone number</u> on your smartphone in case of emergency.

20. Your brokerage's local branch office is another <u>backup</u> resource.

Chapter 6 Answer Key

1. Trading style includes the days and amount of time spent trading, the markets traded, and the average <u>duration</u> of each trade.

2. A trading style that may be well suited to some traders may be too <u>stressful</u> for others.

3. Different trading styles are better suited to some <u>markets</u> than others.

4. <u>Scalpers</u> are traders who take quick profits on sudden price breakouts.

5. Day traders are <u>intraday</u> traders.

6. Gambling is a form of <u>entertainment;</u> trading is a <u>business.</u>

7. Day traders thrive on <u>volatility.</u>

8. Some day traders use Fibonacci retracement lines for the placement of <u>entries</u> and <u>exits.</u>

9. Floor trader pivot point lines show <u>support</u> and <u>resistance</u> levels.

10. These traders make common use of protective stops and one or more <u>profit targets</u>.

11. Most day traders keep their hand on the <u>mouse</u>, ready to scalp and exit in an instant.

12. A trader whose trades remain active for two or more days is called a <u>swing</u> trader.

13. Swing traders use the same <u>price</u> <u>charts</u> and analytical skills as day trades.

14. Swing traders typically begin their research by looking at <u>weekly</u> price charts.

15. A key is to follow a set of <u>trading</u> <u>rules</u> to guide them through the trading process.

16. Long-term traders buy and <u>hold</u> securities for extended periods of time.

17. A LEAPS trade typically remains active for more than a <u>year</u> .

18. When buying an option, time decay <u>erodes</u> premium.

19. The Greek symbol <u>Theta</u> is a measure of time decay.

20. Trade income received inside an IRA or 401K account is tax <u>free</u> .

Chapter 7 Answer Key

1. Technical analysis is used with randomly generated data based on <u>trader</u> <u>sentiment.</u>

2. Examining a company's underlying financial condition is part of <u>fundamental</u> analysis.

3. The study of <u>historical</u> <u>price</u> data is useful for predicting future price movements.

4. The Gaussian Random Walk and EMH disavow the usefulness of <u>technical</u> <u>analysis</u> .

5. Japanese candlestick charts were first used with Japanese <u>rice</u> <u>futures</u> .

6. A single candlestick shows four price levels: <u>open,</u> <u>close,</u> <u>high,</u> and <u>low.</u>

7. Use multiple charts having different <u>time</u> <u>intervals</u> .

8. A doji candlestick is formed when the opening and closing price are the <u>same.</u>

9. Some traders use the shapes of <u>candlesticks</u> to predict a price reversal and breakouts.

10. Finding a definite price <u>trend</u> is an important first step in chart analysis.

11. A sequence of lower lows and lower highs indicates a <u>bearish</u> price trend.

12. A historical support level is also called a <u>demand</u> zone.

13. Trade what you <u>see</u>, not what you think, fear, feel, hear, or hope.

14. Stock prices tend to remain between established <u>support</u> and <u>resistance</u> levels.

15. Securities are <u>overbought</u> at resistance and <u>oversold</u> at support.

16. In an upward–trending stock, a bull flag signals an <u>entry</u> <u>opportunity</u> for a bullish trade.

17. It would be naïve to believe that popular chart patterns <u>always</u> <u>work.</u>

18. Two classifications of chart patterns are <u>reversal</u> and <u>continuation</u> patterns.

19. The double–top, triple–top, and head and shoulders are all <u>reversal</u> patterns.

20. The bullish flag and cup with <u>handle</u> are continuation patterns.

Chapter 8 Answer Key

1. Chart studies are also referred to as odds <u>enhancers.</u>

2. When shorting a stock, a protective stop is placed <u>above</u> the limit entry price.

3. <u>Momentum</u> is the speed at which the market moves.

4. Volatility is a result of high <u>trading</u> <u>volume.</u>

5. Comparing price momentum of a stock to its index is called <u>beta</u> weighting.

6. Four momentum oscillators include the CCI, MACD, RSI, and <u>Stochastics</u> oscillator.

7. The exponential moving average places more weight on the most <u>recent</u> price points.

8. MACD is an acronym for moving average convergence-divergence.

9. The ATR(14) shows the average price range over the past 14 days.

10. Two volatility measures include historical and implied (or current) volatility.

11. Current volatility is an excellent measure of trader sentiment.

12. When IV is at 50%, it is halfway between the high and low of HV.

13. The acronym VWAP stands for volume-weighted average price.

14. The VWAP is the average price at which most of the trading has occurred.

15. One standard deviation is 68.2%. It is a measure of price volatility and trader sentiment.

16. Many option traders use the standard deviation as a probability measure.

17. The Bollinger Band envelope is 2× the standard deviation above and below the SMA(20) centerline.

18. The envelope of the Keltner Channel study is 1.5 × the ATR(14) above and below the SMA(20) centerline.

19. The TTM_Squeeze signals a price breakout when five red dots appear on the axis line.

20. The Fibonacci value 1.616, which abounds in nature, is called the golden ratio.

Chapter 9 Answer Key

1. A DAY order expires at the end of the trading day.

2. The GTC order stands for good till canceled.

3. A GTC EXT is a GTC order that may execute during an after-hours trading session.

4. An EXT order is a day order that may execute during after-hours trading.

5. The 1st trgs All order is triggered when <u>one</u> <u>order</u> is filled.

6. A Minute order type automatically <u>cancels</u> after a specified time interval.

7. An <u>OCO</u> order type closes all other working orders when one is filled.

8. The <u>Blast All</u> order immediately submits all orders to the market.

9. In a 1st trgs Seq order, the <u>first</u> order must fill before the second order is sent.

10. If a trader wants to fill an order immediately, a <u>market</u> order is used.

11. Limit orders will only fill at a price <u>equal</u> <u>to</u> or <u>better</u> than that specified.

12. Protective stops should always use a <u>GTC</u> order type.

13. Going long or short means <u>buying</u> or <u>selling</u>, respectively.

14. Selling ten Boeing 150 October 2017 call contracts is written: <u>−10 BA Oct 17 150 CALLS.</u>

15. This option contract expires on the <u>third</u> <u>Friday</u> of October 2017.

16. Buying five Boeing 140 October 2017 put contracts is written: +5 BA <u>140 Oct 17 PUTS.</u>

17. The most conservative limit entry is called a <u>distal</u> entry by some traders.

18. Traders often manage their working bracketed by <u>sliding</u> stops.

19. NEVER slide a <u>protective</u> <u>stop</u> for a greater loss.

20. If a bracketed trade moves into profit, slide your <u>protective</u> <u>stop</u> above the entry.

Chapter 10 Answer Key

1. An option contract is a <u>time</u>-<u>limited</u> contract between two parties.

2. When a call or put option contract expires out of the money, it favors the <u>seller.</u>

3. The shaded portions of an option chain include strike prices that are <u>ITM.</u>
4. The midpoint between the Bid and Ask price is called the <u>Mark.</u>
5. The trader pays premium when trading a <u>debit</u> spread.
6. The trader receives premium when trading a <u>credit</u> spread.
7. The two option contract styles are called the <u>American</u> and <u>European</u> style.
8. The <u>American</u> style option contract can be exercised prior to contract expiration.
9. The S&P 500 and NASDAQ financial index options are <u>European</u> style options.
10. Financial index options are <u>cash</u> settled rather than security settled.
11. Most option traders who trade LEAPS usually buy <u>call</u> <u>options</u>.
12. Delta displays a decimal value at each strike price. Delta is used to calculate the change in premium value for a <u>$1.00</u> change in the price of the underlying security.
13. The Mark is interpreted as the <u>market</u> <u>price.</u>
14. The most conservative probability metric is Probability <u>Touching.</u>
15. Open Interest is important because it is a measure of <u>liquidity.</u>
16. Option sellers should sell inside <u>60</u> days.
17. Shorter times till expiration increase risk for option <u>buyers.</u>
18. The first option premium calculation formula is known as the <u>Black-Scholes</u> formula.
19. The Bjerksun-Stensland model was developed to calculate <u>American</u>-Style options pricing.
20. Trading permissions are used to govern options trading levels and corresponding <u>risk</u>.

Chapter 11 Answer Key

1. Weekly options expire on Fridays of <u>each</u> <u>week</u> except for holidays.
2. Monthly and quarterly option contracts expire on the <u>third</u> <u>Friday</u> of the month.
3. Debit spreads require a trader to pay <u>premium</u> upon entry.
4. Long-term options cost <u>more</u> than short-term options.
5. Buying a call in anticipation of a price rally is a <u>bullish</u> strategy.
6. When a call becomes ITM, the call buyer can either <u>sell</u> or <u>exercise</u> the call contract.
7. Many option traders are not interested in holding <u>stock</u> or <u>ETFs</u>.
8. Stocks are more susceptible to <u>price</u> <u>drops</u> in a bear market.
9. When selling a call, the trader's goal is to collect premium without being <u>exercised.</u>
10. Selling a naked call requires the highest <u>level</u> <u>trading</u> <u>permission</u>.
11. A short call expires <u>worthless</u> if it remains OTM through contract expiration.
12. Buying one or more put options is a <u>bearish</u> strategy.
13. Many traders sell OTM puts for <u>premium</u> <u>income.</u>
14. When buying premium, the total amount put at risk is the price <u>paid.</u>
15. Three probability values include ITM, OTM, and <u>Touching.</u>
16. Probability values are especially important to <u>option</u> <u>sellers</u>.
17. The column headed by Vega represents the effect of <u>volatility</u> on premium value.
18. The little-used Greek letter Rho represents rate of <u>interest.</u>
19. The effect of a $1.00 change on option premium is represented by <u>Delta.</u>
20. The Greek letter Gamma controls the rate of change of <u>Delta.</u>

Chapter 12 Questions

1. Greek letters are commonly used in <u>mathematical</u> <u>equations.</u>

2. The Greek letters used to calculate option <u>premiums</u> were first used in the Black-Scholes formula.
3. An English word that fits the meaning of Delta is <u>difference.</u>
4. A fitting Greek letter for Rate of Interest is <u>rho.</u>
5. Both *Vega* and <u>volatility</u> begin with the letter **V**.
6. The strike price closest to the money has a Delta value close to <u>.50</u>.
7. Delta values <u>increase</u> as call strike prices become deeper ITM.
8. Vega values are <u>highest</u> ATM.
9. Delta values become smaller as call strike prices move <u>farther OTM.</u>
10. Delta values for ITM puts are <u>negative.</u>
11. Put Delta values increase as strike prices move <u>farther</u> OTM.
12. Gamma values of calls are highest when <u>ATM.</u>
13. A negative Theta value shows the daily <u>decline</u> in premium value at each <u>strike</u> price.
14. Gamma values are higher when an option contract <u>nears expiration.</u>
15. Vega is the measure of a 1% change in the volatility of the <u>underlying</u> <u>security.</u>
16. Vega values are always <u>positive.</u>
17. *Extrinsic* (time) value is the exiting of <u>premium</u> with the passage of <u>time.</u>
18. *Intrinsic* value is calculated as the net difference in value between two <u>strike</u> <u>prices.</u>
19. Rho is rarely considered by some <u>option</u> <u>traders.</u>
20. When interest rates are high, Rho can introduce a new source of <u>risk.</u>

Chapter 13 Answer Key

1. <u>Emotion</u> can be a trader's enemy.
2. Never slide a stop when a trade is <u>going</u> <u>against</u> <u>you.</u>
3. Your rules work when you lose a <u>planned</u> <u>amount.</u>

4. Pet <u>symbols</u> are also among the taboos traders engage in.
5. Those hot tips you get from the so-called "gurus" on TV are <u>worthless.</u>
6. Instead of taking the advice of friends and family, trade what you <u>see.</u>
7. Being a <u>pig</u> often happens when a trader is unwilling to settle for a 50% profit.
8. Trading should be run like a <u>business.</u>
9. The charter of a trading business should be underpinned by a set of <u>trading rules.</u>
10. Rules make your scanning and trading processes more <u>efficient.</u>
11. Different strategies usually have different <u>trading rules.</u>
12. Write ten topics to include in your trading rules:
    a. Trading <u>hours</u>
    b. Market <u>sentiment</u>
    c. Acceptable price <u>range</u>
    d. Acceptable trading <u>volume</u>
    e. Acceptable option <u>premium value</u>
    f. Acceptable <u>risk</u> based on probabilities and Greek values
    g. Reward–to–<u>risk ratios</u> (for bracketed entries)
    h. Minimum <u>Open</u> Interest levels on option chains
    i. Acceptable IV% for each <u>option strategy</u>
    j. Acceptable times till <u>expiration</u> for long and short option trades
    k. Acceptable <u>P/L</u> level for exiting a position
    l. Acceptable option strategy based on price charts, IV%, <u>risk,</u> and bias
    m. Maintain <u>trading records</u> with chart bias, entry, exit, and P/L data
13. The highest market volatility is usually during the <u>first</u> and <u>last</u> trading hours of the day.
14. Option traders sell <u>short-term</u> contracts and buy <u>long-term</u> contracts.

15. Add IV%, ATR(14) and Volume columns to your <u>watch lists.</u>

16. Option traders check statistical <u>probability</u> and/or <u>standard deviation</u> values.

17. Position size is a major part of <u>risk</u> <u>management</u>.

18. <u>Alerts</u> can send e-mail or text messages to smartphones.

19. Some trading strategies avoid <u>earnings</u> <u>release</u> and <u>dividend</u> dates while some use them.

20. Many option sellers can make more premium by <u>churning</u> rather than holding till expiration.

Chapter 14 Answer Key

1. You must have the highest options trading <u>permission</u> to enter uncovered trades.

2. Try the strategies presented in chapter 14 on <u>paper.</u> Find and use those strategies that work best.

3. The first step in scanning is to compile a <u>watch</u> <u>list.</u>

4. A <u>risk</u> <u>profile</u> shows possible profits or losses based on an option setup at different prices of the underlying stock for all days between trade entry and expiration.

5. The short call is a high-risk, <u>uncovered</u> option trade. It includes the sale of an OTM call.

6. The cash-covered short put is a <u>credit</u> option strategy.

7. A long call option trader is <u>bullish</u> and buys an ATM or slightly OTM call in anticipation of a price rally. The risk is the amount paid for the option contract(s).

8. A long put option trader is <u>bearish</u> and buys an ATM or slightly OTM put in anticipation of a price drop. The risk is the <u>amount</u> <u>paid</u> for the option contract(s).

9. A covered call is a <u>bullish</u> strategy in which the trader buys an <u>OTM</u> <u>call</u> and sells a farther OTM call in anticipation of a price <u>rally</u>.

10. The bull call spread is also called a <u>vertical</u> <u>spread</u> or a call spread. It buys a call and sells a farther OTM call.

11. The bull put spread buys an OTM put and sells an ATM put in anticipation of a price <u>rally</u>.

12. The debit spread trader must have a strong <u>bullish</u> bias. The maximum loss is the cost of <u>entry.</u> The goal is for both call legs to become deep <u>ITM</u>.

13. An iron condor is a <u>premium</u> <u>collection</u> strategy. It includes a short put and a short call and a farther OTM long put and long call.

14. A <u>jade</u> <u>lizard</u> includes one naked short put, one naked short call, and one long call.

15. The short strangle is a high <u>risk</u>, limited <u>reward</u> premium collection strategy.

16. A covered short strangle includes the ownership of <u>stock.</u>

17. A long strangle anticipates a strong <u>price</u> <u>movement</u> in either direction.

18. A long straddle is similar to a long strangle but it uses <u>identical</u> put and call strike prices.

19. The strip is an unbalanced bearish strategy because it buys a <u>two</u> <u>times</u> more puts than calls.

20. The strap is a mirror image of the <u>strip</u> strategy. More calls make it a <u>bullish</u> strategy.

21. A ratio spread uses a different <u>number</u> of either put or call contracts at two different strike prices.

22. Diagonal ratio spreads use different <u>expiration</u> <u>dates</u>.

23. The long guts option strategy buys an ITM put and an <u>ITM</u> call. Due to the high entry cost, this strategy requires a strong price breakout to be profitable.

24. The equity collar spread is often used as a <u>stock</u> <u>hedging</u> strategy.

25. Butterfly spreads include four option contracts and are limited <u>risk</u> and <u>reward</u> strategies.

26. The calendar spreads are limited risk, limited reward, <u>neutral</u> bias strategies.

27. The diagonal spread is another <u>time</u> <u>spread</u> that combines a long and a short call or a long and a short put. The long legs use <u>longer</u> <u>term</u> option contracts than do the short legs.

28. A long ATM call and a short ATM put is an example of a <u>synthetic</u> <u>long</u> stock.

29. A short ATM put and shorting 100 shares of stock is a <u>synthetic</u> <u>short</u> <u>call</u>.

30. A short ATM Put and long 100 shares of stock is a <u>synthetic</u> <u>long</u> <u>call</u>.

31. A long call and shorting 100 shares of stock is a <u>synthetic</u> <u>long</u> <u>put</u>.

32. The Gamma-Delta neutral spread is similar to a <u>ratio</u> <u>spread</u> that includes shorting a stock to neutralize <u>Delta</u>.

33. Three of the financial index symbols commonly shorted: <u>SPX</u>, <u>NDX</u>, and <u>RUT</u>.

34. The <u>VIX</u> volatility index is used with the S&P 500 financial index.

35. If exercised, a financial index option contract must be settled in <u>cash</u>.

36. SPX strangles involve the sale of SPX <u>calls</u> and SPX <u>puts</u>.

37. The market falls <u>faster</u> than it rises; put premiums are <u>higher</u> than call premiums..

38. For a trader to buy SPX calls, the trader must have a strong <u>bullish</u> bias.

39. Instead of buying SPX puts, a trader may prefer to buy <u>SPY</u> puts due to the high cost of SPX options.

40. The trader may finance a long SPX put by <u>selling</u> an SPX put.

Chapter 15 Answer Key

1. Futures have been in use for more than <u>2,000</u> years.

2. Many traders buy and sell <u>commodity</u> <u>futures</u> on a daily basis.

3. Excluding speculators, futures contracts are traded between producers and <u>processors</u>.

4. Financial index futures are called the <u>e-mini</u> futures.
5. Options on futures are <u>less</u> <u>expensive</u> than options on the underlying indexes.
6. Options on futures are sometimes used as <u>hedges</u> to offset loss.
7. Long put e-mini options are used to hedge against a drop in the price of the corresponding <u>financial</u> <u>index</u>.
8. Hedges <u>gain</u> <u>value</u> as the hedged security loses value.
9. The symbol for the SPX futures contracts is <u>ES</u>.
10. The e-mini future contracts expire in March, June, <u>September,</u> and <u>December</u>.
11. Future contracts use alphabetical <u>suffixes</u> to represent contract expiration months.
12. The e-mini futures contracts are <u>American</u> style.
13. The symbol NQ–M_represents the <u>NASDAQ</u> e–mini futures contract that expires in <u>June.</u>
14. The symbol for the S&P 400 mid–cap futures contracts is <u>EMD</u>.
15. Most futures speculators buy and sell futures contracts much like shares of <u>stock</u>.
16. There are <u>50</u> shares per ES option contract.
17. The short duration of weekly options reduces <u>risk.</u>
18. Pattern day trader minimums <u>do</u> <u>not</u> apply to trade e–mini options.
19. Trading a short put on an e–mini future is similar to trading a short put on the SPX <u>index</u>.
20. The market price of the SPX and the underlying ES e-mini future may be <u>different.</u>

Chapter 16 Answer Key

1. A trader's patience and consistency can lead to <u>financial</u> <u>independence</u>.
2. Most traders start with <u>small</u> <u>accounts.</u>
3. Growth requires traders to husband their <u>resources</u> in a conservative manner.

4. Check the setup <u>parameters</u> in chapter 14 before entering a trade.

5. The short OTM put is a <u>premium</u> <u>collection</u> strategy.

6. Use the short OTM put with a stock or ETF that you are willing to <u>own</u>.

7. This strategy should be used with highly <u>liquid</u> stocks and ETFs.

8. Premium is higher when IV% is high; Probability ITM should be ≤ 30%.

9. The covered short strangle requires the ownership of <u>stock.</u>

10. The short strangle includes a short put and a <u>short</u> <u>call</u>.

11. Trading the same strategy over and over is called <u>churning</u>.

12. The most vulnerable part of a covered call is the ownership of the <u>stock</u>.

13. Keep churning a covered call until the <u>stock</u> is called away.

14. The primary goal of the iron condor strategy is to collect <u>premium</u>.

15. The iron condor includes <u>four</u> separate option legs.

16. Butterfly spreads can be balanced, <u>unbalanced</u>, and broken <u>wing</u>.

17. A LEAP option contract may expire in one to <u>three</u> <u>years</u> from the time of entry.

18. The long strangle buys one OTM call and one <u>OTM</u> <u>put</u>.

19. The long straddle buys one <u>ATM</u> call and one <u>ATM</u> <u>put</u>.

20. Long straddles and strangles depend on a strong movement in the <u>price</u> of the underlying.

Test Your Options Knowledge Answer Key

1. The <u>Mark</u> value is midway between the Bid and the Ask values.

2. We trade options because they provide financial <u>leverage</u> and <u>flexibility</u> when compared to trading stocks.

3. The at the money value of <u>Delta</u> is close to 0.5 for call options.

4. Gamma dictates the rate of change of <u>Delta</u>.

5. Gamma's value is <u>highest</u> when ATM.

6. We pay <u>premium</u> when we buy a put or a call option.

7. We like to buy options when the IV% is <u>low</u>.

8. We like to sell options when the IV% is <u>high</u>.

9. Traders usually sell option contracts that expire within <u>56</u> (or <u>60)</u> days.

10. Traders usually buy option contracts that expire in <u>90</u> or more days.

11. Name the five Greeks in alphabetical order: <u>Delta</u>, <u>Gamma</u>, <u>Rho</u>, <u>Theta</u>, and <u>Vega</u>.

12. A change in the value of <u>Vega</u> has the most effect on the price of option premium.

13. <u>Theta</u> measures the decay in premium resulting from the passage of each day.

14. An option contract can only be exercised when the option price becomes <u>ITM</u> (abbrev.).

15. The seller of a <u>put</u> option must pay for the stock if the seller's option contract is exercised.

16. The seller of a <u>call</u> option must deliver stock to the option buyer if exercised.

17. An option contract is said to expire <u>worthless</u> if the strike price remains OTM for the duration of the contract.

18. An active American style option contract can be <u>exercised</u> if the underlying becomes ITM prior to contract expiration.

19. A European style option cannot be exercised prior to contract <u>expiration</u>.

20. The call and put options are both bought ATM when trading buying a long <u>straddle</u>.

21. The strip option strategy buys two ATM puts and <u>one</u> <u>ATM</u> call.

22. A bull call spread includes one or more ATM or slightly OTM long calls and an equal number of <u>short</u> <u>calls</u>.

23. The trader of a bull call spread expects the price of the underlying to <u>rally</u> (or <u>increase</u>).

24. The candle that resembles a plus sign is called a <u>doji</u>.
25. The "shooting star" candle resembles an inverted <u>hammer</u>.
26. A bracketed trade includes a limit entry, a <u>protective</u> stop, and a limit <u>target</u>.
27. The acronym GTC stands for <u>good</u> <u>till</u> <u>canceled</u>.
28. Financial index trades are <u>cash</u> settled.
29. Mathematical studies used on price charts are called odds <u>enhancers</u>.
30. The acronym ATR, as in the ATR(14) study stands for <u>average</u> <u>true</u> <u>range</u>.
31. The acronym MACD stands for moving average <u>convergence</u>, <u>divergence</u>.
32. The outer bands of the Keltner Channel are 1.5 × the <u>ATR(14)</u> above and below the SMA(20).
33. The outer Bollinger bands measure increases and decreases in <u>volatility</u>.
34. The acronym SMA stands for <u>simple</u> <u>moving</u> <u>average</u>.
35. An uncovered short call is considered an extremely <u>dangerous</u> option position.
36. The collar strategy is constructed from 100 shares of stock for each short call and <u>long</u> <u>put</u>.
37. A common reversal pattern found with an up-trending stock is called a <u>bull</u> flag.
38. The double top, triple top, and head and shoulders patterns are all considered bearish <u>reversal</u> patterns.
39. The cup and <u>handle</u> is a popular bullish consolidation pattern.
40. The ES e-mini option contract includes <u>50</u> shares of stock per contract.
41. The ES e-mini futures contract includes four quarterly expiration date suffixes H-M-U-Z. The suffix U represents expiration in the month of <u>September</u>.
42. Futures values are calculated using points and tics. The ES uses four tics per <u>point</u>. Each ES tic has a value of <u>$12.50</u>.

43. Forex pairs use a quote value and a <u>base</u> value. The EUR/USD pair represents the following currencies: <u>Euro/US Dollar</u>.

44. When away from your computer, you can use your <u>smartphone</u> to monitor and manage trades.

45. Every trader should have a <u>backup</u> system in case of a power outage.

46. Brokerages will often reduce commissions for an <u>active</u> trader.

47. An exchange fee must be paid for each <u>option</u> <u>contract</u> either bought or sold.

48. Most traders develop <u>watch</u> <u>lists</u> of stock symbols that they frequently trade.

49. Holding a long list of different stocks in one's portfolio is not considered <u>diversification</u>.

50. When a brokerage account becomes stressed, the trader may receive a <u>margin</u> <u>call</u>.

51. A margin account is used to expedite <u>trades</u> rather than waiting for a trade to settle.

52. The highest option trading level permits option traders to use <u>naked</u> trade strategies.

53. Another word for a naked call is an <u>uncovered</u> call.

54. The short put and the short strangle are both <u>premium</u> collection strategies.

55. Option buyers are not <u>obligated</u> to exercise an ITM position.

56. Option sellers have more <u>risk</u> than option buyers.

57. 68.27% is one <u>standard</u> <u>deviation</u> OTM.

58. When prices are rallying, basing, and dropping, trading volume is the lowest when the prices are <u>basing</u>.

59. The weighted average price at which most trading has occurred is referred to by the acronym <u>VWAP</u>.

60. The Open Interest values on option chains measure liquidity. When liquidity is low, submitted trades may not be <u>filled</u>.

61. Rolling a short call <u>buys</u> the current position and <u>sells</u> another position farther out in time.

62. A <u>diagonal</u> spread is similar to a calendar spread.

63. There are balanced, unbalanced, and broken wing versions of the <u>butterfly</u> spread.

64. Option traders can obtain a discount on the price of a stock by selling an OTM <u>put</u>.

65. Trade what you <u>see</u> and not what you feel, hear, hope, or think.

66. The market opens in the morning at <u>9:30</u> EST and closes in the afternoon at <u>4:00</u> EST.

67. You can trade stocks during <u>extended</u> hours using either <u>EXT</u> or <u>GTC</u> <u>EXT</u>.

68. <u>Scalping</u> is a technique used by day traders to regularly take small profits.

69. Many traders draw <u>Fibonacci</u> retracements on their charts to find likely entry and exit levels.

70. Momentum <u>oscillators</u> are used by many traders to determine overbought/oversold conditions.

71. Stock prices frequently rally off established <u>support</u> levels and drop from established <u>resistance</u> levels.

72. A <u>demand</u> zone is a historical price turning point where demand becomes greater than supply.

73. The acronym OCO stands for <u>order</u> <u>cancels</u> <u>order</u>.

74. Day traders most often use a trading <u>ladder</u> to enter and exit trades.

75. Most day traders use <u>bracketed</u> trades with stops and profit targets.

76. Novice traders typically lack experience and trading <u>education</u>.

77. Delta-triggered stops are more stable than <u>mark</u>-triggered stops.

78. Stocks and ETFs with a narrow Bid-to-Ask spread usually have high volume and high <u>liquidity</u>.

79. The <u>market</u> <u>depth</u> is the resistance to price change based on trading volume.

80. A <u>ratio</u> spread sells more OTM options than the number of ATM options bought.

81. A <u>time</u> spread purchases a back-month option and sells a front-month option of the same underlying.

82. A midcap company is said to have a market capitalization value of between <u>one</u> <u>billion</u> dollars and <u>ten</u> <u>billion</u> dollars.

83. A trader must have a <u>margin</u> account to short a stock.

84. Simulated trading is also referred to as <u>paper</u> trading.

85. Traders close long option positions using <u>sell</u> to <u>close</u> orders.

86. Traders close short option positions using <u>buy</u> to <u>close</u> orders.

87. Traders who short stocks make a profit when the price of the stock <u>drops</u>.

88. Option writers are the <u>sellers</u> of option contracts.

89. Market <u>makers</u> match and fill buy and sell orders.

90. Options <u>exchanges</u>, such as the CBOE, are for-profit companies that transact options trades.

91. The acronym ECN stands for <u>Electronic</u> <u>Communications</u> <u>Network</u>.

92. A <u>neutral</u> spread is used when traders believe the price of the underlying will move sideways.

93. Traders are said to be <u>bullish</u> when they believe the price of the underlying will rally.

94. Traders often avoid company events, such as <u>earnings</u> <u>releases</u>, when they want to avoid a sudden price breakout.

95. The <u>exponential</u> moving average (EMA) places more emphasis on the most recent data points.

96. <u>Market</u> orders fill faster than limit orders.

97. An order that requires the price of the underlying to be at, above, or below a specified price is a <u>limit</u> order.

98. Financial <u>leverage</u> provides a higher rate of return using a smaller amount of money.

99. Long-term Equity Anticipation Security (LEAPS) options are typically used with <u>long</u> <u>call</u> options in anticipation of a price rally.

100. The value from a change in the underlying security is referred to as <u>intrinsic</u> value; the time value that remains in option premium is referred to as <u>extrinsic</u> value.

ALPHABETICAL INDEX

-F-

-G-

–S–

-T-

THE ONLY OPTIONS TRADING BOOK YOU'LL EVER NEED

About the Book — Many people who are unfamiliar with how options work are convinced that trading options is both dangerous and unpredictable. And, indeed, options can carry substantial risk for those who have a limited knowledge of how options work. These same people who fear the use of options regularly risk large sums of money buying and selling stocks and exchange traded funds (ETFs). But when compared to buying and selling options, stocks and ETFs carry much more risk, because they are expensive, unpredictable, and inflexible.

Options are statistically predictable and orderly. Options provide extensive financial leverage and strategic flexibility. In fact, it's not even a contest! For just a few hundred dollars an option trader can control tens of thousands of dollars' worth of stock, ETF shares, a financial index, or futures contracts. And options offer dozens of trading strategies designed to exploit current market conditions. No other financial instrument offers this flexibility. And no other trading venue can provide the same steady financial return.

Author Russ Stultz has an extensive background in both writing and instructional design. This book blends his extensive option trading experience with his instructional design and writing backgrounds. His goal for this book is to take its readers from a basic knowledge level all the way to the application and analysis level of cognition through a series of carefully constructed hands-on options trading activities. When finished, readers are equipped to scan for, analyze, enter, and manage high-probability option trades.

For those readers who are already trading options, this book provides an excellent reference. A large collection of the many popular option strategies are covered in detail. It includes scanning, analysis, optimal setup parameters, entry, trade management, and possible outcomes for each option trade. It also includes a series of self-tests at the end of each of the 16 chapters and a 100-question final exam. Answer keys are provided in the appendix.

About the Author — After writing more than a dozen books for publisher Prentice-Hall, Inc., Russ Stultz founded and served as the CEO of Wordware Publishing, Inc. a Plano, Texas-based book and software publishing company. This is his 55th published book, of which some have been distributed in as many as 18 languages. His most recent book is the 5-star rated, extensively researched first-century historical novel entitled *Legions and Messiahs*. This book was released in early 2015 and is available from Amazon.com in Kindle and paper editions.

After 27 years of growing his company into a thriving three-division diversified corporation, each of the three divisions were sold to competitors. Russ began to look for something to fill his free time. Although he had been trading securities since the 1980s, he wanted to expand his trading skills. He enrolled in several market trading education courses including in-depth technical analysis, futures, options, and advanced options from both Online Trading Academy and Investools. He also conducted thousands of hours of independent study, taught, lectured, and has written extensively about option trading and the use of the thinkorswim® trading platform.